By the same author

Communities of Women: An Idea in Fiction
Woman and the Demon: The Life of a Victorian Myth
Romantic Imprisonment: Women and Other Glorified Outcasts

Ellen Terry
Player in Her Time

Photograph of Ellen Terry, 1888. *Reproduced by permission of the Harry Ransom Humanities Research Center, University of Texas, Austin.*

Ellen Terry
Player in Her Time

Nina Auerbach

W·W·Norton & Company · New York · London

First published as a Norton paperback 1989

The text of this book is composed in Bembo, with display type set in Typositor Centennial
Script. Composition and manufacturing by The Haddon Craftsmen, Inc. Book design by
Antonina Krass.

Library of Congress Cataloging-in-Publication Data

Auerbach, Nina, 1943–
Ellen Terry, player in her time.

Includes index.
1. Terry, Ellen, Dame, 1847–1928. 2. Actors—Great
Britain—Biography. I. Title.
PN2598.T4A94 1987   792'.028'0924 [B]   86-21651

ISBN 0-393-30582-1

W. W. Norton & Company, Inc., 500 Fifth Avenue, New York, N.Y. 10110
W. W. Norton & Company Ltd., 37 Great Russell Street, London WC1B 3NU
2 3 4 5 6 7 8 9 0

FOR MY PARENTS

"And one man in his time plays many parts" =
(And so does a *woman!*)
　　　　　　　　　—Ellen Terry

"Be damned *charming!*"
—Ellen Terry teaching herself Lady Macbeth

Contents

Illustrations

CHAPTER 6

Acknowledgments

Ellen Terry seemed to shed her extravagant generosity on this book as I was writing it, and so I should like first of all to thank her for the places I discovered and the friends I made while I pursued her life. The rare good faith with which associates, old and new, shared with me material and ideas is in part a tribute to Ellen Terry's continuing gift of herself.

I began this book in the beautiful Ellen Terry Memorial Museum at Smallhythe Place, whose curator, Molly Thomas, was a friendly and knowing guide through the many surprises in that quiet farmhouse. Later in my work, Arnold Rood steered me to just the right items in his rich collection of material about Edward Gordon Craig. I am grateful to him for his permission to publish portions of that material and for his pungent, generous, and helpful comments about my manuscript. Wilfred Blunt and Richard Jefferies, of the Watts Gallery in Guildford, Surrey, were congenial and informative guides through George Frederic Watts's life and work. Georgianna Ziegler introduced me to archival treasures that I would never have seen without her zealous sleuthing in the library of my home campus, the University of Pennsylvania.

The following archives, libraries, and collections contributed immeasurably to this book: the Henneke Archives of the Performing Arts at the University of Tulsa; the Special Collections Division of the UCLA Library; the Harry Ransom Humanities Research Center at the University of Texas, Austin; the Henry E. Huntington Library, San Marino, California; the Houghton Library at Harvard University; the British Museum and Library; the Fales Collection, Bobst Library, New York University; the Tucker-Coleman Papers, Swem

Library, College of William and Mary; the Furness Collection and the Rare Books Room at Van Pelt Library, University of Pennsylvania; the Folger Shakespeare Library; the Players Club, New York City; and the Billy Rose Theater Collection at the New York Public Library at Lincoln Center. I am grateful to all their staffs for their patient help, and for their permission to quote material in their collections.

I am especially grateful to Ellen Terry's executor, Walter D'Arcy Hart, for his kind permission to quote all manuscripts by Ellen Terry and Edith Craig included in this book, and for permission to reproduce many of the photographs as well; I am equally grateful to Robert E. Craig for his kind permission to publish all manuscript material and drawings by Edward Gordon Craig.

My wide-ranging search for Ellen Terry and those she shaped ranged beyond archives, though never beyond good words. One of its happiest episodes is my correspondence with Rackstraw Downes and his re-creations, through his parents' photographs and stories, of Edith Craig's Pioneer Players. Sir John Gielgud has provided me with a candid and sympathetic account of Edith Craig as he remembers her. Ellen Terry's daughter, a shadowy and elusive figure, gained contour as I worked, in part through the animating generosity of these correspondents. In the same spirit, through memories and eloquence, Stella Bloch restored Isadora Duncan to life one fall evening.

My warmest gratitude goes to the theater historians I approached as in some sense an interloper in their field, to be greeted with welcome, interest, and help. Many, many thanks to Stephen M. Archer, Michael R. Booth, Russell Jackson, and Cary M. Mazer, not only for their published scholarship, but for their friendship and boundless apt suggestions. My friends and colleagues Betsy Erkkila, Myra Jehlen, Gerhard Joseph, Jeanne Krochalis, Mark Samuels Lasner, Jane Lilienfeld, Jane Marcus, Gerald Weales, Carl Woodring, and Nancy Vickers gave invaluable material and suggestions. The University of Pennsylvania granted me an equally invaluable sabbatical leave, during which this book was written.

Carolyn Heilbrun, Martin Meisel, and Carole Silver read the first draft that became *Ellen Terry, Player in Her Time,* bringing to it the knowledge and illumination, and above all the passionately informed interest, that has made all three secret sharers of this book from the beginning. Mary Cunnane, my editor at W.W. Norton, has appreciated and cheered this interest from the first. I am especially grateful for the infallible instinct that told her when there should be more or less of Ellen Terry's story, and for the faith she kept when its progress seemed to falter.

Many years ago, my teachers Morris Carnovsky and Phoebe Brand allowed me to imagine how it felt to be a Shakespearean actor. Memories of them, and of that imagined life, are part of this book. Most of all, I am grateful to my parents Arnold and Justine, to whom *Ellen Terry* is dedicated, for the good sense and good faith that enabled me not only to imagine it, but to write it.

Ellen Terry
Player in Her Time

Introduction:
The Actress Everybody Loved

"WHY JUBILEE ME?" On June 12, 1906, the rarest talents in the theater gathered in London's Drury Lane to honor Ellen Terry in her fiftieth year onstage. Audiences had begun to line up the day before to cheer the matinee the *Times* called "a theatrical debauch." The account went on: "From shortly after noon till six o'clock they filled Drury Lane with a riot of enthusiasm, a torrent of emotion, till they were hoarse, laughed to the verge of hysteria, and sang 'Auld Lang Syne' in chorus, not without tears." The audience might have stayed forever, but the long, lavish jubilee had to end with the day: on their own time performers might choose to celebrate their work, but at night they had to play on schedule. For Ellen Terry, the day's best gift was the knowledge that she still had a role to play at night, though it was a role she mistrusted: the talkative Lady Cicely Waynflete in George Bernard Shaw's comedy, *Captain Brassbound's Conversion*. If the evening had held nothing but to go home and remember the laughter, the singing, the tears, the celebration would have been too sad for her to endure.

Since she still had work she could smile as relentless blessings paraded past her. The capering daughter of strolling players had grown into "this uncrowned Queen of England"; once she had flung herself about in scanty costumes, but now she stood stiff and grand, swathed in heavy satin; long pointed sleeves pulled down her arms, a heavy train curled around her legs and enclosed them. White lace covered her bodice modestly. Like the jubilee itself, her regal dress embraced and enclosed her. As a child, she had played acrobatic boys; as a hoydenish young woman she had courted ostracism by becoming the mistress of the aesthetic architect, Edward William Godwin. Godwin had faded out of her life, leaving two brilliant, difficult children and a memory that became more perfect as it grew less clear. The wayward girl was herself a memory to the fifty-nine-year-old darling who had turned into a beloved epitome of British womanhood, smiling through a jubilee that commemorated a good woman more fulsomely than it applauded an actress.

The jubilee commemorated as well a century of theatrical heroes. The cavernous vastness of the Drury Lane Theatre was itself a reminder of grandeur: once, Drury Lane had epitomized theatrical grandiosity, but it was too big for the diminished performances of the fastidious new century. Ellen Terry's own theater was the Lyceum Henry Irving had dignified with his high-minded productions of Shakespeare; the Lyceum's six Corinthian columns gave its stately facade the look of a temple, promising spiritual edification within. Drury Lane was less temple than circus. Its house was a dizzying series of circles: the enormous pit, the reiterated round tiers of the boxes, loomed over a proscenium stage that made the far-off actor seem a different order of being from the circling masses of the audience. Like all London theaters, Drury Lane had sacrificed to proliferating pit-benches the apron that had bridged the distance between actors and spectators. Nineteenth-century improvers of Drury Lane's design fed the hungry audiences they assumed would always come.

Drury Lane had been rebuilt and restored many times since its beginnings in 1663, but it had always been at the center of theatrical London. In the early decades of the nineteenth century its primacy had seemed assured. Between 1813 and 1833, it was the theatrical home of the ruffian genius Edmund Kean. Shortly after Kean burnt himself out, his rival and opposite, William Charles Macready, became Drury Lane's luminary and, briefly, its manager. The gentleman-actor who had longed to be a barrister and flagrantly despised his calling nevertheless made the Lane as splendid as the disreputable Kean had done. A grand theater had fostered all varieties of great men, but by the end of the century a new, middle-class audience resented being overwhelmed. No single performer could fill the yawning house: it became the seat of popular spectacles, the pantomimes, melodramas, and extravaganzas a newly solemn theater was aspiring beyond. By the turn of the century Drury Lane, for so long the heart of the theater, became the perfect setting for benefits and jubilees, whose interminable nostalgic glamor both paid tribute to aging stars and, more discreetly, raised money for them. In 1897, nine years before her own jubilee, Ellen Terry had played her last mad Ophelia at a Drury Lane benefit for the music hall star Nellie Farren. Ellen Terry, queen of the stage, wistfully loved the other, less reputable Nellie, whom music halls licensed to be impudently funny while revealing powerful, beautiful legs. Now Ellen Terry's own turn had come to be honored on Drury Lane's huge stage. Like the hallowed theater where her ceremony was staged, she too had become uselessly grand.

In its happy extravagance, its seemingly endless flow of love and money—nearly six thousand pounds was raised for the richly paid but financially exhausted actress—and above all in the tensions that simmered within its triumph, Ellen Terry's jubilee was a fitting climax for the Victorian phase of her long career. In her speech of thanks, she wooed her audiences and her colleagues with her usual skill into assuring her that she would not be exiled from the light: "I will not say good bye. It is one of my chief joys that I *need* not say good bye—*just yet*—but can still speak to you as one who is still among you on the active list—Still in your service—if you please." The loving response she won at Drury Lane did not protect her from the twenty-two wandering, disoriented years that lay ahead. But since Ellen Terry's jubilee looked so much like a happy ending, while it contained so much unhappiness and was not an ending at all, it is a fitting beginning to the story of an actress.

To observers, the sturdy, stily royal figure at the center of the pageant was, in her endearing way, as awesome an emblem of power as Queen Victoria had been. The predominantly female audience, many of whom had stood in line since two o'clock the previous afternoon, saw in Ellen Terry the glorification they dreamt of for themselves; when Ellen Terry herself visited the line to cheer them along, she seemed to invigorate all women who stood patiently, waiting. Her theatrical glory exuded political innuendo. The colonized Irish saw in her jubilee all the unjust imperial autocracy of the mother country. Though she may not be "a really great artist," an Irish reporter writes, "Miss Terry represents the British school of actresses; and her complete and dominating control over the audiences at home and in the colonies is an irrefutable proof of her supremacy in appealing to the national taste and the national susceptibilities." It had been a particularly ominous week for royalty; at the wedding of the British Princess Victoria to the Spanish King Alfonso, a bomb had exploded during the gorgeous ceremonial procession, killing five people. The "complete and dominating control" all British ceremonies seemed to the colonized to wield were, to their regal performers, fragile masquerades of courage.

British journalists sentimentalized Ellen Terry's power into goodness, just as they did England's own power. The *Tribune* and its like wrote of a honeyed woman: "Someone once said to Miss Terry, with reference to her great popularity in all quarters, that he did not believe that she had ever uttered an ill-natured word concerning a fellow-creature. To this she replied, 'Why should I? All the world seems to say kind things about me. I am happy in knowing it; and thus

I love the world and all who live upon it. Why shouldn't I?' "

Why not love everybody? It was her job to reflect back to itself the world that looked at her, and in 1906, the world beamed. Earlier in the year, Herbert Beerbohm Tree, the grandiose actor-manager of His Majesty's Theatre, had consecrated in rolling doggerel

> Britain's pride,
> The genius of the stage personified,
> Queen-like, pathetic, tragic, tender, merry—
> O rare, O sweet, O wondrous Ellen Terry.

She had responded in kind, in Louis N. Parker's lines of rhymed gratitude:

> I want to thank you—all of you—I see
> Through tear-dimmed eyes, your love envelop me,
> Wrap me as 'twere within a shining cloud,
> And I am very humble—very proud—

At Drury Lane, she was wrapped still more closely in enveloping clouds of love, though its expression was less booming: Marie Bancroft had taken over Beerbohm Tree's ceremonial role, and she was too knowing to gush. Like Ellen Terry, she had begun her career in breeches parts: in a theater still outcast from polite society, Marie Wilton's dynamic stage boys had embodied all performers' potential for audacious trespass. Her marriage to Squire Bancroft had metamorphosed her into propriety: as managers, the Bancrofts cannily dressed their theater as a cozy middle-class home that welcomed respectable families. By 1906, the Bancrofts knew royalty; they regularly graced aristocratic gatherings. Squire Bancroft, now a knight, strutted grandly through London's theatrical districts as though he had fathered them; Marie (now Lady) Bancroft emanated all the virtues of an efficient household manager.

Lady Bancroft was a well-chosen Mistress of Ceremonies, for she had been one of Ellen Terry's many makers and discoverers in the early days; but even had she never helped, her hospitable presence gave the occasion a reassuring aura of family happiness. For the *Times,* a familial glow warmed the heart of the jubilee's splendor: "The vast Drury Lane audience, which included, we take it, people from every section of our English society, high and low, rich and poor, learned and unlearned, fashionable and unfashionable, the 'simples' as La Bruyère would say, and the 'habiles,' was united like a family party by this common sentiment [of love for Ellen Terry]. And just there, we repeat, the festivity strikes us as without a parallel."

As she had done so consummately and for so long, Lady Bancroft shed a family glow over a theatricality that had looked unsavory and even dangerous only a generation ago. She glowed not for Ellen alone, but for a clan of Terrys. When, in the first act of *Much Ado About Nothing,* Ellen Terry became her old, adored Beatrice once more, theater and family joined hands to form a single celebratory community. Beerbohm Tree supported her as Benedick and Johnston Forbes-Robertson as Claudio; her son Gordon Craig had placed his genius (if not himself) at her service by designing the scenery and concluding masked dance; but the audience was won by the three generations of Terrys who displayed themselves in the minor roles. Proud red feathers in the program identified family members of all ages; there were twenty-two. The *Times* melted at a family party that made less-than-perfect theater: "But considerations of pure art have, of course, to be waived on occasions like this—wherein the carnivalesque mood is paramount—and the audience was much more delighted to see so many Terrys, big and little, all in a row, than vexed at shortcomings inseparable from insufficient rehearsal. If, however, the players for the most part scrambled through their parts in a schoolboy spirit of 'lark,' they were only in keeping with the wild wayward gaiety of Miss Ellen Terry's Beatrice." A prancing, cavorting family redeemed the "wild wayward gaiety" with which Ellen Terry had frightened people all her life.

Ben and Sarah, her hard-working, unsuccessful parents, must also have strutted invisibly at Drury Lane. Strolling players, itinerant and anonymous, they had made the great stage dynasty Ellen crowned. Ben was a mediocre actor himself, but he conceived his family's glory from the first: he trained his nine surviving children to live and work on the stage, and had the happiness of seeing five of them live his dream. Sarah, grimly beautiful, is a powerful but faintly mysterious figure in Terry family history. Her God-fearing, theater-scorning family looked down on the stagestruck Ben Terry, whom she married secretly with melodramatic flair. Her brief career as a player was crowned (at least according to loyal family legend) by a single performance of Gertrude to Macready's Hamlet. Whether or not this was so, a succession of pregnancies led her to bury "Miss Yerret," her stage self, forever. Her powerful ambition devoted itself to steering her children toward respectability as relentlessly as Ben steered them to the stage. By 1906, Ben and Sarah were dead, but they had imagined perfectly their pride of Terrys, winning approval as well as awe on the stage of Drury Lane. Ben's dream of glory, Sarah's lust for acceptance, had created a theatrical aristocracy who inspired a passionate reverence rarely granted to the real lords and ladies who patronized Terrys.

The Victorian age that glorified them found in family life its image of Heaven. In a world of heartless showiness, families alone offered spaces of saving privacy; good women were privacy's precious custodians. Well-intentioned, anti-feminist Victorians feared that women who asserted their right to roles in the public sphere of education and the professions violated a sacred trust and thus heralded the death of privacy itself. Actresses were dubious figures because they lived publicly, forfeiting anonymity and the home. The contemptuous phrase, "public woman," was used interchangeably for both performer and prostitute. In such a climate, decent men like Henry James's Peter Sherringham in James's theatrical novel, *The Tragic Muse,* succumbed to a helpless horror at actresses because their art makes privacy, and thus humanity, evaporate: "It struck him abruptly that a woman whose only being was to 'make believe,' to make believe that she had any and every being that you liked, that would serve a purpose, produce a certain effect, and whose identity resided in the continuity of her personations, so that she had no moral privacy, as he phrased it to himself, but lived in a high wind of exhibition, of figuration—such a woman was a kind of monster, in whom of necessity there would be nothing to like, because there would be nothing to take hold of."

The beautiful, fertile Terrys saved each other from this appearance of monstrosity: the large clan gave each member a comforting aura of family privacy within the "high wind of exhibition" that was their element. Bernhardt and Duse presented themselves as eccentric solitaries for whom the world offered no kin, but Ellen Terry brought to the stage a family that sheltered and proliferated as bountifully as Queen Victoria's did. Her jubilee Beatrice was appropriately framed by her staunchly supportive siblings, artistic children, and adorable skipping grandchildren. True, there was no legitimizing husband to beam at it all; in fact, she was dreaming of a third marriage; the handsome young American to whom she was trying, uncharacteristically, to cling was causing fury to rock her household. The public loved marriage, but it was generally bothersome to Terrys. Thus, most of the winning grandchildren were as illegitimate as their father, Gordon Craig, had been. Nevertheless, they were charmingly visible, endowing Ellen Terry with the pageant of family that allowed audiences to love her and newspapers to laud her womanly presence despite a life that was a series of trespasses.

The family party of *Much Ado* stole the jubilee, but they shared the stage with mighty names. "Caruso, accompanied by Tosti, sang for her: so did her friend from the music halls, Gertie Millar. Réjane came from France, and Coquelin and his son appeared in a scene from Molière's *Le Mariage Forcé.* W.S. Gilbert presented *Trial by Jury,* his production crowded with celebrities from the theatre and the arts; the Jury alone included Conan Doyle, Comyns-Carr and Anthony Hope." These were only the highlights of the six-hour-long program. As the sun set and the parade of praising celebrities threatened to stretch to the crack of doom, Ellen Terry's jubilee, like her life, seemed to overflow with every treasure the stage could dream or hold. In both, though, there were galling, irremediable absences.

The day of love was undermined by a silent war between women and men. The world outside the theater knew about this war and tried not to speak of it, but Ellen Terry's vociferous children could not be quiet. Edith Craig, her stubborn daughter, would not be lovable. Because Edy was outspoken and, it seemed, always angry, London's theatrical establishment had determined to keep her off the jubilee planning committee. They could do so only by excluding women altogether; they did so. In her speech of thanks, Ellen Terry deferred to the committee's unremitting maleness in one of her delicate and elusive barbs, breaths of sarcasm that were so much more artful than Edy's obnoxious clarity. There was a veiled edge when she thanked the committee who "have done with enthusiasm all that men can do—and more!—to make the wheels go round," an edge that gained point to those who knew that the committee had done its best to exclude women from the entire program. Christopher St. John tells the story in her biographical appendage to *Ellen Terry's Memoirs:*

The press in 1906 made no comment on the extraordinary fact that not a single woman was invited to join either the General or Executive Committee constituted to organize the Commemoration performance at Drury Lane. One interesting result was that the Executive arranged a programme, as nearly as possible all-male. Actresses, with the exception of those belonging to the Terry family, who had parts in "Much Ado About Nothing," were to be represented on the stage only in Gilbert's "Trial by Jury." Theirs not to reason why, theirs but to serve as programme sellers. When the draft programme was submitted to Ellen Terry she could at first hardly believe her eyes! "No, no! It's not possible!" she gasped, and then, assured that it was, could not speak for some time for laughter. An actress-less programme in honour of an actress! What a joke! Ellen Terry could not help relishing it, but to the consternation of the committee she said that she didn't want to spoil the joke by appearing herself! This threat led to the eleventh-hour addition to the programme of a series of tableaux in which the leading actresses in the London Theatre could at least be seen. How ungrateful and tiresome of Ellen Terry not to be satisfied by this concession! She despatched a letter to Mr. Arthur (now Sir Arthur) Pinero, the chairman of the Executive: "Dear Pinny, An amusing notion this, of women of talent appearing in *tableaux* only, but if that has been decided upon by the Committee, I elect, if you please, to appear only in a tableau myself. I couldn't, I couldn't, I *couldn't* do anything else!"

I don't know who or what induced Ellen Terry to change her mind. Possibly it was the evidence that in one number at least, actresses predominated. This was a scene from "The Beauty of Bath," presented by "Mr. Seymour Hicks and *all* the Bath Buns."

Pinero's grudging augmentation of the program exposes the precariousness of the love Ellen Terry won so dearly. As she had done so often, the ever-smiling actress did her best to turn insult into comedy, paving the way for the uneasy peace that allowed the divided jubilee to proceed. Edy, as usual, refused all reconciling transformations. She found no comedy in hate.

On the great day, familiar and beloved writers like Shakespeare and Gilbert shared the stage with a majestic pageant of female tableaux vivants. Edy had arranged them in a fury of activity; she always found her energy under conditions of siege. Edy's women had nothing in common with Seymour Hicks's Bath Buns, or with the choric merry maidens who graced Gilbert and Sullivan's operettas; for the most part, her tableaux were epic and heroic realizations of the solitary might of female rulers. In this grand company, even Queen Victoria and the Virgin evolved from solacing to challenging, even vaguely menacing, figures. "Beginners for the First Act, A Hundred Years Ago, arranged by Mr. James Pryde" paid homage to an earlier, still more beleaguered generation of actresses. Other tableaux were more inspirational still: "Ladies of the Court of France presenting the Oriflamme to Joan of Arc, arranged by Mr. Percy Macquoid"; "Mrs. Langtry in a Cleopatra, arranged by Sir James Linton, R.I."; "Queen Victoria as a Girl in Kensington Palace Gardens, arranged by Sir James Linton, R.I." In "The Blessed Damozel, arranged by Mr. Byam Shaw," the climactic appearance of "Miss Julia Neilson (the Madonna)" eclipsed at a stroke the suppliant male speaker who dominates Dante Gabriel Rossetti's poem. Like the painters who "arranged" them, the participating actresses were the pride of their generation; among them were Pauline Chase, Lena Ashwell, Violet and Irene Vanbrugh, Edna May, Lilian Braithwaite, and Constance Collier. Taken together, though, their tableaux were a quiet call to arms, forcing the audience to look at a world drained of men where heroic women were in command. Excluded from the jubilee until the final flurried compromise, these powerful young actresses formed a proud counterpoint to its romping complacency.

Outside the Lane, increasingly determined suffragists banded in similar proud counterpoint to the mellow jocularity of sanctioned Edwardian society. The government was gracefully turning its back on Emmeline and Christabel Pankhurst's Women's Social and Political Union. The Pankhursts had founded the WSPU three years earlier, hoping it would win the labor movement's support for women's enfranchisement; but in the 1906 general election only Keir Hardy, out of twenty-nine Labour members returned to Parliament, advocated votes for women. In 1906, the suffrage movement was perforce separating itself from governmental promises and processes; between 1910 and 1912 suffragists would embrace a militancy and violence that declared war against men's state, bringing the battle of the sexes into the streets of London. The regnant women so impeccably "arranged" at Drury Lane were one harbinger of a self-sustaining women's army devoted to a mighty Cause.

At the center of her torn afternoon, Ellen Terry embodied both the men's and the women's entertainments, justifying the ideologies that had inspired them both. She smiled, she reconciled, she cast a charm that was her most reliable talent. Her presence reanimated Henry Irving's noble Lyceum, whose beloved leading lady she had been. In the 1880s and 1890s, the Lyceum had elevated the theater from entertainment to institution. All classes united to applaud its spectacular Shakespearean productions; eminent members of all ranks and professions attended Irving's equally spectacular banquets in the Beefsteak Room after the performances. Through Irving's plotting, the theater became respectable and Shakespeare, commercial; through Terry's charm, both could be safely loved at last. Pinero, Beerbohm Tree, and the other men were honoring in her person a theater that exuded the security, the dear predictability, of nineteenth-century society. Its collapse in 1902 had been so final and so sad that no man who loved Ellen Terry could bear to think about the end.

But Ellen Terry also invoked the retaliatory rage of the women the jubilee had tried to exclude. She had always been Irving's obedient subordinate; her private triumph was the grace she shed on vapid roles, a whispered challenge to Irving's reign. In the 1890s, George Bernard Shaw's pugnacious eloquence drew attention to her as the victim of the patriarchal Lyceum as well as its jewel. Joan of Arc, Cleopatra, Queen Victoria, the Madonna, all summoned an Ellen Terry finally freed from Irving's dominion, epitomizing to her disciples a gorgeously restored womanhood, enfranchised into majesty at last.

These tableaux vivants insinuated a threatening note into the celebration, reflecting battles in the larger society and announcing a schism in the British theater whose inspirational force came from Ellen Terry's most ardently believing disciple, Edith Craig. The audience saw Ellen Terry's daughter only as she moved decorously through the family dance of *Much Ado,* but behind the scenes Edy's theatrical career was fueled by a dream of a woman-centered theater that her powerful mother both obstructed and inspired. In the uncertain years to come, an aging Ellen Terry would play more, and sadder, Beatrices, but she would also galvanize by her presence Edy's suffrage productions. The jocular jubilee was Edy's dress rehearsal for a full-blown political theater. Two years later, in 1908, the Actress' Franchise League was founded as an arm of the suffrage movement; for Edy and other leaders, theater and Cause were briefly and unforgettably one. The inspirational spectacles Edy staged, such as Cicely Hamilton's *A Pageant of Great Women,* evolved out of the tableaux vivants at Drury Lane, but suffrage pageants proclaimed a self-generated female grandeur that refused all "arrangements" by respectable male artists. The fissure in Ellen Terry's jubilee program was a hint of separatism to come. Soon there would be no theater able to contain the divisions in the lovable woman and in the sorts of love she aroused.

The tableaux vivants were a discordant afterthought, but the great Eleonora Duse, who, as Ellen Terry gleefully put it, "had come all the way from Florence just to honour me" (*Memoirs,* 276), had been invited from the beginning. Duse did not act, nor did she need to: her still presence exalted the ceremony as it did the tawdry melodramas she irradiated into high tragedy. Ellen Terry was adorable, but Duse was awesome. Her magnanimous appearance consecrated the stage, just as it had consecrated the idea of theater for its compromised nineteenth-century practitioners. For Ellen Terry, who subdued herself to pleasing and who came alive when she was loved, Duse represented an unreachable integrity. Two powerful photographs of Duse hung in her last home, her cottage at Smallhythe; these exude the holy power of personified Art. Like much of Ellen Terry's own career, the jubilee was an exuberant hodgepodge. Duse brought to its shapelessness, its incongruities, its mock-humble pride, the benediction of a higher theatrical power.

The willingness of Duse, who was always ill, to make the long journey reminded audiences that Ellen Terry was an artist as well as a darling, but it also affirmed what they already knew: that everybody, even geniuses, loved Ellen Terry. The well-known feud between Duse and Sarah Bernhardt was a Wagnerian spectacle; Ellen Terry, on the other hand, called Bernhardt "Sally," got on with her, laughed with her, wrote about her shrewdly, and was patronized by her. Duse's mute presence at Drury Lane was a loyal reminder that Ellen Terry was an artist—but not an opponent. Like the divided program, Duse's visitation dramatized Ellen Terry's contradictory achievement. In Duse's company, she too became an icon of solitary grandeur; but she remained as well the comfortable, amenable, and thus safely loved, little Nell.

In the audience and onstage, women were exalting if disrupting presences; the men who had mattered most were gone. In 1906, Henry Irving too would have celebrated his fiftieth year onstage. They had discussed a joint jubilee, but he had died the year before, exchanging Drury Lane extravagance for the sacred pomp of burial in Westminster Abbey. For Ellen Terry, there had always been a partner. It was incongruous to stand onstage alone: "I never forgot for a moment that [the demonstrations of homage and affection] were not for me alone, and that many were anxious to show me honour because I had worked with Henry Irving for a quarter-of-a-century. I represented a chapter in the history of the English theatre, of which they were proud" (*Memoirs*, 275). Larger-than-life eccentrics, such actors as Duse, Bernhardt, and Henry Irving epitomized in their own extraordinary persons the theater that imprinted itself on their countries and their age. Ellen Terry, on the other hand, was always aware of the identities she took from others. Her admission of incompleteness without her overwhelming partner was wise as well as modest: Ellen Terry may have subdued herself to the coloration of her milieu, but she also appreciated that milieu with a subtlety, a shrewdness, and an ultimate respect inaccessible to more self-absorbed performers.

Men's descents and departures were woven into the pattern of her life. Most of her collaborative lovers had become, like Irving, potent memories in crowded theaters. Duse's expansive presence reminded her of the most wrenching absence of all: that of her son Gordon Craig, an artist as pure as Duse, but so far at least, one who shunned audiences. Gordon Craig's defection was more wounding than that of the dead; like Cordelia's to King Lear, it seemed a breach of nature. A self-declared genius with a genius for offending, Craig could not tear free from his self-imposed exile in Berlin. His sister Edy had fought the committee's determination to exclude women; but somehow, Gordon Craig complained years later, the jubilee had in reality left out the men. His complaint carried on the battle of the sexes that had torn Ellen Terry's household from the beginning:

> Somehow this Jubilee thoroughly upset me—because my father, E.W.G. [Edward William Godwin], was forgot—like the Hobby-horse!
> My father, my master [Irving] and I, all loved the same woman—and we all left her for the same reason—a commonplace one: our work called to us, and we went. But we did love her. Strange, it was she who could not follow us. My father died in 1886, my master in 1905, and I still live on—older now than they were when they died. Both died tired out. Of us three, my master was the greatest man. Both he and my father did more for her than ever I did: yet I believe she loved me most: how strange. I alone live on now to write of this. I older than all three. It seems queer to me: it seems all wrong: but as it is an old story, ever being retold and rehearsed, it can hardly be quite all wrong. I was the least of the three, the weakest and the smallest: is that why she loved me most? Yes and no: for in loving

me so much, she loved my father at the same time. This leaving her: what is that? E c h o . . .? Fools will say . . . but what does it ever matter what fools say of those we love?

Characteristically, Craig invents the jubilee he did not attend as an intensely private drama with an all-male cast. But Ellen Terry lives in his oracular half-truths, for like an assaultive theatrical role, he obliterates his mother to recreate her. Craig's visionary community of fathers, masters, and disciples has momentous work; she, who always supported him financially, has none. She "cannot" follow her destiny-burdened men; it is inconceivable to him that she follows a path of her own. In his dream of her she lives only to kill great men. In 1906, Gordon Craig was parading his love affair with the renowned American dancer Isadora Duncan, who had become both mother and sister to him; he trusted that Isadora could not kill. In the theater he had dreamed of founding with Martin Shaw the year before, he made women vanish altogether: "No women in it boy. Only comrades! whish! but we're getting at it." Craig's dream of a womanless theater is the other side of the all-female tableaux vivants that were so palpable an actual presence at Drury Lane.

Ellen Terry did love her son most, not because he stood apart from the other men in her life, but because, as he knew, he was like them: her artist-husband George Frederic Watts, her aesthete lover Godwin, her "master" and theatrical husband Irving, even her epistolary wooer Shaw, all invaded her consciousness to translate it. The son who would claim that his grand mother was a little woman who could not follow him epitomized, in the obsessed presence within his stubborn absence, all the men who had remade and left her. Some of them thought they had broken her heart, but she knew she had never been their victim. Bernhardt and Duse, who were more powerful than she, orchestrated florid romantic humiliations for themselves; Ellen Terry took the dreams of her lovers and added them to her repertoire of possible slaves. Her malleability protected her from invading Pygmalions, allowing her to possess the new Ellen Terrys they made.

Ellen Terry's jubilee epitomizes everything she was; in consequence it was not an unmixed joy. She wrote testily about its falsifications to the actress Audrey Campbell: "This Jubilee business is overwhelming rather—Why Jubilee me?—because I'm 'a great actress' (I'm not) and because I'm 'a Dear'! You know I'm not!" At the time of her jubilee, she was beginning her memoir, *The Story of My Life,* a story that was making her own lifelong hiddenness intriguingly clear to her. Her jubilee speech of thanks begins with a muted boast of impenetrability: "I never felt so strongly as now, that language was given me to *conceal* rather than to *reveal*—I have no words at all to say what is in my heart—I can only trust to my friends on the stage and my friends in the audience to be eloquent for me." Finishing *The Story of My Life* two years later, she used the jubilee as an unstable happy ending, but even here, a note of warning mingles with the show of conclusion: "If I have not revealed myself, (Myself? Why even I, I often think, know little of myself!) I hope I have given a true picture of my life as an actress, and shown what years of labour and practice are needed for the attainment of a permanent position on the stage" (*Memoirs*, 276). "My life as an actress" rests on an abyss and concludes with a graceful acknowledgement of that abyss.

Ellen Terry's intimations of mystery within, of a mobile and opaque self beneath her roles, were the charm that lured audiences; she shot tantalizing glimpses of suppressed identities. A note of wry self-parody hummed within the compliant actress. She added to a signed photograph of herself as Camma in Tennyson's *The Cup*—in which she was at her most picturesquely virtuous— a witchlike self-caricature, sketching herself in a profile that magnified her prominent nose and chin. Among the papers of her later years, her witty "Eulogy to Miss E.T." twists into absurdities fulsome accolades like Beerbohm Tree's. His "O rare, O sweet, O wondrous Ellen Terry" inspires her askew prayer to herself:

> Graceful Charming
> Truth of the truth—
> All Kindness
> Who is like unto thee—
>
> . . . .
> You are first in your Art—!
> YOUR BEAUTY IS DAZZLING!!
> Tragedy-Comedy is wreathed on your brow.
> Actress supreme, there is nobody like you.

The old woman's amused self-sanctification mocks the obedient posturings of the "actress supreme." As Ellen Terry laughed at herself, her elusive wit lent an enticing aura of funniness to all good women.

Like Ellen Terry's entire career, her jubilee was a compound of glory, evasions, insults, and omissions; like that career, it ended in fatigue, but the long pageant was not Ellen Terry's final performance that day. When it was finally done, she traveled from Drury Lane to the Court Theatre and the aegis of George Bernard Shaw, whose seductive letters had for twelve years aimed to woo her out of Irving's paternalistic grip into the buoyant play of his own iconoclasm. After years of dodges and doubts, she had in 1905 consented to play the "tall, very good-looking, sympathetic, intelligent, tender and humorous" Lady Cicely Waynflete in *Captain Brassbound's Conversion*. She was glad to have a theater that was not saying good-bye to her. The short journey from Drury Lane to Shaw's advanced company at the Court took her out of an opulent and tender past into a brash future.

But Lady Cicely, the fruit of their brilliant correspondence, did not work out. Ellen Terry seemed uneasy playing Shaw. She forgot her long speeches; she seemed too sad for Lady Cicely's cocky wit, though when she had played with Irving, she had been too funny for his sentimental pathos. Shavians found her old-fashioned, while her own admirers found Lady Cicely as archly sentimental as the ingenues to which Irving had relegated her—though Lady Cicely admittedly had more to say. After all the excitement of a new beginning, the dawn of Ellen Terry's partnership with Shaw soon led to its polite termination. Like the jubilee, the happy ending that had been so eagerly prepared for and so carefully staged carried within it disappointments, fissures, and irresolutions.

Only the young Virginia Woolf found triumph within apparent decline. As Woolf remembered it, Ellen Terry's aptitude at forgetting Lady Cicely was a shrewd commentary on a silly part: "When she came on to the stage as Lady Cicely in Captain Brassbound's Conversion, the stage collapsed like a house of cards and all the limelights were extinguished. When she spoke it was as if someone drew a bow over a ripe, richly seasoned 'cello; it grated, it glowed, and it growled. Then she stopped speaking. She put on her glasses. She gazed intently at the back of the settee. She had forgotten her part. But did it matter? Speaking or silent, she was Lady Cicely—or was it Ellen Terry? At any rate, she filled the stage and all the other actors were put out, as electric lights are put out in the sun." For Woolf and for many women her age, Ellen Terry's apparent lapses were subtle victories over demeaning roles.

She forgot her lines; "she filled the stage." She was obedient, lovable, helplessly charming; she made the stage collapse. She dithered; she dominated. "Wondrous Ellen Terry" is remembered, and deserves to be, less for her assured and ephemeral successes than for the self-divisions she carried within her and transmitted to the audiences—and to the changing cultures—that half-created her.

IMAGES At the time of her jubilee, everybody loved Ellen Terry, but few critics placed her among the great artists of her age, or even among its overwhelming women: she attuned herself too finely to her beholders to emit the solitary, self-generated power the nineteenth century wanted in a genius. In her own way, though, Ellen Terry was the supreme artist of her age, for she epitomized and gave form to its changing dreams. The sly motto she composed for her jubilee program was her creed:

> "And one man in his time plays many parts" =
> (And so does a *woman!*)

Her "many parts" tell a richer story than did any one of them; from childhood to old age, she mirrored the passing needs of successive phases of culture. Taking the conflicting pressures of her times, she tried to become what others imagined. The infinite willingness of her expansive adaptability made the roles that were her life more broadly revealing than the mere creations of Victorian stage conventions. Like the British novel that flourished in her lifetime, from the mid-nineteenth century through the First World War, Ellen Terry's metamorphoses reflected collective dreams. The vocation of the real woman was to become that corporate creation, a work of fiction. This was not a genius's mission; it was the task of many ordinary women who would never touch a stage.

Her instinct to be all things to all people was her bane and her triumph. In its compound of dexterity and self-doubt, obedience and elusive mockery, Ellen Terry's performance as it adapted itself to changing times was the essence of her life. She did not transcend her age as the single-minded Duse appeared to do, nor did she imprint herself on it like the self-promoting Bernhardt, but her performances of womanliness made her its true abstract and brief chronicle. "I have always been more woman than artist," she wrote disingenuously in her memoir (p. 120). In truth, woman and artist were the same. "The actress everybody loved" may be the greatest artist of all, the funniest and the saddest at once, when her performances are tempered by the relentless clarity and wit of Ellen Terry's own self-awareness.

There were no acting schools in Ellen Terry's day; she learned herself from watching others watch her. She found herself as an artist when she flowered as an artist's model; in pictures she was most mercurially and suggestively alive. This photograph from the mid-1880s displays everything Ellen Terry was and was not. Its decorativeness, its mobile composition, its glorified fabrics that threaten to overwhelm the figure, all form an absolute contrast to the two unadorned photographs of Duse which in her last years Ellen Terry hung as self-reproachful icons in her cottage at Smallhythe.

Beauty of a particularly topical sort looks out at us: the lovely woman offers herself up to the mercurial simplicities of aesthetic design. The pattern of her dress, the delicately contrasting colors of her coat, put her on the verge of fading into the wallpaper. The chameleon Ellen Terry is inseparable from her surroundings: her self-display is her praise of an age. Her self-fabrication is a triumphant blurring of the boundaries between herself and her world. She does not look heroic when she subdues herself to her medium, but her apparently modest self-submergence is an act of supreme understanding. To become her world, Ellen Terry had to know both self and world.

The seemingly self-effacing center of this photograph is the sophisticated pictorial actress who made piercing visual statements through skillful self-arrangement. In 1880, Davenport Adams said of her that "no lady on the modern stage is so much of a picture in herself, or falls so readily into the composition of the larger picture formed by the combinations of a drama." For the artist and collector W. Graham Robertson, her deft adaptation to others' compositions was her essence: "Her charm held everyone, but I think pre-eminently

Photograph of Ellen Terry, 1888. *Reproduced by permission of the Harry Ransom Humanities Research Center, University of Texas, Austin.*

those who loved pictures. She was *par excellence* the Painter's Actress and appealed to the eye before the ear; her gesture and pose were eloquence itself." This "child of the studio," as Robertson called her, learned her art from the model's absorption into others' imagined worlds.

When, in her work, she had to take command, she was adept at disarming subordinates by flowing into her surroundings. Johnston Forbes-Robertson fell under her spell when, as a young actor, he was sent to be interviewed by his potential leading lady: "Presently the door opened, and in floated a vision of loveliness! In a blue kimono and with that wonderful golden hair, she seemed to melt into the surroundings and appeared almost intangible. . . . I was undergoing a sort of inspection, but her manner was so gracious that it soon cleared away my embarrassment" (quoted in Manvell, 86). She dominates by seeming to disappear; her boundaryless submergence in her surroundings is her power.

This eerie ability to melt into something larger and take quiet possession of it may have inspired Henry Irving's cryptic tribute to her performance in *The Amber Heart:* "I wish I could tell you of the dream of beauty that you realized" (quoted in Manvell, 189). The chameleon actress is the carrier of a momentous vision, which she makes real in her person. In Victorian theatrical terminology, a "realization" involves the translation of one art "into a more real, that is more vivid, visual, physically present medium": art forms gain intensified life by absorbing themselves in each other. Ellen Terry became that vividly permeable and realized medium for others' dreams. She seemed incapable of the egoistic self-declaration of an Irving, a Bernhardt, or a Duse, but her very art of shrinking and disappearing gave her a power to realize her medium—a room, a theater, or an age's myths—that the self-proclaimers never acquired.

With instinctive economy, Ellen Terry tells us who she is through the medium of a commercial photograph. But a knot in the center of its composition blocks the Whistleresque flow of identity between person and place: the broken, contorted line where the actress shields her hands from us. Ellen Terry was a large woman, larger than she made herself appear; if she exposed her hands, she feared she would expose herself in her full, unfeminine stature. As an awkward fourteen-year-old, she worked under the management of one Madame Albina de Rhona, a deceptively dainty Frenchwoman. Then and forever after, her hands became her bane:

> Her neat and expressive ways made me feel very "small," or rather *big* and clumsy, even at the first interview. . . . She was a wee thing—like a toy, and her dancing was really exquisite. When I watched the way she moved her hands and feet,

despair entered my soul. It was all so precise, so "express and admirable." Her limbs were so dainty and graceful—mine so big and unmanageable! "How long and gaunt I am," I used to say to myself, "and what a pattern of prim prettiness she is!" I was so much ashamed of my large hands, during this time at the Royalty, that I kept them tucked up under my arms! This subjected me to unmerciful criticism from Madame Albina at rehearsals.

"Take down your hands," she would call out. *"Mon Dieu!* It is like an ugly young *poulet* going to roost!"

In spite of this, I did not lose my elegant habit for many years! I was only broken of it at last by a friend saying that he supposed I had very ugly hands, as I never showed them! That did it! Out came the hands to prove that they were not so *very* ugly, after all! Vanity often succeeds where remonstrance fails. (*Memoirs,* 32–33)

By all accounts, those hands were uncommonly large, powerful, and beautiful, but in fact, on the evidence of photographs that spanned her life, they never came out from their prison: when a camera pinions her, she hides or knots them together, away from exposure.

Ellen Terry's hands revealed a largeness and a power forbidden in women: strength, sexuality, even violence, might curl within them. Charles Reade, the novelist and playwright who was one of her many teacher/patrons (she addressed him as "Daddy"), wrote an exasperated tribute to the largeness she did her best to mask: "Ellen Terry is an enigma. Her eyes are pale, her nose rather long, her mouth nothing particular. Complexion a delicate brickdust, her hair rather like tow. Yet somehow she is *beautiful.* Her expression *kills* any pretty face you see beside her. Her figure is lean and bony; her hand masculine in size and form. Yet she is a pattern of fawn-like grace. Whether in movement or repose, grace pervades the hussy" (quoted in *Memoirs,* 75).

In the nineteenth century, words like "masculine" and "manly," "feminine" and "womanly," make little descriptive sense; they tell us less about gender than about power or the lack of it. Observing her piercingly, Reade found "grace" in "the hussy" because this compound of largeness and strength transformed herself with such dexterity into the woman he wanted to see. *The Man of Destiny,* the ill-starred play Shaw wrote for Ellen Terry in 1895, endows the Strange Lady with the contorted strength Reade mistrusted. Shaw, though, is tender toward her enforced deceptions and concealments: "[The Strange Lady] is very feminine, but by no means weak: the lithe tender figure is hung on a strong frame: the hands and feet, back and shoulders, are useful vigorous members, of full size in proportion to her stature, which perceptibly exceeds that of Napoleon and the innkeeper, and leaves her at no disadvantage with the lieutenant.

Only, her elegance and radiant charm keep the secret of her size and strength."

Ellen Terry kept her secret with less ease than did the wonderful woman Shaw imagined. She never played the Strange Lady, though she was closer to that veiled strength than to the winsome ploys of Lady Cicely, but in the Strange Lady's spirit she shrouded herself by hiding her hands. Hidden or exposed, they possessed the imaginations of those who watched her. Gordon Craig's *Ellen Terry and Her Secret Self* insists for its own reasons that his "little mother" was "a very small person," but even Craig lost himself in hymns to her hands, perhaps because he and Edy had both inherited their power:

> I never knew such a pair of hands—like a physiognomy, they lighted up with expression—looked all sorts of things—and belonged somehow to so long ago. Useful as she made them, they were so much more than that . . . they were indeed beautiful. Not only because of their expression, I think—I cannot tell for certain —but I think they were lovely in themselves. In repose—closed across her breast, they still seemed alive—the hands of *Beatrice, Imogen* and *Portia's* right hand.
>
> She could play the piano well—she touched the notes with much surety, and without assault; her hands could grasp without snatching—ward without a tremor —hold firmly, ready to let go at the first sign—and hold up, sign or no sign.
>
> All her life lay in those strange, fine hands—and when she held the carving fork and knife and showed me how to cut a leg of mutton or a sirloin of beef, I learned from her performance in a trice.

"All her life lay in those strange, fine hands," but throughout her long career she hid them like guilty things. It may have been her legacy of guilt that led her son and daughter to identify their own strange, strong hands, so like hers, with murder. Isadora Duncan describes her lover in the language of Victorian gender that masks diagnoses of power. She recalls Gordon Craig's "almost womanly weakness. Only his hands, with their broad-tipped fingers and simian square thumbs, bespoke strength. He always laughingly referred to them as murderous thumbs—'Good to choke you with, my dear!'" Christopher St. John, a feminist writer whose real name was Christabel Marshall, describes Edy's hand in the same idiom: "Edy has a peculiar square thumb. 'The murderer's thumb' it has been called in jest" (*Memoirs,* 341). It may be that Edy and Ted inherited their mother's fearful self-knowledge along with her hands. As with so many Victorian secrets, Ellen Terry's compulsive concealment intensified the lethal power of the hands which expressed her most potent life.

Ellen Terry knew when and how to hide; she was a creature of deft, involuted, half-parodic adaptive genius. Eleonora Duse's strength was exposed for all to adore and for many to fear. Duse dramatized her single-minded selfhood in the legend that she wore no makeup, and in the iconic power of her expressive hands. In his *La Gioconda* (1899), her sadistic lover Gabriele d'Annunzio wrote a part that required her to sacrifice those hands in order to save her genius husband's statue. To the fury of her devotees, Duse had to play the last act with the engines of her power concealed in voluminous sleeves. Ellen Terry's concealment of her hands won her love in England; Duse's, in Italy, was a publicly lamented sacrilege.

The two unadorned faces of Duse with which Ellen Terry spent the last years of her life embody a proud singleness of being she herself could never attain. No background distracts us; when the young Duse and the old one bring us the gift of her face, it is sufficient. In the 1893 photograph, that grand face is shot from below, making the viewer a supplicant before her gaze. In the same spirit, Duse dominated the Italian theater with an obsessed self-concentration no British woman dared unleash. Like Irving, she directed her own, safely mediocre company, chose her own plays, and made her own public image, with no regard for reporters' convenience or audiences' needs. In her own eyes, she had never been an entertainer; she made others see her as a personification of naked truth; at the end of her life she exuded the sacred magic of a saint.

The naked power of Duse's integrity radiates in the mighty faces with which Ellen Terry lived at Smallhythe. As with Irving's, the divine absoluteness of that power was beyond her. "There have only been two faces on the stage in my time—his [Irving's] and Duse's," she wrote (*Memoirs,* 157). The inscription with which she blessed Duse's 1893 photograph—*"There is none like her—None!"*—was Ellen Terry's private prayer to those she worshipped as well as loved. Both Irving and Godwin received this idiosyncratic chant at their deaths, but Duse was the only woman and the only living being Ellen Terry apotheosized with her wistful tribute to supreme, and supremely dominant, individualism.

Because Duse identified herself so completely with uncompromised Art and so little with audiences, she generated, especially in England, a sacred terror from which Ellen Terry preserved herself, a terror that had a sexual component, as Max Beerbohm admitted:

> True, I see power and nobility in her face; and the little shrill soft voice, which is in such strange contrast with it, has a certain charm for me. I admire, too, her movements, full of grace and strength. But my prevailing emotion is hostile to her. I cannot surrender myself, and see in her the "incarnate womanhood" and "the very spirit of the world's tears" and all those other things which other critics see in her. My prevailing impression is of a great egoistic force; of a woman

Eleonora Duse, from Ellen
Terry's Farm at Smallhythe Place.
*Ellen Terry Memorial Museum,
Smallhythe Place. Courtesy of the
Trustee of the Ellen Terry Estate.*

overriding, with an air of sombre unconcern, plays, mimes, critics, and public. In
a man I should admire this tremendous egoism very much indeed. In a woman
it only makes me uncomfortable. I dislike it. I resent it. In the name of art, I protest
against it.

Beerbohm acknowledged what many less forthright observers felt: the unnerving tension between incarnate power and "incarnate womanhood," which by
definition renounced power and ego. Because Duse was uncompromising, she
received no such grudging but reconciling benediction as Charles Reade's final
"grace pervades the hussy." She drew only prayers or protests.

   All magnetic actresses aroused this hostile tension in the nineteenth century;
many still do. To succeed, they evolved various self-abasing strategies to conciliate their unnerved audiences. Duse groveled publicly before the mad self-
worship of Gabriele d'Annunzio, sacrificing to his swollen, distasteful plays even
her artistic primacy; in penance, perhaps, for this extreme act of penance, she
left the stage for twelve years after their affair and their partnership ended. Ellen

Terry was less extreme; she performed little rituals of conciliation every day. She was wise in the ways of a theater that rewarded women not for egoism, but for alacrity in self-sacrifice: "As a rule," explained a troubled reviewer of *Measure for Measure,* "the heroines of drama extort our admiration by the readiness with which they make sacrifices for those they love."

In twentieth-century America, such Shakespearean actors as Morris Carnovsky distill from their roles a glory that is almost blasphemous: "I've always held that Shakespeare is for demigods, at any rate, super-humans, not ordinary people. . . . [By using the Self] the actor becomes a kind of nugget of power." But for Ellen Terry, a woman and a Victorian who was frightened of frightening people, a dole of self-sacrifice accompanied every triumph of ego. As a result, she awed nobody except those who knew her best. She told reporters that she loved everybody, but those who demanded her love found her aloof and alone in a world of her imagination. Edith Craig, who until Ellen Terry's death separated from her only rarely and wrenchingly, exposes through Christopher St. John the memoir's pious claim that she is "more Woman than Artist":

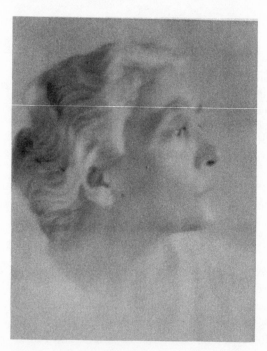

Eleonora Duse, from Ellen Terry's Farm at Smallhythe Place. *Ellen Terry Memorial Museum, Smallhythe Place. Courtesy of the Trustee of the Ellen Terry Estate.*

It is impossible to identify this theoretical Ellen Terry, in whom Ellen Terry herself believed, with the Ellen Terry of fact. Except for a brief period in her youth, her work (like Eleonora Duse, she never spoke of her "art," but of her "work") was always the most important thing in her life. For its sake she "scorned delights and lived laborious days." She imagined she was a home-loving person, yet she spent the greater part of her time nursing her energy for rehearsals and performances in the theatre. She imagined she was a good housewife, yet her home was best ordered when she left its management to others. It is significant that while her domestic partnerships were of short duration, her artistic partnership with Irving lasted for over twenty years. (*Memoirs*, 150).

With shrewd self-distribution, Ellen Terry left the reassuring woman on the stage and brought the artist home. Her "nugget of power," like her hands, was too fierce for the public to see.

She was taught early and well to diminish herself within a look of love, but when she wrote of the stricken Isadora Duncan whom Gordon Craig was in the process of discarding, she admitted that, like her son, she had little but artistic love to give:

> "How can you say you are glad she had gone? I'm awful sorry. How odd you don't find Isadora and her work to be one—If you were alone with her I think her Amazon and spring song, and a little of all she does wd. peep out beautifully —she made me rather wild with her now and again at the Farm, but when we were alone I loved her. One's work is the best part of us all, don't you think Graham? Most folk I've met I've loved their work better than them."

It was in large part Ellen Terry's work to make people love her by pretending she loved them: the artist survived by performing the loving woman, while barricading herself against the grasping need for engulfing intimacy she aroused in others. When we look for descriptions of the actress, we find hymns to the loving woman; when we look in her private life for love, we meet the elusive artist's feints. Living within this precarious exchange of roles, Ellen Terry both experienced and inspired a terror more insidious than Duse's. The fear she continues to arouse is not that of the towering exception whom Cocteau dubbed a "sacred monster," but that of the good woman who is a consummate actress because she is always becoming what she is told to be.

LIVES   Ellen Terry slid into others' visions of her life, but that life was neither orthodox nor conventional: the different messages it transmitted to disparate observers endow it with maddeningly rich and distinctive meanings.

In its enforced, intensifying renunciations, though, Ellen Terry's life tells a universal story, one that divides clearly into acts and scenes.

Ellen Terry was born into the theater and educated by its demands; from her debut at the age of nine to her death at eighty-one, she never stopped acting. When she was sixteen, she had become too dangerously beautiful to play the obstreperous boys in which she had specialized as a child. Angry at a theater that was becoming confined by middle-class respectability, she married the pampered painter, George Frederic Watts, embracing ardently the aesthetic Wonderland of Little Holland House, where his stylish patrons kept him. But Ellen Terry was too rowdy to please her fastidious (and possibly impotent) husband; their brief marriage generated only a series of poignant paintings.

Shortly after Ellen Terry was banished from Watts's circle, she eloped to the country with the dashing, self-absorbed Edward William Godwin, an architect and stage designer whom Max Beerbohm would dub "the greatest aesthete of them all." Her six years with Godwin left her with the rare Edy and Ted and with dizzying memories of a love in nature blessed by art. When, in 1874, she returned to the stage, her marriage and her romance had perfected her artist's eye, though they may not have deepened her emotions: the men she lived with had schooled her in being seen. She used the lessons of their love to make herself the spirit of an opulently pictorial theater, one devoted less to inner truth than to splendid moments of vision.

In her decades of glory, the 1880s and 1890s, Ellen Terry was the leading lady of Henry Irving's spectacularly successful Lyceum productions. She was never given the roles whose power she radiated—even Lyceum Shakespeare subordinated all to Irving, barring her from the mobile comic spirits she seemed born to play—but her very presence aroused dreams of beauty, of joy, of radiant possibilities beyond the scripts Irving mutilated to his own advantage. Her Lyceum years were framed by brief marriages to two handsome minor actors. Charles Wardell (Charles Kelly) gave a legal name to her children, one they quickly discarded; later on James Carew provided a brief barricade against age and increasing helpless dependence on Edy after the Lyceum dissolved. Essentially though, onstage and off, the years of Ellen Terry's greatest fame were consumed by Henry Irving, who as manager, lover, and leading man found in her a cooperative if clear-eyed appendage to his Napoleonic dream of himself.

After Irving's gorgeous palace dissolved, Ellen Terry's omnivorously demanding children led her into an age of Modernism, feminism, and visionary theatrical experiment. Until her death and beyond it, she supported their unorthodox projects, their complex households, with her money, her powerful name, and her regal if waning presence. Blind, intermittently mad, touring indefatigably while steeped in rapturous dreams of the moon, Ellen Terry was in the twentieth century an anachronistic great dear to the public, but for an advanced generation of artists, she was a talisman they fought to possess. Belatedly, in 1925, she was made a Dame Grand Cross; when she died, Westminster Abbey refused to accept her remains. To the end, she lived on the margins of the society that possessed her.

In the seven ages of Ellen Terry's life, changing roles epitomize changing times, but her life, like her art, shows itself in a multitude of perspectives. The publishing history of her memoir, *The Story of My Life,* reveals that story in all its tantalizing openness. The memoir appeared first in 1908; it was written with the unacknowledged assistance of Edy's lover and Ellen Terry's "literary henchman," Christopher St. John. Christopher no doubt helped organize Ellen Terry's brilliantly vivid, if increasingly patchy, account of her life, but the words, and the vision within them, are the actress's own. The feints, the elusiveness, the confusions within its power, make *The Story of My Life* invaluable for its truth to Ellen Terry's experience, if not always to fact.

After Ellen Terry died, she was in danger of being killed a second time by cloying reminiscences of the Terry charm. Edy and Christopher made it their mission to rescue from a patronizing oblivion the powerful woman they knew. Edy founded the Ellen Terry Memorial Museum at Smallhythe Place, which is now under the aegis of the National Trust; Christopher published Ellen Terry's correspondence with George Bernard Shaw as a testimony to the actress's brilliance, wit, and daring. Indefatigable preservers, Edy and Chris redeemed Ellen Terry's distinctive power from the love she felt compelled to win.

The publication of the Shaw letters enraged Gordon Craig. In the same year, 1931, he countered the letters' deft games with his own memoir, *Ellen Terry and Her Secret Self,* invoking a loving, vulnerable, and little mother whom only he had known, whose helpless sweetness was violated and, at the end, imprisoned by Edy's fanatical circle of feminists. Enraged, Edy and Chris published in 1932 their newly annotated edition of *The Story of My Life.* Edy and Chris's colorful, combative notes amplify and occasionally contradict Ellen Terry's own account: they resound with paeans to the grand and strong woman, the powerful artist, whom Gordon Craig had tried to expunge from the world's memory. Even after her death, Ellen Terry continued to play many parts.

She bequeaths to us this phantasmagoria of created selves. Once she became a star, her roles were tailored to her charm, but her life flew apart into warring performances, epitomized in the struggle for possession between her daughter and her son. The passionate controversies and emendations *The Story of My Life* generated place it at the other pole from magisterially self-glorifying memoirs like Sarah Bernhardt's *Memories of My Life: Being My Personal, Professional, and Social Recollections as Woman and Artist,* which also appeared in 1908. Bernhardt leaves no space for controversy in the self-presentation she offers; she proclaims her heroic creed, "I shall never be yielding nor docile," and that is that. Ellen Terry's memoir, like her life, appears to be both yielding and docile, for it gave itself to the dreams of others, while Bernhardt thrust on the world her own dream of herself.

Ellen Terry's powerful letters, too many of which remain unpublished, bring us as close as we can come to the actress's own voice, mercurial and imperious at once. The torrential eloquence these letters let loose, the idiosyncratic, carefully composed system of emphasis and punctuation with which she assures herself she will be properly read, reveal reserves of energy no audience can appreciate, no role can contain, and no biographer has done justice to.

Among the familiar biographies, Marguerite Steen's *A Pride of Terrys* is a shrewd, if gossipy and partisan, account of Ellen Terry and her theatrical family. Steen knew Ellen Terry in her later years; her book is alive with the passionate, if confused, feelings the old woman inspired. Roger Manvell's *Ellen Terry* is the fullest and most reliable biography, though its frugality in quoting Ellen Terry's own letters excises from her life much of its mystery, wit, and torment. Moreover, Manvell, like Tom Prideaux in his later, graceful if doting *Love or Nothing,* writes dismissively and even with revulsion about Edith Craig, who did her best to preserve her mother's spirit for all writers of lives. Unlike his sister, Gordon Craig fathered many fond children to explain his family to posterity. In the long battle between Ellen Terry's children for possession of their mother's memory, Edy has been thoughtlessly vilified, for this withheld woman left no one behind to tell her story. Without that story, though, Ellen Terry's own life loses its meaning and its center.

Ellen Terry's parents trained and taught her, but her profession freed her from daughterly deference: the mid-Victorian actress had the orphan's license to become all she could be. Privileged Victorian daughters had no choice but to become proper ladies; performers had only to please audiences. Each phase in the cycle of Ellen Terry's life was a masterpiece of simultaneous acquiescence in and defiance of what women were told to be. In the 1850s, the child was an acrobatic and hoydenish foil to her ladylike sister Kate: audiences languished over Kate while they screamed with laughter at Ellen's mischievous boys. In the 1870s and 1880s, her lanky, eerie beauty made her the center of an aesthetic cult. No Pre-Raphaelite painted her, but Watts infused her with a pathos so grand that she appeared to incarnate all Pre-Raphaelite divinities.

In the 1890s, when both the Lyceum and Queen Victoria were at the height of their popularity, as Victoria was about to celebrate her own Diamond Jubilee and her new role as Empress of India, a rounder, solider Ellen Terry radiated a queenly benevolence worthy of Her Majesty's own. After the Queen died and the Lyceum collapsed, Ellen Terry's identity veered about as the times did. During those difficult years, she exuded maternal comfort to men like W. Graham Robertson, J. M. Barrie, and George Bernard Shaw, all of whom panted for mothering; at the same time, she became an austere oracle to militant new women. Absorbing the pressures of conflicting times, she wrenched her energy into the shapes that others saw.

Ellen Terry's apparent willingness to give herself up to the obsessed dictates of others—her lovers, her audiences, her managers, her children—allowed her to make of herself a series of wry looking-glass images of ideals others cherished. Since her life was given to acting, even when she seemed most triumphantly herself (as she does in her letters), Ellen Terry took the pressure of her time and showed her age the oddity of its own desires. Her extraordinarily mobile, flexible life tells us more about the successive ages in which she played than their noblest spokesman knew or cared to know.

Stage Child

THE CHILD "I can't even tell you when it was first decided that I was to go on the stage, but I expect it was when I was born, for in those days theatrical folk did not imagine that their children *could* do anything but follow their parents' professions" (*Memoirs,* 8). This Victorian artist knew no moment of consecrated choice, no rupture with family and the past: home and theater, legacy and destiny, were one. From the beginning Ellen Terry saw no boundary separating her from her world, which was all theater, for the mid-Victorian actor was by definition set apart from social sobrieties.

Ben Terry had chosen that isolation, and its concomitant clannish freedom, for them all: the roguish son of a Portsmouth publican, he had fallen in love with the stage. Sarah Ballard, the daughter of a builder and Wesleyan lay preacher, had fallen in love with him. Neither Ben nor Sarah was of theatrical ancestry, but once they joined the itinerant bands of strolling players, placing their crowns and scepters next to the pots and pans in the wagons that were their truest home, they had made the theater their bequest to their children.

Kate, the first girl, was dancing hornpipes onstage when she was three. Ellen, three years younger, was born in lodgings, in Coventry. There was no possible life for her but the dancing Kate's: already, the boys were remote figures. Kate and Ellen both played winning Britannias, but technically, just as they were never quite civilized, neither were they quite English: Ben's family was Irish, Sarah's, Scottish. But Ellen Terry was too engrossed in her roles to imagine herself as an outcast. "My whole life was the theatre, and naturally all my early memories are connected with it" (*Memoirs,* 16).

As infants, she and the others were bundled in shawls to sleep in the drawers of her mother's dressing room: "So it was, that long before I spoke in a theatre, I slept in one" (p. 9). But it was an easy passage from sleeping in a dressing room to speaking on a stage: Ellen Terry made her debut playing Mamillius in Charles Kean's production of *The Winter's Tale* in 1856, when she was nine, though all her life she thought she had been eight: long after her death, Roger Manvell found evidence that she had been born on February 27, 1847, not, as she always believed, February 27, 1848 (Manvell, vi). I suspect that like a pantomime magician, the ambitious and adoring Ben bestowed on Ellen Terry an extra year of childhood, hoping to prolong her stage career and defer the awkward professional transition to womanly roles. Since this transition was to bring her uncommon grief, his sheltering impulse was wise, if confusing.

The fact that Ellen Terry was one year older than she knew may be one source of a certain dislocation that was part of her allure. Her childhood, as she remembered it, was infused with an Alice-in-Wonderland quality of vertigo; she lived in joyous terror, and her body had a vivid life apart from her official identity. Later on, her memory itself began to slide away on its own erratic course; by the time she was fifty, it was anguish to learn new roles, and even the old ones fell away from her unpredictably. Her memory may have begun its askew career when the self she remembered—questioning, rebellious, sexually awake—divided from her public self, a contented child. In this, at least, the stage child with her wild self-awareness was like ordinary girls, who in the 1850s were expected to retain the malleable purity of children throughout their adult lives: the self that felt lived apart from the self others saw. Unlike actresses, though, ordinary girls were forbidden to betray their losses of control.

In the 1850s, the first decade of Ellen Terry's career, the British actor was particularly despised. Macready retired in 1851; there was no longer an ennobling great man to protect the stage from its aura of raffish disrepute. The Evangelical revival licensed ferocious attacks on the actor's calling and morality; to polite eyes, and sometimes to the law as well, provincial actors were still indistinct from the vagrants and vagabonds with whom they had been associated since the sixteenth century. As the Terrys wandered through Scotland and England's northern provinces, playing where they might, Sarah kept the children proper and clean while Ben infused them with a sense of destiny and high art; nevertheless, their strolling life skirted criminality by definition.

One Victorian actor, Peter Paterson, laments in his *Glimpses of Real Life* (1864) the contaminating lowness of his strolling career: "Who but one haunted by a restless burning desire for dramatic distinction would welcome years of poverty, privation, sickness of soul and body, a constant sense of self-imposed beggary, and an internal reproach for frequent acts of meanness not to be avoided, and even dishonesty, which may not be shunned" (quoted in Baker, 131). When Ellen Terry became regal, she clung to these beginnings. Officially beyond the pale, she had made herself at home in an outcast, even semi-criminal theater. Like the orphans and vagabonds in Dickens's novels who made respectable citizens weep (though they were less acceptable in life), she and her fellow stage children played with zest the unschooled and untamed role of wanderers who lacked the nourishing roots and rituals proper families provided.

Snug middle-class children would have looked on Ellen Terry as a wild child had they been permitted to know her, but her strolling brought her a familial allegiance that was deeper and broader than theirs. The mid-Victorian actor lived a life apart. To counter its isolation from far-away normalcy, the theater identified itself with family loyalties and dynastic ties. A typical stock company was a family affair. Its repertoire was family life writ large: "In fact, it is no mere accident that the traditional types of Victorian melodrama corresponded to the age range of the extended family unit: it was a natural dramatic form for companies which comprised children, parents and grandparents" (Baker, 65). But the actor's loyalty flowed beyond kin into the protective network of the actor's community, "the Profession." Unaware of middle-class formulae, actors defined not houses, but their work and their world, as family. Only in the 1870s and 1880s, when respectable society began to accept and absorb the theater, did the sheltering isolation of "the Profession" begin to dissolve.

Ellen Terry grew up in a familial world that neither knew nor cared about its remoteness from institutions. By the time her own children grew up, the Profession had fractured, but in turn-of-the-century America Lillian Gish's touring childhood retained the flavor and many of the routines of the young Ellen Terry's. Lillian Gish's description of her early career is a tribute to a family transcending kinship:

> Perhaps because of the insecurity of their lives, members of the troupe tended to blend into a warm affectionate unit when they were touring. By the time a company had been on the road a month, it was as close as a family, with no social difference between leading players and stagehands. We looked after one another in sickness and helped one another during hardship. If children were well behaved they received affection and protection. Stagehands often read to us from our favorite books. I remember one carpenter knocking down a man for using offensive language in front of me.

At once egalitarian and gallantly protective, "the actor's class" claimed nothing in common with the rigidly hierarchical world outside the theater. Like his trade and his being, the actor's class was protean in its essence. Respectable folk might classify strolling players as vagabonds, or, more kindly, as laborers, but to themselves, offstage as well as on, actors were socially metamorphic. Humble servants, they could explode into royalty on call.

Stage children were charmed and particular vehicles of transformation; in themselves and in their social class, they might become anything. The actor-manager Edward Stirling tells a fairy tale about a stage child whose social metamorphosis is infused with theatrical magic:

> In the house where I lived there once dwelt a poor strolling actress, named Mellon: her little child, a pretty girl, she duly left to the kindly protection of the landlady, who fed Harriet Mellon with her own children, principally upon porridge. Mrs. Mellon, ill-paid, ill-fed, could scarcely keep herself. "Many and many a meal I've given the poor child, when its mother was a play-acting up at playhouse," said the good woman in her garrulous fashion. This little starveling lived to be Duchess of St. Albans. When fickle Fortune smiled, be it recorded to her honour that Harriet Mellon did not forget the humble landlady at Bolton-le-Moors.

Harriet Mellon's rise is the stuff of actors' legends, for she acts in her life the mobile potential attributed to all stage children. Children could transform the actor's class into grandeur, in society as well as onstage. Kate and Ellen acted Harriet Mellon's transformation on behalf of their entire family: when the apparent "little starvelings" succeeded in Charles Kean's company, they provided their family with a London home and with their first house, in Regent's Park, a suburban actor's colony. Their younger siblings were educated, not as vagabonds, but as gentlemen and ladies. In her Lyceum years Ellen Terry shed aristocratic sanctity on the Terrys as lavishly as if she had had a real title; Ben, with his unerring sense of role, nicknamed her "Duchess" when she began to succeed. Ellen Terry, who as a baby slept in dressing-room drawers, never went to school, and who capered about in boys' clothes making people laugh and cry at an age when normal girls were having modesty forced into them, grew up believing that all British society was her theater. Actors, and stage children in particular, looked like exiles from England's class system. In reality, though, they took all class roles as their protean province.

Disreputable to others, "the Profession" was a full world to itself. Its faith in grandeur made it easy for Ben Terry to conceive his dynastic clan, one welded to the theater with a royal sense of lineage, an imperial assurance that self and symbolic identity were one. Kate and Ellen, and then the younger, genteel Marion and Florence, were actresses in their bones. Fred, the youngest and the "golden Terry," became a dashing Scarlet Pimpernel and a colorful actor-manager who in the twentieth century kept the old florid school alive; with his glamorous wife and partner Julia Neilson, he continued the dynasty by producing a new generation of beautiful canny theatrical Terrys. The four brothers who failed to become actors failed, in various ways, at life. They embarrassed the performing Terrys, who sent them money faithfully but rarely saw or discussed them. The Terrys did not sequester their nine children; their family name was their mark of special creation.

Ellen was her father's indisputable favorite; sedate and snobbish Kate belonged to Sarah. The fatigue of poverty, wandering, and incessant pregnancies had led Sarah to abandon her brief career as "Miss Yerret"; her new vocation was sustaining the family; her powerful beauty had fallen away. She was an obstructive and sometimes baleful presence to the boisterous little Ellen; large and disapproving, sewing and counseling caution, Sarah was a harbinger of ominous renunciations. When the family dispersed, as it did frequently in the early years to accommodate Kate's far-flung engagements, Ellen found her freedom by staying with Ben and keeping a messy house for him. They declaimed together in elocutionary bliss; neither cared for houses and propriety when there were so many lives to live, so many people to be.

Instinctively Victorian, Ben and Sarah had assigned themselves traditional roles: Ben was the wanderer, the dreamer, the artistic and sexual experimenter; Sarah was the domestic forbidder. They were a perfect managing team as Ben orchestrated his children's careers, Sarah, their social acceptability. Ellen Terry had no formal teachers; her lack of education mortified her all her life; but between them, her parents taught her more cogent lessons than respectable girls received in the 1850s. With Ben, she expanded; for Sarah, she made herself contract. She hated her mother's lesson, but it was the one she kept relearning.

Ben taught all the children reading, writing, and sums. Ellen Terry's fluent and powerful letters, the handwriting that reflected so vividly the inflections of her speaking voice and the nuances of feeling within her words, were one fruit of Ben's instruction. He fostered her vitality; above all, and on all occasions, he trained her voice: "He never ceased teaching me to be useful, alert, and quick. Sometimes he hastened my perceptive powers with a slipper, and always he corrected me if I pronounced any word in a slipshod fashion. He himself was a beautiful elocutionist, and if I now speak my language well it is in no small degree due to my early training" (*Memoirs*, 11). The public, self-presenting Ellen Terry emerged, as she remembered it, during her cherished times alone with her father.

Her memoir pays a somewhat guilty tribute to the grim mother she had always evaded, but Sarah's less formal instruction cut deep. Like a good woman, she always sewed. When Ben, Kate, and Ellen joined Charles Kean's company, Sarah, who had lost her stage presence, became the company wardrobe mistress and settled into being ingloriously useful. Her granddaughter Edy would sew with Sarah's avidity, though without her propriety. She inherited Sarah's genius for transforming backstage scraps into lovely party dresses, though while Sarah had made exotic materials acceptable, Edy turned common scraps into costumes that were exotic and dashing. Through their sewing, both women played with the shifting boundary that separated the ordinary from the theatrical.

Ellen had learned different transformations from Sarah. She imbibed her mother's political wisdom as duenna, her adeptness at suppressing herself, her woman's ability not to frighten people she might need. Above all, she learned from Sarah, whom she knew only as wardrobe mistress, never as Miss Yerret, how to be useful, a humble enough art for her to boast about it: *"Usefulness! It is not a fascinating word, and the quality is not one of which the aspiring spirit can dream o'nights, yet on the stage it is the first thing to aim at. Not until we have learned to be useful can we afford to do what we like"* (*Memoirs*, 35). One of Sarah's ancestors was the American portrait painter, John Singleton Copley; her mother had been born a Copley, claiming with pride her connection to the Royal Academy. Through her own mother, Sarah might have transmitted despite herself Ellen's most un-humble flair for picturesque self-arrangement, but she was never heard to boast of it. It was Ben who encouraged the glint of wildness that enthralled observers and finally enshrined Ellen Terry on the stage as Victorian England's most loved madwoman.

An unconscious social outcast, the little girl lived with two potent dreams of family: that of the Profession, and Ben's vision of a regnant Terry dynasty within the Profession. Had she been a child of the aspiring middle class, her life would have been locked into a far more restrictive idea of family. Her governess would have told her that beyond the prescribed duties and emotions of a daughter, a wife, and a mother, there was no world and no allowable self.

Certainly, for a girl, there was no allowable work through which family could become a medium of glorification rather than confinement: middle-class men exalted themselves through the work ethic, but for their attendant women, work was a sullying shame. Actresses were shunned, not only because they displayed themselves publicly, but because they revealed themselves publicly, even proudly, as working women. A proper family required incessant care and duty, barring wives and daughters even from the idea of a world outside, while Ellen Terry's hardworking life was consecrated and enriched by a family that was more vision than reality. She wore her rue with a difference, one that would later allow her to make glow with energy the ties that inhibited the respectable women in her audience.

Accordingly, her memoir begins with a gorgeous prison:

> This is the first thing I remember.
>
> In the corner of a lean-to whitewashed attic stood a fine, plain solid oak bureau. By climbing up on to this bureau I could see from the window the glories of the sunset. My attic was on a hill in a large and busy town, and the smoke of a thousand chimneys hung like a grey veil between me and the fires in the sky. When the sun had set, and the scarlet and gold, violet and primrose, and all those magic colours that have no names, had faded into the dark, there were other fires for me to see. The flaming forges came out and terrified while they fascinated my childish imagination.
>
> What did it matter to me that I was locked in, and that my father and mother, with my elder sister Kate, were all at the theatre? I had the sunset, the forges, and the oak bureau. (*Memoirs*, 7)

Here and elsewhere, Ellen Terry shapes her memories with a novelist's suggestiveness. Her memoir moves as Proust's novels do, in tune with the vagaries of the teller's memory rather than external chronology. Events gain in intensity what they lack of logical cause and consequence. The mingled fear and gorgeousness of this little awakening to an attic prison will repeat itself over and over: the wealth of seen things, the power and elation of being seen (the remembered little girl of this beginning is vividly "seen" because the reader cares about the actress), all these visions temper imprisonment. It is the gods' irony as it was Ellen Terry's own despair that she lived the last third of her life on the edge of blindness.

She infuses the gorgeous terror of her own genesis with the vividness of a fictional awakening; the little girl she remembers becomes one of those passionately-identified-with protagonists whose imagined lives shaped generations of Victorian readers. But the child Ellen Terry is stronger than they are. Just as her family was, in the early years, still a half-imaginary dream of conquest rather than the actual institutionalized system of roles and repressions that dictated the lives of non-theatrical girls, so her terror is glorified by her power to make what she sees alive. Using that power, she gives herself the intensity, and the cultural centrality, of a character in a novel.

Ellen Terry was never educated into the mainstream of her culture, but almost magically, she lived its imagination: like fictional children of both sexes, she awakens to self-awareness with a thrill of terror. Throughout her life, the actress would continue to absorb, half-consciously, the destinies of fictional characters with whom Victorian readers lived in intimacy. In the 1850s, imprisonment in attics was such a rich image to women that our own paradigm of the Victorian woman artist has been dubbed the madwoman in the attic. She is, of course, Bertha Mason, the operatically mad wife in Charlotte Brontë's *Jane Eyre,* who sets fires in her husband's mansion to relieve her imprisonment in his attic. In this parable, the attic prison is woman's culture; raging fires are her art. In Charlotte's Brontë's last novel, *Villette,* the incendiary madwoman becomes an actress: Vashti, inspired by the French tragedienne Rachel, is a ravaged performer, simultaneously demonic and divine, whose unleashed passions are so dangerous that fire breaks out while she declaims. Ellen Terry was another large woman who like Bertha Mason indulged in secret, seditious laughter, but she learned to soothe audiences' fears of her fire. Her remembered awakening in an attic surrounded by flames recalls Charlotte Brontë's iconography, but the incendiary madwoman, the dangerous diva, live secretly within the delight of an obedient little girl who works hard and tries to please.

Jane Eyre's Bertha Mason has no childhood we see, but Jane herself begins her story as Ellen Terry will do, by describing the terror of an imprisoned child's awakening to self-awareness. In one of the great Victorian evocations of fear, a little girl looks in a mirror: "Alas, yes [they had locked the door]! no jail was ever more secure. Returning, I had to cross before the looking-glass; my fascinated glance involuntarily explored the depth it revealed. All looked colder and darker in that visionary hollow than in reality: and the strange little figure there gazing at me with a white face and arms specking the gloom, and glittering eyes of fear moving where all else was still, had the effect of a real spirit: I thought it like one of the tiny phantoms, half fairy, half imp[.]"

Ellen Terry imagines herself awakening in the Gothic setting Charlotte Brontë imagined, but she redeems herself from the terror of her own reflection. Instead of looking within, she animates things—the sunset, the forges, and the oak bureau—that console as well as terrify. By bestowing on her setting the power of her own "strange little figure," she soothes the people who shunned *Jane Eyre.* For Ellen Terry was not a foundling in an alien family, trained to service and subservience, dissonant and seething with resentment. She was that rarity, a happy child, if not a peaceful one. She was in union with her world and she tingled with life; that world neither enclosed nor oppressed her, but goaded her into performance. Above all, unlike Jane Eyre and the despised women to whom Jane's story had such incendiary appeal, Ellen Terry lived in her enthralling stage selves. Her power to animate the world she saw was given scope on any number of stages. Play was her work. In childhood, and in later years as well, there was little else she wanted.

The stage child rejoiced in her own all-sufficiency, but to adults she was disturbing. So, however, were most children. The nineteenth century longed to solace itself with faith in childhood innocence, but it was possessed by specters of childhood terror: the scared and scary Jane Eyre is extraordinary only in her situation. Long before Freud epitomized the visions of Victorian culture by schematizing normal childhood development as a series of traumas, Wordsworth articulated at the beginning of the nineteenth century a vision of a child who is both frightening and possessed by fear. Wordsworth's "Ode: Intimations of Immortality from Recollections of Early Childhood" is often carelessly remembered as a sentimental benediction to innocence, but in fact it celebrates a generalized child who is eerily other than humanity. Like the child-monsters who people our own popular literary myths—*The Omen,* for example—Wordsworth's infantine "eye among the blind" appears human only because he is a consummate actor:

> Then will he fit his tongue
> To dialogues of business, love, or strife;
> But it will not be long
> Ere this be thrown aside,
> And with new joy and pride
> The little actor cons another part;
> Filling from time to time his "humorous stage"
> With all the Persons, down to palsied Age,
> That Life brings with her in her equipage
> As if his whole vocation
> Were endless imitation.
>
> (ll. 98–108)

Thirteen-year-old Master Betty was the sensation of London when Wordsworth composed these lines; as Hamlet, Macbeth, and other mature heroes, this weirdly gifted boy outdrew all adult competitors. In 1804, the idea that a child's mobile being should contain "all the Persons, down to palsied Age" that adults become in turn was unsettling but credible. Children were mystifying visitants, whose powers maturity could not contain. Like the imprisoned young Jane Eyre, who in the Red Room casts off her human disguise when her preternatural self confronts her in the mirror, Wordsworth's child-as-actor is a troubling messenger from worlds beyond the acceptable.

The enraptured response of audiences to little Kate and Ellen Terry as they pranced through Shakespeare plays, pantomimes, burlesques, and hodgepodge adaptations from French melodrama would not have recognized itself in Words-worth's still, sonorous poetry, but that rapture was generated in part by the agonizing love and titillating terror of children of which Wordsworth was the best-known spokesman. The ostracism of stage children in mid-Victorian soci-ety, their association with vagrants and vagabonds, their immunity from formal education, find one justification in his enticing but also frightening literary myth in which all children are stage children: strangers among us, they act for their lives. The child capering on the margins of society acts out the secrets of children restrained from performance.

Wordsworth's most closely observed children, though, are boys: the "I" of *The Prelude*, his epic of development, is forced into humanity by Nature's "ministry of fear," while the little girls he writes about are more adept at dying mystically than they are at growing up. In the Victorian literary imagination, girls remain the prisoners of their fearful selves, but there is a certain cosmic terror—the terror that grips Dickens's sensitive boys as well as Wordsworth's —from which by and large girls are barred. The girl's claustrophobia widens into the boy's agoraphobia. Ellen Terry, though, knew all varieties of fear, for the stage had not taught her that she was a girl.

As a child, Ellen Terry believed in everything. Her life was untiring work, and her work was delight. The Keans' company rehearsed from morning until long after midnight; after her own scenes were done, she studied Mrs. Kean and all the adult actors until sleep forced itself on her. She was a fiercely single-minded child who played for her life as well as her livelihood; she was sure that if she were only good enough, she could play anything. At the beginning of her career, she knew no boundaries, and so she imbibed the fears of boys as well as girls, as well as the power of both to frighten others. Her growing up was a development out of the boy's fear of his world, and into the girl's fear of herself.

In 1852, the more reliable Kate joined Charles Kean's company. Kate's success opened the door to her younger sister's debut as Mamillius, the witty little prince in *The Winter's Tale* who after two good scenes languishes to death offstage. Charles was the scholarly son of the great, and greatly dissolute, Edmund Kean; his Shakespeare productions were the edifying result of his untamed father's lust for respectability. According to a famous anecdote, Edmund Kean came home to his wife after his first, electrifying Shylock and cried: " 'You shall ride in your own carriage,' and then, catching up his little son, added, 'and Charley shall go to Eton!' " (*Memoirs,* 12). These words may never have been spoken, but Charley did go to Eton. His father's boast became a legend among Victorian actors, for it captured their yearning for assimilation into the polite society within which they were applauded or ignored as savage outsiders.

As an actor, Charles Kean electrified nobody; his Hamlet has been dismissed as "spluttering and adenoidal." As a manager, he was a model Etonian; he mounted his Shakespeare productions with meticulous historical and archeological exactitude. His *Midsummer Night's Dream* (in which Ellen Terry played Puck) was less a dream than a monument to Athenian culture "in its pride and glory." The souvenir script he sold in 1856, Ellen Terry's debut year, boasted that through Shakespeare, Western culture's great past was restored: "The Acropolis, on its rocky eminence, surrounded by marble temples, has been restored, together with the Theatre of Bacchus, wherein multitudes once thronged to listen to the majestic poetry of Aeschylus, Sophocles, and Euripides, and near which stands that memorable hill from which the words of sacred truth were first promulgated to the Athenian citizens by apostolic inspiration."

What time had destroyed, Charles Kean's archeological Shakespeare had the power to resurrect. Shakespeare's classical phantasias manifest no mission to restore a lofty past, but a guilt-stricken, newly mechanized society was learning from Matthew Arnold's Hellenism to yearn for a long-dead nobility. Charles Kean's scholarly restorations of ages of spiritual grandeur were to bring Shakespeare to popular life throughout the century. Edward Godwin would infuse with aesthetic glory Kean's reverence for the past; Henry Irving would swell that reverence into imperial splendor.

Into Charles Kean's Grecian solemnities pranced little Ellen Terry in baggy tights and sausage curls, dragging a go-cart that was a perfect replica of a child's toy on a Greek vase in the British Museum. "It was my duty to drag this little cart about the stage, and on the first night, when Mr. Kean as Leontes told me to 'go play,' I obeyed his instructions with such vigour that I tripped over the handle and came down on my back! A titter ran through the house, and I felt that my career as an actress was ruined forever. Even now I remember how bitterly I wept, and how deeply humiliated I felt" (*Memoirs,* 16).

Ellen Terry's first fall did not affect her good reviews; nor did her subsequent falls. All her mishaps provided alluring counterpoints to her onstage grace, hints of estrangement from the magnificent surroundings of which she seemed so lovely an emanation, dissonances that made her perfect stage world appear to loom suddenly as her enemy. In her debut and throughout her career, her humiliations endeared her further to her adoring cult, though not always to her

Ellen Terry as Mamillius in *The
Winter's Tale. Ellen Terry
Memorial Museum, Smallhythe
Place. Courtesy of the Trustee of the
Ellen Terry Estate.*

colleagues. Admiring her on that first night were Prince Albert and Queen
Victoria; at the end of the century the Queen would graciously share her
apotheosis with the queenly Ellen Terry. Lewis Carroll was there as well. He
was to bar her from Wonderland, but he never exorcized her, writing of her
that night in his diary as "a beautiful little creature who played with remarkable
ease and spirit."

Carroll found her Puck in Kean's stately Athenian *Dream* to be "the most
perfectly graceful little fairy I ever saw," but Ellen Terry remembered only
clumsy catastrophe. One night, before she had fully ascended to beg the audience's pardon at the end of the play, the trapdoor closed on her toe and broke
it. Imprisoned, she finished her speech between moans, a heroic act of stoicism
for which Mrs. Kean doubled her salary. In Ellen Terry's three years at the
Princess' Theatre, Ellen Kean—who had begun her career as the majestic actress
Ellen Tree—loomed large as the frightening but adored mentor the respectable
restraining Sarah never became. Like Ben, she put Ellen Terry through ceaseless
elocutionary lessons. "No one ever had a sharper tongue or a kinder heart than

Mrs. Kean," Ellen Terry wrote in her memoir. "Beginning with her, I have always loved women with a somewhat hard manner! I have never believed in their hardness, and have proved them tender and generous in the extreme" (*Memoirs*, 18).

Like Ben, Ellen Kean disciplined her not to subdue her, but to further her glory. When, in 1858, Ellen Terry played Prince Arthur in *King John*—a role she inherited from Kate, one which brought her her first triumph of emotional intensity rather than adorableness—Mrs. Kean took on in her own person all the disorienting terror of Ellen Terry's stage world. In a key scene, the wicked Hubert threatens to blind the little prince, who pleads for his sight and his life. Inhibited, no doubt, by the perfect Kate's triumph in the same role, Ellen was paralyzed at the first rehearsals: "Mrs. Kean stormed at me, slapped me. I broke down and cried, and then, with all the mortification and grief in my voice, managed to express what Mrs. Kean wanted and what she could not teach me by doing it herself.

" 'That's right, that's right!' she cried excitedly. 'You've got it! Now remember what you did with your voice, reproduce it, remember everything, and do it!'

"When the rehearsal was over, she gave me a vigorous kiss. 'You've done very well,' she said. 'That's what I want. You're a very tired little girl. Now run home to bed' " (*Memoirs*, 23).

Mortification is triumph. Ellen Terry's first three successes all spring from an intensifying alacrity in disorientation and loss of control: fear is rewarded by applause, money, and sheltering love. Mrs. Kean's training through a love-bringing pain has something in common with Wordsworth's poetic development in *The Prelude:* he stumbles into his own powers through Nature's "ministry of fear." Ellen Terry, who played boys, was learning boys' lessons; there was as yet no one to teach her Jane Eyre's terror of herself and her powers.

Mrs. Kean's methods of violence and her goal of glory seem to immunize the child from the taboos inflicted on ordinary middle-class girls in their seclusion. An average girl was exhorted to banish her superfluous energy, not to invoke it, for she was trained only for a marriage that sanctified her utter dependence on her husband. She learned, thus, to stifle herself, to attract through a veneer of placidity, to appear spiritual and domestic, to look as if she might redeem her future home from the contamination of the marketplace by becoming its untutored conscience; she learned to look like a savior and to do in fact very little. An unsubdued spirit was not only wicked but dangerous, for marriage was a good girl's single urgent task. As late as 1892, a respected clergyman wrote without qualification: "Marriage is a woman's testing and highest function, and it is a culpable remissness not to use the means for the end."

Sarah, disenchanted with the stage, longed to return to respectability through her daughters; her ambition was to marry them well, away from the theater. But she prevailed only with the unimaginative Kate. Ellen Terry's life thronged with teachers; she was never educated single-mindedly into the infantilizing dependence of a proper Victorian marriage. Her inability even to imagine a good wife's sedate seclusion would blind her, in the 1890s, to the power of Ibsen's heroines: she could conceive of no restraint strong enough to generate Nora's inspired flight, Hedda's ferocity of destruction. Yet even as a child, Ellen Terry was not free: in the glory she found through apparent humiliation, she learned a woman's lesson in her own way. Mrs. Kean's rewards for losses of control were looking-glass versions of the sense of destiny instilled in respectable women: they too found success in triumphant mortification. The terror within the promised glory irradiated Ellen Terry's early performances.

Charles Kean wanted his productions not only to impress audiences with their grandeur, but to instill reverence for their cultural past: the stately classical Greece that blended so oddly with Shakespeare reinforced the inspirational Hellenism instilled in public schools, whose virtues Matthew Arnold urged on jaded industrialists. Ellen Terry acted among these inspiring images of high culture, but they did not sink into her imagination. She remembered instead the desolate courtyard where unused sets rested. Looking out of the greenroom window of Kean's Princess' Theatre, she absorbed images of a wasteland:

> I can always recollect the view from the greenroom window. It looked out on a great square courtyard, in which the spare scenery, that was not in immediate use, was stacked. For some reason or other this courtyard was a favourite play-ground for a large company of rats. I don't know what the attraction was for them, except that they may have liked nibbling the paint off the canvas. Out they used to troop in swarms, and I, from my perch on the window-seat, would watch and wonder. Once a terrible storm came on, and years after, at the Lyceum, the Brocken Scene in "Faust" brought back the scene to my mind—the thunder and lightning and the creatures crawling on every side, the *greyness* of the whole thing. (*Memoirs,* 22).

The world beyond the snug actors' community of the greenroom is more memorable than the Acropolis: Kean's high-minded realization of Western culture evokes in one of his most accomplished little actresses visions of waste, Gothicism, and the charnel house. In her golden years, Ellen Terry would move through myriad beautifications of Kean's archeological settings, but she never believed in their noble ideology. Like the child's, the woman's performances fed on civilization's hidden backdrops, on the rats, on desolation, on unacknowledged fear.

As she grew older, blustering actors caught her Gothic imagination. She first saw death in all its overdone grotesquerie when a "pompous, grandiloquent" old actor awakened her in the greenroom: "One side of his face was working convulsively, and he was gibbering and mowing the air with his hand. When he saw me, he called out: 'Little Nelly! oh, little Nelly!' I stood transfixed with horror. He was still dressed as Launcelot Gobbo, and this made it all the more terrible. A doctor was sent for, and Mr. Harley was looked after, but he never recovered from his seizure and died a few days afterwards" (*Memoirs*, 21). Life's and death's performances unite in a horrible invasion of the child's sleep: the theatricality of common events appalls her. The dying old actor was the first of many gibbering, gesticulating men who invaded Ellen Terry's imagination, even when they were not dying.

As a disgruntled adolescent, she saw one of her fellow-actors as the same sort of invading monster, but the beloved light comedian E. A. Sothern lacked the excuse of a seizure:

> I was fifteen at this time [she was sixteen], and my sense of humour was as yet ill-developed. I was fond of "larking" and merry enough, but I hated being laughed *at!* [In fact, she loved it, when she originated the joke.] At any rate, I could see no humour in Mr. Sothern's jokes at my expense. He played my lover in "The Little Treasure," and he was always teasing me—pulling my hair, making me forget my part and look like an idiot. . . . Why I should never have liked Sothern, with his wonderful hands and blue eyes, Sothern, whom every one found so fascinating and delightful, I cannot say, and I record it as discreditable to me, not to him. I admired him—I could not help doing that—but I dreaded his jokes, and thought some of them very cruel. (*Memoirs*, 39)

Ellen Terry is growing up; this time, fear is constrained by guilt. Turning her revulsion from Sothern to herself, she softens her indictment further by invoking a beloved Mr. Howe who played her father in the same production as a type of lovable male authority: "We had a scene together in which he used to cry, and I used to cry—oh, it was lovely!" (*Memoirs*, 39). A benign, weeping actor nullifies a bad, encroaching one; an unreliable humorless self appears to render her vivid fear untrustworthy. As she grows up and the terror that had galvanized the child attaches itself to powerful men, she learns to doubt herself. The future would hold more bullying leading men, and still guiltier fears.

All the cautious restraint her mother instilled rose to discredit her anger, but not all actresses were raised so carefully. In 1848, Fanny Kemble had written with unabashed fury of the horror of playing Shakespeare with the great Macready. With her usual verbal fearlessness, she named the beast cloaked within the stately tragedian:

> Macready is not pleasant to act with, as he keeps no specific time for his exits and entrances, comes on while one is in the middle of a soliloquy, and goes off while one is in the middle of a speech to him. He growls and prowls and roams and foams about the stage in every direction, like a tiger in his cage . . . and keeps up a perpetual snarling and grumbling, like the foresaid tiger, so that I never feel quite sure that he has done and that it is my time to speak . . . I quail at the idea of his laying hold on me in those horrible passionate scenes [in *Othello*] for in Macbeth he pinched me black and blue and almost tore the point lace from my head.

Fanny Kemble's uncensored rage led her on a path impossible to Ellen Terry: growing to loathe "my most impotent and unpoetical craft," she left the stage. To escape it, she married Pierce Butler, an American southerner, only to denounce him as a slave owner; she found her voice as a pamphleteering feminist and abolitionist. When, in the late 1840s, poverty forced her back to the stage, she preserved herself against actors' pinches by playing all the parts, both male and female, in her stupendously successful, if faintly scandalous, readings of Shakespeare.

Ellen Terry never transgressed so openly against her script. Her Memoir describes without comment Henry Irving's disdain of Fanny Kemble, "a lady with an extraordinarily flashing eye, a masculine and muscular outside." Fanny Kemble's fiercely angry Hamlet was beneath the great man's notice: Irving-like, he simply "refused to accept Fanny Kemble's view of the gentle, melancholy, and well-bred Prince of Denmark" (*Memoirs*, 136–37). The child Ellen Terry, who flowered as a boy, grew into a woman no one could dismiss as "masculine and muscular." Macready provides her with an excuse to apologize for her childish energy: her Memoir quotes proudly his forgiving benediction when, as a child, she dashed into him on the way to her dressing room: "Never mind! You are a very polite little girl, and you act very earnestly and speak very nicely" (*Memoirs*, 22).

If she chose, Ellen Terry could speak like as forceful a man as Fanny Kemble, but she did try to be polite, because she believed in what she did. She did not want the terror which animated her imagination to fix itself on her productions, her roles, or her leading men, for all these were the necessities of the work that constituted her only enjoyment and the only world she knew. Thus, as she grew older, she cultivated patches of terror in nature and melodrama, studying Juliet in the Stalacite Caverns—"To me the gloomy horror of the place was a perfect godsend" (*Memoirs*, 30)—and screaming her lungs out for Madame de Rhona as a snake slowly strangled her onstage. She loved the applause her screaming won. "Looking back on it now, I know perfectly well why I, a mere child of thirteen [fourteen], was able to give such a realistic display of horror. I had the emotional instinct to start with, no doubt, but if I did it well, it was because I was able to imagine what would be *real* in such a situation. I had never *observed* such horror, but I had previously *realised* it, when, as Arthur, I had imagined the terror of having my eyes put out" (*Memoirs*, 33).

Her compelling stage terror gave a local habitation to the fear that pervaded her offstage life. Imagination—the faculty she lauded as the actor's greatest asset —funneled her terror into roles where screams were appropriate. At the Lyceum she would settle into playing a soothing foil to Henry Irving's incarnate evil and guilt, writing petulantly as an old woman in the margin of a book about herself: "I wish H. I. had not been always so fond of *'horrors'*!" Buried in her role as comforter, Ellen Terry forgot her own fondness for horrors as a child, when she injected her own fears into the willing souls of audiences.

No rage for justice could separate Ellen Terry from the theater: lacking Fanny Kemble's political audacity, she tried to suppress the fear that had animated her as an actress. Eventually, as a star, she attached her superb antennae for danger to the object she knew best: herself. Stage fright afflicts all actors, but it possessed Ellen Terry with intensifying brutality as she grew into lovableness at the Lyceum. Her captivating description of its approach transmutes into high comedy a visitation that tormented her increasingly as her success increased; it came to paralyze her on openings. Ellen Terry gripped by stage fright is a more poignant, and a braver, figure than Fanny Kemble pinched by Macready, for the victim of stage fright is the victim of herself:

> Stage fright is like nothing else in the world. You are standing on the stage apparently perfectly well and in your right mind, when suddenly you feel as if your tongue had been dislocated and was lying powerless in your mouth. Cold shivers begin to creep downwards from the nape of your neck and all up you at the same time, until they seem to meet in the small of your back. About this time you feel as if a centipede, all of whose feet have been carefully iced, has begun to run about in the roots of your hair. The next agreeable situation is the breaking out of a cold sweat all over. Then you are certain that some one has cut the muscles

at the back of your knees. Your mouth begins to open slowly, without giving utterance to a single sound, and your eyes seem inclined to jump out of your head over the footlights. At this point it is as well to get off the stage as quickly as you can, for you are beyond human help. (*Memoirs,* 34)

The child saved herself from the terror of imprisonment by her capacity to animate "the sunset, the forges, and the oak-bureau"; the woman became the prisoner of her rebelling self. The stage fright Ellen Terry describes is a thoroughgoing self-repudiation: neck, back, feet, mouth, knees, eyes, all become agents of involuntary self-affliction.

Like many ordinary women who wanted to be good and to believe in their lives, Ellen Terry turned her terror inward as she grew up, inflicting herself with fears of herself in an environment she insisted was benign. Stage fright is the disease of the actor's trade, but as she describes it, it suggests as well the hysteria that afflicted homebound Victorian women; its assault differs only in circumstance and dimension from the phobias that paralyzed parts of women's bodies. Ellen Terry was not a lady of leisure; her stage fright was a passing visitation, not, like the paralysis of the official hysteric, a way of life; but it too expressed a terror that originated in her situation.

In 1897 the leading lady frozen in fears of herself recalled with intense nostalgia the fears that had given life to the child's art. She wrote to a reporter on *Lloyd's Weekly Newspaper* about her memories of performing terror: "I was often persuaded to act the 4th Act of King John when I was a child <u>privately</u> before friends = & altho' I never lost control of my feelings when I was playing the scene <u>on the stage</u>, I <u>invariably</u> went into strong hysterics when I had to 'show off' in private = It was very bad for my health I'm sure. However, all hysterical fits left me when I was quite grown up at 15 = If this is worth the telling, tell it by all means only please tell it '<u>properly</u>' & <u>not in my words</u> = Tell it <u>of</u> me & not <u>from</u> me = " She adds in a PS: "I've often wondered about the present day children—whether <u>imagination</u> is as rampant in some of them as it was in me?"

Now "quite grown up," Ellen Terry fears only the exposure of her own perspective (her "own words"): she exists "properly" to be seen, not to see. The self-repudiating woman looks back sadly to the compound of childish terror and imagination: such memories of terror invigorate the mature artist who thinks herself quite free of fear. Her adult fears of herself are more deadening than invigorating, as she admits to W. L. Courtney, the translator of the eerie Undine legend she loved: "The first <u>two or three nights</u> of a new play (as far as <u>I</u> am concerned) are horrible <u>dreams</u>—I'm a terror stricken thing, and whilst some mistaken creatures in the 'house' imagine I am either laughing or crying I am in reality with great fervour praying for sudden death!—any open way from my misery of self consciousness." She concludes this wry confession with a PS marked in strong letters **P r i v a t e :** "What news of the little 'Undine'— Why did I miss that when I was young? Young & alive—"

The self-conscious terror of the adult plunges her memory back to an earlier, galvanizing terror she associates with her lost early confidence and with powerful lost roles.

THE ROLES   Ellen Terry often wrote wistfully of the lost intensity of her childhood. So did many Victorians whose adult lives were more prosaic than hers, but while they looked back to games and freedom, she remembered incessant work, interminable rehearsals that often lasted through the night, strenuous touring, and the military emotional discipline of Mrs. Kean. No protective laws regulated child labor in the 1850s: when, later on, the Lyceum shielded her from strain, she missed the days when she was driven. She missed the constant work and its concomitant terror that animated her world, making her forget herself in its spectacle. Above all, she missed her own credibility as a boy.

The theater into which Ellen Terry was born had been shaped by seventeenth-century whimsicalities. The licensing act of 1737 had made official the precedent set the century before, when only two London theaters, Covent Garden and Drury Lane, had been granted Royal Patents. Thus, only these theaters were licensed to perform the "legitimate" or non-musical drama that flourished without restriction in the provinces. London's many "illegitimate" theaters were forced to limit their repertoire to burletta, opera (including lavishly "opera-tized" Shakespeare), and various forms of popular spectacle: melodrama, bur-lesque, pantomime, and extravaganza. In theory, the two enormous patent theaters were immune from "illegitimate" competition, but in practice they found themselves forced to adorn their productions with lavish music and spectacle in order to fill their large houses. Conditioned by the patent act, London theater had trained its audiences to surfeit themselves on song and spectacle. It had no room for the unadorned dialogue of daily life.

To general relief, the royal restrictions on the theater were partially abolished in 1843, four years before Ellen Terry's birth, but their impact on production remained: the theater in which she was a child was a haven of fantasies, swathing itself in extravagance even when it staged such "serious" dramatists as Shakes-peare. Its primary appeal was popular. Artists and aristocrats condescended to support popular tragedians, but the lower and working classes, the uneducated and the poor, made up the faithful audiences who longed to dream. The middle classes stayed scrupulously away from such haunts of fantasy and sensuous appeal.

London managers would shortly court the strenuously virtuous new rich, but in the 1850s they fed a wearier, hungrier audience with spectacles that relied on impossible transformations. In 1849, Planché's extravaganza, *The Island of Jewels,* concluded with a vast, gilded palm tree opening out into a group of fairies supporting a coronet of jewels; in 1850, his *King Charming* featured "a giant pie with four-and-twenty jeweled blackbirds perched on boughs of silver and precious stones." Common things mutated incessantly into forbidden treasures. But Lucia Vestris, the famous transvestite actress and the manager of Planché's spectacles, presented a still more stunning metamorphosis as King Charming. This canny woman turned magical man appeared in "a pale pink satin tunic embroidered with pearls, Turkish trousers, a turban hat, one mass of pearls, and hung with pendent diamonds, surmounted by a spray of bird of paradise feathers." The extravagance of her costume was a mere symbol of the magic mutations within Madame Vestris's power. Her most beloved trick was her manifestation, again and again, of her own audacious male self.

The transvestism that pervaded the British theater in the nineteenth century is difficult for us to comprehend, particularly since transvestism was considered shockingly obscene in nineteenth-century life. Mid-Victorian men allowed no one to doubt that they were just that. The elaborations of dandyism were morbid eruptions from a decadent Regency past, banished from days when men dressed soberly to express the earnest condition of manliness. Women, in contrast, were all ornateness. Encased in tight laces, bulging with crinolines, their womanliness burst from them in each item of their elaborate costume.

Today, it is chic to dress any which way and to frequent unisex hairdressers, but our child actors remind us to keep to our gender. Twentieth-century stage children like Judy Garland, Shirley Temple, Brooke Shields, and Drew Barrymore were relentlessly feminine from the beginning of their careers. The conventions of movies, and later of television, homogenized even children into embodying the most implacably normal ideals of their audiences. "In signing Judy Garland, M-G-M had bought an extraordinary voice attached to a mediocre body and a badly flawed face. In the next seven years, the voice would be trained, the teeth capped, the thick waist held in by corsets, and the body reshaped as well as possible by diet and massage. In greater or lesser measure, the same things happened to everyone the studio put under contract." In the 1980s, stage children are licensed to be wildly seductive as long as they remain acceptably feminine or masculine. Ex-child star Jane Withers deplores their inhuman normalcy: "They're all plastic, stamped out of a mold. They look and dress alike. It's like they're on an assemblyline." In 1984 Iris Burton, a Holly-wood children's agent, confessed to *People* Magazine: "I hate to say it but kids are pieces of meat. . . . My kids are the choice meat." In our present system, of course, boys and girls are different cuts of meat. Our supposedly permissive culture makes of child actors little policemen, offering visions of delectable uniformity, while Victorian stage children incarnated a dangerous mobility.

In the 1850s the theater was for middle-class people an exotic world apart, playing with forbidden and fantastic possibilities. Ellen Terry and her fellow stage children were prized because they were rare. They were not supposed to inflict their culture's strictures on the audience, but to move that audience beyond itself: Master Betty playing Macbeth at thirteen may appear an abused child today, but in his own day, he was a vehicle of wonderful transforming promises. Before it became respectable, the theater dissolved boundaries, and thus, from the beginning of their careers, actors changed genders with alacrity. It is not surprising that in 1919, Ellen Terry relished the young Laurence Olivier when he played Maria in a particularly dashing school production of *Twelfth Night:* "We lost our Sir Toby owing to sudden illness," Olivier remembers, "and the part was played by a churchwarden's daughter called Ethel McGlinchy, a name which, wisely following the trend, she changed to Fabia Drake. . . . This casting was an odd variation of the Elizabethan tradition: boy was playing girl, but girl was also playing boy." The production may not have been Elizabethan, but it was eminently Victorian, and it must have flooded with memories the womanly actress who, in another time and as a matter of course, had begun her career as a boy.

By 1860, when she was thirteen, she was an adept boy, not only in Shakes-peare, but in vaudeville and pantomime as well. According to her Memoir, she had played Mamillius in *The Winter's Tale,* Puck in *A Midsummer Night's Dream,* William Waddilove in *To Parents and Guardians,* Jacob Earwig in *Boots at the Swan,* Karl in *Faust and Marguerite,* Prince Arthur in *King John* (her indisputable triumph), Fleance in *Macbeth,* Genie of the Jewels in *The King of the Castle,* and Tiger Tim in *If the Cap Fits.* Her William Waddilove was a particularly bold self-transformation, for she had appropriated the role from the famous low comedian Robson, proving that, like Master Betty, she could make the roles of adults her own. She could become a man; she could be impudent, turn somersaults, and strut about in top-boots; but even then, she remembered, she was forbidden to be evil. To her great disappointment, her blonde hair got her cast as the good fairy Goldenstar in the Keans' 1857 Christmas pantomime, instead of as the bad fairy Dragonetta she had longed to play.

Dragonetta haunted her, as would other forbidden roles. In her memoir, she forgets that she did take over the bad fairy later on, dwelling only on Goldenstar's tedious loveliness. As a young mother, she snatched retribution by spitting Dragonetta's curse at her quaking children:

> But on this puling brat revenged I'll be!
> My fiery dragon there shall have her boiled for tea!
> (*Memoirs*, 19)

Ironically, the Christmas after Ellen Terry played her reluctant Goldenstar, the twenty-year-old Henry Irving played her forbidden role at the Christmas pantomime in the Edinburgh Theatre Royal. His own transvestite beginnings, which, unlike Ellen Terry, he forgot as soon as he could, forced on him the wicked fairy Venoma in "The Sleeping Beauty in the Wood." She opens the pantomime with a lovely curse:

> For fifty years, my spells and charms defeated,
> On this old gridiron have I been seated,
> Frizzling and grizzling, and in the rack
> With waiting till the fairy power comes back,
> Of which I was maliciously deprived—
> I wonder how I have the spell survived.
> But by the fire that underneath me burns,
> I think time's up, and all my craft returns.
> Then I'll do all the mischief that I can
> To woman, infant, animal, and man.

Irving's sanctioned mischief, forbidden to Ellen Terry even when she was a child, drew her to him later on, but he refused to share it: their partnership locked her into the role of Fairy Goldenstar she had loathed from the beginning, allowing Irving to frizzle and grizzle to his heart's content. Her one chance at onstage mischief at the Lyceum would be her soft and feminine Lady Macbeth, in whose wickedness only a few shrewd people believed.

Fairy Goldenstar was a harbinger of thwarting loveliness in adulthood, but in 1857 she was a mere distraction from livelier parts. When the Keans left the Princess in 1859, Ben organized a provincial tour for Kate and Ellen that allowed her to throw off the good fairy altogether. Ben's *Drawing-Room Entertainment* held all the joy of her childhood. If she was not quite wicked in it, she was encouraged to be as disruptive as she liked.

As father and entrepreneur, Ben cherished what was wildest and most irregu-
lar in his favorite daughter. He saw her as a star, not as a stricken leading lady
over whom audiences loved to weep. In 1837, as a restless young native of
Portsmouth, Ben had pledged himself to the theater when he saw a juvenile
actress named Miss Davenport being, it seemed, all things. She danced a horn-
pipe, made the audience shiver at her Shylock, then dazzled them with a
phantasia of male and female roles in a piece prophetically entitled *The Manager's Daughter.* Jean Davenport was doomed to immortality as the grotesque
Infant Phenomenon in Charles Dickens's *Nicholas Nickleby,* a twirling, gin-
drinking nightmare of stunted archness; but her versatility aroused Ben Terry,
who was less nervously censorious than Dickens, to imagine an ideal stage
daughter. To Ben's lifelong regret, though, only stage children could become
all things. When in her readings, the crusading and controversial Fanny Kemble
played a Shylock as spine-tingling as Miss Davenport's, the angry woman was
initiating a radical challenge to Victorian scripts: only if they fought could
adults keep faith with stage children's versatility. When Ellen Terry grew up
and left her father's management, she grew into loving pressures to renounce
all her selves.

In "Home for the Holidays" and "Distant Relations," Ellen and Kate played
a variety of roles with the fluidity of Miss Davenport, but by then Kate had
become an adored ingenue to whom Ben's cherished Ellen was an ideal comic
foil. She describes with uncommon relish her performance in the first play as
a dissolute boy who worries his prim sister:

> At this point I entered as Harry, but instead of being the innocent little schoolboy
> of Letitia's fond imagination, Harry appears in loud peg-top trousers (peg-top
> trousers were very fashionable in 1860), with a big cigar in his mouth, and his
> hat worn jauntily on one side. His talk is all of racing, betting, and fighting. Letty
> is struck dumb with astonishment at first, but the awful change which two years
> have effected gradually dawns on her. She implores him to turn from his idle,
> foolish ways. Master Harry sinks on his knees by her side, but just as his sister
> is about to rejoice and kiss him, he looks up in her face and bursts into loud
> laughter. (*Memoirs,* 29–30)

The vulgar rake's loud laughter rang joyfully in Ellen Terry's memory up to
her jubilee, though by then it was a torment to her to keep her pious, inconse-
quential lines in her head. The mocking Master Harry was her dearest legacy
from the father she grew beyond.

Ben groomed his golden child in the image of the versatile, cross-dressing

Jean Davenport, giving her a sense of limitlessness she was false to but never lost. "Duchess, you might have been anything," he would tell the young star with some faint remonstrance later on. The love she won at the Lyceum discomfited him: "We must have no more of these Ophelias and Desdemonas. They're second fiddle parts—not the parts for you, Duchess" (quoted in Manvell, 145). If Ben, who came of age in a freer time, urged her beyond Victorian womanhood, Kate urged on her the constraining virtues womanhood had come to demand, as well as all the love and respect it could win.

Throughout their childhood careers, Ellen emulated Kate; she followed Kate into the Keans' company and inherited her Prince Arthur there. As children, the stage sisters were interchangeable to most of their fans; as young women, they smiled together at their stage-door Johnnys and accompanied each other to elegant parties. The bond snapped only when Ellen married George Frederic Watts, who had been prompted to fall in love with Kate. Kate quickly upstaged her by marrying the prosperous silk mercer Arthur Lewis, who shed benevolent respectability on all the Terrys. Moreover, while Ellen had an eerie and esoteric Pre-Raphaelite wedding, Kate's retirement from the stage at the height of her career was honored by a lavish onstage farewell at which everybody wept opulently.

Kate and Ellen Terry in "Home for the Holidays."

Since Kate was always good, Ellen felt free to be bad—or at least, as bad as she was allowed to be. Kate's assumption of the respectable role their mother played left waywardness available for Ellen. After their marriages, Ellen's separation from Watts and elopement with Godwin, and the bucolic births of Edy and Ted, the rift between the sisters widened, but when they acted together as children their public personalities were in some sense one. The boundaries between them were so fluid that a family story about Ellen's first stage appearance, one that predated even her Mamillius, may have been Kate's story and not Ellen's at all. Ben had gotten Ellen—or Kate—cast as the Spirit of the Mustard-Pot in a Glasgow pantomime, but, in Ellen Terry's account, to Ben's mortification, "when they tried to put me into the mustard-pot, I yelled lustily and showed more lung-power than aptitude for the stage." Because the account features a bad child, Ellen claimed it as her own: "It is *my* mustard-pot, and why Kate should want it, I can't think! She hadn't yellow hair, and she couldn't possibly have behaved so badly. I have often heard my parents say significantly that they had no trouble with *Kate!*" (*Memoirs*, 10–11). When they were little, though, they had not chosen their roles with adult exactitude. Theatrical sisters are popularly supposed to hate each other offstage, but the tension between Kate and Ellen Terry was more complex: their early fusion was so intense that as adults, they could separate only by playing utterly distinct parts.

Photograph of Kate Terry seeing Ellen's face in her mirror.

This ingenious photograph of the two young actresses, in which Kate's mirror reflects Ellen's face, is telling about their relationship, for Kate and Ellen indeed became looking-glass versions of each other. No doubt it became a perpetual embarrassment to the matronly Kate to know that people were searching within her placidity to find her Bohemian sister's face. When at fourteen Kate was acclaimed as the youngest and tenderest Cordelia in stage history, she was already embarrassed by the romping tomboy Ellen. When she was the mistress of Moray Lodge, grooming her daughters toward social success, she shunned her "fallen" sister in the best melodramatic manner. Kate could believe in herself as a lady only, it seems, by exorcizing Ellen; she was no doubt mortified when her scapegrace sister suddenly stepped forward in the 1880s as the great lady of the English stage, outdoing Kate's regal airs and in some finely subtle manner parodying Kate's gentility as well. Diabolically, Ellen continued to take over Kate's roles, acting the lady Kate thought she had become.

When they grew up, Kate's rigidity bought Ellen's freedom, allowing her to experiment with everything her sister was not, but Kate was an impossible model when they were children, for everything seemed easy for her. Unlike Ellen, she had no trouble leaving her boy-roles behind to ravish audiences as Juliet and Cordelia: Kate and her audiences always knew she was a woman, while Ellen had to feel her way into that role. In 1863, Dickens lauded to Macready the effortless continuity of Kate Terry's development: "You may remember her making a noise, years ago, doing a boy at an inn, in 'The Lady of Lyons'? She has a tender love-scene in this piece, which is a really beautiful and artistic thing. I saw her do it about three in the morning of the day when the theatre opened, surrounded by shavings and carpenters and (of course) with the inevitable hammer going; and I told Fechter: 'That is the very best piece of womanly tenderness I have ever seen on the stage, and you'll find that no audience can miss it.' It is a comfort to add that it was instantly seized upon, and much talked of."

Dickens is praising a masterpiece of self-fabrication. In life and in his novels, he would find it wildly impossible, almost blasphemous, for a female character to progress from making noise as a boy to making womanly tenderness in a love scene: only the stage sanctioned such transitions. The womanly tenderness itself is fabricated—it is a "thing," a "piece"—and so it can thrust itself aggressively on the public, rather than offering weary men the saving privacy they required in life. Dickens admires Kate Terry as a stunning artifact, at one with the shavings and stage trappings that surround her, but mid-Victorian players made no such delicate distinctions. As they saw themselves, life and performance were one, and Kate's performance of womanliness was faultless. The effortless perfection with which she passed from male to female roles was surpassed only by her ceremonial passage from the stage to apparent real life.

It was a mark of the Terry sisters' distinction that they both recognized the need to wrench themselves out of noisy boys' roles into womanly tenderness, for in the mid-Victorian theater, transvestism was a vigorous possibility for adult actresses as well as children. Society was changing rapidly, but theatrical conventions seemed eternal and inseparable from popular breeches roles. In our own century, even so powerful a star as Greta Garbo had to defy all the moral machinery of Hollywood before she could play the transvestite Queen Christina, but in the supposedly repressed Victorian age, female cross-dressing abounded in the lowbrow but loved melodramas, pantomimes, burlesques, and other musical extravaganzas. These protracted fantasies have been regularly denounced as mindless, but they remained stubbornly beloved by British families until the austerities of the Second World War truncated them out of recognition. Transvestism and transformation were the heart of Victorian pantomime, a favorite family entertainment. It mandated that a girl play the Principal Boy (or juvenile) and a man play the Dame (the female heavy). By the time of Ellen Terry's birth, the female Principal Boy must have seemed as timeless as pantomime itself, but she was in fact a nineteenth-century addition: the Principal Boy was not made a breeches role until 1815. This innovation made the cross-dressed woman a fixture of the Victorian stage, though she was too threatening a figure to survive the entire spectacle: in the obligatory Grand Transformation that preceded the romantic resolution, in which the characters were changed into the commedia dell' arte types that were their source, a male actor moved into the role of Harlequin. In his untransformed escapades, though, the Boy was proudly female.

Less stylized, more intimately known material gained fresh emotional impact when boys were played by women. In the many popular dramatizations of Dickens's *Bleak House,* the enormous cast of characters was scaled down— omitting much material that may have been too stagy even for the stage—so that the pathetic street urchin Jo shuffled to center stage and became the star. Dickens's massive compound of social denunciation and genealogical confusion became a vehicle for a *travesti* actress: a "Jo-mania" swept Victorian audiences, and in his most popular incarnation, Jo was played by a woman. Many actresses built careers on their pathetic Jo's; Jennie Lee, who played him in 1881, drew tears with him as late as 1921, when she was in her eighties. Boundaries vanished in the theater that society, and even fiction, enforced implacably.

Nellie Farren, who played the Principal Boy at the Gaiety for years, was as loved for her burlesque Gulliver in the 1860s and 1870s as Ellen Terry would be in the 1880s and 1890s for her stately Portia. Her beautiful legs were a cult among Victorian painters, her unflagging vitality, a theatrical legend. In a knowing pun, she claimed to Graham Robertson that she took her energy from her boys' roles: as she aged, he remembered, "she walked and moved as buoy-antly—or as she expressed it, 'boyantly'—as of old." Ellen Terry loved the burlesque Nellie, playing her last mad Ophelia at her Drury Lane benefit. She may also have envied the source of Nellie Farren's inexhaustible energy: in her queenly days, Ellen Terry planned a benefit in which serious actors played burlesque, while burlesque actors played legitimate drama. She cast Nellie Farren as Portia, intimating that she coveted for herself one of Nellie's burlesque boys. Irving, predictably, quickly killed his partner's idea for a Grand Transformation, for he never acknowledged the debt of his own high-minded theater to its lower burlesque relations.

Once it achieved respectability, the Victorian theater became as hierarchical as its class system or the evolutionary ideology of its science. The various forms of extravaganza were loved but ranked low on its scale, and so female transves-tism continued to flourish there. Yet, especially in the first half of the century, it remained a possibility for the loftiest artists. Duse would have none of it, but *travesti* roles were Sarah Bernhardt's favorites, and her most dependably success-ful as well. When the mannerisms of her Marguerite Gauthier or her Theodora wore thin, she remained entrancing as the ethereal boy Zanetto in Copée's *Le Passant,* a role in which she, like Nellie Farren, seemed forever to stay young. The Pelléas she played in 1904 to Mrs. Patrick Campbell's Mélisande in Maeter-linck's dreamy love duet seems to have created a rare lyrical interlude in the stormy careers of both actresses.

Of course, Bernhardt was French, and therefore risqué by definition, but even in staid England, eminent actresses played memorable boys. The forbidding Mrs. Kean, who slapped Ellen Terry into acting, had played an equally forbidding Ion in her youth as Ellen Tree. Macready had grumbled predictably when, in 1836, Ellen Tree had rivaled his own heroics in Talfourd's historical tragedy: "I feel, I fancy, rather *dégoûté* with Talfourd's 'delight' at seeing Miss Tree's performance in the part [of Ion]; if it is the author's feeling that it is the nasty sort of epicene animal which a woman so dressed up renders it, I am very loth to appear in it, and to this notion the author seems to lend his opinion" (27 August 1836; Macready *Journal,* 75). Macready might have been *dégoûté,* but Fanny Kemble had been inspired by Ellen Tree, who impressed her as the only Romeo worthy of her own Juliet. Ellen Tree's unforgotten Romeo and Ion in no way compromised the bristling propriety with which she surrounded herself after her marriage to Charles Kean. When Ellen Terry worked with her, her layers of crinolines were a theatrical joke, for in the name of propriety she refused to remove them even when they spoiled the authenticity of her husband's archeological costumes. At the Princess', Ellen Kean bulged with womanly trappings, but her managerial performance shone with the authority her male roles had brought her. Ellen Terry remembered her as "the leading spirit in the theatre," despite her husband's famous name. She was "at the least, a joint ruler, not a queen-consort" (*Memoirs*, 13). Ion had licensed her to command.

Lucia Elizabetta Vestris, the first woman manager in the British theater, set the pattern for managing women to come by gaining fame in breeches roles. The unbounded erotic appeal of her Captain Macheath and Don Giovanni won a rousing series of tributes in the early 1820s:

> Her very air and style could corrupt with a smile—Let a virgin resist if she can;
> Her ambrosial kisses seem heavenly blisses—What a pity she is not a man.

As an actress, she found herself locked into breeches; audiences refused to accept her as a woman. As one critic put it: "The town ran in crowds to see Madame Vestris's legs, though they had been somewhat lukewarm about her singing, and hundreds who 'made mouths at her' while attired in the becoming dress of her own sex, discovered that her proportions were most captivating when set off to advantage by a tight pair of elastic pantaloons" (quoted in Appleton, 22–23).

When she became a manager, though, her male identity brought her the same authority Ellen Kean would have. In 1831, she took over the Olympic, moving eventually to the Lyceum, where thirty years later Ellen Terry would become so womanly a partner to Irving. Even when Madame Vestris's extravagant productions lost money, her symbolic authority was undeniable. Her first curtain speech at the Olympic evoked her male roles with discreet militancy:

> Noble and gentle—matrons—patrons—friends!
> Before you here a venturous woman bends!
> A warrior woman—that in strife embarks,
> The first of all dramatic Joan of Arcs.
> Cheer on the enterprise thus dared by me!
> The first that ever led a company.

The rakish girl becomes the woman warrior without perceptible strain; the titillating trespass of Madame Vestris's Macheath made her a credible leader of actors, and, by implication, of men, in the world beyond the stage. For over a century, militant female producers like Edith Craig would evoke as their guardian spirit her "dramatic Joan of Arc," but Madame Vestris's immediate managerial successors used the authority breeches roles had given them in subtler, more tactful ways. Mrs. Kean rustled her crinolines relentlessly; Marie Bancroft encouraged the muted decorum of everyday society to invade the theater.

Marie Wilton was the consummate burlesque boy, though by the time she presided over Ellen Terry's jubilee, she had become the consummate gracious lady. She made her debut at seventeen, by which age she was visibly not a child. When she married Squire Bancroft, they became, like the Keans, pillars of respectable commercial management. By the end of the century, Sir Squire and Lady Bancroft strutted through London emanating the lordliness that beamed from Edwardian actors. But in her days as Marie Wilton, her "saucy and amusing" Pippo in H. J. Byron's burlesque, *The Maid and the Magpie,* had not merely simulated masculinity: it had seemed to Charles Dickens to steal the thing itself. In 1858, the same year Ellen Terry played her heartrending Prince Arthur, Dickens wrote to John Forster in wonderment:

> There is the strangest thing in it that ever I have seen on the stage. The boy, Pippo, by Miss Wilton. While it is astonishingly impudent (must be, or it couldn't be done at all) it is so stupendously like a boy, and unlike a woman, that it is perfectly free from offense. I never have seen such a thing. Priscilla Horton, as a boy, not to be thought of beside it. She does an imitation of the dancing of the Christy Minstrels—wonderfully clever—which, in the audacity of its thorough-going, is surprising. A thing that you *can not* imagine a woman's doing at all; and yet the manner, the appearance, the levity, impulse, and spirits of it, are so exactly like a boy, that you cannot think of anything like her sex in association with it. . . . I call her the cleverest girl I have ever seen on the stage in my time, and the most singularly original.

Like most men of his country and class, Dickens needed women to be meltingly womanly. He believed with religious intensity in the doctrine of separate spheres: in their temperaments, instincts, and duties, men and women were virtually opposed species. An "unsexed" woman, like his own Miss Murdstone in *David Copperfield,* was an unholy affront in her very existence. Yet the trespass to which he responded savagely as both man and author moved him to awed admiration on the stage. Marie Wilton's audacious Pippo generated a more profound response than Kate Terry's perfect poise: in Pippo, he admires creation, not fabrication. As a fully autonomous character, Pippo obliterates gender, social taboo, and even acting itself in the plenitude of his independent life.

Even Dickens, who feared unwomanliness as a sign of Armageddon, suspended his horror to applaud un-women on the stage. Pippo must have bestowed some of his transforming power on Ellen Terry's Prince Arthur; he lived on during Mrs. Bancroft's metamorphosis into a manager who was loved and respected at once, even when in the 1860s she cannily purged the theater of some of its wilder fantasies. By the time Ellen Terry played Portia at the Bancrofts' Prince of Wales' Theatre in 1875–76, times had changed; both women had shed the magnetism of their boy-roles. By championing T. W. Robertson's gentle domestic comedies, Marie Bancroft had made middle-class realism the dominant theatrical idiom, enforcing in her actors "refinement, delicacy, a skillful ensemble, and the quiet good manners appropriate to the drawing-room settings of the plays." Fresh from her bucolic retreat with Godwin, Ellen Terry must have chafed at this unfamiliar decorousness. There was perceptible strain between the two women during their common attempt to remake themselves according to social and theatrical transitions.

In the end, though, it was Marie Bancroft who made the theater safe for the middle-class families who in the next decade would sanctify Ellen Terry herself. Marie Wilton, the nineteenth-century theater's most audacious boy, became without visible strain its most benevolent hostess, welcoming prudish patriarchal families into her spruce new theatrical home. The Bancrofts' memoir passes easily and with equal pride from Dickens's tribute to the strangeness of Marie Wilton to her husband's humble acceptance of his knighthood: "the honour which the Queen and all of you have done me should make me a better man." The capacious Victorian theater made many sorts of men, and women as well, formed in varieties of strange ways from normally forbidden beginnings.

Lucia Vestris, Ellen Kean, and Marie Bancroft inherited from their breeches roles the managerial power that the larger society reserved for men. With increasing tactful duplicity, they let their male roles initiate them into male positions of dominance. Why, in this theatrical community where make-believe so effortlessly became real, did Ellen Terry abandon her boy-roles, along with their acrobatic freedom and comic perspective, when she reached a troubled puberty? She did so in part because she was a born actress who had no managerial ambitions. She became a managing matriarch later on only because she had to; she was always uncomfortable in the role. Each phase of her life received its cue from the audiences who transmitted the needs of the age to her, and in the 1860s, those needs were changing. So, accordingly, was the body audiences saw.

In Bristol, in 1862, she played one of her last male parts: Cupid in a burlesque *Endymion*. A young actor in the company described her as an "arch, piquant sprite, full of movement and laughter," but an audience newly conscious of female respectability did not laugh back. For the first time, the fifteen-year-old girl who thought she was fourteen felt a hampering embarrassment at being a boy: "She wore a loose short-skirted sort of tunic with a pair of miniature wings, and of course carried the conventional bow and quiver. Some of the more prudish of the Bristol theatre-goers—the same people who had been wont to roar over the vulgar comicalities of Johnny Rouse—were half inclined to be shocked at a scantiness of attire that even [the manager] himself was disposed to think a little daring."

The performance that was said to "disarm the prude" was forced into a new

Ellen Terry in *Endymion. Reproduced by permission of International Museum of Photography at George Eastman House, Rochester, N.Y.*

note, one that fell somewhere between the defiant child and the womanly charmer: "If I had to describe her acting in those days, I should say its chief characteristic was a vivacious sauciness. Her voice already had some of the rich sympathetic quality which has since been one of her most distinctive charms" (quoted in Manvell, 27). In a girl bred to please, but who lived in a mysteriously changing body which she exposed to changing, newly embarrassed audiences, sauciness and sympathy were at war. This Cupid painfully confirmed the confusions of the year before: "At this time I was 'in standing water,' as Malvolio says of Viola when she is dressed as a boy. I was neither child nor woman— a long-legged girl of about thirteen [fourteen], still in short skirts, and feeling that I ought to have long ones" (*Memoirs,* 32).

In 1862, Ellen Terry/Cupid was "in standing water" not only between boy and girl, child and woman, sauciness and sympathy, but between two sorts of theater that created two radically different audiences—one that wanted to be seduced, another that wanted to be soothed. The uncertain and embarrassing Cupid was already preparing her escape: in 1862 she met for the first time both George Frederic Watts and Edward William Godwin. Each in turn would carry her off to his saving palace of art; each would teach her all he knew about the art of being a woman.

Marie Wilton played Pippo in 1858; Ellen Terry played Cupid in 1862; in 1865, the Bancrofts produced Tom Robertson's *Society* at the Prince of Wales'. A theater offering fantasy and exotic escape was converging inexorably with the known, relinquishing its visions of flight from middle-class domesticity to make itself up as a mirror of that domesticity. Changing theatrical conventions ratified social changes, for by the 1860s, the middle class was not merely an audience to court, but a newly consolidated power in England. The beneficiaries of industrialism, of the new game of business, its newly influential men engaged in missions of purification. They could not wash off their fortunes, but they scourged with purity the women who belonged to them: not only must women be outwardly sanitized from "masculine" sexuality, ambition, aggression, and mobility, but no thought of these tarnished privileges should infect the female mind. In the 1860s, the hoops that covered women's legs reached extremes of enormity; and in that decade, middle-class prudery rooted itself in the arts proper families consumed. Any work that "brought a blush to the cheek of the young person" (who was female by definition) was unfit for home consumption. The theater hoped also to be consumed by these vigorous new rich. Accordingly, it placed itself under constraints that intensified in our own century: a self-contained separate community with its own dreams and codes was reshaping itself to the guilts and fears of alien audiences. Accordingly, Ellen Terry's long-legged Cupid aroused a blush that this young person had never known existed.

The middle-class families Marie Bancroft lured into the theater were made especially uncomfortable by female transvestism because it aroused two demons that threatened the family: aspiration and sexuality. Ideally a woman felt neither, but moral guardians were willing to ignore what she felt as long as she acted pure. She declared her acquiescence most conveniently in her clothes. Feelings could be ignored; words could fall unheard; but clothes bore unmistakable meanings. Whalebone corsets that accentuated breasts and waists; giant bell skirts that obliterated legs but ballooned into a parody of infinite hips; these told the world what a woman was. The assumption of male clothes was an immediate appropriation of male prerogatives.

When, at the turn of the century, cross-dressing became a political declaration through which women dramatized new selves and new privileges, male clothing signaled ideological changes. In the lesbian culture that flourished between the two world wars, within which Edith Craig was a vigorous leader, women cast off conventional dress along with images of a false sexuality. But to Victorian men who were ignorant of feminist codes, women who dressed as boys *looked* disturbingly erotic, particularly as burlesque drew closer to the teasing display we know today. Ellen Terry's long legs told her audience about their desires as well as their fears: they aroused men to erotic reverie, women to dreams of expanded selves. In society, women displayed their upper bodies freely, but their legs were tabooed; a woman's legs onstage made women as well as men aware of embarrassing desires for which public life had no provision and no name. In this embarrassment, sexual and social arousal met, for in a segregated society, a woman's leg was a dangerous fact. Legs were shrouded and hidden in yards of costly material because men had them as well, while men lacked the breasts and white shoulders women displayed so freely. Women could display their differences from men, but not those things their bodies had in common. The very existence of female legs was unnerving because it presumed on the male sphere of activity, mobility, and power.

This evocative music hall program from 1900 juxtaposes a forbidden, theatrical woman with a real one. Pose, costume, instrument, averted face, all emphasize the artifice of the boy/girl; the "real" woman in the audience displays her arms and bosom unself-consciously, while she stares in a reverie suggestive of erotic longing at the inaccessible creature who courts her. Like the two halves of the body, the real woman and the actress seem poignantly disjoined in this drawing, as they were in Victorian life.

Tormented by denials, taboos, embarrassments, and a passionate wish to be reassured about its own identity, the new middle-class audience that went cautiously to the theater in the 1860s did not drive female transvestites from the stage—Nellie Farren made her burlesque success in these years—but it infused transvestism with self-consciousness, both sexual and social. As a fraught character type rather than a gay and natural one, the boy/girl appeared repeatedly and was repeatedly, apologetically, explained away. The confused yearning she inspired was nowhere more apparent than in the Shakespearean productions Henry Irving made smashingly successful in the 1870s. Flocking to Shakespeare, the middle class could absorb culture, learn history, escape to richly mounted dream worlds—and, in most of the comedies, see women's legs at the same time.

Middlesex Music Hall Program, 1900. *Reproduced by permission of the Henneke Library of Performing Arts, University of Tulsa.*

Shakespeare's comic heroines Julia (in *Two Gentlemen of Verona*), Portia (in *The Merchant of Venice*), Rosalind (in *As You Like It*), Viola (in *Twelfth Night*), and Imogen (in *Cymbeline*) all turn themselves into men at a key point in their play. Shakespeare's tragic heroines are confined in their roles: Lady Macbeth asks evil spirits to unsex her, but as far as we see, they never oblige. For an interlude at least, the comic heroines write themselves into new roles. Perhaps because they flirted with the forbidden, Portia, Rosalind, and Viola, who act men for a while but gaily relinquish their masquerade at the end of the play, were loved by Victorian audiences who basked in a transvestism displaced into disguise. None of these women is transformed into a male, as Marie Wilton was. Each remains a woman underneath, claiming male prerogatives only in order to educate the fatuous hero she loves. Such plays challenged Victorian audiences just enough to allay their more far-reaching fears.

Today, some feminists relish Shakespeare's freedom from the constraints of gender, choosing to forget that he wrote his plays for an all-male company: a female girl/boy was inconceivable. In the nineteenth century, actresses wooing their audiences more ardently than they did their lovers were careful to stress their character's womanliness, even when the text licensed them to transcend it: disguised heroines sent coy and constant signals of a feminine instinct that made their male costumes mortifying, assuring the audience that no true woman could be a true man. Henry Irving saw that with such inflammatory material, productions of the comedies must tread carefully: "There is nothing in all nature purer than a Rosalind or an Imogen, and, if rightly treated, these characters are all the more striking from their appearance in male attire; but the slightest departure from the most modest taste, the faintest shade of meretricious, not to say indecorous, dressing is fatal" (quoted in Baker, 101). Thus Irving reassured a lecture audience in 1878, but this careful man never staged *As You Like It*, gave his *Twelfth Night* only a brief run, and deferred his production of *Cymbeline* until Ellen Terry had become so indelibly womanly that no one could see in the forty-nine-year-old actress a credible boy.

Irving was politic to avoid these plays. When they were performed, moralistic critics like William Winter generally praised them for what they failed to do:

> Miss [Mary] Anderson reproduced Rosalind, with all the physical beauty that the part implies, and with its soul of tender womanhood, its rich vitality of changing emotion, its starlight of sentiment, its glancing raillery, and its exuberant mirth. Old play-goers can recall Rosalinds of the Dora Jordan order, who invested the

character with a semi-dissolute air of reckless revelry; experienced persons who knew more of the world than it was healthful to know; elderly experts proficient in theatrical mechanism. . . . But Miss Anderson, superbly handsome as Rosalind, indicated that, beneath her pretty swagger, nimble satire, and silver playfulness, Rosalind is as earnest as Juliet,—though different in temperament and mind,— as fond as Viola and as constant as Imogen.

In short, the acceptable Rosalind is a Rosalind without play. Her comedy is palatable only when it is fundamentally earnest. William Winter praises Mary Anderson wholeheartedly only when she assures him, and his readers through him, that she is not a boy. Shakespeare's comedies touched a cultural nerve that wise Victorian managers were careful to soothe immediately.

In this charged new climate, actresses dressing as men were caught between the Scylla of unwomanliness and the Charybdis of sexuality. Designers of Shakespearean plays had to be careful with their costumes, for these "mustn't remind the audience of the displays of leg that were customary in burlesque and pantomime" (Jackson, 24). Two theatrical photographs from the 1890s show extreme representations of female boys, neither of whom claimed kinship with the other.

Ada Rehan's stern, long-tunicked Rosalind is so laden with male accoutrements that there is no trace of a body underneath. This Rosalind lives in a forest of phallic symbols; the dagger, the spear, the actress's own almost disembodied arms, all create a symphony of long lean objects that distract us from Rosalind's shadowy, contorted legs. The actress's assumed masculinity scatters itself in details of costume, while her feminity is so swathed in decorous accoutrements that it is non-existent. Her costume replaces her body, which, overborne and outweighed, challenges no man's primacy.

Ada Rehan's Rosalind has no legs; Ada Clare's Principal Boy is all leg. Above the waist she is a recognizable woman, feathered and corseted, offering a seductive shoulder. The legs that swing suddenly from the woman's torso must, in the context of nineteenth-century conventions, have given Ada Clare some of the forbidden allure of a mermaid or hybrid creature, for legs were unfamiliar attachments to women's bodies. As a boy, Ada Clare not only shows her body, but reminds spectators that all women have bodies. Ada Rehan's boy-role takes her physical life away; Ada Clare's is a physical revelation. Neither is convincingly male: the first is all disguise, the second, all display. Neither can temper the almost self-caricaturing extreme of the other: Ada Rehan's forest of phallic weapons had no place in burlesque, while Ada Clare's sexuality was banished from Victorian Shakespeare. Still, in what they were and were not, the two Adas

Ada Rehan as Shakespeare's Rosalind, 1890s. *Reproduced by permission of the Henneke Library of Performing Arts, University of Tulsa.*

Ada Clare as a pantomime Principal Boy, 1890s. *Reproduced by permission of the Henneke Library of Performing Arts, University of Tulsa.*

together are tributes to an age's pained dream of forbidden things.

Preternaturally sensitive to that age's changing currents, and, like all actresses, obliged to mimic its ideals in order to be loved, Ellen Terry seems to have realized that her life as a stage boy would end with her childhood: the transvestism that stage conventions still permitted, new cultural conventions blushed at. In time, she trusted that a long career of womanliness would purge from her the comic intensity of playing a boy.

In 1901, she wrote huffily to Gordon Craig: " 'A <u>Man's</u> part'? Why should I play a man? Of course <u>not</u>." She did play a pallid Viola and a noble, though not very boyish, Portia, but never again did she transform herself. Yet lost boys haunted her as she brooded on the *As You Like It* Irving refused to stage. Rosalind is not only Shakespeare's most managing heroine, but his closest approximation to the *travesti* parts in which Bernhardt specialized, for the *travesti* transcends all gender, never unmasking to reveal a single true sexual identity. In just such a way does Rosalind tease the audience when she speaks her epilogue. "My way is to conjure you," she declares, and soon, the figure in woman's dress whom we remember as the boy Ganymede vanishes with the delicate reminder that she is not a woman. And so she teased and conjured Ellen Terry as well.

Some radiantly boyish early photographs remain as ghosts of an Ellen Terry who never evolved, or who was afraid to: an elusive presence, remote and detached, hovering between sexual categories. George F. Watts's haunting painting, "Watchman, What of the Night?," evokes this aloof, androgynous icon. Edy's feminist community in the 1920s, which flaunted its rejection of heterosexual pieties by appropriating men's names as well as their clothes, was in part the next generation's tribute to this lost Ellen Terry. Edy never liked to hear her mother insist that she was "more woman than artist," but in one sense it was true: Ellen Terry's election of womanhood forced her to relinquish the

Ellen Terry, probably 1860s. *Billy Rose Theatre Collection, New York Public Library at Lincoln Center, Astor, Lenox and Tilden Foundations.*

Ellen Terry, probably 1860s. *Reproduced by permission of the Harry Ransom Humanities Research Center, University of Texas, Austin.*

earliest and the most intense incarnation of the art that was also herself. She became famous for her considerateness as a useful actress who accommodated herself intuitively to others' demands, but a perverse regret never left her. As late as 1911, the *Tribune* quoted her: Ellen Terry "has been describing 'Peter Grimm' to her friends and saying that she would like to act in such a piece and in such a part as Mr. Warfield's, if only the gender could be changed." A letter she wrote in or around 1907 to an early Peter Pan, Pauline Chase, is etched with angry parody of the self made in the image of others' love. The stout old lady wheedles the *travesti* actress:

> Dearest little Peter—
> I am longing the last century or so to go upon the stage—tell "Mr. Barrie" I want to play "<u>Tink</u>" at Christmas and as I am a slow study I want the <u>part</u> sent to me quickly [Tinker Bell, of course, has no lines] = You know how I <u>must</u> <u>always</u> be <u>waiting upon some</u> body, and as I have <u>not</u> a selfish husband I should like to be "Tink" and watch over dear pretty Peter Polly Pan.

This wittily self-effacing proposition is a last farewell to a relinquished self who laughs at virtue, who is physically and sexually alive, whose alertness to danger transmutes terror into art. That self moves easily between male and female identities, and waits on nobody.

Ellen Terry claimed never to have "had the advantage—I assume that it *is* an advantage!—of a single day's schooling in a *real school*. What I have learned outside my own profession I have learned from my environment. Perhaps it is this which makes me think environment is more important than education in forming character" (*Memoirs,* 44). From her environment of family, Profession, and the audiences that determined all, she absorbed the fearful life that the lessons of ordinary girls filtered out. The environment from which she learned transmitted complex, symbolic, and unspoken cultural messages through the medium of the arts; she learned what to be and not to be through her sensitivity to applause, innuendo, and silenced fears. Her solitary experiments with terror and gender, her intricate partnership with Kate, protected the rest of the family from the complexities that were her school.

In 1861, she and Kate had toured Ben's *Drawing-Room Entertainment* for two years; it was almost time to give up young Harry's peg-top trousers. She writes laconically: "The time had come when my little brothers had to be sent to school, and our earnings came in useful" (*Memoirs,* 31). As a matter of course, unschooled girls financed their brothers' educations: Emily, Anne, and Charlotte

Brontë gave the same unquestioning, self-negating support to the dissolute and untalented Branwell. On Kate and Ellen's earnings, the younger girls too were sent to a genteel boarding school "for the daughters of gentlemen": Kate and Ellen's success had given even Ben, the strolling player, a loftier role. In accordance with the family's new status, Polly (Marion) and Floss (Florence) converted from Nonconformity to the tonier Church of England. Around the time of this conversion, the itinerant gypsy Terrys bought their first house. Like the theater itself, the Terry family was evolving out of gorgeous, shadowy dreams to a concrete, conforming reality. Ellen Terry, who had learned almost preternaturally, without a real school, to sense unspeakable confusions, initiated the next generation into a society that claimed to have no terrors because it was never confused about anything.

SOME AUDIENCES Kate and Ellen Terry's success as stage children living beyond respectable society propelled their family into social solidity: these two dynamic outsiders gave the boys an education it was assumed would lead them into the professions. They offered the younger girls eligible gentility; for the family that had been itinerant and divided, they bought a home. By abandoning her childhood performances for the role of Mrs. Arthur Lewis, Kate as great lady became the center of this newly genteel family life. Ellen was left outside, alone. It was harder for her to give up her stage childhood. As a social outsider, she had lived in a vivid world of her own, absorbing decorum through an eerie instinct that became part of her private drama. As a boy, she rejoiced in her terror, her licensed derision, her acrobatic body that seemed able to be and do all things at once. Frightening people was a trick of her trade. As a nervous middle-class morality gained social authority, her physical agility became increasingly frightening. A hard-won skill turned into an unwomanly joy in prowess, suggesting an athletic as well as a sexual invasion of a man's world. Part of the unease her body generated came from her transvestite roles, but there was also an aura of the unclean attached to the stage child as such.

With the exception of her father, Lewis Carroll was one of the first men to recognize her. When he saw her debut in 1856, he was still the sober Reverend Charles L. Dodgson. He relished the memory of the limber child, who taught him to love stage children and to champion their professional integrity against meddling child labor laws; but he did not meet her until 1864, when she was Mrs. Watts and he, with the publication the next year of *Alice's Adventures in Wonderland,* was about to metamorphose into the immortal Lewis Carroll. In 1864 he was already afraid of an Ellen Terry who was soon to shock him out of knowledge, but if the ravishing Mrs. Watts was too grown-up for Wonderland, the little Mamillius forever fed his imagination of stage children.

The sensuality Carroll relished in little girls terrified him in adults, but he was one of the few Victorian men before Freud who appreciated children's unabashed eroticism. His photographs and his early writings record its manifestations in little girls with greater love and delight than the censorious Freud was capable of. His writings about stage children defined as precisely as he dared the erotic joy in their bodies from which conventionally schooled children were weaned. A letter to *The Theatre* strategically associates intense physicality with that Victorian guardian angel, "health": "According to my experience, the work is well within healthy limits, and the children enjoy it with an intensity difficult to convey by mere words. They like it better than any game ever invented for them. Watch any children you know, in any rank of life, when thrown on their own resources for amusement, and, if they do not speedily extemporise a little drama, all I can say is that they are not normal children, and they had better see a doctor." Socialized children, he claims, are the true creatures of artifice: "I feel sure that, even now, if one hundred children were taken at random from the highly educated classes, and another hundred from the stage, the latter would show a better average for straightness of spine, strength, activity, and the bright, happy look that tells of health. The stage child 'feels its life in every limb'— a locality where the Board school child only feels its lessons."

With the help of Wordsworth, Carroll's deft Wonderland logic arraigns the dislocations of normal life to celebrate the natural vigor of art: only performing children are true to their vibrant child-natures. In a letter to the *St. James Gazette* about Isa Bowman (his stage Alice) and her sisters, he insists still more passionately that the theater blesses its children by filling their bodies with energy: "I think that anyone who could have seen the vigour of *life* in these three children [at Brighton]—the intensity with which they enjoyed everything great or small, which came their way—who could have watched the younger two running races on the pier, or could have heard the fervent exclamation at the end of the afternoon, 'We *have* enjoyed ourselves!'—would have agreed with me that here at least was no excessive 'physical strain' nor any *imminent* danger of 'fatal results'!" For little girls, the stage is a blessed vocation because it sanctions vigorous, implicitly erotic, physical life: "A taste for *acting* is one of the strongest passions of human nature . . . stage children show it almost from infancy . . . they simply rejoiced in their work 'even as a giant to run his course.'"

Blessing his child-models as the theater did, he photographed them in various sorts of costume when he clothed them at all, inventing games and roles through which he led them with the inventive authority of a professional stage manager.

His Alice is the flexible stage child incarnate, a creature of endless surprising mutations, her body changing as her settings do. Her journeys through Wonderland and the Looking-Glass initiate her, as the stage does, into intensities of terror and joy which she expresses through her mobile physicality. Her metamorphic body allows her to be a pageant of different characters to suit the magic creatures that she meets.

Ellen Terry never played Lewis Carroll's games, but she helped inspire them. When they met, she was too old and complex for Wonderland, but onstage she had given him a dream that was in part her own as well, of a paradise of perpetual stage children who lived with passionate intensity, rejoicing in the work that called forth all the life in their bodies. This brave imagination of paradise is all the more poignant because it was incessantly and increasingly troubled by Carroll's sexual torments about his love of child actresses. In "Theatre-Dress," an unpublished article to which he signed his real name, he condemns in the Reverend Dodgson's scrupulously muffled clerical voice all sexual emotions the theater arouses. Since, he argues, sexual thoughts are sinful if they do not lead to marriage, he denounces even "innocent" costume designers who inflame vulnerable spectators: "but . . . we can hardly say that a painter is innocent, so long as he did not *intend* to suggest evil thoughts, even though the actual nature of his picture be, in average cases, to suggest them; . . . he *ought* to have seen the natural and *probable* effects of his work."

On the face of it, this contorted analogy with painting saves Dodgson/Carroll from implication in the "sinful thoughts" the theater implants, though his own loving photographs of his nude child-friends hover painfully in the background of his indictment. In his rage to purify those he loves, he shelters girl dancers in suggestive ballet dress from the costume designer's "evil": "in the girls themselves I think evil motive is far more rare: I think that in *many* cases their only motive is to earn their wages—and that they neither understand, nor even think about, the possible effect." Elsewhere, in Carrollian joy, he celebrated stage children's vigorous physicality, but Dodgson must protect them from knowledge of their bodies' life, a life that he himself, as an ardent member of the audience, can never forget.

The association among stage children, triumphant physicality, and disturbing sexual threat was not the idiosyncrasy of a Victorian clergyman, tormented with love: in France, Edward Degas' series of studies for *The Little Fourteen-Year-Old Dancer* (c. 1878) evoked a similar mixture of wonder and shock. Degas' Little Dancer is best known as a bronze statue in real ballet dress—a yellow bodice and tutu—who stands in fourth position with her arms behind her, gazing pertly at the viewer. Originally though, the young "rat" (as ballet girls were called) was modeled in wax, in which she appeared so repellently realistic that critics were appalled: "the little student was a *type* of horror and bestiality." Degas' nude studies and wax models of young Marie van Goethem declared still more uncompromisingly that his dancer's life burst out in her body: in the nude statue, the little girl stands with her leg thrust forward, her stomach protruding, with a defiant squint that seems to say, "You cannot deny me." For contemporary critics, such a blatantly held body, such a knowing face, could express only the ignominy of the child prostitute. "Why is she so ugly?" one of them asked rhetorically. "Why is her forehead, half-hidden by her bangs, already marked, like her lips, by such a profoundly vicious character? M. Degas is doubtless a moralist: perhaps he knows something about the future of dancers that we do not. He has picked from the hothouse of the theatre a flower, precociously depraved, and he shows it to us, withered before its time" (quoted in Shackelford, 69).

Most museum-goers today find the Little Dancer adorable; few want Degas to be a moralist; but in her day the stage child proclaimed her physical being with a clarity that spoke to many only of prostitution and perdition. In England, it was harder to formulate such disturbances overtly. For Lewis Carroll, who spoke clearly only in disguise, and then in a twisted language of riddles and teases, even a straightforward denunciation was impossible. He is wonderfully, if obliquely, sympathetic in celebrating the incipient sexuality of stage children, but he draws back into the Reverend Dodgson when he confronts his own vulnerable sexuality as a member of the audience. His pained response when he writes in his own name about the unabashed physicality of the theater drives him back to conventional denials: actresses, and good audiences as well, are "innocent" of bodies, a fantasy that soothed still more distinguished Victorians who lusted for the stage. This theatrical lust, this fantasy of innocence, bestowed on Ellen Terry a childhood brimming with knowledge; but in the end, loving audiences yearned to make her a child forever.

When Charles Dickens moralized about the theater in his own influential person, he shook off the wonderment of his private letters as unequivocally as Charles Dodgson discarded Lewis Carroll's elusive and erotic admiration of play. In the stern "Gaslight Fairies" he wrote in his capacity as editor of the family periodical, *Household Words,* no dazzling transformations cloud his reforming zeal. Shorn of its infinite surprise, the theater, like other institutions, exists only to exploit helpless young women: Dickens sneeringly exposes "that strange world where the visible population have so completely settled their so-potent art that when I pay my money at the door I know beforehand everything that can possibly happen to me inside." The children and stunted

adults who seek out wretched lives as pantomime fairies are, like the factory
hands of *Hard Times,* the fodder of uniformity, not vehicles of astonishing and
dangerous metamorphoses. Like Dodgson's dancers, these victims are reassuringly innocent. Dickens's paradigmatic "Miss Fairy," who represents all abused
stage children and child-like adults, is a virtuous twenty-three-year-old, sacrificing herself for her family: she guards her sister and supports her wicked drunken
father, whom she idolizes, with her pathetic earnings as a Fairy. "A hard life
this for Miss Fairy I say, and a dangerous!" Dickens intones. Miss Fairy is too
pure a victim of a dehumanizing system to exude any disturbing vigor of life
or joy in her body's transformations. A humane society would purge the stage
of Miss Fairies, so that they might consecrate sober homes.

The curl-papered Infant Phenomenon in *The Life and Adventures of Nicholas
Nickleby* has little in common with the dynamic Miss Davenport who inflamed
Ben Terry into imagining all his daughter could be: this simpering, kicking,
pirouetting, and shrieking monster is a manic variant of the stunted, browbeaten
Miss Fairy. Frozen by "an unlimited allowance of gin-and-water from infancy"
into a prison of perpetual, and grotesque, stage childhood, the Infant Phenomenon is bereft of vigor and art: the stage destroys her. Dickens's public writing
admits nothing of the intense vitality Lewis Carroll celebrated and Ellen Terry
embodied. Eradicating what he himself loved, Dickens in the role of godlike
author forbids his stage children to undermine the "normal" suppressions and
sacrifices of bourgeois family life.

It is most bearable for the stagestruck Dickens, who yearned to believe in
family happiness as ardently as he believed in Marie Wilton's Pippo, to associate
stage children with child laborers, orphaned paupers, and other mutilated victims. Only once, in *Oliver Twist,* does he hint at the spell they cast over
middle-class life, and here, Fagin's child-thieves are not literal actors, but adepts
in the dangerous art of an underclass. Still, they study the posturing, charismatic
Fagin, who is costumed as a traditional stage Shylock, as intensely as the Terry
sisters would study Mrs. Kean. They not only steal from respectable gentlemen
like Mr. Brownlow: they ape him, robbing him by their parody of the authority
his dignified strut proclaims. Like Peter Pan's lost boys, they laugh at the normal
and teach the reader to laugh with them, exposing the artifice of virtue by their
thieving games. Like stage children, they have exuberance but no innocence; like
stage children, they are at home in the adult world of money and merchandise;
and when, as one of their company, pure little Oliver laughs for the only time
in the novel, his delight in Fagin's mockery exposes the sham of the normal,
family-made children adults choose to approve. Fagin's child-thieves deftly steal
our own innocence, schooling the reader, as child actors did, in the self-
deceptions of normalcy.

Dickens was true to the lure of child actors only when he disguised it as the lure of thieves. Like Lewis Carroll, he wondered privately at the transformations the public man feared in himself and in society, but in *Oliver Twist,* even when he celebrated stage children's energy safely by making it criminal (as Carroll made it a dream), he barred girls from Fagin's troupe. Kate Terry and Marie Wilton—and later, most dangerously, Ellen Ternan, the young actress who became his hidden mistress—enthralled him on the stage, but they are barred from his novels' play. Nancy, the high-minded prostitute, functions in their company much as J. M. Barrie's motherly Wendy will do in his Never-Never-Land: as an emblem of disapproving domestic Truth, who makes the game dissolve.

In her own childhood, Ellen Terry belonged to this shadowy band of boys. Loved and feared, she was seen as beyond the pale of ordinary childhood; her talent evoked yearned-for images of forbidden things. Born into an exile that was familial and intense, she missed that exile all her life. Unlike the lost children in fiction, she never yearned for a home, for she had many of them, but she did yearn in later life to be lost once more.

Taught by Wordsworth, proper Victorians were supposed to yearn for their childhood, but while they looked back to innocence and shelter, Ellen Terry remembered an elasticity of being that had turned into forbidden fruit. She did not fall into knowledge, but out of it. In the 1860s, that decade of shame and social success, she was exiled from the roles into which she had been so carefully schooled, and which had become her identity. The unself-conscious child was suddenly looked at with new, critically frightened eyes. She had to learn herself all over again.

A Marriage in Art

The stage had betrayed her, but the actress fought for a more expansive theater. Years later, in the obsessed love complaint with which he tried to resurrect his mother, Gordon Craig dolefully remembered "a mother-in-art—which is only one remove from a mother-in-law." Ellen Terry learned early to infuse her love with art: in 1864, when she was almost seventeen, she married the forty-six-year-old neurasthenic painter George Frederic Watts and became his wife in art.

She fell in love with his studio; at first she barely noticed the glum man whose heavy heroic paintings gave her glimpses of a mightiness beyond her silly roles. Watts was an artist of unyielding ambition; the epic grandeur he thrust on even his simplest subjects won him reverence, if not love, from critics and patrons throughout his career. When he was an ennobled old man, G. K. Chesterton wrote affectionately: "He is allegorical when he is painting an old alderman." In 1864, he conducted his quest for a wife with similarly allegorical eyes.

Like Ellen Terry, Watts was haunted by a grandeur his life denied. She did not understand that though he painted grand forms, he was not his own man. Even the wonderful studio was not his own, but an annex attached to Little Holland House, the home of his possessive patron, Mrs. Thoby Prinsep. For Mrs. Prinsep and her stylish sisters, owning artists was a finer accomplishment than collecting paintings. The great man, who, Ellen Terry was sure, would teach her to be great as well, was, like her, a prisoner, and a more willing one than she. The man who seemed so powerful did not release her from false roles, but he did inspire her with a vision of marriage that guided the rest of her life.

By all normal standards, the marriage was a disaster; it ended within a year. Yet Ellen Terry remembered it rapturously, broke down when she parted from "Signor" (as his adoring bevy of women dubbed him), and refused all her life to acknowledge the dark episodes in a year that shimmered like a dream. She loved Watts in art; in retrospect, she loved the entire year whose very torments were the first episode in her legend. Her husband had had little to say to her, but he painted her into her future. Her marriage in art gave birth to the woman audiences would love.

During its short life, though, the marriage exuded hints of intrigue, obscenity, even perversity. At their weekly dinner, the editors of *Punch* amused each other by exchanging ribald speculations about it. There was something lip-smacking in the idea of quivering old men—and the frail hypochondriac Watts looked even older than he was—violating beautiful children. And Ellen Terry was still a child to observers, in part because she took her identity from her well-known stage childhood, and childhood was a rich and dangerous condition in the nineteenth century.

By our standards, nineteenth-century culture infantilized many of its adults, but it had a richer concept of childhood than we do: adults were vivid if inchoate presences in its most memorable children. The boundaries between the child and the adult were tantalizingly fluid: adolescence was not isolated as a separate phase of growth until the 1890s. Lovable grown-ups were endearingly childlike, but at the same time children were perceived as startlingly adult: the legal age of sexual consent for girls was twelve until 1875, when it was raised to thirteen. No experts told parents what a ten-year-old boy or a seventeen-year-old girl should be: if they were not tamed, they could be anything. Adult women were consigned to selflessness, but little girls were rich and strange. In fiction, when they do not die young from the disease of an impossible purity, they *are* their adult selves in perfect because unmastered form. Meg, Jo, Beth, and Amy in Alcott's *Little Women,* Maggie Tulliver in George Eliot's *The Mill on the Floss,* Laura and Lizzie in Christina Rossetti's fantastic poem, "Goblin Market," all are fully formed as children: in their passion, their perplexity, their courage, and their covert eroticism, all these girls are little women. They do not grow into adults; instead, their lives narrow dampeningly into maturity. In the Victorian imagination, the little girl is the woman who is not yet suppressed.

We would call the sixteen-year-old Ellen Terry an adolescent, but her contemporaries had no such reassuring name for her. She was a magically beautiful and vigorous child, brimming with disruptive power like the child prostitutes who swarmed through England's cities. But because she had renounced the stage child's license to be many things and to laugh at virtue, her power in those years was fueled by hate of her new self. She had graduated professionally to "useful" ingenue roles at the Haymarket: Hero in *Much Ado About Nothing,* Nerissa in *The Merchant of Venice,* Lady Touchwood in *The Belle's Stratagem,* Julia Melville in *The Rivals,* Mary Meredith and then Georgina in *The American Cousin.* The famous comedian Sothern was laughing at her and pulling her hair; the greenroom was a wasps'-nest of scandal and intrigue. "Playing ill," as she claims she did in those years, was her only revenge against these new constraints. Her suggestive phrase "playing ill" associates her cramped performances with the sudden invalidism into which non-theatrical adolescent girls threw their forbidden vitality.

For the first time, this angry child sensed her alienation from the Ellen Terry others saw. While she was hating everything, the critic Clement Scott—who was to become the Lyceum's official praiser—was thunderstruck by her hair: "When Ellen Terry played Georgina [in *The American Cousin*] she was a young girl of enchanting loveliness. She was the ideal of every pre-Raphaelite painter, and had hair, as De Musset says, *'comme le blé.'* I always sympathized with Dundreary when he, within whispering distance of Ellen Terry's harvest-coloured hair, said: 'It makes a fellow feel awkward when he's talking to the back of a person's head.' "

The power of her sudden beauty to make men feel awkward did not mitigate the awkwardness it inflicted on her. The stage had given her the power to caper around as a boy, to play godly games with others' laughter and tears; now that she was a beauty she had to stand stiffly, swathed in lovely fabrics, while her hair cast a spell for her. The life the theater had given, it had capriciously taken away. She neither knew nor cared that the vitality of other girls her age was being similarly cramped, in theaters more oppressive and less interesting than the Haymarket. The agile Puck who could "put a girdle 'round the earth in forty minutes" was not born for this diminished life, this hampering loveliness. Like most thwarted girls, she embraced a larger life in the form of a man, but no man could duplicate her father's endowment. Ben had made her a mercurial boy/girl who laughed at piety and whose body could carry her anywhere. The men she loved in the 1860s—G. F. Watts, Lewis Carroll, and Edward Godwin —could make her lovely, but they could not restore her childhood powers.

In 1862 she was ready to fall in love. Eighteen sixty-two was the year of her embarrassing Cupid and her transition to ingenue roles, the year she learned to fear herself and hate her life. It was also the year when Kate became "the stage divinity of her day" in the great theatrical manner: she went on as understudy for a Miss Herbert in an adaptation of Sardou's *Nos Intimes* and became the toast of London. In that unstable year, Ellen Terry met Watts and Godwin, the two men she cast as her rescuers. Watts was sexually shrinking, while Godwin was enthusiastically virile, but in the best fairy tale tradition, both promised to grant her transforming beauty. In 1862, she had not met Charles L. Dodgson, nor had Dodgson turned into Lewis Carroll. When they did meet two years later, it was with ardent expectation on both sides, but though Lewis Carroll neither married nor made love to her, he betrayed most cruelly her hopes for adulthood.

For Clement Scott, Ellen Terry breathed romance, but from the first she had few romantic expectations about men. No doubt because she worked with them so closely, and because she had so many brothers to manage, she never saw men as the morally and intellectually superior beings Victorian dogma claimed they were. She was grateful for their kindness; she longed for the glory to which they had access; but when they behaved badly, she was good-humored because unsurprised. Had she been schooled in Victorian pieties, she would have turned cynical, but the vagabond who learned only from experience never knew that men were supposed to be superior. Her youth had been spent playing boys' roles; it had never been fed with fantasies of male perfection.

PARADISE   From the beginning, the men Ellen Terry loved held out romantic promises of transfigured lives. In Bristol, she met Edward Godwin and fell in love with his aesthetic furniture; Godwin's furniture taught her to fall in love with Watts's paintings. The lovely things both men created and lived among associated them in her life from the first. Both promised to make of the self-hating ingenue their loveliest creation. Together, they made her the spirit of her age.

Godwin impressed her first and prepared her to learn. In 1862, Edward Godwin was a promising young architect in Bristol, intoxicated with beautiful forms from the Gothic and Renaissance past. At twenty-seven, he had won a competition to design the Northampton town hall; schooled by Ruskin, he dreamed of an entire country transformed into his imaginative landscape. His ambition to beautify England did not stop with the facades of its buildings: his most lasting vocational passion, interior decoration, led him to study theatrical and costume design. His articles on the beautification of the stage awakened Ellen Terry to rich possibilities in the work that had grown dreary. The strategic bareness of his own Bristol home was a manifesto of his reforming ideals of taste, defying the ugly clutter with which middle-class Victorians defaced their surroundings. When Ellen Terry attended one of his Shakespeare readings with Kate, his home made the scales fall from her eyes:

> This house, with its Persian rugs, beautiful furniture, its organ, which for the first time I learned to love, its sense of design in every detail, was a revelation to me, and the talk of its master and mistress [Godwin's wife died shortly after this meeting] made me *think.* At the theatre I was living in an atmosphere which was developing my powers as an actress and teaching me what work meant, but my mind had begun to grasp dimly and almost unconsciously that I must do something for myself—something that all the education and training I was receiving in my profession could not do for me. I was fourteen years old at Bristol [she was fifteen], but I now felt that I had never really lived at all before. For the first time I began to appreciate beauty, to observe, to feel the splendour of things, to *aspire!* (*Memoirs,* 38)

For the first time, the gypsy child who had moved from lodging to lodging, theater to theater, was gripped by a vision of home. Godwin's house in Portland Square was more theater than haven: it was a showcase for his own controversial aesthetic ideas, not the setting for intimacy that middle-class homes, with their cozy clutter of family pictures and mementos, wanted to be. The theatricality of its strategic bareness entranced Ellen Terry; throughout her life, she tried to see her homes with Godwin's eyes. Until then, the theater had been her home, but this home was more artful than a stage. When the party read *A Midsummer Night's Dream,* theatrical privacy seduced her utterly. In Godwin's house, she no longer needed to woo alien audiences who had the power to make one hate one's body. The art of the theater, the magic of Shakespeare, were part of his transfigured domesticity.

Portland Square prepared Ellen Terry for marriage, for it beautified privacy with the glamor of the public world. Godwin replaced her father as theatrical guide, a new allegiance symbolized in a dress. He had already seen her Puck; now, as she made the transition to Kate's "womanly" role of Titania, she put her new self into his hands: "Mr. Godwin designed my dress, and we made it at his house in Bristol. He showed me how to damp it and 'wring' it while it was wet, tying the material as the Orientals do in their 'tie and dry' process, so that when it was dry and untied, it was all crinkled and clinging. This was the first lovely dress that I ever wore, and I learned a great deal from it" (p. 38).

Learning her world without a real school, Ellen Terry found lessons in her clothes and the men who saw her in them. Her clinging, aesthetic Titania costume was the first token of womanhood she was willing to accept. In pleasantly scandalous fashion, it repudiated the corsets and crinolines that strangled her body, aligning her with advanced, even iconoclastic, movements of taste. Godwin's tie-and-dry dress not only taught her her style: it symbolized new ways of being a woman. Her hopes for her own future may have been too rosy, but Godwin's Titania costume began a love affair between the arts and the stage that transformed the Victorian theater and consumed the lives of Ellen Terry's children.

The "beauty" with which Ellen Terry fell in love was not merely the watchword of a coterie: it was the emblem of a poignant national dream in the 1860s. Middle-class industrialists had consolidated their power; such self-styled prophets as John Ruskin were teaching them to scourge themselves. Ruskin's denunciation of a green land ravaged by machinery, suffocated in poisonous smoke, crawling with desperate laborers whose native sense of beauty had been starved out of them, was devastating in its eloquence, lacerating in its truth. In the gorgeous laments of Ruskin and his acolytes, a mechanized England learned that it had lost its soul. The countryside would never be clean again; beaten-down factory hands would never retrieve their birthright as independent artisans; but his hearers might save their souls by training their eyes. The fervor with which he exorted them to love art, to learn it, to make it if they could, created the only paradise they had not fouled or destroyed: the capacity to see in all its intensity the beauty of the world they had spoiled.

Artists listened to Ruskin even when he bullied them, and so did industrial magnates, relieved when somebody told them how wicked they were. The Pre-Raphaelite Brotherhood, united only by their ambiguous creed of "truth to nature," had become a cult of the 1850s. The art establishment laughed at their finicky botanical accuracy, whose obsessed precision seemed bent on recording every growth of England's soil before factory smoke strangled the land. The Pre-Raphaelites' weird, luminous colors, their obsession with past worlds that in their stylized, ritualistic half-life had no analogues in history or in the nature they claimed to revere, hinted at bizarre revelations. The joke of the Royal Academy looked earnest to industrial patrons: the quasi-feudal dream worlds of the Pre-Raphaelites found loving homes in the factory cities of Manchester, Birmingham, and Leeds, as frightened industrial magnates with Ruskin's denunciations ringing in their ears bought beauty to save themselves.

In the 1860s, "beauty" rang with redemptive promise as an anodyne to an England ravaged with ugliness, brutality, and killing inhibitions. Aesthetes like Godwin, Morris, and Whistler designed homes not meant for families: they were to be temples of beauty, restoring to daily life a spirit of religious apprehension. Whistler's beautiful Peacock Room (1876–77) is impossible to live in. Its walls are arranged as a large canvas. Its chief inhabitant is not a human being at all, but Whistler's own painting, "The Princess from the Land of Porcelain," whose flat, decorated planes find grander reflections in the room built to house it. The Peacock Room aims not to shelter life, but to enlarge it, publicly proclaiming new visions, new forms, new combinations of space, to surprise a world grown dreary. Striking textures, Oriental screens, handmade chairs, were not, to their devotees, the mere stuff of living. In an age thirsty for restoration, they carried messianic promise.

The Terry family didn't mind industrialism. The theater felt itself timeless; small craftsmen were perishable, but no machinery could replace actors. Ben and Sarah didn't ask Godwin to save them, but they did recognize in him a fellow artist and friend of the stage, one, moreover, of a superior class. "The Godwins represented 'society' to the Terrys, and therefore a desirable outlet for their daughters in contrast to their enclosed lives in the theatre" (Manvell, 32). When, in 1864, Ellen Terry married Watts, it flattered her newly respectable family that aristocrats attended soirees in her new home.

Godwin, who moved to London shortly after his wife's death, attended these soirees regularly as well. Forlorn in her splendid new home, Mrs. Watts was glad to reminisce with him about the theater she had left. This bold-looking adventurer unnerved the fussy Watts; Ellen Terry was to cast the two men as implacable rivals and opposites; but they were more like than unlike in their common pursuit of a vanishing Beauty, a vocation that dispossessed them in Utilitarian, grimly respectable England. Ben and Sarah innocently attributed social power to both men; in fact, both were as isolated in a class-bound nation as Ellen Terry was. They drew to them the dreamers, the discontented, and the spiritually hungry of all classes.

Compared to the theater, though, the new Bohemia both inhabited was an open and a magnetic world. It lived for and on artists, offering a soul-saving beauty that the theater, trying humbly to amuse, was still too modest to claim. Godwin's home and his Titania costume had given Ellen Terry a glimpse of this radiating beauty; Little Holland House, the Palace of Art that moved to the worship of G. F. Watts, was the sumptuous realization of Godwin's designs for a lovelier life.

When, in 1862, Ellen Terry accompanied Kate to G. F. Watts's studio, her life began to blur and swell into legend. Watts's portrait of Kate and Ellen gave that legend its first design: Ellen Terry sprang to life on canvas as the vivid, yet movingly crumpled and clinging girl who invited sympathetic tears. In "The

Sisters," Kate is a hazy characterless mass, present only to be leaned on by the compelling Ellen. Offstage, Kate was a star, but in the studio her supremacy faltered and the scene was Ellen's. Painting became her truth. She could not always believe in artists, but her faith in their pictures guided her life. When she organized her past into scrapbooks, she pasted her wedding announcement under a reproduction of "The Sisters."

It may be that the young actresses were sent to Watts's studio not just to be painted, but to be fallen in love with: the aging Signor had headaches and wanted a wife. Kate, as the eldest and the more refined, is said to have been made ready for him; Ellen accompanied her only as chaperone, but then blazed, Cinderella-like, into possession of painter and painting. Intriguers certainly surrounded Watts, though this particular intrigue may never have existed. The truth lies only in the paintings that survive. Whether or not there was a conspiracy, one seemed appropriate to the tale of a radiant child enmeshed in a ghoulish union, a union in which both partners seemed strangely will-less and immobilized.

If there were plotters, one of them was Tom Taylor, the playwright and popularizing critic of art and drama. Ellen Terry wrote lovingly of him as an early teacher: "Most people know that Tom Taylor was one of the leading playwrights of the 'sixties as well as the dramatic critic of *The Times,* editor of *Punch,* and a distinguished Civil Servant, but to us he was more than this. He was an institution! I simply cannot remember when I did not know him. It is the Tom Taylors of the world who give children on the stage their splendid education. We never had any education in the strict sense of the word, yet through the Taylors and others, we *were* educated" (*Memoirs,* 54). Taylor tutored the magnetic young women by squiring them in society, an initiation as enchantingly freeing for them as getting *on* the stage would have been for a society girl. Privately, Ellen Terry remembered Tom Taylor with some rue, writing of him in the margin of her Memoir: "Sweet fellow: Kate should tell of him for he cared for *her* more than he cared for me" (quoted in Manvell, 336).

As critic and playwright, Tom Taylor was in fact Kate's most energetic patron. He ratified her triumph in *Nos Intimes* by writing a panegyric about it in the *Times;* once Kate was launched, he wrote a series of vehicles for her; he composed her speeches of thanks when she was given a benefit or otherwise honored. But he had not written the scene in an artist's studio where a hoyden emerged from behind the shadow of her perfect sister. To observers, Tom Taylor may have played cynical games with the destinies of both Terry sisters, but Ellen knew only the joy of upstaging, for the first time, his preferred Kate. She never heard his risqué jokes at the *Punch* table about the marriage he had inadvertently arranged. To others she may have been pitied as a puppet, but to herself she was at last a star.

Tom Taylor was only a liaison between the outside world and Little Holland House, the home of Sara Prinsep and her good-natured husband Thoby, an administrator of the India Office who would buy whatever artists his wife wanted for her well-known salons. Watts had been under Prinsep government since 1851: as Sara boasted, the melancholy genius "came to stay three days; he stayed thirty years" (quoted in Manvell, 43). She soothed his gloom, nursed his headaches, consecrated her household (as well as her artist son Val) to his genius: Little Holland House owned an artist only to serve him. When Lady Constance Leslie was initiated, through marriage, into the Prinsep salon, she found a wan and bearded angel in the house: "The Signor came out of his studio all spirit and so delicate, and received me very kindly. . . . Signor was the whole object of adoration and care in that house. He seemed to sanctify Little Holland House" (quoted in Manvell, 45).

Did Sara Prinsep import a wife to fortify the languishing creator in her charge? If so, she, like Tom Taylor, would surely have cast sedate Kate as the bride of the great man she shrouded in opulent reverence. The too young, too vibrant Ellen was too big for the role, but she won it. The Prinseps may have prescribed marriage for their ailing artist, but he found his own love. Watts may not have been brave enough to venture beyond his swaddling patrons, but he was still too authentic an artist to choose a protective wife. When he was sixty-eight, he did choose a wife who was ravenous to serve his greatness, but at forty-six he married the woman the artist could imagine.

In Watts's last years, G. K. Chesterton wrote of his heroic (and, by that time, predominantly male) portraits: "Watts has a tendency to resume his characters into his background as if they were half returning to the forces of nature." Like his cloudy portraits, Watts's cloudy life sank into its own background throughout its course: when Ellen Terry knew him he kept threatening to fade into the setting Mrs. Prinsep gave him. In Ellen Terry's mind, though Mrs. Prinsep hadn't arranged the marriage, she possessed it from the beginning. Mrs. Prinsep was a far more irresistible managing angel than Tom Taylor could ever be, but in her frightening way, she taught the child bride as much as her husband did. For one thing, though Mrs. Thoby Prinsep seemed merely a woman who merged herself dutifully in her husband's name and his life, there were in reality seven of her, for she had been born a Pattle.

By 1862, the eldest Pattle sister had died, but this formidable clan, famous for beauty, poised political acumen in drawing rooms, and swift skill at matchmaking, always imagined themselves as seven sisters. Born in Calcutta and married to civil servants there, they descended on English society in the late 1840s. In a decade of continental revolutions and fearful working-class agitation, when Charlotte Brontë's *Jane Eyre* infected even the most pampered young reader with the alluring danger smouldering in her governess, the Pattle sisters exuded the glamor of early imperial rule: together, these aggressively beautiful sisters personified British power. As Lady Troubridge, one of their many descendants, remembered them: "None of the Pattles suffered from the 'inferiority complex', as it would be called now. Everything they did, said and thought, mattered according to them . . . with their superabundant energy, their untempered enthusiasms, their strangle-hold on life, their passionate loves and hates."

The sole gifted sister, Julia Margaret Cameron, was cast predictably in the role of the family non-beauty. In revenge, this fiercely talented woman stole beauty when she photographed it: "I longed to arrest all the beauty that came before me and at length the longing was satisfied," she said baldly of her art. Like Watts's heroic portraits, the giant cloudy forms of her photographs devoured their sitters' essence; like Sara Prinsep's salons, the photographs engorged the human life that flocked around her. Virginia Woolf was another Pattle descendant—Maria Pattle Jackson was Woolf's maternal grandmother, mother of Woolf's own quietly commanding and painfully beautiful mother, Julia Duckworth Stephen—who was enthralled to the end of her days by the power and the horror of her Pattle legacy. *To the Lighthouse* is a prayer to Pattle beauty and Pattle rule; through the eyes of the fastidious artist Lily Briscoe, it immortalizes with some revulsion the Pattle rage to make marriages. Woolf's Mrs. Ramsay is an impeccably dutiful wife, but like her inspiration Julia Stephen, she shines with the hidden imperial legacy of her mother's line.

With more irreverence, Woolf's witty play *Freshwater* immortalizes her great-aunt's rage to photograph, along with her artist-laden home on the Isle of Wight. Here, the observer who watches Julia Cameron's Pattle rapacity with fascinated horror and finally manages to escape is not the contained artist Lily Briscoe, but the ravishingly young Ellen Terry, who is less an artist than a frisky child of nature. Woolf's Ellen Terry wants only to stop posing and run away, but the real girl was less innocent and more interested in her beautiful prison than Woolf imagines.

When Ellen Terry came under Pattle rule, she had known stage kings and queens: now, she was drawing close to the real sources of power in England. The Pattle sisters forged their beauty, poise, and social skill—virtues that were safely "womanly"—into an iron rule allegedly forbidden to good women. When in 1910 the last but one of them died, the *Times* knew just what to say: "The names of those who were subjects in [their] kingdom would almost comprise the history of [their] time. . . . Whatever may be said, beauty does not pass away. The thought of it is a possession from one generation to another." Ellen Terry had grown up among women who learned to rule theatrical companies by becoming men onstage. Mrs. Prinsep and her sisters were alluringly feminine; they never capered and seemed not to know what legs were; they called their power "beauty." The stage child was used to a community that signaled its intentions in large, direct gestures. The devious new language of the Pattle sisters and their acolytes did not sink into her being until after she had been exiled for failing to learn it.

Watts himself found it natural to languish in the strong arms of his powerful patron. Like many great patriarchal artists of the nineteenth century, of whom Tennyson was the most prominent, he exhorted women to stay in their subordinate place and then dreamed of titanic female divinities into whose control he might lay his poor life. Like Tennyson, though, he was in his depressive magnificence a powerful presence; he was also a stubbornly individualistic artist with vast ambitions which he generally expressed in the mighty abstractions of allegory. In 1881, he described one of his paintings with typical loftiness in the catalogue notes for the Grosvenor Gallery:

> Time as the type of stalwart manhood gifted with imperishable youth, holds in his right hand the emblematic scythe, while Oblivion, with bent head and downcast eyes, spreads her cloak and speeds swiftly toward the tomb.

Like his friend Tennyson, Watts appeared to be a helpless giant straining toward oracular messages: if his audiences propped him up and kept still, he would initiate them into a wondrous Beyond. Impressed by the two geniuses at a Prinsep soiree, Ruskin saw in their common, magnetic neurasthenia the marks of painful journeys to unknown worlds: "Tennyson's face is more agitated by the intenseness of sensibility than is almost bearable by the looker on—he seems almost in a state of nervous trembling like a jarred string of a harp. . . . Watts is very ~~pale and~~ thin—long faced—rather bony and skinny in structure of face features—otherwise sensitive in the same manner as Tennyson's, of course in less degree the thinness being evidently caused by suffering both of mind and body; but not involving any permanent harm to health" (quoted in Blunt, 79).

Watts believed in his own strenuous spirituality and in his patrons' divine mission to attend it, not so much with money as with solace. Endlessly seeking rest, he never saw those patrons as enemies or mocked their pretentions as Whistler did. He had spent his youth suffering in darkened rooms amid a jangle of family problems. In 1843, the gifted young man won a national competition to decorate the new Houses of Parliament with an epic painting of Caractacus being led in chains through Rome. His £300 prize money took him to Italy, where he steeped himself in ancient heroic imagery, and to Lady Holland, the wife of the British Minister to the Court of Tuscany and his first female patron.

Like Godwin, Watts made his name by winning a competition in the nineteenth-century rush to beautify England's public buildings; like Godwin too, his dream of national restoration ebbed into the beautification of his private life. He lusted after a lost Italian grandeur, claiming that he should have been born in fifteenth-century Italy. He was crushed when his epic designs for the new Euston Railway Station were rejected. Weighted with dreams of epic might, he could rest only under female control. As an old man, he passed at last from Mrs. Prinsep's care, only to be taken in hand by a new "agent," the wealthy and energetic Mrs. Emilie Barrington, who was avid for artists. He finished his life being adored by Mary Fraser, his second wife, whose every thought enshrined him. When he died, she built more durable shrines, one in the form of a reverential biography from which Ellen Terry is expurgated. The second, the Watts Monument, is an unforgettable mélange of esoteric symbolism and Celtic mysticism; built by villagers schooled in Ruskin's feudal reverence for beauty, it is still an astonishing imposition on the Guildford landscape. Watts was exactly as old as Mary Fraser's father; in 1864, he was exactly Ben Terry's age; but Mary Fraser mothered the ailing genius more credibly than Ellen Terry could ever have done. Intoxicated with her own potential artistry, Ellen Terry did not know what a wife in her society was.

If she understood neither the man nor the role of his attendant women, she understood vividly his palace of art. When she was an aging woman with a future insecure enough to make her fuss about her legend, she wrote self-consciously about this marriage to Shaw: "I'll never forget my first kiss. I made myself such a donkey over it, and always laugh now when I remember. Mr. Watts kissed me in the studio one day, but sweetly and gently, all tenderness and kindness, and then I was what they call 'engaged' to him and all the rest of it, and my people hated it, and I was in Heaven for I knew I was to live with those pictures. 'Always,' I thought, and to sit to that gentle Mr. W. and clean his brushes, and play my idiotic piano to him, and sit with him there in wonderland (the studio)" (quoted in Manvell, 46).

Ellen Terry believed to the core of her being in a wonderland of "those pictures," but her story of "a donkey" does not all ring true. By all accounts, "her people" (or at least Sarah, who was in charge of marrying) were glad to place her in a world of art's royalty and society's titled; Kate's marriage three years later to the Prinseps' neighbor Arthur Lewis brought her, to "her people's" delight, into the same milieu, a suburban Bohemia spiced with talent and dignified by titled guests. Like the theater, it was motley, but unlike the theater, it was gracious. Little Holland House appeared a better world than theirs, but one not different in kind.

Writing to Shaw, who liked to imagine her as a captive, Ellen Terry created a touchingly vulnerable self, but she had never imagined cleaning Watts's brushes, playing the piano to him, and sitting placidly by him: in 1863, she knew nothing of such subordinate, solacing activities. What she imagined, with all the erotic excitement that was in her, was the explosive activity of posing for "those pictures." The collaborative intensity of such an imagined marriage was indeed her Wonderland.

As she goes on to Shaw, she becomes almost a parody of a violated ingenue: "Then I got ill and had to stay at Holland House—and then—he kissed me—*differently*—not much differently but a little, and I told no one for a fortnight, but when I was alone with Mother one day she looked so pretty and sad and kind, I told her—what do you think I told the poor darling? I told her I *must* be married to him *now* because I was going to have a baby!!!! *and she* believed me!! Oh, I tell you I thought I knew everything then, but I was nearly 16 years old then—I was *sure* THAT kiss meant giving me a baby" (quoted in Manvell, 47).

Really? Or is Ellen Terry teasing the shy iconoclast, letting him believe what he likes about the absurdities of a mid-Victorian childhood, while at the same time trying to seduce this middle-aged young man with a vision of herself as a kissing, killingly innocent child? The woman's coy description glosses over the central fact of the girl's marriage in art: she loved Watts's paintings and she loved the self Watts painted. Ellen Terry's narrative makes herself more deliciously, egolessly innocent than she was, while Watts makes himself more pompous: he wrote to Constance Leslie that he had "determined to remove the youngest [Miss Terry] from the temptations and abominations of the stage, give her an education and if she continues to have the affection she now feels for me, marry her" (quoted in Loshak, 476). In reality, Watts and Ellen Terry shared a dream that neither of them could quite admit: that of creating a new theater through an art that was also an act of love. Through this love, this art, their marriage would glorify them both. It was a brave dream, but not an impossible one.

In the 1860s, the intelligentsia was possessed by the vogue of vision. The *Illustrated London News* had been founded in 1842, allowing the public to look at its age directly, without the filtered abstractions of words. By the mid-1860s, there were such fine-art illustrated magazines as *Once A Week* (1859), the *Cornhill* (1860), and *London Society* (1862). By 1860, only the loftiest novels could attract the public without accompanying illustrations: pictures were gaining an authority the written word was losing. Ruskin had made the eye the organ of holiness; the Pre-Raphaelites had insisted that their own paintings were holy. Holman Hunt's solemnly sacred "The Scapegoat" and "The Light of the World" were not decorations, but icons: an outsize version of "The Light of the World" is still enshrined in St. Paul's Cathedral.

Dante Gabriel Rossetti's models looked profane, but he willed them into holiness: his scowling, strapping women, some soothing, others savage, became goddesses he inflicted on a godless culture, redeeming fallen viewers or blasting them with fear. By 1863, Elizabeth Siddall, Rossetti's wife and his most famous goddess, was dead, but to art connoisseurs, her smoky beauty on Rossetti's canvases continued to reveal unprecedented religious ecstasies. If the undistinguished Elizabeth Siddall could transmit such visionary intensity, surely a beautiful actress who also had compelling hair and a prominent jaw would galvanize the art of seeing.

Watts was the Pre-Raphaelites' contemporary, but he kept aloof from the Brotherhood for ominous reasons: "I hadn't their strength," he said (quoted in Blunt, 62). Nevertheless, he gave his young bride a Pre-Raphaelite wedding. Like many Pre-Raphaelite processions, it was mournful and portentous, at least as Ellen Terry described it later on: "The day of my wedding it was very cold. I can always remember what I was wearing on the important occasions of my life. On that day, I wore a brown silk gown which had been designed by Holman Hunt, and a quilted white bonnet with a sprig of orange-blossom, and I was wrapped in a beautiful Indian shawl. I 'went away' in a sealskin jacket with coral buttons, and a little sealskin cap. I cried a great deal, and Mr. Watts said 'Dont cry. It makes your nose swell.' " (*Memoirs*, 42–43).

The cold, the symphony of muted autumnal colors, the dominance of clothes over the strangely somnolent actors, the painter's distaste for emotions that look ugly to him, all endow the wedding with a spectral aura appropriate to a child who began to see in terror. She wore Holman Hunt's brown wedding gown again in Watts's poignant "Choosing," in which radiant youth turns ardently to a dying world. To solemnize the union, Hunt had made Watts's bride into an emblem of the stern universe, abounding in mystic correspondences, that carried the esoteric meanings of his paintings. Like Godwin's crinkled Titania costume, Hunt's Puritan wedding dress gave Ellen Terry a significance the stage could not hold. Years later, when she had learned that it was not always wise to trust artists' significances, she was amused by her son's irreverence toward this same stern Mr. Hunt: "Ted writes me he had a long talk yesterday (at Liverpool) with Holman Hunt who was stuffing <u>Buns</u> at a tremendous pace all the time he was talking." By the time the much-honored old Pre-Raphaelite was stuffing these buns, his sad brown wedding dress had proved no surer a guide to truth than Ellen Terry's other stage clothes.

Witnessing this gloomy tableau vivant, Ben Terry must have felt far from the mercurial little Miss Davenport who had fired his imagination of a stage daughter. Almost sixty years later, in her notes to her mother's memoir, Edith Craig added more portents still: "The lady Constance Leslie, who was present at the wedding, once told me that the contrast between the atrabilious bridegroom, walking slowly and heavily up the aisle, and the radiant child bride dancing up it on winged feet, struck her as painful" (*Memoirs*, 51). No doubt other spectators were pained; like many of Watts's paintings, the wedding sounds intentionally painful; but "the atrabilious bridegroom" and "the radiant child bride" shared a common consecrating ambition others were blind to. Theirs was no ordinary wedding; it was a ceremonial dedication to beauty.

Passion had not brought them together, but for the bride at least, who felt herself nothing if not an artist, it was no less a marriage for that. Watts's ideas were less clear. Initially he had wanted to adopt Ellen Terry; only later did he decide to marry her instead. His indecision was an index of the fluidity with which the Victorian child and the woman became each other. Had he adopted her, most of his contemporaries would have seen him as a tender bachelor like Charles Dodgson or George Eliot's Silas Marner; because he married her, he became, to many, a monster. A widely repeated tale told of an Ellen Terry seen sobbing on a staircase outside Watts's bedroom on her wedding night. Rampant gossip inflicted Watts with impotence (as it still does). Certainly, he was inexperienced and physically lazy; his loving acrobatic bride, with her ardor to learn and her professional pride in her body, was very likely too much for him. Victorians shuddered deliciously at the yoking of innocence to sour experience, but this abortive union was more truly a sad conjunction of two sorts of innocence, of which the groom's was the more devastating and possibly the more devastated as well.

Ellen Terry may or may not have sobbed on a staircase on her wedding night, but she was encompassed by dire expectations: the world suddenly seemed to be waiting for her to suffer. A sobbing bride was a delectable image. The actress who loved making audiences laugh now had to feed her offstage audiences misery. Having, by society's definition, become a woman when she married, she was never allowed to unlearn this tearful role.

The English have always been drawn to May-January marriages in literature.

Chaucer invented the idiom in his *Canterbury Tales:* "The Merchant's Tale" deals with the marriage of a blooming girl named May to a loathsome curmudgeon named January. Her ingenuity in cuckolding him delights both the gods, who help her along, and the sympathetic reader. *Othello* transposes into tragedy the sexual grotesquerie of age marrying youth. In the nineteenth century, May and January inspired further ironic variations. George Eliot's *Middlemarch,* the great English epic of nineteenth-century life, and Bram Stoker's *Dracula,* where a count older than civilization gorges on blooming British brides, both depend for their power on the obscene sensations evoked by the union of nubile girls and desiccated old men. Readers were especially aroused by spectral bridegrooms clawing sweet virginity to their embrace: the Victorian boom in child pornography and child prostitution suggests that official horrors were underground passions.

Middlemarch, George Eliot's epic provincial revision of *Paradise Lost,* has as its central fall the marriage of an ardent girl to a withered old scholar. The marriage evokes no comic Chaucerian comeuppances, but its Gothic aura of enclosure, necrophilia, and dread lends intensity to all the other marriages in the novel. The tantalizing horror of male age violating and devouring—or, in its impotence, wasting—female vitality and youth cut so close to the Victorian nerve because in its essence, it reflected sedate reality. Even when they were young, men had absolute authority over their brides: prescribed roles made every husband, in his powerful remoteness, a father. Even a young man turned old when he played the authoritative role he was assigned: boyish David Copperfield acquires the weight of years when he attempts to educate flighty Dora into wifehood. The obscene thrill transmitted by May and January marriages cast a sudden light on the comfortable norm.

In the nineteenth century, January might oppress May in many ways, but in others, he helped her to subversion, for he had the authority to teach a wife in an age that barred her from formal education. In *Middlemarch,* Dorothea is attracted to Casaubon because he embodies forbidden knowledge: "The really delightful marriage must be that where your husband was a sort of father, and could teach you even Hebrew, if you wished it." Aching for education, Dorothea has the bad luck to marry a sham scholar who is too curdled with self-hate to teach, but the Casaubon she imagines is, in unorthodox ways, a more romantic figure than the handsome young hero. The Ellen Terry who married G. F. Watts in a somber dress had more in common with Dorothea Brooke than she did with the randy young May in Chaucer's "Merchant's Tale," though her contemporaries—and even Virginia Woolf in *Freshwater*—reinvented her salaciously in bouncing Chaucerian postures. Hungry for wonderful knowledge that was kept from her, Ellen Terry fell in love with a great man who seemed to have the key to everything her life lacked. George Eliot's Casaubon will never write his *Key to All Mythologies,* but Watts's oracular paintings were real keys to empowering truths. Unlike the fraudulent Casaubon, moreover, Watts did teach Ellen Terry "French and German and a little Latin"; he also taught her a new self. The marriage that was clothed in emblems of renunciation held promises of a greater glory than the Haymarket could hold.

As a wife, she spent most of her time working in the Wonderland of Watts's studio: "I was happy, because my face was the type which the great artist who had married me loved to paint. I remember sitting to him in armour for hours, and never realising that it was heavy until I fainted!" (*Memoirs,* 42). *Freshwater* finds this horrifying, but a woman of letters like Woolf never tested her physicality with the exhilarating relentlessness of an actress: for a girl whose body was so perfectly supple, fainting in armor had the same excitement as swooning with passion. Discord came, not in the studio, but in the relentless chic of Little Holland House, which had at first seemed so enticing: "Little Holland House, where Mr. Watts lived, seemed to me a paradise, where only beautiful things were allowed to come. All the women were graceful, and all the men were gifted. A trio of sisters—Mrs. Prinsep (mother of the painter), Lady Somers, and Mrs. Cameron, a pioneer in artistic photography—were known as Beauty, Dash, and Talent. There were two more beautiful sisters, Mrs. Jackson [Virginia Woolf's grandmother] and Mrs. Dalrymple. Gladstone, Disraeli and Browning were among Mr. Watts's visitors. At Freshwater, where I went on a visit soon after my marriage, I first saw Tennyson" (*Memoirs,* 43).

This apparent paradise, crowning beauty, fame, and talent, engineered Ellen Terry's fall. Mrs. Prinsep and her sisters felt the Signor had lowered himself by marrying an actress: the theater did not belong among the arts Mrs. Prinsep nourished so tenderly. For the first time, others forced Ellen Terry to see herself, not as an infinite and boundless creature, but as a lower-class girl of a particularly unsavory sort. Little Holland House moved to fine and subtle class distinctions. It appeared to nestle in the depths of the country, but in fact it was only two miles from Hyde Park; in the same way, its facade of bucolic Bohemianism was threaded with unspoken knowledge and unformulated codes. Edward Cheyney remembered Mrs. Prinsep's Sunday afternoons as a "hornets' nest" (quoted in Blunt, 84). George Du Maurier was still more outspoken about its snobberies and polite lusts. He found its atmosphere "brittle, superficial and immoral": "the nobilitee, the gentree, the literature, politics, and art of the counthree, by jasus! It's a nest of proeraphaelites, where Hunt, Millais, Rossetti, Watts, Leighton etc., Tennyson, the Brownings and Thackeray etc. and tutti quanti receive dinners and incense, and cups of tea handed to them by those women almost kneeling" (quoted in Ormond, 103).

Du Maurier was always sickened by the worship of art. He was touched by Ellen Terry's cavalier exclusion in the midst of Pattle preciosity. To him she was uncontaminated, like his own grand and vulnerable Trilby. In truth, though, Ellen Terry wanted to worship with the rest, but nobody had told her whether she was supposed to bestow incense or receive it.

She was lost in a world where no clear directions were given. It had been assumed that she would leave the stage upon marriage, as did all actresses who married civilians. She had been thrilled to retire, for Watts's studio, she was sure, would lead her to glories she had never known before. Now Mrs. Prinsep, the first woman Ellen Terry had known who did not work, was scourging her with a variety of unfamiliar roles.

Since she spent all day as she had anticipated she would, working in the studio with Mr. Watts, she was not one of the conventional, incense-bearing wives who beautified Little Holland House. Out of the studio, not knowing who to be, she fell back on the stage child who had won so much applause. Like her departed audiences, Mr. Watts loved her body, at least while he was painting it. Mr. Godwin had loved it too: he and his friends were entranced when she leapt down a staircase in one bound. Accordingly, she flung herself about, appearing to the sophisticated guests to be "quite a schoolgirl, and a decided tomboy." One day when she was sullen and bored she casually undid her long hair and flaunted it at the company, to Mrs. Prinsep's horror: the body that had been the life of her art was in Little Holland House an exposure of shamefully low origins. Defiantly, in another outburst of self-display, she is said to have bounded into a dinner party in her controversial Cupid costume. Other versions have her bounding in in tights, or in nothing at all, but since Cupid had taught her the power of her legs to cause consternation, his tunic was more intimately significant to her than her own skin.

The young bride's hijinks sound like those of Dickens's Infant Phenomenon, who gestures and twirls compulsively because the stage child's is the only role she knows. But Ellen Terry was also a woman and an angry one, breaking through the game of innuendo and taboo to flaunt forbidden parts of her body at this select company. She chose her weapons shrewdly, for as Du Maurier remembered it, Little Holland House was anything but modest: "all the women were décolletées in a beastly fashion—damn the aristocratic standard of fashion; nothing will ever make me think it right or decent that I should see a lady's armpit flesh folds when I am speaking to her. . . . Instead of dressing for dinner there, they undress" (quoted in Ormond, 104).

Bosoms and legs, even armpit flesh folds, were acceptably womanly. Legs frightened people, as Ellen Terry knew well, and masses of hair did too. Since she was a married woman, the Pre-Raphaelite "harvest-coloured hair" that enthralled Clement Scott had to be pinned up and hidden. Even on the stage, it had disturbed people. The year before her marriage, the *London Times* had tried, with some nervous reservations, to praise her innocence:

> There is nothing conventional or affected in her performance of the *Little Treasure*, but the young girl of buoyant spirits, kindly heart, impulsive emotions, and somewhat remiss education is presented in her natural shape, free and uncontrolled as her long back-hair. Particularly excellent is her assumption of that perfect confidence which arises from complete innocence of evil. Well may poor Captain Maydenblush be stricken with terror when she makes him an offer of her hand, with an audacity that the most impudent citizen of the *demi-monde* might strive in vain to acquire. (25 March 1863)

"Free and uncontrolled as her long back-hair," Ellen Terry's innocence carried a dangerously knowing audacity. It says much about her appeal in the 1860s that in the iconography of mid-Victorian stage convention, unconstrained back-hair declared not only girlish purity, but female insanity as well.

Outside the theater as well, unleashed hair symbolized dangerous powers of a peculiarly female sort. In the myths fiction and Pre-Raphaelite painting crystallized, woman "achieved transcendent vitality partly through her magic hair, which was invested with independent energy: enchanting—and enchanted—her gleaming tresses both expressed her magic power and were its source." When the Pattle sisters exposed themselves to their guests, they offered a beauty whose power was hidden; Ellen Terry's hair and her legs spoke blatantly of all the frightening things she could be. After her performances in the Pattle sisters' domain, she never declared herself so openly again.

Sophisticated Pattle society was as rigidly divided into male and female spheres as was the non-Bohemian world: Woolf's Mr. and Mrs. Ramsay in *To the Lighthouse* are grandly grotesque heirs of this sexual division. In Little Holland House and Freshwater, all men were by definition great men; women were there to serve these men and to own them. Even Julia Margaret Cameron was licensed to be Talent only in the service of Beauty: her heroic photographs of Tennyson, Carlyle, Watts, and other geniuses laid beauty at the feet of heroes as reverently as other Pattles laid their bosoms, their chic homes, and their scintillating talk. In such company, as in the hated theater, Ellen Terry was once again neither male nor female. Floating somewhere between the sexes, effectively a lodger in the impeccably-displayed Prinsep household, she managed to shock this would-be daring society by replaying her boy-roles, but out of the studio she fit nowhere. Playing a child, though, she was at least exempt from the obligation to strew incense at great men's feet.

Her memoir recalls Gladstone and Disraeli only in fleeting images: "I remember thinking that Mr. Gladstone was like a volcano at rest; his face was pale and calm, but the calm was the calm of the grey crust of Etna. You looked into the piercing dark eyes and caught a glimpse of the red-hot crater beneath the crust" (*Memoirs*, 43). Ellen Terry's own metaphor upstages the great man. As for Disraeli: "The picture melts into one of Henry Irving as Shylock. Both noble Jews" (*Memoirs*, 44). Later, when she and Irving reigned at the Lyceum, they entertained a properly awed Gladstone and Disraeli backstage and in the Beefsteak Room, but the young bride had no intention of being *their* awed audience when they were Mrs. Prinsep's godlike acquisitions. She liked to walk in the fields with Tennyson, who was "so wonderfully simple," but when he began to intone she ran off to play Indians and Knights of the Round Table with his young sons.

Instinctively, she shunned hero worship, the religion of her age. Her memoir never extenuates her self-preserving irreverence. One of its most musical and moving sentences longs for those impossible days "when I was Nelly Watts, and heedless of the greatness of great men. 'To meet an angel and not be afraid is to be impudent.' I don't like to confess to it, but I think I must have been, according to this definition, *very* impudent!" (*Memoirs*, 45).

When she grew up she had to heed the greatness of great men. Irving's Napoleonic attitudes, her own son Teddy's self-adoring demands, became the peremptory facts of her life. But Nelly Watts refused to prostrate herself, and this impudence—not sexual purity, not boredom with art—was her true, blessed innocence. Socially and psychically, she paid the price of her refusal. Her stage child played so badly in polite society that Watts did not escort her to the dinners that fed his shaggy grandeur. Du Maurier raged against this ungallantry, insisting when he married that his own placid, boring wife accompany him everywhere, but it never occurred to Nelly that she should be a cherished satellite.

She faced her new setting with proud bravado, knowing that she and her husband always understood each other in the studio, but her married insecurity announced itself when she wrote. Throughout her life, her extraordinarily mobile and individual handwriting announced her feelings more clearly than her words did. In her years of stardom, the 1880s and 1890s, her letters' distinctive symbols and flourishes, their rich, round characters, are themselves works of art; as she ages, her uncontrolled writing is a cry. To those who come to it from the later letters, Nelly Watts's handwriting is unrecognizable as Ellen Terry's. The thin, stiff characters have none of the dash and expansiveness that seem the birthright of the star (fig. 2.1). The writing, like the writer, is painfully squeezed into itself. Mighty opposites—male and female, artist and wife, child and woman, worshipped and worshipper—all are constricting the bride's identity as they do her letter, cramping her life into a tenuous and desperate activity.

Like other Victorian girls, though more exotically than they, she had married to learn the art of growing up, and she did learn it. Away from the studio, her husband was a hesitant teacher, but his Muses the Pattle sisters composed an Academy in themselves. Sara Prinsep was humorless and jealous, a disheartening contrast to the loved and stentorian Mrs. Kean in the halcyon days at the Princess', but Julia Cameron was undeniably a fellow artist, if a mystifying and indirect one. She was too inarticulate to spell out the codes of her devious world, but her photographs taught vivid lessons. Like Ruskin, the seer of the arts, and like the pictorial theater itself, Julia Cameron instructed the eye. The Keans' archeological Shakespeare productions had taught audiences to imbibe the grandeur of their cultural legacy: they restored in stage pictures Western civilization's ennobling past. In the same way, through pictures, Julia Cameron made Ellen Terry absorb the things she was allowed to be.

In two well-known photographs, Ellen Terry is enshrined, first as mystic child, and then as lovable, because betrayed, woman. When she modeled for Julia Cameron, Ellen Terry beautified the roles life demanded that she play: the eye of the camera was a grand epitome of the watching audiences who from the beginning had given her her being. Off the stage, the passage from girl to woman was demanding incomprehensible humiliations, but when Ellen Terry illustrated Julia Cameron's visions, she understood her role at last.

When, for oracular reasons of her own, Julia Cameron told Nelly Terry she was "the South West Wind From Life," she bestowed on her the amorphous endowment of the Victorian child. The seventeen-year-old-girl resumes her childhood self as a repository of mysterious suggestiveness, sexual and mystical at once. Peering up suggestively from under the weight of her powers, the knowing child lures the viewer into unfamiliar realms of paganism, of fantasy, of dream. Pre-Raphaelite seductiveness suffuses the photograph: like Rossetti's dream worlds, presided over by mystic women, "Nelly Terry" initiates the viewer into strange dangers and pleasures. In Lewis Carroll's photographs of his equally knowing child-friends, their strange seductiveness is housed in familiar domestic settings; "Nelly Terry" is given a magic world of her own. In the 1850s, the Victorian theater was the haunt of similar magic transformations. Julia

Letter from Ellen Terry Watts, 16 October 1866. *Reproduced by permission of the Rare Book Room, Van Pelt Library, University of Pennsylvania.*

Cameron translates the world in which her subject grew up into an attenuated realm of myth, the haunt of the rich and strange. Within its boundaries, and within the magic country of her own stage childhood, Ellen Terry is fraught with powers that are forbidden, mysterious, exotic. When the camera sees her as a woman, though, it forces her into limitation.

When Ellen Terry becomes an adult, her eerie and suggestive promise is bounded by walls and broken into pathos. She was still seventeen when she posed for this well-known photograph: the flexible actress embodies in turn two stages of female life that Julia Cameron sees as rigidly distinct. As the South West

Julia Margaret Cameron, "Ellen Terry." *Reproduced by permission of the Metropolitan Museum of Art, The Alfred Stieglitz Collection, 1941.*

Julia Margaret Cameron, "The South West Wind from Life." *Reproduced by permission of the Metropolitan Museum of Art, Harris Brisbane Dick Fund, 1941.*

Wind, she was an infinite child; here, she is a constrained adult in contemporary (if Bohemian) nightdress, with her wedding ring prominent on the large clenched hand that knots her necklace in a self-strangling gesture. The wall provides solace while closing her into a domesticity as mundane as it can be: the photograph was taken in the Tennysons' bathroom on the Isle of Wight. This wall holds all the decorative implacability of the world that shuts her in once she is a woman. Like Dante Gabriel Rossetti's fallen woman in "Found," who crouches in a similar inhibited posture against a wall, the betrayed young woman finds comfort only in a confining object. Closed in by walls, her pose makes her close in on herself as well: she has shed the expansive child who eyes the unknown knowingly. Julia Cameron both captures and creates the Ellen Terry who supposedly wept on a staircase on her wedding night, using her to dramatize the narrowing betrayal of power, the strangling of magic and scope, that come when a girl grows up.

Ellen Terry illustrates with alacrity a parable of Victorian womanhood that literature of the 1860s also inculcates. George Eliot's Maggie Tulliver is a similar grand and mystical child, associated with mysterious countries and powers, who can grow up only to a world too small to hold her: when she drowns heroically at the end of the novel, she finds her one, remaining opportunity to be grand. In 1865, when Julia Cameron photographed Ellen Terry as child and woman, *Alice's Adventures in Wonderland* appeared. Like the Nelly Terry who is also "The South West Wind from Life," Carroll's Alice has access to magic realms that are also, magically, her own suggestively erotic, infinitely changing body. The loss of Wonderland is the loss of her magical childhood endowment: a little girl is infinite and an infinite lure, while a woman is confined because betrayed by sexuality and marriage, houses and walls. This bleak and fatalistic parable appealed to feminists of the 1860s, who were trying to enlarge women's lives by agitating for access to education and the professions, but it was not feminist in itself: Julia Cameron's photographs, *The Mill on the Floss,* and even Carroll's *Alice* books all suggest that the closing-in of a woman's life is part of the grim cycle of nature, not an inequity a wiser society can correct. When Ellen Terry embodied this fatalistic vision for Julia Margaret Cameron, she had experienced enough narrowing and betrayal to fall into the right self-strangling pose, but she knew that self-strangulation was not all she could do. For a grander, more elastic vision of herself, she ran joyfully to her husband's studio.

As an artist, Julia Cameron had the irresistible éclat of the peremptory Queens in the *Alice* books: she was a whirlwind of energy who forced her subjects into photographs, the Pattles' licensed madwoman. "To me, I frankly own," Lady Troubridge recalled, "she appeared as a terrifying elderly woman, short and squat, with none of the Pattle grace and beauty about her" (quoted in Boyd, 21). Watts, on the other hand, did not have to forfeit Beauty in order to be Talent: for the women who took care of him, threw incense at his feet, and promoted his genius, his art and his erotic appeal were inseparable. In the studio, Ellen Terry never found him grim; unlike Julia Cameron, he brought constantly renewing joy when he painted her. Like her though, if less overtly, he taught through art the sad and stern lessons a Victorian husband was supposed to teach his wife.

Believers in the cautionary tale of May and January condemn Watts out of hand for inadequacy as a husband: his presumed impotence is evoked to explain all manner of loss and unhappiness on Ellen Terry's part. According to the definitions of his culture, though, Watts was a true husband in his own way. He need not have been technically impotent to be sexually frightened of Ellen Terry: so were any number of biologically adequate men in every phase of her powerful life. In the 1860s, a husband was not expected to satisfy his wife, but to teach and to train her. He delegated some of this training to Mrs. Prinsep, to whom he had delegated the minutiae of his own life as well, but in the realm of art he was an authentic and even a loving husband. Not only do his portraits of Ellen Terry have "an air of enchantment" (Loshak, 484), of warm, flexible sensuality unique in the grand generalizations of his canon, but, with all the tenderness of which the artist was capable, they train the model into the poses of womanhood. Through his paintings, Watts played the Victorian husband's role: he created a wife who shaped herself into submission, and he did so with a sympathy he had never known and would never know again. Even later stern detractors find these portraits impossible to condemn. Many writers agree with Edith Craig and Christopher St. John that "his portraits of [Ellen Terry] are among his best works, the only ones which have stood the test of time" (*Memoirs,* 52). Even W. Graham Robertson, her later artist-adorer who yearned to possess an Ellen Terry of his own invention, wrote: "It is curious that Watts, who apparently understood her so little, should have painted by far the truest portraits of E. T." With characteristic disembodied lust, he also wrote of Watts: "To marry Ellen Terry was an absurd thing for any man to do. He might as well marry the dawn or the twilight or any other evanescent and elusive loveliness of nature." But Watts had married a real girl. With all the new, ephemeral tenderness she aroused in him, he created the woman her later lovers would distill into the dawn.

In Watts's paintings as in Cameron's sad, womanly photograph, Ellen Terry lives within enclosures. Within these, however, she is mobile and brilliantly alive as she seems to struggle for more space than the canvas allows. Cameron's

Ellen Terry crumples against a wall, a good woman because a broken one; Watts's contains all the actress's fearful imagination as it fights the encroaching confinement of his compositions. The shrinking space that Cameron makes an inexorable accompaniment to a woman's growth becomes in Watts's vision a nightmare visitation laden with tragic associations.

All Watts's paintings concentrate on Ellen Terry's bust and her face, suggesting mobility but banning motion; like Cameron's photographs, they cut off her legs. In the first version of *Freshwater,* Woolf mocks this persistent leglessness as a fossil from a funny Victorian past: "Legs, thank God, can be covered," Julia Cameron flutters. But Woolf's funny past was Ellen Terry's threatening present, and it was a great boon to learn through modeling how to obliterate, without appearing immobilized, the legs that had embarrassed her onstage and off. Watts taught her to adjust her vitality to Victorian taboos: subduing her acrobatics, she learned to move expressively from the waist up, to generate by turning her back, her head, her wrist, a new sort of vitality, one that was beleaguered and constrained. Watts's paintings cramped her mobility but left intact her fight for mobility. Denying her legs but capturing her yearning for motion, he told his wife without words that he understood her condition in Little Holland House and in the larger Victorian house that was a woman's haven, her prison, and her school.

The haunting "Watchman, What of the Night?"—the painting that made her faint when she posed for it in armor—frames her against a sky that seems to shut in space. This is the only painting we have of Ellen Terry as a boy/girl, and here, her armor and the self-enclosed inwardness of her pose weigh her down, and she has lost her legs. The painting has all the poignance of this lost mobility: the watchman by definition is not a figure of action, but of weighted-down, portentous suspension. The title's question implies an answer; the answer Ellen Terry is about to give seems ominous. Flecks of gold run through the hair, the moon's reflection on the armor, but these seem about to vanish in the swallowing gloom. Watts's vision of quiet doom, of light and vitality engulfed, is reinforced by his title: he originally called the painting "Joan of Arc," under which title Ellen Terry's feminist disciples resurrected it. "Joan of Arc" encourages the viewer to imagine a narrative about beginnings: the night vigil of the boy/girl would end, in our minds, in the dawn of inspired conquest. The new title's humble watchman is vulnerable to being swallowed in night, and so was the wife Watts encouraged viewers to imagine.

The well-known "Choosing" is so ravishing a vision of femininity—it is, in fact, the first purely and powerfully feminine evocation of Ellen Terry that we have—that it seems at first a contrast to the martial watchman. This Ellen Terry

George Frederic Watts,
Watchman, What of the Night?
Reproduced by permission of the
Harry Ransom Humanities Research
Center, University of Texas, Austin.

George Frederic Watts, *Choosing.*
Reproduced by permission of the National
Portrait Gallery, London.

George Frederic Watts, *Portrait of Ellen Terry. Reproduced by permission of the National Portrait Gallery, London.*

wears no armor, but her brown Holman Hunt wedding dress and a small necklace of the amber beads that would become her trademark; she is not preparing for battles but smelling flowers, that most decoratively feminine of activities. Everything tells us that this woman is lovely and could decorate any number of lovely rooms, as she has. Watts's child bride seems at first to elicit a new, almost sentimental softness, one, moreover, with an edifying moral content, for as most critics read the painting's allegory, it preaches modest renunciation of glory: "the rival merits of a showy, scentless camellia and the humble but fragrant violets held close to her heart" compete as emblems of her destiny (Blunt, 107).

Both flowers, though, are dead or dying: the very surge of life with which Ellen Terry grasps them seems to make them wither. This allegory of renunciation makes us less aware of virtue than of sadness; surrounded by dying flowers as the gold-flecked watchman is by deepening night, this radiant girl seems suffocated by the power of her own desire. The funereal aura that encloses her, the surging gesture of hope with which she smells a scentless flower and clasps dead petals to her, abandon her tenderly to menace. The lost Joan of Arc, the engulfed watchman, the betrayed bride, inhabit a common Poe-like universe where vitality is inexorably enclosed.

"Portrait of Ellen Terry" moves the young girl into conjunction with the watchman's dark background, but since in this painting Ellen Terry is no longer a boy, she no longer has the night sky as backdrop; she is set off by a heavy dark curtain of an interior setting. She no longer combats her setting through the evanescent mobility of gold flecks, as in "Watchman," or (as in "Choosing") by the complex contortions of a vibrant girl grasping death; instead, she takes to herself all the light tones in the painting, forming as intense a contrast as she can to her smothering dark background. As in "Watchman," she holds her hands up in a prayerful attitude, but here, her hands do not shield her; instead, they become a further blocking form, inhibiting the movement beyond the frame the rest of her body fights to consummate. Her vividness within the dark and the shapeless; the attitude of terror that blocks its own desire for escape; the semi-scream she seems about to emit; all create for Ellen Terry a subtly Gothic

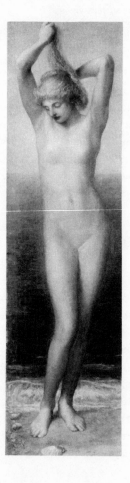

George Frederic Watts, *Thetis.*
Reproduced by permission of the Watts
Gallery, Compton, Guildford, Surrey.

setting. Each painting seems about to strangle the life Watts imagines in her; at the same time, each makes her a hero of vitality, affirming her radiance against a dark unknown. Watts's Gothic endowment externalized the terror she had imagined in childhood, but until she married, had never seen.

Some sketchier paintings are softer and more loving; Watts completed his visions of fear, but left his tenderness incipient. "Knight and Maiden," now lost, is a sweetly sad elegy of May-January love, one Lewis Carroll might have imagined. This knight is bearded and bears some resemblance to Watts; he gazes mournfully down at an Ellen Terry-like maiden who twines around him with the same clinging intensity with which she had twined around Kate in "The Sisters." As David Loshak sees it, he is all patient wisdom, she is "the very embodiment of yielding tenderness" (Loshak, 484). A nude Ellen Terry posed for an early version of "Paolo and Francesca," in which a similar mournful sensuality embraces lovers who in later versions become sexless, sculptural, and remote (Loshak, 485). When Ellen Terry left his house, Watts destroyed a number of his paintings of her. These too may have had a tenderness, a budding sensuality, an emotional fluidity, that were banished from his life when the actress disappeared. Ellen Terry did not model for "Thetis" (c. 1866–89), which he began shortly after she left, but the childish sensuality of the water nymph is reminiscent of the child wife his paintings caress; Thetis is, moreover, a joyful version of the water-haunted Ophelia who was so indelible a part of Watts's imagination of Ellen Terry. In these minor works, he found a home for the tenderness and desire that emerged only fitfully, hedged around by Pattles, in his actual married life.

Watts's loving paintings are moving reminders of feelings denied, but "Watchman," "Choosing," and "Portrait of Ellen Terry" are truest to the Ellen Terry the world came to know: they fixed her image in the public mind while they gave her a new, usable identity. They dramatized the terrors that possessed the stage child, and the fears other girls her age were forbidden to enact; they captured an intensifying aura of doom that attached itself to female vitality in the 1860s, creating a new sort of star; and they evoked Ophelia, the role in which Watts had secretly cast his star.

In Watts's paintings, Ellen Terry became for the first time not only an acceptably lovable woman, but a solitary divinity who acted out her culture's dreams. Watts glorified as well as tamed her, for her incarceration within the frame dramatized a complex new female condition. In the 1860s, a fear of female energy coursed through right-thinking Victorians, but a mysterious aggrandizement of women accompanied this fear: the monumental goddesses of Pre-Raphaelite art had come to haunt the general imagination.

Long before her own suicidal marriage in art to Rossetti, Elizabeth Siddall had inspired this cult of mighty heroines. Her haunting presence in Pre-Raphaelite art whispered of indefinable powers, but at the same time she presented herself as a reassuringly willing victim. The most revealing anecdote about her involves not Rossetti, but Millais: she posed so submissively in a tub of water for Millais' "Ophelia" (1851–52) that she courted pneumonia rather than interrupting the great man to tell him her heating lamp had gone out. Her notorious victimization as a model inspired her glorification into an icon. Her Ophelia floats in a seductively beseeching posture that combines religious ecstasy with helpless sexual receptivity. As a model, Elizabeth Siddall has none of Ellen Terry's dynamic physical expressiveness. She was no actress, and her few mournful paintings fade in comparison to her intense appearance on others' canvases. No struggle disturbs the doom of her Ophelia, but that doom burrowed into the mind of G. F. Watts as he studied Ellen Terry.

Elizabeth Siddall lacked theatrical energy, but the public prominence of her face, her body, her poignant legend, lent new interest to actresses. Ellen Terry was born into a theater beyond the pale of respectable attention, but by the time she married, actresses were newly interesting heroines; in attitudes of proper pathos, they replaced governesses as emblems of all that was sweetly downtrodden in women. Such heroines cannot, of course, act for love of it: as with Dickens's Miss Fairy, the stage is their sacrificial altar. Poverty forces them to act; they have no heart for their performances.

Tom Taylor's popular play, *Ticket-of-Leave-Man* (1863), features such a sweetly reluctant performer. The heroine is a street singer who longs only to stop performing and marry the put-upon hero. In the middle of the play, a philanthropist saves her from the stage by making her a happy seamstress. In 1865, Kate Terry made a great success in this virtuous role. At the height of Kate's popularity, Tom Taylor may have been writing her real happy ending along with his melodramas: her tearful retirement in 1867 to become Mrs. Arthur Lewis acted out to perfection the sentimental plot she and Tom Taylor had exploited so successfully two years before. Taylor's preference for Kate during the period of Ellen Terry's withdrawal into Watts's studio may have been a boon in disguise, for while Watts arranged his wife and model into the pathos that made her lovable, he inflicted no happy endings on her.

Ellen Terry spent a good part of the 1860s retired in a colony of artists: while she was modeling herself according to aesthetes' visions, audiences and actors were drawing closer together. Sentimental actress heroines pined to be non-acting and good, while sensation heroines like Mary Braddon's Lady Audley and Ellen Wood's Isabel Vane (in *East Lynne*) acted ordinary domestic roles with

Sir John Everett Millais, *Ophelia. Reproduced by permission of the Tate Gallery,
London.*

wicked flair. Moralists insisted that actresses were ordinary, while sensation
novelists whispered that all ordinary women were actresses. Both pious and
impious authors were allowing women to imagine themselves theatrically; they
were also training audiences to love Ellen Terry.

Modeling, meanwhile, was preparing her for stardom more imaginatively
than Victorian stock companies, with their rigid typecasting, would have done.
As Watts's model, she posed alone. No one upstaged her or pulled her hair.
There was no need to fight for audience attention: she devoured the imagination
of one man. True, she had to adjust her identity to his vision, but his demands
were mild compared to the sudden whims and inexplicable embarrassments of
audiences; Watts was embarrassed only away from his studio. Moreover, it was
comfortable for her to work intimately with one person. She had spent much
of her early career fitting herself to Kate, learning to be her mischievous
reflection. It was natural to take her being from another. Later on, when she
was Irving's partner, she tried to weave her performances out of the same sort
of artistic intimacy she had known first with Kate and then with Watts, but
Irving never noticed the actors he played with. As queen of the Lyceum, she

felt more abandoned than she had been as Watts's wife and model.

The rapt girl never saw the brutality of art, a brutality which finds consummate expression in Benvenuto Cellini's autobiographical boasts. After making his unfaithful mistress "pose in such discomfort," Cellini alternates artistic with sexual and sadistic punishment: "Then I began to copy her, and in between times we enjoyed sexual pleasures and then, at the same hour as the day before, she provoked me so much that I had to give her the same beating; and this went on for several days; everything in the same pattern, with little variation."

In Watts's studio, Ellen Terry felt she had been elevated to artistry at last, but others made of her a sacrificial victim. George Du Maurier, who was so solicitous when he visited Little Holland House, feared the Cellini in every artist. Years later, when he conceived his Trilby, he remembered Watts's child bride. The Trilby of his illustrations is, like Ellen Terry, large, prominent-jawed, and strangely helpless, placing her contorted power at the service of others' obsessions. She is not literally raped or brutalized, but she is invaded in more sinister ways: her career as artist's model prepares her to be the stricken vessel of men's visions, leaving her vulnerable to Svengali's mesmeric and musical assault on her identity. Like the Ellen Terry Du Maurier pitied, Trilby is not an artist herself, but the innocent victim of artists.

Surprisingly, Woolf's *Freshwater* similarly purifies Ellen Terry. For Woolf, the mature actress subversively "filled the stage," but the child bride is exempted from the life-killing self-absorption with which Watts, Tennyson, and Julia Cameron engulf her. John Craig, an ideal lover Woolf invents, rescues her into healthy Philistinism: he has never heard of Titian, doesn't care about nightingales, loves sex, sausages, and kippers. *All* art kills this ingenue; an ordinariness Woolf laces with lower-class talk is her sole redemption from poisonous artists. Both Du Maurier and Woolf turn the girl who thought she could be everything into a preyed-upon symbol of England's dispossessed.

Woolf could not forget Ellen Terry; twelve years after she wrote *Freshwater* for a private entertainment, she returned to it, to wrestle less farcically with the radiant child's destiny. Never, though, can Woolf imagine Ellen Terry as anything other than a prisoner in Little Holland House. Both versions struggle to provide the heroine with a symbolic redemption beyond John Craig, but neither play implicates her in the suffocating palace of art. In the first *Freshwater* (1923), Ellen Terry elopes with Craig wearing (to everybody's horror) checked trousers. Woolf reclaimed from Ellen Terry's Memoir the laughter and mobility of young Harry in her father's "Home for the Holidays": elliptically, Woolf endows the budding woman with salvation through the return of her boy-self.

The second, more somber *Freshwater* (1935) is closer to the iconography of

Ellen Terry's life. In this play, which is suffused with ominous references to Ophelia and drowning, the violated model has no checked trousers: she leaves with John Craig dressed not as a boy, but as a fallen woman, "painted, powdered —unveiled—," Watts cries (*Fw,* 40). Trying to write a comedy about material she fears is tragic, Woolf gropes for redemption from the sexless, heavy-breathing violations the model endures. She could not imagine what Ellen Terry knew: that modeling itself redeemed her life in Little Holland House, because modeling made her equally an artist with great men.

" 'The marriage was not a happy one,' they will say after my death, but for me it was in many ways very happy indeed" (*Memoirs,* 46). From the time the marriage ended to her death, she insisted stubbornly that she had been happy with Watts. She had never wanted to escape from modeling; she was banished from it inexplicably, like Eve from Paradise. Loshak and Manvell sensibly dismiss as "so much moonshine" the tale of a tryst with Godwin during her marriage to Watts (Manvell, 336). No rescuing Prince broke in, nor did this Sleeping Beauty dream of one. If Ellen Terry's life was a fairy tale, it was one that she composed herself; the heroic figure of her marriage was neither Watts nor Godwin, but the newly conceived transfigured self the artist aroused in her. Outsiders may have said that a model was not an artist, or that she was abused by definition, but Ellen Terry saw her own glory in an artist's loving brush. When Watts died in 1904, her informal eulogy paid tribute to an artist from a fellow-artist who understood: "I am having many <u>letters of Condolence</u> about Signor = He has been <u>wonderful</u>-his work to the very last being his best- They ought to bury <u>him</u> in the Abbey- & near Tennyson-such friends. He refused <u>all</u> 'honours' in his life. it wd be so <u>fitting</u>. <u>Different</u> to Stanley & Millais— fine fellows—but different-different <u>grain</u>-different everything= Your own old Frump." She would not have been the same old Frump in 1904 if Watts had not painted the girl in 1864. Since he never painted anyone else as richly or movingly as he painted Ellen Terry, she deserves the credit for creating him with the same intensity he put into creating her: art bestowed new identities on them both, but hers was never lost. Before she left, he infected her with his dream of Ophelia, the role in which, thirteen years after they separated, England refused to forget her.

In the 1880s and 1890s, her regal years, Ophelia clung to Ellen Terry like a second, hampering self. The dream of her Ophelia began to grow in Watts's studio, haunting non-painters as well as artists. One unidentified woman saw and pitied a girl whose insistent physicality, so disturbing to Mrs. Prinsep and her guests, had all been drained away: "I met her in Holland Park Road, thin as paper and white as a ghost, with drowned eyes. She didn't even hear my greeting; she brushed past me like a broken-winged bird" (quoted in Steen, p. 98). If this Elizabeth Siddall-like ghost with drowned eyes existed alongside the Ellen Terry who flaunted her Cupid costume at dinner parties, it is likely to have been summoned by a modeling session with her husband.

At least one of Watts's Ophelia paintings was begun during the year of the marriage, but none was finished until after 1878, when Ellen Terry had long gone to play Ophelia to Irving's Hamlet. Beauty and pathos give way in these paintings to the dark potency of growing madness: the shadows that hung ominously around the young girl now move within her. In this drawing, done in about 1878 or 1879 from a bland photograph of Ellen Terry as Ophelia, there are no flowers, no love story, and no pretty songs: simply a mental agony that roots itself in the girl's eyes. This Ophelia is gripped by neurosis, not (as Irving would have it) by sweet love betrayed. Whether Watts remembered this tormented Ellen Terry or created her, his drawing illustrates Gordon Craig's cry to Edy in 1915, after a visit to his blind, disoriented mother:

> Mothers eyes!! —
> Still she seems cheerful

The inner trouble blasting the eyes of an Ophelia quite unlike her sweet photograph endows Ellen Terry, who was so frightened in Watts's earlier portraits, with a new and frightening power over the viewer.

Watts's completed Ophelia—for which Ellen Terry posed in an early version —is not half-drowned by her setting, as the model was in "Portrait of Ellen Terry"; she gazes enigmatically from solid ground at the water we know is her fate. She is no longer prettified; Watts stops masking the irregularity of her features, especially the eerie proximity of her elongated nose to her chin. She is no longer an ingenue emanating lovely pathos, but a witch, the power of whose madness erupts in her face.

Virginia Woolf's second version of *Freshwater* features an innocent model whom mad artists are conspiring to drown beautifully. Hearing that Ellen Terry has drowned, even her friend Tennyson declaims: "There is something highly pleasing about the death of a young woman in the pride of life. Rolled round in earth's diurnal course with stocks and stones and trees. That's Wordsworth. I've said it too" (*Fw,* 34). The real Watts also found his model's fate ghoulishly pleasing, but he gave her a mystic stature that belonged to it. The mysterious river her face reflects emanates a sibylline magic that is part of her doom, surrounding her with a prophetic power that aggrandizes the pathetic death the play makes obligatory.

In a haunting oil painted around 1880 from no photograph, that reflective face looks up at us from the bottom of that water, swollen by its own thoughts beyond loveliness or recognition. The final painting in the cycle gives us not Ophelia's romance, but her psyche's invasion of her face. Its drowned and bloated horror is Watts's last wedding gift to Ellen Terry: in her cursed submergence, she gains a magnitude that claims her canvas at last. In the early group, the viewer sees her ominous condition more clearly than she does, and pities it. Here, the Medusa-like power of her anguish grips and drowns the viewer as well: from drawing pity, she evolves to personifying terror. Had the prosperous, seemingly calm Ellen Terry of the 1880s seen this painting, it might have repelled her, but eventually she would have learned the same lesson she had learned before of glorification within horror: when she agreed to become Ophelia, she accepted the horror within that character's glory. Madness was there too. Outsiders celebrated "the indubitably sane Ellen Terry" (Loshak, 485), but those who knew her well knew better.

Watts's Ophelia cycle gave his hoydenish wife the role that would shape her adulthood. Unlike most Victorian husbands, he gave her as well, through pictures, the knowledge of what that role would do to her. This ability to see her newly and to see *with* her as well made Ellen Terry cleave to him as a husband while others were laughing at his supposed inadequacies. She may not have been a wife as others defined it, but to her far greater pride, she had been fellow artist. As she promised at her wedding, she had given her life into Watts's keeping, and she had acted it so well that he had returned it as a beautiful series of painted prophecies. As far as Ellen Terry was concerned, this visionary partnership was marriage. In later years, she would fall in love and she would learn about sex; she would have children and she would be a wife onstage; but never after those ten intense months would she feel married again.

F A L L   Suddenly, and it seemed to her arbitrarily, she was banished: "they" were sending her back to her parents' house. "Wife" was the only role from which she had ever been dismissed. When Eve had been banished from Paradise, God had taught her why she should suffer and repent, but forty years later, Ellen Terry still did not know what she had done:

> I wondered at the new life, and worshipped it because of its beauty. When it suddenly came to an end, I was thunderstruck; and refused at first to consent to the separation, which was arranged for me in much the same way as my marriage had been.
> The whole thing was managed by those kind friends whose chief business in

George Frederic Watts, drawing of Ellen Terry as Ophelia, 1878/9. *Photograph courtesy of the Watts Gallery, Compton, Guildford, Surrey.*

George Frederic Watts, *Ophelia. Reproduced by permission of the Watts Gallery, Compton, Guildford, Surrey.*

George Frederic Watts, *Ophelia's Madness. Reproduced by courtesy of the trustees of the British Museum.*

life seems to be the care of others. I don't blame them. There are things for which no one is to blame. . . . There were no vulgar accusations on either side, and the words I read in the deed of separation, "incompatibility of temper"—a mere legal phrase—*more* than covered the ground. Truer still would have been "incompatibility of *occupation,"* and the interference of well-meaning friends. (*Memoirs,* 46)

During her marriage, Ellen Terry never complained of "incompatibility of occupation": her work as Watts's model may have appeared subordinate in retrospect, but at the time, if it didn't make her equal to Signor, it did make them sharers in beauty's creation. Just as her husband's "well-meaning friends" had invaded their fragile union, so her own friends may have discredited later on the vision of glory she embraced in Watts's studio.

Ironically, she probably never saw in completed form Watts's most triumphantly exalted painting of her: "Joan of Arc, Mounted on an Armour-Clad Horse". In the better-known, more sentimental "Watchman," Ellen Terry was helpless against gathering gloom; Joan of Arc is translated into a flame of irresistible sexual and spiritual intensity. "Joan of Arc" was probably completed after Ellen Terry left Little Holland House; like "Ophelia," also finished after her departure, Joan is prominent-jawed and eerily, almost inhumanly, powerful; she is no longer the pretty, struggling, pathetic Ellen Terry Watts painted from life. Once his wife was gone, Watts paid tribute, through "Joan of Arc," to her dream of a restored and glorified boy-self. That dream had led her to Little Holland House, and Little Holland House had destroyed it.

The painter was brave, but the man could not follow him. No doubt Mrs. Prinsep and his other "well-meaning friends" made it easier for Watts to live without his wife than with her, and ease was more important to him than Ellen Terry could understand. But with the certainty of a teacher as well as an artist, he may have realized too that their work together was over. He had not made Ellen Terry an incense-bearing wife, but he had taught her dynamic suffering.

Since the disgraced girl had nowhere to go, no vision of Joan of Arc prevented her from mourning clamorously. Just before her marriage, she had played Hero, the maligned bride in *Much Ado About Nothing,* whose bridegroom, like Othello, believes slanders against her, berates her, and leaves her for dead. After her marriage, she played Hero in life, growing fond of the role. When she looked back to her Haymarket year in her Memoir, it was her only performance she liked. Even in her annotations to Charles Hiatt's book about her, she writes amid a tangle of self-abuse—"played badly," "played vilely" —"I played Hero beautifully! E. T.=" So she insisted to her dying day and so she probably did, not only at the Haymarket.

Back on the touring circuit with her father and Polly in 1866, she wrote a pseudo-confession to her mother:

> Read this to yr self!!!
> To finish up the night in a pleasant manner, I went to bed and dreamed not of the Theatre (isn't that strange?) but of Mr. Watts!
> I dreamed he was dying, & I woke up in the greatest grief—crying!
> This is the 20th of the month! my wedding day! Married 2 years ago today! & it is such a day. *Pouring* with rain! & altogether wretched!!
> Oh! . . . with all thy faults, I love thee still!
> (Quoted in Steen, 108)

George Frederic Watts, *Joan of Arc, Mounted on an Armour-Clad Horse. Christopher Wood Collection. Reproduced by courtesy of the Shepherd Gallery, New York.*

She had learned Pattle lessons well enough to kill her lost husband only in a dream, waking immediately to tears of contrition and, like a good Shakespearean actress, forcing nature to weep for him as well. Never would she criticize Watts. Instinctively, she assumed his incapacity, as she would her son's later on, making her suffering an art and berating Mrs. Prinsep as the manager behind the man. In 1865, after seeing Kate act, she wrote to her friend Mary-Ann Hall, whom Manvell describes as "a young girl who painted" (p. 58), a letter in which she tries to arrange herself in the pathetic attitudes Watts had taught her, but falls instead into guilty anger:

> Goodbye dear little Marian my clever little (I hate the word *Artist*) Painter: Believe me always, your very loving friend, Ellen Alice Watts, N.B. Better known as Poor Nell.
>
> 'Ah me I am weary, and I wish that I were dead.' No dear Marian I have much to live for *even now*. 'Nil Desperandum' is my motto. I have youth (I'm not very old rather) and I have *great, great hope*—Oh! so much and I can't believe that *all* is lost yet—I have Faith too dear, for I cannot but think that help *will*, must come to me *some day*. Hope—Faith—Two great things—but Charity! Oh Ellen Ellen I'm afraid you have not one particle of that, the most beautiful of *all, all,* feelings or you would not feel *as you do* towards a person of flesh and blood and that person a Woman. God forgive her for I *can not* do so—I suppose I'm very, very wicked to feel so but indeed Marian I think, and think what have I done that she should use me so. God knows, I'd forgive anyone that even *killed* me if I loved them—but 'Hope up, hope ever' and don't be selfish Nell. You are talking to yourself. Pray forgive me, for this is selfishness.
>
> (Quoted in Manvell, 59)

She is Ellen Alice Watts, Poor Nell, Ellen, and selfish Nell: already her simple name has fractured into a multitude of possible beings. Later on, when her suffering is deeper and change is harder, this symphony of names will provide material for tragic bewilderment. Now, like Alice in Wonderland (whose story she may have already read), she sees herself everywhere, talks to her selves, and feels guilty about seeing these selves everywhere.

About Mrs. Prinsep, though—whom she direly dubs "a Woman," melodrama's epithet—she is implacable. Her mother, who when Ellen knew her had no enlarged stage life but only endless babies to care for, had already made her skeptical of women's authority. Kate triumphed over her so easily that she was an alien creature as well as a second self. Though she was faintly ridiculous, Mrs. Kean alone had been worth respecting. The Pattle sisters were more powerful than Mrs. Kean, with none of her grandiosity: they were not regal, but political. She warmed to Mrs. Prinsep only when, at the Lyceum, she herself had become charmingly, whimsically indirect: when, in fact, she had learned to act Mrs. Prinsep offstage. In 1865, she was trying to act "Poor Nell" as Watts had taught her: all evil fell on "a Woman," while men were only great. The fact that she could be like Mrs. Prinsep if she chose led her to work still more strenuously at her offstage role of Hero, the "Poor Nell" she rehearsed so assiduously even when her teacher was gone.

Over the years, she cherished Watts's gifts; as was her pattern, she loved the giver all the more dearly after he receded and she could love the part of him she had taken into herself. Her marriage in art never stopped meaning marriage to her, an ideal she transmitted to her children to glorify and complicate their lives. When, in 1892, her friend Stephen Coleridge planned to see Watts, she wrote to him in rapture: "You tell me you are going to stay awhile with Mr. Watts. The dews of Heaven fall thick in blessings on him. Where? Not at Little Holland House! At Freshwater perhaps? or—where? *Let me know for I like to picture* things." By that time, the man had become absorbed into her own pleasure in picturing things. When he was about to marry Mary Fraser Tyler, she sent a still more potent benediction through Lady Constance Leslie: "Now this is *very* private. See Mr. W. (the dear Signor) for me, and say, he, from first to last, has been a beautiful influence in my life, and that I pray God to bless him. She too I bless for going into his life and cheering it. I have always had a great desire to tell her so, but feared it might not have been seemly in her eyes" (quoted in Loshak, 480–83). Very little was seemly in Mary Watts's eyes that did not tend to her husband's greater glory. She would not have wanted to know that a hoydenish actress had aroused that glory so intensely that even the grandly hideous mausoleum she built could not encompass or kill it.

As Ellen Terry grew tenderer and more appreciative, Watts grew more spitefully frightened of her. When they separated in 1865, he had made a relatively generous settlement on her of three hundred pounds annually for "as long as she remained chaste"; with what sort of feelings did he stop paying it? When, in 1877, she finally requested a divorce to marry the man who would give Godwin's children a patronym, Watts's evidence in the proceedings is the only portrait of Ellen Terry he attempted in a medium that was alien to him: words.

> That although considerably older than his intended wife he admired her very much and hoped to influence, guide and cultivate a very artistic and peculiar nature and to remove an impulsive young girl from the dangers and temptations of the stage.
>
> That very soon after his marriage he found out how great an error he had made. Linked to a most *restless and impetuous* nature accustomed from the very earliest childhood to the Stage and forming her ideas of life from the exaggerated romance

of sensational plays, from whose acquired habits a quiet life was intolerable and even impossible, demands were made on him he could not meet without giving up all the professional aims his life had been devoted to.

That he did not impute immorality at that time but there was an insane excitability indulging in the wildest suspicions, accusations and denunciations driving him to the verge of desperation and separation became absolutely necessary unless he gave up his professional pursuits which was out of the question as he had no independent means and it was arranged by his friends and those of his wife that a separation should take place. That separation took place within a year of the marriage. (Quoted in Loshak, 483)

Obtaining a divorce was at that time as expensive and as difficult as moralistic courts could make it; but Watts's distaste is still bruising. His contempt for Ellen Terry's work, a work that taught his own art so much, transcends any need for plausible argument; so does his accusation that her "insane excitability" jeopardized him professionally: the insane excitability which had always possessed her had galvanized a work she thought they had shared. Watts's deposition banished her all over again, this time from his studio, where she had seen herself as his partner; twelve years later, when her star was rising, he relegated her to the silent inactivity of the wife she had acted so badly.

In their final encounter, five years later, she told him as clearly as she could who she was, what she thought their life had been, and why she loved him. By that time, though, he imagined her only in frozen attitudes and did not want to hear it.

> I saw Mr. Watts but once face to face after the separation. We met in the street at Brighton, and he told me that I had grown! That was the last time I spoke to him. But years later, after I had appeared at the Lyceum and made some success in the world, I was in the garden of a house which adjoined the new Little Holland House, and Mr. Watts, in his garden, saw me through the hedge. It was then that I received from him the first letter that I had had for years. In this letter he told me that he had watched my success with eager interest, and asked me to shake hands with him in spirit. "What success I may have," he wrote, "will be very incomplete and unsatisfactory if you cannot do what I have long been hesitating to ask. If you cannot, keep silence. If you can, one word, 'Yes,' will be enough."
>
> I answered simply, "Yes." (*Memoirs*, 46-47)

In fact, she answered more than simply "yes." In two previously unpublished letters written in the clear, distinctive, and beautiful handwriting of her early maturity, she embraces him "in spirit" as the fellow artist she has always been:

Let the past be, as you say, a story in a book that we have both read. <u>As artists</u> we can still wander hand in hand through the images of the beautiful, and if it can be an encouragement to you and a help to you in striving after real greatness as distinct from mere success, to know that your efforts will be appreciated and honoured by me, do believe that no one has a more intense interest in you.

In 1882, when Watts received this generous but self-affirming letter, his divorce evidence had painted a picture of a wild and contaminated girl who interfered with his great work; he had also cursed her through that work in his succession of tortured Ophelias. The first time she had confronted him as a self-possessed adult, he had responded only with the Lewis Carroll–like accusation that she had grown. He could imagine her life only as something broken, and broken by him. On July 11, 1883, she wrote again, eager to show himself to him as proudly as she had done when she posed:

> It is impossible for me to stay away since you say you desire me to come for what can I see in your request but an expression of your life, of beautiful gentle fondness. When you wrote to me last Easter twelvemonth you forbade me saying anything in answer only <u>"yes"</u>, but in truth your words made me dizzy with exquisite waves of feeling <u>and gratitude</u> and joy. It is impossible for me to get a spare quarter of an hour in the days until July 29 is over my work being incessant. Enclosed is the name and address so you may send the picture and I am vexed and perplexed to think that I can <u>say nothing</u> while the whole wish is so great to desire some word that could thank you and bless you.
>
> Nelly—
> Read between the lines of mine how sacredly I shall hold your letter.

Knowing what he knew of himself and possessed by blighted and stricken images of his former wife, Watts wanted only recrimination from her: loving gratitude scourged him. His answer ignored everything she had said: "I have nothing to add unless I may say that I never for a moment lose the pain of feeling that I have spoiled your life, I have never forgiven myself and never shall." He wanted to hear from her that she was enjoying her success—or perhaps he sought evidence that she *wasn't*—but he could not meet the woman he had never stopped seeing: "perhaps <u>it is</u> better and more seemly that we should not come in personal contact."

When Mary wrote a fat and worshipful memoir after Watts's death, her original subtitle immortalized *The Life Story of a Noble Soul Seeking Beauty, Truth, and Goodness,* but his later life and art were crippled by the awareness that he had fled these saving abstractions when Ellen Terry, who had made herself their personification, held out her arms to him. Until she died, she believed that he had glorified her life, while he insisted that he had spoiled it. That life, which was both glorified and spoiled, must tell its own story, but from this point it is suffused in the coloration of Watts's visions: in his painted realizations of her, he showed her how to act a new Ellen Terry and to recreate herself within the dimensions he imagined.

When she became famous, journalists pounced on Watts as the villain of her legend: he was pinioned by the lovely suffering Ellen Terry he had himself invented. On May 12, 1889, the *Philadelphia Press* ran a long feature on the pathetic Ellen Terry Watts had given the world; his own creation returned to mortify his austere retirement. Purging Nelly Watts of her powerful ambition and her passionate ego, Olive Weston heads her highly colored account:

Ellen Terry the Woman
A Strange and Lovely Being with Many Noble Traits
THE SAD ROMANCE OF HER LIFE
Her First Marriage with the Artist, Watts, and her
Attachment for Godwin, the Architect
Henry Irving's Devotion

Writing the sad romance her audience wanted, Olive Weston turns the singleminded artist who panted after grandeur into a goatish hypocrite:

> She was very young—poor thing!—when she married the great artist, Watts; she had always been on the stage, and her bright, joyous personality had even then begun to attract attention. It was not a love match. She was only 16 and he an old man, who would never have thought of marrying, it is said, if it had not been suggested to him by a friend who lived next door and who the gossips were beginning to talk about, saying that a splendid piece of tapestry which hung in the hall of the room next to her's, when lifted disclosed a sliding panel. So she thought it would be wise to have him marry some raw-boned girl. Ellen Terry was selected as the victim, and the grand lady danced at the wedding.
>
> Neither the old man nor the woman of the world understood this strange girl. In fact, neither thought much about her. She was surrounded with art influences and left to grow by herself. They had made a mistake in their selection and did not know it. She was of a strange, nervous, peculiarly pliable nature, and to live in the midst of all these strange splendors and strange people and strange conversations was a new life to her, a new education, and she gradually grew up to it and, ere long, began to expand in nature, to be unsatisfied with her position, to say to herself, *"I, too, am an artist."*

Of course, there was no intrigue between Watts and Mrs. Prinsep: for her story to be palatable, Ellen Terry must become a sexual as well as an artistic victim. Thus, Weston suppresses the artistic hunger that led her to glorify herself by marrying Watts. Will-less and empty of motive, Ellen Terry is thrust into an evil house to her bane.

> There are many different versions of the final break up. His friends say that a streak of insanity ran through all her actions, that she was so nervous, so eccentric and unconventional, he was at last obliged to put an end to her mad pranks; that on one occasion she actually horrified his guests by coming down to dinner in tights.
>
> Her friends tell that she bore everything as long as she could, and was a martyr to an old man's whims, till at last one day she revolted and left him. . . .
>
> There was a friend of her family, a young architect of great talent. One night he was taken ill in an old house alone, with no one near him and he sent word by a passing boy for some of the family to come round and see him. They were all occupied excepting the young girl, who, without thought went to see him alone; all the world knows that she did not return.

"The sad romance of her life," which Watts first illustrated, transforms him into a loathsome "old man," stripped of his dignity among the Prinseps. He is hardly an artist at all; only a Chaucerian lewd and heavy husband. Ellen Terry is no longer disruptive hoyden, but passive Cinderella; intimations of insanity make her pathos more intriguing. Weston drains her of the theatrical expressiveness that drew her to Little Holland House; in Chaucerian style, she is allowed to leave it voluntarily (which of course she did not), but only to cuckold the repulsive Watts with a virile lover of the same redemptive facelessness as Woolf's John Craig. Watts had never added himself to his poignant portraits of a menaced Ellen Terry. When journalists fell in love with her and cast him as a type of husbandly repulsiveness, he was flayed once again by the life of his own myth. Understandably, the portraits of his later years are as austerely masculine, and as grimly heroic, as he can make them. They will not come to life.

Ellen Terry too was flayed by the creative life her marriage awakened. Doomed to draw tears as Ophelia, she never cuckolded the husband who taught her how to see herself. In his own way, Watts had fulfilled his mid-Victorian duties: like a true patriarch, he had educated his child wife into adulthood. Because he had done it in art, in her own way, Ellen Terry obeyed him ever after.

After she was famous as a pictorial actress, she shed gratitude and grace on the memory of her marriage, but when she was cast out of Paradise she was in a frenzy of despair. Her childhood was gone; as an embarrassing revenant in her parents' spruce new house on Stanhope Street, she had none of a wife's adult authority. She loved Watts still, but she locked her baby brother in a dark cupboard in her rage: Fred never liked her again, not even when they were old and distinguished together (Steen, 102). *Freshwater* makes a comedy out of her elopement with a perfect (because perfectly sexy and perfectly simple) lover; like Olive Weston's inventive account, *Freshwater* plays fairy godmother, bestowing a romantic escape on a heroine who knew no escape was possible. In 1923, Woolf dressed the fleeing Ellen Terry in the checked trousers with which Harry had shocked his prim sister, but the real Nelly Watts could never wear trousers again. Only Fred would inherit them; she couldn't lock him in dark cupboards forever. In 1935, when Woolf tried once more to make a comedy out of Nelly Watts's destiny, she faced the fact that the checked trousers were a dream, giving her the only other costume with which Victorian culture could free such a girl: the paints and powders of the fallen woman. Ellen Terry eventually put on this costume, but marriage did not force it on her: neither Watts nor Godwin persuaded her that the joyful mockery represented by Harry's checked trousers was closed to her forever. Her teacher was Lewis Carroll, the self-appointed guardian of girls' childhoods, and he taught her as both Watts and Julia Cameron had: by making a new self for her in pictures.

Had she remained Nelly Watts of Little Holland House, she would have been licensed to be a child, though a docile one, for the rest of her life, for a proper wife was always a child to her husband's authority. Out in the world, she donned the mantle of that authority and claimed adult status. A castoff wife, though, had no one to control her or to license her adulthood. When the castoff was Ellen Terry, so angry and so assaultively beautiful, this half-child became by definition a danger to children. Lewis Carroll, who had loved her all her stage life, immediately shut her out of childhood when he finally met her.

Lewis Carroll met the Terry family in 1864, when he was still the shy clergyman Charles L. Dodgson. *Alice* had not yet been published to license him as a collector of little girls, and so he gained entry to promising families through his photographs. Eight years ago, Ellen had embodied for him all the stage child's enchanted joy. When he met her at last, during a tense Christmas visit, she was a woman with another name who could only act childhood discordantly. He wrote in his diary a clinical account of a day he nevertheless marked with his token of glory, a white stone:

Polly and Benjamin met me in the hall, and in the drawing-room I found Miss Kate Terry, Florence, and, to my delight, the one I have always most wished to meet of the family, Mrs. Watts. Mr. Tom Taylor called in later to read Miss Terry some of her part in a MS play, and I remained to listen. I was very much pleased with what I saw of Mrs. Watts—lively and pleasant, almost childish in her fun, but perfectly ladylike. Her sister seemed ill and out of spirits. I fancy her gaiety yesterday, and Mrs. Watts's today, were both partly assumed. However, both sisters are charming, and I think it a piece of rare good fortune to have made two such acquaintances in two days. (Quoted in Manvell, 54–55)

By the time he returned with his camera seven months later, the storm he sensed had erupted: Mrs. Watts had returned to embarrass the family. He too had changed, for he was now Lewis Carroll; the success of *Alice* had transformed him from a furtive lover of little girls into their licensed protector. His portrait of the Terry family protects the children sternly from Ellen. She is clothed in black; her hair is tightly combed and knotted; she appears to be the matron among the Terrys. Though Kate is the eldest, she wears girlish white in contrast to her sister's somber, constraining black. Moreover, Ellen's pose isolates her from her family. Carroll groups her with the younger girls, but they snuggle around their father; Ellen leans away from them toward Kate's group, but the window blocks her from them. All the other Terrys lace their arms around each other. Only Ellen, large and alone, is given no one to touch.

Carroll's portrait photographs of Ellen Terry are equally stiff and somber. One shows troubled glimmerings of the neurotic Ophelia Watts would draw almost ten years later; neither hints at the fluid sensuality Watts's art had celebrated the year before. Carroll's grim Ellen Terry is farther still from the enticing child who had become the South West Wind for Julia Cameron; she has nothing in common with the child-friends of Carroll's own photographs, most of whom are creatures of mobile delight. Oddly, Cameron's alert nymphet, the South West Wind of 1864, is infinitely more Carrollian than the restrained Ellen Terry Carroll himself photographed in 1865. Carroll's model shuns life, exuding loss and grief. In 1861, Prince Albert had died; his weeping queen had made deep mourning fashionable. Carroll dramatizes Ellen Terry's newly un-married condition by plunging her into mourning with Victoria, suppressing the acrobatic joy, the fluid eroticism, that had made her glow for him with a little girl's infinite promises.

When he died, his family spread a story that he had been in love with Ellen Terry, living in stricken celibacy because she refused him. He is said to have longed in a lost diary to be her dresser: "I can imagine no more delightful occupation than brushing Ellen Terry's hair." His photographs, though, show

A photograph, by Lewis Carroll, of Ben and Sarah Terry and their children. Ellen and Kate stand in the center by the window.

Ellen Terry, by Lewis Carroll.

Ellen Terry, by Lewis Carroll.

no awareness that Ellen Terry has hair, a body, or the artist's love. Shrouded in dark colors, her hair pinned tightly enough to satisfy even Mrs. Prinsep, she mourns for the fantastic journeys on which only little girls may embark.

In the same year Lewis Carroll immortalized a resilient child who was so much like herself, he descended on Ellen Terry like an iron angel, barring the gates to Wonderland. "[Mr. Dodgson] was as fond of me as he could be of any one over the age of ten," she wrote drily later on. "[His] kindness to children was wonderful. He *really* loved them and put himself out for them" (*Memoirs*, 142–43). His photographs insulated her from that kindness. His adoring intimacy with her sister Florence made her exclusion all the more biting: recreating knowing little Flossie in his letters and photographs, Carroll bestowed on her all the vigor and self-delight he denied her older sister. Flossie reveled in Carroll's courtship and in the animal joy his camera had taken away from Ellen.

Kate was a great star; the younger children had stolen vividness and vitality; Ellen Terry had come home only to be the untouchable negation Carroll photographed. She did not know that he meted out love to all little girls at the same time as he plotted to withhold it. In 1876, he would write to Marion Terry about his adored, all-licensed Flossie: "Love to Flossie—unless she prefers to be called 'Florence,' in which case I will modify the love, and substitute sincere regards." Ellen Terry knew only that this loved and gentle man perpetuated the denials, the punishing humiliations, that made up adult life. Had Lewis Carroll photographed her differently, had he allowed her into the Wonderland that held so many of her own stage dreams, the outcast from Watts's studio—that other Wonderland—might not have decided to play a fallen woman. When she threw herself into that role, she gave kindly Mr. Dodgson the shock of his life. He would make her pay for it when she came back.

When Ellen Terry ran off with Godwin, she threw off the dark clothes of Carroll's photographs, unpinning her hair as defiantly as she had done at Little Holland House. She refused to mourn a vitality she had never lost. Instead, she made her own Wonderland. After all, as her signature began to insist, Nelly Watts had really been baptized "Ellen Alice Terry," and not Poor Nell at all. The two vivid children she produced made cruelly clear just what sort of Wonderland this grown-up Alice had claimed as her birthright. When Charles Dodgson learned what Mrs. Watts had done, he erased her from his life, deigning to write to her only once she was properly, if briefly, married. Their subsequent relationship lived the photographs he had taken almost thirty years earlier. When she emerged as the Lyceum's proudly respectable queen, he scourged the middle-aged woman in myriad ways by barring her from the childhood she still longed to re-live. This time though, she responded humbly.

The letters he wrote to Ellen Terry in the 1890s are not Carrollian gems, but

Dodgsonian sermons laced with unspoken accusations of uncleanness: "Once I wrote to you about *Faust,* and was so unfortunate, I fear, as to vex you a little by a remonstrance (probably very unskilfully worded) about the 'business' in the chamber scene. I only allude to it again because I noticed the other day, that you have quite altered the 'business,' and now wholly omit what I had feared might make some of the audience uneasy. Would you mind telling me, some time, whether the alteration is a permanent one, or merely an accidental difference that day; and, if permanent, whether the change is connected at all with my letter?" The offending "business" involved a scene in which Ellen Terry's Margaret began to undress; Carroll claimed that it pained the little girl who accompanied him. Ellen Terry remembered sending a *"furious"* response: " 'I thought you only knew *nice* children,' was all the answer I gave him. 'It would have seemed awful for a *child* to see harm where harm is; how much more so when she sees it where harm is not.' " But his scourge never left her: "I felt ashamed and shy whenever I played that scene" (*Memoirs,* 142). Despite the many favors he had demanded of her, Carroll in the clerical role of Dodgson felt licensed to press his point, forcing the actress to feel her own alienation from the denying child who deserved his love.

When he was not flaying her with his child-friends, he pressed them on her. Some of them, like Dolly Baird, were no longer children, a further rebuff to the forty-seven-year-old actress who had never stopped wanting Wonderland. Dorothea Baird would shortly play Trilby, a role Ellen Terry had in part inspired, in the wildly popular stage adaptation of Du Maurier's novel. She would marry H. B. Irving, the son of Ellen Terry's own stage husband. Now Lewis Carroll was asking for a bounty that shut her inexorably away from Dolly's youth: "Now I have a favour, to ask you. (What a lot I've asked of you, and what a lot you've granted!) I have a very nice girl-friend here, aged about 20. She has set her heart on going on the stage. She has a good many things in her favour. She is a very fine handsome girl, with plenty of spirit and energy. . . . *Would* you mind naming a day and hour, when you would see her for a few minutes? I would most likely come with her; but my life is *very* busy, and she might have to go alone."

Ellen Terry always said yes to these requests. The allowable pleasure she gave this non-child brought her, in return, a lesson: "I want to thank you, as heartily as words can do it, for your true kindness in letting me bring Dolly behind the scenes to you. You will know, without my telling you, what an *intense* pleasure you thereby gave to a warm-hearted girl, and what love (which I fancy you value more than mere *admiration:* I know *I* do!) you have won from her." Only when he writes *to* children *about* the actress does he recapture his sinuous sense of play. For his child-friends, Ellen Terry is a piece in an endless game, but for

Ellen Terry herself, the energetic children he paraded through her dressing-room are emblems of renunciation. Isa Bowman, the first stage Alice, makes the lesson explicit. When Ellen Terry coached her a bit, Carroll began his letter of thanks: "My *dear* old friend," rubbing in his salutation with the whimsical reassurance: *"(N.B.* 'old' doesn't mean 'old in *years*' but 'old in *friendship*'!)" The sweet penance continued: "and so you have found out that secret—one of the deep secrets of Life—that all, that is really *worth* the doing, is what we do for *others?* . . . And so in your case, dear friend; I believe that it is real joy to you to know that you are filling, full to overflowing, Isa's little cup of happiness; and yet there is no shadow of *selfishness* in what you are doing, but that it is pure, unadulterated, generous *kindness."* Each favor he asks demands that she be no-self when she meets the all-self of his child-friends.

In 1865, she had defied his photographs to make herself an adult Alice, but when he demanded penitence, she performed it. She writes to him as a great lady, but her letters carry undercurrents of apology for unstated trespasses. She admits incessantly that she is "spoiled," taking on Watts's word about her life. "Yes-- 'like Christine Nielson' I'm quite spoiled by the Americans, but then I was spoiled before I went to America by ~~injudicious friends~~ dear delightful sweet people, friends, who will I hope continue to do so till the end of the chapter=" About a photograph that Dodgson failed to obtain for her, she writes: "I hope you'll trouble no more in the matter. I'm dreadfully spoiled by everybody, and it will <u>do me good</u> to 'want something' and not be able to get it. An unusual sensation="

The would-be Alice whose onstage escapades helped Carroll formulate his dream of Wonderland writes to him as a chastened child, holding out her faults for his salutary disapproval. Finally, as so many others did, Carroll writing as Dodgson absorbed Ellen Terry's life into his own morality. When in 1894 he wrote to the mother of twenty-year-old Dorothea Baird to determine whether the actress was sufficiently pure to do favors for Dolly, he told a tale of a girl with nothing in her of Alice. The avid child becomes a pious victim of circumstances. Dodgson's is not the story Ellen Terry wanted her life to tell. It is certainly not the tale into which she wanted Lewis Carroll to write her. More systematically even than Olive Weston in her "sad romance of Ellen Terry's life," Dodgson drains his heroine into a pallid victim:

> When she was scarcely more than a child (17, I think), a man nearly three times her age professed to be in love with her. The match was pushed on by well-meaning friends who thought it a grand thing for her. From the first, I don't think she had a fair chance of learning her new duties. Instead of giving her a home

of her own he went on living with an elderly couple and the old lady was constantly exasperating the poor child by treating her as if she were still in the school-room and she, just like a child, used to go into fits of furious passion.

[As Mrs. Watts, Ellen Terry showed no desire to learn household duties. Like Olive Weston, Dodgson strips all glory from her marriage in art to make the story suitably pathetic.]

Quarrels began at once and very soon a separation was agreed on. He cynically told his friends that he found he had never *loved* her; it had only been a passing fancy. He agreed to make her an annual allowance so long as she lived respectably.

This she did for a while, then she rebelled and accepted the offered love (of course without ceremonial of marriage) of another man.

I honestly believe her position was, from her point of view, this:

"I am tied by *human* law to a man who disowns his share of what ought to be a *mutual* contract. He never loved me and I do not believe, in God's sight, we are man and wife. Society expects me to live, till this man's death, as if I were single and to give up all hope of that form of love for which I pine and shall never get from *him*. This other man loves me as truly and faithfully as any lawful husband. If the marriage ceremony were *possible* I would insist on it before living with him. It is *not* possible and I will do without it. [As we shall see, it was the essence of their idyll that neither Godwin nor Ellen Terry thought about marriage.]

I allow freely that she was headstrong and wild in doing so [as his Alice had been when she pursued a White Rabbit that talked]; and her only real *duty* was to accept the wreck of her happiness and live (or if necessary die) *without* the love of a man. But I do not allow that her case resembled *at all* that of those poor women who, without any pretense of *love,* sell themselves to the first comer. It much more resembles the case of those many women who are living as faithfully and devotedly as lawful wives without having gone through any ceremony and who *are,* I believe, married in God's sight though not in Man's. [After she left Little Holland House Ellen Terry was married in nobody's sight, even when she had occasional husbands.]

A lady (wife of a clergyman) to whom (before I would introduce her daughter to my friend) I told this story said "She has broken the law of man; she has *not* broken the law of God."

She lived with this man for some years and he *is* the father of her son and daughter. Then came the result she must have known was possible if not probable and which perhaps her mad conduct deserved; the man deserted her and went abroad. [It is more likely that Godwin felt deserted by her in multiple and complex ways.]

When her lawful husband found out what she had done, of course he sued for and got a divorce. Then of course she was, in the eyes of the law, free to be legally married and if only the other man had been as true as she, I have no doubt, meant to be to him, they would have gotten married and it would have gradually been forgotten that the children were born before the ceremony.

At this time I held no communication with her. I felt that she had so entirely sacrificed her social position that I had no desire but to drop the acquaintance. Then an actor offered her marriage and they were married. It was a most generous act, I think, to marry a woman with such a history and a *great* addition to this generosity was his allowing the children to assume *his* surname.

The actor's father, a clergyman, so entirely approved his son's conduct that he came from the North of England to perform the ceremony. This second marriage put her, in the eyes of Society, once more in the position of a respectable woman. And then I asked her mother to ask her if she would like our friendship to begin again and she said "yes." And I went and called on her and her husband.

What a story for the author of *Alice* to write about the Puck who showed him all that little girls dare to be! In 1865, the year *Alice* was published, Lewis Carroll began his long betrayal of all the qualities he had relished on the stage. Once he had cast Ellen Terry in such a story, there was no childhood left for her, and thus (as he saw it), no sexuality, imagination, adventures, or play; no life, in short, but only pious gestures.

As she aged, forgetting the betrayal and remembering only the art, "Wonderland" became her word for all the paradises she fought to recapture: her boy-roles, Watts's paintings, the garden whose key Lewis Carroll withheld. Writing to the American Shakespearean scholar Horace Howard Furness in 1911, she translates herself into an Alice who is also Lewis Carroll, holding the key:

> In spite of myself I leave Wonderland (America) without seeing you—the day I had set aside to <u>chance</u> finding you at yr home I was too ill to budge from my bed= & so - - . . . I'm told you are about starting to see yr grandchild - how lovely it would be (for <u>me</u> at least) if whilst you are in London I might take you & the child to some nice place like the Zoo (<u>for instance</u>)—I know every inch of the gardens & the animals are brought out at un-usual times if certain child-friends of mine wd like to see them--

This is the Ellen Terry Carroll refused to write. There is no trace of the gracious lady to make this invitation a secret penance: Ellen Terry offers herself so gaily that I suspect she forgot about it by the time Horace Howard Furness arrived in London expecting a trip to the zoo. Recapturing her mobility as she writes, she becomes in turn the enchanted child leaving Wonderland and the Carrollian enchanter making wonders for special child-friends. In her mind at least, she can open Wonderland's gate for herself. By 1922 she spent much of her time there. Writing in shaky script to her old friend Ella Casella, she smiles from within the forbidden paradise: "I am with Peter Pan & in the woods all day —. . . It is Fairy Land--& in the evening . . . oh Lor' a mercy but it is Wonderland= Nellen." Denied her rightful role in Lewis Carroll's imagination, her own imagination restores to the old lady the childhood that artists stole.

In 1867 she had not found her word for what was lost. She knew only that family and stage had combined in an incomprehensible betrayal and she hated them both:

> If I had been able to look into the future, I should have been less rebellious at the termination of my first marriage. Was I so rebellious, after all? I am afraid I *showed* about as much rebellion as a sheep. But I was miserable, indignant, unable to understand that there could be any justice in what had happened. In 1866 I returned to the stage. I was practically *driven* back by those who meant to be kind —Tom Taylor, my father and mother, and others. *They* looked ahead and saw clearly it was for my good.
>
> It *was* a good thing, but at the time I hated it. And I hated going back to live at home. Mother furnished a room for me, and I thought the furniture hideous. Poor mother!
>
> For years Beethoven reminded me of mending stockings, because I used to struggle with the large holes in my brothers' stockings upstairs in that ugly room, while downstairs Kate played the "Moonlight Sonata." I caught up the stitches in time to the notes! This was the period when, though every one was kind, I hated my life, hated every one and everything in the world more than at any time before or since. (*Memoirs*, 47–48)

She was the sewing Cinderella, Kate, the privileged artist: in both theaters, that of home and the more obvious one of the Profession, the years of Ellen's dispossession were those of Kate's glory. Effortlessly, Kate had become a star, and just as effortlessly, she was going to be married, and well married. Arthur Lewis was not an artist, but he liked to gather artists around him in his lovely home, Moray Lodge. Kate would retire there when she married: she was infested by none of her sister's turbulent confusions between marriage and art. Try as she did to cast off Ellen, though, she could not escape their looking-glass identities: Moray Lodge, where she would be so perfect a hostess, was right across the way from Little Holland House, where Ellen had been so rude a guest. Moray Lodge was also famous for chic Bohemian entertainments dotted with titles—even the Prince of Wales had come to hear the Moray Minstrels—but

Kate planned to curtail these all-night parties when she presided.

Her farewell performance as Juliet aroused thunders of love. Nobody in Little Holland House missed the departed Nelly, but according to the *Times* at least, the entire world would miss Kate:

At the conclusion of the tragedy, in the course of which Miss Terry was called for at the end of each act, except the fourth, when the good taste of the more intelligent part of the audience suppressed the demand, Miss Terry came on before the curtain in obedience to a thundering summons from every part of the house, and almost overcome with the combined excitement of the part and the occasion, stood for some moments curtseying and smiling under the showers of bouquets and the storm of kindly greeting. Nor when she had retired with her armful of flowers—looking in the white robe and dishevelled hair of Juliet's death scene, as she used to look in Ophelia—was the audience satisfied. Again Miss Terry was recalled, and again she appeared to receive the loud and long-continued plaudits of the crowd. Then the stalls began to clear. But the storm of voices and clapping of hands continued from the pit, boxes, and gallery, through the overture of the farce, swelling till it threatened to grow into a tempest. The curtain rose for the farce; still the thunder roared.

One of the actors, quite inaudible in the clamour, began the performance, but the roar grew louder and louder, till at last Mr. Phillips came on, in the dress of Friar Lawrence, and with a stolidity so well assumed that it seemed perfectly natural, asked, in the stereotyped phrase of the theater, the pleasure of the audience. *"Kate Terry!"* was the reply from a chorus of a thousand stentorian voices; and then the fair favourite of the night appeared once more, pale, and dressed to leave the theatre, and when the renewed roar of recognition had subsided, in answer to her appealing dumb show, spoke, with pathetic effort, a few hesitating words, evidently the inspiration of the moment, but more telling than any set speech, to this effect:—"How I wish from my heart, I could tell you how I feel your kindness, not to-night only, but through the many years of my professional life. What can I say to you but thanks, thanks and good-bye!" After this short and simple farewell, under a still louder salvo of acclamation, unmistakably proving itself popular by its hearty uproariousness, the young actress, almost overpowered by the feelings of the moment, retired with faltering steps, and the crowded audience poured out of the house, their sudden exit *en masse* being itself one of the most flattering tributes to the actress whose last appearance had drawn them together.

Each faltering step led Kate to the virtuous rewards of virtue. She had even taken time to participate in the loving conspiracy to drive Ellen back to the stage—she was clearly safer there than at home—by writing a surprisingly ungracious recommendation to the manager Benjamin Nottingham Webster, whose son was to be Ellen's staunch counselor in her bad years: "It is quite immaterial to me in what way *right* is done, but I certainly consider some acknowledgment is due of my sister—and can't help thinking it has been too long delay'd."

Right was not done in Kate's way, though she was sure she knew the way, having become in turn everything that the oracles of her day told a woman to be. When she ascended a stage again in 1898, she aroused none of the excitement of her farewell Juliet in 1867. She had done everything right, but after all, she had chosen the wrong role: "Unluckily, the part that she had consented to play offered her few opportunities, the lady she represented being simply a sweet and gentle wife and mother, with a pleasant presence, a delightful smile, and a voice (the sweet voice of days gone by) characterized by very winning tenderness. In itself a charming part, but not one that gave scope for acting" (Pemberton, 119).

Even in her days of sewing and hating, Ellen Terry had known in her bones that Kate's good part did not give scope for acting.

Love and the Heart of the Country

When Ellen Terry was "practically *driven* back" to the stage, acting aroused a hysteria in her from which she was never subsequently free. On dutiful days, she controlled it, but on wicked ones—which came increasingly often as she grew older—she didn't bother. During the hated time on Stanhope Street, the artifice of acting came dangerously near the lie of her life. She was a wife and no wife, a daughter and no daughter: as a wife, she had been a daughter, but now, living with family disapproval, she was too knowing a wife to be anybody's protected daughter again. Her non-marriage had even dissolved her stage identity. She had lost her name: managers now billed her as "Nelly Watts" or "Mrs. G. F. Watts." She protested against this net of falsification by committing the actress's cardinal sin: she laughed onstage. In later years, her laughter—or "fooling," as she called it—captivated audiences while it irritated her fellow players. Through laughter, she told a truth too fearfully rich for words about the absurdity of her roles.

When she played a single performance of *The Hunchback* in 1866, she diagnosed her laughter to Mary-Ann Hall as if it were an illness: "I was so very nervous, and oh wretchedly unwell—on the stage I *laughed* as you know, but when I reached my dressing-room I cried with pain in my side." Stardom would transform her guilty hysteria into contagious subversion: "Of her it may indeed be said, She was born to speak 'all mirth and no matter,' " Clement Scott wrote fondly. "I have seen her sit on the stage in a serious play and literally cry with laughing, the audience mistaking her fun for deep emotion; and actors have told me that in the most pathetic scenes she had suddenly been attracted by the humorous side of the situation and almost made them 'dry up,' as the saying goes."

Ellen Terry's great moment as young Harry had come when she looked up into Kate's virtuous face and burst into loud laughter, but the winsome ingenue was forbidden to see funniness in virtue. Her comedy bubbled up as an intensifying hysteria, her only weapon against the pathos engulfing her roles. The funny woman who cried with contagious laughter at her supposedly serious emotions fought in the only way she knew the absurdity of her new self.

In 1867–68, she joined the Wigans' company. The formidable Leonora Wigan took her in hand to cure her of her fidgeting and fooling: " 'Stand still!' she would shout from the stalls. 'Now you're of value! Motionless! Just as you are! *That's* right!' " (*Memoirs,* 59). Too many women had told her she was of value only when she was still. Her mother and Kate, the Pattle sisters, now Mrs. Wigan, all had combined to muffle her into womanly motionlessness. They had all failed; she could not stop her laughter. When Mrs. Wigan hissed her sharply from the audience to cure her giggles, she was terrified but unregenerate. She had wanted grandeur, scope, beauty, art; they demanded placidity. Whether women had hard manners or sweet ones, they conspired to reduce her. As she still loved Signor, so she hoped to be saved from stillness.

At the end of that angry year, she played opposite Henry Irving for the first time. On Boxing Day, the Wigans brought in the intense young actor to play Petruchio to her Kate in Garrick's abridged version of *The Taming of the Shrew.* Having tried vainly to keep Ellen Terry still, Mrs. Wigan imported Henry Irving to be her tamer in play. At twenty-nine, Irving was just beginning to taste success. He had endured ten years of strenuous obscurity in Edinburgh, Dublin, and England's northern provinces, where he played any part that was thrown at him, high or low, comic or tragic, woman or man. On lucky nights he awed audiences, but he had never made them love him. By 1866, he had played 588 roles, but the London success he craved eluded him. Finally, in November, it came. His Rawdon Scudamore, the villainous roué in Dion Boucicault's melodrama *Hunted Down,* chilled audiences and critics alike by its understated evil. When, a year later, he was cast opposite Ellen Terry for the first time, he was gripped by the hope that his long wait for glory might be ending at last.

The play was portentous, but Ellen Terry was too restless to read her destiny.

She did claim later on that Irving talked the language of a taming world: "He had no high opinion of *my* acting! He has said since that he thought me at the Queen's Theatre charming and individual as a woman, but as an actress *hoydenish!*" (*Memoirs*, 61). If Irving did use this word, he joined the armies of female forbidders who were doing their best to still her by expelling her boy-self.

Irving did not look like a tamer to her. He was so ravaged by the success that never came that he touched her as a man who was, in his way, a fellow prisoner: "Henry Irving at first had everything against him as an actor. He could not speak, he could not walk, he could not *look*. He wanted to do things in a part, and he could not do them. His amazing power was imprisoned, and only after long and weary years did he succeed in setting it free" (*Memoirs*, 61).

The Wigans' production of Garrick looked to her like Little Holland House all over again. Mrs. Wigan, like Sara Prinsep, embodied all cruel authority, while Irving, like Watts, was sympathetic because in chains. Her mistrust of women in the 1860s, her emotional affinity with powerful men whom she made kindred spirits rather than tamers, may not have been politically shrewd, but it helped her toward a freeing vision of her own artistry. Mrs. Wigan had tried to constrain her, but Irving's own constraint made her gratefully aware of her ease: "Many of his defects sprang from his not having been on the stage as a child. He was stiff with self-consciousness; his eyes were dull, his face heavy" (*Memoirs*, 61). She cared little that they both "played badly": she remembered that his self-consciousness worked against his taming role and made her feel free.

Irving's obsession with the theater, which in 1867 gripped him with paralyzing intensity, also assured her that she was alive. Their single performance inspired her first proclamation that she was more woman than artist: "His soul was not more surely in his body than in the theatre, and I, a woman who was at that time caring more about life and love than the theatre, must have been to him more or less unsympathetic" (*Memoirs*, 61). The girl who had married in art now disentangled her life as a woman from that art: "love and life" would free her from ridiculous roles. She was about to betray the stage with the man she loved. If she sensed that this abandonment to love would be another sort of performance, one fuller and more complex than Katherine and the others, she never said so.

Her artful dissociation of herself from Irving's single-minded ambition persisted during their spectacular partnership later on, encouraging spectators to love and patronize her. Little Holland House had taught her that it was dangerous for a woman to make large artistic claims: women served mighty men beautifully, and only male grandiosity won approval. After her expulsion, she poured a good deal of artistic energy into a repudiation of artistic ambition. It was some kind of triumph that when she was famous, many men found it impossible to see her as an actress at all. Laurence Irving's biography of his grandfather describes *Katherine and Petruchio* by diagnosing the woman knowingly and ignoring the collaborative artist: "She herself, humiliated and frustrated by the mockery of her marriage to Watts, was longing only for the fulfillment of her womanhood in domestic life."

She *was* humiliated and frustrated, she *did* long for fulfillment of her womanhood, but her alienation was encompassing: in houses as well as on the stage, she was humiliated and frustrated by the roles she had to play. She dreamed of grander stages, grander houses, and above all, grander performances. Like most biographers of actresses, Laurence Irving limits his analysis to her offstage life, ignoring her intense responsiveness to the theatrical roles that were her primary education: these taught her what to be in private. Even when her plays betrayed her, even when she fled the stage to make herself grand through love—as she had done with Watts and was soon to do again with Godwin—her roles were the self she knew most intimately. The actress was always the origin of the woman, though the woman learned to shield the actress strategically from the mistrust of sincere spectators.

In 1867, Ellen Terry was humiliated and frustrated not only by her failed marriage, her dreary and anomalous situation, her relative obscurity, but by *Katherine and Petruchio* itself: the anticlimax of her first performance with Irving arose in part from the insult of Garrick's adaptation, an insult she could not formulate, though she protested against it by playing badly, and one that intensified the insults inflicted on her in society and at home. Her role as Shakespeare/Garrick/Irving/Mrs. Wigan's tamed hoyden crystallized all the lessons she was trying not to learn, all the women she was fighting not to be.

Shakespeare's early farce, *The Taming of the Shrew*, makes brutal material into a witty game. Its comedy demands that the railing, rebellious Katharina be mastered by her husband like a wild hawk. Petruchio, her trainer and bridegroom, claims absolute possession because he is a man: "I will be master of what is mine own: / She is my goods, my chattels; she is my house, / My household stuff, my field, my barn, / My horse, my ox, my ass, my any thing" (*TS*, III, ii, 231–34). With consummate tact, Shakespeare transmutes this predictable farce about power and submission into a comedy about the delights of education. Like Jane Austen's heroines, Kate wins mental freedom as she submits to dependence; her growing warmth and flexibility persuade the audience that for a woman at least, inner freedom lies in outward submission. Like Jane Austen's *Emma, The*

Taming of the Shrew lives on its rich tensions between the heroine's recurrent humiliations and her inward growth. A female and comic variation of Shakespeare's tragic kings, Katharina gains when she abdicates the treasures hidden in her own mind and heart.

David Garrick's 1756 *Katherine and Petruchio,* which displaced Shakespeare onstage for more than a century, has none of this witty dialectic between humiliation and growth: Petruchio breaks Kate down, and that is that. Garrick's abbreviation dispossesses the heroine not only of her complex centrality, but of her best lines. In Shakespeare's play, Kate sees the light when Petruchio eyes the sun and exclaims provocatively: "Lord, how bright and goodly shines the moon!" All at once, she realizes that objects may be what one wills. Her sudden illumination inspires an acquiescence that brings her close to Juliet's imaginative appropriation of all bodies and heavenly bodies: "And be it moon, or sun, or what you please: / And if you please to call it a rush-candle, / Henceforth I vow it shall be so for me" (*TS,* IV, v, 13–15). By contrast, Garrick's Kate says laconically, "I see 'tis vain to struggle with my bonds." In the same spirit, Shakespeare's Kate makes a long speech of public submission at the end: humbled, she is allowed to hold the stage for the first time. Garrick's Petruchio takes over most of this peroration while Kate listens in reverent stillness, murmuring only such accompaniment as: "Nay, then I'm all unworthy of thy Love, / And look with Blushes on my former self." Garrick's Kate loses not only her primacy, but her words and her soul. In 1867, after more than a hundred years, she was still more palatable to audiences than was Shakespeare's indigestibly many-sided heroine.

"*Stand still!* Now you're of value! Motionless! Just as you are! *That's* right." So Garrick in the voice of Henry Irving told her when she acted; Mrs. Wigan when she rehearsed; Watts when she posed; Mrs. Prinsep when she sat in drawing rooms with the other wives; her mother and Kate when she came home to play a humiliated daughter. When she played Garrick's Kate badly in a holiday matinee, all these tamings rushed together. The laughing audience's festivity was madness to the actress. Shortly afterwards, while playing in a "comedietta" called *The Household Fairy*—no doubt in a role similar to the one Garrick's Kate was expected to play once she had learned to blush at her unworthy self—she ran off with Edward William Godwin to an untamed world beyond families and beyond theaters. She had married in art; sick of it, she would love in nature.

FALLEN WOMAN Before she became intoxicated with Watts's studio, Godwin's house in Bristol had taught her to associate home with settings more beautiful than any theater could provide. His architectural designs did not end at exteriors: with scrupulous love, he designed furniture and costumes as well. Godwin offered Ellen Terry not only love, but sumptuously arranged privacy. Fallows Green, the house he built for them in Harpenden, nestled in the enticing quietness of the southern English countryside, but its interior swathed its inhabitants in the exotic beauty of Japan. Ellen Terry wore blue-and-white cotton to match the decorative scheme; their daughter Edy pattered about in kimonos. No one barked orders to be still. All life was suffused with the sensuous glow of God's countryside and Godwin's interiors.

Ellen Terry's flight was her one great leap beyond the boundaries of her life. In abandoning *The Household Fairy,* she abandoned the family and the theater that had become so entangling. Six years later, she returned to both, transfigured. Her marriage to Watts had given her a poignantly lovable self; her love affair in Godwin's ravishing world gave her an untamed and defiant glow that her long subsequent years of useful service to an increasingly patriarchal profession would never extinguish. At twenty-one, while other young girls were declaring themselves adults by submerging themselves as wives, Ellen Terry cast off household fairies and, for the only time in her life, composed her own drama.

Godwin was almost irrelevant, though she loved him all her life. She had chosen not only a man: she had chosen a self at last. Since she could not imagine a self that was independent of the roles her culture constructed for women— and since, as Virginia Woolf realized when she re-wrote *Freshwater,* Ellen Terry could not return to childhood and play young Harry again—she became a fallen woman, scandalous and blessed. It was a brilliantly right decision.

Later on, people who loved Ellen Terry tried to explain away this one act of wholehearted disobedience. When she became a matriarch, her daughter Edy never dared disobey *her.* Characteristically, when Edy and Christopher St. John wrote explanatory notes to Ellen Terry's Memoir, they placed on the irascible Ben and Sarah the burden of responsibility for the trapped girl's flight:

> There is no proof that Ellen Terry left the stage in 1868 without hesitation, and voluntarily. . . . Who would wish to pry into the secret places of Ellen Terry's heart? But the story that she ran away from her family and the stage at the dictates of love is not the exact truth. The parents of the youthful Mrs. Watts were, in spite of their association with the stage, in spite of their having begun their married life unconventionally with an elopement, eminently Victorian in their standards of conduct. An indiscretion of Nelly's—it is said that when Edward Godwin was ill, she stayed to look after him one night instead of returning home—led to a domestic scene, that often acted scene which ends in a door being slammed on an erring daughter. [Marguerite Steen repeats this story, which Manvell, p. 336,

dismisses as "so much moonshine." For years it served as a convenient family justification of the key events of Ellen Terry's wild years.] The sequel was that Ellen Terry "set up house" with Edward Godwin somewhere in Hertfordshire. One reason for her abandoning the stage at the same time appears to have been that she had incurred the disapproval of all the friends who had interested themselves in her career as an actress. She may have been influenced too by a genuine wish not to be a source of embarrassment to her family. Her sister Kate, through her marriage, now occupied a social position of some importance. The conclusion that Ellen Terry's retirement was to some extent forced on her is not fantastic, and quite compatible with her statement that she did not regret it, and for a time was blissfully happy. (*Memoirs*, 63–64)

Edy and Chris wanted to present a single-minded artist, not a woman who abandoned herself to love in the years when her beauty and energy were at their zenith. But no one forced Ellen Terry into exile: while her life with her newly genteel family seems to have been intolerable to her, many girls her age lived more desperately at home and never considered running away. Nor was love alone her motive. Her flight was her own route to an artistic self-creation both family and theater denied her, a route more circuitous and devious than the blunt Edy and Chris, who were so intolerant of Victorian by-ways, could understand.

Lewis Carroll's excuse was more tender, familiar, and conventional; her apologists were fond of it. He asserted, as we have seen, that Ellen Terry could not marry Godwin only because she was still technically married to Watts: "If the marriage ceremony were *possible* I would insist on it before living with him. It is *not* possible and I will do without it." But as far as we can tell, she spoke no such speech. By definition, marriage played no part in her country life, which thronged with Godwin, night skies, soft animals, and the food she was learning to cook erratically: "beautifully made, well-cooked vegetables, and pastry like the foam of the sea," as well as an odd-smelling chicken whose "in'ards" she had neglected to remove (*Memoirs*, 67). Finally, there were the incomparably brilliant Edy and Ted, with their piercing mystical observations that took her breath away. Marriage had nothing to do with these discoveries, and further-more, it would destroy the fallen woman she had found such bounty in becom-ing.

In 1868, fallen women were acquiring a glamor in the Victorian imagination that common prostitutes had never had. The prostitutes who were rampant in London and other industrial cities turned their femaleness into their profession. Common snobbery still associated them with actresses: both were "public women" whose bodies and whose simulated emotions were the tools of their trade. Actresses of Ellen Terry's generation, who exalted themselves as artists, shuddered at the association; by the 1860s, carefully genteel divas like Helen Faucit, Marie Bancroft, and Madge Kendal were protesting against the prostitute's shadow on them. From the actress's perspective, prostitutes were sordid and exploited laborers whose helpless enslavement to their "profession" had nothing to do with the noble art of the stage. By the 1880s, a tough-minded genteel generation had transcended this indignity. Worried Victorians had more trouble exorcising the prostitute's specter from the traditional wife's sanctity, for wives too were often deprived of choice when they sold their bodies and their sometimes simulated emotions to men who were shopping.

Fallen women were something else again. Even when they suffered, they were the antithesis of wives. Officially they existed to be shunned, but secretly—unlike prostitutes—they inflamed the imaginations of "good" women, among them actresses. Fallen women were not in thrall to a dismal trade; they were visionaries, like *David Copperfield*'s Little Em'ly or Tolstoy's Anna Karenina, who flung themselves beyond the protective boundaries of paternalistic society. According to Victorian popular mythology, their sin always involved a sexual trespass; inevitably, this same mythology decreed, they doomed themselves to an ostracism followed by ghastly death; popular prints showed them drowning in the foul Thames. In art at least, for all their woe, their sin licensed them to live and suffer on a grand scale that diminished respectable wives and daughters. When she fell from a life hemmed in by restrictions and taboos, a woman might find her fall the only avenue by which she was allowed to grow.

East Lynne, Ellen Wood's wildly popular novel about a fallen wife, sent a thrill through the wives of England when it exhorted them to resist the impulses it recognized so acutely: "Oh, reader, believe me! Lady—wife—mother! should you ever be tempted to abandon your home, so [in an "abyss of horror"] will you awake! Whatever trials may be the lot of your married life, though they may magnify themselves to your crushed spirit as beyond the endurance of woman to bear, *resolve* to bear them; fall down upon your knees and pray to be enabled to bear them; pray for patience; pray for strength to resist the demon that would urge you to escape; bear unto death, rather than forfeit your fair name and your good conscience; for be assured that the alternative, if you rush on to it, will be found far worse than death!"

Really though, Isabel Vane's alternative is an emotional exaltation, a fluidity and expansiveness of being, that dwarf her ritualistic punishment and self-punishment. The fallen woman was permitted a virtuosity that had hitherto been allowed only to actresses. It was no wonder that real actresses, as well as homebound women, were drawn to this titanic outcast. The fallen woman glorified sexuality and redeemed love from married deference; the enormity of her sin allowed her to live enormously and to die memorably; in her, the ordinary woman took on the grandeur of the actress, while the supposedly shallow actress acquired the emotional depth ordinary women were supposed to have. Falling turned domestic life into a theater.

Since Ellen Terry was technically a wife when she ran off with Godwin, the exhortation of *East Lynne* was meant for her. It didn't quite fit, however. She had never sanctified a real home; she had never even lived in one. Her family, like the theater they mirrored, were just learning to ape respectability, and doing it badly. The world beyond their control was no abyss of horror; she knew she would be happy in the country with Godwin. The taboos of her day were stage furies that did not touch her life.

If any one fallen woman taught Ellen Terry how to be an exile, it might have been Alexander Dumas' Marguerite Gauthier. The heroine of *La Dame aux Camélias* (1852) also begins her play as a glamorous outsider—though she is a courtesan, not an actress—who falls only when she falls in love. She too celebrates her love by fleeing to the country; artful nature consecrates that love and lets her blaze into stardom. In the 1880s and 1890s, Bernhardt and Duse would vie publicly and gloriously over which of them could play Dumas' tender courtesan most heartrendingly. By that time Ellen Terry was enshrined as a good woman, paying only furtive tributes to the lady of the camellias: when a biographer of the great French actress Rachel complained that as Marguerite Gauthier, Rachel dwarfed the other characters, Ellen Terry testily defended in the margin of her book both actress and role: "because she (the actress) was great, and they (the rest) were small." In the privacy of the heart of England, she too had played Marguerite Gauthier and been great, loving gloriously in the country and leaving small people behind.

She knew she was choosing a role, one that forbade her to forget that she was still married to Watts. Where we expect a description of Godwin, her memoir substitutes a ghoulishly funny account of her drowned double. Through this mysterious corpse, Ellen Terry initiates herself into the role of fallen woman, tortures her parents, and remarries Watts, all at once:

> My retirement was a very different one from my sister Kate's. I left the stage quietly and secretly, and I was cut off from my family and friends.
>
> Then a dreadful thing happened. A body was found in the river—the dead body of a young woman, very fair and slight and tall. Every one thought it was my body.
>
> I had gone away without a word. No one knew where I was. My own father

identified the corpse, and Floss and Marion, at their boarding-school, were put into mourning. Then mother went. She kept her head under the shock of the likeness, and bethought her of "a strawberry mark upon my left arm." (*Really* it was on my left knee.) That settled it, for there was no such mark to be found upon the poor corpse. It was just at this moment that the news came to me in my country retreat that I had been found dead, and I flew up to London to give ocular proof to my poor and distracted parents that I was alive. Mother, who had been the only one not to identify the drowned girl, confessed to me that she was so like me that just for a second she, too, was deceived. You see, they knew I had not been very happy since my return to the stage, and when I went away without a word, they were terribly anxious, and prepared to believe the first bad tidings that ever came to hand. It came in the shape of that most extraordinary likeness between me and that poor soul who threw herself into the river. (*Memoirs*, 65)

This bizarre compound of art, nature, and theater sets the scene of Ellen Terry's fallen life. Through the medium of "that poor soul who threw herself in the river," she dramatizes her role as fallen woman. At the same time, she laughs in its face, casting off retributive wretchedness to thrive in the country. The poor corpse becomes her instrument of revenge against her family, even against the good little sisters her childhood earnings keep safe in genteel school. Only her sharp-eyed mother refuses to confuse the wayward Nelly with a poor corpse; with the same pitiless skepticism, the sharp-eyed Edy who is soon to be born will see through her charades later on. The poor corpse is the pathetic self she was learning to play so adroitly.

For the drowned girl recalled the haunting creatures Watts created. His well-known painting, "Found Drowned" (c. 1850), aggrandizes another poor corpse, that of a fallen woman dredged from the river, sprawled in a monumental crucified position; a single star looks down at her. One account of Ellen Terry's elopement has her announcing her flight to her family by attaching to a photograph of Watts the prophetic words, "found drowned." She cast off Watts's allowance, but her rebellion conformed to his iconography. Her bizarre account of her drowned double realizes while it seems to repudiate her husband's starkest painting.

Ophelia was still more vivid than Watts's grand and nameless corpse; she too followed Ellen Terry to the country. On the face of it, her sedate life with Godwin had little in common with Ophelia's lunatic pageants. Before the children were born, they saw scarcely anyone in their tiny cottage at Hertfordshire. In the periods when Godwin was traveling on architectural commissions, they barely saw each other; Ellen Terry rose dutifully with him at six and proceeded to manage the house, the little maid, the garden, the throngs of animals. When Godwin was there, she played his helpmate with ardor, copying his designs in delicate watercolors and reading Shakespeare with him, not as a star, but as a research assistant for his ambitious articles, "Architecture and Costume of Shakespeare's Plays."

In December, 1869, fourteen months after their elopement, Edy was born. Her father ennobled her as he did his buildings, by imagining her as a revenant from the deep past: he named her Edith after Eadgyth, daughter of Godwin, Earl of the West Saxons (Prideaux, 78). Ted's birth in 1872 prompted Godwin to build for the family their beloved house, Fallows Green, whose medieval facade covered interiors that were startlingly Japanese. Fallows Green brought all Godwin's loves together. The fallen family seemed as durable as the trees that watched over its growth.

But Ophelia was a spectral presence, for she was central to the Victorian iconography of fallenness. She begins her life in *Hamlet* as a product of the sick court, kept artifically—perhaps even questionably—pure by her suspicious father and brother. When the tormented prince excoriates her as a liar and an actress—"God has given you one face, and you make yourselves another" (III, i, 149–50)—she embraces an insane pastoralism. Her madness is strewn with flowers and haunted by rustic sex. Under its spell, she no longer belongs to the court; she gives herself to the country as Ellen Terry did. When she drowns —and she is the only character in this corpse-strewn play who manages to die outdoors—she is both submerged by nature and reborn into it. Ellen Terry's discovery of love and sexuality in the country imitated Ophelia as consummately as it did Marguerite Gauthier.

As yet there was only proxy madness there, brought by the Mrs. Rumball who looked after the children: "[Boo] was the wife of a doctor who kept a private asylum in the neighbouring village, and on his death she tried to look after the lunatics herself. But she wasn't at all successful! They kept escaping, and people didn't like it. This was my gain, for 'Boo' came to look after me instead and for the next thirty years I was her only lunatic, and she my most constant companion and dear and loyal friend" (*Memoirs*, 68–69). Safe in nature, Ellen Terry abandoned herself happily to Boo's keeping.

After Ellen Terry died, Edy veiled this period piously: "Who would wish to pry into the secret places of Ellen Terry's heart?" Even if we did wish to pry—and we do of course—no letters or photographs survive from her six-year idyll. Buried seductively among trees—not in the sort of sham suburb that enclosed Little Holland House and Moray Lodge—Fallows Green was a temple of art in nature. Within it, and sometimes, one suspects, outside it as well, Ellen Terry was assured that her long, perfected body was not meant to be embarrassing; as her instincts had always told her, it was a treasure in which art and nature blessed each other and taught her how to bless a lover at last.

She would remember with pride her self-forgetting devotion to Godwin, but she may have been more immersed in her own sensations than she was in her lover. Marguerite Steen's witty account questions Ellen Terry's ability to minister. Steen contrasts Kate's fierce absorption in the role of matron with the abstractedness within Ellen's "absolute devotion." Carelessly, she drifted and dreamed through Godwin's meticulously arranged rooms:

> [Kate] regulated her own life no less strictly than she regulated that of her staff; an hour for needlework, an hour for baby Katie, an hour for conference with the cook, butler and parlourmaid, an hour for rest—so that when Arthur Lewis came home from his office in Conduit Street he found a smiling, *soignée* young wife, prepared to entertain or be entertained, to go to "the play," with perhaps a supper party to follow, or enjoy "a little music" at home with a few chosen friends.
>
> Sister Nelly, also heavy with child, cooked abominable meals for her lover, invariably forgetting some essential ingredient, or letting the dish burn while she petted the animals, or wandered along the hedgerows, gathering autumn leaves and berries, which she was idly arranging while Godwin craved for his supper. For "staff" she had a rough girl who knew as little as herself about cookery, and was equally forgetful. There would be no fuel, or no oil in the lamps; no water drawn from the pump, and a litter of lifeless ash on the hearth. [Steen also claims, p. 134, that Ellen Terry forgot to pay the bills.] And upon this joyless scene would arrive a tired, chilled, nervous man, having made the journey from London in an unheated third-class carriage. Nelly would sit up to all hours, making tracings and transcriptions from his current notes. Was Godwin to be blamed if he longed at moments for a buxom, brainless mistress who would produce a blazing fire and a succulent steak and leave him, in the long night watches, to get on with his own work? Like many of his kind, he wanted to eat his cake and have it. He wanted the inspiration of Nelly's beauty, her iridescent presence, and expected her at the same time to minister to his (admittedly not exigent) material needs.
>
> Wholly self-centered, he took it for granted that this young, beautiful and gifted companion would devote herself to his interests, be grateful for the favours he bestowed (at his convenience) upon her, and act round the clock as his housekeeper, cook, amanuensis, and partner of his bed. He never recognized the crying need in Nelly, after her disastrous marriage, of tenderness and care. Of both he was incapable. He was, according to his lights, "in love" with her; but love, to Godwin, carried none of the connotations it implied to a romantic and sensitive

girl. A monumental egoist, taking feminine adulation for granted, his increasing professional prestige gradually took precedence of his attachment to Nelly. (Steen, 122–23)

Ellen Terry's domestic daze rings true, though Steen's indignation against the heartless Godwin mitigates her heroine's equal self-centeredness. Despite her later pride in having lived for another, Ellen Terry was in the country to let nature grow in her, not to keep house. Once more, she and Kate were mirror images: in her early years of marriage, Kate had turned into the household fairy Ellen had plunged into nature to escape. Godwin seems far less egotistical a companion than Steen implies. The aesthete for whom every room was a temple of beauty may have found Ellen Terry's sloppiness less enchanting as the years went on. Moreover, the exigencies of his work in London, his long journeys in that unheated third-class carriage, suggest that living in the heart of the country brought him some discomfort. For as long as they stayed there, though, Godwin did his game best to play the role she assigned him.

For all the rapture and romance he brought Ellen Terry, we know that role better than we do the man. The shadowiness that dogs him is one requirement of that role. Armand Duval, the hero of *La Dame aux Camélias,* satisfies the audience through a similar shadowiness: he lives obligingly to catalyze Marguerite Gauthier's extravagant rebirth. Edward William Godwin was a well-cast lover, for his best-remembered achievement is the inspiration he gave his more famous aesthetic contemporaries. His sole biographer attributes to Oscar Wilde a cryptic sonnet to Godwin that begins by crowning "A man of men, born to be general king, / By frank election of the artist kind, / Attempting all things, and on anything / Setting the signet of a master mind" (quoted in Harbron, 185). This "general king," though, has no one attribute that gives him contour. In the same spirit, Max Beerbohm dubbed him "the greatest aesthete of them all," but singled out for commemoration no particular work. Godwin was a superb midwife, not merely to Ellen Terry, but to an audacious generation of art-worshippers who paid generous tribute to the leader they overshadowed. Edy and Ted, to whom he was no more than a powerful shadow, assumed his catalyzing role. Heroine of a coterie when she died, Edy bullied and galvanized a generation of feminists who became distinguished in the British theater; Gordon Craig, the mysterious begetter of theatrical Modernism, accepted wryly from his obscure retreat the tributes of famous men.

Godwin had not aspired to ignite others' masterpieces. He wanted to be not only an acolyte of beauty, but its sole source: "In his own person and practice Godwin tried to unite all the arts; he disliked the title architect as too limited"

(Harbron, 39). He dreamed of transforming not only England's public buildings, but its privacy: houses, rooms, furniture, textiles, clothes, all aroused his fever to beautify. He designed homes for Wilde and Whistler—neither of which has survived as he conceived it—but he could not touch his country. His influence never approached that of William Morris, who aspired similarly to beautify all facets of British life: Godwin lacked the private income that allowed Morris to organize the guilds that made his books, furniture, and textiles. Haunted by other ages, he became a learned antiquarian, particularly of his native Bristol, but never a national restorer. As commissions for public buildings diminished, he turned to theatrical design, where, in miniature, he realized his dream. He had hoped to renew England; in 1886, his ambitious production of Sophocles' *Helena in Troas* constructed for a select audience a restored ancient Greece. For a short time and in a limited space, Godwin built a nation.

A contemporary photograph shows a trim dandy with melancholy, recessive eyes. His withdrawn face takes animation from its jaunty beard, a dapper hat and pocket handkerchief. In itself that face is sad and strained; accessories give life to the man. Like his photograph, Godwin never gained focus apart from the objects that moved him. Perhaps because he could never gather his energies

Edward William Godwin.

effectively, he became the prey of violent rages and mysterious breakdowns that intensified as he grew older. Knowing him meant knowing his frustrations, his explosions. As a domestic presence, Harbron compares him to that paragon of irascible Victorian fatherhood, the Reverend Patrick Brontë, who was said to have cut up his wife's gowns when black moods descended. Edy was six when Godwin left the family. She remembered his rages. Teddy, who was three, forgot them.

When Teddy became Edward Gordon Craig and plunged into a quest for his elusive father, he found only his own feelings of loss and some dead facts: "Mr. Harbron's book on E. W. G. is carefully done, and only after much patient research. Most of the information it contains was unknown to me—but I know the truth about E. W. G. through my blood and bones." Craig's memoir goes on to transcribe a bare chronology of Godwin's career, which has no glimmer of human or particular "truth." No matter how frantically he embraced his own blood and bones, Gordon Craig would never know his father. He transmitted this mystery to his own sons, to whom Godwin became an unattainable image of ideal fatherhood in art. The shadowiness that darkened Godwin's life became his most effective legacy to the son and grandsons who needed gods.

In Ellen Terry's memoir, Godwin is no more than an occasional name who never comes to life. In 1908, a tenacious Victorian discretion made her excise him from her rural idyll. In her own account, she lives, cooks, and gives birth in a strangely intense solitude: "I was very happy, leading a quiet, domestic life in the heart of the country. When my two children were born, I thought of the stage less than ever. They absorbed all my time, all my interest, all my love" (*Memoirs,* 62). As she describes them, her six years produced a fuller intercourse with nature than with any living man. There was reality in this reticence. As bills and bailiffs troubled their retreat, and (no doubt) as babies cried unbeautifully, Godwin spent more and more time in London, leaving Ellen Terry and the children alone in a countryside as eerie and sinister as it was romantic. Godwin's absence from her memoir is false literally, but not emotionally. Ellen Terry never doubted that she was the star of her own rebirth. In her life as in literary incarnations of fallen women, her lover was less a memorable man than he was an unforgettable agent of her own empowering change.

His advent does alter her memoir, but more in its form than its content. Once she falls in love, her narrative method changes: she moves from bold and powerful vignettes to suggestion and indirection. With the loss of girlhood, she casts off direct presentation, telling the truth but (in Emily Dickinson's words) telling it slant. Accounts of men who occupy only a moment in her life combine to form a secret portrait of Godwin, of whom she cannot speak directly. Envy and anger predominate in these sketches, as they did, perhaps, in her memory of love.

Her first sketch is a portent from her stage childhood. The little girl is picked to walk on in *The Merchant of Venice* with a scene-stealing basket of doves. In 1875, the woman would play a scene-stealing Portia in a *Merchant* where only a few connoisseurs appreciated Godwin's gorgeous mounting. "The other little boys and girls in the company regarded those doves with eyes of bitter envy. One little chorus boy, especially, though he professed a personal devotion of the tenderest kind for me, could never quite get over those doves, and his romantic sentiments cooled considerably when I gained my proud position as dove-bearer. Before, he shared his sweets with me, but now he transferred both sweets and affection to some more fortunate little girl. Envy, after all, is the death of love!" (*Memoirs,* 21). Is Ellen Terry's story of the jealous chorus boy a veiled account of Godwin's abandonment many years later? Godwin left her household after their sole collaboration, the Bancrofts' *Merchant of Venice,* in which his scrupulously reconstructed Venice set off her regal Portia. Godwin was destined to inspiring obscurity; Ellen Terry went on to fame. A short time after their separation he married his student, Beatrice Philip, who would never dwarf his designs. Had he, like the envious chorus boy, refused to share more grown-up sweets with the beloved who eclipsed him? A wry anecdote from Ellen Terry's childhood carries glimpses of an envy that may have been the death of a love she could not write about directly.

In 1866, before joining the Wigans' company, Ellen Terry went to Paris for the first time with an unidentified friend who may have been Godwin. She describes the trip hastily—even her first sight of Bernhardt is only sketched in —but she expatiates in surprising detail on the indignities jealous little French-men inflict on noble women. The most telling of these vignettes may contain undercurrents of a violence nearer to home, that of Godwin himself:

> The friend who took me everywhere in Paris landed me one night in the dressing-room of a singer. I remember it because I heard her complain to a man of some injustice. She had not got some engagement that she expected.
> "It serves you damn right!" he answered. For the first time I seemed to realise how brutal it was of a man to speak to a woman like that, and I *hated* it. (*Memoirs,* 57–58)

The eruption of this sudden and seemingly inconsequent anecdote shortly before Ellen Terry's veiled account of her elopement may cast into dramatic disguise a complaint she could not make directly. Like the brutal Frenchman in her story,

Godwin was moody, jealous, psychically if not actually violent. After their separation, she wrote of him: "He is apt to brood and imagine all kinds of ills which do not exist. . . . He never was happy—he never will be." He flailed out at others in part because the work that drove him brought him no power beyond the limited spaces he controlled absolutely. Like Watts's studio, like the Wigans' stage, the garden in Harpenden held beautified rage against Ellen Terry's energy. Only in Parisian disguise could she tell tales of gifted, splendid women, galled by injustice and humiliated by little men. Only through writing of another country could she express her own hate of the hate within the shining love that transformed her life and glorified her memories.

If Godwin loved her jealously, he was jealous not in the conventional way of her fidelity, but of her potential for a life outside their retreat. Gordon Craig would be gripped by the same jealousy. His love for his mother took the form of rage at the "E. T." who swallowed up his "Nelly" and swept into the world: "E. T. was always getting in the way of my mother . . . I continue to speak of them as two, because although one and the same person, they were leagues apart . . ." His desire that Mother have no identity beyond his ken and control did not check the proud declarations of independence with which he left her repeatedly. His father had done the same thing before him. When Ellen Terry wrote about her one great love affair as a solitary retreat where she communed unreservedly with nature, animals, and her children, she was not false to love. Godwin's presence was erratic, his sympathy uncertain, but he aroused in her the rapture that enabled her to love herself without audiences.

His legacy was the deep countryside of England, a countryside that in the 1860s awoke painful longings in many Victorians because it seemed to be on the brink of extinction: urbanization, suburbanization, and industrialism were turning England's green world into an achingly loved memento mori. She had first discovered that world on the happy tour when she played young Harry and laughed at everything: "Oh, those delightful journeys on the open road! I tasted the joys of the strolling player's existence, without its miseries. I saw the country for the first time. . . . When they asked me what I was thinking of as we drove along, I remember answering: 'Only that I should like to run wild in a wood for ever!' " With Godwin she could do so. Loyalty to those days with him would inspire her to accumulate property in the country and, finally, to die there.

The country was her new family. Some claim waspishly that she played at country living "like Marie Antoinette in the Trianon," but she never covered her unease at the lonely distances, at the mice that ran down her dress, at the animals that loomed at her or that had to be killed. Fear of the country intensified her life in it, just as fear had electrified her Prince Arthur when she was little. The country enthralled her because she was not a child of nature. Even when, as an aging woman longing for peace, she moved into her beloved farm at Smallhythe, she didn't pretend to adore its primitivism: "It's pretty rough at the Farmhouse! 'The simple life' <u>indeed</u>! but at least there's a jolly big Bath there —" The country was not always her friend, any more than Watts's portraits were, but like them it enlarged her imagination of the things she could be.

W. Graham Robertson's adoring account makes her self-consecration in nature more sexless than it was, but his incantatory prose is true to her fundamental solitude: "She learned in her sorrow to creep close to the heart of Nature and to draw from it help and comfort, in her joy to turn to Nature for an answering smile." In truth, her country life was a discovery of physicality: like Lawrence's Lady Chatterley, she learned in Harpenden to touch things that were alive, after having been trained to bestow her own imagined life on stage properties. She learned impalpable majesty only as an accompaniment to things she could caress. According to Robertson, her unnamed companion taught her how to make her thoughts great: "For one whole night . . . you must lie out in the fields alone and watch the sky from dusk to dawn."

An attentive student of nineteenth-century avenues to holiness, she did let the night change her, even though she probably did not lie alone in it: "What she had learnt that night she could not tell; she could not remember, but she *knew,* and the knowledge remained with her. What she had learnt was something of proportion, something of rhythm, of reverence, of melody—she could not formulate, only feel, but the memory never faded, and all through her life she found courage and peace in a vision of stars passing across the sky above Fallows Green." In *The Prelude,* the responsive young Wordsworth has similar experiences; these make of him a virtuous man and a bard. They apparently made Ellen Terry something of a witch, for she became "a daughter of the night, . . . loving the moon with a strange ecstasy which I have never met with in another."

Even in this most private time, Ellen Terry acted dreams that were not entirely her own. Wordsworth had made himself Nature's priest to later generations; even Victorians who had never bothered to read him knew that solitude in Nature awakened great and holy thoughts. Later, less austere writers put lovers in the landscape, but they left its essential solitude undisturbed. Even *Lady Chatterley's Lover* (1928), whose scandalous veneer masks a cry of nostalgia for anachronistic and vanishing forms of love, makes Mellors a more dependable catalyst to Constance Chatterley than he is a companion: nature and the arousal of her senses compose a healing process that restores her more to herself than to him. Dreams of love did not free themselves from Wordsworthian exhortations to solitude. Often, in literature, when a beloved is there at all, that presence becomes Nature's agent, coupling the lover with the landscape.

The most intensely imagined Victorian lovers are solitary figures who sink rapturously into the natural world. In the melodramas that bred Ellen Terry, the fallen woman is rarely separable from her iconographic punishment, suicide by drowning. Poetry transmutes melodrama's retribution into a baptismal exaltation that lures *all* lovers. In one of Tennyson's characteristic, vividly erotic lyrics (1830), Mariana, an obscure and largely silent character in Shakespeare's *Measure for Measure,* acts an inner drama in which her lover smites her with the shadow of his absence, causing her mind to dissolve in a landscape that realizes her own hungers and fears:

> And ever when the moon was low,
>   And the shrill winds were up and away,
> In the white curtain, to and fro,
>   She saw the gusty shadow sway.
> But when the moon was very low,
>   And wild winds bound within their cell,
>   The shadow of the poplar fell
> Upon her bed, across her brow.
>   She only said, "The night is dreary,
>   He cometh not," she said;
>   She said, "I am aweary, aweary,
>   I would that I were dead!" (ll. 49–60)

For Mariana and a host of amorous characters, love works its own transformations alone; a beloved is needed only fleetingly, to set them in motion. Love bestows not companionship, houses, and heirs, but solitude, madness and symbolic drowning in the non-human world that waits to swallow consciousness.

Victorian love literature subverted official ideologies of strenuous progress. Dreams of drowning, of flight, of forbidden pleasures in strange lands, of solitary extinction in quiet nature, held an erotic attraction that the things readers were supposed to want did not inspire. Work, family, and duty, those bricks of civilization, won devotion, not desire. When Ellen Terry fled to the country, she lived the longings of her audience, becoming the women in poetry and fiction whose dangerous passions they had shared. Even when she exiled herself from the theater, her fidelity to the thwarted imaginations of people who did not act justified the rapturous reception she received when she returned to audiences.

Her submergence in love and nature lived the erotic escapes of literary heroines, but this actress whose only school was experience attuned herself to her age not by reading about it, but by living in it and feeling its dreams. From childhood, she had learned to sense what people sitting beneath her in the dark wanted her to be; her work was to become that woman, no matter what in her was amputated or denied along the way. Her life in Harpenden acted out a longed-for and impossible ritual in the 1860s, one that was particularly alluring to frustrated men.

The powerful dream Ellen Terry lived was not, in literature at least, a woman's dream. Weary men like Tennyson wrote about weary women whose consciousnesses were obliterated in lush landscapes, but women rarely thirsted to have their minds extinguished. Teachers, preachers, and doctors routinely exhorted women that mental activity would make them ill: freedom lay in forbidden energy. Women writers conveyed erotic excitement by imagining a sharper consciousness, an intenser awareness, than authorities prescribed. Perhaps because her idyll was shaped by others' longings, Ellen Terry left Harpenden with surprising alacrity when the time came to go back to work. Like many men, Gordon Craig wanted her to cling to her retreat, censuring her resilience: "E. T. worked on. Strange to realize now that she did not kill herself [when Godwin left]. Is it that she was made of more clay than spirit?" (*Index*, 21).

She had lived the intensest love she could imagine; she had given it the holiest and most beautiful settings; but she had never acted a peculiarly female dream of love in which the meek subordinate evolves into the ruler of her broken master. Charlotte Brontë's *Jane Eyre* and Elizabeth Barrett Browning's *Aurora Leigh* are love stories whose erotic power comes from the woman's refusal to drown: both Jane and Aurora gain social, intellectual, and sexual energy as their oppressive lovers diminish. At the end, both heroines guide their blinded husband/masters tenderly: eroticism clings to the illicit alertness the women acquire when their powerful men are maimed. Love is consummated in mastery, not escape. Later, when she was beautifully useful to Henry Irving, Ellen Terry began to learn this dream, but the twenty-one-year-old girl could conceive no feminist alternatives to her illicit pastoral. Being a fallen woman stretched her defiant imagination to the limit. Besides, this particularly flexible role not only shocked her tamers: it could be accommodated at need to the selfless idioms of the Victorian wife.

Her six years with Godwin allowed her to defy convention while at the same time she certified herself as a good woman: "If it is the mark of the artist to love art before everything, to renounce everything for its sake, to think all the sweet human things of life well lost if only he may attain something, do some good, great work—then I was never an artist. I have been happiest in my work when I was working for some one else. I admire those impersonal people who care for nothing outside their own ambition, yet I detest them at the same time, and I have the simplest faith that absolute devotion to another human being means the greatest *happiness*. That happiness for a time was mine" (*Memoirs*, 66). This is the sort of womanly piety that made Edy and Christopher St. John wince; in their annotations to Ellen Terry's memoir, they do their best to excuse it. Ellen Terry's "absolute devotion" to Godwin is certainly debatable; their love affair was a glorious retreat for her, but for him it was a source of exhaustion, financial anxiety, and professional sacrifice. In Ellen Terry's lifelong self-creation, though, her six years of love in the country allowed her to become a recognizable woman without being tamed into self-obliteration. She could glory in an exemplary female identity while retaining young Harry's license to laugh at virtue. That happiness for a time was hers indeed.

Ellen Terry may not have lived for Godwin, but when he was there, she did, joyfully, live with him. Accounts of her life repeatedly describe her happy journey in the pony-cart to meet him at the railway station, and her frequent forlorn returns in the gathering dark when he failed to arrive; once, a drunken rustic leaped into the pony-cart, forcing her to fight him off with her whip. These pathetic anecdotes of abandonment ignore the strain of the long commute on Godwin, who was trying unsuccessfully to support the growing household; they also ignore the freshness and the freedom from routine Godwin's absences brought to their love story.

But Edy and Ted were always there, part of the landscape and its spirit. In 1872, when Ted was born, Godwin's entry in the local birth registry rechristened Ellen Terry with a flourish: "Eleanor Alice Godwin, formerly Watkins." Here were new additions to her cacophony of names. "Watkins" teasingly evoked "Watts," while it also rebaptized her with a common country name, giving her roots as well as houses in the heart of the country. "Godwin" was the dream name that was neither hers nor the children's. "Alice," her own middle name, also evoked the child who found her own way into the garden with no help from Lewis Carroll. "Eleanor" came to be more than a variant of "Ellen." In later years, Godwin's playful invention would haunt her signature as the ghost of the bold girl who was gone, and also of the Eleonora Duse she could never be. Her son's birth, like that son himself, gave her treasures that turned bitter as the years passed.

Virtuously, she claimed to have lived for Godwin, knowing he had never asked for that. She could never have guessed how consumingly she would live for Edy and Ted. Estranged from her family when they were born, she put into her love for them all her need for Terrys, as well as her mystic faith in the half-invisible Godwin. Technically, they were neither Terrys nor Godwins, but over the years they would become her second self: even when they were estranged from each other, together they were Ellen Terry's definitive teachers and her most ruthless audience. Because they were illegitimate, they had special claims, which multiplied uncontrollably as they grew up. In 1895, when Ted was becoming as cavalier a father as his own father had been, she wrote luridly to him of her sacrifices for motherhood at Harpenden:

> *Do you see the doubled responsibilities which await you in the near future?* Give up dreaming of the future, and make your *bread and butter for today.* The rest will follow *if you do this now—not else!* . . . You will have your wife—you *will* have your children—Well, they are joys—then work for them, deny yourself other joys—*books,* and *pictures,* and feed and wash them—yourself—*I* did—and it did me more good than any other thing. They are helpless—when *you* were helpless I was your servant—I had no servants for you—and I cooked and baked, and washed and sewed for you—and scrubbed for you, and *fainted* for you, and *got well again for you,* as my mother did for me—You talk and talk, and don't *do* —"He who would rule the day, must greet the morn—There is no hour to lose." (Quoted in E. A. C., 95)

Of course she had servants in Harpenden: there was "Boo," as Edy had named Mrs. Rumball, and then her niece "Bo," both of whom spent their lives in Ellen Terry's household. Moreover, the robust young "Eleanor Alice Godwin, formerly Watkins" is unlikely to have fainted often. But the sacrificial agonies with which she embellished her children's babyhood were to come in the future. In 1895, trying to goad the son she saw as lazy, Ellen Terry was also girding herself to face the worst of her children.

In popular iconography, the illegitimate child was the fallen woman's badge of shame, the permanent manifestation of her sin. But to their mother, Edy and Ted were miracles of brilliance and discernment, who seemed, like herself as a child, strangely unencumbered by innocence. Visitors expecting conventional adorableness found these aesthetic prodigies intolerable. Like deities, they referred to themselves in the third person, as "Miss Edy" or "Master Teddy" (Steen, 127). They lived in a stylish Japanese nursery; Edy wore little kimonos and Teddy white piqué suits; they looked only at Walter Crane picture books and played only with wooden toys: mechanical toys, like frilly dolls, were "vulgar." Raised in seclusion, Miss Edy and Master Ted were not stage children like their mother, but like her they lived in a world meant only for them, which they guarded jealously and never quite left.

To Ellen Terry, Edy, the oldest, was the unquestioned fount of extraordinariness, a fact both of them remembered sadly later on. It was Edy who transfigured the garden, bringing in "minute bunches of flowers all the morning, with the reassuring information that 'there are lots more,' or, on digging up a turnip, cried: 'Miss Edy found a radish. It's as big as—as big as *God!*' " It was Edy who disapproved of circuses (and continued to do so), crying, when a clown pretended to fall from the tightrope: "Take me away! take me away! you ought never to have brought me here!" (*Memoirs,* 68). On a trip to Normandy, it was Edy who listened alone to choir practice in a cathedral and then admonished the adults who came to fetch her: "Ssh! ssh! Miss Edy has seen the angels!" (*Memoirs,* 69). Both mother and daughter accepted this pipeline to Heaven as Edy's birthright. As Edy grew older, she feared above all that her mother would stop believing in the angels she saw.

Edy was called Edy all her life, but Teddy swelled into Edward Gordon Craig; Edward Anthony Craig, his favorite son and future biographer, got his cast-off nickname, "Teddy." He was "a greedy little thing," not given to oracular remarks (*Memoirs,* 70); primarily, as everyone remembered, he was fat. Ellen Terry's most extended anecdote about his childhood concerns his inability to recite one of Blake's *Songs of Innocence,* while Edy prompted him disgustedly and made things worse. Yet as Edy saw him, he was born with the power to betray, for this soft little lump was the family heir.

Women had guided Ellen Terry's own family: Kate and Ellen's tireless performances as children shed security and gentility on all Terrys. In the 1870s, Marion and Florence, the younger sisters, were just beginning their stage careers, while the three oldest boys were floundering as usual, more or less disastrously; Fred was still too young to redeem the Terry brothers. The girls were the doers, the achievers, the forgers of their own and others' lives and identities. Nevertheless, in deference to some command beyond her own experience, Ellen Terry set Teddy apart as the boy. In the early days Godwin swathed Edy in tenderness, yearning to protect her from the world's ugliness. He was relatively indifferent to Teddy, who was born after the idyll had begun to come apart, yet after he left, Ellen Terry raised the boy alone to be his father's child. In 1894, she sealed the mystery by sending him some writing by his "Father, by Edward (Call him always so - one, or the other - Altho' I call you Ted I always think of you as 'Edward'=)." She insisted that this material was given "To you only & afterwards to be burnt."

Ted was only symbolic heir: Godwin soon had another, proper son. But symbols in that family were more magical than money. Gordon Craig always ached to return to the Harpenden he was too young to remember, though when they were all together there he had done little but eat. When, at the conclusion of *Ellen Terry and Her Secret Self,* he has his mother die, he throws himself into death with her in order to regain a paradise that was always less hers than his own: "She sat up suddenly—opened her eyes—fell back and threw off fifty years as she fell. She became twenty-five to look at—and in truth, she became once more little Nelly Terry, back again at Harpenden with little Edy and little Teddy and the one she loved better than all the world" (p. 197). Always, when he was little and big, Teddy did love his unknown father better than all the world.

Edy hated him after he left; she shunned becoming his heir. Gordon Craig remembered with horror the day when Edward Godwin suddenly erupted out of the Dantesque universe in Edy's mind: "I shall ever remember one day in 1878, she asked me if I would like to see a portrait of my father—whom I had not seen since I was three years old and could not remember—and instantly she whipped out a terrible drawing someone had made for her, of a fiend with long teeth and claws and a tail, and said: 'There—that's him!' That was meant as kind" (*ETSS,* 59).

It was not meant as kind, but for Edy, it was true: her father brought evil to her paradise. In a letter whose contents would reverberate through their lives, Ellen Terry claimed that Godwin had tried to kidnap Edy, bringing about their final estrangement. Around 1875, she wrote to a Mr. Wilson:

> In all gentleness and kindness of feeling, I must beg you not to act as mediator between Mr. Godwin and myself. Our separation was a thing agreed upon by *both* of us many weeks before it actually took place. The first steps were taken by *him* and I certainly am much astonished to hear that he professes any strong feeling in the matter. Part of our compact was that we should always maintain a kindly, friendly relation to one another—He has since Tuesday last made this an IMPOSSIBILITY. He tried by unfair means to get my little girl from me (I *had offered* to let him have the boy) and I now distinctly refuse to hold any communication whatever with him.
>
> I do feel sorry that he is ill—Glad that he has some good friends—may he CONTINUE to appreciate them through his lifetime. I thank you for many kindnesses you have shown me and my children but I thank you still more for the fact that you are Mr. Godwin's friend now. . . .
>
> If Mr. Godwin's friends knew his temperament as I do and the effects of change of scene on him, they would advise his leaving London and *staying with friends,* for a time at least. He should not go alone as he is apt to brood and imagine all

kinds of ills which do not exist. You say in your letter—*"I really fear for his reason"*—When I knew him in his home life 13 years ago I had the same idea, and at that time he had *an utterly sorrowless life*—a devoted help-mate—success—friends—*everything*. He never was happy—he never will be. If you choose to show him this letter I will find no objection. At the risk of being called utterly heartless I again say I will hold no further risk of communication with Mr. Godwin, and I also say that this hard behaviour on my part has been brought about entirely by his own rash conduct since the last time we were together on Taviton Street.

(Quoted in E. A. C., 47–48)

Godwin's "rash conduct" was his final violent attempt to preserve the beauty to which his life with Ellen Terry was dedicated. Edy incarnated all the preciousness of the past. She was born in the first and freest year of their union; her piercing mystical observations had peopled their Eden with angels. Godwin's perverse refusal of "the boy" suggests that in Edy alone, he cherished his own purified capacity for vision, but his desperate and clumsy abduction attempt locked his daughter into her childish fears of him. His chosen child hated him; the rejected Teddy was maddened by the legacy the women in the family had thrown away.

Later on, clear-eyed Edy did her best to purge herself of her father's mysticism, while Teddy yearned to make himself into his father's child exclusively. His inheritance from Godwin became his illness: he too nursed cruel and tormenting moods which (along with his mother's "insane excitability") drove him into savage frenzies of mistrust in the most peaceful and promising of circumstances. Whether Godwin was fiend or savior, his absence possessed his children in a way he had not possessed Ellen Terry—or thought of doing so—when they lived together. His departure transformed him ironically into a preternaturally powerful man.

Edy re-made him into a fiend, but he was not Edy's only fiend. Even though he did nothing, her soft little brother was equally Satanic, because while she saw God everywhere, Teddy was loved and important. She was aware of his subtle supremacy, and thus she was as passionately aware of herself as a woman as she was of God in the garden. When she heard Teddy whining in his usual cowardly way about being afraid of the dark, she hit him on the head with a wooden spoon and exhorted him "to be a *woman!*" (*Memoirs*, 68). Naturally, at such a possibility, Teddy was more afraid than ever.

Ellen Terry had never imagined saying such a thing, and with such pride. At Edy's age, she had been transported beyond all limitations when she played boys; she had turned to her father for inspiration and adventure, and guiltily shunned her correct mother; even when men were cowardly or unreliable, they had always held the keys to the pride of life. Edy's loyalty to her gender was not the first lesson Ellen Terry learned from her daughter, but it was the most difficult and perplexing one.

As adults, Edy and Ted looked back to Harpenden as a paradise to recapture, but (unlike George Eliot's equally divided Tom and Maggie in *The Mill on the Floss*) they never dreamed of recapturing it with each other: they were alienated from each other long before their final rift over their dead mother's letters to Bernard Shaw. Edy looked hard, and frightened people, but it was beyond her nature to fight for herself; Gordon Craig fought with everybody, but he was a soft survivor at heart. Opposed as they were, though, Edy and Ted were haunted by identical specters of the nineteenth-century family romance: the lost garden of childhood, the incomparably, elusively beautiful mother, the invisible and so omnipotent father. As adults, they were defiantly modern, but their dreams were Victorian.

Ellen Terry had never had such familial dreams. As a child, she had had no home. Her parents were never towering figures, but colleagues that she left in the wings. Her mercurial father never shaped her fears of onstage mishaps, rats in the alley, vividness and vertigo, people laughing at her, the wideness of the world. The vagabond had known no consecrated, bounded space that would possess her all her life. Used to grand vistas, new cities, new audiences, long separations within her family, she never understood her own effect on her children in their enclosed rural childhood. She was enraged that because of her, they remained children beyond their proper time.

Edy and Ted were her only lasting souvenir of the country. The woman whose first memory was of "a large and busy town" where "the smoke of a thousand chimneys hung like a grey veil between me and the fires in the sky" raised country children, a fact that altered all of their lives and may have altered the history of the British theater as well. Wordsworth had told generations of disciples that truth rested in the heart of the country; Victorian fallen women like Ellen Terry had grown grand enough to search for it there; but for all the quests of poets and prophets, unreality suffused the British countryside as cities grew in power and prestige, and industrialism triumphed over feudal longings. In their common, lifelong attraction to productions that could never be staged, experimental and impractical methods, amateurish and eccentric theaters—all so different from their mother's inveterate professionalism—Edy and Ted were forever drawn to pastoral utopias. In Ellen Terry's visionary, undisciplined children, the anachronistic unreality of the country defeated the city's bracing professionalism. When she abandoned *The Household Fairy* for love and nature, she had never expected to return with two free spirits she would have to support for the rest of her life.

Like Wonderland, Harpenden existed to be left and mourned forever. Godwin could not pay the bills. Despite the increasing time he spent at his London office, there were not enough commissions for Gothic town halls or Japanese interiors (his real love) to keep a family of four living in beauty. In 1871, his partnership with Henry Crisp dissolved in a fatiguing tangle of legal claims and counterclaims. Finally and fatally, Godwin's own inveterate carelessness about money led him, and Ellen Terry as well, to lose even those bills they were able to pay. Their lovely life had become as draining as respectable households were.

When the bailiffs became too pressing and everything began to wear thin, Ellen Terry returned to the stage. With both of them working in London, Fallows Green had to be relegated to a summer house; the family moved to the city. They remained together for over a year, but in 1875, after *The Merchant of Venice,* Godwin drifted away. Adorers like Lewis Carroll were quick to vilify him, taking Ellen Terry to their hearts because they assumed she was betrayed. She was more easily lovable when she appeared to be Godwin's floral maiden at heart. Olive Weston's distorted but revealing article in the *Philadelphia Press* (12 May 1889), which sentimentalizes so tellingly her marriage to Watts, makes her love story palatable by turning Godwin into an ambitious villain, while Ellen Terry becomes a paragon of self-sacrifice:

> For many years they lived together in the country, and were very happy in that complete oblivion of the world which only artists can feel who are completely wrapped up in their art and in themselves—but he was very ambitious, he was petted and praised by noble ladies, his work led him into many of the finest houses of London as counselor and friend, he had walked through crowded ball rooms with coroneted duchesses on his arm, and his soul began to yearn for the flesh-pots of Egypt, to feel that he was not appreciated, that his life was too narrow for him.
>
> She watched it grow day by day—she did everything she could to make him happy, and when she saw the end had come said nobly, without quarrel or reproach: "I know—you want to marry a rich wife—well, do not let me stand in your way." He protested, but the time was not long before the society pages had to chronicle his marriage with a rich widow.

Ellen Terry would become the most highly paid woman in England and consort with titled admirers at the Lyceum, but Godwin never became rich, nor did he try to. The society pages took no notice of his marriage to Beatrice Philip, his twenty-one-year-old student; no trace of worldliness led him to marry this young woman instead of Ellen Terry. Like Watts, he wanted comfort, drifting to a girl who had made being an artist's wife her career; when Godwin died at the age of fifty-three, Beatrice's vocation led her to marry his friend Whistler.

Ellen Terry continued to fret about Godwin's poverty, which was as native to him as his art. In 1890, she wrote one of her many eulogies of Godwin to the son who had no other legacy: "It [the Northampton Town Hall], and heaps of other work he did afterwards, shd have made his fortune, but he was very careless of money and wasted it and died very poor— But there was no one like him, none—A man born long before his time— Of extraordinary gifts, and of comprehensive genius— Until lately you have had so little understanding of the world, I have not been able to speak with you of many things but when you come back we must have some nice long *quiet* talks—and you will *understand,* and *feel,* I am sure" (Quoted in EAC, 73).

Ellen Terry eulogized Godwin's genius to the end of her days, but their six years together changed his work more than it did hers. After they parted, he relegated architecture and interior decoration to secondary interests; his most admired work was done in the theater. He never abandoned public buildings and houses, but his fellow architects felt he had defected, and thus commissions became sparser than ever. As one of them mourned during his work on *The Merchant of Venice:* "Whereas the loss to the profession of those who are continually crying out for better buildings and design, cannot be too highly estimated when the *most accomplished living architect in England is expending his tried powers over the trappings of a play*" (quoted in Harbron, 106). But Ellen Terry had taught him that "the trappings of a play" could be a means of grasping history. The most enduring product of his Harpenden years, the thirty-two articles on "The Architecture and Costume of Shakespeare's Plays" (1874–75), delineate in a more searching and sophisticated manner the archeological Shakespeare Ellen Terry had absorbed from the Keans. His Venetian *Merchant of Venice* placed Ellen Terry in a meticulously accurate Italian Renaissance. When their parting became final, he designed sets and costumes for other productions. His most memorable, though quirky, achievements were the two pastoral productions of *As You Like It* he staged in the Surrey woods in 1884 and 1885. Lady Archibald Campbell, his Orlando and patron, elevated Godwin's Pastoral Players to the status of a formal society. They went on to stage more ambitious blends of nature and art, but none recaptured his life with Ellen Terry at Harpenden. That life lured Godwin away from public buildings: to the end of his days, he haunted the theater, struggling to marry its artifice to nature. As Watts could neither live with Ophelia nor expel her from his art, so Godwin pursued for the rest of his life Ellen Terry's medium. His pastoral *As You Like*

It would have given her Rosalind an ideal setting, but by 1884 Shakespeare's Forest of Arden where Rosalind ruled had become another of Ellen Terry's forbidden Wonderlands: Henry Irving would not be credible in it.

As an artist, Ellen Terry was less true to Godwin than he was to her, but the woman who performed herself tirelessly made their six years together the shrine of her life. Her apparent renunciation of art, her abandonment of herself to privacy and devotion, her "fall" that put her beyond the pale of family and polite society, were the crucibles that forged her into a magic presence when she returned to the stage. From that time on, no one billed her as Nelly Watts. She was Ellen Terry forever.

Godwin's lessons were less visible than Watts's, but they were pervasive and indelible: the aesthete finished the education into womanhood that the artist had begun. Godwin was her last formal teacher, though he left her hungry to learn. Her marginal comments to her biography of Rachel include the following suggestive remark, one that tells us more about her own development than it does about Rachel's: "The following her art seems to have educated her—& her observation—her art friends—her travels—all to have developed her. I'd like to know those who loved her—they must have taught her." Love was Ellen Terry's only available teacher, and she embraced it hungrily, especially after her imagination had recreated it. Edy and Christopher St. John write shrewdly about Harpenden's role in her intricate self-creation as actress and woman, seeing it less as a retreat than as an ingeniously innovative theater:

> Graham Robertson's statement that at Harpenden Ellen Terry was far from the theatres, and all concerning them, is a romantic exaggeration, since Godwin was there, with the theatre in his head and heart. However, it appears that as time went on Ellen Terry herself romanticized these days, at least when she was speaking of them to a romantic listener. Some puzzling discrepancies in the impressions she gave different people, equally intimate with her, of her experiences, thought and feelings, in her retirement, may be explained by the ease with which she could always identify herself with different people's conceptions of her character and temperament. To put it more clearly, it came naturally to Ellen Terry to dramatise herself. So there are hundreds of Ellen Terries, all genuine in their way, for there was in this extraordinarily rich and varied nature an abundance of material for their creation. (*Memoirs,* 74)

For the rest of her life, and whenever she chose, Godwin inspired her to create herself as a woman in love, and to recreate him in various attitudes of perfection. Marguerite Steen claims that she said of him later on, "You cannot go on caring about somebody in whom you no longer have faith" (p. 136), but as the years passed she regained faith because she forgot his hysterical behavior and remembered only her own aroused emotions. Men who had barely been born when Godwin died swore reverently that "Godwin was to remain her only real love," that Ellen Terry was a "one-man woman" who "loved Edward ever." Once she knew she would never see Godwin again, her love for him became the lodestar of her life.

When she heard of his death, she is said to have cried out her favorite eulogy—"There was no one like him" (Quoted in EAC, 60)—and she eulogized him to Gordon Craig in the same vague but intense words. But to Bertha J. Bramly, she wrote only of herself and the children when he died, for by then Godwin had already become a phantom: "I couldn't write in answer to your last letter—Edward Godwin died just then & I have been finished by that. I shall seem well soon, I think, but I didn't know how terribly it would alter me. I went on at my work for a time but broke down at last & sent for Edith to be with me. Selfish & wrong but I couldn't help it— I think I shd have lost my wits from misery—I'm all right now. Edith did that — She & Ted are with me now . . . Ted my boy has altered lately—looks rather shy now sometimes & is much quieter. Edith the same rum queer old Frump!"

Godwin's death absorbs him forever into his own extraordinary power to change her, a power that was always more real to her than the man. She wrote the next year to Audrey Campbell of Godwin's power manifesting itself even in the alphabet: "Such strange things have happened here - (of which we don't speak to Boo, remember) a letter came one evening with E.W.G. outside the cover. I could never, tho' I lived for centuries, see those letters in combination, with out a sadness, & a thrill, but I opened the letter carelessly thinking it most likely to be asking for an autograph— 'twas from his nephew!—who is here in N. Y. the living image of his uncle—but without his brains—A nice sweet young [man] of 25 — he is a clerk here in a Bank — has married a very pretty nice little Irishwoman, & --------here they are now come to tea. Strange the whole thing, isn't it?" Godwin towers in imagination to measure the strangeness of an ordinary world of banks and tea. Like Shakespeare's Cleopatra, whose Antony has swelled beyond human magnitude in death, Ellen Terry finds "nothing left remarkable / Beneath the visiting moon" (*A & C*, IV, xv, 67–68). Godwin has no contours, but his very amorphousness proves that the commonplace can be transcended, and once was.

When she writes to her philistine friend Clement Scott, Godwin becomes a vaguer and more sacred force: "With a woman, it is the Father of her children who lives for her in the middle of her heart—the holy of holies." Finally, as the world grows dim and an alien decade begins, Godwin falls into place with other dear ghosts. Her 1920 New Year's Day letter to Graham Robertson is a pageant of losses:

> Your Greeting was a fine Bird
> (A fine Greeting—)
> Mine is not even
> fine words! but
> I loves yer—
> Along with my very
> best Dears— with
> Edy & Ted & the
> children—& Edward
> & Henry—
> —but I'm feeble=
> just sorter bat-
> tered=

It suited Godwin to dissolve into a phantom lover, for to Ellen Terry and their children—and to his aesthetic contemporaries as well—he had always been more a force than a man. Watts had altered the Ellen Terry the world saw, but Godwin infused himself into the way she saw the world and lived in it. His reverence for the beautiful nurtured an inhumanity that lurked within her charm, encouraging her to write to Stephen Coleridge from Yorkshire: "Yes, isn't it wonderful that beautiful places don't make the people beautifuller in mind and body too. The beauty of Durham Cathedral which I saw the other day, for instance. I never did see such ugly folk as the Durham. I think they are all sense less."

Through Godwin she submerged herself in nature. The great lady could never do that again, but her hunger for country cottages allowed her to possess the landscape. Writing to the painter Joe Evans about her acquisition of Tower Cottage, she conceives imperial excursions on the simple, sexual country life she has lost:

> One cannot dream a wonderful Dream & tell it in cold blood, & so I cannot tell you in words my dearest Joe of this place I'm writing from, nor of how happy I have been in it the last 5 weeks—but you must must come. There's no friend I have in America who could love it as you could—Mr. Winter I think wd like it very much= but you could see it & paint it— . . . Down a little Garden path from this Bay Window is my Look-Out—& what we see from that Look Out

—Best of all times, on August nights with a full pale moon—I cannot tell of it, only on the <u>horizon is the Sea</u>, a mile away across the flat &-----No. I can't word it nor paint it, but thank God <u>I can see it!</u> — & you cd see it better! "Think of that" as Tessman says= It is just a dream of a dream—from my Look-Out= ... P. S. I'm not quite sure whether you know that this Cottage is <u>my very own</u> <u>freehold!</u>—bought & paid for out of my little play "Nance Oldfield"—I'm a "landed Proprietor"—It seems to me splendid!!!

Her rage to buy cottages did not enable her to recapture the past that devoured her children and haunted their father's *As You Like It,* but it did allow her to control her memories of that past and to rebuild it as her imagination dictated. She no longer had to wait apprehensively in the pony-cart for Godwin, for once they parted and she became grand, he was always inside her.

Above all, he made her glorious because through him she became a fallen woman, a role that allowed her to love his body and her own. It was almost certainly a sexual glow that transfigured her when she returned to the stage. In the mid-1870s, she exuded too powerful a glory for any tamer to quench it. The short period before she joined the Lyceum displayed a hoydenish ingenue transformed into an overweening presence. Being fallen allowed her to glow, to expand, as good wives like Kate could not. Soon Irving would make her, onstage at least, as proper a wife as Kate was in Moray Lodge, but Godwin had let loose the power that made her seem too large and too knowing for that role: she played it, but she laughed at it. In helping her to become an outcast, Godwin had in part restored young Harry's license to laugh at virtue. That gift alone consecrated him in her imagination.

She had little patience with long novels in her comfortable years, but if there were fallen women in them, she put up with tedium. Writing to Audrey Campbell of Dickens's *Dombey and Son,* she praises the fallen and stagy Mrs. Dombey, who has won few admirers in her day or our own: "<u>We</u> found "Dombey & Son" (especially Son) a trifle heavy—a trifle dull, & <u>not</u> a <u>trifle</u> too long!—Skip was the word= but the Nipper - <u>Edith</u> Dombey - Carker [her wicked would-be seducer] - & dear Mr. Toots we all adored="

When she writes to Audrey in darker, more frightening years, another fallen wife brings her temporary rejuvenation:

Oh, darling how terrible about poor Evelyn's husband= - -- but he <u>must</u> be better now—? it wd be too fearful= And Bessie too, to have been so <u>very</u> ill —what dreadful things seem to be in the air— Miss Harries writes me Boo's head is bad, which frightens me= & so I'm writing to her now—The quieter she is the better—never going out is <u>best</u> for her= I hope I'll hear she's well again soon or I shall worry= . . . Ah--my eyes are dreadful today. Did I tell you how bad they have been? Remember <u>Boo</u> <u>is not to know</u> = & they are improved - but I was frightened for they <u>are</u> really necessary for one's work= Fancy if I could not see you!!!—I think Jude the Obscure is--- ------dreadfully shocking now & again (sometimes <u>unnecessarily</u>) but I think it is <u>magnificent</u> - finer than "Tess." & I do think <u>never</u> was there a truer <u>life painting</u> than the portrait of '' **S u e** '' = But oh, <u>what</u>-a-pity-he-is-so-coarse= <u>on purpose</u> it seems to me now & again—"

The joy and energy she had gained from playing a fallen woman in life had made her so beloved that she could never be fallen on the stage: only in private had she competed with Bernhardt and Duse as Marguerite Gauthier. When she read novels, though, glorious fallen women stalked once more through the hidden theater in her mind. She never told her correspondents that all of them lived in her body and looked out at the world from her eyes.

RISING STAR The story she told about leaving Harpenden had nothing to do with her attempt to become the author of her destiny by creating herself as a fallen woman. Charles Reade starred in it as her bluff male rescuer; enthusiasts immediately wrote it into her legend.

One day I was driving in a narrow lane, when the wheel of the pony-cart came off. I was standing there, thinking what I should do next, when a whole crowd of horsemen in "pink" came leaping over the hedge into the lane. One of them stopped and asked if he could do anything. Then he looked hard at me and exclaimed: "Good God! It's Nelly!"

The man was Charles Reade.

"Where have you been all these years?" he said.

"I have been having a very happy time," I answered.

"Well, you've had it long enough. Come back to the stage!"

"No, never!"

"You're a fool! You ought to come back."

Suddenly I remembered the bailiff in the house a few miles away, and I said laughingly: "Well, perhaps, I would think of it if some one would give me forty pounds a week!"

"Done!" said Charles Reade. "I'll give you that, and more, if you'll come and play Philippa Chester in 'The Wandering Heir.' "

He went on to explain that Mrs. John Wood, who had been playing Philippa at the New Queen's, of which he was the lessee, would have to relinquish the part soon because she was under contract to appear elsewhere. The piece was a great success, and promised to run a long time if he could find a good Philippa to replace Mrs. Wood. It was a kind of Rosalind part, and Charles Reade only exaggerated pardonably when he said that I should never have any part better suited to me!

(*Memoirs,* 69)

This anecdote colors Ellen Terry's life with key motifs from the popular theater to which she was returning: the appealingly helpless woman who triumphs only accidentally and through indirection; the active blustering man who solves everything by saying "Done!"; the happy ending ("the kind of Rosalind part") that is something of a lie, though a lucrative lie. Onstage and off, these wove themselves into her new London self.

Godwin lived on with her in London, on Taviton Street, for over a year, until he designed for the Bancrofts the *Merchant of Venice* in which Ellen Terry felt for the first time the elation of the conqueror; then he disappeared. Effectively, though, she abandoned Godwin as teacher/lover when Charles Reade in his hunting clothes took her in hand on that country road. Harpenden had sequestered her from men's fashionable idioms in the 1870s. She needed a man who would teach these to her.

"Dear, kind, unjust, generous, cautious, impulsive, passionate, gentle Charles Reade" (*Memoirs,* 71) became her manager and her mentor after her immediate success in *The Wandering Heir* and its successor, his old melodrama *It's Never Too Late to Mend.* Reade's fractious, paternalistic disapproval might have come from his own smashingly successful play, *Masks and Faces* (1852). This melodrama about the great eighteenth-century actress Peg Woffington takes its energy and fun from the dazzling series of roles the actress plays in life, but its pious ending confronts the actress with a sincere wife who inspires her to renounce her deceitful artistry. Reade's novelization puts it baldly: "She flung her profession from her like a poisonous weed."

Reade's Ellen Terry exudes the same poisonous fascination. Widely quoted after their publication, his notebook descriptions of her trust neither woman nor artist: they depict a demon child who draws the author to her against his judgment. The distaste beneath Reade's affection is eminently of its time: "Ellen Terry, a character such as neither Molière nor Balzac, I believe, had the luck to fall in with. Soft and yielding on the surface, egotistical below. *Varia et mutabilis,* always wanting something 'dreadful bad today,' which she does not want tomorrow, especially if you are weak enough to give it her, or get it her. Hysterical, sentimental, hard as a nail in money matters, but velvet on the surface. A creature born to please and to deceive. *Enfant gatée, et enfant terrible.*"

Reade is her first author to fling her back to childhood, but this new childhood is no longer magically versatile: it is a condition in which she can do no right, for every activity betrays her spoiled nature. At a later date, he relented enough to add to the above: "This was written while she was under the influence of ——— [Godwin, no doubt]. Since then, greatly improved: the hardness below is melting away. In good hands a very amiable creature, but dangerous to the young. Downright fascinating. Even I, who look coldly on from senile heights, am delighted by her" (quoted in *Memoirs,* 75).

Like Lewis Carroll, Reade insulates her from childhood's charm while treating her as a wicked child who needs to be controlled. An earlier Ellen Terry would have chafed against this sort of disapproving paternalism, but the Magdalen returning to a proudly proper theater could afford no further defiance: she was glad to put herself into Reade's "good hands," lovingly addressing her letters to "my dear papa." She may have grown bored with Godwin's sensual tenderness, his insouciance about money and plans, the easy way he let himself be taken care of rather than taking care: his pocket diary from their years together consistently names her "mother" (quoted in Prideaux, 83–84). Charles Reade's high-handedness relieved her from worrying: however hectoring he was, he managed her into a restored career. After Ellen Terry's death, Edy found a piece of paper written in her last years and labeled "My Friends." Charles Reade's name headed the list; Bernard Shaw's was directly underneath (*Memoirs,* 76). Godwin may have been her holy of holies, but he was not part of her final benediction on men with whom she was not intimate, but who goaded and stung her into her future.

In this period when she was building a new life after her retreat, she searched rather feverishly for fathers. Her meetings with Ben and Sarah were tense; Kate was estranged from her entirely. The papers had remained loyally silent about her six illicit years; the story began to leak out, in various sentimentalized shapes, only after she had become, with Irving, so grand and irreproachable a star that no trespass could take away the love she won. In the 1870s, the public knew only tantalizing whispers about her six-year retreat. In the Profession itself, though, she was a returned recreant with much to be forgiven. She may have searched for a father to punish her. Certainly, she was tired of mothering.

Reade's collaborator Tom Taylor had preferred Kate in the old days, but in these new ones he was happy to sponsor Ellen and write plays for her; he would do the same for the younger Terry girls when their turns came. She adopted Tom Taylor as her new father as ardently as she had Reade: "I was very fond of my own father, but in many ways Tom Taylor was more of a father to me than my father in blood. Father was charming, but Irish and irresponsible. I think he loved my sister Floss and me most because we were the lawless ones of the family! It was not in his temperament to give wise advice and counsel. Having bequeathed to me light-heartedness and a sanguine disposition, and trained me splendidly for my profession in childhood, he became in after years a very cormorant for adulation of me!" (*Memoirs,* 91).

In other words Ben refused to see his shining daughter as an *enfant gatée.* He was no Victorian, while she had to try in her own way to become one: she turned from his helpless pride to the "wise advice and counsel" of men who saw it as their birthright to manage women. Her multiple and cavalier replacements for the father who had never wanted to tame her, who saw her rarity and treasured it, gave her an adaptability she did not transmit to Edy and Ted. Their allegiance to the Godwin they didn't know was unyielding. They could conceive of no replacements. Whether he was savior or demon, they had no father before him.

If Ellen Terry wanted to be punished, *The Wandering Heir* itself was a good beginning: its professional rewards carried private recantations for her transvestite days. Philippa, the "kind of Rosalind part," disguises herself as a boy (Philip, of course) but love comes to mortify her. Reade's novelization dwells on her guilt and shame:

> [H]er breast was torn with doubts, and fears, and shames, for which my reader, who has only seen her fitful audacity in boy's clothes, may not be quite prepared. She was now all tremors and misgivings, and paid the penalty of her disguise. Under that disguise she had fallen in love with James Annesley; yet inspired him with no tenderer feeling than friendship for a boy. That knowledge of the heart, which an inexperienced but thoughtful woman sometimes attains by constantly thinking on its mysteries, told her that between love and friendship there is a gulf, and that gulf sometimes impassable. Philip might stand forever between James and Philippa.
>
> And, besides this, for a girl to wear boy's clothes was indelicate; it was condemned by law, it was scouted by public opinion. James Annesley, even in this humble condition, had shown a great sense of propriety; and she felt, with a cold chill running down her back, that he was not the man to overlook indelicacy in her sex, much less make an Amazon his wife; and now, as she had learned with her sharp ears, the story he had told her was confirmed, and he was the real Earl of Anglesey; and all the less likely to honour a Tomboy with his hand. For three whole days she had longed and pined to speak to him; yet fear and modesty had held her back. She could not bear to be Philip any more; yet she dreaded to be Philippa, lest she should lose even Philip's place in his regard.

"Wise advice and counsel" of this sort was a subtler scourge than Garrick's *Katherine and Petruchio* had been, but times had changed since she had been so easily angry: she had run away and returned to a theater that was mobilizing in its service the sanctimonious might of Society. She accepted uncomplainingly the fact that her triumphant return required her repudiation of her happiest stage self. Her memoir mocks an abortive project in this period "for me to star as Juliet to the Romeo of a lady!" (p. 95). The Ellen Terry of the mid-1870s found such aberrations inconceivable, thereby forgetting her loved and harsh mentor Mrs. Kean, who as Ellen Tree had alone moved Fanny Kemble to imagine a true Juliet; she also brushed aside the great American actress Charlotte Cushman, who had played a warm and seductive Romeo to her sister's Juliet. Her own boy-self was as ruthlessly forgotten. In dismissing rumors of her rivalry with Marie Bancroft, she places Mrs. Bancroft in the great transvestite and managerial tradition of Madame Vestris, while she herself (Ellen Terry implies) is not only no manager, but has never played a breeches role! (*Memoirs,* 99)

By the 1870s, the squeamishness Ellen Terry had sensed twelve years earlier had triumphed: the idea of a woman's trespassing beyond her gender as society defined it was not merely uncomfortable, but dangerous. Even organized feminism had taken to heart the shame Charles Reade makes his Philippa feel: women who fought to enter the great, implacably male universities and to enter the professions on the same terms as men felt (or expressed) a disapproval as strong as Charles Reade's at the idea that educated women might become "unsexed": the potent essence of womanliness, they insisted, was fettered and not preserved by ignorance and incompetence. Women countered men's jealousy of their own prerogatives by proclaiming a new pride in their womanliness: aping men was not merely unseemly, but disloyal. The proud heroine of Charlotte Brontë's *Villette* (1853) anticipates this new mood. When Lucy Snowe is forced to play a man in a school play, she does so only from the waist up, accepting a cravat but staunchly refusing breeches. Far from hampering her, her skirts galvanize her into a passionate performance: she can fling herself into her role because she has been true to her own, female identity. When *Villette* appeared, it was incomprehensible to most readers and distasteful to the few who understood it, but its heroine, an unmarried working woman, was a harbinger of a new militant self-acceptance among women: instead of challenging accepted boundaries of identity, they transmuted familiar limitations into a new, exhilarating strength. Like Edy exhorting the sniffling Ted to "be a *woman,*" they did not want their heroines to betray themselves by aping their oppressors, but to find the joy and glory that were the unshackled essence of femaleness. All manner of new audiences would applaud Ellen Terry's remorse when her Philippa could no longer bear to be Philip.

She had missed six years. There had been changes, tightenings-up, a new self-consciousness in the theatrical community; the stage, now in league with the larger society, needed to remind itself as well as its audiences that men were men and women, women. She too had to learn all these new things, but through it all, what a joy it was to be back! The country was lovely, but the country was—not home. Her new caution even inhibits her autobiographical expression of her delight at returning: her memoir's chapter on Charles Reade concludes with an anecdote about a transplanted circus goat. Only through the role of a goat could Ellen Terry admit that rural life, even love, were simply not acting:

> All the time, while Charles Reade had been fashing himself to provide every sort of rural joy for his goat, the ungrateful beast had been longing for the naphtha lights of the circus, for lively conversation and the applause of the crowd.
> You can't force a goat any more than you can force a child to live the simple life. . . . Rachel's sentiments were of the same type, I think. "Back to the circus!" was his cry, not "Back to the land!"
> I hope, when he felt the sawdust under his feet again (I think Charles Reade sent him back to the ring) he remembered his late master with gratitude. To how many animals, and not only four-footed ones, was not Charles Reade generously kind, and to none of them more kind than to Ellen Terry. (*Memoirs,* 73–74)

Charles Reade rescued Ellen Terry from privacy and returned her to audiences, but Marie Bancroft rescued her from Reade's melodramas and returned her to art. The Marie Wilton who had played breathtaking boys was now bringing domesticity into theatrical fashion: with her dignified husband Squire Bancroft, she had taken over the Prince of Wales' Theatre and made it the home of Tom Robertson's middle-class, cup-and-saucer comedies. No longer was the stage haunted by disturbing transformations: for middle-class audiences, the Prince of Wales' was a reassuring replica of home. As one woman remembered it: "It was the prettiest, most charming little house imaginable, for it was . . . all upholstered in palest blue, and there were little antimacassars over the backs of the chairs in the stalls, boxes, and dress circle. While antimacassars may not sound artistic to modern ears, they were the fashion then, and very clean, lacy, and pretty they looked in the theatre."

Marie Bancroft had learned femininity. With it, she made her theater reassuring to a new public who condescended to be entertained only if they found the entertainment wholesome. But by the 1870s, domestic realism was overfamiliar even to family-centered audiences: the Bancrofts wanted to try a Shakespeare. Charles Reade had gone hunting in the country and found Ellen Terry there only by accident, but Marie Bancroft walked quite deliberately to the arty if depleted house on Taviton Street, which brokers had stripped of all the domestic properties audiences at the Prince of Wales' liked:

> "May I come in?"
> An ordinary remark, truly, to stick in one's head for thirty-odd years! But it was made in such a *very* pretty voice—one of the most silvery voices I have ever heard from any woman except the late Queen Victoria, whose voice was like a silver stream flowing over golden stones.
> The smart little figure—Mrs. Bancroft was, above all things, *petite*—dressed in black—elegant Parisian black—came into a room which had been almost completely stripped of furniture. The floor was covered with Japanese matting, and at one end was a cast of the Venus of Milo, almost the same colossal size as the original.
> Mrs. Bancroft's wonderful grey eyes examined it curiously. The room, the statue, and I myself must have seemed very strange to her. I wore a dress of some deep yellow woollen material which my little daughter used to call the "frog dress," because it was specked with brown like a frog's skin. It was cut like a Viollet-le-Duc tabard, and had not a trace of the fashion of the time. Mrs. Bancroft, however, did not look at me less kindly because I wore aesthetic clothes and was painfully thin. She explained that they were going to put on "The Merchant of Venice" at the Prince of Wales's, that she was going to rest for awhile for reasons connected with her health; and that she and Mr. Bancroft had thought of me for Portia. (*Memoirs,* 84)

The tableau is arresting: two women who began their careers as stage boys meet in a more decorous time. Marie Bancroft's elegant Parisian black, Ellen Terry's aesthetic disarray, are two of the very few non-bourgeois costumes they can wear in an age that was increasingly obsessed with boundaries and proprieties.

The respectability Mrs. Bancroft has learned to ape is as trim, as artifically homelike, as her stage sets. When she holds out her hand inviting Ellen Terry to ascend her adorable stage, her understated gesture is more momentous than Charles Reade's bountiful, blustering "Done!": as mistress of ceremonies at Ellen Terry's jubilee in 1906, she will welcome her to immortality with the same prim efficiency. Now, she brings Ellen Terry both to Shakespeare (whose heroines she has never played) and to stage domesticity. For the rest of her life, Ellen Terry will revere the former as her paramount teacher, and try, for his sake, to fit herself to the latter.

She writes her letter of acceptance in the eager, daughterly manner she adopted after leaving Harpenden: "My work will, I feel certain, be joyful work, & joyful work should turn out good work, & then you'll be pleased, & I shall be pleased at your pleasure, & it wd be hard if the good folk "in front" were not pleased." Her new lust to please everybody lasted as long as the century did. Willingly, she repudiated old trespasses and tried to stop fighting her roles. She did this in part for Edy and Ted; in part as an act of contrition for running away; and in part because she had run away twice, first to art and then to nature, only to find herself confined in lovely prisons. Neither prison would take her back. The theater was her home.

The Merchant of Venice was not a commercial success—its Shylock was weak, and in 1875, Irving's striking Hamlet had only just begun to create a new vogue for Shakespeare—but artists flocked to its sumptuousness, and after Ellen Terry's star rose, the production became legendary in memory. In Godwin's conception, the play had no single star: his aim was the apotheosis of Venice itself. Using as his source Cesare Vecellio's *Abiti, Antichi, et Moderni di tutto il Mundo* (1589), he insisted that sets, costumes, and props be both accurate and gorgeous: Charles Kean's high-minded archeological reproductions were elevated to aesthetic glory. Oscar Wilde would parody Godwin's scrupulous literal-mindedness. Godwin's solemn suggestion that "Portia would do her shopping probably at Padua, and would therefore follow the fashions of the main land" became Wilde's teasing claim in 1888 that Ellen Terry's serpentine Lady Macbeth is "sure to do her own shopping in Byzantium." But audiences schooled in Ruskin's *Stones of Venice* and the Brownings' love songs to Italy saw their dream country realized before their eyes: authentic history glowed with Titian's sensuous magic.

An actress less adept than Ellen Terry would have been lost in the production's glamor, or would have fought vainly to upstage it. Having learned on her pulses the ways of art and artists, she turned herself effortlessly into an epitome of Godwin's golden Venice. At Harpenden she had dressed to match his Japanese rooms; he had stage-managed her union with nature; now, through him, she expanded into all that a city could be. The ease with which she adapted herself to stage pictures was the most useful lesson her artist-lovers taught her; in life she failed to become the women they imagined, but on the stage she absorbed herself into those women perfectly. Her eerie ability to become her setting would impress even William Archer, who despised Irving's Lyceum and all it stood for: "Whatever her absolute merits in a part, she always harmonizes as perhaps she alone could with the whole tone of the picture. She gives their crowning charm to the fabrics of South Kensington." Her effortless interchangeability with her stage world transfigured her first when she became the Bancrofts'—and Godwin's—Portia.

She knew just how unique her success was, and she knew the precise moment it descended. Fittingly, her consecration came not in the famous Trial Scene, but in Portia's one moment of utter humility. The heroine of *The Merchant of Venice* is a brilliant and beautiful heiress whose dead father has decreed that she may wed only a suitor who chooses the right one of three caskets. Handsome Bassanio, who may be a fortune hunter, passes her father's test. Like a more accomplished and polished Katharina, Portia instantly makes herself nothing but his:

> You see me, Lord Bassanio, where I stand,
> Such as I am: though for myself alone
> I would not be ambitious in my wish,
> To wish myself much better; yet, for you
> I would be trebled twenty times myself;
> A thousand times more fair, ten thousand times
> More rich;
> That only to stand high in your account,
> I might in virtues, beauties, livings, friends,
> Exceed account; but the full sum of me
> Is sum of something, which, to term in gross,
> Is an unlesson'd girl, unschool'd, unpractised;
> Happy in this, she is not yet so old
> But she may learn; happier than this,
> She is not bred so dull but she can learn;
> Happiest of all is that her gentle spirit
> Commits herself to yours to be directed,
> As from her lord, her governor, her king.
>   (*MV*, III, ii, 150–67)

More humility follows. Playing a similar scene in Garrick's *Katherine and Petruchio*, she had wilfully played it badly and hardened in her determination to leave the stage. She had learned to play it well since then, and to welcome its rewards:

> I had had some success in other parts, and had tasted the delight of knowing that audiences liked me, and had liked them back again. But never until I appeared as Portia at the Prince of Wales's had I experienced that awe-struck feeling which comes, I suppose, to no actress more than once in a life-time—the feeling of the conqueror. In homely parlance, I knew that I had "got them" at the moment when I spoke the speech beginning, "You see me, Lord Bassanio, where I stand."

"What can this be?" I thought. *"Quite* this thing has never come to me before! *This is different!* It has never been quite the same before."

It was never to be quite the same again.

Elation, triumph, being lifted on high by a single stroke of the mighty wing of glory—call it by any name, think of it as you like—it was as Portia that I had my first and last sense of it. (*Memoirs,* 86–87)

She had been tamed at last, and she loved the love it won her. "Every one seemed to be in love with me!" (*Memoirs,* 88). That too was the language of the conqueror.

But five years later, at the Lyceum, even this triumphantly humble scene was to draw withering criticism from a prim young American. Henry James had just moved to England, and was eager to teach it tradition. London loved Ellen Terry; he found her "school-girlish." Her Portia was not a lady:

Miss Terry's mistress of Belmont giggles too much, plays too much with her fingers, is too free and familiar, too osculatory, in her relations with Bassanio. The mistress of Belmont was a great lady, as well as a tender and a clever woman; but this side of the part quite eludes the actress, whose deportment is not such as we should expect in the splendid spinster who has princes for wooers. When Bassanio has chosen the casket which contains the key of her heart, she approaches him, and begins to pat and stroke him. This seems to us an appalling false note. "Good heavens, she's touching him!" a person sitting next to us exclaimed—a person whose judgement in such matters is always unerring.

This person of unerring judgment was none other than the notorious and unsexed Fanny Kemble, who might legislate decorum to Portia, but who had dared, in her readings, to play a bloodcurdling Shylock! It was easy for those who had so many roles available to preach restraint in one.

It was galling to be told, when she had conceded so much, that she was still not a lady—especially when the teller was Fanny Kemble, and especially when the great John Ruskin agreed that Portia should stand *much* further off from Bassanio. Her memoir worries at this criticism, citing the mighty Dr. Furnivall as her ally (pp. 145–46); as late as 1903, she continues to argue against so drearily quiescent a Portia: "I like this idea [that the song in the Casket Scene might contain a hint to Bassanio] . . . And why shouldn't Portia sing the song herself? She could make the four rhymes, 'bred, head, nourished, fed,' set the word 'lead' ringing in Bassanio's ears. A woman of Portia's sort couldn't possibly remain passive in such a crisis in her life" (*Memoirs,* 152).

Neither could a woman like Ellen Terry, whose own proudly sexual energy, whose initiative in inventing herself, had lifted her on the mighty wing of glory and given her the feeling of the conqueror.

Would she never be still enough to please?

Our Lady of the Lyceum

THE WOMAN In one of her many scripts of *Hamlet,* Ellen Terry recorded next to Ophelia's name the most important decision of her life: "Monday. 30 December 1878 = My first appearance at Lyceum." In the beginning of Act III, Scene i—the "nunnery scene," where Hamlet denounces Ophelia and all women, as her spying father and the lying king watch her humiliation—she inserted a tender note from Henry Irving:

> My fairest — sweetest
> Loveliest Ophelia
> Only this
>   Your Hamlet.

"Only this," and what more could there be? Everyone who loved her and whose love she needed imagined her playing two roles that were really one: Henry Irving's stage wife, and Ophelia to his celebrated Hamlet. For the rest of her life, this composite identity would bless and shackle her. Her partnership with Irving, her willing subordination within it, was the reward of her education. Under his generous protection, she became famous as a womanly actress who could be safely loved at last.

As Irving reinvented her, Ellen Terry exuded sanctity. So, under his generalship, did the theater itself. Irving could will the theater into grandeur because he had not been born into it, and so had never learned its outcast code: his undistinguished father, whom he barely referred to, might have been a traveling salesman or a caretaker or both. His mother, a ferociously holy Methodist, never forgave her son for embracing the wicked stage. If Irving's crusade for the actor's respectability was a strategy for regaining his relentless mother's acceptance, it failed; she despised his work until she died. Like the culture heroes of Samuel Smiles's *Self-Help,* that Victorian bible of strenuous success, John Brodribb was given nothing: he made himself Henry Irving with no family blessings, and with no endowments of voice or physique.

At forty, he assumed the management of the Lyceum and hired Ellen Terry; his daunting apprenticeship in Ireland, Scotland, and the provinces had prepared him for leadership. Unlike the spoiled and demanding child star, whose birthright was the stage, the young Irving had found no part too base for him, for the theater was his dearly won holy ground; but once Ellen Terry became his employee, their roles were ironically reversed. He never forgot the week he was booed in Dublin because he had replaced a popular favorite: the humiliating memory bristled from him every time he addressed cheering audiences with ineffably sardonic dignity as their "respectful, grateful, and affectionate servant." In reality he made servants of everyone who entered his theater. Even after conquering London, he knew audiences too well to entrust his identity to their approval. Ellen Terry learned herself from everyone who watched her; no one but himself possessed Henry Irving.

His Rawdon Scudamore had brought his renown, but praise was unreliable: in the years after he played his awkward Petruchio to Ellen Terry's Katharina, he searched out routes to power. In 1871, he seized that power: playing at the Lyceum under the lackluster management of "Colonel" H. L. Bateman, he persuaded Bateman to produce *The Bells.* As the guilt-stricken murderer Mathias whose mask of respectability fails to shield him from specters of his sin, Irving terrorized London audiences into reverence. *The Bells,* an adaptation from Leopold Lewis's French melodrama *Le Juif Polonais,* was a typical staple of the non-Shakespearean English repertoire, whose lifeblood was pirated French ephemera. In Irving's hands, though, *The Bells* took on the admonitory resonance of Dickens's *Christmas Carol,* becoming a searing parable of the guilt that lacerated all respectable men. Mathias became the quintessential Irving role—during his last illness, he played it despite doctors' warnings—because in it, the actor underwent agonies of remorse on behalf of the virtuous men whose respectful, grateful, and affectionate servant he declared himself to be.

The Bells estranged him permanently from his wife Florence O'Callaghan, who despised the theater as robustly as his mother had done. She had subdued her loathing of his vocation until the night of his triumph, when she burst into a short, stinging performance that rivaled his own: "Are you going on making a fool of yourself like this all your life?" They were riding home after the elated opening-night celebration. Irving stopped the carriage, got out, and never saw her again, leaving her to implant her hate in their sons Henry Brodribb and Laurence. Mathias had lost him his family, but it put him in the way of gaining his first theater: *The Bells* had made him the power behind Bateman's company. He could become whatever he wanted; soon, he would make a host of actors become what he wanted them to be.

His Hamlet in 1874 won astonishing praise, even reverence, for the artist; still more astonishingly, it made money for the Lyceum. In 1875, "Colonel" Bateman died obligingly; his widow took over the management. Irving bided his time until he could raise enough money to buy her out. Meanwhile, he endured her untalented daughter Isabel as his leading lady. Isabel, the pawn of her mother's ambitions, was ashamed of acting and longed to become a nun. Eventually, she became one, but first, she fell embarrassingly in love with the monkish Henry Irving. A few years later, when he was sure of his power, Irving would play a superbly munificent husband to Ellen Terry, but when he was still an employee of the Lyceum, he could not bear the presence of the dependent Bateman women, who waited only to lavish on him theatrical and domestic happiness. He felt nothing but relief at their dispossession once he had finally borrowed enough money to take over the theater himself. At the cost of ungallantry, he had achieved his imperial goal: that of producing Shakespeare in his own theater. The addition of Ellen Terry to his orbit would make his glory indestructible.

The Bells that had rung in his fame were French; so was his great hero Napoleon; pirated French fustian remained a staple of his Lyceum repertoire. Nevertheless, under his management, the Lyceum was as purely English an empire as Victoria's own. Ellen Terry obligingly fitted herself to his patriotic chauvinism, becoming the "genial Britannia" Max Beerbohm mocked gently at the turn of the century: "She is always, whatever she does, the merry bonny English creature with the surface of Aestheticism—always reminds me of a Christmas-tree decorated by a Pre-Raphaelite."

As a child, Ellen Terry had belonged to no country but the theater. Her Irish father had taught her all she could be, while her Scottish mother had reminded her of all that life forbade. "Craig," her children's patronym, adopted into her family a Scottish dialect that declared allegiance to her mother's origins. Ellen

Terry's calling and her family made her an outsider in her mother country, but Henry Irving turned her into a mirror of every dear Englishwoman. "He made an honest woman of the theater," and of Ellen Terry as well (Prideaux, 206). But only because she was an actress in her essence could she become Irving's "genial Britannia": bred to the stage and schooled in painters' visions, she embodied with ease the respectability Irving had forfeited in his mother's eyes when he became an actor. Her presence was vital to the Lyceum because it authenticated his productions with artists and aesthetes; her Portia and Olivia swelled the audience with her own adoring cult; but most important, Ellen Terry epitomized the theater Irving aimed to transform into Britannia. She was born to the world that had lured him; his mission was to assimilate that exotic community into powerful, polite Victorian society. When she understood what he wanted, Ellen Terry did her best to civilize the theater in her person.

Until the turn of the century, most actresses were stage children like Ellen Terry, while actors were generally, like Irving, self-made invaders from the outside world. Squire Bancroft saw in his own marriage the pattern that shaped the Victorian theater:

> Often as I went to the play, dearly as I loved the theatre, until I tried to become an actor I had never known one, and very rarely had even seen one off the stage. And so it has been with many of my comrades, Henry Irving, John Hare, Charles Wyndham, W. H. Kendal, Charles Coghlan, John Clayton, Arthur Cecil, Johnston Forbes-Robertson, William Terriss, and E. S. Willard, as also with some of a later generation, a few of whose names pass at once through my mind, Herbert Beerbohm Tree, George Alexander, Cyril Maude, Arthur Bourchier, Lewis Waller, and Charles Hawtrey—all of whom, I believe, were as unconnected with the theatre as I was. The law of compensation has in this way often served the stage: many men whose gifts and talents have wooed the Cinderella of the arts might, but for their lack of means, have embarked in other callings. On the other hand, Marie Bancroft, Madge Kendal, Ellen Terry, Winifred Emery, Ellen Farren, and Mrs. John Wood were all, so to speak, brought up in theatre-land.

This is an orotund way of admitting that women did not have the freedom to choose the stage as men did: as in the larger society, women were what they were born to, while men elected to become greater things. At the height of her fame, Ellen Terry encouraged a generation of well-bred girls to become actresses: her simple, smilingly seditious welcome toppled the barrier that segregated nice women from stage children. In 1878, though, Ellen Terry stood alone; her seasoned loveliness must have personified to Irving everything he had ever wanted. He had been in love with an actress ten years earlier—another Nellie, Nellie Moore, who had died hauntingly young—but otherwise, he had known only virtuous women like his mother and his wife, who despised the only work that made him real.

Ellen Terry embraced men's inventions of her, but Henry Irving was irremediably alienated from women: the more nobly they claimed to love him, the more woundingly they tried to destroy his only real self. Even Isabel Bateman had loathed the stage, aspiring, like his mother, toward a pious life. Ironically, once he had forced her out of the Lyceum, his management shed on it a ritualistic intensity and a holy stillness redolent of the Church she had pined for. Ellen Terry too had fled acting, but she could not abandon the only life she knew. When Irving bought the actress and possessed the woman, she was so purely a product of the Profession that devoured him that he must have felt himself at last making love to the spirit of theatricality itself.

Ellen Terry's legend has her becoming Irving's "wife" on that momentous December 30, 1878, the night of the Lyceum debut that was also her first Ophelia. As she does when she describes her elopement with Godwin, she surrounds the consummation with portents of disaster, loss, and drowning. Her loss begins with her audacious refusal to wear white in the mad scene:

> "In the last scene [the mad scene] I wear a transparent, black dress."
> Henry did not wag an eyelid.
> "I see. In mourning for her father."
> "No, not exactly that. I think *red* was the mourning colour of the period. But black seems to me *right*—like the character, like the situation." [Irving has her present this idea to his production advisor, Walter Lacy]
> You should have seen Lacy's face at the word "black." He was going to burst out, but Henry stopped him. He was more diplomatic than that!
> "Ophelias generally wear *white*, don't they?"
> "I believe so," I answered, "but black is more interesting."
> And then they dropped the subject for that day. It *was* clever of him!
> The next day Lacy came up to me:
> "You didn't really mean that you are going to wear black in the mad scene?"
> "Yes, I did. Why not?"
> "*Why not!* My God! Madame, there must be only one black figure in this play, and that's Hamlet!"

I did feel a fool. What a blundering donkey I had been not to see it before! (*Memoirs*, 123–24)

On the stage and off, she continues to learn her roles from her costumes. Her sumptuous Fairy Goldenstar dress had taught her the consolations (if not quite the rewards) of goodness; her Cupid tunic had taught her that her body frightened people; her brown Holman Hunt wedding dress taught her that she personified woman's holy sadness; Godwin's Titania costume taught her that even when her body was no longer childish, it could feel enchantingly alive. Through the forbidden black Ophelia dress, she learned the limits of her partnership with Irving: she could expect no parity. The godlike actor-manager would be both stage husband and fellow artist, but they were to be in nothing alike. In the Lyceum, as in proper families, woman's nature had nothing in it of man's. Tennyson's moral in *The Princess* was the new code of the stage: "For woman is not undevelopt man, /But diverse" (VII, 258–59). On the stage as in society, man's role was the hero, woman's the sweet server. Ellen Terry obediently went mad in the conventional white dress, thereby regaining an innocence she had never had before.

The lost black costume was indeed a mourning dress, not for Polonius but for herself: when she played Ophelia at last, she renounced her comedy, her capacity for mobile self-invention, to support Irving's high seriousness and mighty self-absorption. She could not stop mourning when the curtain fell. Possessed by an awareness of failure, she ran to the Embankment to drown herself. A modern biographer, one less hampered by decorum than Ellen Terry was, takes up her story:

> There was not a dissenting voice. Only Ellen was not there to take her curtain call. She felt she had failed, and sped off, like the mad girl she had studied, towards the Embankment with the intention of drowning herself. She was followed and brought back to her house at Longridge Road by Mrs. Rumball ("Boo") . . .
>
> After midnight Henry Irving came back to reassure her. In the emotions of the moment she became his mistress. It was the beginning of a long professional and emotional partnership. Ellen needed Irving's drive and the stability which this gave her, and Irving needed her magic. Hamlet had rescued Ophelia.

This highly colored account rings true iconographically, even if it heightens the facts: Ellen Terry's Ophelia, dressed properly in virginal white, carries self-destructive images of failure and drowning. Mad thoughts and loving submergence in Irving consummate her performance and save her from its consequences. When she had run off with Godwin and they found her drowned double, she had bounced back home to assure everyone that she had not drowned like the "poor corpse" who initiated her into fallenness. Now, Irving and Ophelia were initiating her into respectability. In that role, she *did* drown, though Boo saved her from the Thames.

There has been debate about whether Henry Irving was technically Ellen Terry's lover; the discussion is suffused with the chivalrous embarrassment that dogs biographers of Victorians. It seems indisputable that they played in their lives the flexible love that suited them more than their public union. In 1878, both were married. The vindictive Florence refused to grant Irving a divorce, thereby licensing the bachelor existence, centered in the theater and his clubs, with which he was most comfortable. The love affair he played with Ellen Terry endowed both their lives with the look of intimacy and the feel of stability; intermittent lovers, they acted the conventional marriage that was so alien to them both. That "marriage" predictably dissolved with the Lyceum in 1902, but by that time Ellen Terry had gotten used to playing a wife: she had taken into herself the noble self-mutilations the role required. Christopher St. John's brief biography, written five years after the dissolution of Irving's empire, is in part an epitaph for all good women: "Her generous soul seems always to be crying out, 'Let me serve!' "

Ophelia was the role by which, according to Christopher, she "abandoned . . . all chances of empire." Civilians made a cult of Ophelia, but many theater people agreed: in the hierarchy of the old stock companies, the leading lady was assigned the role of Gertrude, while Ophelia was relegated to the female juvenile. Moreover, in 1878, the thirty-one-year-old Ellen Terry was on the edge of being too old for Ophelia, though Irving, nine years older, was just reaching ripeness as Hamlet. Generous and sensuous Gertrude, with her several loves, might have suited Ellen Terry more than the clinging Ophelia, but Irving could not cast his stage wife as his mother: he had hired her to be daughterly. She had not begun her career crying "Let me serve!," but Irving's *Hamlet* taught her myriad readings of that line. By the end of the play, it almost seemed real to her.

The role that made Irving choose her as his partner was not Portia, the great lady of Belmont, but Olivia, a winsome stage daughter. On March 30, 1878— exactly nine months before her Lyceum debut—she opened in the first role she had ever created: Olivia, in W. G. Wills's sentimental adaptation of *The Vicar of Wakefield*. At thirty-one, the unrepentant fallen woman captured the general public by playing a seduced innocent. One scene was particularly acclaimed: "Only an artist of distinct genius could have ventured upon the impulsive abrupt movement by means of which she thrusts from her the villain who has betrayed her, and denotes the intensity of her scorn for him, the completeness of her change from loving to loathing." Too robust to be seduced and too free-hearted to loathe anyone she had loved, Ellen Terry won her public when she learned to ape virtuous revulsion.

Her Olivia was a great child whose true mission was to bless her father, the gentle Dr. Primrose. Clement Scott remembered her Olivia as the household fairy she had run to Harpenden to escape becoming: "When we talk of the Ellen Terry manner, and her indescribable charm, may I ask, were they ever better shown than in the scene where Olivia kisses the holly from the hedge at home, and then hangs it on a chair and dances around it with childish delight?" (quoted in Pemberton, 168). Irving may not have bothered to see this childish delight for himself; he knew that this seductive presence was just what the Lyceum needed to offset his own chill intensity. Like a good daughter/wife, Ellen Terry would win the audience's love, while he, like a proper father, would arouse its fear and awe. Moreover, she was, as Graham Robertson called her, "the Painter's actress." She could become a dream of beauty, while he was grotesque, and knew it: his long fleshless legs, his disjointed walk, his dissonant voice, needed Beauty to make them endurable; to make them stand out, he needed the aesthetic setting her trained eye oversaw. While the real Ellen Terry adopted and discarded fathers profligately, the adoring stage daughter was invited to the Lyceum in a union that seemed to some as ghoulish as the child's marriage to Watts: "That vivid woman . . . , physically and mentally young for her years, was yoked with a skeleton, of love and art" (Steen, 232).

That union made Ellen Terry famous, but Olivia, like many of her best characters, transplanted poorly to Irving's Lyceum. In her annotations to Charles Hiatt's *Ellen Terry and Her Impersonations,* she writes ruefully beside his account of her 1878 *Olivia:* "Played very well then." Irving's insistence on playing the Vicar in regular revivals only intensified the discordance of youth and innocence in this grand woman. In 1885, the impatient young George Bernard Shaw deplored her parody of an ingenue:

> Miss Ellen Terry tries very hard to reproduce her old Olivia; but the very effort does away with the apparent spontaneity that was once so fascinating. It is inevitable that her representation of the dawn of womanhood should be a little more artificial than it was; but there is no valid reason why such memorable points in the old Court performance as the glimpse of Olivia's face as she passes the window in her flight should be replaced by the monstrous improbability of her opening the lattice widely and kissing her hand several times to her father.

Playgoers who have never seen Miss Terry in this part should not lose the opportunity of doing so; but those who have tender recollections of the original Olivia will keep away from the Lyceum. The spectacle of Miss Terry imitating herself, and overdoing it, would not compensate them for the disappointments which they would suffer in the play.

Had Ellen Terry played her original Olivia to Irving's Dr. Primrose, Shaw would probably have grumbled at that as well: from the beginning of his career as a drama critic, he saw no wrong in Ellen Terry for which he did not hold Irving's Philistine tyranny responsible. He could not know that to begin with, the role was stunted and infantile compared to the dynamic little beings she had played as a real child. Despite criticism, as she aged, grew tired, and gained weight, she played Olivia with obedient regularity whenever Irving wanted her to. Dutifully, she squeezed herself into Irving's innocent daughter; dutifully, this demonic man made himself benevolent, though once when he was in the wings he was heard to "Baa-aa-a" disgustedly like a sheep at his own mildness. For the most part, audiences wept delightedly through all this wrongness. The history of Olivia epitomizes Ellen Terry's career at the Lyceum. The part that brought triumph when it was fresh clung to her like a succubus, veering close to embarrassing caricature as the years went on; she gained wealth, security, and love by resolutely miming an innocence her curious education had never given her. And like so many good women, she thought nobody would find her out.

During the run of the first *Olivia,* she married Charles Wardell, a fellow actor in the play, whose stage name was Charles Kelly. This brief marriage was her last attempt to cling to the freedoms that were her birthright, before she placed herself under Irving's control. Most biographers wish she had married the intense young actor Johnston Forbes-Robertson, who had been in love with her since her years with Godwin. Wardell was Godwin's opposite, "a manly bulldog sort of man" (ET quoted in Manvell, 99). More soldier than actor, he was still more violently jealous than Godwin of her talent and success. By the time they separated in 1881, he was a drunkard. Fred Terry claimed blithely that his sister had put her suitors' names in a hat and pulled out Wardell's by the luck of the draw, but Fred had never believed in Ellen Terry. She could no longer lock him in closets, but he disliked her even more now that he was an actor himself. Like a good sister, she had introduced him to the Bancrofts and gotten him his first real part in her vehicle, *New Men and Old Acres.* To his mortification, his voice had cracked onstage; instead of covering up, she had imitated him pitilessly and drawn a laugh. During her years with the Bancrofts, Ellen Terry shone with repentant conciliation for her defection to the country. Her flash of savagery toward her dashing little brother was equaled only by her savagery toward the dashing boy she was trying to suppress in herself. At the Lyceum, she would deflect her fury from the powerful Irving, letting her handsome son feel the lash hidden in her sweetness. In 1878, Fred had no reason to say romantic things about this second marriage and third apparent love. Charles Wardell's marriage would be dangerous for him.

The rest of the family didn't care whom Ellen Terry cast as her husband: it was the role that mattered. Once she was married, the rift with the Stanhope Street Terrys was healed as though it had never been. Grandparents, uncles, and aunts of whom they had never heard swooped down upon the newly christened Edy and Teddy Wardell, though their proper little cousins at Moray Lodge remained scrupulously aloof. Even Charles L. Dodgson was willing to visit, and all because a man had lent her his authority. In 1878, the Terry family was still supported by its girls: Polly and Flossie, now Marion and Florence, were building promising careers in the provinces. The women of Ellen's generation made the name of Terry famous, but only a man could bestow on her a name powerful enough to make the family whole again. Charles Wardell's name was ambiguous enough to suit this mobile, slippery clan: the Charles Kelly they claimed to know, whom Ellen Terry wrote about in her memoir, was a stage fiction: only the alien and ungainly "Wardell" could give Edy and Ted legal and familial substance. Since the real Godwin was unnameable, the children quickly divested themselves of the stranger's "Wardell"; they felt at home only with the stage names they made for themselves.

Most biographers assume with Charles Dodgson that Ellen Terry married only as a "concession to respectability" (Manvell, 137), but sexual vitality probably motivated her as well. Edy and Chris state stiffly but aptly: "No doubt one of her motives then for deciding to marry was a desire, in her children's interests, to regularize her position. Yet it is conceivable that she was strongly attracted by Charles Wardell. All through her life the man of brains competed for her affections with the man of brawn" (*Memoirs*, 116). This is a nice (or not so nice) way of suggesting that Ellen Terry preferred Wardell sexually to Forbes-Robertson and the rest. Godwin's aesthetic education had been a sexual education at its heart. Forbes-Robertson thrived on complicated emotions; in the 1890s, he would have a protracted, tormenting love affair with the malevolent Stella Campbell; only art and the theater satisfied him fully. Henry Irving, who was to pry Charles Wardell out of her life, was alive only when he acted, and in those hours, no matter who shared the stage, he was always alone. His determination to cast himself against type as Ellen Terry's lover heightened his isolation in his own discomfort. Great actors did not rest well in their bodies.

Ellen Terry and Henry Irving in *Olivia*. *Ellen Terry Memorial Museum, Smallhythe Place. Courtesy of the Trustee of the Ellen Terry Estate.*

Ellen Terry liked "the man of brawn"—lusty, comfortably physical men like Charles Wardell, Frank Cooper (a young actor with whom she was infatuated ten years later), or James Carew, her third husband—because she enjoyed her own vigorous body, despite others' inexplicable fears. Victorian men were licensed to find "outlets" for desires home did not fulfill, but Victorian women needed ingenious rationalizations when they embraced the same comfort.

Probably because she liked Wardell physically, she liked acting with him, and traveling with him as well. After *Olivia* closed, and then in the summers of 1879 and 1880, they embarked on a series of strenuous provincial tours. It was her last happy taste of the early itinerancy before the gates of the Lyceum closed on her. The Lyceum toured in cumbersome state: Irving's was the first company to transport not skeleton productions, but its entire cast, along with opulent sets and costumes, all the way to America; he prided himself on his heavy journeys. When, after 1902, Ellen Terry toured alone, her trips were increasingly disorienting and surreal. Charles Kelly lacked the majesty Irving would bring to touring, but on the road and onstage, she was comfortable with him. In 1880, in Leeds, she played her first Beatrice to his Benedick in *Much Ado About Nothing*. Later, with Irving, her Beatrice became celebrated, but she always insisted that it never rose to that unheralded performance in Leeds, when she had a handsome Benedick who was "perhaps better for the play" than the painfully slow and stately Irving (*Memoirs*, 115, 172). Easy physicality, gypsy comradeship, were some casualties of Irving's reign. Pointedly, he did not invite Charles Kelly to join the Lyceum. Ellen Terry's brawny, now superfluous husband drank more and more. In 1881, they separated; in 1885, he was dead.

When Ellen Terry exchanged Charles Kelly/Wardell for Henry Irving as her partner, she replaced a real (if ill-fitting) marriage with a stage union that was adulterous but scrupulously proper. She also exchanged the ease with which she had acted, traveled, and loved for a rigidly constrained role. Gordon Craig pronounced his mother "not a marriageable person—because she was too passionately the servant of the stage" (*ETSS*, 47), but he admitted that at the Lyceum, she played an impeccably subservient stage wife:

> If anyone had shown inspiration in Irving's company (and I believe the whole company will agree with me when I say that no one did this but Ellen Terry—her sole apology being that she couldn't help it), he would promptly have been sacked.
>
> Ellen Terry only retained her place in Irving's company because it was plain to see what efforts she was making to suppress herself—and having that tact of the clever woman, she did really keep her place.

After she left Harpenden, her life fractured in multiple ways. The untameable woman split off from the womanly actress who was daughterly, wifely, and motherly at once; love in art split off from the feel of love. As Watts's wife and Godwin's mistress, she had believed ardently in the generative union between sexuality and creation. Wardell/Kelly tried lumberingly to provide that union, but the single-minded Irving upstaged him utterly. Their love affair also upstaged the simplicity of physical fact; like the Lyceum, it was a created dream. Irving's overpowering imagination of their acted marriage groomed her for her epistolary love affair with his rival, George Bernard Shaw, in the 1890s. She and Shaw made love only in letters; only after the letters had subsided did they meet in embarrassment. At the same time, to avoid confronting the body that housed Shaw's glorious voice, she hungrily pursued Frank Cooper and then James Carew. Her life was not split simply between "the man of brains" and "the man of brawn," as Edy and Chris put it: she reflected the split in her society, whose women were groomed to display themselves as enchanting pictures of perfection while they were forbidden to speak about the bodies that transmitted their felt experiences. After Harpenden, her divided romantic impulses dramatized the widening gulf between her roles and her sensations. Onstage, she grew younger and more adorable every year. As her acting grew less like enhancing herself and more like lying (and as her children became more draining and demanding), the dream of love that had once embraced all the world became her sole means of defending her own truth against a world that lied about her. Her weak defense had no chance against Henry Irving's potent dream of his "sweetest, loveliest Ophelia."

England too had no defense against Henry Irving's dream. From his unpromising beginning as John Henry Brodribb, an awkward young man with an ugly voice, he dreamed not only his own glory, but that of the British actor in his person. In the previous stage generation, his great predecessors Fanny Kemble and William Macready had come to loathe the stage: ashamed of strutting and fretting, they longed only to rise above their roles as mountebanks. Macready retired to play a gentleman, while Fanny Kemble threw her histrionic passion into political activism. Both remembered the great Edmund Kean, his Napoleonic rise and swift decline into groveling, drunken buffoonery. Kean was a genius but no hero to a more careful generation that aspired, in its own ways, to live nobly: heroes and actors could only encumber each other.

In reaction, the stage generation that came of age during Victoria's reign dreamed of serving a theater as noble, as worthy of reverence, as the mighty pageant of British history. As early as 1856, Irving wrote to a Mrs. Wilkins: "The names of Shakespeare, Garrick, Kemble, Macready, and many others show that they were and are the companions of the master spirits of the ages, and rank as gentlemen and scholars among Royalty and the aristocracy. [Edmund Kean, who was no gentleman but only the greatest actor of them all, is significantly omitted from Irving's list of honors.] A person may be as moral and good in that as in any other walk of life. There is much prejudice against it in our circle of society, and that is wearing off as the world grows wiser, but in the higher ones they [actors] are considered equals." Irving taught his fellow actors to revere the royal family less as patrons than as spiritual kin; to exalt acting as an art as heroic as the painter's; to dream of a national theater that would unite the stage with the state.

In the 1860s the Bancrofts had lured middle-class audiences to the Prince of Wales' by designing stage pictures that were reassuringly like their own homes; by the 1890s, leaders of fashionable and intellectual life flocked to Irving's first nights at the Lyceum. When Irving appeared as a distinguished speaker, and later received honorary degrees, at England's great universities, entertained royalty and political leaders at the Lyceum, played before the Queen at Windsor, and finally became the first actor on whom she bestowed a knighthood, he displayed his honors as symbols of an assimilated caste. With Irving at its head, the Profession had evolved from an outcast group of vagabonds to an acknowledged arm of Empire.

By the time he possessed his own theater, Henry Irving had been hissed, mocked, and despised by his intimates and by strangers; he had abased himself energetically in low comedy, pantomime, and burlesque; he had lived without a home; he had forfeited his wife and sons. Through it all, he had dreamed not only of acting, but of power. His obsessed autocracy, his fierce control over every aspect of production, his unremitting centrality onstage, transformed the role of actor-manager: the complementarity of such overseeing couples as the Charles Keans and the Bancrofts was lost forever. The woman had been the true manager in both partnerships, but Ellen Kean and Marie Bancroft were shrewd enough to efface themselves publicly on behalf of their pompous, less intelligent husbands. Irving, like God, moved alone: no woman's *noblesse oblige* propped up his government. He was the most powerful of the great managerial patriarchs, who graced the theater with images of political and divine leadership. As Martin Meisel puts it:

[T]he great [English] actor-manager was by definition both the visible mark for all eyes, and a heroic will extending through a vast and cumbrous organization. In their theatres, the likes of Irving and Tree were both high priest and visible god, the heroes of every occasion; and theatres and productions were designed to magnify their impact. The [primacy of the actor-manager] repeated, in the house of illusion, the experience of history.

It did not escape some of the spectators, notably Tolstoy, Shaw, and Napoleon Bonaparte himself, that the heroic will on the stage of history, the historical Man of Destiny, was also an actor-manager, for whom the arts, theatrical and pictorial, were prime instruments for the creation of a satisfactory heroic persona, and its promotion into glory.

During Irving's great decade, the 1880s, he reflected his country's national, mystical, and religious dream of a hero. As Disraeli was urging his countrymen to extend England's empire through India and Africa, so Irving, who was said to resemble Disraeli, built a splendid empire in London to show the way. In an age when organized religion had become a torpid anachronism, and sophisticates flaunted their doubts, Irving exuded the sanctified magnetism of the churchmen of England's great days: Shakespeare's Cardinal Wolsey, Tennyson's Thomas à Becket. Irving's reverent assistant Bram Stoker placed the Lyceum at the heart of a last remnant of belief: "I often say to myself that the Faith which still exists is to be found more often in a theatre than in a church." Under Irving's guidance, the theater had indeed evolved away from the seaminess of the bordello to take on the reverent stiffness of a house of worship.

More and more, in the 1880s, wits, writers, and even women were feeling free to mock patriarchs. George Meredith's *The Egoist* (1879) pointed the way, for it showed that the pervasive laughter of the comic spirit can diminish a lordly man to the nothing he is. Oscar Wilde, who haunted the Lyceum in its early days, would soon set London laughing at all earnest authorities. In a decade of irreverence, of sophisticated silliness, Irving fortified his audience's faith in great men. The theater that revealed itself as a gorgeous little England allowed nobody to doubt the omnipotence of its patriarchal "Guv'nor."

Edy and Ted had no father, but they grew up in a more rigidly patriarchal household than did many non-theatrical children in the 1880s: the Lyceum family adored the male authority many real households were learning to laugh at. Edy, who had no doubt that she hated her true father, seemed unimpressed by Irving's grandeur; she liked him, felt free to criticize and advise him, played small parts deftly, and in 1899, designed with great pride the costumes for his production of Sardou's *Robespierre*. But Gordon Craig could never forget the vision of male power the Lyceum instilled. When he was in exile, he glamorized his days as a juvenile in the company, consecrating the Lyceum as "our house," an ideal patriarchal family: "We hear of the *partnership* of Irving and Ellen Terry, as meaning that both had the same power—it was no such thing. There was only one head of the house, and it was Irving. This house was the Lyceum Theatre, which was head of the English Theatrical world" (*ETSS,* 152). Power, for Craig, is power over others. Though he sequestered himself loftily from theatrical politics and performances, he never stopped praising Irving's genius at imposing himself on others and controlling them. In the 1920s, the actor-manager he saw as the perfect strong father swelled in the arena beyond the family into the perfect strong statesman: Benito Mussolini. "The only immense enthusiasm I have seen of recent years is that displayed by crowds of men and women on catching sight of Signor Mussolini. I mean that is the thing I call enthusiasm . . . nothing less than that is worthy of the name. . . . Irving could arouse it, both in the theatre and out of it. Out of the theatre it was controlled, in the theatre it was frantic" (*HI,* 22. First ellipsis EGC's). In the same heroic, covertly political vein, Bram Stoker's reminiscence regularly depicts Irving towering above thundering crowds. The strong man of the Lyceum restored England's faith in strong men everywhere.

Like his productions, Irving's lavish banquets in the theater's Beefsteak Room epitomized his dream of an England united under his own protection. His guests' chic is less astonishing than their diversity: "It was said that for a quarter of a century the Lyceum became part of the social history of London. Celebrities, visiting foreigners, statesmen, travellers, explorers, ambassadors, foreign princes, potentates, poets, novelists, historians, representatives of all the learned professions, industrialists, sportsmen, pretty ladies of fashion, less decorative philosophers and scientists, and Irving's old friends from the early days of the theatre —the cream of London's life all drifted through the Lyceum's private entrance." On crowning occasions the Prince of Wales appeared with his Marlborough set in tow; one evening Irving gave little Princess May of Teck a dainty birthday party (Bingham, 224–25). Bram Stoker declares categorically: "The range of his guests was impossible to any but an artist" (I., 310). Irving's kingdom of art was indeed a visionary Camelot, transcending, because it lived in a theater, the abrasions of political reality. Like all art, Irving's banquets were founded on exclusions: the poor and the paupered, the angry and the dispossessed, the unbeautiful and the untalented, went unfed. As often as not, women went unfed as well. Ellen Terry often played Irving's gracious consort and hostess, but just as often, at the Lyceum and elsewhere, she was banished with the other women while Irving toasted the less gifted male mainstays of the Lyceum family: Stoker, W. G. Wills, Joe Comyns-Carr, Hawes Craven, and the rest. Irving's kingdom extended its largesse to women as it pleased, but like Camelot, it was essentially a company of men who moved to Irving's vision and believed in it.

Ellen Terry never believed. She was more comfortable in her mock family than she would have been in a real one; she honored Irving; she "doted on his *looks*" (quoted in Manvell, 351). She was paid not only handsomely but, what was still more important, regularly; the unreliable Godwin, and the children he left her, had taught her to value security. Above all, after six obscure years, she relished fame and centrality. In her early days, even when she had played well, she was a vagabond: after being cheered in one city she would move on to a new one where she was again a stranger. At the Lyceum, audiences knew her over the years: like characters in fictional serials, she had come to matter to them as a changing constant in their lives. Moreover, she was at last mistress of her own house without having to run a home. Women, especially fallen women like herself, were told to crave a home: the Lyceum was her first one with a solid foundation. It was not the Wonderland Watts's studio had been; it had none of Harpenden's lush expansiveness; but it was the appointed goal of all her wandering.

When she was a wife at Little Holland House, she had expected, in her childishness, to be glorious; instead she was made to cover herself, to keep still, to serve posturing men who were famous. At the Lyceum she looked wistfully back to that early period "when I was Nelly Watts, and heedless of the greatness of great men." Now she was a woman whose household depended on a great man's good will; because he was everywhere, and because he was Irving, she had to heed him all the time. Her only revenge was to watch him relentlessly and to analyze him unsparingly. She examines him recurrently and compulsively in her memoir, as if he were a dream she could neither understand nor forget. Until his death, when she rises to the eulogies at which she is becoming so expert, she writes with an admiration chilled by irony: "It has been said that when Henry Irving had the 'advantage' of my Ophelia, his Hamlet 'improved.' I don't think so. He was always quite independent of the people with whom he acted" (*Memoirs*, 102).

> He was an egotist—an egotist of the great type, *never* "a mean egotist," as he was once slanderously described—and all his faults sprang from egotism, which is in one sense, after all, only another name for greatness. So much absorbed was he in his own achievements that he was unable or unwilling to appreciate the achievements of others. I never heard him speak in high terms of the great foreign actors and actresses who from time to time visited England. It would be easy to attribute this to jealousy, but the easy explanation is not the true one. He simply would not give himself up to appreciation. Perhaps appreciation is a *wasting* through a generous quality of the mind and heart, and best left to lookers-on, who have plenty of time to develop it. (*Memoirs*, 119–20)

Irving's blindness disquieted the actress whose happiest performances grew out of collaborative intimacy with a teacher or partner. She fought her solitude by watching him with an attentiveness he was incapable of returning. She kept a diary devoted to him, which Edy and Chris appended to her memoir under the title, "About H. I." Its passionate (but never reverent) scrutiny of the actor is laced with sardonic exposures of the man:

> H. I. is odd when he says he hates meeting the company and "shaking their greasy paws." I think it is not quite right in him that he does not care for anybody much. . . . Quiet, patient, tolerant, impersonal, gentle, *close,* crafty! Crafty sounds unkind, but it is H. I. "Crafty" fits him. . . .
> Indifference is personified in H. I.
> He has faults, but still such an over-balancing amount of virtues, that he is quite one of the best and most remarkable men of his time.
> He is a very *gentle* man, though not in the least a *tender* man.
> *1897.* Very odd. He is not improving with age. . . .
> *February, 1898.* For years he has accepted favours, obligations to, etc., *through* Bram Stoker! Never will he acknowledge them himself, either by business-like receipt or by any word or sign. He "lays low" like Brer Rabbit better than any one I have ever met. His hold upon *me* is that he is INTERESTING no matter how he behaves. I think he must be put down among the "Greats," and *that* is his only fault. He is Great. Constantine, Nero, Caesar, Charlemagne, Peter, Napoleon, all "Great," all selfish, all, but all INTERESTING. Interesting, but terrors in the family. (*Memoirs,* 270–71).

"He is Great." These were the words with which (as Chris put it) Ellen Terry abandoned all chances of empire. These brief fragments of her brilliant portrait leap with the intensity of her study of H. I., but her very intensity tacitly accepts the role of watcher: like Mrs. Prinsep and Julia Cameron, she has made herself a passionate student of great men. What she really wants, one feels on reading these descriptions, is to *play* Henry Irving: the pertinacity with which she deepens and embellishes her characterization is that of an actor building a role point by point until the character springs to life in his entirety. Of course that role, like so many, was forbidden: she was hired to be useful to Irving, to mediate between the great man and his company, his audiences, his sons, to woo with charm the multitude he depended on and despised. She was not licensed to become him.

The useful actress was first of all a wife. Unlike Mrs. Kean, she was beautiful and beloved, but she had none of Mrs. Kean's authority over the company. Times had changed, and the theater had changed still more: as Irving reinvented

Haverly Theatre program for the Lyceum
production of *The Merchant of Venice*.
*Reproduced by permission of the Henneke
Library of Performing Arts, University of Tulsa.*

Globe Theatre, Boston, program for the
Lyceum company tour, 1885. *Reproduced by
permission of the Harry Ransom Humanities
Research Center, University of Texas, Austin.*

Lyceum Theatre program for *Faust*, 1886.
*Reproduced by permission of the Harry Ransom
Humanities Research Center, University of
Texas, Austin.*

it, it was a glamorous bulwark against unbelief. The public persona he created might have illustrated Milton's nostalgic tribute in *Paradise Lost* to the primacy of unfallen man: "He for God only, she for God in him." The cover of this program for *The Merchant of Venice* drops no hint that Ellen Terry's Portia humiliates and dispossesses Irving's Shylock: the play is forgotten as she, placed demurely beneath him, gazes down at her own humility, while he eyes the heights in exaltation. At least until the turn of the century, Ellen Terry never received billing equal to Irving's at the Lyceum: the actor-manager's name blazoned itself alone on the cover, while inside, his partner was acknowledged only by being set off from the rest of the cast. When they toured the more egalitarian America, however, Ellen Terry received an equality of billing England denied her. American democracy claimed to be as enlightened about women as it was about everything else; its intelligentsia was ostentatiously conversant with feminist ideas; Ellen Terry was presented to America as Irving's proud equal, and was billed accordingly, while the hierarchical English loved her for her womanly subordination.

And the English did love her mercilessly. Shaw's *Pen Portraits and Reviews* exalts the power over her age she achieved through being loved:

> The part she has played in the life of her time will never be known until some day—perhaps fifty years hence—when her correspondence will be collected and published in twenty or thirty volumes. [These fifty years have come and gone, and to our loss, no such volumes have appeared.] It will then, I believe, be discovered that every famous man of the last quarter of the nineteenth century —provided he were a playgoer—has been in love with Ellen Terry, and that many of them have found in her friendship the utmost consolation one can hope for from a wise, witty, and beautiful woman whose love is already engaged elsewhere, and whose heart has withstood a thousand attempts to capture it.
> (Quoted in Manvell, 185–86)

Some obscure men—and many many women—were also in love with Ellen Terry in the last decades of the century: her effect was most enduring on those who were not famous enough to have their letters collected. It is impossible, however, to recreate that powerful figure today; her stage presence elicited abstract rhapsodies, not precise descriptions. She is celebrated most consistently as a picture, one that is living and kinetic, but, nevertheless, remote and confined: she is magnetic but not quite real. She had been groomed for stardom in a theater that took its identity from painting. In Michael R. Booth's reconstruction: "To look at the stage as if it were a painting was an automatic response in Victorian audiences, and to make the stage look as much like a painting as possible was equally a habit among managers and technical staff." But, he adds, even in such a context, Ellen Terry's status as living picture was unique: "No performer in the history of the English stage has ever been considered in quite these pictorial terms."

The visual power of her presence was so overwhelming that it obliterated her performances. Even W. Graham Robertson, her most rapturous admirer, remembers only a mystic haze. After painting an extended word picture of her glorious golden Portia, he admits that Irving's Shylock (which he did not admire) remained with him more vividly: "The memory of the Lady's Portia (oddly enough, I never saw it again) is like a dream of beautiful pictures in a scheme of gold melting one into another; the golden gown, the golden hair, the golden words all form a golden vision of romance and loveliness; but of Irving's Shylock I seem to remember every movement, every tone." Ellen Terry is a still vision to be dreamt of: she does not act so much as she elicits reactions in the viewer. All her energy concentrated itself on achieving this remote catalyzing power.

When Irving watched *The Amber Heart* from the front of the house, he celebrated her as a distant reflection of abstractions within abstractions: "I wish I could tell you of the dream of beauty that you realized" (quoted in Manvell, 189). In 1925, when she made her last stage appearance in Walter de la Mare's *Crossings,* Christopher St. John evoked her mystic presence in terms of worship eerily similar to Irving's. The vividly physical hoyden aged into a holy ghost: "The vision of this fragile creature, far advanced in years, yet somehow not old, tremulously gliding across the stage with loving arms outstretched, all earthiness purged away by time, the spirit of beauty, rather than beauty itself, filled the spectators with a strange awe. A long sighing 'Oh!' arose from them all, and the sound was a more wonderful tribute than any applause I have ever heard" (*Memoirs,* 308). This Ellen Terry is less an actress than a priestess, whose magic body is a conduit to mysteries still holier than her own. The religious awe Ellen Terry aroused found its crispest expression in Oscar Wilde's affectionate nickname: "Our Lady of the Lyceum."

An icon drinks the life of others; it cannot celebrate its own life. Irving was so painfully deliberate a presence that he immobilized Ellen Terry even in her most mercurial roles. As Shaw observed, with some bias but more truth: "To him, professionally, Ellen Terry was only the chief ornament of his theatre. Besides, his method was so slow that it was almost impossible to act with him. She had to stop too often and wait too long to sustain her part continuously when he was on the stage." The most evocative of Oscar Wilde's three sonnets about her is a hymn to her performance in W. G. Wills's *Charles I*. She is not acting, but waiting stilly as the world moves and makes noise around her:

In the lone tent, waiting for victory,
She stands with eyes marred by the mists of pain,
Like some wan lily overdrenched with rain;
The clamorous clang of arms, the ensanguined sky,
War's ruin, and the wreck of chivalry
To her proud soul no common fear can bring;
Bravely she tarrieth for her Lord, the King,
Her soul aflame with passionate ecstasy.
O, hair of gold! O, crimson lips! O, face
Made for the luring and the love of man!
With thee I do forget the toil and stress,
The loveless road that knows no resting place,
Time's straitened pulse, the soul's dread weariness,
My freedom, and my life republican!

Mrs. Wigan, with her exortations to "*Stand still!* . . . Now you're of value!," would have commended the Ellen Terry of Wilde's sonnet. If her heart was not still, but trembling with suppressed energy, she had succeeded in hiding herself from discerning spectators. To be useful to Irving, she had to let him become the theater's prime mover.

Irving also turned himself into a painting, as Henry James noted with distaste: "He is what is called a picturesque actor; that is, he depends for his effects upon the art with which he presents a certain figure to the eye, rather than upon the manner in which he speaks his part." No one, though, could imagine Irving as still, or mistake him for a reflection of abstract and unearthly beauty, for he was painter as well as painting. Ellen Terry's wonder at his Charles I encompasses both creator and created portrait: "His stateliness - gentleness - *his atmosphere of dignity* could never be told of. Every inch a King. So pure - so unasserting - so lofty, simple - Holy = I mean H. I. - as the King = I have lost myself looking at him and half doubted its being Henry. It surely was the best Van Dyke portrait - moving and speaking - alive. His hands - his face - his bearing - Nothing - nobody cd describe and do any justice to the subject - but thank God I've seen the noble bit of work" (annotated *Charles I* script quoted in Manvell, 126). Painter and painting merge in the pure, lofty, even holy figure of the self-crowned Henry Irving.

Charles Kean's archeological productions began a theatrical evolution of which Irving's moving and speaking Van Dyke portrait was the culmination:

living paintings glorified the stage. In the 1880s, the Bancrofts had left behind their pleasant genre paintings at the Prince of Wales'; they had taken over the Haymarket to transform its enormous stage into an actual living picture. They encompassed the stage with "a rich and elaborate gold border, about two feet broad, after the pattern of a picture frame, [which] is continued all around the proscenium, and carried even below the actors' feet" (Percy Fitzgerald, quoted in Meisel, *Realizations,* 44). An increasingly respectable theater made itself up more and more consummately to resemble the highly fashionable medium of painting. Charles Kean and Edward Godwin had put art to the service of historical accuracy, but by the 1880s, the mystique of art swamped edification. Prestigious painters like Lawrence Alma-Tadema and Edward Burne-Jones designed Lyceum productions; their visual integrity meant more to Irving than fidelity to mere historical fact. The popular Aesthetic catchphrase, "Art for Art's sake," made Beauty answerable to no tedious representational accuracy. The Lyceum abandoned bourgeois drawing-room realism to recreate history as a figuration of titanic artists.

Irving, the paramount artist, towered over the famous painters he hired, for he created a new cosmos on a living canvas. Michael R. Booth's description of *Faust* (1885) illuminates Irving's entire achievement: "He overmastered not only by his acting, . . . but by making a spectacle of himself, by his superb sense of colour, design, composition, space, and light—the skills . . . of a painter as well as those of an actor and manager." Irving's reign and Terry's charm made the hegemony of pictorial theater so overpowering that sensitive novelists feared for their own medium: drab-looking words that painted only fragile inward pictures. "The theatre just now is the fashion, just as 'art' is the fashion and just as literature is not," Henry James wrote gloomily in 1879 (*SA,* 119), incidentally explaining his obsessed animus against the "picturesque," and stunningly popular, Lyceum.

At every opportunity Irving insisted on his role as maker of his canvas as well as object within it. Like those of our own film directors who have been consecrated as *auteurs,* Irving's name dwarfed all others on the programs; moreover, after each performance, he deliberately broke the pictorial illusion to address the audience in his own proudly humble person. As an actor, he maintained his dynamic centrality by specializing, not in heroes, but in electrifying villains. Nobody believed Irving in love. His miscast Romeo to Ellen Terry's equally miscast Juliet was received with polite, though faintly derisive, incredulity. His creed was that of Shakespeare's Richard III: "And therefore, since I cannot prove a lover, / To entertain these fair well-spoken days, / I am determined to prove a villain / And hate the idle pleasures of these days" (I, i, 28–31). As a villain, he was unforgettably mobile. As Shylock, Eugene Aram, Mephistopheles, Mathias, the perverse and sadistic Synorix in *The Cup*, Iago, Macbeth, Iachimo in *Cymbeline*, he aroused audiences to frenzies of empathy and fear that led ironically to his canonization as England's most respectable actor. Like Dickens, he won acclaim by turning himself into the twisted outcasts audiences feared, coming forth at the end, as Dickens did, to remove the frightening mask and extend the reassuring hand of deferential fellowship. Respectable audiences accepted him as a somewhat scary brother because he played out their fears of themselves and of the grandiose imperial world they were afraid that they had made.

Gordon Craig's brilliant description of Irving's Mathias resurrects an actor at the opposite pole from the Ellen Terry who was so often, but so vaguely, evoked. Ellen Terry made herself into a concentrated catalyst for the half-understood images that haunted spectators, while Irving imposed himself on audiences through a sequence of pantomimic, almost imperceptible but unforgettably vivid gestures:

> By the time the speaker got [his line] slowly out—and it was dragged purposely —Irving was buckling his second shoe, seated, and leaning over it, with his two long hands stretched down over the buckles. We suddenly saw these fingers stop their work; the crown of the head suddenly seemed to glitter and become frozen —and then, at the pace of the slowest and most terrified snail, the two hands, still motionless and dead, were seen to be coming up the side of the leg . . . the whole torso of the man, also seeming frozen, was gradually, and by an almost imperceptible movement, seen to be drawing up and back, as it would straighten a little, and to lean a little against the back of the chair on which he was seated. [There is more minute description of Irving's movements throughout this first scene. Craig concludes:] and *one* of the movements of the immense and touching dance closes—only one—and the next one begins, and the next after—figure after figure of exquisite pattern and purpose is unfolded, and then closed, and ever a new one unfolded in its wake. (*HI*, 56–58. ECG's ellipsis)

Neither Gordon Craig nor anybody else has described an Ellen Terry performance with such obsessed precision. She has been transmitted to us from the Lyceum as a generalized icon, while we inherit an irresistibly vivid Irving made up of countless mesmerizing, though almost invisible, motions.

To those who studied Irving most reverently—Gordon Craig and Bram Stoker—the source of his power was less artistic than occult. Craig places his art not in the context of theatrical tradition, but in relation to the "profound thoughts of Mesmer, and . . . the most surprising powers of Cagliostro" (*HI*,

105–6). Like Du Maurier's mystic Svengali, like the Mussolini Craig applauded later on, Irving possessed others' minds so intensely that he linked the theatrical to the supernatural. Bram Stoker reacted with still greater violence. Hearing Irving read "The Dream of Eugene Aram," he was overwhelmed by hysteria, though, he insisted, "I was physically immensely strong" (I, 32). As Irving's manager, hero worshipper, and fountain of geniality, Stoker studied his master with the appalled fascination his hero Jonathan Harker would later direct on the suave, aristocratic vampire, Dracula.

For Stoker, Irving's portrayals of great men were triumphs of witchcraft as well as mesmerism: "He did not merely look like Dante—he *was* Dante; it was like a veritable re-incarnation" (I, 273). His awed description of Irving reading Tennyson's *Becket* at Canterbury Cathedral, the very site of Becket's martyrdom, evokes a power that is sacred and diabolical at once: Irving's reading for the benefit of the Cathedral Restoration Fund becomes a mediumistic rite whereby the actor engorges the spirit of the dead saint. When Irving died, poor and on the road once more, in the lobby of a Bradford hotel, both newspapers and Stoker's reminiscence made much of the fact that his final onstage words had been Becket's: "Into Thy hands, oh Lord, into Thy hands." Through Irving's powers Becket lived and died once more. For his most devoted acolytes, Irving did not merely represent heaven and hell: he incarnated them in his own mystic person. To believers, his powers extended beyond the artistic to the political, and beyond politics to the magical and cosmic.

Believers knew that Ellen Terry's "marriage" to this magus empowered her as well, just as in *Dracula,* Lucy and Mina, the vampire's brides, acquire metamorphic powers that are at once infernal and celestial. Ellen Terry may or may not have cared for Stoker's mythmaking—without exception, literature concerning the Lyceum is silent about *Dracula,* keeping Stoker in his place as Irving's relentlessly genial factotum—but those who were moved to awe at Ellen Terry's very appearance shared Stoker's reverence for his master's kingdom. Later, when Ellen Terry acted without Irving, the legend of her charm would cloy and cripple her performances, but within his aegis, a charm descended on her that lent magic to her every appearance. Irving's holy circle made her less an actress than an object of belief, but as the years went on it became harder for her to descend into a merely secular theater. Like Mina in *Dracula*'s final scene, Ellen Terry froze into her magic circle, immobilized and adored.

To believers, including disparagers, Irving was utterly unlike other men. His triumphant grotesquerie faded to normality in photographs and disappeared altogether in portraits, but it leaped out in caricature. In that assaultively individualistic medium, the subject *is* his idiosyncrasies: there is none like him.

Caricature of Henry Irving as Hamlet. _Reproduced by permission of the Harry Ransom Humanities Research Center, University of Texas, Austin._

Portraits, which aim to be more generalized and typical, obliterated Irving's unholy charm. Of the several that were attempted, Irving and his circle approved only the portrait by Jules Bastien-Lepage, which despairs of capturing the occult actor to settle on the whimsical comrade. The actor who invented himself as a living portrait faded out of existence when painted by anyone other than himself. In 1910, Ellen Terry donated the Bastien-Lepage portrait to the National Portrait Gallery, where, utterly dwarfed, it hangs beside Sargent's grand apotheosizing painting of her Lady Macbeth. Their portraits reverse the balance of power that defined Irving and Terry's partnership. Ellen Terry dwindled to vacant prettiness in caricature—her own irreverent sketches of herself are witty exceptions—but in portraiture she assumed myriad lives. When they acted together, the intractable Irving obscured her adaptability, but now, in portraits, we can see Ellen Terry's metamorphoses, while Irving's power survives only in his disciples' dark myths.

Always, there was something perverse about Irving, something not only crafty but cruel: Bram Stoker's devout reminiscence expunges the sinister, invasive magnetism that made his Dracula another unforgettable Irving caricature. As time went on, Ellen Terry too, in her own way, became increasingly perverse onstage. She fooled, she fidgeted, she forgot her lines, and worse, she acted herself forgetting lines. In the late 1890s, young Margaret Webster watched her intensely. Her parents, Ben and May Webster, were junior members of the company; May, who would later become Dame May Whitty, was one of Ellen Terry's young protégées and confidantes. Margaret Webster remembered countless performances of *King Arthur* (1895) "when everybody played a kind of merry-go-round with the lines while the erratic Nell chased some speech that had eluded her." For those who knew how to look, the real play was Ellen Terry subverting her scripts.

Had the perverse tendencies in Irving's exemplary stage family been unleashed, the Lyceum, so determinedly wholesome, would have taken its place with the other theatrical aberrations that overran London: the corrosive nonsense of Oscar Wilde, the unforgiving social exposures of Ibsen, the domestic case histories of Henry Arthur Jones and Arthur Wing Pinero (a graduate of the Lyceum company), in which Stella Campbell was so seductively neurotic. Towards the end, the Lyceum was going mad, but Irving allowed nothing neurotic to contaminate its majesty. Until the end, it remained true to the epic grandeur of Irving's self-exaltation.

His resistance to contemporaneity infuriated William Archer and Shaw, who cast the Lyceum as a fortress of reaction against Ibsen's revolution, but Irving was wise to place restraints on his own dark power and on the anarchic energy of his stage wife—the "insane excitability" that had unnerved Watts when she was a girl. The Lyceum's comparatively innocuous repertoire remained stubbornly the same: a Shakespeare cut and tailored to Irving's dimensions alternated with historical pageants and familiar old French melodramas like *The Lady of Lyons* and *The Corsican Brothers*. Shaw fumed at his Shakespearean scripts—"He does not merely cut plays; he disembowels them. In *Cymbeline* he has quite surpassed himself by extirpating the antiphonal third verse of the famous dirge. A man who would do that would do anything—cut the coda out of the first movement of Beethoven's Ninth Symphony, or shorten one of Velasquez's Philips into a kitcat to make it fit over the drawing room mantelpiece"—and spluttered against a repertoire that had no room for his own or his Ibsen's iconoclasm. But a modern Irving who tried to understand the human psyche, or one who respected probing modern playwrights, could never have built an empire. Neither could a Disraeli who respected the new, still inchoate, nationalist movements around the world.

Because of the restraints and repressions Irving built into it, the Lyceum became a unifying force in British society. Because it was fashionable, it ended forever the quarantine that had isolated the actor from acceptable humanity. Henry James, who thrived on isolation, wrote sourly about the passing of a prejudice that had demeaned actors through the ages: "Plays and actors are perpetually talked about, private theatricals are incessant, and members of the dramatic profession are 'received' without restriction. They appear in society, and the people of society appear on the stage; it is as if the great gate which formerly divided the theatre from the world had been lifted off its hinges" (*SA*, 119–20). Even William Archer, who did his best to mock Irving out of existence, admitted that the Lyceum was a rare point of union in a fractured society, as the novels of Dickens had been: "An amusement which was formerly 'worse than wicked—vulgar,' has now become better than respectable—fashionable. But the Lyceum is more than fashionable, it is popular. There is probably no artistic institution in England which unites all the classes as it does." Bram Stoker imagined his master as a vampire, but Irving's true mission, and his greatest stage trick, was his persuasive conviction that the actor, who had been ostracized for centuries, was a common and harmless human being.

When Irving's knighthood became official, Ellen Terry could express her sense of exclusion to Gordon Craig only through the words of the company: "The good folk at the Lyceum (who have no more logic than Cats—) think 'it's too bad' that 'birthday honours' fall only to Henry's share, & so they have dubbed me 'Lady Darling' with which title I'm well content." Irving's title was traditional and imperial, while Ellen Terry's girlish one was improvised by the theatrical community that bred her. Only belatedly, in 1925, did she exchange this paper crown for a Dame Grand Cross, and by then she had lived beyond the world for a long time.

Theatrical coincidence pursued Irving: on the day his knighthood was announced, Oscar Wilde was sentenced to two years' imprisonment and hard labor for acts of gross indecency. The patriarch and hero might be called "Sir," but simultaneously, the flagrant homosexual, the creator of a remorselessly theatrical theater that laughed at heroes and imperial boasts, the champion of the grotesque and the artificial, saw prison doors open for him while all his plays in London closed at once. The theater had become respectable, but theatricality would never cease to be an offense.

With his weird physical mannerisms and his obsessed ambitions, Henry Irving was more eccentric than Oscar Wilde could ever be, but he had mesmerized people into believing that he exemplified a proud national tradition. When Irving's became the first statue of an actor to be erected on Trafalgar Square, he was fittingly purged of the Mephisophelean glow, the dynamic oddities, that won him his fame. The statue stands today as a momento of the British theater's crusade for irreproachability. It is indistinguishable from surrounding lofty monuments to political dignitaries, unrecognizable as Irving, but, swathed in its academic robes, it looks unyieldingly noble.

Ellen Terry's "marriage" to Irving did not duplicate her marriage in art to Watts, for he was too aloof to play with her. She missed artists, for they looked at one rather than testing their own mesmeric powers. She admitted unabashedly to Anna Held: "Just think! Burne-Jones is coming to The Tart [her nickname, it seems, for *The Amber Heart*]!! I'd sooner please him than anyone after Mr. Irving (who, by the way, never notices, I do believe!!!!!)" In that as in many things, their marriage was eminently Victorian. Though it was never legalized, it was the marriage that concluded all Victorian novels, bringing not only a noble mission the wife may serve, but security, money, and a solid home. According to Manvell, Ellen Terry received by the early 1880s "probably the highest salary earned by a woman in Britain during the late nineteenth century —£200 a working week, together with lump sums acquired from benefit performances." But the cost was her exotic autonomy, her immunity from ordinary life: "She was dependent on [Irving] for her security and livelihood, as virtually all women of that period were on a husband" (Manvell, 297, 143). For the first time in her life, she was taken care of, though to fight her protectedness, perhaps, she gave her money away with increasing profligacy as she grew older.

In George Eliot's *Middlemarch,* which was published seven years before Ellen Terry joined the Lyceum, the ardent heroine Dorothea Brooke longs to serve a great cause. Too intense and grand for the roles provincial life allots her, this earnest creature with nothing to do epitomizes all the perplexities of the novel. Her high-mindedness leads her into a disastrous marriage to a mean-minded pedant she imagines is Milton; when he dies, she falls in love with his mercurial cousin Will Ladislaw. Will becomes an "ardent public man"; Dorothea embraces her destiny of virtuous anonymity, submerging herself in her family and leaving a mission to Will. This happy ending unsettles readers with great expectations, but Dorothea recedes out of the action before her complaints can join theirs. In its own theatrical idiom, Ellen Terry's Victorian marriage to an ardent public man lived Dorothea's destiny. Hers was the happy ending every woman was supposed to want, and all good women deserved. A responsive daughter of her culture, Ellen Terry adapted its plots to her life, but unlike those of fictional heroines, that life did not fade away when a hero took her in.

It was impossible to belittle her gains: she had acquired not only security, but citizenship in the larger society that had despised theater people. As Henry

Irving's stage wife, she had become star and great lady in a leap. Kate was now a portly and proper matron who had faded into obscurity like Dorothea Brooke; Ellen had all Kate's love and accoutrements without having to renounce her fame or to play a wife all the time. Moreover, there was Shakespeare, whom Irving had made popular all over again. In no other theater could she play Portia, Beatrice, Ophelia, Lady Macbeth, in exacting, sumptuous productions that audiences cared passionately for. Still, like Dorothea Brooke's, Ellen Terry's happy ending disturbed spectators. Her energy seemed wasted at the Lyceum, her comic spirit extinguished. As with Dorothea Brooke, though, nobody could say just what it was Ellen Terry ought to have done.

In these years, she began to announce herself as a useful actress, one whose only ambition was to serve. Even on the margins of Charles Hiatt's book about her, she writes next to accounts of her ambition: "Never had 'ambition.' " "Not at all. I was a paid servant and had to, at least try to do it=" In the 1860s she had exalted her own artistry, but now it could not be disentangled from the art of being a good woman. By the 1880s, every good woman knew what Ellen Terry's word meant: "USEFUL. It was becoming the new watchword of the times [around mid-century], a goal for women more important even than good looks, marriage, or sexual fulfillment." Women with ardor who aspired to be more than frivolous ornaments—women, in fact, like George Eliot's Dorothea —longed to be "useful" as a way of affirming their energies without announcing dangerous ambitions that would arouse the opposition. By the 1880s, Ellen Terry had absorbed the argot of restless women in the world beyond the theater; but when so powerful a person called herself "useful," the word's timidity, its false modesty, stood suddenly revealed.

Moreover, the word had dreary connotations in the theater, as Ellen Terry knew well, for it evoked the sad specter of the permanent utility man or woman in the old stock companies, of whom *Oxberry's Dramatic Biography* wrote: "Once establish a name for utility, and you throw down all hopes of eminence in the profession" (quoted in Donohue, 74). It was this dead-end dreariness that suffused Ellen Terry's sense of herself at the Lyceum.

Writing about *The Dead Heart* to Audrey Campbell, she finds it hard to be a good sport about being useful to two heroes, for her son is now a soft-faced juvenile in Henry Irving's house: "All went well the first night of the play. Henry is quite wonderful in it - I knew how well it wd suit him = Ted made a most promising beginning & tho' mine is a beast of a part, it is very important to the play that it shd be played carefully = & so I come in usefully = !!!" She concludes disconsolately: "I can't write now about the play, & I've no other news—but I do wish I cd get away to fresh air somewhere, the last months day

& night at the theatre has made me sick of it." Around this time, she writes still more self-depreciatingly to her American friend Elizabeth Winter, wife of William Winter the powerful dramatic critic: "Dear Willie = <u>High up</u> Willie [Winter] - I love him— & wish I had 2 grains of his nature in me to make my material mass finer — sweeter = There is Fortinbras I know, but I've always hated him whilst acknowledging his use, but oh, the 'useful'ness of the dreamers to the do-ers — <u>that</u> shd be insisted upon —" The very sound of the virtuous word "useful" arouses all her sadness and self-discontent.

Surprisingly, her private letters about Irving are mellower than her Memoir, but they too convey an anger that denies itself, an intense subterranean complaint that is neither formulated nor banished. Some of his love notes to her survive:

> Soon – soon!
> I shall be near you on Sunday.
> God bless you my only thought
> Your own till death
> (Quoted in Manvell, 246)

Her letters about him, though, are at best tolerant and dispassionate: "Well, we have had our holiday & it stands us in good stead now. Directly Henry begins his work, he is to me the most wonderful creature under the sun - but when he is <u>holidaying</u> he's but a mortal man, & I don't think much of him!" "Henry & I get to understand each other better every day, I think = I think mistakes come, of fancying people too perfect! — I don't think Henry as perfect as I used, but he is **I k n o w** much more lovely than any other I have met." Charles Wardell had been dead for almost four years when she wrote this last, determinedly well-adjusted letter to Elizabeth Winter. With him had died the time when play and work had merged happily, without explanation and without strain.

To Marion, she is explicit about their liaison, its coziness, and her own subordination within it. Writing from Chicago, she is a lover who never forgets that she is also an employee: "This is the first time Henry & I are staying in different Hotels & we are both dull for that—but I cd not stay in the middle of the City, and he took his rooms 2 months ago=" As if to counter any intimation of indifference, she adds: "Henry never <u>never</u> was so sweet & kind & <u>unselfish</u> as he is now to me= Long may it <u>last</u>!" His new sweetness may have been the harbinger of his sexual and emotional withdrawal from her in the 1890s, when the Lyceum's power was waning, an aging and tense Ellen Terry was hard to cast, and iconoclasts like Shaw were laughing at his empire and all it stood for. Sensing, perhaps, an ominous change, Ellen Terry tries to preach womanly resignation to her little sister, but her hungry ego takes over: "God bless you my sweet little sister & keep you well, & happy & <u>content</u> - 'Content is our best having'= I'm always quite content when I have everything I want!!!!!="

This letter encapsulates her devious life in this period: she turns her own sweetness into a parodic game, makes assertions and denies them, releases and repudiates an anger that found full expression only in her "H. I." diary. Like those of all subordinates, her emotions ricochet back on herself: they don't dare reach her unconscious employer. Four years later, when the partnership is fraying, she tells May Webster what she has never told Irving: "I see the papers say he & I have 'quarreled'—the blithering idiots! Ain't they clever?—It takes 2 to quarrel--& <u>he won't!!</u> I've tried for 19 years & he just **w o n ' t !**"

Irving loved h̄er, but he heard nothing she said. Had the quarrel come, nothing would have changed, for her real quarrel was not only with him, but with her own roles, and it was the quarrel she had always had. She had learned only to be devious, irresistibly sweet and then, changing like an opal, sweetly savage. She was at her most devious in the intense correspondence with George Bernard Shaw that began in 1895, when she was forty-eight. She let him rage against Irving in his letters and in the *Saturday Review,* cooing over him but siding neither with him nor against him. When he tried to make her declare her allegiance, she fell back on the Poor Nell she had learned so long ago: "Ah, I feel so certain Henry just hates me! I can only *guess* at it, for he is exactly the same sweet-mannered person he was when 'I felt so certain' Henry loved me! We have not met for years now, except before other people, where my conduct exactly matches his of course. All my own fault. It is *I* am changed, not he. It's all right, but it has squeezed me up dreadfully, and after the long pause of illness [surgery on her eyes], I went back last night, weak and nervous, but looking well and acting well, thank the Lord. Only for the first time not glad to go back to my dear work" (November 7, 1900. *A Corr.,* 281).

Despite her disciplined self-suppression, Irving did leave her in the end. In 1898, when the Lyceum was collapsing of its own weight, the stricken man turned beyond the theater for comfort: his last lover was not Ellen Terry, but the journalist Eliza Aria. Like Watts and Godwin, he found a quieter woman with whom he could die; for all the charm Ellen Terry shed, she could never play a solacing wife. At Irving's funeral, Eliza Aria produced for him an enormous pall of laurel leaves that engulfed the coffin, while Ellen Terry exuberantly brought him back to life in her response to condolence notes: "For 'thoughts & Remembrance— <u>Thank you</u>. It is just as you say — S u c h a passing! He hated illness & weakness — finished his work & then went quietly away. With <u>distinction</u> to the last = the Hub-bub is glorious to me — he would have <u>loved it</u>! & I do - for him = Like Watts, Irving lived at the end with a woman who would turn his death into art, but he found himself as an artist when he shared the stage with a woman to whom hubbub was glorious.

Ellen Terry's letters to the young Gordon Craig are more dynamic and forthright than are her stagily coquettish letters to Shaw, but as far as they concern Irving, their divided burden is the same: she holds Irving up as a hero to the undisciplined boy, but at the same time she exposes—even parodies— his tyrannical narrowness. A complaint from America swivels into an exemplum:

> It was quite killing about Henry. Knowing this was a terrific big theatre I begged & prayed that I might be "let off" the first night in Boston because of my voice & that Miss Emery might play Margaret - No - he was like iron - like a rock about it, & I got mad & said "I do think that if your son, or your mother, your wife the idol of your heart were to die on the stage through making the effort to do the work you wd let it happen." "<u>Certainly</u> I would," said he to my amazement! I expected he wd say, "Oh, come now, you exaggerate"—so now I know what to expect. He certainly wd <u>drop</u> himself, before he'd give in, & there my lad is the simple secret of his great success in everything he undertakes. *He* is most extraordinary.

The warning within this earnest tribute is that Henry Irving is a monster. With such a mother painting such a portrait, Gordon Craig could do nothing but flee the essential madness of his sort of success. As with her letter to Marion, Ellen Terry concludes by sliding away from her own pious homilies into a witty declaration of hunger:

> The Lord be merciful to me
>   A sinner
> Who wants her dinner—
> And doesn't get thinner—

In another letter, she frees Irving from his monster role to use him as the vehicle of a piercing truth, one which guided her own life more than it did his. When

Gordon Craig was a young actor on tour complaining about his parts, she shared the accumulated wisdom of her life cloaked dutifully in Henry Irving's words:

> Oh, Ted, you're quite wrong in thinking that either Henry or I ever went touring and playing big parts before we played little ones, and we <u>never</u> either of us went touring <u>on our own account</u> until about 15 or 16 years ago—We played in provincial <u>engagements</u> parts like Hero & Claudio— Nerissa & Lorenzo—(or Gratiano) and then minor parts in all the melodramas . . . and all the <u>bigger</u> parts in <u>Farce</u>, but go on tour with the responsibility of our own company we never did. You say "the art has not changed, tho' the times have—Henry says the man who sets himself <u>against</u> the times in an Art as old as the dramatic art wd be a fool, and get left!

At any rate, such a woman would be a fool. Irving set himself against the times again and again: he did play every role he was given in his provincial apprenticeship, but his dream of staging Shakespeare in his own theater, the grandiosity of his vision of himself as actor-manager, were mad until he made them work commercially: until his 1874 Hamlet, Shakespeare had been box-office poison in London. Like him, Gordon Craig set himself bullishly against the times (as Edy could not); his reward was not commercial success, but canonization as a theatrical saint. Ellen Terry's advice to her son is woman's wisdom, the same experiential acumen that told her to be useful at the Lyceum. It is the advice Lady Macbeth gives to her husband, who understands it no better than Gordon Craig did: "To beguile the time, / Look like the time" (I, v, 64–65). Ellen Terry's insistence that Lady Macbeth was not bad, because she was Everywoman, may have sprung from her lived understanding of these lines.

The highly strung, tautly feminine Lady Macbeth she played in 1888 was to be her richest, most searing commentary on herself in the role of womanly actress. Her brilliant notes survive, but she lost heart when her performance failed to communicate all she meant it to: in her memory, the Lyceum itself declined after *Macbeth* (*Memoirs*, 179). Had Lyceum audiences been attuned to the confession she was making, Lady Macbeth alone would still not have given her adequate expression for the tensions, the terrors, the sense of fracturing, that gripped her during her years of glory. Even in her early Lyceum years, as Marguerite Steen alone among her biographers describes them, she was in a state of incipient uncontrol: "In 1883 she was thin as paper, in spite of eating heartily, usually sleeping well, and rarely ailing. [By the next decade, she was barely sleeping, complaining incessantly of illnesses, and on the way to being fat.]

Veering constantly between the wildest of high spirits and deep depression, she would, in the present day, be said to be heading for a breakdown" (p. 184).

These are the years in which she begins to sign her letters in a phantasia of different names. Sometimes these are simply the names of her characters—her letters to the paternalistic Stephen Coleridge often come from "LIVIE" or "OLIVIA"—but more generally, and for the rest of her life, they designate her own mercurially shifting incarnations. The old "Nell" that has always been her nickname takes on a perverse life of its own, suggestive of Little Nell, Dickens's moribund paragon in *The Old Curiosity Shop,* and of everything in Ellen Terry herself that is stunted and adorable. It loses itself by blending into her own name and becoming "Nellen," or it represents the hateful contrary of the "Eleonora" (or "Eleanora" or "Ellen Nora") she wishes she were—the great Duse, strong in her identity, useful to no one but God. In 1907, she signs herself to Graham Robertson:

Signature of a letter from Ellen Terry to Walford Graham Robertson, 24 December 1906. *Reproduced by permission of the Huntington Library, San Marino, California.*

Yrs affectionately
Eleanora—Nell—?
PS. I note "Nell" now, with you—not "Eleanora"—I
wonder have I dropped from Eleanora to Nell—or risen
to Nell from Eleanora?—

This follows her declaration of dependency with which she announces her third marriage, to James Carew—"I couldn't be alone any longer"—suggesting that she has fractured into "Nell," womanly and dependent, and "Eleanora," transcendent and brave, who must now be cast off.

Sometimes, for reasons she alone knows, she changes identities in midsignature. Like characters in a play, the separate names assume the autonomy of separate selves. Irving had cast her in the nebulous and generalized role of his stage wife; to compensate, "Lady Darling" became a cast of female characters in herself. Some of the other names she gave parts of herself over the years were: Old Nell, Old Gandy, E. T., Nellen T., Nelena, Nellian, Nell Nell, Your old Wattles, Godmother E. C. [Ellen Carew], Awful Ellen Louisa, Ellen Alice, Eleanora Alicia Terry, Granny Nell, Muddlepated Ellen, E. A. Terry [to Oscar Wilde], Nellchen, L. N. T. [this visual pun, with which she signed herself in 1900, has infantilizing associations. Might it also designate Little Nelly Terry, who is also Dickens' Little Nell Trent?], Your Frump, Ever the horrid same Old Frump, Your Own Old Plumb Pudding, Your loving Old Crosspatch, Your Old Winkle, Your loving old Jubilee Ellen, Your old Hoighty-toity, Your old Nuisance, N. T., Your Sweetheart
Your old
  Hen—
  ———
  N.!!

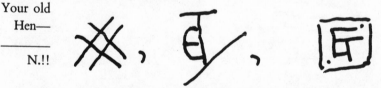

To Shaw, she is mostly E. T., to match his predictably uniform G. B. S., but her other names pop out occasionally. When he innocently addresses her as "Ellen," her supposed real name, she responds with a confusing symphony of signatures:

Good-bye.
NELL (or NELLEN)
not Ellen! (9 Sept. 1896. A Corr., 44)

In her brief married periods, she dutifully assumes her husband's name, though sometimes she explicates it with her own: "Ellen Terry = Wardell." To Mabel

Malleson, she signs her married name but explains the accident embarrassedly as a lapse into businesslike impersonality:

$$\frac{\text{Ellen Carew} =}{(\text{ E . T . })}$$

Across this divided signature, she writes apologetically: "How stupid! – thought I was signing a cheque!!"

Her married names perplex her more than do the endless beings she makes of herself. Unlike Charles Wardell or John Brodribb, she never carried the confusing burden of a stage name; the entire Terry family bore their simple and distinctive patronym proudly; but like many women without stage identities, she exploded into the many selves her life denied. As she became a household name, she lived increasingly in those parts of herself the public, possessed "Ellen Terry" did not encompass.

As she kept hatching new selves, so she found herself behaving in ways Ellen Terry had not authorized—or fearing she had. After she becomes a star, her letters are full of contrition for half-imagined misdeeds: "You called too, my aunt tells me when I was from home, & she also says that I was very rude to you!! Was I? I cant believe it, however. I am exceedingly sorry if such is the fact." "A horrible thought crossed my mind that I have not replied to yr kind invitation for the 3rd May! — if I have written before pray excuse this second letter =" To Elizabeth Winter, Irving's gracious hostess dithers out an invitation that keeps running away from her:

> Hamlet — I mean Mr. Irving — asks me to ask you, to be so sweet & kind as to come to dinner on Sunday with him - The dinner hour is ------- Mercy!! I don't know!!! but sure sure 'twill be 7:30 or 8 - & you cd come here first perhaps, for a dull ten minutes & we cd go in together.
>
> The place of meeting is Delmonico's — & I will put on a white ~~frock~~ dress & you'll put on a pretty one (with a bit of pink somewhere, for that colour becomes you), & we'll all be Lords & Ladys - !!

After restoring herself to dignity by signing her full name, she clarifies everything by adding: "This is an invitation to a dinner!!!" She ends, though, by muddying the waters once more: "P. S. = I think a good many people are coming on Sunday."

Sometimes, when life's amenities escape her, it is more frightening than funny, as she writes to an unidentified "Mildred": "What did I do to you last time I was in Boston that makes you unkindly keep away from me now? —

I was very ill when I was here before, so perhaps I offended you— Did I — ? But perhaps you're frightfully busy --- ?" To Oliver Madox Hueffer, the brother of Ford Madox Ford, she writes nervously in the same vein: "I am somewhat afraid that I have offended yr mother—(please don't trouble her with my fears) ⌇⌇⌇⌇⌇⌇ I remember how I wrote her a very flippant, silly note, being at the time hovering between flippancy silliness and neuralgia! If I had not laughed I shd [have] wept — and the idea that she shd be offended with me, me who wd grieve to give offense to any of yr kith and kin really distresses me.＝Please don't waste her time by telling her all this rigamarole, only you will know, and if I'm right in thinking my ass-ical letter affronted her, and you wd tell me "yes," I'd write to her a line."

As Ellen Terry's career and her public identity became controlled by Irving's spectacular brand of patriarchy, the self she had always believed she possessed began to fly apart. By the mid-1890s, before she was fifty, this child of the stage could barely learn new lines or retain the old ones. Her private and her public roles had never been separate, and now both were too ridiculous and incoherent to stay in her head. Even before her eyes gave out, her Lyceum letters tell of illnesses, of breakdowns, of cures at Margate spas: this "Queen of every woman," as Manvell calls her, began to share the malaise of every woman, the ineffable, gnawing knowledge that something was wrong in a supposedly wonderful life, and that the wrong must be rooted in her body.

Guilts and anxieties invaded her sleep, though never Henry's. During one of their trips to Berlin, she wrote to Audrey Campbell of his complacent rudeness to fellow actors: "Henry has slept well! slept in the boat, slept in the train - slept (I conclude) at night in his bed, & slept—oh, hasn't he slept—at the Theatre—1st 2nd 3rd 4th & 5th Acts, sound asleep! I was delighted, only a little envious (since I can't sleep,) until, when the popular favourite of the Deutchen Theatre was slowly, & softly, dying to music, a great snore from our box somewhat un-nerved the general company." Compulsively awake to Henry's guilt, she takes on the anxiety he is too powerful to have to feel. The previous year, while working on Lady Macbeth, she had written to this same Audrey: "My dear I can't sleep yet.—which you confess is provoking!—" Around this time, she wrote in her Macbeth script next to the line, "Methought I heard a voice cry 'Sleep no more'": "The most awful line in the play, if one realizes what it means to his guilt-burdened mind. Poor wretch, he does not sleep after this" (quoted in Manvell, 195). Elsewhere, she writes simply: "Shakespeare knew what it was not to sleep!" So, it seems, did she. Her mind was burdened with the guilt of a life denied.

Like Kate—Shakespeare's Kate as well as her sister—she had become every-thing they told her to be. Secretly and repeatedly though, the Ellen Terrys she created in private resurrected her suppressed boy-self. She boasted in her Memoir that from childhood, she and Kate had learned all the female parts of all the plays they were in, but her annotations to her Lyceum scripts claim as well roles she was forbidden to perform: those of Shakespeare's men. Often, in fact, her notes for the male characters blaze with excitement, while (with the exception of Lady Macbeth), those for the female roles (her own included) are perfunctory, curt, or sardonic.

A script of *The Merchant of Venice* begins with a note on Antonio's opening line, "In sooth I know not why I am so sad": "laughing at himself—gently & sadly." Her *Macbeth* scripts are not limited to the extraordinary analysis of Lady Macbeth that led her to understand so much—perhaps too much—about herself: they range restlessly, probingly, about the play and into supposedly minor male characters. Irving, of course, limits his commentary to his own Macbeth. Most of it is self-praise through glorification of the character: "When you pause— pause with eloquence." "Lofty — manly, heroic." "A man of action—of overpowering strength and resolution." In contrast to these heroic boasts, Ellen Terry lives the multiple voices of the whole, writing of the opening chant: "like a soul howling dirge"; "it sounds just like the high wind." After the witches vanish in I, iii and exposition begins, she writes: "Ross and Angus are important parts to make the play alive."

Of II, i—a scene between Macbeth, Banquo, and Fleance, in which she did not appear—she writes: "This scene shd look a strange wild affair—half torch light, half day-light & frightened half-dressed people huddling together." In the moving, and generally cut, V, i, where Macduff hears of the slaughter of his wife and child, Ellen Terry plays a wonderful Macduff on paper. She translates his eager questions to the male rebels: "is my sweetheart as lovely as she was? Love in saying the word 'Scotland' shows here=" When Macduff hears the horrible news, Ellen Terry provides him with a precise, balletic expression of agony as it strikes in turn his eyes, mouth, arm, elbow, and hand. *Macbeth* is traditionally unlucky to produce, and it is not a play she claimed publicly to prefer, but the intensity with which she threw herself into the spectrum of its characters, the look and sound of its world, is an artistic translation of her feelings about the guilty enterprise on which she had embarked with Irving.

In 1896, feeling some compunction about Ellen Terry, Irving put on *Cymbeline* for her. Imogen, its heroine, is Shakespeare's gorgeously spoken version of Chaucer's patient Griselda. The astonishingly loyal wife of the weak and gullible Posthumous was some atonement for Rosalind: at least she had beautiful speeches. Ellen Terry's commentary, however, makes little of Imogen, who receives such perfunctory directions as "smile" and "be sweet," together with a series of hieroglyphic suns to mark emphasis; she emerges as more object than character. When, in IV, iv, the three virtuous rustics who shelter her when she is dressed as a boy carry her on supposedly dead, Ellen Terry directs them: "They shd all <u>look</u> & <u>look</u> & <u>look</u> at her =" There is only one telling comment about Imogen herself: "I care for somebody that isn't *worthy* of me, because *nobody that's worth* me *cares* for me" (quoted in Webster, 178). This disenchanted exposure of an exemplary wife has no place in Shakespeare's romance; once again, the actress knows too much for her role. She reserves her theatrical appreciation for villainous men. At the end of III, i, she marks the loutish Cloten's line appreciatively "!!!" and adds: "How clever for acting = & Humourous." When the villain Iachimo (Irving, of course) steals lewdly to the sleeping Imogen, Ellen Terry steals with him, ignoring her sleeping beauty self: "*try* and remove something from a sleeping person & you'll find your heart beating & hear the noise [—] you'll feel faint & have to sit down. Good business."

Her *Hamlet* scripts say something about Ophelia, but not much; that little is tinged with sardonic dismissal, with none of her empathy for Macduff and Iachimo. When, in II, i, Ophelia describes Hamlet's bizarre behavior, Ellen Terry translates: "I've just been sitting by the kitchen fire & fell asleep." Irving staged *Hamlet* as a touching love story—his sweet prince gazed longingly at Ophelia even when the play made him excoriate her—but beside Ophelia's reverent tribute to him ("O, what a noble mind is here o'erthrown!"), Ellen Terry writes only: "a kitten." When, in the play scene, Hamlet in his hysteria interrupts the actors and Ophelia comments vacuously, "You are as good as a chorus, my lord," Ellen Terry pinions this girl who is supposed to be herself: "Nothing on a stick!" In the margins of her scripts at least, she could abuse the poignant self that artists saw.

By contrast, Claudius's first address to the court gets the rousing and witty translation: "Britons never never never will be *slaves.*" Her notes on Hamlet himself veer between excited empathy and disgust. In her notes on the play scene, Hamlet springs to vigorous life. When the players enter, she writes: "chucks up his hat to the back in a frenzy." When the Player Queen vows eternal fidelity and Hamlet comments, "If she should break it now," her note gives Hamlet a poignance and depth she never allows Ophelia: "To Ophelia, looks at her & grows sad." His great defense of his integrity to Rosencrantz and Guildenstern after the play might have come from the soul of Ellen Terry: "Why, look you now, how unworthy a thing you make of me! You would play upon me; you would seem to know my stops; you would pluck out the heart of my mystery; you would sound me from my lowest note to the top of my compass; . . . 'Sblood, do you think I am easier to be played on than a pipe?

Call me what instrument you will, though you can fret me, yet you cannot play upon me" (III, ii, 379–89). Ellen Terry writes beside this moving self-affirmation: "Dropping all humourous banter—& <u>blazing</u> out." Ophelia, that "nothing on a stick," has no such mystery to preserve against spies and fools.

The fair Ophelia does not appear in the closet scene between Hamlet and Gertrude, but Ellen Terry studied it. Of course she was loved too much for her to play a guilty, sensuous woman; no matter how old and ripe she became, she was Ophelia. In the margins of her script, she was also Hamlet in his anger:

> working it up tremendously—excitedly—
> <u>the laws of Climax</u>
> tremendous pause = Great change
> then whisperingly [to the Ghost], "Save me . . ."

These notes may want to immortalize Irving's performance, but their emphasis on speed, excitement, "the laws of Climax," and "great change" does not sound Irvingesque. By all accounts, Irving's Hamlet was slow, deliberate, too lofty to make the familiar stage points, too noble (like his Shylock) to assault the other characters or be cruel. What begins to materialize in these margins is the ghost of Ellen Terry's own Hamlet, excited, mercurial, enraged, unplayable and unplayed.

In one script at least, one initialed "H. I." (indicating that Irving used it), she dares to assault the sweet prince himself. In his first, cutting speeches, affirming his honesty against his corrupt mother and her court, Ellen Terry writes irreverently: "Ugly & fat. Looks a beastly <u>tempered</u> man—not a sad one." The grand "To be or not to be" is marked: "Jolly bad Theatrics." Irving is too high to quarrel, but in the theater of her imagination, she can mock his Hamlet, bring it low, and breathe her own life into it. Similar lightning-like barbs dart through other scripts. Like Tennyson's *Idylls of the King,* Comyns-Carr's *King Arthur* forced her Guinevere to prostrate herself at King Arthur's noble feet. Shaw fulminated against this hideous affront: "As to Miss Ellen Terry, it was the old story, a born actress of real women's parts condemned to play a figure as a mere artist's model in costume plays which, from the woman's point of view, are foolish flatteries written by gentlemen for gentlemen. . . . What a theatre for a woman of genius to be attached to!" (*Shaw's Dramatic Criticism,* 11). For Ellen Terry, the "mere artist's model" could not be separated from the "woman of genius." She understood her role from within. Knowing it too well to attack it, she inverted one of Arthur's more sanctimonious speeches into a bitter truth about her womanly self:

'Tis the base mind
That lightly may forgive the thing that's base,
Using God's gift of mercy as a cloak
For shameful sin.

Ellen Terry blazes out: "Then women must be very base="

If she felt that like Lady Macbeth, she had a lot to be forgiven, she also had a lot to forgive. Repeatedly, she lashed out at Henry, and repeatedly, she lapsed into solicitude, as she does here to Elizabeth Winter: "I thought you & Henry were coming here together, but he appeared here directly after I last wrote to you, & told me he must be alone because of his confounded splendid work 4 days afterwards he started for Norfolk - I think he looks worn out but such work! Unceasing for him & they say (altho' I can't believe it) he is no longer a boy!"

She never admitted it openly, but it cut more deeply that she too was no longer a boy, and thus (according to Victorian definitions) no longer mobile, grand, "*blazing* out." The old, now disreputable transvestite theater had become in memory a discipline within which she could be all things. Her only tribute to the boy she once was was buried in the delicacy with which she caricatured her adorable women onstage, and audiences loved her so suffocatingly they refused to notice.

But some of her friends guessed. In 1889, she was delighted when the remnants of the old theater rose up in a transvestite burlesque of the mighty Lyceum *Faust:* "Henry did not care for burlesques as a rule and in this one he particularly disliked Fred Leslie's exact imitation of him. Face, spectacles, voice—everything was like Henry except the ballet-skirt Leslie wore. Marie Linden gave a really clever imitation of me as Margaret. She and her sister Laura both had the trick of taking me off. I recognized the truth of Laura's caricature in the burlesque of 'The Vicar of Wakefield' when as Olivia she made her entrance, leaping impulsively over a stile!" (*Memoirs,* 188).

Her memory may have slipped here: Margaret Webster says that Fred Leslie's partner was not Marie Linden, but Nellie Farren, her friend and forbidden double, who played ravishing Principal Boys in burlesque (Webster, 148). It was Nellie Farren whom she had envisioned playing her own Portia in a burlesque *Merchant of Venice;* she of all actresses would have been delightfully alive to the strain of self-parody in the relentlessly innocent Margaret. Ellen Terry was delighted to be seen through at the Lyceum, but Irving took himself painfully seriously. He was a world-builder now; his comic, transvestite beginnings were gone forever; Fred Leslie drove him into a fury. He went so far as to kill Leslie's act, only to be further scourged: "A few nights later Fred Leslie reappeared in ballet skirts, his completely bald and masked head wrapped in folds of gauze; by silent mimicry of Irving's gait and gesture he got the last laugh and louder applause than he had done for his original misdeameanour" (LI, *HI*, 518). Mockery, trespass, and transvestism might be banished from the Lyceum, but they adhered in the theatrical imagination to which Ellen Terry was so angrily, helplessly bound in her years as Lady Darling.

She maintained her allegiance to it by playing men's parts in the margins of her scripts, and also by assuming their voices in her letters. She was obedient when she sent autographs embellished with wise saws by Portia or Beatrice, but her letters speak repeatedly in the voices of Shakespeare's male characters, usually his villains. As she got older and crises intensified, Iago-like boasts of self-sufficiency became her talisman. At the Lyceum, she was a servant and a useful employee who saw herself with unrelenting honesty: "I have always found it hard to find my inferiors. He was sure of his high place" (*Memoirs*, 120). When she was writing, though, she could be all things.

To Joe Evans, in a relatively happy time, she inserts the fraternal Hamlet into her holiday letter: "It's Christmas Day—God bless you my brother—my good friend - I'll change that name with you." To young actresses, she sends not Hamlet's cry of friendship, but Iago's boast of self-sufficiency, though in the context of *Othello* these words are brashly irreverent: the villain delivers to the corrupt gull Roderigo a message Ellen Terry loved. His line reads in its entirety: "Virtue! a fig! 'tis in ourselves that we are thus or thus" (I, iii, 322–23). Ellen Terry turns this blasphemy into a prayer for power in her Christmas letter to Audrey Campbell: "Now mind you are Merry at Xmas, & that you are happy in the new year = ' 'Tis in ourselves that we are thus—or thus.' " She paraphrases this bold wish to Janet Achurch before an opening: "Brava Janet - Another success = for I'm sure before I go, I shall like you in this - 'in ourselves are triumph or defeat=' " With no strain, she makes Iago's creed her own and gives it to the women she wants to invigorate. The blatant self-regard from which Irving's leading lady appeared immune becomes the legacy she sends a new generation of actresses.

At the beginning of World War I, Iago becomes her inspiration once more as she tries to buoy Pauline Chase: "Don't idealize the future in your thoughts too greatly—we are all mortal! You must carry your own sunshine with you & dispense it freely.—'It is in ourselves that we are thus or thus'—Do keep jolly, & be just the duck you are now always." The impious self-trusting tenacity of this recurrent advice has little in common with the selflessness of the useful actress, or even with Portia's high-minded "quality of mercy" speech she recited so often: her female disciples receive from her not sweetness or nobility, but a code of power, persistence, and survival.

In a still more frightening time, as she leaves on an Australian tour with war raging all around, she laces her farewell letter to Graham Robertson with Hamlet's despairing gallantry: "I feel strangely indifferent to be or not to be, but I shall in all [seriousness?] I assure you, provide myself with a good lifebelt, & a German dictionary— & shall hope to find courtesy, as I have all my life, from any strangers I may meet on my journey, & I pray I may meet you, & all others I love, in some dear garden where only Friends & flowers inhabit— I hope you are well—as well as the well-est among us— for sure we are all ill—ill at these numbers." Only Hamlet's cry to Ophelia is adequate to express the Great War; even Shakespeare's triumphant heroines have no words for the world of fear into which she travels.

Her final terror lay within. To describe it, she could find only the words of Hamlet's usurping uncle, King Claudius. Writing to one "C. C." in thick, penciled scrawl from within the clouds that swallowed her mind at the end of her life, she becomes her last male villain:

> Only, with Hamlets' Papa
> I say
> "My words fly up, my
> thoughts remain below"
> and I - - - ---- ------ ----
> Forgive me. I can scribble no more= . . .
> I am just going to the sea - for a week to brace up my
> scatter'd brain-box. . . .
>
> > God be with you
> > Yours yours E. T.
>
> Please excuse
> Pencil----& confusion of
>   my wits.

In crises, her forbidden roles renewed and enhanced her as the acceptable ones never had. Her letters to Gordon Craig in the 1890s are riddled with apprehension: she can see the end approaching, and the darkness beyond the end. There is no Iago to fortify her, but only the Ophelia her son was so sentimental about, to frighten her further. "If I'm not at the bottom of the sea I wonder where I shall be this time next year! The look forward for me is pretty blank—I don't mean in the theatre that's nothing—I care for that least of all.— . . . the

dwindling of Love is the only thing to be feared in this world I am sure of that
=" But everything was theater, including the love she played with Henry.
When that theater foundered five years later, Ophelia was no help. She could
not be Iago to her son; only younger women understood that voice; and so she
became Ophelia to convey helpless terror: "Then there's Edy & you & all the
children & all the troubles------oh dear. I hope all may be well but I cannot
choose but ~~weep~~ fear—a mighty deal=" The lost <u>As You Like It</u> provides no
more courage than Ophelia. Rosalind can become only her symbol of despair
at all things: "it's all too late for 'Rosalind'= so little <u>pluck</u> & 'attack' left in
me=a wearier <u>machine</u> is E. T.=" She had stayed at the Lyceum to play
Shakespeare's heroines, but in times of trouble, they gave her no sustenance; they
only added to her fear.

She had lost more than roles for love. In her good years, the acrobatic girl
had grown fat: Rosalind was banished, not only by Irving, but by Ellen Terry's
own, suddenly alien body. "Fat is fatal to romance!," she wrote grimly
(*Memoirs,* 87), but for a Victorian woman over thirty, it was lovable and safe:
fat made a woman motherly, regal and solid like Victoria, safely immobilized.
She sketched her own changing face as it lost contour; her sharp chin, her
piercing look, become in full face blandly benign. A soft woman frightened
nobody by bounding about with her wicked legs exposed; she stayed still. And

Drawing by Ellen Terry, 1886.
Reproduced by permission of the
Folger Library.

so did Ellen Terry, angry, tense, and frightened, feeling herself growing beyond control, sensing retribution and disaster. After all, Henry Irving had made her a lady.

And after all, there was Shakespeare, who loved her more than Henry ever could. Generous and consecrating, he lived in her imagination more pervasively than any other teacher-lover: "My friend, my sorrow's cure, my teacher, my companion, the very eyes of me" (*Memoirs*, 304). When Henry died Shakespeare gave her talismanic words to write in her diary. For once, they were a woman's words, and they set both partners free:

> 13 Fri. 1905— Henry died today—
> "& now there is nothing left remarkable beneath the
> visiting moon"—
>
> Cleopatra—

Once Irving was dead, she bestowed on him unreservedly the greatness she had mocked during their life together, for his death freed her to play, if only privately and on paper, a role impossible in the Lyceum, and one she thought she didn't want: the comic, imperial, infinitely varied and subversive Cleopatra, Shakespeare's only heroine who is the controlling agent of her story. To the end of her life, Ellen Terry's unacted parts inspired her to announce a glory she recognized only fitfully in the roles she did play.

THE ROLES   Her intensifying discomfort during her twenty-four years with Irving came from more than her bad part: the ideology of hero worship that exhorted Victorians to prostrate themselves before self-aggrandizing men had always made her instinctively suspicious. She prayed to no man she knew, but she did bow before the great dead: Shakespeare exuded a holiness, an absolute authority, she conceded to no living man. The Lyceum, for all its abuses, had allowed her to consecrate herself with his women, and to nineteenth-century celebrants, Shakespeare's genius realized itself in these glorified women. Henry Giles, an American rhapsodist, claims that Shakespeare's heroines are vessels of a sacred womanly essence transcending time, change, and history: above all, "his genius intervened through all the inward life of womanhood." Most critics cared less for his heroines' transcendence than for their mobility, for a humanist age wanted humane divinities. Victorian critics worshipped Shakespeare because he avoided absolute bardic claims—a polite eschewal of personal or ideological intervention that Keats called "negative capability"—and because he created abundantly living characters, all of them intimately knowable, but, in their essences, tantalizingly elusive as well. *The Girlhood of Shakespeare's Heroines* (1850), Mary Cowden Clarke's popular series of tales, invents for each heroine a formative, unfolding life before the play. Clarke's origin myths pay homage to the open-endedness of Shakespeare's heroines, their potential for incessant self-creation. Ellen Terry embraced their mobility in the same way: "Has there ever been a dramatist, I wonder, whose parts admit of so many interpretations as do Shakespeare's? There lies his immortality as an acting force. For times change, and parts have to be acted differently for different generations. Some parts are not sufficiently universal for this to be possible, but every ten years an actor can reconsider a Shakespeare part and find new life in it for his new purpose and new audiences" (*Memoirs,* 87).

To Victorians, this very mobility and historicism were holy. German higher critics like David Fredrich Strauss, whose *Life of Jesus, Critically Examined* George Eliot had translated into English in 1846, argued for the historical relativism of Scripture: the Bible Strauss explicated evolved from a vehicle of timeless revelation to a human document whose myth was decomposed and recomposed over the centuries. Many found it frightening to contemplate the Bible as a book made by humanity and time, but as its authority weakened, that of the deeply human Shakespeare intensified, precisely because he transformed himself through time.

The humanity and historicism that threatened the Bible somehow sanctified the Bard: the myth of Shakespeare's plays as an eternal legacy, transmitted by a succession of generations through civilizations that came and went, made their author more than man. Henry Curling's novel, *Shakespeare; The Poet, the Lover, the Actor, the Man. A Romance* (1848), has the reverence of a life of Christ. Its Shakespeare is more than poet, lover, actor, or man. A peasant who shelters him on his journey to London cherishes his stool and his plate "as relics, never to be used by others, for God forgive me, but I think, as I recollect his words, that yonder man was something more than mortal."

Matthew Arnold celebrates Shakespeare's Olympian if good-hearted elusiveness more tersely, in a sonnet that begins: "Others abide our question; thou art free. / We ask and ask, thou smile'st, and art still." This supreme humanity that manages to elude the rigidity of human definition inspired women in particular with visions of freedom. Ellen Terry, the foremost Shakespearean actress of her day, may have been in thrall to Irving's Lyceum, as Shaw insisted, but as she imagined herself, Shakespeare released her into self-creating glory. Her *Four Lectures on Shakespeare* borrow a statement from Coleridge that is not, for her, hyperbole—though she qualifies it—but the truth on which she predicated her career: "In Shakespeare all the elements of womanhood are holy."

She had inherited this faith in part from the florid mysticism of the Romantic movement. When, in 1827, a vapid Drury Lane actress named Harriet Smithson played a breathtaking Ophelia at the Odéon, making her a cult heroine for a generation of French Romantic artists, the *Figaro* explained the cause of her transformation as "something supernatural at the heart of Shakespeare." Two novels in Ellen Terry's library at Smallhythe, both written long after her own Shakespearean days, continue the consecration: Wilfrid Blair's *The Death of Shakespeare* (1916) imagines a holy man dying a martyr's death among Pharisees and Philistines; his only consolation lies in his immortal characters, who come to him and ease his death. Clemence Dane's *Will Shakespeare: An Invention* (1921) imagines a similar inspired soul, delivered from his shrewish, mundane wife by the characters who summon him to tell their stories. Like Joan of Arc inspired by her voices, the holy Shakespeare is a chosen spirit, ratified by supernatural visitations.

Cynical colleagues thought that Irving's magnificence had raised Ellen Terry to an eminence she would never have achieved alone; her sister Marion, after all, was a finer, more elegant and careful actress, but she had "no Irving to lift her to glory" (Steen, 149). But Ellen Terry and other believers knew that Shakespeare was the source of whatever glory she had; Irving had only given her the plays. When he did so, he lifted her to a radiant country that was also, magically, her birthplace. When she brought her Shakespeare lectures to America, the *New York Times* acknowledged her dual citizenship: "One had the queer impression that she who is speaking was herself one of Shakespeare's women . . . , and, that in the native country of them all, his creative mind, she had met, and talked with, and lived with them all."

Over the years, as she was increasingly patronized in England, she believed more intensely in that other country and in the characters who had lives that were unimpeded and separate from her own: "I'm so glad I Portia (I never do such things.) didn't ~~wink~~ close one eye at the wrong man, & that it was you in the stalls after all." Irving found his Heaven when his statue took its place among England's dignitaries, but hers was a mergence into beings who had always been realer than she was: "be quite sure [she wrote to a Charles Coleman in 1902] that the red roses you gave to 'Portia' so long ago made ~~her~~ me a little better—a little happier in the getting them, as of course it made you a little happier in the giving them = I've gotten over the wishing I were 'Portia'— &, (as I shd cease to be, I verily believe if I had not some hope) I nowadays think that in 'another & a better world than this' (!) I may (?) open my eyes & say, 'oh Bottom how art thou translated!!!' & find no E.T. left! but some creature begotten of Portia Beatrice Imogen Rosalind Volumnia Cordelia Ham-

let Cesar <u>Silvius</u> !!!—& I'll say looking at some old Photograph (!!) 'that's
me!!! <u>Was</u> me - **H a v e n ' t** I improved?!! **'W o t r o t ' ! ' '**

This lovely consummation in which there is *"no E. T. left"* translates Ellen
Terry's Hell into her Heaven: her dissolution into myriad characters with other,
funny names becomes, through Shakespeare's embrace, achieved artistic beati-
tude. In this visionary faith, renunciations and suppressions are redeemed by her
translation into Hamlet along with Rosalind, Caesar and Silvius with Beatrice.
The intensity of her belief explains some of her more reactionary statements in
the early 1890s: "I . . . love Portia and Beatrice better than Hedda, Nora, or
any of [Ibsen's] silly ladies." "I prefer presenting to an audience, and living
familiarly with, Queen Katherine and Imogen rather than with Dr. Ibsen's
foolish women." In the same issue of *The New Review*, Henry James celebrates
Ibsen's advent as a particular boon for actresses. Like Shaw's, James's progressi-
vism makes Ellen Terry look more closed-minded than she was. In 1895, when
she was in *King Arthur*, a particularly flaccid and dated heroic romance, she was
trying to look beyond the Lyceum. She filled Comyns-Carr's script with angry
comments: "1st entrance <u>Dreadful</u>"; "<u>Not</u> good"; "Oh Lord!—When Joe is <u>not</u>
inspired he is hidebound! & shy = The whole of this page for instance is useless
=" Into this script she inserted a touching enumeration of writers beyond
Irving's control, perhaps a reading list from one of her advanced children:

> Ibsen
> Strindberg (Sweden)
> Materlinck (Belgium)
> Fletcher (England)

But her disenchantment never touched Shakespeare. Ibsen may have opened out
women's future, but Shakespeare brought grace precisely because he had seen
all that was old and true in England. It had taken centuries of faith to lift Ellen
Terry to her actress's Heaven.

Like Ellen Terry, Shakespeare's heroines had begun their stage lives as boys,
to mature into instruments of grace for women. It was possible that they cast
their spell only in England. The great Duse saw little in the heroines, though
she was interested in playing Macbeth and Lear: in her opinion Shakespeare "had
not written primarily or even adequately for women: he was an actor's dramatist, against whose heroic masculine figures no actress could hold her own except
in such rare instances as Portia, Cleopatra, or the tenuous Juliet." Theatrically,
Duse was right, and the Ellen Terry who wrote herself into forbidden male roles
knew it, but Duse could never feel the power of an English myth.

Like Duse, Gordon Craig believed in Ibsen and in a future that would create a different, modern sort of actor, but he also lived with his mother's faith in the glorious perpetuity of Shakespeare's women as peculiarly English divinities. His eulogies to his little mother ring false, but for a flickering instant he restores Ellen Terry to life when he laments, in modern times, the death of her Heaven: "I had hesitated to speak of these beings [Cordelia, Ophelia, and Imogen], lest their names should signify nothing in 1931. They certainly seem to have vanished from our world—gone away suddenly. Were you to ask an acquaintance, 'Have you seen *Imogen* lately?' it is possible that the reply would be, 'No—but I saw Lady Mancatous only yesterday.' So *Imogen* is dead and gone, and no one need be sorry for her. Perfectly splendid—*she's* out of it—hurrah for death, and glory to those who are lost" (*ETSS*, 167).

Few people other than her son understood Ellen Terry's belief in the glorification and grace shed on her by the women she played, who had a life far better and more vivid than her own. The most intent spectators saw in her performances not Portia's emanation descending on the Lyceum, but the ghost of another Ellen Terry, rarer, freer, and funnier than the woman who was making herself assiduously useful on the stage.

She dreamed of death as a comic triumph, releasing her into union with her unacted parts, but in her actual Shakespeare performances, comedy was rare. In compensation, Irving allowed her to gallop through two farces, *Nance Oldfield* (which he bought for her) and *Madame Sans-Gêne* (which she reputedly hated and couldn't learn); but their large-scale, full-length productions were slow, stately, and ritualistic. Laughter would kill the reverence Irving wanted, so it was banished even from comedy. Even his worshipful grandson admits: "In jilting the comic muse, [Irving] was guilty of a grave breach of promise" (LI, HI, 441). He had been a blazing comedian in his early days, but, associating laughter with ridicule, he hated to hear it. Ellen Terry mourned, and was mourned, most vehemently. William Archer did not recognize her as an icon: "I have yet to allude to Mr. Irving's masterstroke as a manager—the creation of a tragedienne in Miss Ellen Terry. The British public has accepted her with acclamation in that character, thus justifying Mr. Irving's choice, which is all I am here concerned with. To those who in tragic parts, demand more than graceful attitudes and a sing-song recitation, it must seem a pity that this most charming of all our actresses of comedy should have been translated into a sphere in which she is so far from home" (Archer, 100).

Her lost comedy haunted her. "I would always rather make people laugh than see them weep," she wrote (*Memoirs*, 254), but she was easier to love when she was pathetic, just as she had been at Little Holland House. In her *Four Lectures on Shakespeare,* she abandoned the conventional categories of comic and tragic heroines for her own unorthodox terms, "triumphant" and "pathetic," hinting implicitly that comedy and triumph were synonymous. Irving's stateliness was a weight on her, imprisoning the swiftness that was the essence of her acting. "Pace is the soul of comedy, and to elaborate lines at the expense of pace is disastrous. Curiously enough, I have met and envied this gift of pace in actors who were not conspicuously talented in other respects, and no Rosalind that I have ever seen has had enough of it. Of course, it is not a question of a swift utterance only, but of swift thinking" (*Memoirs,* 79). She wrote of swiftness, of triumphant comedy, but as Margaret Webster deduces from one of her scripts, onstage, Irving clogged even her Lady Macbeth: "The emphasis on Macbeth's weakness grows in [Ellen Terry's] second set of notes; because of Irving, one wonders, or in spite of him? Her notes about him stress her own love of speed, as against his slowness and deliberation: *'Please* quickly.' . . . *'Please* at once.' . . . 'a look please like lightening will help me here' " (Webster, 142–43). Her protest against his resolute restraint on the rhythm she needs is charged with sexual as well as artistic frustration. The girl who was sure love and art were one had become the woman helpless to stop both from going lame and sour at once.

Even her Beatrice in *Much Ado About Nothing* was more joyful imagined than seen. Her line, "there was a star danced, and under that was I born," was quoted over and over again to describe the irrepressible Ellen Terry. According to Clement Scott, Hero's description of Beatrice's approach—"For look where Beatrice, like a lapwing, runs / Close by the ground, to hear our conference" (III, i, 24–25)—had in it all Ellen Terry's swiftness. But at the Lyceum, Irving's Benedick was at best a gesture toward *noblesse oblige,* not a mercurial performance matching her own: "When Irving put on 'Much Ado About Nothing'— a play which he may be said to have revived for me, as he never really liked the part of Benedick—I was not the same Beatrice at all [as she had been in Leeds with Charles Kelly]. A great actor can do nothing badly, and there was very much to admire in Irving's Benedick. But he gave me little help. Beatrice must be swift, swift, swift! Owing to Henry's rather finicking, deliberate method as Benedick, I could never put the right pace into my part." (*Memoirs,* 127).

Moreover, she continues, the insertion of vulgar traditional "gag" into the climactic church scene strangled Beatrice's great outburst of rage against her slandered cousin. Her sudden, explosive "Kill Claudio" and "O God that I were a man! I would eat his heart in the market-place!" were trivialized by the farcical coda Irving insistently—and most uncharacteristically—interpolated at the end of the scene:

> *Beatrice.* Benedick, kill him—kill him if you can.
> *Benedick.* As sure as I'm alive, I will!
>   (quoted in *Memoirs,* 217)

It was a relief even to play with his understudy. When, in 1885, Irving fell ill in Boston, a member of the company recorded in his journal that the church scene sprang to new life: "I never saw her play the scene in the cathedral when Beatrice tells Benedick to kill Claudio with such fire and energy" (quoted in LI, *HI,* 450).

Always, Irving stifled the life in her, but it was not only inflexibility, or even competitiveness, that led him to drag her down: once again, as he had when they first played together, he was taming a shrew. Independent and assaultive, Beatrice disturbed Victorian middle-class audiences; they liked heroines who suffered, not termagants who attacked men. If they must have a Beatrice, she had to be womanly, and thus earnest, beneath her comic aggression; a palatable comedy underscored the "profound seriousness of Beatrice and Benedick" that underlay their dangerous duels of wit. Irving dragged Ellen Terry's Beatrice down to the place where audiences could love her without fear. He did so to promote the high seriousness of the actor, but always, always, there was another Beatrice and another Ellen Terry who really did run like a lapwing.

Even Godwin's golden Portia, the sumptuous personification of the Venetian Renaissance, subdued herself to Irving's single-minded intensity: Irving's unremittingly tragic Shylock threw her joy awry. In the trial scene, the grim weight of his martyrdom crushed her comic triumph. Shortly after opening, Irving cut the luscious Act V, over which Portia presides in her harmonious Belmont empire; he replaced it with a short, pathetic play. Instead of reigning over the comedy, she became a still sterner justicer than her antagonist: "In 'The Merchant of Venice' I found that Henry Irving's Shylock necessitated an entire revision of my conception of Portia, especially in the trial scene, but here there was no point of honour involved. I had considered, and still am of the same mind, that Portia in the trial scene ought to be very *quiet.* I saw an extraordinary effect in this quietness. But as Henry's Shylock was quiet, I had to give it up. His heroic saint was splendid, but it wasn't good for Portia" (*Memoirs,* 128).

Whether, in her opinion, the heroic saint was good for Shakespeare emerges between the lines of her advice to Gordon Craig: "No - No beard or any 'get up' for Shylock. Just think of the Jew's <u>temperament</u>, his cunning - his cleverness - his <u>desire for revenge</u> - & show them the <u>inside</u> of the man. I wd sooner you had read Gratiano-" Her son should play the Henry Irving she lives with, clever and cunning and bruised, not the scene-stealing, self-ennobling tragedian who called himself Shylock at the Lyceum.

That Shylock immortalized Portia, not as the triumphant prime mover who scintillated at the Prince of Wales', but as a stern agent of anti-comedy. Thomas Bailey Aldrich's sonnet, "Ellen Terry in 'The Merchant of Venice,'" commemorates Portia's conversion out of comedy. Only then does Shakespeare's holy mind deign to consecrate her:

> As there she lives and moves upon the scene,
> So lived and moved this radiant womanhood
> In Shakespeare's vision: in such wise she stood
> Smiling upon Bassanio; such her mien
> When pity dimmed her eyelids' silken sheen
> Hearing Antonio's story, and the blood
> Paled on her cheek, and all her lightsome mood
> Was gone. This shape in Shakespeare's thought has been!
> Thus dreamt he of her in gray London town;
> Such were her eyes; on such gold-colored hair
> The scholar's jaunty velvet cap was set;
> So stood she lovely in her crimson gown!
> Mine were a lucky cast, could I but snare
> Her beauty in a sonnet's fragile net!

This bloodless avenger is indeed "snared" by a widely circulated engraving whose grim and heavy Portia stares accusingly at the viewer. Her marmoreal figure is as massive as the law book that is its emblem. Within its stoniness we can find faint hints of a desire for flight—Portia's cap is perched on her unruly hair at an imperceptibly askew angle, her finger is curled with a touch of self-parodic gentility, and her expression is less noble than it is woebegone—but these are mere glimmers of Ellen Terry's old comedy within an enforced, massive immobility. This Portia no longer darts and shimmers with the color Godwin gave his spirit of Titian's painted world. Millais painted her as sternly and in the same spirit, in large heavy masses of uniform color. His Portia is a columnar figure among columns, gazing sadly at the sins of a world she is not part of, more spectator than star.

"Portia is the fruit of the Renaissance," Ellen Terry wrote in *Four Lectures on Shakespeare,* "the child of a period of beautiful clothes, beautiful cities,

Engraving of Ellen Terry as Portia. *Reproduced by permission of the Harry Ransom Humanities Research Center, University of Texas, Austin.*

Sir John Everett Millais, *Portia. Reproduced by permission of the Metropolitan Museum of Art, Wolfe Fund, 1906.*

Photograph of Ellen Terry as Viola in *Twelfth Night. Reproduced by permission of the Furness Collection, Van Pelt Library, University of Pennsylvania.*

beautiful houses, beautiful ideas. She speaks the beautiful language of inspired poetry. Wreck that beauty, and the part goes to pieces" (p. 116). But Irving's management translated Portia from Godwin's aesthetic arranger to a grim accuser. The glittering chatelaine of Belmont subdued herself to sadder, if nobler, womanhood.

Viola in *Twelfth Night* is bittersweet, not buoyantly comic, less an arranger than an instrument of the action. About Irving's ill-starred *Twelfth Night* in 1884, we know only that Ellen Terry acted wanly due to an infected thumb, remaining seated through most of the few London performances; that Irving's Malvolio was too painful to be funny; and that in an outburst of anger remarkable at the Lyceum, the opening-night audience hissed at the curtain call. The play was soon taken out of the repertoire. In the nineteenth century, *Twelfth Night* was an obscure and faintly disturbing play; its love scenes brim with overt homosexual tenderness. Onstage and off, nobody seems to have liked it, hardening Irving's resolution not to allow comic reversals to subvert the mission of his stage.

But this doomed production bequeaths to us a rare photograph of Ellen Terry taken during the play, not in a studio. In it, we see what so many Victorians exalted in all her Lyceum performances but failed to describe: the eerie rapport between the actress and her setting. Retaining her fluidity and seemingly unconscious of place, Ellen Terry seems to grow out of the rock that menaces her, figuring in her body the desolation of the scene. Left alone by Irving, spinning incessant new identities, she infused the energy that had nowhere to go into the stage properties among which she lived. She had at last become suitably still, bestowing her vitality on a world of objects.

She seems not to have missed Viola, but the mobile, managing Rosalind she seemed born to play became her private symbol of comedy, of physical intensity, of everything she had been promised and denied. Claiming that there was no part in it for him (the melancholy Jacques being too small and Touchstone too undignified), Irving barred *As You Like It,* along with much else, from the Lyceum. Hoydenish and independent, Rosalind was still more inflammatory a heroine than Beatrice; privately, Irving might have thought the play as wrong for his "sweetest, loveliest Ophelia" as it was for himself, or, if it was not wrong, he preferred not to know it. But though Ellen Terry never played Rosalind, she wove Rosalind into her public identity.

In 1898, she wrote in bold pen in the margins of Charles Hiatt's book about her: "I wish H. I. had not been always so fond of 'horrors'!" Underneath, she adds in smudged and timid pencil: "Then we might have played 'As You Like It.' " When Hiatt mentions Rosalind, she notes: "Alas! The part I shall never have the happiness of acting="; she adds to his index of her roles: "Never Rosalind. Alas!" Her *Four Lectures* are more publicly outspoken: "I have been Beatrice! Would that I could say 'I have been Rosalind.' Would that the opportunity to play this part had come my way when I was in my prime! I reckon it one of the greatest disappointments of my life that it did not! In my old age I go on studying Rosalind, rather wistfully, I admit" (p. 97).

She admitted it freely, almost obsessively, to others, as if she could not exist authentically in their minds without being imagined as Rosalind. In 1894, for example, she wrote to the great Shakespeare scholar, Horace Howard Furness: "Could you have forgiven yourself or cd I ever have forgiven you if you had called public attention to Ellen Terry in plain clothes & spectacles, sitting alone & undefended at your discourse?! ⋀⋀⋀ but the honour of being mentioned by you as a <u>possibly</u> good Rosalind <u>(when I am over the Leas & far away)</u> is not to be undervalued!!—<u>I have never played the part</u>, & have longed for centuries to make the attempt. However the time is past & gone—& if you suggest I might have done well I am comforted = Farewell in every place ="

In the end, Rosalind became more indelibly a part of Ellen Terry than she might have done had *As You Like It* been staged. When Irving gave her a *Cymbeline* in 1896, it seemed the safer choice, though by that time she was old for Imogen. The suffering wife was more palatably pathetic a Victorian heroine than were the boy/girls who take their plays into their own hands. As Paula S. Berggren explains:

> Imogen's career explicates the transition from the comedies' resourceful virgins to the romances' beatified mothers. The nineteenth century preferred Imogen to the earlier heroines because her male disguise discomfited her, but if she lacks their high spirits, she has good cause. Even before Posthumous casts her off, in the simple act of marrying him she has set herself within a framework none of the boy-women had to cope with. The tomboy vivacity of the unmarried woman does not become the wife, who has already narrowed her choice of the options that a Rosalind is free to explore. . . . An extension of her husband rather than an autonomous object of desire, Imogen has chosen her disguise name wisely—Fidèle.

But Irving's safe choice returned to haunt him: Ellen Terry's power as this compliant heroine summoned the restless ghost of the forbidden Rosalind. Even the conservative *Atheneum* used Imogen to reproach Irving: Ellen Terry's revelation of new strengths reminds the reviewer that "we have not yet gained from the superbly endowed and most winsome artist all that we have to hope. That she has not already been seen in Rosalind is a matter for surprise and complaint; that she shall be seen as Constance [in *King John;* she never was] is a matter for hope and supplication."

T. Edgar Pemberton and Clement Scott were similarly moved by her Imogen to rhapsodies about the lost Rosalind. As Pemberton quotes Scott, a dependable friend of the Lyceum: "It may be heresy to the old school to hear an actress interpolating asides and adding remarks and breaking in upon the text with charming gestures, but Ellen Terry does it and every one loves her for doing it. . . . but when we get to the Fidèle scenes then came the revelation, the touching of the heart, the true tears. There was only one remark in the house, 'Oh what a Rosalind she would have made!' And many added, 'and ought to make' " (quoted in Pemberton, 284–85).

Ellen Terry's fooling is a performance within a performance, invoking the banished women within a sanctioned one. "Miss Terry is a model Shakespearean boy; there is no doubt about that, and has both laughter and tears at her winsome command," Pemberton exclaims, but he goes on to evoke, not the embodied Imogen, but the imagined Rosalind: "The loss of such a Rosalind to the stage as Ellen Terry would, and must have been, has ever formed a subject for regret with her warmest and most enthusiastic admirers. If ever woman lived who displayed in advance the temperament of Rosalind, it was Ellen Terry. What affection she would have shown for Celia," and so on, as he goes on to laud, point by point, her non-existent performance (p. 286).

Her own tormenting, superfluous energy seems to have summoned Rosalind to a stage where no Rosalind was allowed: as if by magic, the tearful Imogen/Fidèle aroused in receptive spectators visions of the laughing Rosalind/Ganymede. It was not Lyceum audiences alone who found in Rosalind forbidden wonders: Shakespeare's bold cross-dressing girl became, for England's homosexual elite, a symbol of visionary liberties their own country forbade. In 1891, Oscar Wilde allowed his dangerously beautiful Dorian Gray to fall fleetingly in love with an actress who, as Rosalind, beckons him toward magic delights:

> But Sibyl! You should have seen her! When she came on in her boy's clothes, she was perfectly wonderful. She wore a moss-coloured velvet jerkin with cinnamon sleeves, slim brown cross-gartered hose, a dainty little green cap, and a hawk's feather caught in a jewel, and a hooded cloak lined with dull red. She had never seemed to me more exquisite. She had all the delicate grace of that Tanagra figurine that you have in your studio, Basil. Her hair clustered round her face like dark leaves round a pale rose. . . . I forgot that I was in London and in the nineteenth century. I was away with my love in a forest that no man had ever seen.

In the same spirit, Virginia Woolf's *Orlando* (1928) features a hero whose name evokes Shakespeare's Forest of Arden, and whose ability to incarnate all modulations of gender is similarly forbidden in ugly, heavily patriarchal Victorian England. The role the Lyceum forbade Ellen Terry contained everything advanced souls were forbidden to become. The banished Rosalind that haunted her admirers became more powerfully associated with Ellen Terry than the acceptable parts she did play, bestowing on the actress an oblique and peculiarly Victorian sort of victory: her vivid non-performances teased her audiences into imagining a wealth of forbidden things, all the fooling, fun, and swiftness of thought the Lyceum could not contain.

As the years refused to allow Rosalind's incarnation, she came more and more to stand for Ellen Terry's banished comic spirit and integrated self, for all of her wounding disjunctions from her roles. The hidden triumph within her pathetic roles was her increasingly subtle and fine performance of this very disjunction. As far back as her Bancroft days, she had given Shaw "an impression of waywardness; of not quite fitting into her part and not wanting to; and she gave no indication of her full power, for which the part offered no scope" (*A Corr.,* xx–xxi). That first, disappointing performance Shaw attended was the one she refined so effectively over the years. When he was dramatic critic of the *Saturday Review,* the very sight of her goaded him to rage against the patriarchal stupidities of Irving's Lyceum, but he was confident that his rage was his own discovery: he never knew it was Ellen Terry's own subtlest effect. Her life had been composed of treasures that were suddenly, inexplicably forbidden; as delicately as she could, she acted her losses.

Comedy was the loss that encompassed them all, and the loss was not hers alone. Since she returned from Little Holland House, she had tried to fight the impulse to drown her plays in laughter: as queen as well as hoyden, she knew that laughter was her only weapon against her roles. Like a true Meredithian patriarch, Irving crowned her by submerging her comic spirit, but if Ellen Terry's impulse to laughter had not been mutilated into pathos, she would probably never have become a triumphant heroine.

Despite her famous boast, Queen Victoria *was* amused, but only by men: comedy was regarded as more dangerous in women than sexuality was. Dickens, Disraeli, Matthew Arnold, Gilbert and Sullivan, Lewis Carroll, Edward Lear, Oscar Wilde, won love and blessings for their antic nonsense; even Teufelsdröckh, the sage in Carlyle's revered *Sartor Resartus,* expresses his prophetic afflatus in a gargantuan laugh. But the age's revered women—Florence Nightingale, George Eliot, Charlotte Brontë, Harriet Martineau, the queen herself—made themselves look sternly serious. Their martyred, militant heroines were Antigone, Cassandra, Joan of Arc; they cared no more for Rosalind than Irving did. Stella Campbell explained the phenomenon wickedly. In many ways she became Ellen Terry's successor in the 1890s; she was the loved culture heroine of a new, neurotic age, who was to inherit the love of both Forbes-Robertson and Shaw. In her best style, she touched the fear that underlay the Victorian taboo: " 'Do you know why God withheld the sense of humor from women?'

she asked [a solicitous dinner partner] winningly. The gentleman replied that he could not guess. 'That we may love you instead of laughing at you,' she replied sweetly."

Here and often, Mrs. Pat told the truth to her bane: like most enlightened women of her generation, she scorned Ellen Terry's apparent acquiescence and the indirect, finely tuned sedition within it. But Ellen Terry's almost inaudible protest—so rarefied that audiences mistook it for their own—won her more acolytes than did Stella Campbell's cruel exposures. Yet each knew the dangerous secret, one that Elizabeth Bennet in Jane Austen's *Pride and Prejudice* had also confronted when she mused about the powerful man who loved her: "He had yet to learn to be laught at, and it was rather too early to begin." These words had been written in 1813; throughout the century, it remained "too early" to laugh at powerful men, or at the women they wanted to see. By the 1880s, some advanced men were accepting abuse from angry feminists demanding their rights; they modestly admitted having too much power, but they feared ridicule's disenfranchisement. Readers of novels agreed to be mangled and chastened with Charlotte Brontë's Rochester, or drowned with George Eliot's Tom Tulliver and Grandcourt in floods of female ire; it was not insulting to be depicted as an autocrat justly brought low. Pain and rage were fair weapons, but a woman who laughed was a woman who went too far.

Women tended to be equally uneasy about comedy: feminists wanted reparation, not transcendence. In fiction by women, light-minded characters like Hetty Sorrel (in *Adam Bede*) and Ginevra Fanshawe (in *Villette*) are generally expelled from the noble heroines' perspectives. The essential funniness such characters find around them threatens to trivialize—or worse, to evade—the pain and anxiety true women endure. For both patriarchs and their most eloquent victims, oppression was more comfortable than comedy: both knew how to talk about the roles of master and victim, but from a woman at least, they could not face a laughter that transcended and subverted all roles. It was not Henry Irving alone who muffled Ellen Terry's comedy. A funny woman who cries with secret laughter at her supposedly serious roles was as alien to struggling women as she was to conceited men. The comedienne Ellen Terry might have been, instead of the beloved woman she was, hovered over the theater like a poltergeist, hinting to all who entered of identities beyond the acceptable.

The Lyceum cast itself as the guardian and epitome of the larger theater of Victorian society. Licensed Rosalinds appeared on stages with less weighty responsibilities: *As You Like It* was a popular play, if one that required gingerly handling. The American actress Ada Rehan was one of the century's most popular Rosalinds. Caught in pathos, Ellen Terry cast Ada Rehan in Kate's old role, as a second, unattainable self. In 1878, the same year Ellen Terry became Irving's Ophelia, Ada Rehan had joined Augustin Daly's company; in 1890, during one of their American tours, Irving leased the Lyceum to Daly. As manager, Daly loomed over Ada Rehan as her creator, but onstage she acted with John Drew, whom Ellen Terry described wistfully as an authentic partner: "With what loyalty he supported Ada Rehan! He never played for his own hand but for the good of the piece" (*Memoirs*, 225).

Would such a partner prove as addictive as Irving had? Ellen Terry wrote nervously to Graham Robertson that she was certain she and Ada Rehan would become "excellent friends" if they could meet for more than five minutes at a sitting. She goes on to wonder whether either of them is capable of standing alone onstage: "but it was a doleful day for each, I shd say, when John Drew & Ada Rehan ceased to act together = & she must miss it most. A woman would, I'm sure = If I didn't act with Henry he'd forget perhaps in a year (?) But I shouldn't = —"

In still more doleful days, when the fifty-three-year-old actress is forced to romp through yet another *Olivia,* she watches an Ada Rehan who has become, like Rosalind, too triumphant to acknowledge her:

> It appears to me positively shocking that I am obliged to go back & play such a part as Olivia "at my time of life," & my baby brother to play my lover! =
> I saw Ada Rehan walking in the street below the window I was looking from = (I feel sure she does not like me by the way—) She was looking well & handsome—she is touring around the states =

She mourns her subordination by making Ada Rehan her perfect reflected self, just as Daly and John Drew combine to become Irving's. Her memoir's generous praise of both describes Daly's productions as the opposite of Irving's: "His productions of Shakespeare at Daly's were really bad from the pictorial point of view. But what pace and ensemble he got from his company!" (p. 225).

As far as was possible in the 1890s, she avoided meeting Ada Rehan, perhaps trusting the folk superstition the Pre-Raphaelites had revived, that meeting one's Doppelgänger means death. Characteristically, Ted had offended Daly, giving his mother an excuse to lie low. On New Year's Day, 1895, she wrote affectionately from Philadelphia (a safe distance): "Happy new year to you my dear Ada Rehan - from my heart I wish you your hearts desire — I wd dearly have liked to go and see you when I was in New York, but the remembrance of what a naughty boy my son was to Mr. Daly prevented me — (but when we are young — boys or girls — we are always 'naughty,' & to most of our friends — I think we <u>get different</u> - a little better or a little worse!)" Ellen Terry had gotten different and better; she saw her banished boy-self flourishing in the actress she feared confronting. On another occasion, when Daly sent her tickets to a box to one of Ada Rehan's London performances, she sent Edy ("my girl") to applaud and congratulate in her place. By that time Edy, who was indeed her mother's girl, was learning to outface the disappointment that greeted her when she stood in for Ellen Terry.

Always, she wants to feel the feelings of the actress she shies away from: "Was in London yesterday I was flying about doing one or two things for the new play & who should I meet but Ada Rehan! as fresh as a sweet-pea, & merry - as --- as merry!! - (tho' she always seems to me a sort of <u>merry-sad</u> = She is very attractive.—wonder if she's happy. I do hope so - Someone once said I was 'incureably (inc<u>u</u>rably) happy' — so <u>that's</u> all right, since folk know all about other folk's's's feelin's — <u>that's</u> all right=" Grappling with her own mirror reflection, she finds it impossible to consider Ada Rehan's emotions without questioning her own. As with herself and Kate, and always to her own disadvantage, Ada Rehan is Ellen Terry in reverse. Above all, Ada Rehan is the lost boy/girl, preserved and triumphant, in contrast to her own womanly, ground-down self:

> I feel like a bit of leather [she writes to Ada Rehan], & what is the good of "a bit of leather" sending to you, but I do send over this line to tell you that I love you, or rather <u>shall</u> once more when I <u>can</u> love or hate or feel anything at all — about the 24th I guess — Some, I think, are <u>born tired</u> - I'm one of 'em.
> . . .
>
> Yr affectionate
Bit of leather
ET= =
>
> Congratulations on yr success as "Viola" - I wish I had seen it — I never could play the part myself a bit properly. It seems to me you will always have to play <u>boy</u>-girls!!!

After an elaborate apology for Ted—"He is such a dear <u>Donkey</u>, & at the <u>obstinate</u> period which has come to him rather later in life than with most boys" —she concludes again, only to add two days later: "I'm glad John Sargent is painting <u>you</u> as <u>yourself</u>."

But what is Ada Rehan's "self"? Ellen Terry can see only the boy/girl that the "bit of leather"—the Viola with the swollen thumb, the Rosalind manquée —incarnates in dreams and in the dreams she inspires. Her Sargent self was not that dragged-down woman, but it was that woman's vision: Sargent's mermaid-like Lady Macbeth, crowning herself (not her husband) in a frenzy of unsanctioned ambition, embodied (she said) "all I meant to do . . . — but I never achieved what he painted." Is Ellen Terry's self the bit of leather or the transfigured, aspiring queen? In the private drama underlying this wary, complex correspondence, Ellen Terry tries to touch her triumphant Rosalind self, but fails because, in deference to Irving's script, she casts herself inexorably as a pathetic heroine.

For better or worse, Ellen Terry became Ophelia—a role she did not like, in which she did not like herself. Her *Four Lectures* brim with generous affection even for pathetic heroines, but she denies her embrace to this insufferably "timid" girl: "Her brain, her soul and her body are all pathetically weak." Only "incipient insanity," suggesting that "from the first there is something queer about her," makes Ophelia interesting (pp. 165–66). Her fearful distaste was exacerbated by Watts's insinuation of the poor mad thing into her own identity. Gordon Craig's adoration was still more irritating, for it made Ophelia seem to stick to her through the generations like a fate. Even as a child, he wrote a tender letter of farewell to

Sweetest - butifulest & Kindest & Bestest =
"OPHELIA"

When he was a man, he saw her mad scene at a Drury Lane benefit for Nellie Farren and was enthralled by her acting for the first time:

> The whole of my fabric was rent and consumed, like the fabric in a dream. I could not compare my notions [of Ophelia] with hers, because mine were all scattered and she hadn't any—she had no notions—she was the thing itself.
> All was faultless—and all I could do was to look and listen and look again, and murmur in between times a prayer for forgiveness.
> This was revelation—more powerful and far more beautiful than on that first night of *Mistress Page*. When the curtain came down, the thought left with us was not "That's the way to do it," [the praise to which her comedy had aroused him], but "It is the only way to do it." (*ETSS*, 172)

His commemorative woodcut elicited only a tart response from her: "You know best whether the Ophelias <u>reduced</u> wd come out well- I shd scarcely think so- & I don't call it one of yr best=" But Gordon Craig's best-known Ophelia woodcut is indeed one of his best. Craig pays homage to the stark tonal contrasts of Watts's "Portrait of Ellen Terry," to his vision of encroachment and enclosure; like Watts, Gordon Craig pours all his loving art on an Ophelia associated with an expansive sky, from which she is barred by black and menacing forms and ruthlessly blocked space.

To her fellow actors as well, Ellen Terry was somehow one with Ophelia. Unlike Beatrice, Ophelia was not born in a merry hour; she did not skim the ground like a lapwing as she moved; the identification was less obvious and more malignant. Stella Campbell brought it cruelly home. Mrs. Pat had inherited Ellen Terry's wild dissonance—the desperate onstage fooling with which she fought contamination by her roles, the insane excitability that in her case erupted into unmistakable breakdowns—but she despised Ellen Terry's accommodations, her subservience to Irving, her coy adorableness; her Ophelia-ness, in short. In 1897, she played not so much a fair Ophelia as a truly mad one to Forbes-Robertson's acclaimed Hamlet; closing in for the kill, Shaw used his praise of that production to expose Irving's meretriciousness. As with Ada Rehan, one of Ellen Terry's own, more privileged doubles had replaced her at the Lyceum. On the night she and Irving attended, the dark-haired Mrs. Pat paid tribute to her other self by playing half her Ophelia scenes in a "blonde Ellen wig" (Peters, 160). Watching her own performances and her protective empire deteriorate, appalled at any identification of herself with Ophelia, Ellen Terry did not receive graciously this wicked glimpse of herself in a ruder generation's mirror. But the "Ellen wig" would not come off. When her own early suitor, Johnston Forbes-Robertson, parted bitterly from Mrs. Pat at last, his final contemptuous valediction exorcised the blonde and the dark woman together: " 'Oh yes,' he remarked [when Stella's name was mentioned], 'that little woman I was living with—that Ophelia' " (quoted in Peters, 180).

Ophelia lived mysteriously beyond her role: pathetically weak as she looked, Ellen Terry could not shake her off. Her essential power lay in her madness, intimations of which clung to Ellen Terry. As early as 1889, in her demonstrably unreliable *Philadelphia Press* article, Olive Weston had gossiped about the actress's mental disarray: "She is of a too-nervous, changeable, hysterical nature to be really happy with anyone. She needs constant change to amuse her and occupy her mind. Even at a dinner party she can not sit through the entire meal, but has to get up between the courses, flitting from one room to another to examine the pictures, the bric-à-brac, the decorations, talking nervously and gayly all the time. She is fascinating like an opal." Rumors of her instability circulated throughout the 1890s, particularly among those who sought to explain her increasingly bad parts and her apparent rift with Irving. Laurence

Irving hints darkly at her later deterioration (p. 628); Margaret Webster gives a sinister account of a rehearsal of *King Arthur:* "As usual, Miss Terry worried about the lights. May [Webster] managed to get offstage for a moment and rushed to the stage manager. 'For God's sake get that lime on her,' she said, 'or she'll go mad!' There was a soft little chuckle from the darkness and a voice remarked drily: 'Better get it right, Loveday. Don't want her to go mad, y'know. Pity.' It was Irving" (pp. 174–75).

In the 1890s, insanity and neurosis were claiming the stage. Ibsen's Hedda, Pinero's Mrs. Tanqueray and Mrs. Ebbsmith, sprang to discordant life in Stella Campbell's taut and tormented performances. Henry Arthur Jones's *The Masqueraders* (1899), whose heroine Dulcie was written for Ellen Terry but played by Mrs. Pat, relies on stage directions like the following: "[Dulcie] *flings herself wildly round, half dancing, and drops her head into HELEN's lap sobbing.*" In

Edward Gordon Craig, Ellen Terry as Ophelia.

stylishly advanced fiction, Hardy's Sue Bridehead in *Jude the Obscure* lives on the compelling edge of sanity, as does the ardent feminist Lyndall, in Olive Schreiner's *The Story of an African Farm* (1883). At the same time as Freud was publishing his early case histories in Vienna, Englishwomen whose lives toyed with madness became emblems of a new, abrasively modern decade. Whispers of a mad Ellen Terry allowed even Irving's strenuously wholesome Lyceum to take on the coloration of its age.

She fought to preserve herself, but she could not withhold her amused respect for the power in Ophelia's madness. A mad scene in Chicago lifted her to the sort of surprising triumph she had known when her Portia abdicated to Bassanio at the Prince of Wales': "I ran to the stage in the mad scene, and never have I felt such sympathy! This frail wraith, this poor demented thing, could hold them in the hollow of her hand . . . It was splendid! 'How long can I hold them?' I thought: 'For ever!' Then I laughed. That was the best Ophelia laugh of my life" (*Memoirs*, 215. ET's ellipsis).

Rosalind's sane laugh would tell the audience too much, but Ophelia's mad one is licensed to command. At the Lyceum, Beatrice lost her swiftness, and Portia her glittering rule; the reign of madness alone allowed Ellen Terry to emulate Irving's Napoleonic command of the stage. Even before they became objects of clinical fascination in the 1890s, madwomen were seen as mystic and marvelous beings a powerful literary myth had invested with special powers. When Watts painted Ellen Terry as a sane and healthy girl, she was overpowered and at bay, but the mad Ophelia dominated his canvas. Mary Cowden Clarke endows this frailest of maidens with prophetic afflatus: as she is about to meet Hamlet for the first time, "the rose of Elsinore" is stricken with a vision of the king's murder and all the ensuing anguish. The tragedy is refracted not in the noble mind of the sweet prince, but in the magic glass of an Ophelia divinely mad from the beginning of her story. Alone among Clarke's heroines, Ophelia shares her role with Shakespeare, the seer of the action.

As early as 1827, when the hypnotic Harriet Smithson displaced Hamlet from his own tragedy, this frailest of heroines assumed iconographic power on her own account. Harriet Smithson barely spoke French; Parisians remembered her Ophelia as virtually a mute role. Like Stella Campbell in the 1890s, she was adored for authentic insanity rather than memorable acting: "Miss Smithson has shown us true madness in Ophelia; despite the efforts of our own actresses and perhaps through the failings of our authors, we have never seen it before" (The *Corsaire*, quoted in Raby, 177). Hugo, Delacroix, and Berlioz (who married her) seized on her "true madness" as their symbol of an erotic and aesthetic awakening that soared far beyond her ancillary role in Shakespeare's play: as

Harriet Smithson invoked her, Ophelia became the type of French Romanticism. Delacroix painted her as a harbinger of Romantic transformations, barebreasted like his personified female Liberty, suspended between air and water as she is between humanity and divinity, reality and myth. This later Ophelia by Madeleine Lemaire is a Dionysian spirit of natural and sexual renewal, invading enfeebled civilizations to transform them. Hamlet—and *Hamlet*—destroy her, but in French Romantic revisions, Ophelia is reborn and redeemed as a symbol of revolutions in nature and art, obscuring the tragic posturings and long speeches of the tragic hero to hold the stage wordlessly and to seize the viewer's spirit.

Ellen Terry never bared her breasts; looking thoughtful with a lily, she seems aloof from this visionary cult. Yet her Ophelia transmitted hidden symbols and prophecies. From the myths of Romanticism to Watts's dark obsessions and the fascinated psychologizing of fin-de-siècle sophisticates, Ophelia's self-transfiguring madness was more appealing than Hamlet's portentous soliloquizing. Mad, Ophelia bore the trumpet of a prophecy; drowning, she mingled mystic worlds with familiar ones, joining a host of compelling hybrid women, water nixies, mermaids, lamias, serpent women, and Undines, who haunted Victorian dreams of a new dispensation.

Undine, like Peter Pan, was the center of a late Victorian cult; Ophelia could never be as sinister as these equivocal pagan invaders. Born to the sea, Undine has the power to steal souls and to control storms and tides. Like Hans Andersen's little mermaid, she impetuously relinquishes her magic to marry a handsome mortal. He betrays her and breaks her heart, forcing her to murder him by returning to her true primeval identity. Ophelia, especially as a quasi-mute role, teases the spectator into imagining that she has an Undine-like other-worldly identity the play refuses to show us. Ellen Terry longed for that self. "What news of the little 'Undine,' " she wrote ruefully to the adaptor of the German version of the legend. "Why did I miss that when I was young? Young & alive —"

It was her fate to miss all the things she made her characters hint she could be. Hamlet contented himself with insulting Ophelia. He never whispered to her such supplicant prayers as those of Undine's false husband: "Make me not mad with terror in my hour of death. If thou hidest a hideous face behind that veil, raise it not. Take my life, but let me not see thy face!" Hamlet had forgotten Ophelia's face by the time he died; he thought only of Horatio. And so of course, the mute Ophelia could never acknowledge her power in the words of Undine, striking her hearers with terror: "My tears have been his death." Undine drew her power from hints within Ophelia, but she had been given a

Eugène Delacroix, engraving of *The Drowning of Ophelia*.

Madeleine Lemaire, *Ophelia* (1880s); engraving
from George William Norris' illustrated
Hamlet (1907). *Reproduced by permission of the
Furness Collection, Van Pelt Library, University
of Pennsylvania.*

Photograph of Ellen Terry as Ophelia. *Reproduced by permission of the Furness Collection, Van Pelt Library, University of Pennsylvania.*

play of her own, and that made all the difference.

"This frail wraith, this poor demented thing" lent her apparent pathos and her buried power to Ellen Terry's non-Shakespearean roles at the Lyceum: Margaret in *Faust*, Lucy Ashton in *Ravenswood*, fair Rosamund in Tennyson's *Becket*, all obediently resurrected the Ophelia audiences loved to watch suffer. Ellaline in Alfred C. Calmour's *The Amber Heart*, one of the only plays in which Ellen Terry starred without Irving, is a diluted Ophelia with a trace of Undine, but she lacks the mythic suggestiveness that gives Ophelia intimations of Undine's power. Instead of magic, Ellaline possesses a baby-like innocence dependent on her mother's charm, an amber heart, which grants her immunity from the pangs of love. Capriciously, she throws the heart into the lake and falls woundingly in love. In her big scene, she is accordingly half-mad and preparing to drown herself:

> *Ella. (with a wild laugh).* Aye, Aye, I'm mad, but all my
>   woes are gone;
> I see a way to endless rest and peace;
> I'll lay me down beside the precious heart
> That I have lost. Hush! The rushes call on me.
> I come—I come! My grief will soon be o'er. . . .
> I must not stay. I come, sweetheart, I come!
>   *(Laughs hysterically, and, as she is running off, end act II)*

Her second act curtain speech is a red herring, for in the end Ellaline has both her innocence and her amber heart back; Ellen Terry's enforced evocation of Ophelia, evident in contemporary illustrations, is the only raison d'être for this play. *The Amber Heart* replaces woman's demonic magic with an embalmed and stunted innocence, but Burne-Jones didn't mind, for he found in Ellen Terry's Ellaline a magic he needed to believe in. After seeing *The Amber Heart* for the third time, he wrote Irving: "It is a most inspiring work to a painter—and Miss Terry's performance a revelation of loveliness. It is not acting—it is a glimpse into Nature itself. Is there any one like her? I think not. I had not been in a theatre for twenty years before I went to see 'The Amber Heart'" (quoted in Pemberton, 263–64).

For Burne-Jones at least, Ellaline/Ellen Terry gave *The Amber Heart* a mystic ritual's sacred power. Back in 1880, Henry James had said Ellen Terry possessed "a face altogether in the taste of the period, a face that Burne-Jones might have drawn" (*SA*, 143). In 1895, Irving hired Burne-Jones to design *King Arthur*. Both men knew that for Ellen Terry's Guinevere, psychological realism was out of the question. She could not play a mature, disobedient, and sensuous woman, even though she was one, but only a Guinevere translated into Ophelia, who is herself translated into a mystic, hieratic spirit of nature. Because Ellen Terry's Ophelia was so resonant a creation of artists, the artists who designed Lyceum productions translated her every possible character into Ophelia's emanation.

She was so compelling that, like all mystic symbols, she banished probability. Another figure of embalmed innocence, Margaret in W. G. Wills's *Faust,* has little to do but be pure and betrayed; as she grew older, Ellen Terry begged Irving repeatedly to find younger actresses to fall victim to his devilish plots;

" The Rushes call on me! I come – I Come –!

Ellen Terry: (Amber Heart:)

Drawing by Pamela Colman Smith of Ellen Terry as Ellaline in *The Amber Heart. Reproduced by permission of the Harry Ransom Humanities Research Center, University of Texas, Austin.*

Edward Burne-Jones, costume design for the Lyceum production of *King Arthur*, 1895. *Ellen Terry Memorial Museum, Smallhythe Place. Courtesy of the Trustee of the Ellen Terry Estate.*

Edward Burne-Jones, costume design for the Lyceum production of *King Arthur*, 1895. *Ellen Terry Memorial Museum, Smallhythe Place. Courtesy of the Trustee of the Ellen Terry Estate.*

Ellen Terry as Margaret in *Faust.* *Reproduced by permission of the Harry Ransom Humanities Research Center, University of Texas, Austin.*

but no one else was right for his ambitious dream. In the last act, Ellen Terry's Ophelia-like presence, mad and in chains in her dungeon, provided a magically still counterpoint to the frenzies of creation with which Irving—as Mephistopheles and as Mephistophelean actor-manager—created his own, breathtaking Heaven and Hell. Without her chained energy, his Satanic schemes would lose their meaning.

From a theatrical perspective, Ellen Terry was overwhelmed, not only by Irving's dictatorship, but by her own visual freight of symbolic significance. But arts and ideologies beyond the theatrical had endowed her with a prophetic magic that was stiller and less self-proclaiming than Irving's. Because it spoke primarily to acolytes, it had a deeper power than his strenuous creative adventures. Because that power was so blatantly misused, she helped Irving become convincingly diabolical.

In chains at the Lyceum, her very presence whispering of forbidden and expansive roles, Ellen Terry touched a chord in the most dynamic women of her day. Her quality onstage of distraction, of barely suppressed laughter simmering in loveliness, aroused a discontent more perfect performances would have left dormant. Like Dorothea Brooke, Ellen Terry evoked more than she was allowed to be; the inadequacies of her Lyceum roles aroused visions of suppressed possibilities and stronger lives. Virginia Woolf's *Between the Acts* articulates the promise Ellen Terry held out to women by sharing their thwarted condition while appearing to transcend it. Mrs. Swithins, a member of the audience, pays tribute to the itinerant director of female pageants, Miss La Trobe, whose character is Woolf's tribute to Edith Craig: " 'What a small part I've had to play! But you've made me feel I could have played . . . Cleopatra!' . . . 'I might have been—Cleopatra,' Miss La Trobe repeated. 'You've stirred in me my unacted part,' she meant."

This moment of understanding between thwarted women, onstage and off, crystallizes Ellen Terry's bond with the women in her audience. Her compelling presence in secondary roles inspired women to imagine their own unacted parts, the laughter it was still too early to indulge, the triumph betrayed into pathos. Her self-subduing usefulness to Irving spoke more painfully to women of their own condition than the most regal Cleopatra would have done.

Her own subordination may have inspired her to extend herself to subordinated women beyond the Profession. According to Marguerite Steen's typically jaundiced account, she opened the gates of the Lyceum to a flood of women living empty lives in the outside world: "Girls who had made a *succès fou* in London drawing-rooms yearned to extend the orbit of their triumphs. Impassioned for Ellen Terry, they made the Lyceum their Mecca. It was not difficult, through friends or relations, to make acquaintance with the divine Miss Terry (herself, by then, a figure in Society) and, through her, to get a walk-on at the Lyceum—to the disgust of young women dependent on such work for their livelihood. According to an old actress, the wings 'stank of debs and Debrett,' and the patience of authentic members of the Company was much tested by these frivolous invaders, on whom it was impossible to impose the discipline of the theatre" (Steen, 162).

In her ruder moments, Ellen Terry might have felt that the wings of the Lyceum stank sufficiently without debs and Debrett. Her twenty-four-year performance as Irving's wife brought her closer to ordinary women than she was to other actresses, whom she envied, even when they were less successful, because they were freer than she. Her generous sympathy for aspiring women extended beyond actresses whose names we know—such as May Whitty, Margaret Webster, Violet Vanbrugh, Lena Ashwell, Edith Evans, Pauline Chase, and Lynn Fontanne—to affect a generation. When she allowed debs to walk across the Lyceum stage, she did her part toward ending the hegemony of stage families like her own, and allowing normally bred women to work in the theater. "Increasingly after the 1890s actresses were the daughters of vicars, stockbrokers and civil servants." Ellen Terry opened the door to them. Restrained from a larger life herself, she inspired other women to look for one, despite the Irvingesque heroes who blocked their way.

The Lyceum had glorified and stunted her at the same time: she could never be the transcendent being Bernhardt and Duse had become. The two continental "queens" were actor-managers in their own right, playing parts tailored to their grandeur in companies that existed only to support the star. Neither knew the women in their audience, but each in her way claimed to speak for them. Neither spoke in Ellen Terry's way, but in their own, both were right. Bernhardt lied for all women forced to live by pleasing, while Duse told their grand hidden truth.

Bernhardt describes the aftermath of one of her usual intoxicating triumphs: "Some of the *artistes* were very delighted, especially the women, for there is one thing to remark with regard to our art, the men are more jealous of the women than the women are among themselves. I have met with many enemies among the men comedians and with very few among the women. I think that the dramatic art is essentially feminine. To paint one's face, to hide one's real feelings, to try to please and to endeavor to attract attention, these are all faults for which we blame women and for which great indulgence is shown. These same defects seem odious in a man."

Bernhardt manages to eat her cake and have it, blaming women for the acting subservience demands, and glorifying herself for the same enforced attempts to please. But that glory is a product of woman's necessary self-concealment, allowing her to speak out about her own, and all women's, lies. Duse makes herself a vehicle of the truth these same despised women are forced to hide. Her embrace of women is more indirect than Bernhardt's—she perceives them only through the medium of her characters—but it is no less absolute. In 1884, she wrote to the Marchese d'Arcais:

> Acting—what an ugly word! If it were merely a question of acting I feel that I could never have done it, and could never do it again. But the poor women in the plays I have acted so get into my heart and mind that I had to think out the best way of making them understood by my audience, as if I were trying to comfort them. . . . But in the end it is generally they who comfort me. How and why and when this inexplicable reciprocity of feeling between these women and myself began; that story would be far too wearisome and difficult as well—if I were to tell it fully. But this I can say: though everybody else may distrust women I understand them perfectly. I do not bother whether they have lied, betrayed, sinned, or whether they have been lost from their birth, once I feel that they have wept and suffered while lying or sinning or loving. I stand by them, I stand for them, and I burrow, burrow into them, not because of any thirst for suffering, but because woman's capacity for sympathy is greater and more many-sided, gentler and more perfect than man's.

Each makes herself an epitome of women, Bernhardt of their lies, Duse of their truth. Both divas form their art out of woman's degradation, transcending and exposing it at the same time. Because they know they are grand, they dare to speak the unspeakable.

In her great years, unlike them, Ellen Terry did not feel great; she lived her subordination too intimately to articulate it fully. Because she was visibly silenced onstage, and then because she kept losing the silly words she had, she gathered to her the resentful compliance of the women in her audience. She was closest to them when she fooled and forgot her lines. Virginia Woolf remembered her letting her part slide away, as Shaw's Lady Cecily expanded into Ellen Terry: "She filled the stage and all the other actors were put out, as electric lights are put out in the sun." No mere obedient performance could exude that burst of power.

In Woolf's own phrase, Stella Campbell had to kill Ellen Terry as the angel in the house, the eternally good woman the female artist must either destroy or, to her own destruction, become. Yet even she sank into rapture when Ellen

Terry's Imogen conjured worlds beyond the script: "When she entered I felt she had come from the moon: when she left the stage I was sure the stars were greeting her. No one has ever had her magical step—that extraordinary happy haste, that made you feel she must presently arrive at the gates of Paradise. The evening I saw her as 'Imogen,' she forgot her words, and—giving a delicious look at the audience and then towards heaven—spoke three times in a voice that melted your bosom, this word: 'Beyond—beyond—beyond—' There was no 'Beyond' in the text, but it was the loveliest word I ever heard, and described her 'Imogen' " (quoted in Peters, 138).

This plangent improvised "beyond" has within it all Bernhardt's lies, and the essence of Duse's deep truth. Because it was not simply triumphant or pathetic, but a forbidden interpolation, it crystallized Ellen Terry's message to the women she let dream of their unacted parts. But it was ironic when women began to adore her mistakes: when she had burrowed into Lady Macbeth to speak for them, they hadn't cared at all.

"MY POWERS OF BEING BAD." Like most younger women, Stella Campbell loved Ellen Terry not for what she was, but for the "beyond" she summoned: caught in pathetic roles, she evoked a largeness beyond them. The parts she played, fitfully and alone, on the margins of her scripts contained all the energy, anger, wit, and passion that in the company were reserved for Irving. But she had not set out to be an artist in the margins or despite her lines. When she played Lady Macbeth in 1888, she had tried, like a true artist, to give the role the contour of her experience; subverting it had never entered her mind.

The year before, Irving had rejected *As You Like It* for the Lyceum, along with *The Tempest, King John, Antony and Cleopatra, Timon of Athens, Richard II,* and *Julius Caesar* (*Memoirs,* 231). Rosalind was gone and the walls were closing in. Lady Macbeth would have to be the part she made her own. While she worked on it she was in terror, not only because on the face of it she was miscast, but because it was her first Lyceum role to address her forbidden selves. For once, Ellen Terry did not "play" her part; she transfused it with her own audacious interpretation. Shakespeare's "fiend-like queen" became the vehicle for everything she had learned about being a woman.

She had been good by definition since she became Irving's stage wife; Lady Macbeth allowed her to think about being bad. Her mind went back to Goldenstar and Dragonetta, the two pantomime fairies she had played when she was little. In her Memoir she remembers only being trapped in the good Goldenstar, but when she wrote to Clement Scott while she was studying Lady Macbeth, twenty-one years before her Memoir appeared, her bad Dragonetta was vividly present. She may, she tells him, have played the good fairy Goldenstar, but she is sure she played "afterward the <u>bad</u> fairy — something-or-other. . . . I <u>do</u> remember one thing clearly. That having made a success (!!!) as the <u>bad</u> fairy, I—doubting my powers of being <u>bad</u> in a play, <u>before</u>, immediately set to work & studied the words of—LADY MACBETH!!!"

Lady Macbeth was her grown-up Dragonetta. Playing her meant crossing that enticing line into being bad, the line Henry crossed to such acclaim every time he played in *The Bells* or *Faust*. But for a woman, it was difficult to know what being bad meant. Ellen Terry had been bad when she ran off with Edward Godwin; she became good again when she married Charles Kelly, although she had been cruel to Kelly, while she had given herself to Godwin with all the generosity that was in her then. Popular novels like Thackeray's *Vanity Fair* had the same sort of trouble with its bad woman. Becky Sharp and many other Victorian anti-heroines are comic spirits; they have Ellen Terry's wit, mercurial rapidity of thought, adeptness at moving in and out of roles. Like Ellen Terry, Becky Sharp plays everyone life has her play, and like Lady Macbeth, she plots a murder at the end. But, Thackeray makes us wonder, are quicksilver, funny women really bad? Or is Amelia Sedley, Becky's virtuous if infantile foil, whose hero-worshipping dependence saps the vitality from men, the truly murderous woman? Becky and Amelia might have stood in for Eleonora and Nell, Ellen Terry's two selves, or for her old fairies Dragonetta and Goldenstar: good and bad women were uniform types in the nineteenth century. Almost always, they raised tantalizing questions. Finally, Ellen Terry decided that the wickedest woman she knew was her own onstage self. In their hearts, Goldenstar and Dragonetta were the same.

Lady Macbeth's great witch-like soliloquy, in which she summons dark spirits to take her femaleness away, raises the same sort of puzzlement about a woman's power of being bad:

> Come, you spirits
> That tend on mortal thoughts, unsex me here,
> And fill me from the crown to the toe top-full
> Of direst cruelty! make thick my blood;
> Stop up the access and passage to remorse,
> That no compunctious visitings of nature
> Shake my fell purpose, nor keep peace between
> The effect and it! Come to my woman's breasts

And take my milk for gall, you murdering ministers,
Wherever in your sightless substances
You wait on nature's mischief! (I, v, 41–51)

Victorian commentators debated at length about whether unnatural spirits answered Lady Macbeth's invocation, but Ellen Terry had no doubt: no spirits came, because no spirits had to. Lady Macbeth needs no unsexing to make her wicked; in her poise, her murderousness, her rage for power, and her untiring usefulness to Macbeth, she is "all over a *woman*." The womanly actress would tell audiences about herself.

Most audiences wanted Lady Macbeth to be a virago, not a woman. A virago was the adult equivalent of a hoyden. According to the *Oxford English Dictionary,* its primary meaning in the nineteenth century was "a bold, impudent (or wicked) woman," but it carried a more approving meaning as well, though one labeled *"rare"*: "A man-like, vigorous, and heroic woman." The *OED* quotes a sentence from the *Nineteenth Century* that plays the heroic meaning against contemporary disapproval: "[Vittoria Colona] was a virago, a name which, however misapprehended now, bore a different and worthy signification in her day" (1885). In the 1880's, a woman who was "man-like" or "unsexed" was not heroic but horrible. "Woman" was so restrictively defined that Victorian vocabulary was rich in words for such aggressive female monsters; monsters cast no shadows on good homes. A century earlier, Sarah Siddons had played a famous Lady Macbeth as a bloodcurdling virago, fascinating in her hybrid grandeur, unrecognizable as a woman. The stage tradition she exemplified thrilled audiences without implicating them in domestic evil.

Like Ellen Terry, though, Sarah Siddons wrote about a role she never played. Her notes on Lady Macbeth ignore the virago on behalf of a woman "fair, feminine, nay, perhaps, even fragile," "captivating in feminine loveliness"; at the end, her "feminine nature, her delicate structure, it is too evident, are soon overwhelmed by the enormous pressure of her crimes" (quoted in Manvell, 192). Sarah Siddons's unacted part sanctioned Ellen Terry's interpretation of a Lady Macbeth whose powers of being bad were the same powers that made her impeccably feminine.

This captivating creature who stayed within approved boundaries was safer imagined than performed, as Sarah Siddons may have known: if Lady Macbeth was not a monster, she exposed a side of woman's nature that most men and many women did not want to know about. Most commentators expelled the character summarily from woman's sphere. Henry Giles, who found the heart of Shakespeare's genius to be his exalted identification with women, made no

Sarah Siddons as Lady
Macbeth. *Reproduced by
permission of the Furness
Collection, Van Pelt Library,
University of Pennsylvania.*

room in that celestial company for a Lady Macbeth who "stands before us divested of womanly tenderness: as such she is prepared for treason and murder" (p. 152). Even the iconoclast Frank Harris agreed: "Lady Macbeth is not one of Shakespeare's happier creations. It is impossible to make a woman credible to us by lending her a man's resolution and courage." The virago may be repulsive or heroic; she is never female. Since Shakespeare's genius reveals for all time the truth of woman's nature, it follows that his Lady Macbeth must be a monster or a man.

Sarah Siddons's notes, so tantalizingly at odds with her performance, reinforced Ellen Terry's instinct about good women. There were other, isolated doubters. G. Fletcher's article in the *Westminster Review* (March 1844) rejects the monster in favor of a loving wife deceived in her husband. In *The Girlhood of Shakespeare's Heroines,* young Lady Gruoch is a "little Amazon" with a "masculine spirit," but she is also "singularly delicate," and unlike the traditional virago, she has "golden locks." Mary Cowden Clarke's Lady Gruoch bears a suggestive resemblance to Mary Braddon's sensation heroine, the would-be murderess Lady Audley, who is also demure, ruthless, and smiling. But Lady

Audley needs no masculinity to be a killer: her compliant womanliness makes her bad and mad at once. In Bram Stoker's *Dracula,* the blonde, super-feminine Lucy, who collects marriage proposals and clings adoringly to men, becomes a more horrible vampire than does her friend Mina, a stalwart career woman who swells into the majesty of a saint when she is vampirized. Lucy, a sleepwalker like Lady Macbeth and a dear, giggling English rose, might be Bram Stoker's tribute to his adored Ellen Terry's most audacious performance.

These adorable feminine killers might have learned their characters from a real Victorian murderer, Madeleine Smith, who, when she was tried for poisoning her lover, became like Ellen Terry a cult heroine to flocks of obedient girls whose dreams she acted out. Before murdering her lover, Madeleine deferred to him in approved fashion: "I have a very poor opinion of my sex. There is no doubt man is a superior being and that is the reason why I think a wife should be guided and directed in all things by her husband. I get few ladies to agree with me—they all think Woman is as good and clever as man. I allow there have been many clever women, but a Book written by a woman never makes the same impression on my mind as one written by a man."

This is Ellen Terry's Lady Macbeth: not the unnatural woman, but the pliable one who makes herself into all the sweet things she is told to be. In her notes, Lady Macbeth smiles incessantly: "Smile. Devil" (quoted in Manvell, 358). She coaches herself to tempt Macbeth in the same words with which the actress must often have walked onto the Lyceum stage: "Be damn'd *charming.*" She wins him to murder not by bullying, but by pleasing: "Now see = now here is a beautiful plan which your wife has thought all out (the hellcat)" (quoted in Manvell, 195). "Play with his hands and <u>charm</u> him."

Her reading extended her insight beyond the play: in her library at Small-hythe, there are articles that not only show Lady Macbeth to be feminine, but generalize upon the Macbeths until they become female and male paradigms. Joe Comyns-Carr's "Macbeth and Lady Macbeth: An Essay" gives Ellen Terry's interpretation a scholarly format. Not only does it find Lady Macbeth to be "truly and typically a woman," but the play becomes "a sublime study in sexual contrast." Her concentration of will, "finer instinct," and retrospection complement his male infirmity of will and apprehension. F. A. Leo's *Shakespeare Notes* uses the two characters in the same way, to epitomize gender distinctions. Ellen Terry underscored his discussion heavily: "She was very skilful in management and ready in contrivance, as women are apt to be; while Macbeth was wanting in both these qualities, as men generally are." This Lady Macbeth is no longer beyond the pale of womanhood; she has become the type of a good woman: "Her part is simply that of a woman and a wife who shares her husband's ambition and supports him in it."

Ellen Terry's ambitious project was not merely to show Lady Macbeth as *a* feminine woman: she was *the* feminine woman. The unnatural schemer who plotted murders if she could not execute them illuminated the familiar qualities of all women and wives. Ellen Terry found Ibsen's Hedda Gabler petty and drab, but her Lady Macbeth places the bourgeois wife in the same sinister perspective the malevolent Hedda does. Her stage marriage to Henry Irving had made her the pattern of all wives everywhere. As Lady Macbeth, she would speak to and for them.

Her notes may be unactable, particularly in an opulent Lyceum production, but if they do not tell us what Ellen Terry did as Lady Macbeth, they reveal with astonishing pungency everything she felt about being a woman in the 1880s. A woman's task—and it is often a mad one—is to love men: Lady Macbeth "is full of womanliness" because she is "capable of <u>affection</u> - she <u>loves her husband</u> - Ergo - <u>she is a woman</u>-and she knows it, and is half the time <u>afraid</u> whilst urging Macbeth not to be afraid as she loves a <u>man</u>. Women love <u>men</u>" (Quoted in Manvell, 195).

This note half-expresses her trouble about Edy, along with fears about the veracity of her own womanly love of her "husband," Irving. At nineteen, Edy was as fiercely loyal to her femaleness as she had been as a child, when she exhorted the whining Teddy to "be a *woman*"; but like the child, she showed no sign of loving men. What did that make her? What did her own dark anger make Ellen Terry herself, of whose hidden emotions Edy was so preternaturally aware? Above all, what kind of love, and how much of it, would satisfy a man that she was womanly enough to be a woman?

It is a chore to love the Macbeth her notes construct, a husband far from the "lofty—manly, heroic" character Irving thought he was playing: "A man of great *physical* courage frightened at a *mouse*. A man who talks and talks and works himself up, rather in the style of an early Victorian hysterical heroine. His was a *bad* nature and he became reflected in his wife. M. must have had a neglectful mother – who never taught him the importance of self-control. He has *none!* and he is obsessed by the one thought *Himself*" (quoted in Manvell, 194). Her self-obsessed son Gordon Craig lurks within this analysis: he did talk hysterically and work himself up, he had just been expelled from his school in Germany, and, she had begun to fear, he was manifesting a nature irreparably bad. Had she neglected him through all her torrents of adoration, not only for the Lyceum, but in negligently allowing him to be born without a father or a name to give him character?

This supposedly objective sketch of Macbeth has the contours of other men she loved, most notably the heroic Irving she pinioned in her diary. Lady Macbeth's essential tragedy is not her unwomanly ambition, but her womanly faith in this spurious hero: "A woman (all over a *woman*) who *believed in Macbeth,* with a lurking knowledge of his weakness but who never *found him out* to be nothing but a brave soldier *and a weakling,* until that damned party in a parlour – 'Banquet Scene' as it is called. Then, 'something too much of this' she says and gives it up – her [un?]mistakable softening of the brain occurs – she turns quite gentle – and so we are prepared for the last scene madness and death" (quoted in Manvell, 194).

Is the ominous gentleness a harbinger of the soft, mad, and womanly end she feared for herself? As Ellen Terry sees *Macbeth,* regicide is a mere background distraction from the essential female tragedy of misplaced belief in a man society makes up as a hero. For this proper wife, "Macbeth preyed on her mind more than the deed" (quoted in Manvell, 362), for she is neither violent nor a virago: "She loved her babies and she could not kill the man who looked like her Father. (Woman)." "All women are clever at *contriving* merely," adds an Ellen Terry whom Irving's heroics had forced into sardonic inactivity (quoted in Manvell, 358). This exemplary woman whose life centers on a supposed man of action lives her intensest life retrospectively. Ellen Terry's authority for this womanly symptom is the popular novelist Ouida: " 'The danger told on her *now that it was past* – as it does most commonly with women.' *Ouida* ('Under Two Flags')" (quoted in Manvell, 364).

This Lady Macbeth could be Shakespeare's Kate *after* Petruchio has tamed her: her tragic virtue is her faith in her husband. But, because she is so consummate a woman as Victorian culture defined the species, she craves power before love: "Yes, Lady M. was ambitious. Her husband's letters aroused intensely the desire to be a Queen – true to woman's nature, even more than to a man's to crave power – and power's display" (quoted in Manvell, 194). A queen herself, and an ambitious one, Ellen Terry knew whereof she spoke. In some mysterious way, womanliness purchased power; it had done so when she played her first Portia, and had risen to glory when she yielded to Bassanio all she had and was. She formulates this connection only in relation to Lady Macbeth, leaving it dormant and unexpressed in her Memoir. One of her *Macbeth* scripts includes a ringing annotation Manvell does not quote: "There's such authority doth hedge a—'Queen!' " This gleeful line transposes Claudius's empty boast in *Hamlet:* "There's such divinity doth hedge a king, / That treason can but peep to what it would, / Acts little of his will" (IV, v, 123–25). Instead of divinity, Ellen Terry exalts self-generated individual authority, as she does when she gives herself and her woman friends heart by quoting Iago's counsel of self-sustainment. The power she sees as Lady Macbeth's ruling, and always womanly, passion is not sanctioned, but self-bestowed. The usurping queen who is "all over a *woman*" can be exalted only by her will. Macbeth is too cowardly to consecrate her, and God will not.

In her *Macbeth* notes, for the first and last time, Ellen Terry told her own story through and not beyond the character she played. Lady Macbeth admitted none of the mercurial comedy in which the actress was most at home, but neither did Our Lady of the Lyceum: Macbeth's wife became the vehicle for her account of a Cinderella who was so *"damn'd* charming" that she became a Lyceum queen and lost her identity when she did so. Her performance could not say all this; neither, in her letters, could she; but in her incessant explication of Lady Macbeth, she never stopped trying to confess. Aware that she had failed to make audiences believe her, she turned to critics. Clement Scott and William Winter were Irving's loyalest journalistic advocates in England and America; neither could see his charming partner as Lady Macbeth. In her drive to explain Lady Macbeth to them, Ellen Terry tried vainly and desperately to explain good women as well. Two days after the disappointing opening, she wrote Clement Scott a long letter marked "Private":

> After feeling miserable a bit, about what you were going to say (for of course I guessed it — having just about enough wit to keep myself warm) I must confess I laughed, when I read what you did say. You have hit the blot!—"an empty & a barren cry"—**i n d e e d i t w a s ,** when I called on the spirits to unsex me—I acted that bit just as badly as anybody could act anything = [Could she have acted the soliloquy badly because her Lady Macbeth has no need to be unsexed?]
>
> It was most kind of you to suppose that I could act Lady M — you write from that point of view, which itself is a very great compliment = For my own part I am quite surprised to find I am really a useful actress - for I really am!! to be able to get through with such different parts as -----
>
> Ophelia - Olivia - Beatrice - Margaret - & Lady M-
>
> & my aim is usefulness-to my lovely art, & to H.I. This is not a very high ambition - is it? but long ago I gave up dreaming & I think I see things as they are (especially see myself as I am, Alas!) & off & on the stage only aspire to help a little= ---Mind you though Mr. Clement, although certainly I know I cannot do what I want to do in this part, I don't even want to be "a fiend"-& won't believe for a ~~moment~~ can't believe for a moment that she did "conceive" that murder = that one murder of which she is accused = Most women break the law during their lives, few women realize the consequences of that they do to day = In my memory I have facts, & I use them for (not for my "methods" in my work that's where I fail dismally in this—but for) reading women who have lived, & can't speak & tell me = **I a m q u i t e t o p f u l l o f—**

(not direst cruelty I hope but)—<u>womens secrets</u> = (& I have <u>my own</u>!!! & my women - my friends — were <u>not</u> wicked---& <u>you say</u> <u>I'm</u> not = !!!

I do believe that at the end of the banquet, that poor wretched creature was brought, through agony & sin to repentance & was <u>just forgiven</u>—

Surely did she not call on the spirits to be made bad, because she knew she was <u>not</u> so <u>very</u> bad? <u>I'm</u> always calling on the spirits to be made <u>good,</u> because I know I'm not good - not <u>strong</u> in good, although all the while <u>desiring</u> it above all else. No- she was not good, but not much worse than many women you know — me for instance - My hankerings are not for blood, but I think I <u>might, kill</u> for my child, or my love <u>blindly</u> — & see & regret & repent in deepest sincerity after — You would have <u>laughed</u> the other night though - the man at the side put the paint — the "blood" — on my hands, & in the hurry & excitement I didn't look, but when I saw it I just burst out crying = I don't believe you think I'm very bad - <u>I am</u> - Perhaps when I tell you I loved, you won't believe it, when at the <u>same time</u> I tell you I broke the law <u>& forged</u> for my love - I tell you I <u>did</u> love, & forged - said money was owed by him to me when it was not - in order to get it again <u>for him</u> of course - Do you think I thought that wicked <u>then</u>? I thought it was <u>right</u> — I couldn't have done it with my baby at my breast if I had seen it <u>as I see it now</u> — you say I can't be Lady M. whilst all the time you see I am quite as bad ----- Don't have me hanged drawn & quartered after this ---- You are quite right I can't play Lady M - but it's because my <u>methods</u> are not right. & oh, nothing is right about it yet. To be consistent to a conviction is what I'm going to <u>try</u> for =

Her confession of a guilt all good women share takes urgency from its underlying insistence that, for all her girlish modesty, she is an artist. Her urgency increases as she begs Scott to obliterate her declaration. Wryly, she steals Mathias's well-known curse in *The Bells* ("Into the fire, Jew, into the fire") to dramatize the evil everyone cheered in Irving, but denied his stage wife:

If you don't put this into the fire <u>this moment</u> may my eternal cuss fall on you! "<u>Go</u> into the <u>fire</u> Jew - <u>Go</u> into the <u>fire</u>"-- Now I've my work before me haven't I? I've not slept for a month, properly, & these fogs frighten me - I wish I didn't act, or you didn't <u>write</u>, then perhaps I might see something of you = Forgive this horrid scrawl which is written to <u>assure</u> you I am a <u>real</u> bad person, & yet somehow in the person of Lady M have contrived with evident subtlety, to make you think I can't <u>assume</u> bad, 'cos I'm good! Don't you think it's all rather humourous?—

It's good of you to have "<u>let me down easy,</u>" but I care more for what you think, than because you say it to others in print =

Was it not nice of an actress she sent me Mrs. Siddons shoes. (not to <u>wear</u>, but to keep with me-) I wish I could have "stood in 'em="! She played Lady M. (<u>her</u> Lady M. not Shakespeares & <u>if I could</u>, I wd have done <u>hers,</u> for Shakespeare's Lady M. was a fool to it - [In Ellen Terry's shorthand, Sarah Siddons's Lady Macbeth is the virago and Shakespeare's is the womanly wife] but at the same time I don't think I'd even care to <u>try</u> to <u>imitate her imitators.</u> I wish I could have seen Helen Faucit in the part—I <u>do</u> believe <u>she</u> was the <u>rightest</u> - although not to be looked at by the side of the portrait of <u>Siddons</u>, as a singly effective figure - Can you ever forgive me, or can I ever forgive myself this long horrible scrawl?

Ah, but I do wish you & yours a happy new year -

On the margin beside her signature, Ellen Terry scrawls in swelling letters: "Fire - Fire - **F i r e !**"

Like her performance, this urgent if uncontrolled letter wants to say more than it does about herself, Lady Macbeth, and the women who *"have* lived, and can't speak and tell." Writing to a man and a critic, the terse, bold annotator scatters into a girlish creature who dithers about how bad she is, but turns out (like Ibsen's Nora) to have broken the law only on behalf of love and service: power and its display go unmentioned. She transposes her brutally bold awareness into the voice Clement Scott expects from Irving's leading lady. Like most audiences, he cannot see that her very dithering and devotion, her modest protestations of usefulness, represent the Lady Macbeth she sees as Shakespeare's.

The most striking fact about this letter is that it was written at all. She had no need to cajole Clement Scott, a friendly critic, but Lady Macbeth released her from silence: for the first time, she needed to tell the truth about being a woman, if only in the disguise of Lady Macbeth or of her own disarming idiom. When *Macbeth* traveled to America, she wrote a similar letter to William Winter before the opening, insisting for the only time in her career on an integrity of conception that transcended her need to please:

It is not a very pleasant prospect for <u>me</u>— For I rather anticipate folk will hate me in it = Everyone seems to think Mrs. McB is a <u>Monstrousness</u> & <u>I</u> can only see that she's a <u>woman</u> - a mistaken woman - & <u>weak</u> - not a Dove - of course not — but <u>first of all</u> **a w i f e** = I don't think she's <u>at all clever</u> ("Lead Macbeth" <u>indeed!</u> — she's not even clever enough <u>to sleep!</u>) She seems shrewd, & thinks <u>herself</u> so, at first to a certain point, about her husband's character but oh, dear me how quickly he gets steeped in wickedness beyond her comprehension = <u>try how hard I may</u> I <u>cannot</u> perceive that Madame Sarah Bernhardt is a "thin woman" — "an eel" — that the sun shines upon us at midnight, or that Lady

Macbeth was a monstrous fiend who urged her little husband against his will to be naughty. Only I have to act the thing tomorrow & I just <u>shake</u> -- 'cos I haven't courage to do firmly what lies so plainly before me - I wish to goodness I cd see you tomorrow <u>morning</u> some time = I always leave everything to the last moment — for 2 years I've wanted you to tell me things about Lady M. <u>to help me with her</u>—I don't mean in the <u>Paper</u>—<u>but for myself</u> I can scarce <u>endure</u> feeling as I do, so infirm of purpose = No - not quite <u>that</u> — infirm **o f d e c i s i o n** - to try to do what is <u>expected</u> by <u>so many people</u> <u>or to do what I want to do</u> - <u>That</u> is the question = Forgive my mad scrawl = <u>So</u> selfish it seems - & even if <u>tomorrow</u> (Tuesday) you can't find time to help me before I do it let me have a little of yr loveliness <u>some</u> day this week, before I <u>finish</u> the part - so I may <u>try</u> <u>ways - & methods</u> — I'm so excited at playing the horrid part = Of course I'd like to be liked in the part— but that's <u>nothing</u> by the side of being sure of <u>what I'm going to try for</u> = It appears obvious I shd ask Henry! —but I'd sooner trouble you — for you have a better knowledge of <u>womanfolk</u> at least it is almost ludicrous his ignorance on that one subject—He has I think never given ~~that subject~~ it his consideration(!!) or doubtless he wd be better informed = This is just a cry for help to you my dear friend & you will forgive the [illegible] scrawl, and my not being able to say what I want to say for indeed today (& always before this play comes on) I'm "off my head a bit" & wretched — Such a hot stuffy day too!

In both Lady Macbeth letters, Ellen Terry's "cry for help" is really a cry to be taught. Since she left the Keans', she had lived among teaching men; when she was young, being taught had been a form of lovemaking; but after she joined the Lyceum at the zenith of her power and energy, they had begun to refuse. Henry never directed her: while he ordered the rest of the company about, he assured her that she was a vision of loveliness just as she was. Did they think she had no more to learn now that she was tamed into a wife at last? Had it all been an education merely to un-learn, or to not-know? So Edy might say, but was Edy a woman, or another teaching man in disguise?

In thrall to Irving's greatness, William Winter was no more helpful than Clement Scott had been, or than Irving was himself. All three were certain they knew her; none cared to hear Lady Macbeth's lessons to women. Scared into the sort of gentleness and "softening of the brain" she diagnosed in Lady Macbeth, she apologized to William Winter three days later, excusing her excitement as insanity: "Ah yes - you are most kind but you must have thought I had eaten of the insane root, or that I was tipsy!!! to scrawl those lines to you = Forgive me It was disgraceful - unpardonable & so you will pardon me = As <u>you</u> will be — But I'll trouble you with a few questions when we meet, even now — but I'll be temperate - "

The Lyceum was not the sort of theater that would let her tell her own story: perhaps there was no such theater. Some reviewers were kind, while others were amused, but kind or jocular, none of them understood that through Lady Macbeth, she was composing a legend of good women. The women she spoke to and for were equally dense; they began to understand only when the urgency of her message had ceased to torment her and she started to fool. Irving was courteously uncomprehending even when, later on, she offered herself as the prescient Fool in *King Lear:* he merely insisted, as she knew he would, that Cordelia was her only role.

Even while she was playing it, her Lady Macbeth had only a hazy existence to most spectators. The *Morning Post* had seen the woman whose reality had gripped her as a Pre-Raphaelite phantom: "A creature so spiritual, so ineffable, has never perhaps been put on the stage. Is this Lady Macbeth? Who shall decide? That it is not the Lady Macbeth of tradition or of Mrs. Siddons we know. It is scarcely a Lady Macbeth we realize. It is, perhaps, one of which we have dreamed" (quoted in Manvell, 201). Critics may have dreamed it, but to Ellen Terry, Lady Macbeth's story had been more painfully vivid than all the roles for which she had won love. She began to wonder what about herself was real and what was a dream—the womanly woman she had made herself, hungry for power and investing her faith in a weak and cruel husband, or the phantom others insisted she was? Perhaps Lady Macbeth had been a tangible and compelling dream, and only ghosts of women were real.

Her father knew how important it was that she had played as she did: Ben always understood what was unique. Her role at the Lyceum depressed him, but *Macbeth* inspired him to write his only letter of enthusiastic approval that we know of in her glorious years: "Nelly dear your performance of Lady Macbeth was *fine* . . . Don't allow the critics to interfere with your own view of the part . . . There will be thousands who will think otherwise, and, who knows, but that the experts may, before the end of the run of the piece, be converted . . . It was a grand performance of a most intellectual conception. . . . My joy was prodigious: Always your loving Daddy" (quoted in Manvell, 201). Her first teacher-lover, the one who had known all along what she could be, was not a stern enough patriarch to suit the present age, an age in which no woman could afford to ignore her critics. Once she was grown, Ellen Terry realized that her father loved her too much for his opinion to count.

John Singer Sargent also understood Lady Macbeth, though he could paint her only by isolating her from Macbeth, from Irving, from the stage, and even from Shakespeare. Frenzied for power, exuding forbidden magic, Sargent's "Ellen Terry as Lady MacBeth" stands alone. Sargent's first sketch was compara-

John Singer Sargent, "Ellen Terry as Lady Macbeth." *Reproduced by permission of the Tate Gallery, London.*

tively decorative: encircled by bowing ladies, Lady Macbeth bursts out of her castle in a swirl of motion and drapery. After Ellen Terry had posed for some time, he discarded pageantry for the grand upward thrust of the single figure who, in defiance of Shakespeare's play, crowns herself with Napoleonic ardor.

"It was a satisfaction to me that some people saw what I was aiming at," Ellen Terry wrote. "Sargent saw it, and in his picture is all that I meant to do" (*Memoirs*, 233). But had she acted what Sargent painted, she would no longer have been womanly, for Sargent saw the undisguised rage for power within the exemplary wife. This Lady Macbeth gives no thought to her husband, transforming herself, as Irving did, into the author of her own majesty. In *Aurora Leigh*, Elizabeth Barrett Browning's epic of a female poet's development, Aurora begins her career by crowning herself with laurel leaves in a gesture of similar self-authorizing defiance. Both Aurora Leigh and Ellen Terry's Lady Macbeth emulate the avid self-consecration with which Napoleon snatched his own crown: "When Napoleon seized the crown from Pius VII at Rheims and placed it on his own head, he was attacking the most venerable patriarchy in Europe, substituting for an 'apostolic' descent of royal power a self-authorizing kingship . . ." In Ellen Terry's equally self-authorizing note, the Lady Macbeth Sargent sees unfurls herself: "There's such authority doth hedge a—'*Queen!*' " In Sargent's painting, Ellen Terry is neither Shakespeare's queen nor Irving's, for she rises into possession of her unsanctioned, forbidden, powerful self with a boldness she dreamed of but never realized. Watts had painted her into a pathetic heroine. Sargent, discerning her lust for forbidden roles, painted her into the triumph she could not act, though it encompassed "all that she meant to do."

For the duration of the painting, Lady Macbeth had a life beyond the Lyceum. When she descended on Tite Street in full costume to pose, Sargent's neighbor Oscar Wilde saw a self-complete and glorifying divinity like the Shakespearean characters into whom Ellen Terry hoped to die, come to make a myth of the street: "The street that on a wet and dreary morning has vouchsafed the vision of Lady Macbeth in full regalia magnificently seated in a four-wheeler can never again be as other streets: it must always be full of wonderful possibilities" (quoted in Manvell, 201). Even when she was gone, Wilde's house held visions of her, for Edward Godwin had decorated it with the help of James Whistler. When she posed for Sargent, Ellen Terry returned to the haunts of the artists who taught her to be a woman in the days before Irving incorporated their visions and her own artist-made self into his empire.

Her costume also recalled those early days of beauty and self-love. Alice

Comyns-Carr designed it: at Ellen Terry's insistence, she had replaced the usual ostentatious theatrical costumes with dresses Godwin might have made, simple, clinging, and crinkled, evoking the artful ease of the Grosvenor Gallery. Ellen Terry had always learned new selves from her costumes; this dress gave her her richest, most significant, if also her saddest, self. Alice Comyns-Carr made her a woman warrior steeped in pagan myth: "I was anxious to make this particular dress look as much like soft chain armour as I could, and yet have something that would give the appearance of the scales of a serpent" (quoted in Manvell, 198). Her dress, at least, played the dangerous Undine she could suggest but never be. To make it brilliant, "it was sewn all over with real green beetle-wings," which made Ellen Terry a creature who was militant, serpentine, and alien to the human species. The Everywoman she claimed to be playing was thrust by her dress into other, magical realms; she had no place in her play. As Oscar Wilde saw, the creature of Alice Comyns-Carr's imagination evoked a climate beyond the British Isles: "Judging from the banquet, Lady Macbeth seems an economical housekeeper, and evidently patronizes local industries for her husband's clothes and the servant's liveries; but she takes care to do all her own shopping in Byzantium" (quoted in Manvell, 198).

The lesson within Ellen Terry's Lady Macbeth dress was that it did not belong to Lady Macbeth. The costume dramatized, not the wife Ellen Terry tried to play, but her unspeakable alienation from that role and from the world of the Lyceum in which she moved. Her one faintly Scottish accessory was a blood-red cloak Irving quickly snatched for himself; without it, she glittered through the play like a creature from another sphere. Ellen Terry had tried to play the women in her audience, but Alice Comyns-Carr dramatized only the lost powers that possessed their souls; this serpent-woman looked like nothing they could recognize. Such a wife fit into no play. She came alive only when she was alone, not acting but telling herself to an artist, just as Watts's trusting bride had done.

If the beetle-winged dress fitted any role, its sinuous amalgam of serpent and Amazon belonged in Egypt, as Oscar Wilde saw: Shakespeare's Cleopatra, that elusive comic queen who becomes all things, might wear it with ease. "I could not see myself as the serpent of old Nile," Ellen Terry claimed (*Memoirs,* 231); her *Four Lectures* dismiss Cleopatra as a "wanton" and (the kiss of death) a pathetic heroine; but in Sargent's exultant portrait, the beetle-winged costume makes her a Cleopatra her own imagination dreamed and denied. She could express Irving's death only in Cleopatra's great wail of mourning and magnitude; Rosalind haunted her, but the serpent of old Nile possessed her despite herself. As with Virginia Woolf's Miss La Trobe, Cleopatra stirred her to a

Edward Gordon Craig, *Lady Macbeth. A Drawing, Theatre Arts Monthly,* 1928.

grand expression of her unacted part. The Lady Macbeth dress, and Sargent's crowning vision of its meaning, were definitive embodiments of Ellen Terry's disjunction from her assigned roles, and her grasp of a visionary mobility, an imperial comedy, beyond the boundaries of any stage she knew.

Gordon Craig's vast theatrical designs might imagine spaces large enough for his mother to play in; but in 1928, the year of her death, he defied her magnitude by dethroning Sargent's imperial serpent-queen. Craig's Lady Macbeth is a lunatic and a beggar, not a self-possessed, self-defining queen. In a letter to an actress, he lauds his drawing as an apotheosis of degradation:

> Now I am afraid I may horrify you by the drawing I've made of Lady M herself during her sleep-walking— . . . Because it's ugly. It makes her ugly — it makes her untidy — she slops along in straw slippers, slipped into night after night. She is not impressive, she is merely almost daft and uncouth.
> I've seen a woman of forty-five – grey, old-looking as eighty, walking as in sleep or plodding along – voice *husky* as that of a drunken man – growling continually like a dog: TRAGIC as a Shakespeare thing is tragic: As a Japanese ghost picture is tragic: . . . get some to look at.

And if I saw such a perfectly enchanting woman like Lady Macbeth of Act I changed to a horror of Act IV, I should feel I was looking at something Shakespearean.

This growling horror in straw slippers strips Ellen Terry's Lady Macbeth of both grandeur and recognizable humanity; moreover, in his cruelest stroke of art, Gordon Craig forces her to devolve back into Ophelia. Long ago, Irving had unnerved her by trying to transform her into Ophelia in the sleepwalking scene: "The hair to my mind should be wild and disturbed, and the whole appearance as distraught as possible, and disordered" (quoted in *Memoirs,* 233). In memory of his mother, Gordon Craig stripped off her beetle-winged dress, threw away her crown, and scorned Sargent's apotheosis to resurrect the sleepwalker Irving had told her to be. The woman who had lived with robust intensity only in her unacted parts was shattered into phantoms by her son and by men who felt themselves to be her sons.

Motherhood and Modernism

"THE WOMAN'S LOT OF PERPETUAL MOTHERHOOD." Even when he was young, Gordon Craig chewed at his past mercilessly in the same spirit with which he venerated long-dead theaters: things were grand to him only once they were lost. Ellen Terry let the past rest. Sometimes its intensity flashed into her memory and made her wistful. Once her life became dull she enjoyed reliving vivid experiences, but it never occurred to her to analyze them: she imagined her life not in a coherent sequence, but in scenes. Only once, in an undated scrap of a diary, was she driven to question what she had always thought she felt:

> Always loved a dog or a cat
> better than a doll. Maternal?
>
> Doll
>
> No. I think not.

By then, though, it didn't matter what she felt, because she had become a portrait of a mother in everybody's sight.

Motherhood had been her glory in Harpenden: the brilliant children were a mystic chorus to the wonders of nature and to her own wonders. When she returned to the theater and to London, and Godwin vanished from the household in which he had always been peripheral, motherhood sealed her new power: Edy and Ted provided the motive for a female household that ran itself happily, aesthetically, and as it liked. There was no authorizing, regulating paterfamilias: the domestic routine was arranged around the actress's eccentric schedule. After he became Gordon Craig, Teddy remembered with loathing and guilty longing the "house of women" that had possessed his little self: from Harpenden there were Boo, his mother's companion, and Bo, his own and Edy's nursemaid; then there were the grotesque governess Miss Harries; Mrs. Cole the schoolmistress; Edy and her friends; and of course Mother, who at once presided over, glorified, and evaded the domestic routine.

Longing for a father to assure him of his own manhood, Gordon Craig rebuilt this hated house of women over and over until his death at ninety-four; he was never without clusters of mistresses to coddle, support, and care for him; those who asked for support and care in return, like Isadora Duncan, were deftly replaced. When he grew up he learned that groups of women could be controlled and artfully humiliated, but the power of his mother's household remained inviolate to him. He sensed its retaliatory menace. Motherhood was the only power Henry Irving had not taken away from Ellen Terry, and to her children at least, she wielded it with ferocious grace.

These children, both (as their mother saw them) brooding so oddly on their gender, learned from her about the sorts of power they could claim. Invaded by women, Teddy turned to the Lyceum, Irving's patriarchal kingdom, for a grandiose display of male autocracy. Edy was enthralled with her fatherless childhood home. It made male authority unreal to her forever: Ellen Terry shielded her daughter with her own grand person from the wearing experience of subordination. For Edy, women were the reality of the world, even if women made her own world smaller and smaller as the years passed.

Had there been no Edy and Ted, men would have venerated Ellen Terry as a mother nevertheless, for Victorian women, no matter how unorthodox their lives, were enmeshed inextricably in the imagery of family; even childless women who had earned authority were most safely revered as a peculiar species of mother. In the 1890s, George Bernard Shaw and W. Graham Robertson vied with each other in their worship of Ellen Terry as their own private mother goddess; when, in 1907, the fifty-nine-year-old actress married James Carew, who was more than twenty years younger than she, she acted the myth of a new and passionately filial generation of men. But none of these men cared how she brought up her children: Edy and Ted were fractious irritants to be gotten out of the way so that they themselves could strew incense on Ellen Terry's maternity. Her role as a mother was impersonal, aggrandizing, and infinitely reassuring as well to men who coped with powerful women only by calling them maternal. Her actual children, abrasive and inglorious, impeded the rituals she inspired.

But whatever men wanted of her, Edy and Ted were her intensest life. Unlike many actresses, she never secreted her children away to protect her age or her image; she displayed them proudly, even compulsively, until they left her, or tried to. When they were off at school, she wrote and talked about them; when they were too old to trail in her wake, she secured for them small parts at the Lyceum. Their constant presence in Irving's empire gave her her own proud plot of ground; she was fortified by the two brilliant hostages from the house of women she directed in a quiet counterpoint to his kingdom. Moreover, Edy and Ted were the banners of her early rebellion: their open illegitimacy was her boast while it festered as their shame, especially Ted's. These rarities were proof of the integrity, the creative energy, the Lyceum was draining away. They also testified to her male self, for like a proper Victorian father, she was prepared to give the world to her own. In giving them the Lyceum, she tried to do so. Was it her fault that the world frightened them?

In 1884, she spread out America for Ted. Ill and lonely during the second of the Lyceum's epic American tours, she suddenly cabled loyal, stuffy Stephen Coleridge to "bring over one of the children." She must have known Stephen would choose Teddy, for he was her son's appointed guardian. Unhappy everywhere, the twelve-year-old boy was ecstatic at being lifted out of school and into glory. Was Teddy chosen over the older, more independent Edy as a compensation for his lost legacy, as a tribute to his superiority as a boy, or in an attempt to heal something wrong within him? Gordon Craig never heard the lurid story of parental rejection, in which his mother *"had offered to let [Godwin] have the boy,"* only to see the father refuse his son in his mad lunge at the daughter who hated him. Somehow though, that unknown episode contained the poison that seeped through Gordon Craig's privileged life. In the new world that was supposed to sweep him beyond this past, he found all the blessings Ellen Terry had to give.

In the America his mother arranged for him, Teddy realized for the first time how irresistible he was. At his hotel in Pittsburgh, little girls in captivating pinafores fluttered around the boy who "looked like a peach," but he held himself temptingly aloof. In Chicago, he was given his first speaking part with the Lyceum Company—Joey the gardener's boy in the first act of *Eugene Aram* —and had his first set of theatrical photographs taken. *Index to the Story of My Days,* the bilious memoir that appeared when he was eighty-five, reproduces a photograph of the angelic child with a hoe who gazes intently at an unseen spot in the distance beyond the frame; the boy's soft, sardonic superiority taunts the viewer who is too limited to follow the child's gaze.

Crude and enthusiastic, Ellen Terry's America roused Teddy to his first awareness of the glorified self that vindicated and solaced his embattled life. But years later, when he was floundering and fighting with everybody, his mother urged him to take his iconoclastic designs to technologically sophisticated producers in the new world; despite the proud excitement of his tour with her, he refused to return to America.

In 1904, Gordon Craig left England forever and burrowed into a succession of venerable cities and ancient villages. His one indisputable theatrical achievement, the *Hamlet* he staged for Stanislavsky's Moscow Art Theatre in 1912, grew out of a pre-revolutionary Russia remote in every way from America's aggressive modernity. America's power was tangled in his mind with the power of his mother. Italy, the only country where he claimed to feel at home, was too disordered and impoverished to support Gordon Craig or his theaters, but he could dream that his father's elusive legacy was bestowed on him there at last: he was living in the country Edward Godwin's meticulous Shakespearean reconstructions had attempted to restore bit by bit. He could never control his mother's power as he had seen it unmediated in America. Shaw and others might adore that power, but it had seared Teddy too intimately for him to be anything other than a refugee from its country.

He was right to imagine America as an emanation of Ellen Terry: when the Lyceum was beginning to fossilize and thwart her, when she was too depressed and tired to want to act, she was roused by the dynamic new world Irving's kings and heroes could not rule. Her paean to the Brooklyn Bridge as an idea beyond human imagination might be a tribute to the designs of Gordon Craig: "There were no trolly cars on it then. I shall never forget how it looked in winter, with the snow and ice on it—a gigantic trellis of dazzling white, as incredible as a dream. The old stone bridges were works of *art*. This bridge, woven of iron and steel for a length of over 500 yards, and hung high in the air over the water so that great ships can pass beneath it, is the work of *science*. It looks as if it had been built by some power, not by men at all" (*Memoirs*, 216). So does the art of Gordon Craig. It was reasonable to imagine that he would flourish in this wealthy country that loved monumental, inhuman machines, but since his mother had put him there, he would not dream his dream there.

For Ellen Terry, as for many English citizens, including the expatriated Henry James, enlightened America at the turn of the century appeared to be a country of women. As in her own household, women clustered freely together, with no need to apologize to male authorities. When she played in Boston, she exchanged affectionate visits with Sarah Orne Jewett and Annie Fields, whose "Boston marriage" (as New Englanders discreetly called it) was the center of a household more unapologetically female than her own. The journalist Joseph Hatton analyzed the un-English excitement with which New England women received her:

> She captivated the women, all of them. It is easier for a clever woman to excite the admiration of her sex in America than in England. A woman who adorns and lifts the feminine intellect into notice in America excites the admiration rather than the jealousy of her sisters. American women seem to make a higher claim upon the respect and attention of men than belongs to the ambitious English women, and when one of them rises to distinction they all go up with her. They share in her fame; they do not try to dispossess her of the lofty place upon which she stands. There is a sort of trades-unionism among the women of America in this respect. They hold together in a ring against the so-called lords of creation, and the men are content to accept what appears to be a happy form of petticoat government. So the women of Boston took Ellen Terry to their arms and made much of her.

This trades union of talented women who relished his mother with a stinging indifference to masculine superiority may have given Teddy a disturbing revelation of the community his own home was on the verge of becoming. In America, the powers the Lyceum forced Ellen Terry to suppress expanded alarmingly, and so did the power of her motherhood. Even Edy learned this later on: when she joined her mother on the tense 1895 tour, after the Lyceum had begun to come apart, their feverish relationship came to a dangerous crisis. America brought out the frightening force that had always been hidden in Ellen Terry's motherhood, a fury Englishmen were better equipped to subdue because their country had lived with mothers for so long.

Englishmen adored mothers as long as they had no selves. As Victorian culture celebrated it, motherhood was the sacrificial essence of womanhood, not a biological fact or a particular relationship with real children. Their native altruism made mothers of all women: innate unselfishness diluted a mother's power. When Gordon Craig was not lashing out in print at his dead mother's mistakes in raising him, he hymned her idealized, all-giving memory in true Victorian fashion. His "Annex" to *Ellen Terry and Her Secret Self* attacks Shaw's unchivalrousness in publishing the private letters of so helplessly tender a woman:

E.T. was one of those motherly women—and there are more than a few, though perhaps few who possess a richer fund of love to give to others. It is a wonder how these great ladies—spite of their own troubles, of which they have enough —are able to strengthen all those men who once arouse their deep sympathy. . . . all's one to such wonderful women, for the simple reason that to them we are all of us just children—and the naughty ones are often preferable to the good. All we have to do is to pout, and they love us.

G.B.S. pouted ever so pretty, and so E.T. "loved" him. (Annex, *ETSS*, 14–15)

Craig's "Nelly's House – The Theatre Itself" elevates this beacon of a mother into the guardian of the entire British populace: "E.T. belonged to a large group of public servants whose duty it was to look after the British Public. It was so different in those days to these – for she felt she had a responsibility – the Public in a sense were her children, to be helped a bit."

From the time her son was little, Ellen Terry knew that his adoration was a way of denying her. In the year of her death, Gordon Craig met his old schoolmaster from Heidelberg College, the school from which he had been expelled at sixteen. Had he listened, he would have received a lesson from the dead. The schoolmaster remembered speaking to Ellen Terry "about my 'progress' & then said 'Your son worships you' & she replied 'no – the mother he worships is in Heaven' – & I find it so unusual that he should have remembered this so exactly." Ellen Terry's sophisticated self-assertion was rare in Victorian mothers, but Teddy's sort of worship was common: many men worshipped their mothers, and mothers in general, in order to send them to Heaven while they were very much alive. Even if they were not famous actresses, they might become too powerful if they were not shrouded in celestial selflessness. The most conventional guides to Victorian women exalted maternal power in potentially subversive language, though their ideal mothers veiled themselves reassuringly in altruistic attitudes. Isabella Beeton's indispensable *Book of Household Management* begins by encouraging the wife who studies it to glorify herself: "She ought always to remember that she is the first and the last, the Alpha and the Omega in the government of her establishment; and that it is by her conduct that its whole internal policy is regulated. She is, therefore, a person of far more importance in a community than she usually thinks she is. On her pattern her daughters model themselves; by her counsels they are directed; through her virtues all are honoured;—'her children rise up and call her blessed; her husband also, and he praiseth her.' "

Writers like Isabella Beeton exhorted mothers to see themselves as towering over society, reducing fathers to passively praising children. Legally, fathers controlled the family finances, activities, and destiny as absolutely as Irving controlled the Lyceum, but mothers were credited with mystic power over souls. Gordon Craig had no father to show him the limits of that power: it burned into him unmediated. Night after night, he watched his mother engorge audiences, even when she fooled or acted pathetic. In the theater, she was under Irving's jurisdiction, but in her own household, Ellen Terry was truly the Alpha and the Omega Isabella Beeton claimed that all women had the potential to become.

A mother's power was exalted and obliterated at the same time. Victorian novelists acted out social confusions, more often than not refusing to grant a mother tangible existence. Dickens's good mothers are generally fading or dead. In his own household, Dickens continued to believe that motherhood was a role of magical power and human nullity: he vehemently denied his participation in the incessant pregnancies of his unloved wife. They were her own doing entirely, a trick to distract him from his work. In the twentieth century, Gordon Craig adopted Dickens's creed with a Bohemian twist: compulsively impregnat-ing many mistresses and one wife, he found in his swarms of children excuses to desert the mothers who perversely made them. This peculiar mythmaking exalts a mother's power beyond biology into witchery, but it does so to bar the real woman from the male world of significant concerns.

In novels, the traditional courtship plot ends with the heroine's marriage: she is a mother only in some limbo beyond the story. Women writers did not challenge the convention of maternal invisibility. They kept mothers out of sight not because they feared maternal power, as so many men did, but because motherhood was a dispiriting emblem of the loss of power, the fading out of self, from which they tried to guard their heroines: for the most part, mother-hood was the unquestioned destiny, not the choice, of women whose lives were prescribed from childhood. Few chose it with the enthusiastic awareness of possibilities that Ellen Terry felt in her fallen years, and women, like men, wanted to read about that time of life when choices are possible and the future is a tantalizing mystery.

Charlotte Brontë's Jane Eyre and Elizabeth Barrett Browning's Aurora Leigh are two intrepid culture heroines who have only the wariest association with mothers. Both are tormented by monstrously obstructive foster mothers who strain to break the heroines' spirits in the service of femininity. Both are inspired by the dead mothers whose spirits offer mystic inspiration in moments of crisis: the task of each is to elude her restraining mother-on-earth so that she may achieve the stature of her invisible mother-in-Heaven. Neither Jane nor Aurora becomes a mother herself until after her story fades beyond excitement: they are intrepid and solitary travelers when the reader knows them. Their stories warn women implicitly that mothers are at best fitful and invisible presences in life's significant pilgrimages.

In relation to her own mother Sarah, Ellen Terry accepted this warning, but she knew too that unwed mothers exuded a powerful charm precisely because it was less easy for them to be relegated to Heaven. To official moralists, they were loathsome outcasts; to liberal philanthropists, they were appealing victims; but they could be heroes in art. Their motherhood entailed no meek acquiescence in a common destiny: it was a gesture of ennobling defiance. In *Aurora Leigh,* the violated working girl Marian Erle expands into grandeur when she has an illegitimate child: even the awesomely aloof heroine learns to worship her. Ordinary mothers had done what they were told, but women who trespassed into unwed motherhood were aggrandized—at least to many artists— by their bold and self-defining choice of a destiny. In Ford Madox Brown's powerful "Take Your Son, Sir!" an angry and inviolate fallen woman demands that her lover acknowledge his child. In most novels, mothers float over the action like spirits, but though Brown's fallen mother has the halo of a Madonna, her maternity is aggressively biological: the arrangement of her drapery gives her the air of plucking her child from her womb. The mirror that exalts this audacious creature into a gigantic Madonna frees her from male authorization: its reflection so dwarfs her lover that he could not possibly obey the title's command, for his baby is bigger than he is. This fallen woman is a monument of physical and spiritual power unalloyed by the self-renouncing selflessness of ordinary mothers: the child that is supposed to shame her licenses her dominion.

Ellen Terry, who learned herself from Pre-Raphaelite art, thrust Edy and Ted at the world with the physical and spiritual bravado of Ford Madox Brown's fallen Madonna. She too dwarfed the men who were supposed to support, possess, and govern her children: like the cottages she bought, Edy and Ted gave her an empire to rival Irving's. When she was young, they intensified her mobility by endowing her with new, infinitely interesting identities that were at once alien and her own: if she ruled them well, they might reconcile the male and female roles that warred for possession of her own performance, tearing her life apart. For ordinary women, motherhood was a commandment to self-suppression, but Edy and Ted, nameless and unlicensed, promised infinite expansion. Her children possessed her like the characters she played, and with the imaginative intensity she used onstage, she took them into herself.

As she grew older, they gave her an anchor in time that she desperately needed; without them, she was in danger of forgetting how old she was. Like all actresses and many women, Ellen Terry feared aging into diminished roles,

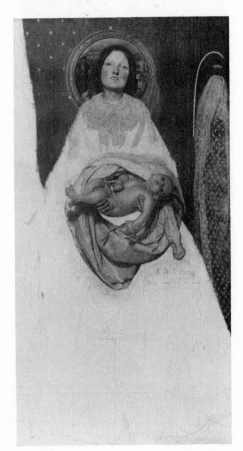

Ford Madox Brown, *Take Your Son, Sir! Reproduced by permission of the Tate Gallery, London.*

but in the nineties, the mad fluctuations of her age at the Lyceum were more disorienting than the natural changes that came with the years. After her death, an obituary notice in the *Philadelphia Inquirer* quoted her suspicion that her life "in some way [seemed] to have passed as a dream." She goes on to dream her actual onstage development: "If I had devised creation, I would have had everybody born old and year by year grow younger, finally to pass away in innocent infancy."

In a sense, the actress really was born old, to grow younger and more innocent year by year. She was always slightly unsynchronized with her official self, for she was a year older than she knew. The stage child, though, had been mercurial and shrewd, freer than the adults she laughed at and controlled. When, at thirty-one, the woman was growing into self-delighted strength, she became fixed in the public mind as the innocent Olivia; thereafter, even when she evolved into stage motherhood, she grew younger and sweeter as the years passed. Her roles embalmed her in virginal youth or childlike old age, allowing her to be anything but the rich and powerful woman she was. Edy and Ted redeemed her stunted performances by embodying the powers and prerogatives of her real age.

At forty, she became Ellaline in *The Amber Heart,* who can survive only as an emotional baby: growing up drives her mad, and with the audience's tearful approval, she reverts to childish babble at the end of her play. She had already become *Faust*'s achingly innocent Margaret, who in similarly approved fashion grows up only to be driven mad. Ellen Terry's *Faust* annotations translate Margaret's emotions into a reverie whose faintly self-mocking simplicity verges on baby talk. When Margaret is falling in love, the actress writes:

Happy

Just satisfied, <u>pleased</u>.

comfortable—at more

Content—

ease — In the <u>domestic</u>
speeches losing thought of
who it is she is speaking to

unconscious-

until Faust kisses her hand.

In the climactic love scene, she scrawls all over the page in increasingly swollen letters: "Happy - Happy - H A P P Y ' ' ; "Happy - Heaven - Certainty." Her final H A P P Y is written in letters so huge that they dissolve into cloud-like squiggles. When Margaret dies penitent on her final line, Ellen Terry directs herself to "shriek like a <u>child</u>!" While Irving as Mephistophelean actor-manager vaunted his transcendence of human limits, Ellen Terry reverted contrapuntally to pre-consciousness and pre-adulthood; her implausible childishness tempered audiences' fears that Irving was more than man. The child's Puck had never been as determinedly infantile as the woman's Margaret.

Only a year or so after *The Amber Heart,* Irving bestowed on Ellen Terry the actress's kiss of death: he cast her as a mother, and moreover a mother to her own son, wrenching her from babyishness to maternity with just a scrap of a life in between: "Here I was in the very noonday of life, fresh from Lady Macbeth and still young enough to play Rosalind, suddenly called upon to play a rather uninteresting mother in 'The Dead Heart' " (*Memoirs,* 235). Mother-hood, which was to glorify her in life, drained her to a lovable shadow on the stage: her act of loving, self-extending defiance became her professional doom.

In 1893, she and Gordon Craig starred in the sprightly Lyceum curtain-raiser, Charles Reade's *Nance Oldfield,* a sentimental improvisation on the life of the great eighteenth-century actress. Gordon Craig, a poetic youth, pours romantic devotion on the star, who teases him out of love by playing hoydenish tricks —the very sorts of tricks that had won love for Ellen Terry in her early years —persuading him to write a play for her instead of wooing her. The pseudo-filial reverence Gordon Craig poured on his mother onstage anticipated the prolix passion of George Bernard Shaw, who had sent her his first letter the year before. When, in 1895, their epistolary duet began in earnest, Shaw seems to have learned from *Nance Oldfield* exactly what kind of stage son to play to Ellen Terry's wise and winsome cosmic mother. Shaw called Reade's play "wicked frivolity," but it was not the only time he would steal his characters from the Victorian drama he pretended to despise, nor was it the only role he would snatch from Gordon Craig. His *Candida* recasts Reade's rueful love story between a feverishly aesthetic youth and a mother-figure who is a fountain of generous, bittersweet wisdom. His letters dictate that Ellen Terry meet his own youthful ardor with Candida's tender restraint, but after disciplining her for the role, he withheld it from her onstage.

It seemed to others natural for Ellen Terry to pass from Irving's innocent daughter in *Olivia* to Gordon Craig's all-giving mother in *The Dead Heart* and *Nance Oldfield:* at the Lyceum as in middle-class culture, dutiful daughters guaranteed the primacy of fathers, while self-renouncing mothers paid tribute to the grandeur of sons. Only a few women were beginning to complain that they were allowed no life in between these two cramping, inescapable roles. When, "in the very noonday of life," Ellen Terry found herself playing "a rather uninteresting mother," that role preserved her in audiences' eyes from disruptive adventures and sexual aggression. It also preserved the synthetic youth the Lyceum had given, for loving mothers, like good daughters, had renounced the capacity for growth.

After 1890, lovers of Ellen Terry were delighted to applaud a mother who was at the same time unchangingly young: her stage childhood had allowed her to leap over the boundaries that enclosed the lives of proper little girls, but her stage motherhood shut her out of the life cycle. Shaw was only the most articulate of the sons who adopted her as their all-powerful, baby-talking, virginal Madonna. In 1906, he commemorated her jubilee with a poem celebrat-ing her immunity from a change that might let her outgrow her role:

Oh, Ellen was it kind of Fate
To make your youth so thrifty
That you are young at fifty-eight
Whilst we are old at fifty?

Though for our sakes you strive to seem
A tiny little older—
To be the woman of our dream
Yet leave our grandsons colder,

They love you too. Change plays its part
In every known direction
Save your imperishable art
And our unchanged affection.

Ellen Terry and Edward Gordon Craig in *Nance Oldfield.*

> Joy be for ever by your side
> And roses all your bedding!
> Our stage could have no dearer bride
> To grace its golden wedding.

Graham Robertson was another self-adopted son, but one less voracious than Shaw: he comforted, cherished, and babied the actress as she aged and grew sad. Nevertheless, his memoir ends with a tribute to an Ellen Terry identical to Shaw's, one who is fixed beyond life's cycle:

> My friendship with Ellen Terry thus passed through several phases. We began, of course, as the Goddess and the Little Boy: not that Miss Terry ever considered herself a goddess, but I naturally regarded her in that light. Then I became a bigger boy and was admitted to a greater intimacy, though still, very properly, "kept in my place." Then I caught her up and for a glamorous few years we were contemporaries; discussing things together from the same age-point, having "larks" together as two young people with high spirits and a sense of humour. Then I began to draw away from her; my years increased, hers did not. I became almost respected. Finally I settled down into the old Family Solicitor, sent for in moments of difficulty, consulted on family and other matters and confided in generally. (*Life Was Worth Living*, 338)

This was not all. Ellen Terry did initially float across his vision as an unearthly golden Portia whose glory aroused the collector, but within twenty years she was clinging to him as she never did to Shaw, yielding up her growing madness and sadness to his imperturbable solace. Above all her adoring pseudo-sons, Graham Robertson witnessed the devastation of the real woman within the static Ellen Terry he commemorated, but he could not believe in the woman he comforted.

Both Shaw and Robertson evoke an Ellen Terry who is ageless and magically young, immune from the developmental cycle that governs men. Like the transcendent sorceress in Rider Haggard's *She,* which was published just when the cult of Ellen Terry was reaching its zenith in 1887, this imagined woman incarnates extremes of age and youth; she is divorced from the natural rhythms within which men mature and die. In 1892, at a banquet in the Beefsteak Room, Sarah Bernhardt claimed as woman's divine right this magic immunity from time: "Over the supper-table in the Beefsteak Room that night talk turned on age, and the effect it had on acting. Irving remarked sadly that old age must come to us all, but Sarah, leaning over the table to Nell, said, 'My darling, there are two people who shall never be old - you and I.' "

Bernhardt, who ruled so effortlessly and absolutely, made agelessness a blessing, for she had lost no selves. No one made her an uninteresting mother: she would play Phèdre, Marguerite Gauthier, the boy Zanetto, and the nineteen-year-old Joan of Arc until her death at seventy-eight. Ellen Terry had lost the boy-self of her childhood; all other losses followed from that. Denied the comic freedom of maturity, she could never forget that she had aged, and she bled for everything age had taken away. To be frozen into the young-old self she was becoming meant exile from everything she wanted to be. Sarah's transfiguration was Ellen Terry's blight. Bernhardt's triumphant assurance that she would never be old was part of the isolating inhumanity Ellen Terry analyzed:

> On the stage she has always seemed to me more a symbol, an ideal, an epitome, than a *woman*. It is this quality which makes her so easy in such lofty parts as Phèdre. She is always a miracle. Let her play "L'Aiglon," and while matter-of-fact members of the audience are wondering if she looks *really* like the unfortunate King of Rome, and deciding against her in favour of Maude Adams who did look the part to perfection, more imaginative spectators see in Sarah's performance a truth far bigger than a mere physical resemblance.
>
> It is this extraordinary decorative and symbolic quality of Sarah's which makes her transcend all personal and individual feeling on the stage. No one plays a love scene better, but it is a *picture* of love that she gives, a strange exotic picture rather than a suggestion of the ordinary human passion as felt by ordinary human people. She is exotic—well, what else should she be? One does not, at any rate one should not, quarrel with an orchid and call it unnatural because it is not a buttercup or a cowslip. (*Memoirs,* 168–69)

Ellen Terry's popular consecration brought her into a complicity with "ordinary human people," with men's dreams and women's disappointments, that autocratic actresses like Bernhardt transcended utterly. Clement Scott must have thought he was being kind when he wrote of her, "Women who have inspired men with love, or loyalty, or homage, or respect, should never be allowed to grow old," but just because she had inspired so many men, Ellen Terry knew that Scott's blessing had cursed her. She did not want to grow old, but she did want to grow. Her children would have to grow up for her.

She could always play the dear little woman audiences saw, though her performances teetered ever more dangerously toward scorching self-parody. Even more than her own hungry son, Shaw lusted for the perfect mother. When she feared, rightly, that she was losing him, she played her trump card without hesitation: "With your 3 (or 30?) love affairs on, and the Fabian, and the *Saturday* and the etc. etc. etc., you must be full up and it's not my moment. I'll wait until you 'need' me, and then I'll mother you. That's the only unselfish love. I've never been admired or loved (properly) but one-and-a-half times in my life, and I am perfectly sick of loving. All on one side isn't fair." Shamelessly, she concluded: "Goodbye child" (13 October 1896. *A Corr.,* 75).

Mothers were supposed to be unselfish, and she was trying not only to make this bold young man love her, but to wheedle his *Candida* from Janet Achurch. As he had described it to her, it was "THE Mother Play"; it was also (perhaps: he had not let her read it) the perfect vehicle for a career beyond the Lyceum. Her winning declaration of unselfish love was an audition for a part Shaw would not let her win, no matter how well she played it. By 1896, she was adjusting to the realization that offstage as well, the rewards motherhood had promised could not be won, for the better, the more altruistically, she played, the more humiliation lay in store: her son's omnivorous demands were becoming frightening, while Edy's every gesture toward independence hid a knife. Accordingly, while pouring out material indulgences, she unleashed a surprising savagery toward the children who could neither go nor stay, a savagery that had been growing from the beginning of their lives. It was directed against her own thwarting, all-giving mother-role as well as against her children.

She had always talked about motherhood in two voices. Writing to Elizabeth Winter, whose son has died, she hymns an angel-mother and a dream child, but when her own, vigorously living children enter the letter, so does cutting ironic disapproval:

> but Lizzie darling girl give [the surviving children] the happiness of being able to look back & remember their mother at her best — pretty & bright — for you are so pretty my dear when you are bright for a while — & so dear all ways you must be to those who know you even a little = I love you Lizzie so. I love you dearly - & I pray for you - but you can't care for that can you? I care - & do & hope & hope I ever may - Some day you'll see your Angel-boy again — who knows, perhaps in Viola or the others --- but if you count him gone he'll never come - Lizzie sweet Lizzie be strong & be pretty for the sake of Willie & the children — but oh, I feel for you & with you— . . . The children are home & are very good & well & Ted grown in 6 weeks wonderfully tall — I wish his brain developed! Edie has tried her very best I'm sure at her "exam," & I will try to be content even if she does not "pass" —

The pretty mother of a dead child is to live lovingly for others, keeping faith in heavenly reunions. The flesh-and-blood mother of children who are all too vividly alive is galled by faults and failures. Confronted with Edy and Ted's dependencies and demands, which became more clamorous as they grew, Ellen

Terry had more and more trouble believing in herself as a mother at all. In life as on the stage, she was not the woman she played.

She subverted her own associations with the role by fooling, just as she had fooled to evade her own mother when she was a boy/girl. Writing to Graham Robertson of his own adored mother, with whom he lived in unsullied intimacy until she died when he was forty-one, she casts herself and Graham as irrepressible children. She will not share the stage with the authoritative Mrs. Robertson: "I am extra sorry about not coming tomorrow because of your Mother being with you= Her presence would perhaps have made us behave a little more proper-like---(No - I don't believe that by the way!!)" Fallen and in Harpenden, she had thrown herself into unwed motherhood with triumphant ardor, but now that the role was "proper" and was closing in on her, the idea of herself as a mother became too funny to bear.

In 1906, three months after her jubilee, her stage life circled back to its origin: she appeared in *The Winter's Tale* once more. In 1856, she had played for the Keans the pert little boy Mamillius who dies offstage too soon. In Beerbohm Tree's lavish production, she played Hermione, the stricken mother and nobly suffering queen. Hermione was not technically her last prominent role, but with the exception of a nostalgic cameo as Juliet's Nurse in 1919, Tree's *Winter's Tale* was her last major London production: thereafter she appeared primarily on her own tours and in quasi-amateur performances. Her evolution in *Winter's Tale* from boy to martyred queen recapitulated her career.

Hermione is crowned by the injured dignity that characterizes Shakespeare's later heroines. Like Imogen in *Cymbeline,* she is a martyr to the mad jealousy of a husband to whom she is a paragon of loving faith throughout her ordeal. Finally, presumed dead, she is consecrated beyond suffering and time by becoming a work of art. Her loyal serving-maid unveils a statue of her which comes alive to bless the kneeling company: her forgiving benediction heals and unites her lost daughter and her penitent husband.

Of all Shakespeare's women, Hermione comes closest to the unselfish, all-healing mother of Victorian convention. As with the image of Ellen Terry, a magical art preserves her from time and change. Suffering makes her more queenly still; in her apotheosis as a statute, she exudes the still wizardry with which the pictorial actress had irradiated the Lyceum. It was a perfect valediction for Ellen Terry. One critic was sufficiently awed by the ending to write: "Miss Viola Tree [as Perdita] need not fear that we shall accuse her of superstition when she kneels and implores Hermione's blessing, for we see Ellen Terry not only as a great actress, and a great personality, but as a great religion" (quoted in *Memoirs,* 284–85).

But in 1906, Ellen Terry was almost sixty, and weary of blessing people. She

Ellen Terry as Hermione in *The Winter's Tale*, 1906. *Reproduced by permission of the Furness Collection, Van Pelt Library, University of Pennsylvania.*

had wanted to be a powerful mother, not a forgiving one. She had wanted to make art, and art was paralyzing her. She did not feel graceful and gracious, but awkward and hampered. With some shame and more pride, she told Graham Robertson that she had subverted Hermione's apotheosis, if not her own: "A dreadful thing - I laughed last night!! as the statue! & I'm laughing now! Who cd help it! With Leontes shouting & Paulina shouting they just roared so I cd not help it! ∿∿∿∿ oh, Graham I was rather glad — for I've not been able to laugh at all lately (& that's downright **w i c k e d**) but I'm so afraid I may do it again if they will shout!!— You see (as a statue) I don't look at 'em - I only hear them - & it's excruciatingly funny= I'm mad at myself—"

Laughter had been her weapon against pathos; now it became her weapon against the veneration of mothers, a form of worship which in the supposedly sophisticated new century was taking on a feverish intensity. Her laughter did not dispel her ardent, silly worshippers, nor did it convey the absurdity of a mercurial artist enshrined as a statue. No laughter could restore the roles she had lost. Perdita in *The Winter's Tale,* the lost princess turned shepherdess, a sweeter version of the pastoral arranger Rosalind in *As You Like It,* symbolized those lost roles. Mobile, outspoken, something of a nature goddess, Perdita contains the ardor and the audacity of new-blown womanhood; Shakespeare has her preside over the middle of the play. Both *Winter's Tale* and Ellen Terry's London career began with Mamillius and ended with an all-transfiguring Hermione. She had missed Perdita as she had missed the center of her stage life. As a darling child and an ageless, consecrating queen, this womanly actress made herself "a great religion," but *Winter's Tale* was a reminder that she had only rarely and fitfully played a woman. The lost space in the middle of the play was the emblem of her unacted parts.

When she was real, ritual maternal benedictions alternated with protests against her role, just as they did when she was a statue. She directed her most scorching protests to the men in the family. After she died, these men recreated her as a self-sacrificial darling who existed only to love them, but her letters deny the statue her descendants worshipped. While she was working on her womanly Lady Macbeth and brooding about her own womanliness, she wrote impatiently to unstable young Teddy: "I should love to have you home here for the holidays but I fear I cannot - must not - for it will be just in the thick of my work & I want <u>helpers</u>, instead of children who <u>need</u> help. The quicker you mature my dearest lad the better." In wounded revenge, Teddy never did.

To the next Teddy, Edward Anthony Craig, Gordon Craig's favorite son and spiritual heir, she wrote with an affection laced with the same anger. By then, she was "Granny" to her son's flocks of children, for whose support he had made her responsible: instead of motherhood ending like a role in a play, there always seemed to be more of it. Now the children's children were having babies: "Did I send the news that Rosy [Gordon Craig's first child] has got a big boy baby? he is called <u>David</u> Le Brasseur = Rosy thinks he's lovely but I shd rather say, <u>a fine male specimen!!</u> So far he doesn't squall <u>much</u> & I don't see much of him — I like babies when they are more grown up! . . . I wonder what you will be settling down to soon? Easel pictures are not much over the land = I shd like you to be an <u>Architect</u> so much—to apprentice you to a man like Mr. Tipping of 'Country Life,' for a couple of years, to see how you liked it = It wd help you anyhow very much with your drawing=------<u>& you are</u>

getting on!! [Edward Craig was then fourteen]."

The son and son's sons who wrote about "Granny" as a fountain of nourishing love forgot the note of sardonic complaint that defined the woman who did not think herself maternal; they cherished only the statue's generous largesse. Her suggestion that this new Teddy become an architect carries an implicit wish that he revert back into Edward Godwin, so that Granny might return to the time when motherhood was a brave self-declaration, not a thankless performance in a play that never ended.

As the role engulfed her, her own denied mother began to haunt her. Gordon Craig remembered a surreal moment when she garbled a speech from *Robespierre* into beginning: "I never had a mother, Mr. Vaughan" (*ETSS,* 150). In a sense, though, she had garbled biological absurdity into confession, for Sarah Terry had never been real to her. Like those fiery heroines of fiction, Jane Eyre and Aurora Leigh, Ellen Terry might have envisioned a true, inspiring mother in Heaven, but the actual mother who had done her best to trim her into social acceptability had been a figure to evade. Ellen Terry had been her father's girl from birth: only Ben had urged her beyond decorum and into her own powers. Yet when he died in 1895, she did not say good-bye with one of her characteristic dashing obituaries. Perhaps because she knew she had disappointed him when she became good, she said, as far as we know, nothing at all; she rehearsed *Cymbeline* and threw herself into her letters to Shaw.

It had been different in 1892, when Sarah died: she had so fallen apart that she needed a leave of absence from the Lyceum. When she returned, Irving solicitously filled her dressing room with daffodils "to make it look like sunshine" (*Memoirs,* 260). In her time of mourning for the mother she had never accepted, she reappraised the sisters she had taken for granted: her womanly role was leading her to see women newly. Her mother's death became a test of her own and her sisters' strength. She assumed at first that she and Kate were the strong ones, as they had been in childhood, and described accordingly to Ella and Nella Casella the communal deathwatch that gathered around their mother:

> The last 2 hours there has been a kind of crisis, & any of us who are strong are useful now & again to turn her over.
>
> Kate has gone away for awhile, as she is the chief night watcher, & I am much stronger than either Marion or Floss, & dare not leave until Kate comes back.

When it was over though, Sarah's death taught Ellen that all the Terry women were strong:

My poor little Floss was so broken up—but she & Marion too—are magnificent in hard times—they are not only sunshine women. Little Floss for 7 hours without moving on her knees, & with her little white wax fingers moistening the poor lips—& speaking cheerfully to her of the children.

What one can go through with, without bursting! (Quoted in Steen, 215)

In 1892, motherhood was beginning to determine Ellen Terry's own identity, onstage and off, as it would do for the rest of her life. Just when she might have learned from Sarah, that powerful, proper, opaque woman died, abandoning her wildest daughter to a role she had never prepared. Her death was an occasion to celebrate her legacy of strength. Ellen Terry was primed to value Sarah's sort of strength because she was realizing how much women had to give up.

Ellen Terry's relationship to her sisters—and to Fred, the single successful brother—had always had a competitive edge. At the Lyceum, she was a model of self-effacing, unambitious service, but in the family, she had no need to act good. She had scarcely taken the younger girls into account during her turbulent years: they had been secluded in boarding school learning to be well-bred. They gained focus when they evaded the proper marriages they had been raised to aspire toward and followed their older sisters to the stage; they also came alive as possible rivals. The shared strength Ellen Terry commemorated at their mother's deathbed did not let the sisters trust each other easily.

Florence was the undisputed favorite because she was the gayest and the kindest. She was also, like Beth in Louisa May Alcott's _Little Women,_ the least ambitious: she obligingly supported Ellen as Nerissa in _The Merchant of Venice,_ toured with Charles Kelly after Ellen had discarded him, and stood in for both Marion and Ellen when they called on her. After her marriage, she moved cheerfully into amateur productions. Like Beth, she loved family life and enjoyed waiting on her brilliant sisters, and like Beth she died young. When peritonitis caused by premature childbirth killed her in 1896, a humanizing spirit left the circle, but its strength survived.

Marion Terry, withheld, self-contained and understated, absorbed all her boarding-school lessons: Ellen was a disheveled queen, but Marion made herself memorable playing titled ladies. Fastidious spectators like Kate's daughter Kate Terry Gielgud dubbed Marion the true Terry of the age, for she had discipline and refinement; but Sir John Gielgud has always written of his great aunt Ellen with a shrewd respect for her primacy, onstage and in the family. It was Marion, though, who exalted the Terry lineage. When, in the twentieth century, she revived her Mrs. Erlynne in Wilde's _Lady Windermere's Fan_ (1904) and played an elegant Mrs. Higgins in a revival of Shaw's *Pygmalion* (1920), she persuaded a more democratic generation that the Terrys were the last emanation of an age of pure breeding and theatrical refinement. Ellen enjoyed spreading lurid stories about her untouchable sister, inventing a love affair between Marion and strutting old Squire Bancroft that was intended to scandalize London (Steen, 259–60). When they were grand old ladies nagging at each other, Marion was still mortified by Ellen's boisterous manners. In the end, it was not Kate but Marion Terry who made herself into Sarah's perfect daughter, for it was Marion's stage aristocrats that made the Terry lineage magnificent.

The younger girls might be loved and mocked, but for Ellen, Kate was always the yardstick of reality, though they would never be close again: the lifelong search for the perfect partner that had carried Ellen Terry to George F. Watts, Edward Godwin, and Henry Irving before Edy ended the search was in its origin a quest backward to her early days with Kate. They remained mirror reflections of each other, though Godwin had driven them apart forever. Even in Ellen Terry's stardom, she continued to play Kate's old roles. Back in 1862, when Kate starred as Fechter's leading lady, she had played an acclaimed Ophelia to his Hamlet at the Lyceum; when in 1878 Ellen Terry began her Lyceum career in that role, she may have hated it, but she came into her inheritance. Moreover, in 1866, Henry Irving himself had had his first London triumph playing Rawdon Scudamore in Dion Boucicault's *Hunted Down;* Kate Terry had been his leading lady. Though she had always disapproved, Kate continued to pave the way for Irving's Lady of the Lyceum.

Kate and Ellen had always been the solidly successful sisters, the ones the family leaned upon, but they lost their empires simultaneously just before the turn of the century. In 1898, Arthur Lewis's firm went bankrupt; sumptuous Moray Lodge, the center of the family that had promised security forever, had to be left. The four pampered daughters, who had been raised to be ladies and to avoid their disreputable Craig cousins, all went to work. Mabel became an actress and added "Terry" to her patronym; when Arthur Lewis died in 1901, her sisters adopted the name as well. The name Kate had discarded in 1867 to fulfill her great expectations was now restored to bring glory to the humbled family.

In the same year, 1898, the Lyceum began to go: ill and despairing, having lost his extravagant sets and costumes in a fire for which he was underinsured, Irving gave up the management of the theater to a syndicate. This abdication was the beginning of the end: a few years later, like Arthur Lewis, Henry Irving declared himself a bankrupt. The estranged sisters, who had begun their lives on the road and then passed into great houses for what looked like forever, returned to the road once more. In Ellen's ironic account, Irving's dissolution of their partnership inspired his only suggestion that she play *As You Like It:*

> He wrote and asked me to go down and see him at Bournemouth. I went, and found him looking much better. He wanted to tell me that not only was he broken in health but he was what is called "ruined." At which word I refused to shed tears, for, said I: "As long as you and I have health, we have means of wealth. We can pack a bag, each of us, and trot round the Provinces. Yes, and go to America, Australia, India, Japan, and pick up money by the bushel, even were we to take just the magic book of Shakespeare alone with us." I then asked his plans, and he astonished me by saying: "That's why I asked you to come to Bournemouth. (He might have written, but no; he'd not *write* that.) I propose—have in fact written to the managers—going round the English provinces with a very small company, and playing 'The Bells,' 'Louis XI,' 'Waterloo,' and perhaps another play." Long Pause. I didn't think it *possible* I heard aright. *"What* plays?" said I. "Bells, Louis, Waterloo," he said irritably. "Well, and where do *I* come in?" said I. "Oh well, for the present, at all events, there's no chance of acting at the Lyceum." (He looked exceedingly silly.) "For the present, you can, of course, er, *do as you like!"*
>
> I felt—a good many feelings! At top of all came amusement to save the situation. "Then," said I, "I have in plain terms what Ted would call 'the dirty kick out'?"
>
> "Well—er—for the present I don't see what can be done, and I daresay you —" I cut him short. "Oh, I daresay I shall get along somehow. Have I your permission to shift for myself, and to make up a tour for myself?" "Well, I can hardly say." "Until Christmas next?" "Yes."
>
> (*Memoirs,* 271–72)

Irving did call her back at the last minute, but as with Moray Lodge, the empire had died only shortly before the man. Kate was too proper to suggest, in the words of her irreverent sister, that Arthur Lewis "looked exceedingly silly," but both sisters knew that protective men had failed to protect. Heroes were perishable, if not silly; for both, the role of mother survived husbands and their fragile fortresses. As they had discovered when Sarah died, and again with Floss's death, motherhood ruled everything. It was even strong enough to kill the women it had glorified and the lives it had created.

Ellen Terry was not born knowing how to be a mother, any more than she was born a stage boy. Her children were too intimate, too fractious, too eccentric, to teach her that role, so she apprenticed herself to that master son,

George Bernard Shaw. She received her first series of letters from him in the year Sarah died: they were stern and wheedling at the same time. He chastised her for frisking through *Nance Oldfield:* she was "the woman who OUGHT to have played [Ibsen's] the Lady from the Sea" (5 July 1892; *A Corr.,* 10); but at the same time, he let her know she was sacred to him. In response, she addressed Shaw with the benevolent babyishness audiences relished in mothers, though she would never dare use it to her own son: "Thank you. Thank you. *Thank* you for all your beautifulness" (4 July 1892. *A Corr.,* 8).

To Shaw, even when he was wicked enough to insult Irving and the Lyceum, she was all mercy and grace; to Gordon Craig, who loved the Lyceum even when he ran away from it, she played an avenging justicer, pouring money on him while searing him in her letters with terrible truths. Accordingly, when her true son cast her as a mother in 1903, he thought not of the angelic Candida or the infinitely healing Lady Cicely Waynflete, but of the Valkyrie Hiördis in Ibsen's *The Vikings,* a demonic goader of men. When, in 1931, Edy and Christopher St. John published her correspondence with Shaw, Gordon Craig's wild rage at the book may have been his protest against the baby-mother who blessed Shaw with a tender indulgence he himself was never granted.

The motherhood Shaw demanded was a new role in a world far from the Lyceum: emancipated modernists like himself dreamed of displacing society's patriarchs by enthroning all-wise, all-embracing mothers who would rule a saner and a tidier world. As he imagined that world, though, Shaw always placed himself above those mothers, criticizing their excesses and telling them very tenderly what to be. At their most lovable, they were teasingly childlike. Introducing the body of the letters to the reader of *A Correspondence,* Shaw gives his own account of the triangle between Irving, Ellen Terry, and himself: "If we take it that a clever woman's most amusing toys are interesting men we must admit that Ellen Terry was fortunate in her two dolls. How far, and for what moments, they were anything more to her (and after all, one can be very fond of dolls, as Ibsen had just pointed out) must be gathered from the correspondence" (p. 14).

Never, even when she was suffocating with suppressed rage, did Ellen Terry see Henry Irving as her doll. He was cruel, silly at moments, inadvertently funny, but in art as in the Lyceum family, he was the absolute power in her world: she might deride the man, but his authority was never in question. Never could she have played with him, even had she liked dolls (she didn't). She gradually replaced Irving her stage husband with G. B. S. her stage son, but like her real son, Shaw was more player than plaything: he seemed adorably needy, but when you asked him for help or demanded justice from him, he bolted. When Ellen Terry, like the age itself, began to listen to vulnerable sons instead

of paternalistic husbands, these sons arranged her dispossession from the sheltering empire that had led them to pity and adore her.

Shaw was never her doll, but his flirtation with that role was a sign of his
emancipated Modernism. His manifesto *The Quintessence of Ibsenism,* which he
sent Ellen Terry when their correspondence began, argued that Ibsen's new
drama was inseparable from the new woman's revolution. Shaw exhorted her
to throw over self-sacrificial obedience in order to govern the foolish little men
who had bullied her, but he gave her nothing to replace the tamers who had
constituted her audience and her intimates when she was learning her roles:
ignoring the defining prohibitions that had formed women, he did not see why
they refused to free themselves according to his instruction.

Like many men of his generation, Shaw appropriated for his own purposes
feminist complaints against patriarchal marriage and second-class citizenship. His
advocacy of women's rights was colored by delightful dreams of his own: he
peopled his utopia with grand emancipated goddesses who would take care of
him with the dispatch of conventional Victorian mothers, but who would talk
intelligently as well. His idiosyncratic amalgam of Modernism, Socialism, Ibsenism, and Feminism would save Ellen Terry from the "ogre's den" of Irving's
patriarchal Lyceum. He made dire prophecies about actresses who refused his
saving creed. A few months after he and Ellen Terry began writing letters in
earnest, he devoted a *Saturday Review* column to Ada Rehan, Ellen Terry's
envied alter ego, whom Shaw characterized remorselessly as a festering victim
of Daly's unenlightened management:

> And it strikes me forcibly that unless Miss Rehan takes to playing Imogen instead
> of such comparatively childish stuff as Julia [in *Two Gentlemen of Verona*] or even
> Helena [in *A Midsummer Night's Dream*], and unless she throws herself into
> sympathy with the contemporary movement by identifying herself with charac-
> teristically modern parts of the Magda or Nora type, she may find herself left
> behind in the race by competitors of much less physical genius, just as Barry
> Sullivan did. . . . Five years hence she will be still more rhetorical and less real:
> further ahead I dare not look with Barry Sullivan in my mind. There is only one
> way to defy Time; and that is to have young ideas, which may always be trusted
> to find youthful and vivid expression. . . . With Grandfather Daly to choose her
> plays for her, there is no future for Ada Rehan. (13 July 1895. *Shaw's Dramatic
> Criticism* 99–100)

In thrall to Irving's idea of a stage family, Ellen Terry had yearned toward Ada
Rehan and Augustin Daly as perfected selves: Ada Rehan had flourished as a

boy/girl under a manager who respected his company, not as foils and subordinates, but as an ensemble, autonomous and alive. Shaw's prophecy proved true nevertheless, as Ellen Terry may have sensed it would: Ada Rehan's career faded utterly when Daly died. Shaw's magisterial announcement of doom about an actress she had envied reinforced Ellen Terry's fears about herself at the Lyceum. As hungry to learn as she had been when she entered Watts's studio, she did her best to obey Shaw and to have "young ideas" for which she would find "youthful and vivid expression," even if that meant talking baby talk to her savior.

Shaw was in his own way as old-fashioned as Watts, though he exhorted her to emancipation rather than pathos: he too wanted to define the woman he worshipped. William Archer's review of his *Plays Pleasant and Unpleasant* diagnosed the Pygmalion within the acolyte: "It is exceedingly difficult for a man to see a woman objectively, because a woman, even in the most superficial and conventional relations, is very largely what a man makes her. The converse, of course, holds good to some, but not to the same extent. Mr. Shaw has gone through life seeing Shaw women, because women who were probably quite different both before and after, became Shaw women the moment they entered his sphere of magnetism, his 'aura' " (quoted in Peters, *Shaw*, 245–46). In 1864, the limber girl had flung herself into the Wonderland of Watts's paintings, but in 1898, the weary woman was confused by Shaw's floods of words and his dearth of beautiful things for her to look at; becoming a Shaw woman meant learning the rules of an alien game. Eager for a future, though, she gathered her energy once more and played with all her spirit.

The famous correspondence aroused bitter controversy when it was published. Gordon Craig and Graham Robertson were appalled at its supposed invasion of privacy, but Edy and Chris were confident that it would redeem the witty and literate woman they loved, who had been sentimentalized out of existence. The women were right; Ellen Terry survives today chiefly through the Shaw letters; but in these letters she is bewildered and bemused, uncertain what he is asking her to be, an Alice in Wonderland where all the wonders lie just beyond her reach. Shaw repeatedly promises delights and withholds them: he stimulates her with roles in his *Man of Destiny, Candida,* and *Caesar and Cleopatra,* all to culminate in a new, modern love story of Shaw's own devising. Yearning for a life beyond the Lyceum as she had yearned when she met Watts for a life beyond her vapid ingenue roles at the Haymarket, she passed through yet another cycle of fulfillment offered and denied. Shaw's sweet words led her once more through the pattern of her life; with the same inexorability, *Captain Brassbound's Conversion,* the one Shaw play in which she did appear, forced her back into the arch, adorable Lyceum tricks from which he had promised to release her.

About *The Man of Destiny,* his Napoleon play, Shaw wrote to Bertha New-combe, another woman he had teased into loving him: "My correspondence with Ellen Terry, the blarneying audacities of which would fill you with envy could you read them, has ended in an offer from Irving to buy the Napoleon play. . . . I stipulated for production this year; this was declared impossible and next year proposed, upon which I suddenly and elusively slipped away from business into a thousand wild stories and extravagances and adorations (I really do love Ellen), which are at present on the way to her" (1895; quoted in Peters, *Shaw,* 168). Shaw plays a Machiavel on paper, but his maneuvers outsmarted himself and Ellen Terry together: he won her, but lost the Lyceum. Irving optioned *Man of Destiny* but delayed production in his best tantalizing Shavian manner; when, in his column and in private, Shaw poured barbs and taunts on him, he produced another Napoleon play, Sardou's *Madame Sans-Gêne,* in which Ellen Terry, in a part Réjane had made famous, frisked about as a spunky washerwoman who becomes a spunky duchess.

Had she been a real Shaw woman, Ellen Terry would have enjoyed the quarrel between two silly men who loved her, but she was an actress, and she was devastated at losing the Strange Lady: it was losing Rosalind all over again. In *The Man of Destiny,* the Strange Lady has mystic and mobile powers anticipat-ing those of Woolf's Orlando: her abundant being exposes the futility of Napoleon's imperial dream, making of this great man an implicit anti-hero whose befuddlement was, no doubt, repugnant to Irving. Her "lithe tender figure is hung on a strong frame . . . which perceptibly exceeds" that of the men in the play. She is woman, man, and witch in turn: "Only, her elegance and radiant charm keep the secret of her size and strength." The Strange Lady was the self the Lyceum had suppressed, restoring the mercurial transvestism, the mystery and power, of her early years on the stage. Just as Ibsen's Lady from the Sea, whom Shaw harangued her that she "OUGHT to have played," would have restored the dangerous Undine who peered out intermittently in her sweet Ophelia and Ellaline, so the Strange Lady would have animated the Rosalind-self who was fading irrecoverably.

Ellen Terry's grief was incomprehensible to both Irving and Shaw. Their energy went into fighting each other. After Irving returned the play, Shaw wrote to Ellen Terry with a Mephistophelean glee worthy of his antagonist: "Dont bother about The Man of Destiny. Watch the fun and chuckle. Leave them to me. Haha!!!" (17 April 1897. *A Corr.,* 139). Irving was having an equally good time dictating pompous letters. It was only Ellen Terry who had lost once again the self she had been losing all her life.

When she re-read the first edition of her memoir, the Rosalind within the Strange Lady dictated her criticism of the character sketch of Shaw: "This is jolly poor of 'such a man as Orlando'" (quoted in *Memoirs*, 265). But after the Strange Lady, Ellen Terry was never Shaw's heavenly Rosalind again. He did write love epistles to her as fatuous as Orlando's, but they were not hung on trees, and they were directed to a mother. From the beginning, he had tempted her with *Candida* by invoking the Virgin Mother. He promised that she and Janet Achurch (for whom *Candida* was written and who eventually played it) should perform the role on alternate nights because "you and Janet are the only women I ever met whose ideal of voluptuous delight was that life should be one long confinement from the cradle to the grave." "Of the two lots," he mused on, "the woman's lot of perpetual motherhood and the man's of perpetual babyhood, I prefer the man's I think" (28 August 1896. *A Corr.*, 33–34). He had every reason to do so, for the Strange Lady, along with all the other Ellen Terrys whose champion he claimed to be, has no place in the nursery vision of the sexes that came to dominate his love letters.

Gradually, Candida, Cleopatra, and Shaw himself retreated into dreamland. It became clear that the letters were not a prelude to a meeting, but the meeting itself; like an Irving-Terry performance, they were their own reward. Once Shaw had cast Ellen Terry as his epistolary if not his actual Candida, he directed her to say wise and womanly things about his love affair with the wealthy Charlotte Payne-Townshend, whom in defiance of his iconoclasm he married in 1898; Ellen Terry obliged. As she came to understand what he wanted of her and to settle into her letters, her tactful charm aroused the great Modernist to a proposal so indecent that it might have come from Lewis Carroll:

> I am particularly tedious at present in this midnight solitary journey, wanting to sleep, and yet to sleep with you. Only do you know what the consequences would be? Well, about to-morrow at noon when the sun would be warm and the birds in full song you would feel an irresistible impulse to fly into the woods. And there, to your great astonishment and scandal, you would be *confined* of a baby that would immediately spread a pair of wings and fly, and before you could rise to catch it it would be followed by another and another and another—hundreds of them, and they would finally catch you up and fly away with you to some heavenly country where they would grow into strong sweetheart sons with whom, in defiance of the prayerbook, you would found a divine race. Would you

not like to be the mother of your own grandchildren? If you were my mother
—but I have a lot of things to say and we are at Redhill already. (14 June 1897.
A Corr., 158–59)

So much for the adventure of Ibsenism that promised so bold a life, such a wealth
of grand roles. Irving restricted her, but he never demanded to be her baby or
to watch her make love to sweetheart sons. The end of this letter is particularly
galling, for in 1897, Shaw's delicious dream was coming true: in that year,
Gordon Craig abandoned his wife May for a young actress, Jess Dorynne,
leaving Ellen Terry to take care of May's alimony and their four children. His
desertion of May began a cycle that would indeed make Ellen Terry mother
to her own grandchildren, as her son deposited more and more of them in her
support and care after impregnating and deserting their economically powerless
mothers. The reality was less titillating than Shaw's reverie. Had Candida
materialized, or any of the other roles he dangled before her and then withheld,
many fears about the future would have been allayed. Trouper that Ellen Terry
was, though, she played mother to her grandchildren with all the gusto and
charm Shaw assumed were sincere.

Until the letters waned, Shaw avoided a meeting because he feared that a
physical encounter would break the spell of their words and his dreams. He met
Edy instead, and he saw her often. Ellen Terry never played Candida, but Edy
did play Prossy in the first production of Shaw's play. Later on, unfriendly
observers labeled Edy a man-hater, but in her mother's prime, Edy was Ellen
Terry's only associate who got on with both Irving and Shaw. She admired both
with friendly irreverence, while they respected her without awe. It was her
brother who explosively alienated Irving and Shaw in turn.

By the time Shaw came into Ellen Terry's life, Edy had become adept at
standing in for her mother offstage. She knew she disappointed everyone when
she first appeared, but she knew too that she was an easier companion than the
glamorous mother. It was no trouble to stand in for her with Shaw and to
scrutinize him with interest; Edy may have recognized the preening, frightened
man within the prophet. One night, Shaw visited their Barkston Gardens
apartment to read *You Never Can Tell* to Edy and her friend Satty Fairchild.
Ellen Terry, to whom he had tantalizingly refused to read the play, was off
entrancing the Lyceum. Edy could imagine her mother's frustration at being
trapped onstage while her ungainly daughter basked in Shaw's mysterious
presence. Edy did not charm; unlike her mother and brother, she hid herself.
Her dark hair was always gathered away; her thin mouth was pulled shut in
a ruminative line; her small, penetrating eyes looked as if they saw secrets. That

evening, she looked inscrutable, at which she excelled, paying so few compliments that, Shaw complained, she might have been married to him for twenty years.

After he left, the young women diagnosed him coolly as "just the vainest flirt": "He'd coquet with a piece of string," added the unseduced Satty (quoted in Peters, *Shaw,* 187). Edy was not a powerful mother to Shaw; he was not a powerful manager to her; and so they let themselves begin to know each other. In her secret "About H. I." diary, Ellen Terry could be as knowing as Edy and her friends; she had many of the same sharp thoughts; but everything in the experience that had been her education stopped her from showing the remorseless accuracy with which she saw things. Had her daughter's generation been given another world, one in which felt truths about men could be spoken?

Edy was rude, but Shaw liked her; she lowered the fever of his incestuous longings. Later on, when even his signature was worth a great deal, he gave Edy his own and her mother's letters to publish; he endorsed her experimental productions, and learned from them, as long as she lived. When Shaw liked her, Edy won for the first time something her mother coveted. She, not Ellen Terry, knew how it felt to talk to that piratical man.

At the turn of the century, Ellen Terry and Edy were locked in a death-dance of fierce mutual identification: they could neither reconcile nor separate. Needing to keep Shaw to herself, Edy told her mother that he "could not bear her" after their first constrained encounter at Janet Achurch's *Captain Brassbound* in 1900. Ellen Terry believed this and was devastated; for fifteen months, the letters stopped. She had known since her Lady Macbeth in 1888 that her roles were strangling rather than enhancing her, but she could not stop playing them. Just because she had played so consummately for Shaw in her letters, she had known he would loathe her physical presence. Worst of all, she feared she had inspired Shaw's loathing just when she was beginning to need him.

In 1900, Ellen Terry was particularly vulnerable to her self-appointed teacher. She was cast adrift in a new century that flaunted its modernity and youth. Irving was ill and floundering; their solid house had fallen; soon there would be no money, while dependents were always coming. As she wrote to Ted with an urgency and directness Shaw never heard from her: "I hope all may be well but I cannot choose but ~~weep~~ fear a mighty deal=" It was not only money that was going: love, growth, and physical excitement, all were lost. Always, there had been men who loved her enough to tell her what to be. Soon there would be no self to love and no men left. Her father and Edward Godwin were dead. Henry no longer had anything to teach. Even the Lyceum's loyal champions, the critics Clement Scott and William Winter, to whom she had tried so fervently to explain the revelations of her Lady Macbeth, had fallen out of authority.

For years, Clement Scott had celebrated her in adoring prose; suddenly, in 1897, he published a mad attack on the theater's contamination of female purity. His abuse of actresses cost him his job; it also shook Ellen Terry's trust in her charm. Had she been contaminated in his worshipful eyes all along? William Winter, America's most confidently pontifical critic, also lost credibility through his vitriolic attacks on Ibsen and the new drama. In a widely repeated gaffe, he warned the actor Richard Mansfield not to appear in such sordid, immoral works as Ibsen's. As with Clement Scott, he lost his influence immediately and irrevocably.

No authority remained for Ellen Terry in the onslaught of new things: Shaw and his new empire were destroying all her teachers. Even Shaw himself was not so much teaching her as forcing her to be his mother, though she was only eight years older than he. But if Shaw turned away, there would be no one left but her children to guide her into the new century, and she was afraid of the roles her children wanted her to play.

Shaw's approval meant even more to her because the great Duse was the only actress of her own generation to have won it. During her Shaw period, she began to sign her letters "Eleonora," though the "Nell" she couldn't shake off made her identification with Duse another vivid but unacted part. Shaw cast Duse as his and the future's exemplary New Woman. He dismissed Ada Rehan and, by implication, Ellen Terry herself, because in his opinion, not even the greatest actress could transcend the defective authors and managers who created her: "Every woman who sees Duse play Magda feels that Duse is acting and speaking for her and for all women as they are hardly ever able to speak and act by themselves. The same may be said of Miss Achurch as Nora. But no woman has ever had the very faintest sensation of that kind about any part that Miss Rehan has yet played" (13 July 1895; *Shaw's Dramatic Criticism*, 99).

Virginia Woolf would feel that Ellen Terry spoke for all women when she discarded Shaw's own cloying Lady Cicely to let her native power radiate, but to Ellen Terry herself, such praise for fooling and forgetting was inconceivable. She revered Duse as unquestioningly as Shaw and her children did: obediently, she tried to imagine Nell as a noble Eleonora. Yet, apart even from her genius, there was something in Duse Ellen Terry could never become: like the puritanical Shaw, like (as she sometimes feared) her own intractable son, Duse hated the theater that kept her alive. Something in Duse, and in the new generation that was rushing to sanctify her, reminded Ellen Terry of the moralists of her childhood who were repelled by the human exposure of acting. Duse's calling had always seemed to suffocate her. On New Year's Eve, 1893, she had written to Boito at the end of a tour: "One who has lived in PRISON, he, yes, he can understand me. One who has lived in darkness, under ground, without the oblivion of the dead. . . . He who has lived bound hand and foot, biting the gag and without screaming—he can understand, yes, if tonight I yell, it's over, it's over."

No Terry could write about a tour with such unalloyed anguish. For Terrys, acting was life. If the roles were bad, one suffered one's reduced self just as non-actors did; but since offstage life was also composed of roles that one played to the best of one's ability, the theater was no more a prison than the world was. Even to an aging and fearful Ellen Terry, the world was grand, and acting was all things: to extinguish acting was to strangle life itself.

It seemed, though, that the architects of the new theater did want to exterminate actors; Duse lent her self-mortifying authority to their cause. Her own son, who wrote about replacing actors with marionettes, quoted Duse's indictment at every opportunity: "To save the theatre, the theatre must be destroyed, the actors and actresses must all die of the plague. They poison the air, they make art impossible. It is not drama that they play but pieces for the theatre. We should return to the Greeks, play in the open air; the drama dies of stalls and boxes and evening dress, and people who come to digest their dinner."

Certainly playing in the open air was magnificent. Ellen Terry longed to play Rosalind in the *As You Like It* Godwin staged in a wood for the Pastoral Players; in the country she crept out at night to dance to the moon in her nightgown. But since actors made themselves one with nature as well as scenery, why should they die of the plague? Duse was exalted, of course; only when Duse stood with her onstage did the tiring pageant of her jubilee become transfigured; but something in her nature recoiled from a theater that glorified Duse at her most austere.

Shaw too had something lethal in his love. His tirades of words seemed somehow to silence her. She too hung back from a meeting, preferring to act in her letters the woman he liked; like him, she sensed that it might be better to leave unacted the new roles he boasted about so fulsomely. But in 1905, she agreed at last to do *Captain Brassbound's Conversion:* in life as at the Lyceum, her parts had run out. In 1903, she had tried to go into management, placing herself and the Imperial Theatre in her children's hands; the result had been catastrophic. After ten years, she was free at last to be Shaw's woman; she had to be that woman; she tried to ignore her mistrust.

Captain Brassbound's Conversion is a tour de force for an actress. Set in

Morocco, it features the irrepressible Lady Cicely Waynflete mothering, fussing, and eventually taming a group of hostile Moroccans and British imperialists. Her ministrations and example are supposed to elevate Captain Brassbound beyond acquisitive imperialism, but there are sinister undercurrents within his exemplary conversion. At one point, before he has fully succumbed, he cries to Lady Cicely: "Damn you! you have belittled my whole life to me." Such, from one perspective, is the equivocal mission of all Shaw's women. He had originally given the play a Shelleyan title, *The Witch of Atlas,* but by the time it went to Ellen Terry, Lady Cicely had become too lovable for so ominous a name. Shaw wondered whether *The Angel of Atlas* would do, but then he resigned himself to making his heroine simply an angel.

Ellen Terry hadn't liked the play when she first read it in 1899: "I believe it would never do for the stage. The two parts, the man and woman, are right; but that *bore* Drinkwater! Mrs. Pat for Lady C! . . . Some day, spite of your saying you won't, you'll be pushed by everything within you to write more plays and then (I'll be grown up *then* certainly!) perhaps one will fit me" (3 August 1899; *A Corr.,* 245). Her actress's instinct was right: the play was hostile to the stage, to her stage at least. There was nothing to look at, only torrents of words that proved a torture to learn. Watts, Godwin, and Irving had made her a vehicle of extraordinary visual power, but their training had spoiled her for learning lines. Her notorious failing memory was in part simply a rusty one, for words had meant little in her non-Shakespearean performances at the Lyceum. The symphony of Shavian talk that called itself theater undermined the powers her life had given her.

"It's not the sort of play for me in the least," she had told Shaw definitively, but she could not grasp a key fact: that to Shaw—and to so many others who believed they loved her—she would never be more "grown up" than Lady Cicely was. Even Edy insisted that her mother *was* Lady Cicely, especially in the strange cold lovelessness which lurked within her charm. Edy loved Lady Cicely/Ellen Terry's confession: "I have never been in love with any real person; and I never shall. How could I manage people if I had that mad little bit of self left in me?" Certainly Ellen Terry thought she loved people: if she didn't, why would so many people love her back? Yet even her maid joined Edy's assault: "Excuse me, but Lady Cicely is *so* like you! She gets her own way in *everything—just like you!*" (quoted in Peters, 263). In recent years, though, Ellen Terry knew she hadn't managed people well at all. Around the house she got her way perhaps, but not in all the theaters that composed the world. All she cared for, she had lost. She could never believe with Shaw's heroines in inexorable triumph.

When Shaw received her rejection, he excoriated her as a "woman with no religion." He harangued her at length about Lady Cicely's anti-imperialist power: "I try to show you fearing nobody and managing them all as Daniel managed the lions, not by cunning—above all, not by even a momentary appeal to Cleopatra's stand-by, their passions—but by a simple moral superiority. . . . Here is a part which dominates the play because the character it represents dominates the world—and you think it might do for Mrs. P. C.!" (8 August 1899. *A Corr.,* 248). Shaw talked her down and made her feel stupid, as he did with most people. But when, five years later, she saw nothing but to do the play after all, Shaw's exhortations had become a bitter joke, for by then she was sure she didn't dominate the world. She was now the needy one, "fifty-eight, weak-eyed, buxom, jowly, gray streaking the straw-blond hair—a woman poised awkwardly between lost youth and the grace of age" (Peters, *Shaw,* 288). This untriumphant heroine came hoping to redeem a series of devastating losses. Shaw, who a few years ago had been afraid to be in the same room with her, had meantime grown mighty in the world of the theater. It was not merely theatrical success that had given him authority: his deepest dreams were beginning to haunt others' imaginations.

In 1905, the public liked mother goddesses. The avant garde had heard feminist denunciations of patriarchy and its gods; mothers, whom the Victorians had scarcely written about, became for the Edwardians a rich subject. As *Captain Brassbound* shows, mothers were an attractive solace to escalating international tensions; at home, they were an effective scourge of patriarchy. Moreover, the solitary little girls who were radiant presences in Victorian literature gave way to little boys: Barrie's Peter Pan, Kipling's Kim and Mowgli, became emblems of Edwardian experience. Even absent parents matter more to these brave boys than they did to such mid-Victorian fictional girls as Carroll's Alice. Like many of them, Peter Pan yearns for a mother's kiss while fearing it will destroy him. Boys' needs and dreams endowed mothers with formidable power. In life, women like Lady Cicely did not defeat military officers; they did not even confront them; but Modernist mythmaking claimed to prophesy a new dispensation. The cult of the boy proclaimed that the time of The Mother was at hand.

Ellen Terry had begun her partnership with Irving as shrew to his tamer. In 1905, Irving was dead; she was cast as tamer at last. The role terrified her. She had spent so many years learning to be pathetic while exuding a wicked triumph within that pathos; now she was told to subdue important men just by mothering them. In 1905, her own motherhood had utterly, irrecoverably humiliated her. She knew that she could not win Shaw's game. She knew too that she had to make him like her.

She had played victorious mothers before; few had believed in them. In *Coriolanus*, Irving's last Shakespeare production, she had played a Volumnia no one had liked. Gordon Craig's ill-starred production of Ibsen's *Vikings* made her a savage mother who goaded men to glory. In Christopher St. John's translation of a Dutch play, Herman Heijermans' *The Good Hope*, she was a peasant woman whose pious compliance with a rotten shipping system drives her husband and sons to their deaths. In all three plays, her noble intentions made her a killer of men.

Her last play before *Brassbound*, James M. Barrie's *Alice-Sit-by-the-Fire*, was, like Shaw's, a vehicle for her. Barrie's Alice is no savage idealist, but a dear wily woman. She is as far as she can be from the curious voyaging Wonderland Alice whom Ellen Terry had inspired. Barrie's Alice is an adorable, managing mother who tricks her children (and the audience) into loving her. Of the Alice who, like Lady Cicely, was supposed to be herself, Ellen Terry wrote dismissively: "I was never happy in my part, perhaps because although it had been made to measure, it didn't fit me. I sometimes felt that I was bursting the seams!" (*Memoirs*, 258). The woman she had played for so many years was worlds away from the woman she felt herself to be.

In 1895, Henry James had offered her *Summersoft*, her first benevolent mother play. In the 1870s and 1880s, anticipating Shaw by many years, James had written devastating criticisms of the fatuity of Lyceum spectacle, deploring as Shaw would do the widening gap between pictorial theater and literature. Because he too opened vistas on a wider world than Irving's, Ellen Terry secretly liked her severest critic: "I am sending you a very clever article by Henry James on Rostand," she wrote to Audrey Campbell in 1901. "Henry has not read it but wd call it spiteful & jealous — I don't believe that, but do read it - it is so very clever & interesting." She claimed to like *Summersoft* as well, but she never played it: no doubt its talkiness daunted her. James's Mrs. Gracedew is a garrulous, adorable American widow who brings salvation to a fine old English house: mothering its occupants, she talks the heir out of his radical delusions and into a true veneration of his legacy. "Your house is a kind of altar!" she cries. "You've got [the past] in *trust,* and oh! we have an *eye* on you. You've had it so for *me,* all these dear days, that, to be grateful, I've wanted to do something. Tell me now I shall have *done* it - I shall have kept you at your *post!*" Like *Captain Brassbound, Summersoft* glories in talk; both take revenge on the pictorial theater by inundating actors and audience with words. Mrs. Gracedew has more sentiment than Lady Cicely—she is allowed to marry the man she converts— but she is essentially the same character, an irresistible mother of the world whose "heart wisdom" (as Shaw called it) reforms nations and saves souls.

James, Barrie, and Shaw saw Ellen Terry as a triumphant heartwise mother, getting her way with a hint and a smile, but Ellen Terry never knew this woman. By 1905, her own son was gone. She had long lost faith in the power of mothers, and her own power was a dead stage dream. Because Lady Cicely was farther from her experience even than Ophelia had been, her fidgety and abstracted performance disappointed everybody except people who didn't like Shaw. Everybody was polite, but everybody knew she had lost the game.

Only Max Beerbohm spoke out: "Miss Ellen Terry was duly vivacious last Tuesday. But she was, also, very nervous. She was often at a loss when it was most necessary that she should take her cue instantly. And in the relief of having remembered her cue, she often spoke with disastrous emphasis. . . . Her nervousness not only marred Mr. Shaw's conception; it marred the performance of the other parts, and communicated itself, I am sure, to the whole audience. I draw attention to it because I should not like those of the rising generation who saw the performance to imagine that Miss Terry was within measurable distance of her best; and that is an impression which the criticisms of most of my colleagues would be likely to foster."

She had been born to act; now, again and again, acting was destroying her. Lady Cicely had lost Shaw, just as Hiördis had lost her own son; but there was nowhere else to go. She began rehearsals in terror, knowing what the result would be, and so she fell in love with James Carew, a burly American actor in the company. As Shaw saw it, she "simply proceeded to put James Carew in her pocket," but it always pleased Shaw to invent powers for her. Really, she clung to Carew as a shield against her failure to be the "Ellenest Ellen" of Shaw's overpowering letters.

In 1905, Edy had surrounded herself and her mother with a colony of advanced women; disapproving observers interpreted her sudden and brief third marriage as an attempt to escape Edy and her militant, monstrous circle. But the handsome, uncomplicated James Carew was her last attempt to salvage her vitality against the devastating anticlimax of her meeting with Shaw, and to excite a love that redeemed her from Lady Cicely's contrived and impersonal manipulations. James Carew might have been a barricade against her daughter, but she also cast him as savior from the emptiness of the Shaw woman.

Her letter to Graham Robertson from Pittsburgh announcing her secret marriage in the America that had always empowered her is less concerned with engulfing women than it is with the men who are abandoning her. In this letter she relinquishes Shaw's real beloved, her Eleonora-self, on behalf of the pathetic Nell her Victorian apprenticeship had taught her to play. "I babble all this to you [about Edy's disapproval of her marriage to Jim] because you are the one *man-friend* I have. . . . I couldn't be alone any longer. Then, a Miracle! Jim loved me—! told me so— & meant it!—it is true!! a Miracle! I have always believed in miracles= I love him."

She loved Jim when he let her cast him as her defender against the woman Shaw insisted on seeing, who was all-saving, all-powerful, and loveless. More appropriate than a world of managing mothers to the Ellen Terry of the twentieth century is her identification with a King Lear who madly sees the lie of his supposed power: "in America they held their arms to me more than ever! They flattered and fooled me to the top of my bent." Her marriage is her farewell to Shaw's dream of that power: "I note 'Nell' now, with you — not 'Eleanora' —I wonder have I dropped from Eleanora to Nell - or risen to Nell from Eleanora?—"

James Carew protected her from comic triumph to initiate her with grace into her true role in Shaw's script: that of mendicant. They spent months playing *Captain Brassbound* in the provinces, but Jim's promotion from Captain Kearney to the title role only emphasized his awkwardness. Ellen Terry besieged Shaw with pleas to cast her husband—and incidentally herself—in more plays, but her former suitor was on his way and she had had her chance: in his intellectual empire at the Court, where his primacy was modeled so carefully on Irving's at the Lyceum, there were to be no more parts for her. The end of their correspondence finds Ellen Terry playing with searing humility the role in which Shaw had cast her all along: "I wonder shall I ever act in a Play of yours again! I know you didn't like me in Brassbound, and indeed I didn't like myself, but sometimes nowadays I feel as if I *could* act! But that's only in Moon-y time, when the Marshes all look silver, and I feel very calm and happy" (28 August 1910. *A Corr.*, 323). " 'What can you do'? (Thank you for asking.) Why let me play a fine part written by you so I may abide in England!" (18 March 1911. *A Corr.*, 325). The Britannia Irving had so patriotically enthroned was shooting all over the colonies on tours, begging his enemy's pleasure so she might live in the England she had once personified.

At a time when she was far from triumphant, plays about triumphant mothers besieged her. She had become powerful at the Lyceum by playing pathetic roles; now that she felt defeated, plays demanded that she be powerful. When Maurice Magnus, her son's manager, sent her an experimental play, her refusal was quietly sardonic: "The incident dealt with wd. never—never be swallowed here if I coated it ever so thickly with my 'sweet! personality.' So few things possible for me now-a-days, it seems a pity to reject this — but - - - I Know - Is a modern comedy floating around on the lines of 'A Scrap of Paper'? - (that was taken from the French) a duel of wit between a man & a woman — the woman winning (She always does — in Plays ! !) I'd like the man to win - & the love interest was carried on by younger folks - I feel certain you will find something for me — in time — but time has wings."

As time whipped by and her life closed in, she became bitterly sensitive to the chivalrous irony that allowed women to win in plays. She realized with some amusement that in life, the man had always won, even before she had known there was a duel. Irving had known; he had nothing but sad contempt for victorious little mothers. When she had taken over the Imperial, leaving him to sail for America without her, he had written: "Poor dear, she has been absolutely under the influence and spell of her two children—who have launched her on a sea of troubles" (quoted in Prideaux, 250).

She had always accused Irving of being cruel to his own sons, to the sensitive Laurence in particular, but his cruelty was consistent: for all his egotism, for all the roles they had played and made each other play, he had scorned to act the selfishness of a son. Because the Lyceum had had no place for that kind of selfishness, she had failed to recognize it when it found her.

TEDDY   If, as Irving claimed, Gordon Craig launched his mother on a "sea of troubles," he did so because he hated her for casting him adrift on that sea, away from the whole and healing spot that rested just beyond his memory. Shaw played a game where fathers were abolished and mothers inherited the future; Gordon Craig, lacerated by the lack of a father, saw mothers (as his own mother personified them all) as the guilty guardians of a past they had wantonly ravaged. He knew only the parents who had been too large and perfect for him to know. The old man reconstructed a life in which everything ebbed back to those vanished figures: "For to please women became my deepest real delight – and one or two I did please. Yet often I felt it was all acting – not real – for real was Father and Mother, and see where that reality led me to!" (*Index*, 164).

A mother was not a role, but the origin and end of all roles. Like his American contemporary Eugene O'Neill, Gordon Craig cast his parents as his single psychic reality, making masks and shadows of everything outside their orbit. But O'Neill's plays were a continuing exorcism of indelible memories; Gordon Craig's workroom teemed with unfinished projects because he could not begin to exorcise the parents he could not remember. He fancied himself as Hamlet: had his mother killed his father? Certainly, when they refused to talk about him, her house of women killed Edward Godwin's memory. He had known no man beyond that terrible, that murdered, absence: "The 'impediment" came from the union and separation of E. T. and E. W. G. For my father might – would – have taught me what I had to discover for myself. . . . In spite of all the love and tender sympathy I now feel for Father and Mother, I do feel certain that mothers are not the right people to bring up their sons" (*Index,* 152).

He never stopped worrying at his deprivation. In the myth he made of his life, his mother's fall had brought doom: not the fall that led to his own birth, but the fall that came when she listened to Charles Reade's Satanic blandishments and left the garden of Harpenden to return to the London stage. That fall not only destroyed both father and son; it was the fall of the British theater as well: "I only see . . . the loss of the unity achieved by E. W. G. and E. T. when they came together. I see this and have for years felt it, and regret the lack of *strength* in E. T. and E. W. G. For with patience, a place, control and unity, these two would assuredly have brought to our Theatre something remarkable, even unique. Without E. T., H. I. would by no means have been lost. . . . Without E. T., E. W. G. was without . . . almost all" (*Index,* 72. Final ellipsis EGC's).

Throughout his life, Gordon Craig tried to conjure his father into being in order to nullify his mother's power to harm. He refused to attend her jubilee "because my father, E. W. G., was forgot – like the Hobby-horse!" (*Index,* 287). He dedicated *Ellen Terry and Her Secret Self* to his father, as if that spectral authority lay hidden in the secret self he needed to believe his mother had revealed only to him. In 1901, when he was almost thirty, he had a dream about his father so vivid and sad that it took on the tone of a visitation. The dream began with weeping, drowning, and separation, ending "in a huge theatre" with the dreamer's annihilation in overwhelming parental love: "And I looked into the great audience once more in search of something . . . and there I found a smile for which I had waited, it seemed ten thousand years—Into it I fell and knew nothing more but heard two voices whisper 'My Son'—and felt four arms laid over my shoulders——" (quoted in EAC, 142).

In Gordon Craig's revision of Genesis, he stood—like Shaw, like O'Neill, like so many daring and dashing men of letters—fixed in center stage as a perpetual son, perpetually grasping at the parents who struggled to escape his needs and demands. The generation that emancipated itself from duty, from the taboos of respectability, from the unwholesome lust for sexual purity, the first generation that dared learn about itself from Freud, clung to swollen fetishes of its parents with an obsessed intensity incomprehensible to supposedly inhibited Victorians.

Gordon Craig made no accusations against his father: it was his mother who had abandoned Godwin and wholeness at once. Observers generally romanticized Ellen Terry as the abandoned partner, for a woman was more easily loved when a lover had rejected her. No one who made a myth of that distant love affair wanted to know that Ellen Terry and Godwin had parted because in the course of time, their lives diverged. Their life together had always been an interlude away from urban reality: it became a static image of healing perfection only when that reality became intolerable.

The intolerable genesis that made Gordon Craig ache for a garden he could neither remember nor recover was his galling knowledge that women had made him. Even his grand patronymic was female in its origin: when he was sixteen, he had become "Edward Gordon Craig" in an impressive christening service, but Edy had given his name to him, not his father. Vacationing in Scotland in 1883, the family cruised past Ailsa Craig, a craggy little island off the Glasgow coast. Rough and imposing, Ailsa Craig was a favorite Pre-Raphaelite beauty spot. William Bell Scott's 1860 oil painting emphasizes its rugged solitude. When Edy saw the crag, in Gordon Craig's account, she snatched its name for her own. Ellen Terry's children were Craigs forevermore (EAC, 57).

Edy herself forfeited responsibility for her name. In her notes to her mother's Memoir, she characteristically obliterates herself from the scene and expunges the audacity of claiming a mountainous island's name. In Edy's account, the dramatis personae are Irving, Ellen Terry, and Teddy, not the Ellen Terry, Edy, and Teddy whom Gordon Craig described to his son. "Craig" becomes her mother's invention entirely: "What a good stage name! . . . A pity *you* can't have it, Ted. I shall give it to Edy" (*Memoirs,* 195). Brother and sister had different imaginations of their genesis, but in neither's account does Gordon Craig name himself: like a traditional appendage, he takes his sister's name, though he makes it sound superb. Whether his mother or his sister bestowed it, his crowning name, like his life, was to his profound discomfort not his own or his father's, but a woman's.

"Craig," a self-bestowed and gutteral bit of Scottish dialect, was the only durable name Ellen Terry's children ever had, and it belonged to a rocky peak jutting out of the ocean. In the family too, Edy and Teddy were rugged islands: they had never been Godwins or Terrys. "Wardell" was a brief conventional disguise, one with no human content: at home as well as in the theater, the father who had once played a bit part in Ellen Terry's household was "Charles Kelly." Like the uprooted century to which their productions gave form, Edy and Ted began life fresh and unique, cut off from the mainland, with no dragging inheritance. Ellen Terry remembered herself as a visionary child locked in a room, but her own children were free.

Perhaps because even his self-bestowed name was not his own, Teddy could not rest as Gordon Craig: in *The Page* and *The Mask,* the periodicals he founded and ran virtually by himself, he burst into a chaos of names. His son locates "sixty or seventy pseudonyms" in his writing (EAC, 19). "John Semar," "John Balance," "Julius Klassen," "Jan Van Holt" and the rest are not simply names, but quarreling, fractious characters, each with his own appearance, personality, and—sometimes—signature (EAC, 242). None of these selves was female; otherwise, they were vividly distinct. In her letters, Ellen Terry too fractured into distinct, warring, proliferating selves with different characteristics and signatures. As her role as Lyceum stage wife rigidified, she threw her imagined life into this medley of selves: they were the vital confusion of her unacted parts. Her son's warring, multiple selves became his public reality. The incoherence of Gordon Craig's persona brought into the light, in all its wit and rage, Ellen Terry's secret self.

Capricious and assaultive, Gordon Craig evolved into a perpetual goading presence in the twentieth-century theater, but the work that obsessed him was realized in no theater: the decomposition his mother revealed only privately and selectively consumed the career of her son. Between 1900 and 1902, he attracted the attention of the English avant garde with three operas he staged with Martin Shaw—Purcell's *Dido and Aeneas* and *The Masque of Love,* and Handel's *Acis and Galatea.* Then came what Shaw might have called his two "Mother Plays": *Bethlehem,* Laurence Houseman's Nativity play, which he designed in 1902, and in 1903, the heartbreaking production with his mother of Ibsen's *The Vikings.*

William Bell Scott, *A View of Ailsa Craig and the Isle of Arran. Courtesy Yale Center for British Art, Paul Mellon Collection.*

Thereafter, though he lived heartily until 1966, he staged no more productions in England. His theatrical career effectively ended after the *Hamlet* he staged in 1912 for Stanislavsky's Moscow Art Theatre. He spent most of his time constructing vast dreams of theaters no building designed by man could encompass. His abstract grandiosity might have found a home in the mechanized epics of cinema, the new century's paramount art form that was coming of age along with Gordon Craig, but he shunned inventions other than his own as fearfully as he avoided America. Like Hamlet, he made himself a riveting work of art through his profound inability to act. Like his mother, he became a legend through the haunting influence of his unrealized productions and unacted parts, though his books made of his unfulfilled dreams inspiring realities for later directors. His very art had begun as a matricidal plot, but he succeeded only in inheriting the role of the mother he had meant to kill.

All his necromancy went into restoring his father's life. When, in the 1890s, he was on the verge of success as an actor, he abandoned the career his mother had tried to build for him, turning to Godwin's sphere of production and design. He reprinted his father's articles and, by his own account, adopted their aesthetic, though he quietly discarded the antiquarian passion for historical accuracy that had inspired them. For Gordon Craig as for his hero William Blake, vision was not a saving activity in itself, sensuous and complete, but a path to imagined unseeable worlds beyond history and humanity. Like Godwin, he read Ruskin carefully, but only to deny Ruskin's Victorian exaltation of the visible world. Around 1898, when the visionary theater he dreamed of instituting was becoming his overriding reality, he wrote to Edy:

> It might put more water into the gentlemen [the editors?] if in your Fortnightly review article you quoted the old Ruskin—
> "The modern stage is ruined by its *realization* of scenery which is contrary to all noble art.
> A picture whether on canvas or on the stage should give an idea, not its realization."
>
> John Ruskin

They mind their P's & Q's better when the old greybeard pops up with his hammer.

At the Lyceum, realization had been all: Irving's wizardry made living pictures, transporting spectators to opulent foreign lands. Never, beyond the Lyceum, could one inhabit Shakespeare's Italy or *Faust*'s hell. In her halcyon time as a pictorial actress, Ellen Terry was the Lyceum's supreme realization, epitomizing in her person artists' visions of rare places. Henry Irving's tribute to her Ellaline—"I wish I could tell you of the dream of beauty you realized and were"—pays tribute as well to the dynamic tension between Ruskin's "idea" and the living woman who makes it humanly real by taking it into herself.

Blake might have called the animate expression of Ellen Terry's realizations a consecration of the "human form divine," but in the name of Blake and of his father before him, Gordon Craig conceived a theater free of the human mediator on whom realization depends. If England would provide him with such a theater—but England never did—then perhaps he would be free of the mother who had realized his being and possessed it.

The Art of the Theatre, Gordon Craig's great text, first appeared in 1905, the year of Irving's death; an expanded edition was published in 1911. This combative book, the first edition of which was cast entirely as a Platonic dialogue, became the handbook of theatrical Modernism throughout Europe. In it, the stage director is exalted to godlike status in the company; he is not so much the actor-manager Craig observed in Irving as the dreamer of the dream actors obey. Over the years, Craig refined his vision of actors beyond flesh and blood. In 1908, he conceived the über-marionette, a grand, inanimate, perfectly controlled creature who rises, in Craig's evolutionary dream, to replace the actor: "The über-marionette will not compete with life—rather will it go beyond it. Its ideal will not be the flesh and blood body but rather the body in trance—it will aim to clothe itself with a death-like beauty while exhaling a living spirit."

Patiently, Craig reassured his disciples that the über-marionette was neither a ghoul nor a golem, but a human actor whose art is refined to a peak of perfection; yet his vision of theatrical transformation is steeped in anti-humanity. The über-marionette will never realize an idea: he is already an idea incarnate. Never will he fool onstage, forget his lines, or create a delicately angry self within his assigned role, as Craig had seen his mother do so often and so seductively. The über-marionette is entirely the stage director's creature. His performance cannot protest, but only obey.

In Craig's frontispiece for *The Art of the Theatre,* as in all his designs, grandiose masses open into glimpses of the illimitable. Its structural principle is one of Craig's motifs: tiny figures toil foolishly and heroically up mazes of steps. His explication of this idea is his creed: "Quite an impossible scene, that is to say, impossible to realize on a stage. But I wanted to know for once what it felt like to be mounting up impossible ladders and beckoning to people to come up after me." As usual, his explication is disingenuous: it is there to muddle our perspective, not to clarify it, for in his drawing neither artist nor viewer knows

Frontispiece, Edward Gordon Craig, *The Art of the Theatre.*

how it feels to mount impossible steps. We share nothing with the silhouetted little climbers; we become instead the steps, the vast ascents, the dwarfing masses. Like all the models and designs he guarded so jealously, Craig's frontispiece to his most influential book allows the artist to assume the teasing vastness of God.

The volumes Craig wrote in his long exile elaborate on *The Art of the Theatre.* The modern theater he envisions is classical in its transcendent control, ancient in its origins; it aims to restore the holy imperturbability of religious ritual. Shaw had tried to use Ellen Terry as a beacon to the new woman in the new century; Craig dreamed of obliterating her in the service of remote, and nobly masculine, gestures of salvation. But underneath his magisterial calm seethed a rage to destroy. Isadora Duncan's notebook sketch for an article on his work —an article Francis Steegmuller suggests that Craig himself dictated—isolates the holocaustal impulse his stateliness masks:

> This book seems to me to contain in little the bomb for an immense explosion of all things which exist as we know them in the theatre. An upheaval so general and so deadly at first it presents to our mind's eye the entire theatres of the world suddenly heaved sky high in the air together [with] pieces of buildings, shreds of

their scenes, tatters of their costumes and finally separate legs, arms, bodies—yea, heads of their actors shooting through the air in one wild, chaotic bang! What if this bomb explodes, the last days of Pompeii will seem a scene of mild Sunday amusement in comparison with [the] last days of the theatre as threatened by the flaming torrent of lava from this new Vesuvius Theatre Destroyer. Oh! the comparison is very good—only, the lava of Vesuvius destroyed [and] covered with ashes thousands of feet deep, did it not, a beautiful city and the remains are still beautiful. But when the present great incubus, the present theatre, is destroyed, the ruins, poor, ghastly ruins . . . will show us but the tell tale weak foundations of the one great ugly chaotic threat fraud of today and we will scorn this poor weak remaining foundation and cart away the rubbish leaving clear space. . . .

Step up Mr. Thrower of deadly bombs, step up Mr. Vesuvius Theatre Destroyer, step up Mr. Edward Gordon Craig, we have cleared away the last remaining tatters. Step up now and show us—*what's* to happen next.

The thrower of deadly bombs lies within the empty calm of the designs: these designs are majestic revelations of a decimated world. When Gordon Craig fled England in 1903, he evolved a prophetic vision of a world stripped and drained; its desolation awed a Europe heading for war. Ellen Terry mourned all her life her son's empty visions, in which it was impossible to play, for she knew she had somehow inspired them by driving him away to desolation.

Almost from the first, Ellen Terry sensed something wrong in her son, and made the mistake of trying to drive it out. She wanted Teddy to have the education she had been denied, but to his schoolmasters she sent nervous apologies for unspecified flaws. Her letters to a Mr. Wilkinson, written when he was eleven, is ingratiating and apprehensive at once; it hints at his embarrassment out of her household of women and in a community of other boys.

> I hope most earnestly that you have not found Ted to be either a bad, or a hopelessly dull, boy. It makes me very happy to realize he is with you. . . . Ted's letters make me quite comfortable about him. He quite appreciates his master, & his lessons - altho' mingling with so many boys seems rather to appall him! & I gather he would wish life were all master & lessons & no boys!
>
> I would not have troubled you with this letter, except that I am sure you will kindly pardon my desire to know that Teddy my boy does not give very much trouble.

Ellen Terry writes in the linear and constrained script of proper little Nelly Watts, not in the gorgeously eccentric writing that evolved in her years of stardom: the flourishes, the idiosyncratic emphases and marks of punctuation that became seismographic equivalents of her speaking voice, are abandoned before the authoritative educator to whom she has given her boy. She masks herself out of fear of what he will see, in herself as well as in Teddy.

Writing two years later, in 1885, to her friend Bertha Bramly, she abandons caution to express her fears:

> If you <u>knew</u> the trial it is to act night after night in this heat this tearful part [Margaret in <u>Faust</u>]— & rehearse in the daytime= Too tired to sleep . . . It troubles me greatly that Ted is going on month after month & doing no patient work — he is so strong & well — & so terribly self willed — he is <u>such</u> a good fellow but so ~~silly~~ unwise & intractable=
>
> Oh, <u>Work, work</u> until one drops from fatigue— <u>anything better</u> than theorize— Talk — & not <u>do</u> = It's bad in a woman, but terrible in a man= Oh, I'm tired=

Already, she discerns and deplores the man Ted would be, the explosive theorist unable to manage in the practical community of production. Already, too, she punishes him with contemptuous disapproval for the male privileges she showers on him as a matter of course. Raising her son with all the tokens of superiority, she lacerates him—and, in his unformed person, all great men—for his inability to deserve his power.

At the same time as she criticized Ted's helplessness, she piled indulgences on him, making him more helpless still. These were her contrary ways of warding off her unformulated knowledge that something was wrong. When Ted was fourteen, she took the children to her Uxbridge cottage; Irving drove down for dinner and returned to London. When she was alone, she wrote in her diary a cryptic announcement of inner deformities: "That which is crooked cannot be made straight, and that which is wanting cannot be [illegible]." She had always associated the Uxbridge cottage with Ted, perhaps because it had originally been a pub; when he married May Gibson in 1893, she gave it to him. Her oblique diary entry casts into authoritative Biblical cadences her intense awareness of the doom lurking within the boy to whom she tried to give everything. She both feared this doom and courted it.

She never let him forget her own pains and exertions. Never, though he was a lordly son, could he have lived her life: "<u>Try hard</u> not to be kept in darling. You see that's their way of punishing, & we must all be punished to push on our intelligences a bit—Mrs. Kean used to punish me—but I'm better for it <u>now</u>, I know. . . . Now darling boy let me hear from you <u>very often</u> — & try to think that a little suffering is good for all of us. Anyhow good or not suffer we must — <u>all</u> of us. You'll know some day that your poor old Mum has had a great share, & when she was quite young too—only 17 years old! & lots afterwards, too! So just work away darling—peg into your studies, & then you <u>will</u> have less to battle with later on-" The suffering she prophesies may or may not make one "better": at bottom, it has no moral meaning beyond its own overwhelming existence. The sixteen-year-old Ted is only a year younger than was his "poor old Mum" when she suffered, and, she implies, he is ill-equipped to endure what she did. Her dire autobiographical hints establish no kinship with the nervous schoolboy; they seem designed both to terrify and to exclude him.

After enumerating instances of her generosity to him, she goads his male superiority: "Now what have you got for me - I'm a woman- you're a man- you should try to give me more than I have you - Have you given me more hard work? or a victory over your little temper?" Irving, as usual, swells into a fearsome example: "We are slaving at rehearsal. Henry is at rehearsal every day at ten o'clock - & generally sticks there for 5 hours. He is the wonderfullest man - & his is <u>the</u> way to succeed. With all his great powers & popularity he says, work- work- work - & he **D o e s** 'work, work, work'! says, & does it too." The money her son "let . . . slip unheeded through buttery fingers," and which she tried feebly to ration, is given with a sharper sting: "I think this will help you - you weak little boy - . . . all you have to do is learn to be strong - strong for <u>honour</u> & for the <u>right</u> - <u>& you will!</u>"

Ted didn't learn to be strong for honor and for the right, nor did he grow into the self-made Victorian man Henry Irving was: he was a bomb-throwing modern who always found someone to take care of him. In 1888, when he was sixteen, he confronted his mother with his first grand self-defining gesture: he had been expelled from his prep school, Heidelberg College. He wrote not as a strong man, but as his mother's boy, for he had learned to twist the idiom of Victorian melodrama to make himself a self-parodying victim almost as appealing as her own Ophelia:

Dearest Mother:
    I dont know how to begin this letter = I am a stark staring fool! I must be! At least I feel very like going mad!
I suppose Laurence [the headmaster] has written to you. [He had.] I went out with 2 other boys at 11 o'clock at night on my bicycle & the others on bicycles. We went for a long ride for about 18 miles and returned at 4 oclock in the morning. Laurence was waiting up for us & next morning said I was to go & the other two

need not! The thing is that I was in the wrong to go out at all. But as Laurence will say except for that I did nothing.

Please don't think too badly of me just when I want a friend = You cant tell my agony of feelings when they said I must go = Please write to me — do please!! And for gods sake dont worry yourself about me = I can and will do anything I can possibly do = If you think me not worthy — why then I'll shift for myself. But what ever happens dont worry or distress your self = I am a fool! Grandpapa is very kind — very kind — too kind = I know I dont deserve any help or pity not one little scrap but my punishment was almost (and is) past bearing — Its impossible to describe my feelings = I knew it would make you ill — Oh! I am sorry — I am! I am! When I went out I never stoppd to think or if I had I could not have thought it possible to send me away — like a culprit — from school!

Oh please write and tell me if you are well again! Dont write me a bad account I could not bear it — I cant go on — Darling good bye.

Ben, to whom schools meant nothing, laughed it off as a boy's prank; Ted's guardian Stephen Coleridge was in despair. Ellen Terry made no fuss, but her dire prophecies had been fulfilled, and in the middle of *Macbeth*, always an ill-omened play. She had always known something was wrong with Ted: now only he of the three malefactors had been expelled, and moreover, despite Stephen Coleridge's indignant threats and her own blandishments, Mr. Laurence refused to have him back. Teddy had not made her ill—though in some perverse fashion within his tears and pleas he seemed to want to do so—but he did make her fear for them all. Perhaps Henry could help: at the theater, he was God, arranging everything. He had always been kind to Ted; when Edward Godwin was dying in a hospital, Henry had even taken the boy in for several days. She had always held him up to Ted as a pattern of heroic manliness, in the best wifely and motherly fashion, with only an edge of parody. Near despair, she enrolled Ted in her own school, the theater where she had learned her life. He was apprenticed at the Lyceum.

Like the money she never stopped sending, this reprieve was a cruel reward: bringing Teddy into Irving's protective orbit put beyond his reach forever the Victorian virtues of fortitude and self-reliance she never stopped preaching to him. The Lyceum provided only an illusory happy ending for son as well as mother. Ted felt the power of Irving's grandeur only after it had died. At the time, his failures at school rankled. Flogged, perhaps, by the ghost of his scholarly father, Ted never forgot the ignominious end of his education. His mother had known only one school, the stage, which for her was as large as the world. Gordon Craig's life was a quest for a school that would teach all he needed to know. Like his authorizing father, like the theater he never founded, the school that would realize his ideas never existed on earth.

Later he spun a myth of the Lyceum as his true school, casting Irving as his grand and all-wise "Master," but at the same time he denounced it for not having been a school like Heidelberg College: "There should, of course, have been a school connected with the Lyceum Theatre, a place where those who were beginners could study, could be clearly and slowly trained, directed by masters neither too pedantic nor too go-as-you-please. The only school we had was the stage of the theatre in rehearsal time and during the performances . . . So that the Lyceum 'school' was the old one known as the school of experience." In print, he nagged his mother incessantly for her casual assumption that acting could not be taught: "You will know that I am following up that which you assert—that acting cannot be taught, that it has no laws; that, obviously, if this is true it is no art." He never forgave the theater for refusing to act his lost school, or for its intractable indifference to his own pedagogic transformations.

Like his father's, his writings take authority from a tone of schoolmasterly precision. In *The Art of the Theatre,* the stage director's manner is more fitting to the lecture hall than the greenroom:

> The first dramatists were children of the theatre. The modern dramatists are not. The first dramatist understood what the modern dramatist does not yet understand. He knew that when he and his fellows appeared in front of them the audience would be more eager to *see* what he would do than to *hear* what he might *say.* He knew that the eye is more swiftly and powerfully appealed to than any other sense; that it is without question, the keenest sense of the body of man. The first thing which he encountered on appearing before them was many pairs of eyes, eager and hungry. Even the men and women sitting so far from him that they would not always be able to hear what he might say, seemed quite close to him by reason of the piercing keenness of their questioning eyes. To these, and all, he spoke either in poetry or prose, but always in action: in poetic action which is dance, or in prose action which is gesture.
>
> ### PLAYGOER
> I am very interested, go on, go on.
> ### STAGE-DIRECTOR
> No—rather let us pull up and examine our ground. (pp. 141–42)

And so he does, for several pages. The smell of the lamp that suffuses Gordon Craig's prose is his favorite stage trick, restoring not only his erudite father, but the school that had banished him. At the same time it allows the writer to incarnate his stern Master Irving who, in his actual Lyceum days, had had little interest in the lazy boy.

When he was living in Italy, his father's dream country, and coming into majestic middle age, he began to dream of founding a school himself. The idea had haunted him since 1903, but now it possessed him. In 1910, he wrote in his daybook: "I want time to study the Theatre. I do not want to waste time producing plays—for that is vanity—expensive—unsatisfying—*comic*. I know something about my art after twenty years study. I want to know more. I want to know enough to be of use to those who can *do* more" (quoted in EAC, 261). He glorified his theatrical stasis as his mother had done at the Lyceum, by protestations of usefulness to others. His school would redeem the gifts he had wasted; it would restore the Edens that had cast him out, replacing family, college, and Lyceum in one comprehensive community: "A body of picked men will take charge of the School when it is erected, and conduct researches into every aspect of the three elements—Sound, Light, and Movement—of which the Art of the Theatre is composed" (quoted in EAC, 180).

In his original dream, the school was all-male, as a challenge, perhaps, to the all-female suffrage pageants Edy was staging so successfully for the Actress' Franchise League. A manuscript dated "Feb., 1915" contains a grudging recantation of his ban on women:

> If at the end of the first years work I find that the women working in the school have worked well but if at the same time I find they have chattered about each other, and have behaved like cats - or have spoiled the men - or have failed to understand what is needful then out they must go - all of them. & the school goes on its way without them & their sex.
>
> If I prove them unworthy it will be a great grief to me. But it shall never be said that women were excluded & not given a chance in this work.

By 1913, when the short-lived school was founded, Gordon Craig was bitterly aware of women's power to "spoil the men." All his life, his mother had showered protection and indulgence on him, poisoning these gifts with taunts at his weakness. His mistresses protected him more tenderly until he cast them off in a rage at his own dependence. No wonder he feared the dangers of women in a school meant to restore, with the help of his father's spirit, his own spoiled manhood.

In 1913, time had gone forward but his dreams had retreated. Elena Meo, his loyalest and most loving mistress, was living in London next to the drawing offices William Godwin had occupied in 1874; Gordon Craig was inaugurating his school in Florence in an open-air theater, the Arena Goldoni. With a flourish, he offered it to his mother on her sixty-sixth birthday: "I bring it to Her as a birthday offering, fully recognizing that I owe its fulfilment largely to her unwavering and helpful encouragement" (quoted in EAC, 284). Nothing could be a more incomprehensible gift to the mother whose country he could not share than this rarefied, woman-mistrusting, impractical school. His birthday present was a symbol of his own healed obsessions, but their losses were not the same, and hers cut so deep that no school could restore them.

Of course, the school could never be realized. There were omens before the disaster: on April 19, he learned that Deirdre, his daughter by Isadora Duncan, had drowned in Paris, along with Patrick, Isadora's son by Paris Singer. He steeled himself against tragedy's contamination by his refusal to join Isadora in Paris. More and more, like his many families, the school became a bastion against outside life: elaborate rules forbade the students to communicate with non-initiates in the world. In London, Elena moved into Godwin's old rooms, but her talismanic retreat did not work. War was declared; the school closed the next day. In 1917, the Italian government requisitioned the Arena Goldoni for military purposes. After that, though he lived for almost fifty more years, Gordon Craig was sealed off from either learning or teaching.

The closing of the school symbolized the closing of all the doors his mother had opened. She had brought him to the Lyceum in an act of grace that seemed to open the world for him: "Life really was beginning for him in earnest [in 1889]. He had failed miserably at all his schools, but now, as by magic, he had suddenly won a 'scholarship' to the Lyceum Theatre!" (EAC, 66). But, as Marguerite Steen states flatly, "Irving did not care for him and frequently mocked him" (p. 197). So absolutely his own, self-made man, Irving was unnerved by the next generation even if they acquitted themselves well. Ellen Terry wanted to control the young, but Irving only wanted them to go away. When Ted did join the Lyceum, he began by involuntarily inflicting on Ellen Terry the "tears & dullness" of the uninteresting mother in *The Dead Heart*. Her letter to Elizabeth Winter exudes a resentment more sweetly cloaked than Irving's:

Good — & since it's best he begins to work so young (just 17 -) I'm rejoiced he begins at Henry's lovely theatre - for the lad is too young & sweet & fair to send unprotected against puzzlements, & tempting ills, & too old for a perambulator & Miss Harries to await him at the stage door after his work — As it is, I shall be his "Miss Harries", & his perambulator will take him home — or my "rattletrap" will instead, & he won't know it!! & won't want to fly with his silly, weak dear wings — Lord! how we intrigue for our young! — I only do it in a kind of simple, half frightened fashion though, & as I believe <u>under direction</u> for "whatever is is right", & the house of cards we build up, goes down so often it's terrible to fix one's wishes <u>too</u> hard to one point =

She was, with reason, "half frightened." She had initiated her undisciplined son into a fraught situation. Irving, whose implacable mother had forced him to do all his intriguing for himself, no doubt resented this fuss about Ted's "weak dear wings." In 1895, he would resent still more Ellen Terry's clamorous advocacy of his own son Laurence; like Othello's, his murderous instincts against his supposed rival swelled beyond control as his stage wife forced the man's cause on him.

But, as he always did, Gordon Craig aroused antagonism on his own. He was unnerved by his mother's blunt letter of welcome and advice, a letter that was worlds away from the adorable maternal deviousness Barrie and Shaw would make her creed:

<u>Now remember</u>, I have the <u>highest hopes</u> for you, & the <u>fullest trust</u> in you that you will now aim high, and always endeavour to do your best in your new calling = You'll find many temptations but <u>with help</u> & determination to <u>go right</u> instead of <u>wrong</u>, you <u>will</u> go right - <u>will succeed</u> — <u>will remain a gentleman</u> — & your Mammy's own lad—with the respect of everybody in the theatre - & the affection too, I'll be bound.

Be simple-truthful-& industrious & as straight as a die & <u>you'll never get into trouble</u> but if you go <u>ever so little out</u> of the straight, <u>you will</u> get into trouble = One thing to remember—It's very <u>difficult</u> to go <u>quite</u> straight always, but directly it <u>begins</u> to go wrong <u>go back</u> & set it right = To have a friend is a good thing in need - but <u>friends</u> to stick by one, & "hide the fault they see," are not common as blackberries. They must be <u>tried</u> for years before one can be sure of them—Such a friend <u>I</u> will be if you want one in any difficulty - a cleverer friend than <u>younger</u> ones could be, if they wanted to, ever so much, for I have <u>great</u> <u>experience in suffering</u> & great belief in <u>endeavour</u> to be straight, & no belief whatever in fundamental evil - evil right away down deep-I fear you have not shown much strength hitherto—when I was young I was weaker than I am now — & suffering has made me stronger, but I've always found a helping hand, a loving, helping hand the best thing in the world in a difficulty—Now here's mine ready for you & <u>don't forget</u> it— & <u>never fear me, I love you</u> & that means

everything as you'll find—Remember by the way to always say "Mr. Irving"
in the theatre— not "Henry"— (27 August 1889. Quoted in EAC, 66–67)

This formidable and apprehensive letter did not ease Ted's new life. Because his
mother demanded of him the searing honesty she herself was forbidden; because
she punished boys by forcing them to be heroes; because she resented playing
his mother; and because she loved him intensely; he did fear her. When he left
the Lyceum the following summer to go touring on his own, she did not scruple
to tell him he had disappointed his mighty employer:

> You will get on quite well during this tour, & be quite happy if only you keep
> your head, on all occasions = I suppose you were very nervous on the Caleb night
> [his opening]-I hope so - or I'd not give 2d for your chances as an Actor = you
> must send me a lot of papers & I'll keep them all for you . . . I must see them
> —all—Henry is surprised you haven't sent me more. Good & bad notices I want =
> Don't tell other people the houses aren't full-only me = Remember = Don't write
> many letters (except to me!!!) I implore you at first, but think all the while, all
> you can of your work - I fear Henry doesn't believe you think of it at all!!
> He says you have "natural ability" but have no idea of what work even means,
> so far -

To the impatient Irving and his jealous sons, and to the rest of the company
as well, Ted appeared shamelessly indulged. He was an anomalous presence in
the Lyceum, for during the same years, Irving's own sons were being sternly
schooled away from the theater. Their mother had raised them (with imperfect
success and at Irving's expense) to despise their father and to shun Ellen Terry
as a scarlet woman. When Ted was expelled from Heidelberg College, Harry
and Laurence Irving were doing dutifully well at Marlborough School. They
longed for the forbidden stage, but Harry was to be trained for the bar, Laurence
for the Foreign Office. Only in the mid–1890s, when Irving could no longer
finance their ambitious professional schooling, did he relent, with bitterness, and
allow his boys to join him in the theater. Terrys bred each other for the stage,
but when H. B. and Laurence Irving joyfully followed their father there, their
presence dramatized his defeat.

For the respectable Irving boys, Gordon Craig epitomized everything they
were forbidden to be, but "his perambulator," as Ellen Terry called the Lyceum,
was the most bruising school of all. He endured no more plain speaking after
he fled England: he reminisced grandly about his house, the Lyceum, and his

Master, Irving, flattered by adoring choruses of children, mistresses, and disciples. But Margaret Webster remembers him cruelly as the butt of the company:

> "Stop the train! stop the train! I'm Ellen Terry's little boy!" This, according to Edy, had been young Teddy's furious reaction to the sight of a train leaving Winchelsea station just as the children arrived there. The Gordon Craig who now rejoined the Lyceum company was not unrecognizably changed. . . .
>
> Craig was never noted for his modesty and he was not the most popular actor in the theatre, especially with the "supers." In the battle scene [of *Cymbeline*] he and Ben [Webster] had to fight their way, shoulder to shoulder, through serried ranks of embattled walk-ons. One night Ben became aware that he was being prodded from behind with a spear, bashed on the head with an ax, pushed and jostled by the troops at his rear beyond the call of duty. At last he turned around and hissed furiously, "What the hell do you think you're doing?" The army wavered and stopped. "Very sorry, sir," whispered one of them. "We thought you was Mr. Craig."

The Websters never knew that Ellen Terry tormented him as systematically as the supers did: swaddling him in public, she gouged his ego privately. She had lashed her little brother Fred with the same flashing savagery when, after bringing him into the Bancrofts' company, she mimicked his breaking voice onstage. Fred would become famous playing a man with a double life: the Scarlet Pimpernel, an apparent fop who is really a hero. Behind Ellen Terry's taunts lurked a terror of her son's burgeoning double life: the public Gordon Craig of the flaring capes and dashing felt hats looked like a cross between Henry Irving and the Scarlet Pimpernel, but in his secret self, she feared he was the helpless fop the Scarlet Pimpernel only pretended to be, fleeing from trouble and exertion to hide in the arms of strong women.

The charmed circle of the Lyceum was alive with traps for the soft boy; these fed the fits of terror about enemies and plots that possessed him as he aged. When he left the Lyceum to play a Hamlet of his own, and finally abandoned acting altogether for the comparative anonymity of printing, production, and writing, no one but his mother seems to have missed him. He refused to look back after his wounded departure, neglecting the Lyceum's gala 1902 Coronation performance of *The Bells*. Ellen Terry wrote in vain: "Hope you are not ill? Why were you not at the Lyceum gathering last night? Write Henry a line, I think, or it is an affront from your age to his" (quoted in Prideaux, 247). His only response was his absence, in 1905, from Irving's kingly funeral in Westminster

The young Edward Gordon Craig.
*Reproduced by permission of the Harry
Ransom Humanities Research Center,
University of Texas, Austin.*

Self-portrait by Edward Gordon Craig in a
letter to Edith Craig, 1898. *Reproduced by
permission of the Harry Ransom Humanities
Research Center, University of Texas, Austin.*

Drawing of Henry Irving as Man of the World. *Reproduced by permission of the Harry Ransom Humanities Research Center, University of Texas, Austin.*

Drawing by Edward Gordon Craig, probably of Henry Irving. *Reproduced by permission of the Harry Ransom Humanities Research Center, University of Texas, Austin.*

The aging Edward Gordon Craig. *Reproduced by permission of the Harry Ransom Humanities Research Center, University of Texas, Austin.*

Abbey, and his more flagrant absence in 1906 from his mother's golden jubilee, that long, lavish farewell to the theater experiments like his own were murdering.

Only after he had settled into exile did images of the Lyceum fuse with dreams of Harpenden as a lost and golden patriarchal home. He could not remember the father he prayed to, and so he adopted Irving as Godwin's visible realization; he made himself a man by copying his Master. The round, smooth boy who took his contours from the shaming house of women recreated himself in Irving's image as he came into his own. In 1898, he sent Edy a sketch of his new self in the hat and cloak that were to become his trademarks. The drawing of this new man evolves out of an Irving who had himself realized his most vivid life in drawings. Carefully, feature by feature, Gordon Craig turned himself into his adoptive father, a role Irving detested in his true home, the theater, though he played it good-naturedly offstage. This drawing by Gordon Craig could be either himself in his familiar costume, or the Irving whose vivid image never left him. When he is a grand patriarch himself, Gordon Craig continues to borrow himself from his Master, though Irving would never have sanctioned the nervous, inward-turned, self-blocking gesture: the mannerisms live, but Victorian expansiveness is gone forever. Still, to his own satisfaction, Gordon Craig effectively remade himself beyond the house of women in the image of the male God he had failed to please. In the 1960s, pilgrims to Gordon Craig's protected retreat at Vence were greeted by a reverend old man jauntily brandishing Henry Irving's walking stick. The "Mr. Vesuvius Theatre Destroyer" who set out to kill the gorgeous school that mocked him had become the puppet of the past.

He turned to figments of men for salvation, but in his mother lay all his fears. James M. Barrie and George Bernard Shaw did their best to make a mother's power so kittenish and devious that its triumphs were mere manipulative stage pranks, but when the mother was as strong and mutilated and angry as Ellen Terry, the children who lived with that unmediated power saw nothing to patronize. After the disaster of *The Vikings,* Gordon Craig fled her country, punishing women in her image but unable to bear the sight of her. He had been her captive male all along; when she could not be angry at Irving, or Charles Reade, or Godwin, he was there. Pseudo-sons who loved Lady Cicely dismissed her fierce Volumnia as miscasting, but her real son had felt a fury the stage forbade her to show.

Her marginal notes to *Coriolanus* show a penetrating understanding of a mother who needs heroes to assuage her rage. In her note to Act V, Scene iv, after Coriolanus has suicidally yielded to his mother's command, Ellen Terry prophesies the effects of her own motherhood: "She knows it's mortal to him - he goes back to certain death - but ROME IS saved!! Then his 'good report' will be her son - & she will train 'the poor Epitome' to be like the shadow of her son." Gordon Craig's "good report" from far corners of Russia, Italy, and France did become Ellen Terry's son, but it was a poor pleasure to raise her grandchildren in his wavering shadow.

The "little mother" he invented later on had been bigger than anybody but

Ellen Terry as Volumnia in *Coriolanus. Reproduced by permission of the Furness Collection, Van Pelt Library, University of Pennsylvania.*

himself knew. The funny drawing of Edy spurning him he had done at seventeen swelled suddenly into an Ellen Terry grown beyond control. But his cartoon told a painful truth. Again and again, his mother and sister had combined against him: when he was sent off to school, a freemasonry sprang up between them that no one could break. The home he had missed bristled with subtle taunts and too-shrewd criticisms. His first Hamlet drew a mortifying letter from his mother: "I was surprised to hear <u>not only</u> from Edy that you don't <u>look</u> well as Hamlet!!—" Edy's sisterly amplification followed:

My dear Boy=
   I was told <u>not to say</u> I had been to Hereford or I should certainly have written before = I liked it very much & I clapped to the echo - in fact so much that I thought they would have turned me out = Try & do <u>without</u> music when you die as they dont do it well & mind & have the lights <u>off</u> the back cloth when you say "'Tis now the witching hour of <u>night</u> etc." I liked your long cloak very much but the hood is either too small or it looks it & is not becoming also you

Yrhalo has dropped a bit! -

Drawing of Edith Craig by Edward Gordon Craig, 29 July 1889.
Reproduced by permission of the Harry Ransom Humanities Research Center, University of Texas, Austin.

look so fat in HI's clothes - couldn't you put them on a bit tighter or neater or something?

Gordon Craig took his Hamlet with deadly seriousness: it was the play he staged for Stanislavsky, the noble, disinherited prince he *was*. Could his later profundities blot out his mother and sister coolly telling him he looked fat in the role?

It was nothing new: the two reinforced each other in undermining his entire visionary life. Even when Edy was a young music student in Berlin, her intransigent practicality had the power to reduce him. When they tried to collaborate on a play, she wrote: "About the play= I'm not quite clear as to what you mean but as far as I can see, the new arrangement makes the play longer which is what we want to avoid-not? Anything I think after the 'Thank God' of Norwich when he is ill, would be an anti-climax or else that scene (where he is in bed) would have to be sacrificed & have no definite conclusion= I'm writing the whole play out in a book so as to see how it reads= Send me your m.s.s. of the 2 & 3 acts= the first ones= About the scene you sent either it must be a huge stage or the people must play between the arch & the wall & keep jumping over the partition= It's very pretty but unpractical. It might be used as a back cloth painted, & nothing built out="

Edy's literalness, her insistence on seeing what was and was not there, made him want to retreat from her eyes. His mother warned him about this tendency to retreat. Fearing for his work because of "the lack of cultured criticism" in his ambience, she sent him a lesson he could never accept: "It's not enough to criticize oneself." These two women who would not go with him, who saw through his efforts so remorselessly, would haunt the enemy world from which he fled when he hid his drawings, his screens, his puppets and model theaters, even from his devoted son Teddy. He, and he alone, criticized himself, screening his theaters from the eyes that had watched him in England. Always, the cruelest and the sharpest eyes belonged to women.

His vocation as a womanizer had more rage in it than love: he rejoiced in playing sultan to clusters of uncritically adoring handmaidens. His pleasure climaxed when the babies he fathered gave him an excuse to abandon their mothers. Before World War I, he effectively abandoned even the loving Elena Meo, though in imagination he always blessed her as his spiritual wife: until she died in England in 1957, she lived mostly with Ellen Terry, and with her own daughter Nellie after 1928, while Gordon Craig founded and abandoned other households in Italy and France. When he deserted his women and children, he endowed himself with his father's power of leaving; he also entangled his mother (though at a safe distance) in his complicated erotic life, for her cottage at

Smallhythe was the retreat for many of his discarded families. His compulsive scenario forced his most penetrating critic to play the dear little woman who lived in a shoe.

As early as 1893, when he insisted on marrying his former Harpenden neighbor May Gibson, Ellen Terry saw the writing on the wall. May gave him a pretext to defect from the Lyceum's impending American tour, but after she had rescued him from America's abundance and space, he stopped liking her. In 1897 he left May and their four children for Jess Dorynne, and the cycle began. He had married May and the rest to his mother, not himself: Ellen Terry paid May's alimony and supported the new children (and several of their mothers) for the rest of her life. The woman who had been so grand that she left him crying alone in the dark (*Index*, 6) now had so many of his children that she didn't know what to do.

Even in their best days together, she had tended to swoop on him with a faintly savage distaste. She sent him a bizarre blessing when he was seventeen: "You certainly are of an age to take reverent care of a book now, & you <u>must</u> read= . . . I conclude with a blessing upon your fair tho' fat-ish 'chops', & a suggestion that you have yr head shaved—I mean cut off—I mean yr <u>hair</u> <u>cropped</u> quickly, so that you can train it against the heavenly hour when <u>we</u> twain shall happily meet - it will cool yr BRAINS." His new family aroused the same distaste, which she expressed even to outsiders like Audrey Campbell: "Mr. Alfred Austin has come & gone — so has the family of Craig! (it was not with unmixed sorrow I said farewell-----but the <u>baby</u> is just <u>Perfect</u>!!" When crisis came to them two years later, she wrote unsympathetically to Audrey: "I fear Ted & M are beginning to awake from their dream —('The old story Madame — The old story') & I'm very unhappy about them - but <u>hush</u>! for I wd like neither Boo, Harries, or such like to know & I'll <u>tell</u> you when we meet= I have always been prepared for a good deal from T̄. & M. but--------"

She was more outspokenly exacting to Ted and May themselves. May, whom she robustly disliked, did provide a convenient focus of blame for Ted's irresponsibility: "Tell Ted if he doesn't get some engagement soon, I'll,—well I know what I'll do=May you shd think of <u>that for</u> him & of nothing else= Why don't you urge him to be up & going?—for you & yours." Since it didn't matter what either woman thought or said, she abandoned herself to terrible prophecies she knew would be ignored: "At my time of life with my regular work to do I *must* expect *help* from you, rather than all these added little worries and added responsibilities. . . . I look upon this £3 per week as helping May and your babies, and *you must not put it to any other use*—and for yourself you must make your own living. . . . *Do you see the doubled responsibilities which await you in the near future?* Give up dreaming of the future, and make your *bread and butter for today.* The rest will follow *if you do this now—not else!*" (1896. Quoted in EAC, 95). Her enraged interference was a desperate attempt to salvage her own future, for if Ted chose to spend his energy falling in and out of love with large families, her own life was at risk. In these years when her son's paternity was strangling her, Shaw commemorated her as the triumphant vehicle of a mother's powers.

Things got worse after May was discarded. Ellen Terry preferred Jess to May, but Jess too was allowed only to adore him, not to remake him. Ellen Terry watched helplessly the frenzies of indulgence that would destroy him in the theater, despite the brilliant work everyone assured her he was doing: "You must not dictate to people in power=I've stuck at rehearsal in my early days 'till past 3 in the morning of the 1st performance & again in the afternoon until too late to leave the theatre!!= Really you are too silly Ted in some things . . . **W i l l** you not 'hold you still'? This is going on & you are getting no practice! & all nonsense- The name you'll get=" When he wanted to stop publishing *The Page* without refunding the subscribers' money, she wrote frantically: "A contract is a contract & whoever on either side breaks it is **d i s h o n o u r a b l e**, & I can't get over my horror of that for you =I want to be so proud of you all around=think-think- think- Your 'contract' with May you have chucked upon me - for myself I don't much care, but that you shall not care just kills me=Don't break more contracts outside in the open, for other people wont treat it as I do when they come to know it ="

Everything Ellen Terry had won came from her talent for becoming what people thought she was; now a child who flouted his audiences was suffocating her. She envied his license to be bad; she hated him for making her pay for his trespasses, not only with her earnings, but with her life. Wearily, she invited him to the opening of *Coriolanus,* the last Shakespearean production Irving staged at the Lyceum, not (she said) because she wanted him to see her as a fierce mother, but because his presence would relieve the world: "To be sitting very quietly at some good public places wd put to bed what so many people are saying - that you are insane . . . & it is only business people we heed how they think= & business people swarm on first nights="

Sometimes, as he deposited broken pieces of his life one by one into her lap, she became so angry that she was frightened of herself, didn't know what she had said, and tried to conciliate him: "I enjoyed being with you much but sorry I was ill & a trouble rather=" "Forgive me last night=I was not in the least

vexed or angry (as I suppose I seemed to be-) only just muddle-brained &
confused. I feel **a w f u l** lately if I'm with more than one person at a time
- Explain to Jessy =" Were other mothers selfless and forbearing? The more
fools they! "I know how very unhappy [Jessy's mother] must be feeling = as
I shd be in her place, until years had proved the integrity of the man to whom
my daughter had given herself-and the knowledge that the man had already
many ties & responsibilities, which ties & responsibilities he had simply 'chucked
up,' wd not give to my mind the peace which shd fall upon me when I sought
my downy pillow = . . . Jess says her mother won't get angry!! How wonderful
& really admirable of her ="

   Ellen Terry could not imagine being as tactfully restrained with her children
as she had to be with the public: Edy and Ted were her anchor to reality, her
repositories of emotion, the sole allowable recipients of her anger. Audiences
could be offended and even driven away, but never sons, particularly this son
whose helplessness had already enmeshed her in so many ensnaring tokens.
Accordingly, when Gordon Craig showed all the symptoms of sending Jessy the
way of May, Ellen Terry unleashed on him a gorgeous symphony of rage on
behalf not of Jessy alone, but of all women degraded by selfish, silly men. Her
writing in this long letter is bold and clear, beautiful and strong:

   ''A m u s e'' me? (you & J -) You Flat Iron - you idiot -------- I can
find no name to tell you what I think of your intelligence = = = you are doing
your best to miss your salvation - your fortune that lies before you — your whole
happiness & by that I mean J. & with all of it at your feet you are— so blind,
with jealousy, vanity, discontent & obstinacy you don't see it --- you refer I
suppose when you speak of "amusing" me, to the evening when I laughed at your
saying I had no love for you? — If you cd only have known the weight you
lifted from me, as you said that, for then I knew that you were jealous, & feeling
wretched, which indeed you shd feel at the work your foolish obstinacy has done
in simply driving J. from you — I felt when you said that (she "had no love for
you") that all was not yet lost --- & that you did love her — & were not callous
as she thinks, but only jealous without knowing it = Now consider --------
she has done everything a woman can do for three years to prove her love for
you - spite of your outrageous ungentleness & selfish inconsiderateness — She
longs for you to be with her - I can't get a word from her upon any other subject
but you — you — you = & no one but a really unintelligent person cd fail to
know her entire devotion & adoration of you - (I am blind sometimes but not
so blind as not to see this laid out like a Map before me —) You love her —
you have said so & I believe you —(the scrap of paper in my bag the comfort

it has been to me —) **A m u s e** me — you! You torture me - as you have the other poor souls who have loved you — for all the heartbreak you have caused & are causing me — you have never appreciated any of the love you have had thickly thrown upon you =

Ellen Terry goes on to pride herself on the gift she has publicly forfeited, a gift that will ruin her with her son: her native honesty.

When I used to pour out just what I thought of you — with intent for your happiness solely before my eyes ---- you simply fled— That was your usual pretty unreasoning trick to avoid anyones implorings or advice — Then, knowing how words of any kind but flattering words, make you impatient (& I wouldn't give those) then I tried to be not so serious with you — avoided speaking of your affairs & only just shouldered your difficulties time after time you ungrateful son - hoping you might take the chances of love, & fortune that have presented themselves before you, & which you have only blindly kicked aside - & after all, & the last few months intenser suffering than I have ever experienced for myself you think you "amuse" me!! If you cd see my ragged old heart — Do you know nothing --- have you no perception =

I keep from advising J. by one word about you - (in fear of causing a wider breach -) but in spite of the cowardly way in which you put the fault upon her shoulders, I know you love her, & I entreat you not to lose her - Heavens --- she's not granite -- you will wear all the beauty of her character out, by your constant unreasonableness -- You could not wear my love out but that's because you are your Father's child, & because of the blood being the same -- yours & mine =

The abused Jessy in whom she has seen herself dissolves into the mother who does not know how to play the role assigned her:

Blind one - can't you see the dilemma I am in **n o w** about you? (This is another subject.) I shd think you could see, but perhaps you dont — (!!) Great Heavens — how can one make you see the very nose upon your face? — This is my dilemma — you are in a tight corner again in regard to money — Now what am I to do? The same I have done before, again & again? — Is that for your best good? — I'd do it if I knew it wd be the best — but as J. is doing now, I feel I ought to change my method for you, which had failed & failed **& f a i l e d**, & try some other way — Dont you see that we are two devoted women who long to be friends & show our friendship to you, & that nothing we do seems to have the slightest effect upon you — or to be of any

benefit whatever for your happiness? — I've tried not to speak, for well I know
how every word may mar instead of mend — but here am I at my age finding
all my love not understood by you in the least, that you think I am "amused"
by the case of Edward & the Rebellious J, & all the while you are both doing
your best way to kill me - At my age . . . (with my repeated failures in regard
to you, in mind) . . . At my age I am taking a leaf out of the younger womans
book. I will change my plan & try another way with you about your business
affairs — Unless you will be plain with me & tell me what to do for you ---
point out the way **y o u c a n s e e** for me to help you — in business
— with regard to J. with regard to any thing on earth for you & your better
having — I'm getting very doddery so I'll end — one thing Dont dare to say
or even think that I say or think lightly for one moment about you or Edy =
or J — or your children - You are all heart of my heart - breath of my body
— Mother-

Perhaps this letter is Ellen Terry's most complete performance, but in it she lost
her audience by unleashing her secret self. This torrential accuser is not the soft
"Nell" Gordon Craig created after she died, but a woman who had always cared
for herself and who had always seen more than she was supposed to. She had
been tactful with Henry, she fluttered and crooned over Shaw, but she let the
son whose blood she shared feel the power she could not show. In forming this
helpless, wasteful, exploitative boy, she had made a parody of all the men who
had insulted women and abused the privileges they had never deserved. In
payment for pouring money on him, she poured out as well the honesty she
could not express publicly, making him listen to the woman she was forbidden
to act. Her reiterated outraged "*amuse* me?" half-confesses to the sin the Lyceum
had imperfectly suppressed: once again, and this time with dire results, she had
seemed to laugh at a man.

Edy was teaching her about women's rights, and she was learning more from
the frighteningly empty future that was to be the reward of her years of
usefulness. She was learning, too, from the helplessness of the women her son
abandoned: they saw no way of supporting themselves and their children alone,
without a man. Was there in truth no way for women? Her son was making
it impossible not to learn searing lessons about the men those women needed:
"But I am self-respecting & don't like rude rough manners - & so when you
are rough, I just feel as if I curl up & tumble down from you, like those rum
little insects which roll themselves into a ball = I believe in my soul you feel
tenderly but I have never seen you behave tenderly to any woman = . . . To
start with, **I c a n n o t u n d e r s t a n d a n y m a n** = I

give it all up - I have in my long life been of great service to many women - clever & fools, they have come to me, I have helped them, advised them, & several have been bettered & made happier all - through - me = That's something = "

Her children were teaching her too much, too intensely. When they were growing up, she had lived in the theater, but now that they were grown and she had less to do, they twined around her with insistent, stinging intimacy. She was learning too much about the men and the women she had played when she was a star. Now that there was no Lyceum and only the mother was left, she tried to put all her intensity into that ill-defined role. She had blighted her son by showing him her truth. To keep him, she put herself on his stage.

By 1903, Gordon Craig had staged three innovative and acclaimed productions with Martin Shaw; no prophet whispered that this promising beginning would become in retrospect his greatest sustained achievement on the English stage. Like all his work, *Dido and Aeneas, The Masque of Love,* and *Acis and Galatea* were both striking and strikingly uncommercial; Ellen Terry did her best to bring in audiences by playing *Nance Oldfield* as a curtain raiser. Craig waited for West End offers that never came; he cursed the old-fashioned theater; and he turned to his mother, its darling. In 1903, the old world, the Lyceum, was crumbling, and Shaw, the new, was playing with myriad projects; she too was waiting for a future that never began. She had written out her rage and her son's wounds had closed sufficiently for him to beg her to go into management with his productions. The theatrical Terrys had been bred to play together; she took over the Imperial Theatre, which was attractive but out of the way, and agreed to stage Ibsen's early play, *The Vikings of Helgeland.* She was to play the formidable Hiördis.

The Vikings called down on them that disaster that had hovered at least since Gordon Craig joined the Lyceum fourteen years earlier. The play was turgid and operatic, with none of the searing contemporary relevance people expected from Ibsen; Hiördis was a still more unsympathetic mother than Volumnia. The bleakness of Ibsen's pagan north did not lend itself to novel visual effects as well as Purcell and Handel's music had done. When, in 1900, life had looked better, Ellen Terry had seen all the dangers of the collaboration: "I fear it wd be quite impossible . . . I shall probably go on fairly much the same as now, with H. as long as he wants me. **And he will want me as long as he is!** you can be quite sure of that= . . . I shd not feel at all inclined to be entirely in the hand of my dear old rash & inexperienced-in-business-ways boy Ed'ard!! = In other words I fear we cd not work together = " But in 1903, the old way was no longer there; her son had put himself in her hands, which were as inexperienced in business ways as his own; through Ibsen's script, they acted once more the fraught drama they had made each other play at home.

Only Gordon Craig knew that *The Vikings,* not *Candida, Alice-Sit-by-the-Fire,* or *Captain Brassbound,* was Ellen Terry's real mother play. *Bethlehem,* the Nativity play he had staged the year before, had allowed him to enthrone the Madonna-Mother he longed for; *The Vikings* licensed him to manage the formidable mother he had. Its Egil, Hiördis's child, is a despised cipher and (his mother initially thinks) a bastard. She denounces him in martial language: "Egil is weak; one can see he is no freeborn child. . . . Doubt not that shame can be sucked into the blood, like the venom of a snake-bite. Of another mettle are the freeborn sons of mighty men. I have heard of a queen that took her son and sewed his kirtle fast to his flesh, yet he never blinked an eye. *(With an evil look.)* Dagny, that will I try with Egil!"

Gordon Craig, who was not a freeborn child, knew how much his mother enjoyed such torturing tests of strength. The audiences who doted on Ellen Terry had never seen her taunting men, straining to make of them the heroes she was forbidden to be, goading them with mockery for not being great. At the end, after her rage for supermen has wrought havoc among the Vikings, the terrified Egil watches his dead mother lead an army of ghostly warriors. Death allows her a grandeur of her own, independent of the men she has flayed. In staging *The Vikings,* Gordon Craig presented to the public the warrior Ellen Terry he alone knew. Of course, no one understood, and least of all his mother. She thought as she struggled through her role that she was helping him as selflessly as she always had: her secret self was a secret even from her.

Like the play, the production was rent by a struggle for authority. Ted felt infantilized and conspired against by Ellen Terry and Edy, who was working on the costumes; the actors could not keep their feet on his rocky, dimly lit set; they could neither see nor be seen through their masklike helmets. Groping about through the dark, the tensions, the general discomfort of modernity, Ellen Terry could not realize the Hiördis she had been to him all his life. Like Shaw, Gordon Craig had dreamed of escorting her into the modern world, but like Shaw he could not do it: if there were more changes left in her, her sons could not arouse them. In a panic, he wrote a letter which he never sent, pleading with her for his authority. Like the letter he wrote when he was expelled from school, it entices her into his pain and powerlessness:

Dearest Mother. A word in time saves much misunderstanding. I have now finished designing all the scenes & dresses for Vikings & have mapped out some of the "situations" as these are called — but still it all seems to me as unlike my work & what I have always striven for in work, as can be.

This is unsatisfactory for the production - & we will lose all unity - (by production I dont mean picture only-)

If you & I were the only two who had a single say in the matter, all would be perfect - provided we worked like one — as we should do the play would grow quietly & quickly & straight — whereas its present growth is

It is not understood that you & I are doing this play together — I feel already that I am not doing it at all — that is deadly. but I am trying the position of artistic suggester only by sufferance ---- probably the last position you want me to think I fill. I am not at all useful in such a position — for heaps of reasons which we both know — one reason specially strong just now,—that of losing belief & affection for the work in hand . I do not feel responsible,—I cease to worry about the work,—& one scene or another — and colour or another — one dress or another, one emotion, movement, or intention or another seems to me a matter of indifference if it can be changed & altered without any consideration & by a momentary idea occurring to any of us.

You on your part say that you will not be at all like the part - and be able to touch it — perhaps also the result of losing heart.—

I believe you are right & more than that — you will be unable to act or appear at all unless you can devote all your time to the part.

Why not leave all the rest to me - I do know that never yet will you have had such an accompaniment such as I could give you if I were not tied. But [illegible] in one moment I am thinking of the work & the next moment wondering if I ought not to think of what you think you want — & so over goes the apple cart.

I do honestly believe that this was an opportunity —& is still if I may have free play — but at present my work is damned out & out for slowly & surely an entirely foreign element is creeping into it. you fear for it - rush to its aid - & whoops over goes the cart again. Bless you I know you mean every help in the world but somehow it muddles me & I lose my head -

It's like an overanxious & kind prompter giving one the word when one hasn't forgotten it but is merely making a carefully considered pause. It is not as if I were new to the business of stage director & rather enjoyed it as a pose —

Its old work to me & all the first fun of it, — the fun of the toy - is over & gone long ago.

I don't know whether this letter will do any good — anyhow you'll read into it nothing I do not intend — but it may help if only it makes us work together — you & I only — oblivious - <u>thats</u> the end — oblivious of anybody else & of anything else except the PLAY.

Then it will b̲e̲ the event I believed it <u>could</u> be.

But he never let Ellen Terry read the letter that was to unite them with the play. There could be no partnership when Gordon Craig cast his mother so rigidly as the ferocious Hiördis, with himself as the weak little Egil. With her there he could never claim controlling authority; his mother was manager, it was she people would come to see, all her money was invested in this production. Once more, the stage had sullied his vision.

To justify her son and keep him near her, Ellen Terry tried to believe she could play Hiördis, though in her heart she knew that audiences would pity their miscast darling. She had never listened to her own uncensored Hiördis-like voice: "You take everything lightly & go on & on, & leave all the <u>women</u> you are connected with to bear the pains—& I̲ am the one you make suffer most. If you were a <u>weakling</u> I wd take charge with enthusiasm but <u>why</u> shd you be so unmanly & <u>look so like a man</u>?" She did have glimmerings that Hiördis might allow her to speak out as she had tried to do through Lady Macbeth so many years before: "Then a part like that for me wd be like 3̲ Lady Macbeths. It's superb—& I'd like to — but I'm afraid I could not get̲ at it-could not do it = but it's wonderful - & as I <u>think of</u> it I feel like getting up <u>& trying</u> — but nobody wd believe me in such a part & I'm too old now to experiment - <u>handicapped</u>" (19 Nov. 1902. Quoted in EAC, 174).

The Lyceum had taught her too well: it had sealed the womanly actress permanently away from the complete woman, handicapping both forever. Irving had forbidden her to be Hiördis, and now she was afraid of that self, and so she failed her son and their new theater. She wrote out her remorse in her diary in writing that was wild and askew: "Play went splendidly tonight-Ted's work <u>all through</u> <u>magnificent</u> = As for me — it's awful to play what I can not do---I can not play H— 'for nuts,' think it is because I don't understand her. Can't <u>look</u> the part even. All the work—truth exp—in vain I fell short — . . . What shall we do—? Ted's work is so beautiful . . . he is the only good thing. All the artists come— & are delighted— <u>General public</u> <u>don't</u> cue for play—<u>nor me</u>." Unable to rest, she retold the story, this time focusing on her own role in the disaster: "1st performance of Ibsen's 'The Vikings'= All played well & all went well until 3rd Act when I forgot most of my words & the whole thing went to pieces. The last act took a terrible time to set, & at the end a friendly enthusiastic audience applauded what I'm afraid will prove an 'artistic success' only."

The useful actress seemed once again to have sacrificed herself for a man, but she had also been doing her best to control that man. In the end, she undermined him by her floundering performance. Max Beerbohm, who admired Craig extravagantly, wrote about the production with chivalrous disapproval: "For the art of Ibsen and the art of Miss Terry our admiration has not been intensified, but the stage-manager-scene-painter-of-costumes-and-all-the-rest-of-it looms up illustriously with laurels on his brow. On the first night Miss Terry led Mr. Craig before the footlights (or rather, the place where the footlights were before Craig swept them away). It would have seemed more correct, really, if Mr. Craig, with an air of grateful acknowledgment, had led Miss Terry."

In desperation, she revived *Much Ado,* as she had wanted to do all along, with her son's new, ingeniously designed church scene. This time there was no need for her to play Cassandra, for the disaster was plain. She spelled it out to Ted: "It will mean ruin to me if this play don't succeed and I shall close the theatre and finish up on the following Saturday if things don't go smoothly on the Tuesday--It wd mean ruin to me if this Play don't succeed, for I should with that play [The Vikings] be losing about £150 or £200 a week--& for you it would be ruin, as making 'impossible' from an all round point of view to do Craig's beautiful work. . . . To get through this season quietly without obvious disaster must be our united aim" (quoted in EAC, 175).

It was ruin all around. Ted took his revenge by hating *Much Ado:* "Each time I see it a viler gaiety is added—speech is noisier & action floppier—thought infrequent, and taste unknown" (quoted in EAC, 176). He brooded, he fathered babies, he avoided creditors, he began to plan his school. He blamed his mother, her management, her friends, for the failure with which he had infected her. To her son, she had always been a triumphant heroine. Now she was part of his world of loss. The next year, he moved to Berlin, leaving Ellen Terry with six of his children to look after. He stayed abroad for the rest of his life almost by accident, returning to England only on painful visits. He had gotten away from his mother at last, freeing himself from her truths to become part of the host of men who recreated her according to their beliefs. He too had become a man.

She had lost her son by acting (or failing to act) the mother he saw. In 1905, with Lady Cicely, she would lose Shaw in the same fashion. Did they leave because she had played their parts badly, or because she had played too well? Whichever was the case, her torn life would never heal. And they saw only themselves. Ten years later, she was pleading and wheedling the powerful Shaw for a part. He thought only that Teddy was draining her money again, not that she was an actress who needed to act. The actress launched into a bitterly compressed defense of sons and the sorts of illumination they brought:

> My dear friend neighbour, you must not trouble your dear heart for a moment about me in that way, for I am really quite rich! My worldly possessions positively hamper me! I could get on nicely without them (but having them there's no being without them). I am grateful for the loan of your light which shows me that I see a little all the while. I see how unintelligent I am. That fact is so near me, that I must be careful I don't break my heart against it. But your flashlight shows me one or two other usefuls, and after a little more plodding in hope, all may be well. [So the mad Ophelia also hoped.] Thank you, very dear friend, for the loan of your light. My eyes pain me. Good Lord, my poor eyes! Teddy is afloat now, and my son all along has been my sun. Without the warmth of him many a time I would have died and died, I know! When I cannot see I'll get dear little Barrie to adopt me! Thank you for writing me so kindest and helpfullest a letter. (12 November 1913. A Corr., 329)

Did the light sons cast pain and finally blind her poor eyes? After Gordon Craig left and Shaw outgrew her, she did not take refuge with dear little Barrie: she turned to an even tenderer young man, Graham Robertson, a sometime artist and passionate collector. She knew he would never hurt her, for he cherished the precious things he acquired.

After 1903, when the storm broke and Gordon Craig left England, Ellen Terry lost her mobility: the woman who had been a living picture turned into a statue, alien and adored. Her jubilee in 1906 froze her into a memento mori; so did her valedictory Hermione in the same year, even though she had laughed as the statue.

The artist William Rothenstein was her son's passionate acolyte. After *The Vikings,* he thanked Ellen Terry profusely for her service to Gordon Craig and to the theater through him: "You have been so brave and good to Teddie. I am so delighted he has been able to show you how wise you have been; I am sure that in a very short time he will have won that foremost place in the modern theatre he already has shown his right to" (quoted in *Memoirs,* 267). Rothenstein's lithograph of Ellen Terry is his—and his generation's—image of the woman he thanked. She is static, sad, and inward-turned; Graham Robertson would name this Ellen Terry "Our Lady of Sighs." Her fixed abstraction and clenched pose suggest that she might brood forever as she is brooding here, in contrast to the pictorial actress of 1881, whose stillness resembles a pause in music. As Camma in Tennyson's *The Cup*—a production Edward Godwin helped design—this Ellen Terry sits in a pose similar to Rothenstein's: both are seated, looking beyond or away from the viewer to the right. But Camma's eyes, her face, her gesture, are intensely mobile. The early, pictorial Ellen Terry has been frozen in the middle of a burst of energy; the later woman freezes into herself.

The marmoreal turn-of-the-century Ellen Terry reaches one extreme in Graham Robertson's portrait, which he nicknamed "Ellen Terry in Heaven." This stony-faced woman is not only immobilized, but enskied: she seems to be undergoing a permanent ascension. The lily that accompanies her is as distant as it can be from the encircling flowers in Watts's "Choosing," though for Robertson "Choosing" was the most sacred icon of his Lady. Watts's young girl is almost smothered by the flowers that simultaneously dramatize and deny her intense hunger for life. Woman and flower gaze remotely at each other in "Ellen in Heaven," each inviolate in cool celestial lifelessness.

Ellen Terry's tender association with Graham Robertson in the last three decades of her life was both a diminution and a return. Robertson's loving care of "the Lady" he liked to imagine as a fairy visitant finished the attenuation from woman to dream that Irving had begun and Shaw had perpetuated. Nineteen years her junior, Robertson never knew the hoyden Irving had tamed. His Ellen Terry had no being beyond the Lyceum:

> Her loyalty to Irving never faltered; she well knew how unapproachably great he was. As to her career being sacrificed to him—does anyone in their senses suppose that she would have gained her unique position without him? She had little ambition—no "push"—little business capacity. She loved to serve and would always have served *somebody*. Luckily, her keen artistic perception led her to serve the right man. . . . After E. T. left Irving (by mutual arrangement because she could no longer play juvenile lead), after she was "set free" as Shaw would put it, what happened? Nothing in particular. She put on *The Vikings* to please Ted, she played in *Brassbound* to please Shaw (and played by no means well), she played in *Alice sit by the Fire* to please Barrie, and in *Pinkie* to please me. *Hermione* was not of her best, and her brilliant Mrs. Ford [in Beerbohm Tree's *Merry Wives of Windsor*, 1902; in fact Ellen Terry played Mistress Page to Madge Kendal's Mistress Ford] was launched *before* the parting from Irving. Irving and she were the perfect combination—each supported and inspired the other. (10 Nov. 1931. *Letters*, 260–61)

William Rothenstein, lithograph of
Ellen Terry. *Reproduced by permission
of the Harry Ransom Humanities
Research Center, Department of
Iconography, University of Texas,
Austin.*

Ellen Terry in *The Cup. Reproduced
by permission of the Harry Ransom
Humanities Research Center, University
of Texas, Austin.*

Tender custodian of a past he could barely remember, Graham Robertson never realized how well the stage had trained the wild child: as an actress, it was her duty and her talent to please everyone who had a play. He stripped his ethereal Ellen Terry of her incarnations as boy, as dangerous child, and as fallen woman, but he restored a dearer past that had never been hers: when Graham Robertson took her in, he gave her her garden.

He spent his happiest days at Sandhills, his estate near Witley in Surrey, where he presided over a profusion of flowers, dogs, and art treasures. His widowed mother was his dearest love and closest companion until she died in 1907, when he was forty-one. He collected Blakes, Rossettis, and children: like Lewis Carroll, he gathered little girls and reproduced them, though this old-fashioned connoisseur painted his child-friends rather than photographing them. He wrote a series of books for a little girl named Binkie whom he had lost: her family left the neighborhood when she was five. One became a whimsical play, *Pinkie and the Fairies,* which Beerbohm Tree staged magnificently in 1908. Ellen Terry did not play a fairy, but the kindly Aunt Imogen. She read a nostalgic epilogue which began:

> Babyland and Fairyland
> Lie so near—so near each other.
> By the stretching of a hand
> Is the gulf between them spann'd:
> Baby Sister, Fairy Brother,
> Meet and greet upon the strand.

Ben had trained his stage daughter to speak clearly and beautifully: not until she was adored as a mother did she learn the language of the nursery. When Graham Robertson adopted Ellen Terry as his dream mother and dearest child, he made for her the sort of Edenic shelter she had, in Harpenden, given her own children to their bane, though she had never lived in it herself. The stage child had no use for protective shelters; Lewis Carroll had barred the fallen woman from the garden he dreamed; now she was grateful to be made welcome.

In 1900 she had bought her own Tudor cottage at Smallhythe Place, on the marshes in Kent. She had made of the cozy place a little estate, but her dominion exacerbated the tensions of home: there were her son's children to care for and his mistresses to placate, while next door at Priest's House there was Edy, always solicitous and in a rage, accompanied by strange demanding women who wanted one to be grand for them. Sandhills brought peace and a past she had never wanted before. It was rough with a roughness she remembered, for its owner

Walford Graham Robertson, "Portrait of Ellen Terry" (nicknamed "Ellen Terry in Heaven"). *Ellen Terry Memorial Museum, Smallhythe Place. Courtesy of the Trustee of the Ellen Terry Estate.*

had made it a shrine to a distant decade: "I blush at your polite allusions to the luxuries of Sandhills. May you be forgiven. Sandhills—stuck fast in the sixties —gasless, electric lightless, bathroomless, motorless. Well, it suits me but most folks wouldn't thank you for it. It is of my date and we get on well together. But to you, accustomed to 'all modern improvements', it must have come as a mild shock" (6 October 1915. *Letters,* 29).

Graham Robertson's reverence for the home of his childhood restored to Ellen Terry her marriage in art and her one great love affair. She remembered the hopes for love and art that had transfigured Little Holland House; she recaptured the power and joy the country had given her when she slept under the sky. Her country homes in the sixties, before Henry had frozen her into womanliness and fame, now seemed to hold all that had ever mattered. Of course there had been flaws. At Little Holland House, everyone had criticized her; at Harpenden, Godwin had brought intervals of excitement, but like Teddy he bolted when she needed help. Sandhills restored the touch, the smell, the feel, of the sixties, but it banished all the disappointments. For the first time, she felt taken care of. She had never been a child before.

Gladly, she let Graham Robertson exempt her from being human. He explained her by saying she was really a fairy; he wrote reams of praise to "the

Ellen Terry, 1907.
*Reproduced by permission of
the Furness Collection, Van
Pelt Library, University of
Pennsylvania.*

real Ellen Terry, the Fairy Lady with the wonderful message of beauty from that country East of the Sun and West of the Moon." Her son had published these words in *The Mask,* his beautiful, costly magazine whose first issue had contained his hectoring *Letter to Ellen Terry.* He had worried in it about things she had said about acting years ago; then it ended: "We have talked about this, I think, but not so much in detail as now." But of course when he wrote from Italy and printed the letter in *The Mask,* he flaunted the fact that they were not talking—only he was—and that they would never talk in detail again. She preferred to be a fairy. It was truer to write that she lived East of the Sun and West of the Moon than that she talked in detail to her son.

It mattered less and less where she lived, she could imagine more and more, go back and forward in time or out of the world altogether, because after 1915 she was almost blind. Her eyes had pained her for years; people tended to blame her (or her men) for it. Some said she had strained them copying Godwin's drawings late at night; others blamed the gaslight at the Lyceum, which Henry had refused to replace with electricity even when gas had become old-fashioned. Perhaps because it brought those days closer, part of her clung to her blindness:

when, in 1915, she could put off cataract surgery no longer, she is said to have destroyed her sight by prematurely throwing off the bandages, "impatient of the darkness" (Steen, 322). Perhaps, as she intimated to Shaw when she wrote that her son was the sun of her life, she knew she had seen too much and wanted a protective dusk between herself and the world. In some photographs from the early twentieth century, she has the blank look of the shell-shocked.

As early as 1896, when she had had a preliminary treatment for cataracts that blinded her temporarily, she wrote to Shaw: "You cant imagine how I'm looking forward with delight to being blind for a short while. Folk are so sympathetic to a blind woman, and I shall have to be taken care of instead of taking care of folk" (7 July 1896. *A Corr.,* 27). With Graham Robertson, that dream came true. Just as she could no longer quite see the world, the world in Graham's person could not quite see her, nor could it hear her, and that was comforting.

For a long time, the world had not seen or heard her. At her jubilee, the *London Times* had paid tribute to her wholesomeness in a neurotic climate: "For half a century Ellen Terry has been appealing to our hearts. Whatever the anti-sentimentalists might say, that is the simple truth. She is no 'intellectual' actress. Nor is she 'a bundle of nerves.' Her way is and always has been the way of heartiness. A creature of the rudimentary, full-blooded, naïve emotions, she excites these emotions in us. Natures like this, no less on the stage than off it, are the natures that do not arouse an interested curiosity or a thrilling wonder or a weird sense of fascination so much as that simple, homely, yet all-powerful sentiment which the world is agreed to call love" (*London Times,* 13 June 1906). Her most perceptive chroniclers still imagine that depression was a rare and startling invader of her constitutional good cheer (Peters, *Shaw,* 216). Yet her confession to Ella Casella is outstanding only in its fervor: "I've seen lots of fun here but I am changed—oh dear, oh dear—I am never any thing now but in the depths of down-ness!!—if you know where that is! I pray you don't!"

In her letters from the 1890s and after, depression is a motif, but nobody believed her, just as they never believed she was ill. "Don't be down Bessie dear — How 'down' we all are — East wind I guess!" "My eyes are very bad & I must leave off writing - My everlasting love to you sweetheart - I hope you are as brightly shining as ever — My star has stopped dancing I'm afraid — but ------ who knows what is, & what isn't, when they are as tired as I am =" The Lyceum had slowed down her mercurial Beatrice; eventually Beatrice deserted her altogether. Four years later, her flight inspired a more ominous lament: "My star is tired out & I fear will never dance again — 'Heaven take my soul & England keep my bones -' Perhaps gentle England will patch me up again! It is so difficult to get dead ="

In 1897, not even Ted could deny his mother's state of mind to Edy: "Mother seems [really?] depressed. I suppose it's one of us - or both. I wish I saw a way to do what would brighten her up a bit. I cannot get a paying engagement yet & cannot keep it when I do get it - & you cannot get married or settle down (naturally) & all together we possess the cause of all her worries & can produce no remedy." Ted's diagnosis was more Victorian than Ellen Terry's disease. She was dragged down by her children's continued dependence; beyond that, her comic spirit was confronting to its horror the lie of all happy endings: "& after all my life working I want things to go smoothly - they'll have to - or I shall break down."

They didn't, and she did. In the year of The Vikings, she half-prepared Graham Robertson: "I hope you have not got 'the blues'—all my friends seem so depressed— many of 'em nearly kill me to be with them & I fear catching the complaint! A fine gift from the fairies a cheerful temperament!!" But the fairies' gifts didn't always last. Playing Lady Cicely amid the preparations for her jubilee, she wrote to Audrey Campbell: "I cannot write but the merest scrawl - for I am so ill - 'Cap. B--' over & I was awful - I think - however I've been let down with much gush instead of rotten eggs!⊤ but anyway I'm dead nervous - & a crazy head - . . . I'm ill anyway=" The next year she gave her growing illness a name no doctor has bettered: "I'm in a very queer condition just now - suffering from Ditheration of the brain I think-"

The date of Ellen Terry's first breakdown is unknown, but in 1912 Graham Robertson received a letter scrawled in pencil that must have been a great shock to the fastidious man who believed so tenderly in gifts from the fairies:

> Dearest Graham, In a difficulty I turn to
> thee - !
>
> ___
>
> I am in a "Home"-for a Rest-Cure- & I never was
> so tired in all my life—which I shall certainly end! if I
> don't get out of it, soon!!!!!!! -
>
> ___
>
> (Who says I'm not Irish? - !! -)
>
> ___
>
> This Home belongs to a Miss Pollock. It's a nice home
> a good home I feel sure - for those who don't know what a
> home is, -----------
> I've been here just a month — Last week I was half dead but
> now I am hungry The food here is good - too good! I want
> something devilish! And now I come to you!! to the point.
> Two slices of real tasty Ham — Lovely! — In fact anything tasty! A rotten egg

or sausage wd be acceptable, but
for the present . . . do tell Mrs. Cave that a few slices
of her delicious Bacon cut thin, & all ready for Cooking
wd make a man of me! — (At the present moment I'm a distinct failure as a
woman)

This place is one of Miss Pollock's Homes = (The Pollocks)
My heart has always "brought me to grief" — & now it
has brought me here-

Only about 5, know I'm ill. Please don't mention the
unimportant fact - bad for business. I'm just "away"—
Abroad — or "at the Farm" —
I'm not ill now — but I was —
But no matter - the point is **B a c o n** — !
(Don't put me off with Shakespeare) A 1 lb & 3 oz of your best fat back for pity's
sake my Graham — Direct it here to Mrs. Carew [she goes on to give the address.]
Mark it immediate & save my life. (They'll think it's
Pollock as has done it, but you & I, & Mrs. Cave will
know better!

This under the eyes of the Nurse - who never sees anything

I'm all right as they say—but must not write - 2 more
weeks & then the Farm! I **know** how Sandhills has
been looking Pale yellow & blue & grey & green & Heaven!
--- I want to come later for a few days ---

No more scribbling

Of course you are well - at Sandhills — my love to you
& all the other dogs Especially Bobs & now I'm going
to sleep = Nell.
2:30 p.m.
I mean it about the Bacon - Please =

There is nothing beautiful about this unembellished pencil-scrawled madness: there are no floral gifts, no musical drownings, no searing revelations about self or society, but only unappeasable hunger. The letter has no inflections or apologies; it doesn't try to please. When she was a queen, Ellen Terry made her letters the visible equivalents of her speaking voice and, in their subtle visual

variations, mobile objects of beauty like Gordon Craig's screens. At times—
perhaps when she wrote as a man—the letters became larger, more linear, full
of heavy defiant strokes. The letter in which she begs for bacon is stripped of
any life beyond hunger and monotony.

There had been rumors of her madness since the last days of the Lyceum. One
article from 1897 was called "Eccentric Ways of Ellen Terry" (she was said to
powder her nose between dinner courses and to collect eyeglasses); another, from
1899, was shocked by her "indifference to her appearance on the stage"; a third
condemned Irving's unmanly remark that Ellen Terry was "no longer able to
retain the lines of characters she undertakes to portray, the plain intimation being
that she is losing her reason." When the Lyceum that had been her prison fell
apart, she could no longer collect herself. For years artists had beautified her with
madness; when it finally came, it made her life less beautiful, but simpler. She
scaled her attention down to rest and food. After her years of wide-ranging
exuberant letters to Mabel Malleson, Edy's former teacher, she narrowed her
final letter to a single almost desperate request. She begins by thanking her for
a chicken and asking for another:

> I enclose a £1. bill & shall be glad if you will send me a few other Farm goodies
> in any shape of something so very good to eat = Some of us, are not well, &
> the Drs orders to take a great deal of nourishment is difficult to carry out by those
> of us who are old & unable to fight for food! — a smallish piece of fresh Pork
> — or good bacon, or some cream, wd. be of such service to me just now — a
> dear woman who has served me with her best [years?] is very very ill, & I want
> to feed her for one - My Edy cooks quite splendidly but we find it difficult to
> find good sure food - & we are both very busy = . . . Do what you can for me
> to make me fatten my poor friend — & to fatten me too—I'm frightfully thin!

Graham Robertson babied her into this new reduced awareness of her hunger.
When she was away—off her head or on lonely, increasingly strenuous tours
to the provinces, Australia, or America—Sandhills embraced her memory as a
cozy paradise, restoring the lovely places she had lived in when she was beautiful
and a girl and a boy in the 1860s: Little Holland House; Harpenden; and Alice's
garden, better than all.

Once she and Graham Robertson got used to her strange trips, she wrote to
him about them with her old vigorous interest. Half-away, she reminisced in
1914 from a hotel in Melbourne, Australia: "I think Bobs was more with me
than he was with you! For I kept on mixing him up with 'Joy' when my head
went a bit silly, & I thought I had him at the Farm = I cd think of nothing

Ellen Terry to Walford Graham Robertson, 21 March 1901. *Reproduced by permission of the Huntington Library, San Marino, California.*

Ellen Terry to Walford Graham Robertson, 6 September 1906. *Reproduced by permission of the Huntington Library, San Marino, California.*

Ellen Terry to Walford Graham Robertson, 14 May 1912. *Reproduced by permission of the Huntington Library, San Marino, California.*

but Dogs for a long while—they were much easier to think of than people =
& I babbled of Snob - Winkie — Charley - Fussy - Drummy & Bossy as well
as of all my <u>later</u> Ducks- (<u>Dogs</u> -)" In the middle of the letter, her sprawling
writing stiffens, becoming angular and tense like that of the unsure Nelly Watts:
"I'm quite sane now & hope this will find you well & hearty as it leaves me
at present."

Graham Robertson was always loving, always discreet. He wrote about Ellen
Terry in Fairyland and never mentioned bacon. He loved her because he saw
no comedy in her; Shakespeare's Beatrice had always repelled him. By the time
he took Ellen Terry in to Sandhills, her star had truly stopped dancing. When
she died, he wrote an obituary tribute to a heroine as pathetic as any Watts had
made and loved:

> They talk of her "charm" and "brightness" as if she were a revue girl or a film
> star—even Agate seems to wonder how she could have so far abated her brilliance
> and gaiety as to play Ophelia. Gaiety—it seems strange to me. In her great period
> she exhaled a wistful sadness, a tender pathos which used to make me wonder how
> she could play bright parts. Her eyes were always infinitely sad. Perhaps that was
> why she succeeded so wonderfully in scenes of too great happiness—happiness that
> was "fey" and must forebode sorrow. Imogen's joy as she reads the false letter,
> Juliet's joy as she dances off laughing to sorrow and death. She was always to me
> "Our Lady of Sighs"—of a beautiful sadness in no way akin to the doleful dumps
> of Duse or the tragic splendor of Sarah—the sadness that is in the eyes of
> Botticelli's angels. (24 June 1928. *Letters,* 207)

But Graham Robertson had never known her in the funny days she relived in
his old-fashioned garden.

While Ellen Terry moved gropingly around Sandhills, her son searched
through Germany, Italy, and France for the source of the theater. Like Graham
Robertson, like most artists of his intensely modern generation, he was lured
to the deep past. From Italy, he besieged his mother with postcards of gentle
Madonnas and lectured her about remote origins:

> This next number [of *The Mask*] contains an interesting
>   surprise about the origin of Cubism.
> I don't suppose even Edy knows where it started.
> They all think these things so <u>new</u>—
> And the roots are so <u>old</u>
> & the modern buds so poor.

Graham Robertson had written a more modest *Pinkie* book about a similar alluring regress through fairy tales: "The children were 'carried away by a book' and first find themselves on Robinson Crusoe's island, where they trace the footprints of Cinderella in the sand. Then they work back through the fairy tales to the Greek and Egyptian myths and finally come to the 'Fairy Islands of the West'—the original Sun myth—and wake [in the garden of the Hesperides] with 'shining fruit of Magic Gold' in their hands" (3 November 1923. *Letters*, 115). Men who feared and adored Ellen Terry as their mystic source associated their revelations with those of ancient religions. In his *Back to Methuselah*, even Shaw allowed his aggressive topicality to fade into the primal imagery of religious myth. While newspapers exclaimed over Ellen Terry's "genius that never grows old," more intimate adorers venerated their mother goddess along with alien and unimaginably ancient objects.

Gordon Craig lived more and more comfortably among primeval shapes and forms, but he never imagined himself as an exile. He learned neither French, German, nor Italian, waiting always for England—and Ellen Terry—to call him back and grant him omnipotence. He focused his ambition on Herbert Beerbohm Tree, who had inherited and inflated Irving's pictorial grandeur. In the decade of her Modernist experiments, Ellen Terry also appeared in three of Tree's swollen productions at His Majesty's. Craig gave her her mission: she was to bring him to His Majesty's as she had brought him to the Lyceum twenty years earlier.

> There is no Art Theatre in London.
> There is one in Moscow, St. Petersberg, Berlin, Paris & Krakow.
> These exist without doing harm to other theatres, and
>   are in use as sources for ideas.
> I want Tree to work with me towards the founding of
>   such a theatre in London.
> Only I can do it. . . . but not unless I have an older
>   man's influence to back whatever talents I bring
>   to the work,
> I wrote something of this to Whelen (Tree's secretary)
> Not a word as answer.
> You have now the opportunity of using your influence
> to a blessed end (for a hundred reasons). So speak
> with Tree seriously about it and do [not] leave him
> until you have convinced him and made him promise to
> do something in the matter.
> I will not write more at present.

Beerbohm Tree invited him to design *Macbeth,* but the play cast its usual bad spell. Craig tried to control the production and was quickly fired; assuming his scenic models were the usual theatrical ephemera, Tree casually destroyed them. Gordon Craig responded with clamorous attacks and a lawsuit. His friends persuaded him to settle out of court, but he had isolated himself irreversibly from the English theatrical establishment. As with *The Vikings,* it was an issue of authority: he was not a mere designer of sets, but the invisible God of the play's world. His vision of the stage director was as messianic as that of his American contemporary D. W. Griffith, who exhorted actors that his new medium would transform the world: "We've gone beyond Babel, beyond words. We've found a universal language—a power that can make men brothers and end war forever. Remember that. Remember that, when you stand in front of a camera!" Sinking in visions of the deep past his father had reconstructed so methodically, Gordon Craig had no camera and no peacemaking medium to offer actors; he preached only his own primacy. As the years passed, he scaled his efforts to the masks, puppets, and model theaters he built for himself, which illuminated no strangers' eyes.

His mother and Edy received the same sort of letters he had written at school, always enumerating errands to be run and things to be sent. Ellen Terry received regular requests for money, clothes, and books; she was also asked to be an inexhaustible source of contacts. In an elated moment he instructed her to write to J. P. Morgan and request that he serve on the executive committee for the school at the Arena Goldoni. Edy was to publicize and distribute *The Mask* and to contribute her expertise on theatrical costume to various money-making schemes:

> Shall we do a big work together. There's no one else to do it so far as I can see, and I certainly could not do it alone—though perhaps you could. An Encyclopedia of costume for the theatre in about 6 volumes, I mean a thundering big work, which shall be the standard book on the subject. . . . we should see the book complete in less than three years and should taste some of the *profits* before then, & for ever after. It would cost about £2-2-0. 1st edition popular editions coming out long after. I should think it would be possible to print 2000 copies. . . . But its a good task dont you think so Edy & *money* Editha & a little nest egg for the future—What do you say

Gordon Craig was not loftily indifferent to his mother's goal for him of fame and fortune: he repeatedly, unsuccessfully assaulted her world of success. He brooded about it; in his heart, he expected miracles from it. He saw himself in

Dickens's Mr. Micawber, but he could not consign himself to that character's visionary seediness:

> Reading David Copperfield
> for 1st time --
>   Mr. & Mrs. Macawber !!!!!
>   What a pair.
>   What good fortune they deserve.

Only after he was unimaginably old did his professional withdrawal turn him into an icon of integrity and a seer of a purer theater. For most of his life, his imagination was haunted by the dream of success he had fled.

When he was not sending Ellen Terry on errands, he wrestled with her ghost in print. In 1913, probably with the help of her "literary henchman" Christopher St. John, she wrote a book about the Russian ballet with sweet illustrations by Pamela Colman Smith, who had made drawings of Lyceum productions; in it she loyally echoed her son's precept that dance is the holy origin of theater. His various personae in *The Mask* responded by excoriating the Russian ballet with intensifying virulence. *The Mask* reviewed an early version of her Memoir still more virulently, claiming that its only use is to drive gifted young men away from the theater:

> by the way in which [the memoirs] reveal the narrowness of the theatrical brain, the limitations of the theatrical outlook, they will, also unwittingly, help the Art itself. How? Why, because the younger men, reading these pages, will feel more insistently than before the imperative need of escaping from the triviality of the stage world, from the artificiality of its atmosphere. The stage world as drawn by Miss Terry would not be a tiny one for a *public person* but it is a tiny one for an *Artist . . .* and it is artists that the theatre needs. The world of the Stage is one in which men may crawl or climb, but never fly. The Art of the Theatre is the only art which exists in such an atmosphere. All the others spread their wings. But discontent with existing conditions is a necessary prelude to their reformation, and it is in arousing this discontent in the younger workers in the theatre that Miss Terry's memoirs will be of service to the Art.

Hamlet was the most effective medium of return to his abandoned country and his old battles. His 1912 production for the Moscow Art Theatre was, in the overweening primacy of the central character, a compelling caricature of Irving's. Even more shamelessly than Irving's, the Hamlet Craig imagined blotted out the other actors with his titanic self. As Craig describes the first court scene, only the hero's consciousness is alive:

> You see the stage divided by a barrier. On the one side sits Hamlet, fallen, as it were, into a dream, on the other side you see his dream. You see it, as it were, through the mind's eye of Hamlet. That which is behind him is molten gold. It is the Court of the King and Queen of Denmark. It is the grotesque of a vile kind of royalty. The King speaks . . . as if he were an automaton, his jaws snap on the words, he grunts them out ferociously. If you will read the words of the play, you will see that they are pure caricature and should be treated as such. It is not an actual thing—it is a vision. The barrier which divides Hamlet from the Court is what you will, but to him it seems to be like the shrouded graves of his hopes, amongst which lies his father's body—murdered.

His Hamlet is his own dream of himself dreaming his past. Here, he pictures himself brooding over his lost father at Henry Irving's court, the Lyceum. He becomes Irving's towering Hamlet while isolating himself from Irving his stepfather-king. In his Moscow years, he expunged Gertrude from his dream, but Ophelia goaded him to fury. A transcript of a forty-five-year-old conversation with Stanislavsky conveys his blinding, unfathomable rage:

> C: [Ophelia] must be both stupid and lovely at the same time. That's the difficulty. S: What do you mean—should she be a negative or a positive type? C: She ought rather to be indefinite. . . . S: It might be more tactful to make her attractive and pleasant generally on the stage, but to show her as stupid in some places. Would that do? C: Yes, but I think that, like the whole family, particularly in this scene, she is a terrible nonentity. It's only when she is beginning to go mad that she gradually becomes more positive. . . . I have no liking at all for Ophelia. The only ones I find attractive are Cordelia and Imogen. [Stanislavsky worries that Craig's reduction of Ophelia destroys the tragedy] C: I don't see that. She is a small, petty creature. S: Then why did he love her? C: He loved only his imagination, a woman of his imagination.

The Hamlet Edy and his mother dismissed as fat achieved his revenge. As an old man, he evoked his Hamlet-self for the last time, but this time he allowed his mother to play Gertrude: "I too had lost a father – I too saw my mother married to another – I exaggerated these things then and supposed my stepfather might well have poisoned him in his orchard at Harpenden as he slept. And sleeping, vanished" (*Index,* 162). In his mind and on his stage, the play pursued him as a masque of spectral presences: "Today I am an aged Hamlet – that matters not – that brings me only nearer to the ghost again – but this time there are the two ghosts. He and she. I cannot say if they are happy or unhappy" (*Index,* 163).

The most sustained and best-known work of Gordon Craig's long exile took life from his rage against his mother and his fear of the ghosts she unleashed. Her intrigues for him failed; her lessons of honor and strenuous professionalism made him hate her; her money incapacitated him; but her anger flayed his imagination. The women who replaced her, Isadora Duncan and Elena Meo, resurrected yet again the fury-mother who drove him, personifying the Eleonora and the Nell that fought within her.

Musing about his omnivorous sexuality, the old man lifted it out of the sphere of human relations to cherish it as art:

> It distressed me – those sudden attacks [of desire] bewildered me – and only much later on I saw some relation between sex and creative ability in my work – and this somehow made my peace with sex.
>
> It is a huge power which, properly guided, lends its strength to the creative artist – this is very certain. What else it assists I cannot say – but wrongly dealt with it damages those who attempt to crush it. It is not a thing to quarrel with – you must make friends with it. (*Index,* 7)

Ellen Terry too had begun life prepared to rejoice in the generative ecstasy that united love and art: Gordon Craig had been born out of that dream. Sadly, she had seen them divide: her art had become a consuming fiction, while sexuality had been relegated to a furtive corner of her expansive life. Gordon Craig was a man and a modern, and so he was free to live out his mother's dream for as long as he liked: his flamboyant and compulsive love affairs became his most visible artistic enterprise. Domesticity bored him. His mother took care of all that, freeing him for the erotic raptures of love and creation. His best-known love affair, with Isadora Duncan, realized the dream Ellen Terry had forfeited.

According to the legend Isadora wove out of their first meeting, Gordon Craig rushed to her dressing room after seeing her dance in Berlin. He was enthralled by artistic recognition: "They are my *décors* and my ideas! But you are the being I imagined in them. You are the living realisation of all my dreams. . . . I was the one who saw and invented you. You belong to my scenery."

My Life, Book Topsy, his Isadora diary, takes violent issue with Isadora's account (Steegmuller, 21–29). The words she quotes ring true, though, for Henry Irving might have spoken them to his mother. *Book Topsy* dwells less on Isadora's dancing than on the haunting familiarity of her presence:

> The expression of her face changes & seems to me to be at times the faces of very many women I have known. . . . Each day I suddenly recognize a familiar face in hers— or a familiar voice— It's queer.
>
> I think she is really Aphrodite—which accounts for it. (Quoted in Steegmuller, 21)

Isadora was not Aphrodite, and Aphrodite didn't account for it at all. His memory of her dancing recalls the dynamic stillness his mother had incarnated in the Lyceum's living pictures:

> Quite still . . . You might have counted five, or even eight, and then there sounded the voice of Chopin again, in a second prelude or etude; it was played through gently and came to an end and she had not moved at all. Then one step back or sideways, and the music began again as she went moving on before or after it. Only just moving—not pirouetting or doing any of those things which we expect to see, and which a Taglioni or a Fanny Elssler would have certainly done. She was speaking in her own language—do you understand? her own language: have you got it?—not echoing any ballet master, and so she came to move as no one had ever seen anyone move before. The dance ended, and again she stood quite still. (Quoted in Steegmuller, 23)

Isadora's presence, like Ellen Terry's, overwhelmed her performances. A former student remembers her as Gordon Craig did: "Her very presence was so moving that it's hard to say what she did. The music seemed to come out of her—she was its source." The revolutionary dancer and the pictorial actress evoked powers greater than their actions.

Isadora not only recalled Ellen Terry: she worshipped her. In the account of their first meeting that so offended Gordon Craig, Isadora succumbs not to his assurance that she is "the living realisation of all his dreams," but to the "wonderful words" with which he makes himself known:

> "I am the son of Ellen Terry."
> Ellen Terry, my most perfect ideal of woman! Ellen
> Terry . . . ! (*My Life*, 180)

Whether or not he actually presented himself as Ellen Terry's son, his rage at her account is understandable, for as she tells the story, from the beginning of their love affair and throughout its course, Ellen Terry's awe-inspiring image dwarfs her temperamental, somewhat "feminine" son. Gordon Craig gives the impression of "a certain almost womanly weakness"; his mother embodies womanly strength. She is not Shaw's child-mother or the "Nelly" of *Ellen Terry and Her Secret Self* or Graham Robertson's "Our Lady of Sighs." To Isadora as to many woman artists of her generation, Ellen Terry incarnates an almost primitive grandeur:

> Ellen Terry was then [the 1890s] in the full maturity of her magnificent womanhood. She was no longer the tall, slender girl who had captured the imagination of Watts, but deep-bosomed, with swelling hips, and a majestic presence, very different from the present-day ideal! If audiences of to-day could have seen Ellen Terry in her prime, she would have been besieged with advice on how to become thin by dieting, etc., and I venture to say that the greatness of her expression would have suffered had she spent her time, as our actresses do now, trying to appear young and thin. She did not look slight or thin, but she was certainly a beautiful example of womanhood. (*My Life,* 63-64)

Isadora's repeated paeans to Ellen Terry's magnificence hint that the real object of her abandon was her lover's mother. She aroused herself by fantasies of family: "Here before me stood brilliant youth, beauty, genius; and, all inflamed with sudden love, I flew into his arms with all the magnetic willingness of a temperament which had for two years lain dormant, but waiting to spring forth. Here I found an answering temperament, worthy of my metal. In him I had met the flesh of my flesh, the blood of my blood. Often he cried to me, 'Ah, you are my sister.' And I felt that in our love was some criminal incestuousness" (p. 182).

Isadora was certainly not his real sister, the coolly critical Edy who always saw more than she should. As he imagined Isadora, she was the mother and the sister who saw only through his eyes; as Isadora imagined him, he was the male incarnation of a grand female principle to which she was consecrated. Throughout their love affair, each willed the other to become Ellen Terry. Isadora came closest to obeying: after Gordon Craig made her his all-sharing sister, she became the all-providing mother he was trying to escape. This new woman, he was sure, would never dare despise him.

Like Ellen Terry, Isadora supported him in style. Like many women of the day, Gordon Craig put so rare a value on himself that others felt honored to work for his care. At the end of 1904, he wrote contentedly in *Book Topsy,* "We go to St. Petersburg, Moscow, Hamburg, Dresden, Cologne, Breslau, Frankfurt — together— she dancing and I doing little— resting and being happy with her" (quoted in Steegmuller, 53). As she whirled about on long, confusing tours, her letters were eerily reminiscent of those Ellen Terry wrote to her sedentary son at school. Like Ellen Terry's, beneath their veneer of complaint, they are full of excitement: "Dear— I am passing a river. I don't know the name but the flowing waters are quite *black* & the banks covered with snow make the most amazing contrast— stretching off in great desolate fields with here & there a black forest patch— It might be the river Styx— and my poor soul ready to cross to the land of shadows. Dear you would like to see it— what a picture for you— I'm being borne away away— The clouds are flying past— Am I transformed to a great bird flying always North— I think so—" (quoted in Steegmuller, 32).

Like a traditional wife, Gordon Craig became the still point in Isadora's mobile life. As a man, of course, he had no need to simulate the egolessness his mother had assumed at the Lyceum: as the years went on he became angrily possessive of Isadora's career, insisting that the unstable Maurice Magnus manage her work as well as his own. When Isadora was ill and exhausted after the birth of their daughter Deirdre, his demands that she dance for his support became peremptory and brutal. The more she supplied, the more he was lost in clouded recriminations that she had betrayed his work. Brooding over his past, he annotated a draft of one of his letters to her: "Written in Florence 1907 to I.D. in Germany who had promised to support the work & who had made a tour with that end in view— PROMISED ME! It was the 1st time I had told her I would prepare some theatre thing if she would help a little— & she promised" (quoted in Steegmuller, 254). It was his mother all over again: the more she gave, the more impossible it became to support his omnivorous need. Unlike his mother, Isadora did not accompany her payments with lashing accusations. She was only puzzled at a certain murderously draining quality in her beautiful lover: "I have no strength when I am near you– I only want to fly into you & die" (October 1907. Quoted in Steegmuller, 163).

Like Ellen Terry, Isadora used her talent and success to make theatrical contacts for her grumbling genius; like Ellen Terry, she was thanked by accusations that she was forcing him into sullying compromise. She brought him together with Max Reinhardt, Constantin Stanislavsky, and Eleonora Duse. In predictable sequence, he impressed and alienated each in turn. His mother's art fed on collaboration, but Gordon Craig could not stomach it. His most tangible achievement, his Moscow Art *Hamlet,* was the fruit of Isadora Duncan's matchmaking; even this did not lead to continued collaboration with Stanislavsky. His work for Eleonora Duse was more characteristic of his professional associations: it began in elation and ended in fury. Duse, whom he had worshipped as a saint of the new theater, joined forces in his mind with his mother, Isadora, and the unnamed cabal of stupid and dangerous women who threatened his primacy.

They met in Florence, in the summer of 1906. Duse had just returned from London, where she had gone to grace Ellen Terry's jubilee, the ceremony Craig had so conspicuously missed. They chose to put on Ibsen's *Rosmersholm*. Craig's set ignored the play's domestic realism: it was an audacious evocation of the colossal, abstract, post-human forms that haunted him. All was wonderful at first. Isadora was as tactfully devious a liaison as Ellen Terry would have wished. A typical Craig diatribe—"Tell her I won't have any damned woman interfering with my work!"—reached Duse in Italian as: "He says he admires your opinions and will do everything to please you" (Weaver, 276, citing *My Life*).

Duse was enthralled by the set: in it she saw the new spaces, the new theater, she had pined for. The handful of performances she played in Craig's decor have become legendary, but the grand beginning was abortive. The set did not survive her first tour: at Nice, it was cut down to accommodate a smaller stage. As with Tree, Craig the artist was maddened by the irreverent exigencies of the theater: his tantrum expelled him from Duse's company. Gladly, he had used her authority to scourge actors: "they poison the air, they make art impossible," she had said rightly. Now, she had revealed herself as a woman of the theater. She had gone over to the enemy.

Over the years she became increasingly confused with his mother. In the summer of Ellen Terry's death, Gordon Craig wrote for Duse (who had died four years earlier) the obituary tribute he withheld from his mother. Against the evidence of his and everyone else's senses, he claimed that the stark Duse was a secret comedienne trapped in a weeping age: "We took her to be a melancholy woman; and she, with her infinite spirit of humour, took herself as we labelled her." He lauded "that divine sense of humour which blazed in this fine lady and permitted her to indulge her public." These words were perversely wrong about Duse, but they were the perfect eulogy for Ellen Terry, whom his surrogate Graham Robertson had let die in pathos.

He could no longer see the difference, for his mother, Duse, and Isadora (who had died in 1927) were merging as the governing specters of his mind. In 1928, the year his mother died and he gave her secret comedy to Duse, he had a weird visitation that appropriated the opening of *Macbeth*. His three women materialized as the three witches:

The play begins – will you three lend me your aid? – You, Isadora, you, Eleonora, and you Ellen Terry, nearer to the angels than are most humans and nearer to the fiends than are most angels. You should be women, yet your genius forbids me to interpret that you are so.

To have known you . . . and now to call on you –

Ring up the curtain – let us make infernal hay while the moon shines.

The three preside in a mystic procession over a theater of mighty ghosts, "advancing to the deliberate and natural rhythm which only three such beings can move to without a word said in explanation, nothing planned and nothing lacking – only an increased astonishment swelling in us all. Even Voltaire does not smile, but is rapt." They proclaim their reign through stillness, finally summoning the fiend-like queen who is both womanly and utterly triumphant:

There is no motion: then what is it that holds us? – their presence alone.

It is of Macbeth they are speaking – of a man who is too weak to catch the nearest way – but who has a wife.

It is this wife they are concerned with, though they speak of him.

The fragmentary vision of demonic women coming to proclaim their reign, seen by a man who saw himself as "too weak to catch the nearest way," is the source of Gordon Craig's fearful rage against the women who possessed him. He was prone to such visions of triumphant women. In 1907, he had sent Isadora, who was becoming increasingly abrasive to him, a mad diatribe against female power:

Woman as a rule being the most material packet of goods in this earth, makes a good effort to kill the Desire for an Ideal.

So she could create Peace Congresses— and is now creating Socialism and is trying to break the man of his worship of king— monarchy— stars and gods— that he may have no other gods but HER.

And she will succeed until she reaches the artist and then she will utter a shriek and like the Sphinx— will throw herself off the Cliff—

(17 October 1907. Quoted in Steegmuller, 266)

These political references come oddly from a man who lived in Europe as an expatriate through two world wars, aware of no cause but his own: he dreamed of supreme power while shunning all alliances. Like Shaw, he had visions that transcended politics of demonic women returning to control the new century; thus, like Shaw again, he did his frightened best to control the women he knew.

He tried to write Isadora into being little, as he would do with his mother, explaining her (and incidentally Duse) to a Dutch actor named De Vos:

> At one time I *dreamed* that Isadora was by nature (or even perhaps by love) bound up with this labour of mine— this fight for the freedom of our theatre— & had she liked she could I believe have taught me to do better what I am doing only to the best of my own ability—
>
> But little Isadora is very little & very sweet & weak & she has to do whatever her impulse tells her to do at the moment. And sometimes it is one thing, sometimes it is another— & all that she does is right— & then besides she has her sister & her school which absorb all her time & attention— & then too she has to keep moving— first to Berlin— then to Moscow— then to Munich & then to Stockholm— So how can she have time to think quietly about anything — or to work with me—
>
> Madame Duse too.
>
> (13 or 14 February 1908. Quoted in Steegmuller, 290)

Like Duse, all-powerful, all-little, all-betraying, Isadora was in the end absorbed into the ghost of the mother who grew larger as he tried to forget her. When, in 1913, their daughter was drowned in an accident, Isadora lost her identity entirely in his eyes. Deirdre's drowning was an odd triumph for the Ophelia-ghost George F. Watts had unleashed on the family so many years before. Isadora eulogized her less as Gordon Craig's child than as the mystic consummation of her own union with Ellen Terry: "Shortly after, I discovered—and there could not be the slightest doubt about it—that I was pregnant. I dreamt that Ellen Terry appeared to me in a shimmering gown, such as she wore in 'Imogene,' leading by the hand a little blonde child, a little girl who resembled her exactly, and, in her marvelous voice, she called to me—'Isadora, love. Love. . . . Love . . .'" (*My Life,* 188).

Deirdre's birth does not dispel the dream, but realizes it: "Deirdre was now running about and dancing. She was particularly lovely, and a perfect miniature of Ellen Terry, which was certainly due to my thoughts and admiration of Ellen" (p. 228). Years before, when Ellen Terry had run off with Godwin, a drowned girl who looked like her had arisen to frighten her family: the drowned double had suffered the fallen woman's traditional death, while the escaped ingenue exulted in the country. This Victorian iconography lived to haunt the next generation. Kathleen Bruce, who stayed with Isadora during her pregnancy, claims that while she was carrying Deirdre, she tried to drown herself (Steegmuller, 148). In 1913, the "poor corpse" who was Ellen Terry's double was also her granddaughter, and the actress herself was sinking in madness and memories. Ophelia had unleashed herself on the confident modernism of an emancipated generation.

Her death released in the father who had barely known her a flood of blame that finally found its source:

> Never need she [ostensibly Isadora] have lost her loved children had she realized that to have children entails having obligations. *Someone* must care for them— & that someone is always MOTHER. This truth she never seems to have faced up to— She let them be looked after by governess or whoever was at hand— the joy & the pain (if pain there be) of doing all that herself she seems to have missed. Never could they have died as they did die with their MOTHER watching. She simply failed to watch— & I believe her grief loses its worth since it was her own fault. It was a punishment of the gods? was it— there certainly is something Homeric in it— but somehow her tears do not grieve me— they make me cross with her.
>
> (Notebook entry. Quoted in Steegmuller, 330)

The terrible MOTHER infuses herself everywhere, swallowing in her magnitude both Isadora and Deirdre. As an artist, Isadora perpetuated herself in a series of schools, while his own school closed almost immediately, but as a woman, even this most vivid presence in his life dissolved in the memory of the Ellen Terry he could not bear to see.

Beautiful, loving Elena Meo never competed with Ellen Terry's specter: she lived in harmony with it. From their elopement in 1902, which he staged to resemble his mother and father's, Elena settled down tenderly, whenever he let her, to being his "Nell." Elena was the daughter of a painter; she was a trained professional violinist when, at twenty-two, she met Gordon Craig; but thereafter, he and his work became the vocation that displaced the convent of which she dreamed. For all the holiness of their love, Elena and their children Nelly and Teddy (his father's future biographer, Edward Anthony Craig) spent more time with Ellen Terry at Smallhythe than they did with Gordon Craig. Two world wars provided a convenient reason to separate. Both isolated Elena from him in England, but when World War II ended, he did not send for her; they barely met again. When, in 1957, Elena died, Nelly moved dutifully to Vence to care for her father until he died in 1966. He never married Elena, despite the dictates of the Catholicism that gave her life meaning, but in his mind she was his wife because she played for him the Nelly he had always wanted.

The pious, submissive, uncomplaining woman who lived with his mother in domestic seclusion sanitized his past and made it comforting. Elena's letter of condolence to Isadora Duncan documents the family confusions in which she was entangled: "From your letters to Ted I feel that you perhaps did not get the letter I wrote you at the time of your trouble— or perhaps as I signed 'Elena,' & not 'Nelly' you may have thought it was Ted's sister— but Nelly is only a pet name of Teds & my mother-in-law." She signs her letter "Elena Craig" (19 June 1913. Quoted in Steegmuller, 324). Elena obediently played a role Ted's past had conceived, but unlike Ellen Terry, she harbored no grand Victorian visions of fallen women in their empowered defiance. With no sanction but her own imagination, she always insisted on playing a wife.

In the same spirit, Gordon Craig's favorite children played boys and girls and nothing else: they were taught the boundaries of their gender as his mother had never been. Like Ellen Terry and Isadora, Elena had two children, a girl and then a boy; onstage at least, they knew who they were from the first. During World War I, as part of a benefit in support of Lena Ashwell's Concerts at the Front, Nelly and Teddy appeared in E. V. Lucas's *Ellen Terry's Bouquet*. The skit took its humor from the immutability, even in childhood, of male and female roles. Teddy, as the boy, gives orders as a matter of course:

> T.   *I'll* be the *compère*.
> N (Wistfully). Yes; I thought you would.
> T (Self-righteously). It's not because it must be someone good. Nor is it "just my selfishness" again; it's merely this – that *compères* must be men. *Compères* are always men and *commères* girls; we make the jokes; while you – you
>   (Nelly still discontented)
>   sup with earls. You ride in cars and wear the loveliest dresses
> And colonels toast your beauty at their messes.
> N (Not yet satisfied). But you have all the lines.
> T.   Of course. Whoever
> Heard of a girl both beautiful *and* clever?

Ellen Terry's Bouquet is a sad distance from the *Drawing-Room Entertainment* in which, under their father's management, Kate and Ellen Terry had flashed instantaneously from male to female, youth to age, laughter to tears. When Nelly and Teddy Craig were onstage, they asked no disturbing questions about children and adults, boys and girls: all they were, they proclaimed. The war that signaled the twentieth century's emancipation from the limitations of Victorianism gave us an enlightened and an emptier world, but it was also a world that dared to think it knew the differences between boys and girls, men and women.

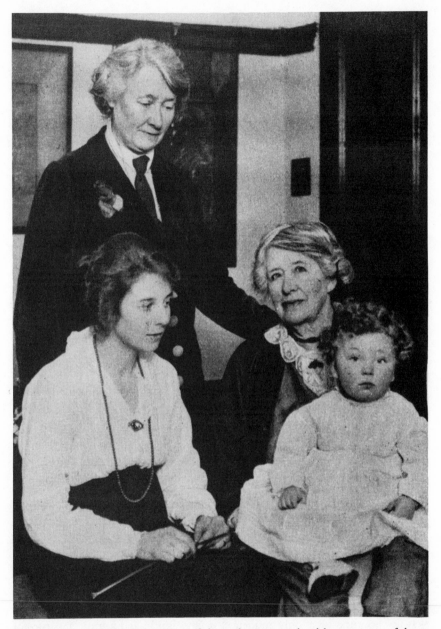

Ellen Terry with three generations of descendants. *Reproduced by permission of the Harry Ransom Humanities Research Center, University of Texas, Austin.*

That iconoclastic Bohemian Gordon Craig gave Nelly and Teddy no rich and confused childhood selves they would have to spend their lives unlearning.

Ellen Terry, that adored *grand-mère* of the *Bouquet,* settled rather vacantly into her public role of "Granny" and "old dear." Irving seemed far away, but then he had always been far away. The obituary she had given him in her Memoir was an ironic contrast to her own slow death: "Henry Irving belonged to England, not to a family. England showed that she knew it when she buried him in Westminster Abbey" (*Memoirs,* 263). Insofar as England honored the living Ellen Terry after World War I, it did so because she belonged to a family. A syndicated photograph enshrined her as the mother of a dynasty, but the photograph cannot hide Ellen Terry's apathy or Edy's new controlling role as head of the family.

Deirdre, her physical reincarnation, had drowned, but in Nelly Craig she briefly saw her work reborn. Chris and Edy remember the child as an artist her family suppressed:

> [Ellen Terry] soon recognized that although the boy at this time had the greatest desire to act, and was more teachable, the girl had more natural talent for the stage. Ellen Terry's conviction that "poor old Nenny," as she often called her backward pupil, was a born actress, did not seem strange to those who noticed how completely the dull, rather apathetic child, less graceful and charming than little Teddy in real life, was transformed in the theatre. The few appearances on the stage she made in early youth justified Ellen Terry's belief in her vocation. She was never to follow it however. In 1907 both children returned to Italy with their mother, and any chance Nellie had of wearing her grandmother's mantle was destroyed. Teddy suffered less from the change of environment.
>
> (*Memoirs,* 305)

E. V. Lucas's skit was played offstage as well: whatever "poor old Nenny" wanted to be, she was raised to become her father's consummate Nelly and his last audience. Aged into delicious malevolence, Gordon Craig died illuminated by his patient golden daughter.

In the 1950s, pilgrims came to Vence to adore this giant of the theater who had so few productions to his credit, but who had authorized so many grandiose visions. Kenneth Tynan saw nothing but a prophet and a wicked boy: "There was no bitterness here: only resilience, magnanimity, and a great appetite for joy." But an American reporter felt the angry isolation that had governed his life: "Oh, it's so good to talk with someone again. It's very lonely for me here. I really don't like living where I am. . . . Strange, how things go; most people

Edward Gordon Craig with his daughter, Nelly Craig. *Photograph by Arnold Rood, reproduced by permission of Arnold Rood.*

must think I'm dead by now. Let them. If only they gave me my theatre!" (*New York Times,* 8 September 1957).

Nelly grew intimate with the consuming rage he had absorbed from his mother: "I wish you would die—drop down in front of me now" was his ritual response to her nursing. His imagination, she claimed, "ran away with him. He had it for work—that's why his work was so wonderful. But in his daily life he would imagine all the wrong things. He saw shadows and at times he thought I was trying to poison him! He imagined people hated him and were trying to 'do him in.' Papa said 'I will not buy a new suit, they (the clothes) will kill me.' " She never became an artist, but she had one triumphant claim: she believed she had tamed her father. "Teddy does not like [the publication of the Gordon Craig-Isadora Duncan manuscripts]– he thinks that it makes father too 'cheap' — & I think so also— but that's what Father was like with all women, except me. I kept him in his place— that is the only way that I could live with him!"

Gordon Craig left no legacy but rage and the infinite promise of the theater he had never been given. Like Ellen Terry, he made himself a legend by tantalizing audiences with the things he had not done. Like her, he wrote about them, but not in letters or in the margins of scripts: eloquently, irascibly, he published the sorts of protest his mother only whispered. Over the years, the influence of his books defeated his contemporaries' success. "Had he directed more, perhaps he would have written less, and in an ephemeral art it is the documents which endure," his disciples argue (Walton, 155). His baleful withdrawal brought him theatrical salvation in the end.

Only Edy saw him plain: she always had. During World War II, when the family was unable to reach him, she solaced herself with reminders of the artful self-preserving genius that lurked under his impolitic veneer: "Of course Ted had his best public always in Germany & one country doesn't seem to matter to him more than another = . . . he never would make a will & everything would have gone to May in South Africa where ants would very likely have eaten the books & prints - He has I believe encouraged the idea that he is a harmless lunatic, when he doesn't want to do what he is told to do [i.e., he will save himself from working for the Nazis]."

Edy was right about everything, including the will: Gordon Craig died intestate and his estate went automatically to his legitimate children, not to Elena's, though he died crying to the devoted Nelly: "I love you, I love you, I love you and Teddy" (*The Last Eight Years,* 37). It was his last wicked abandonment of the world that had frightened him out of his senses.

Edy, who would not be Nelly for him, frightened him most of all. She saw through things other women believed in, or said they believed. He could call Isadora his sister because he imagined he invented her, but Edy eluded his art: "There will be an opportunity some day to write of our friendship – Edy's and mine. When we were quite young at Hampton Court and here at Winchcombe and later when we acted together at the Lyceum – in Merchant of Venice and in Olivia and still later when I began to produce operas – and then long after when we were much older – I hope I shall be really able to write the very things I hear in the wind and see in the trees – which remind me of my sister – I had but one" (*Index,* 77).

Gordon Craig never did write about Edy, and neither, in the course of her long life, did anybody else.

Edy's Women

Edy always saw plainly. Unlike her brother, who loved to invoke cloudy mysteries, Edy did not speak until she knew what she had seen. Her mother remembered her eerie silences:

> Until she was two years old she never spoke a word, though she seemed to notice everything with her grave dark eyes. We were out driving when I heard her voice for the first time:
> "There's some more."
> She spoke quite distinctly. It was almost uncanny.
> "More what?" I asked in a trembling voice, afraid that having delivered herself once, she might lapse into dumbness.
> "Birds!" (*Memoirs,* 67–68)

Crouching alone during choir practice in a French cathedral, Edy was so certain that she had seen something better than birds that she shared her vision with her parents: "Ssh! ssh! Miss Edy has seen the angels!" (*Memoirs,* 69). As she grew older, she saw more, but she told about it sparingly.

Safety lay in seeing, but the "dour child" shrank from being seen. In photographs, she is not reborn for the camera, as her mother and brother were, but stares it down in an attempt to rival its primacy as watcher. Watching was her power. She had seen how eyes could remake her mother, whose very being melted into the self that others saw. As Sybil Thorndike remembered acting under Edy's direction: "Edy had an eye like—well, whatever has eyes sharpened extremely."

Her sharpened eyes, her mistrust, her unfeminine self-command, all branded Edy as the only charmless Terry. When, at the turn of the century, Edy emerged as the center of a colony of advanced women with a culture of their own, lovers of Ellen Terry deplored her imprisonment in Edy's unnatural, female world. Marguerite Steen's distaste was shared by most observers. It sets the tone for Ellen Terry's future biographers: "At every hour of the day the place was seething with women. Some of them [Ellen Terry] liked, and tolerated others. It seems curious that there was no one to protect Ellen Terry from these female cohorts, most of whom owed their acceptance to Edy who, heading her band of feminists, waving her banner of Women's Franchise, sponsored their intro-duction to Ellen Terry—who could not have cared less whether or not women had a vote, though she pretended, to please Edy. . . . The result was that the men in whose company Ellen Terry had formerly taken pleasure were scared by this female bodyguard from battling into her presence" (Steen, 305).

Edy let this condemnation stand, and it has stood largely uncontroverted to this day. Unlike her brother, she had no descendants to tell her story or to transmit to biographers the Ellen Terry she wanted to perpetuate. When, with Christopher St. John, she edited her mother's Memoir and her letters to Shaw, she had the self-obliterating grace to let Ellen Terry live again to perform her own story. Unlike her brother, she made a style out of obscuring herself. She worked tirelessly on experimental productions no books immortalize; she never wrote about herself, while Gordon Craig wrote about little else. After her death, a band of women collaborated on *Edy,* a volume of appreciative essays, whose distribution was as local as Edy's life. There is no other book about Edy and her circle, though Shaw urged Christopher St. John to write one. The woman her associates said was "always right" let herself become a chapter in others' more ornate narratives.

Edy and Ted were intimately alike, though they played different roles. Both lived in terror and suspicion—the mother who had aroused so many of their fears had herself come to self-awareness in gorgeous terror—but as a man, Gordon Craig felt licensed to flee an annihilating world and to immortalize his odyssey, while Edy simply steeled herself against the murder she saw in others' eyes. Gordon Craig built monuments to himself that outlasted his enemy, the theater; Edith Craig immersed herself in the incessant work of practical produc-tion without a thought for a life after death. Shaw's wry epitaph is scarcely exaggerated: "Gordon Craig had made himself the most famous producer [direc-

Edith Craig as a child. *Ellen Terry Memorial Museum, Smallhythe Place. Courtesy of the Trustee of the Ellen Terry Estate.*

Drawing by Edith Craig in a letter to Anna Hollaender, ca. 1890. *Reproduced by permission of the Folger Library.*

tor] in Europe by dint of never producing anything, while Edith Craig remains the most obscure by dint of producing everything." Like the good women she thought she scorned, Edy veiled herself from the lethal distortions of public life. Her mother had taught her the art of hiding herself, and helped her by hiding her in a star's obliterating radiance. Like Richard III, Edy could not play a lover, so she found herself playing a villain. Her mother, the woman everybody loved, had left her no role but that of the woman everybody hated.

Accepting that role was her own choice: she did put Ellen Terry in prison, as her critics charged, though it was a prison her mother had built for them both, the sort of prison Lear had dreamed of building for Cordelia. After Gordon Craig fled England in 1903, Edy gradually assumed the guardianship of her mother's stricken life. Christopher St. John, the woman writer with whom Edy lived from 1899 until her death in 1947, remembered the shifting balance of power between them: "Edy seemed to me the wise mother, and Ellen Terry the wayward child. A child Edy would not spoil," she added in dark allusion to Ellen Terry's own fatal misgovernment (Adlard, 29). Edy was not always her mother's wise mother, but she saw things no one else admitted, shielding from exposure a mind that was blurring as inexorably as her eyes. Cultural prejudice cast her unfairly as a manhater: some men were always admitted to her mother's sanctuary, but they were judiciously selected and monitored. Edy had watched all her life her mother's dangerous tendency to become the self that others saw; she tried to stiffen the identity that was growing more pliable year by year. Men's approving eyes sapped strength away. She guarded her mother from them with no more ferocity than she guarded herself.

She had put Ellen Terry in prison, but that was where she had always been. The child had realized herself in a locked attic her vision made gorgeously consoling; throughout her life, the roles into which she had fit herself provided the same sort of effulgent arrest. Only when she played Ben's girl/boy had they been expansive enough for her. Watts had rescued the ingenue only to remake her as the poignant captive of his lush canvases. Godwin had given her fallen woman a glorious pastoral setting, only to imprison her in his own selfish violence. (So Edy imagined him. She had no way of associating her own shadowy nature that shrank from exposure with the temperament of the father she loved to hate.)

The Lyceum that gave Ellen Terry immortality had been the most gorgeous prison of all. In making her beloved it had stolen her comedy: she left it chastened and subdued, eyeing "the depths of down-ness," guided by a star that had stopped dancing. Shaw cast himself as her rescuer into Modernist comedy, only to ensnare her in new humiliations and constraints and then abandon her.

The Vikings her son designed was no less draining and oppressive. Edy never forgot her brother's contempt for the women on its crew. After their mother died, Gordon Craig's recreation of her as one of his "little" women in *Ellen Terry and Her Secret Self* was a mad attempt to slaughter her memory and imprison her spirit in the name of manhood. Ellen Terry, the most loved woman in England, among the wealthiest and most seemingly powerful, has passed in her glorified life from prison to prison. This was the pattern from which Edy and Chris shaped their annotated, expanded version of Ellen Terry's Memoir.

They transmitted their Ellen Terry to younger, more aesthetic feminists. In 1930, Vita Sackville-West moved to Sissinghurst, only seven miles from Small-hythe, with her family of elegantly androgynous men. The community at the Priest's House, whom Vita dubbed "the Trots," were illuminated with Ellen Terry's enthralling memory. In 1933, Vita introduced the Trouts to her lover, Virginia Woolf. Woolf knew the actress only through the shrines her daughter was building, but through Edy, she conceived Ellen Terry as one grand type of imprisoned Everywoman. Her prose builds a redemptive shrine to stand beside Edy's shrine at Smallhythe:

> Something of Ellen Terry it seems overflowed every part and remained unacted. Shakespeare could not fit her; nor Ibsen; nor Shaw. The stage could not hold her; nor the nursery. But there is, after all, a greater dramatist than Shakespeare, than Ibsen, or Shaw. There is Nature. Hers is so vast a stage, and so innumerable a company of actors, that for the most part she fobs them off with a tag or two. They come on and they go off without breaking the ranks. But now and again Nature creates a new part, an original part. The actors who act that part always defy our attempts to name them. They will not act the stock parts—they forget the words, they improvise others of their own. But when they come on the stage falls like a pack of cards and the limelights are extinguished. That was Ellen Terry's fate—to act a new part. And thus while other actors are remembered because they were Hamlet, Phèdre, or Cleopatra, Ellen Terry is remembered because she was Ellen Terry.

Woolf's Ellen Terry, like Edy's, is so grand that all roles imprison her. At the end of her life, Edy did her best to redeem her mother's sorrows by making a prison that fit the dimensions of her dreams as Edy perceived them: she would free the woman within the good woman, as she tried to do in the costumes she designed. In this most loving, most hopeful of prisons, Edy waited for her mother "to act a new part," the role within the role she had always slyly promised.

Everything Edy's generation had trained her to expect fed her faith in the female millennium her mother's new part would inaugurate. The suffragist Emmeline Pethick-Lawrence recalled the soaring spirits of young women who came of age in the 1890s: "It was a wonderful thing at that period to be young among young comrades, for the ninth decade of the last century was a time of expansion and vision. In spite of sordidness and insecurity in the lives of the poor, everything was on the upgrade. . . . It was an era of religion and faith, and at the same time of intellectual challenge. We read, discussed, debated, and experimented and felt that all life lay before us to be changed and moulded by our vision and desire."

The new century that beamed on the horizon promised to exalt women while it immobilized men. Gordon Craig talked, boasted, floundered, and fought, moving from here to there, possessed by annihilating visions of a theater no one could work in, punishing the women whose phantoms mocked and drove him. Edy had no desire to flee the world; she longed for the power and energy her brother abused. When he tried to discredit the Terry-Shaw correspondence on which she and Chris had worked with such passionate faith, she wrote about him to Shaw with withering contempt:

> I feel I ought to grovel on my knees before you for all the trouble that I've brought on you. All this spluttered spleen that is pouring out of Teddy makes me & most people sick but I think it's killing him with most of his friends= I hope I shall not have to see him again= How can anyone write so many misstatements & willful lies & get away with it—but I hope you wont do anything less than annihilate him or laugh at him. Loud & long. What am I to do? I feel like doing both but my attempts would be so feeble. I should only look a fool: I am really sorry for him—he's done himself no end of harm & he must have such an unhealthy brain & soul that it must be torture to him: Please forgive me.

Gordon Craig's rage epitomized his heedless hate of all the gifts and talents of the world.

Gordon Craig longed for a garden; Edy made one. Unlike him, she never wrote nostalgically about the pastoral wholeness of her days with her parents, but when Ellen Terry bought the Farm at Smallhythe and gave Edy and Chris the adjacent cottage they named "Priest's House," Edy threw herself into transforming a flat potato-patch into a spreading garden that still exists. A converted Catholic who labored to transmute all worldly sensations into spiritual truths, Christopher remembered a transfigured Edy in a garden that was doubly consecrated because they had made it themselves. Dismayed by its scruffiness, Chris was illuminated, through Edy, into a vision of holiness: "Yes there was Edy, on the doorstep, gazing at [the garden] in ecstasy. 'Oh, how lovely it all is!' she called out, moving her arms up and down in a jig, laughing and weeping, streaming with light. My eyes were opened. 'Of such is the Kingdom of Heaven'" (Adlard, 34).

She and Christopher cultivated Ellen Terry with the same transfigured diligence they applied to their garden, clearing a space where she could recreate herself. Yet she yearned for a world outside as she had always done, writing wistfully to Graham Robertson: "I think pretty nearly every day of the quietest peacefullest spot on the earth— & that's Sandhills—" Edy labored, she needed Edy there, but Edy could not reconstruct the houses and gardens that had promised the world in the 1860s. Edy's causes could never become her as did Graham Robertson's art, his dogs, his house and garden that enshrined the past. She was too old to imagine the future Edy cultivated, though she had inspired it herself.

Ellen Terry aged clinging to her daughter and denying her; she had done the same thing when Edy was young. She had grown strong fighting women who tried to invade and diminish her, beginning with her mother, and then Kate, when they tried to make her proper. Mrs. Kean had slapped her into sobbing well; she was succeeded in Little Holland House by Mrs. Prinsep and Julia Cameron, who in their own formidable ways had slapped her harder to make her cry still more beautifully. The men who loved her—her father, Watts, Lewis Carroll, Godwin, Charles Reade, Henry Irving, Bernard Shaw—had all promised rescue into freedom, but their freedom had never been hers. Like Gordon Craig, who worshipped only the mother he put in Heaven, they had loathed and betrayed the real woman in their hearts. Women had known her; that was why they slapped her. Now here was her daughter, reflecting and restraining her like the others, and she could not, from the beginning, let Edy go. She was ready to learn what her mother and the rest had tried, through their slaps and punishments, to teach. It was her son's business to leave, she had furthered that business when she drove him away, but she would keep Edy as guide and truer self, even if it meant obliterating her. Before Ellen Terry became Edy's prisoner, Edy was hers. Helplessly loving, Edy read her mother's dream and obliterated herself with the same care she put into making her garden and her shrines.

When she was twenty-one, she drew a picture for Anna Hollaender, the wife of her piano teacher in Germany. The drawing, and the letter that accompanied it, are revealing in their dogged self-effacement:

I didn't write to you yesterday but I drew this instead in bed. Nothing of importance has happened except that we went to the Lessing Theatre last night & saw "Fall Clemenceau" not very well acted = The play isn't much as an acting play but the novel is very good. Today we went to the Exhibition & went in the Theatre Bergweks & Diver pond = It is a very good exhibition but we were not there long enough to see everything. We saw chocolate being made & Mr. H. bought you a piece & Miss B gave me a piece for a bit = It was awfully good = Quite fresh & rather soft. Today another singer was there & the mother of the big singing lady = But nobody of any importance comes = I haven't had a word from Mother now for 14 days & more = I'm very sleepy now & want to sleep so good-night. [But Edy apparently sees to her mortification that she hasn't filled the page, so she doggedly produces more stiff and choppy sentences. She writes "Candle light" before the bottom third of the letter.] At least I hope you have a lamp now = Mr. H. is reading poetry to Miss Becker in the dining room = [illegible] and Heine etc. with expression & as I don't understand a word & my arm (left one) feels bad I'm going to sleep = Edy.
PS. Mr. H. has pains in his knee & cant walk without trouble & pain & he wont go to Ashof = Tell him he must = It's the same [illegible German word] knee.

Ellen Terry's letters dance with fun and joy even when she declines an invitation: her refusals promise treasures. Edy's stiff, withheld communication interests in its very colorlessness; it aims, not to delight, but to fill the page at any cost. The faint pencil in which Edy writes is a cloak of invisibility. Her accompanying drawing is more revealing still. A vividly colored Ellen Terry and Teddy stand on the right with the Beckers, calling "Come over!!!" The Hollaenders stand on the left, asking, "Shall we?" Next to them crouches a shadowy Edy, drawn in the faint pencil of her letter. She explains her ghostly self by the cryptic caption: " 'I' was an afterthought."

In her work, she was equally unwilling to draw herself boldly. Even her ardent admirers could not define what this tireless woman of the theater *was:* was she pianist manquée, actress, costume designer, producer (our "director" today), manager of her mother and custodian of her memory, or, most accurately perhaps, tyrant at large? When Ellen Terry was dying, the *New York Times* solved the problem of Edy's anomalous theatrical identity by announcing that "Miss Terry's daughter, Edith Craig, who is a prominent theatrical producer, has abandoned her work to care for her distinguished mother" (19 July 1928). When Edy herself died, the *Times* was vaguer still, identifying her grandly—and meaninglessly—as a "Veteran of the Stage," then collapsing into Shaw's magnificence the identities of mother and daughter alike: "Daughter of Dame Ellen Terry, to Whom George Bernard Shaw Wrote Love Letters, Dies" (28 March 1947).

When she died as when she drew herself, Edy had no realized identity. Those who worked with her, like Margaret Webster, fought her obscurity by giving her all the identities the theater can bestow: "I know now that I have done many things because of what I watched her do—set a light, angle a rostrum, drape a cloak, compose a picture on the stage; my eyes and hands learned these things. She made me understand what craft meant in the theatre. She knew everybody's job, from the author's to the usher's. From all she exacted workmanship, to all she accorded value" (Webster, 280). Edy could do everything but announce herself. Her father had transmitted the impulse to extinction; her mother had brought it forward. It was the legacy even actresses had to inherit and transmit.

Edy drew herself faintly in life; after death she was further obliterated. Christopher St. John, her faithful lover and family chronicler who survived Edy by thirteen years, burned Edy's papers shortly before her own death in 1960. Christopher made it her literary mission to perpetuate great women through artful presentation of their papers: after preserving Ellen Terry by editing her Memoir, her Shakespeare lectures, and her letters to Shaw, Christopher was appointed literary executor for the composer Ethel Smyth, whose first biography she duly wrote from the material bequeathed to her. Yet she became the posthumous executioner of the woman to whom she was closest. Whether Christopher's bonfire was a response to Edy's expressed wish, or a gesture of murderous irony, we shall never know, but Edy's lost papers are true to her obscured life. The girl who drew herself in the act of vanishing was perpetuated only in the reminiscences of a small, determined circle of women, and in her mother's absorbing life.

But to those who knew Edy in her maturity, she was as vivid as her mother and as triumphant a worker: she remained in Ellen Terry's orbit, not out of infirmity, but because, like other women of her generation, she saw salvation in female communities. Born in 1869, she inherited an unwavering faith in a "woman-controlled space" (Vicinus, *IW,* 7). The previous generation had institutionalized this saving space in the new woman's boarding schools, colleges, and religious sisterhoods; Edy and her associates expanded and empowered woman's space in the messianic vision of the suffrage movement, whose corporate transforming power Edy dramatized in the plays and pageants she staged for the Cause. Isolated from each other by the crushing restraints of family duties, late Victorian women dreamed of remaking society through union with each other. Ellen Terry, who played all roles for all watchers, had become a community in her mobile self, but Edy's watchful generation mistrusted the power of women who stood alone to change the roles they played. Together, women might transform humanity.

Women's schools, colleges, and sisterhoods, the later settlement and suffrage movements, all offered alternatives to a patriarchal family that truncated women's identities by allowing no life but marriage and economic dependence, no activities beyond the self-denying ministrations of daughter, wife, and mother. The new women's institutions made a power base opposed to the family, while slyly defining themselves in pious familial language. They talked of tenderness and modesty, of service and sacrifice, while dreaming of grand transformations. They exhorted their members to selflessness and whispered promises of glory.

Edy, though, had been born into the world of women her generation fought its fathers to join. Moving by her own devious route, Ellen Terry had already evaded the patriarchal family, making of her home an autonomous female space that won Edy's prize for her in advance. Her house of women pursued Gordon Craig like avenging furies; he died far from it but still protesting in terror, "I'm afraid to be hurt"; but his demons were Edy's glory. She had no forbidding father; her brother ran away from her; even when she saw Ellen Terry as a strangling presence, she could not leave a mother who represented everything advanced ideology exhorted women to be.

Ellen Terry had moved in childhood from lodging to lodging; until her own earnings bought one, she had had no family home to escape. Since she began life without enclosures, unlike other mothers, she had no qualms about letting feminists educate her daughter. Initially she had the radical idea of sending Edy and Ted to school together: in her home as in her roles, her overriding and unrealized aim had always been to unite the girl and the boy. The children began their schooling in London under Mrs. Cole, "a lady with ideas which in the 'eighties were considered advanced. She was a supporter of the new women's movement, and thought that girls ought to have as good an education as boys" (*Memoirs,* 192). At home power and pride were in the air one breathed, but Mrs. Cole initiated the children into a formidable new world.

Their schools, like their lives, quickly divided them. Edy became a boarder at Mrs. Cole's when the Lyceum went on its first American tour; Ted began his disruptive career at a series of boys' academies, interrupted only by the sudden summons to America that mortified Edy for years afterward. America did not prevent his ignominious expulsion from Heidelberg College, but it did crown his privileged position at home. Edy began to lose heart when she graduated from Mrs. Cole's school to that of her sister. Mrs. Malleson was a still sterner feminist, whose mission it was to prepare her girls for Girton, Cambridge's most demanding and prestigious woman's college. Mrs. Malleson did not dream of expelling Edy—unlike Ted, Edy was not an enemy of groups, though she grew into a tyrant within them—but she could not make Edy thrive.

Ellen Terry worried about her daughter as well as her son, but she met Edy's faults with comparative resignation. She did not take arms against them; she simply wrote ingratiating letters to the Mallesons—with whom she corresponded for the rest of her life, though Edy seems to have lost contact with her teacher as soon as she could—alerting them to Edy's defects:

> I send you my girlie again - It seems to me that <u>slothfulness</u> is her difficulty — or rather <u>our</u> "difficulty" in regard to her, for she seems unconscious of the "<u>difficulty</u>"!! I <u>do regret regret</u> regret being unable to see you & talk with you about her - & I regret the lost treat of being with you a few days in your own beautiful home for my <u>own</u> sake - however you will I'm quite sure be glad to know that I had a "perfectly lovely time",—never before such a real happy holiday & that I am much stronger & better in health for it - Edie will tell you (perhaps!!!) how <u>she</u> enjoyed herself. Mr. & Mrs. Carr <u>seemed</u> to enjoy it, & as for the dear Vicar [Henry Irving]; he was a picture of perfect content, all the while — even when one of us lost £60 for him! . . . Still I don't think Mr. Goodwin [Edy's drawing teacher] has seen what she seems to me to do so ~~well~~ much best - She, one moment, scribbles so vilely, & the next, draws so well (<u>Slothfulness.</u>) — One thing I shd much like to get (myself) some drawing from her once a week - I will offer her <u>a prize</u> for every half dozen careful drawings she sends me - . . . Edie is sorry to leave us - but longs to see you all again - "Joy Poole" is a great delight to her - & we joke her about "<u>trouty</u> Pool-e" — the dear thing she is so <u>very</u> serious over a joke. I hope you'll <u>not think</u> we have spoiled her during the time she has been with us - I try not to - & I hope she will not trouble you <u>too much</u>. Poor Miss Mabel I fear gets the worse part of her — for which I am very regretful.

Few students would want their teachers to receive such penetrating letters from their mothers: the Mallesons learn not only of Edy's slothfulness at work, but of her sluggishness in responding to family jokes. But Ellen Terry withheld from her daughter the heroic yardstick with which she measured Teddy. In 1885, around the time she charmed Mr. Malleson into an awareness of Edy's slothfulness, she wrote in despair to Bertha Bramly: "Oh, <u>work, work</u> until one drops from fatigue — <u>anything better</u> than theorize— Talk—& not <u>do</u> = It's bad in a woman, but terrible in a man=" Edy never had Ted's power to bring grief; thus, even after her sloth fell away, Ellen Terry had less joy in her as well.

She was apprehensive from the first about Edy's attempt to enter the world of institutions and authority. After criticizing Ted for his own poor performance at school, she continues doubtfully: "Edie is at work to pass for Girton. It's 'a <u>coiker</u>' to pass, & I shd say her spelling—like yours—wd have to improve first—however Mrs. Malleson says 'she can pass easily'—& as all Mrs. Mallesons girls are Girton girls, she <u>ought</u> to know." Edy may have been able to pass easily, but she didn't. Two years later, Ellen Terry wrote with false cheer: "[Edy] can <u>pass</u>, if she wants to, the Senior Cambridge Exam = & of course it would be splendid to have done it - & I'm <u>sure</u> she can do it, if she tries again =" But Edy never became a Girton girl.

Girton was the first of the pioneering female communities from whose weighty embrace Edy backed away. Emily Davies had founded the college in 1872, after a bitter struggle to retain the men's curriculum undiluted. Girton's unyielding claims for the female intellect made it a bleak and strenuous encampment within a hostile environment: Cambridge had been forced to educate women, but it denied them comfort, as well as official degrees. Mrs. Malleson must have instilled in Edy Girton's lonely, embattled ethos, the high seriousness of pioneering academic women who were always proving their earnestness to snickering men. Edy's "slothfulness," her mother's careless joy, the creeping sententiousness of the Lyceum in the late 1880s, all led Edy to shy away from grimness as a kind of death. Jolly actors found her dour; associates who refused to accept her leadership found her, like her brother, impossible; but she needed fun around her. Unlike the militant women of her generation, Edy had not the heart for a fighting life. And though they never acknowledged it, the women's colleges of the 1880s were training their students for battle.

In 1928, the year of Ellen Terry's death, Virginia Woolf delivered two elegant feminist discourses at the Cambridge women's colleges; these became her famous manifesto, *A Room of One's Own.* Lightly, Woolf denounces the penitential joylessness academic women endured. Their deprivation is manifest in bad food: "Here was the soup. It was a plain gravy soup. There was nothing to stir the fancy in that. One could have seen through the transparent liquid any pattern that might have been on the plate itself. But there was no pattern. The plate was plain. Next came beef with its attendant greens and potatoes—a homely trinity, suggesting the rumps of cattle in a muddy market, and sprouts curled and yellowed at the edge, and bargaining and cheapening, and women with string bags on Monday morning." After more unappetizing observations, Woolf concludes: "The human frame being what it is, heart, body and brain all mixed together, . . . a good dinner is of great importance to good talk. One cannot think well, love well, sleep well, if one has not dined well. The lamp in the spine does not light on beef and prunes."

In Girton and Newnham, the bad food Woolf deplored was a badge of honor as well as a stigma of poverty. While enforcing apparent humility, it put a generation of women in trim for a battle on streets and in prisons, whose most

effective weapon would be hunger strikes. Fasting in jail, resisting the violation
of force-feeding, militant suffragists in the first decades of the twentieth century
won—not the vote—but their own self-possessed and conquered bodies.
Through starving they achieved the triumph of spirit over appetite, initiating
them into the exalted and transforming loneliness of perfect purity. Beef and
prunes had not given young women ease, but it had taught them what they
could withstand, and the glorification they could, in consequence, achieve.

In the 1880s, when Mrs. Malleson was preparing Edy for Girton, women's
education was inextricably associated with aptitude in starving. It was not the
body alone that was disciplined: the comic imagination as well was subdued,
the same imagination with which Ellen Terry had endowed the female community of her home with a freedom no man had granted. Her mother's play would
always, for Edy, represent woman's freedom. When, at the height of the suffrage
battle, a new community of women sprang up at Smallhythe around Edy and
Chris in Priest's House, with Ellen Terry living through the hedges at the Farm,
their communion produced the food Edy could not do without. The food her
mother offered lured her with the savor of play:

> A Filet of Veal=
> To be, or not to be cooked today?— Rather a heavy night meal— I can't come
> up to Cottage [Priest's House] today. Will you eat early here—[the Farm] or have
> the fatted Calf tomorrow or — what? Just tell me, that's all=

Edy's retreat from the race for Girton led to more significant withdrawals. After
leaving the Mallesons, she studied music in London, then, in 1888, moved to
Berlin to study the piano with Alexis K. Hollaender; it was his wife who
received Edy's thinly penciled self-portrait. Her year in Berlin led friends to
assert later on that her rheumatic hands had prevented her from following her
true vocation as a pianist, but she was as dispirited at the piano as she had been
in school. Around 1889, when Edy was twenty, Ellen Terry wrote the Hollaenders one of her ominously ingratiating letters, apologizing for the "defective
nature" that shunned definition. The exam she mentions is probably Edy's
second attempt to qualify for Girton:

> **P r i v a t e**=
> Thank you for another dear letter = Do pray believe that, no matter what the
> result is, of the exam, that I know you have both done everything — & more
> = You are two dear creatures & I never can repay you for the loving care of
> my child = & now about Edy herself—

Do not think her unfeeling or ungrateful - she loves you both — but it is so <u>natural</u> that very young people kick up against steady work - it's <u>very naughty</u> , but natural = About Edy returning let us not <u>yet</u> say anything = <u>not yet</u> = I certainly <u>intended she should do so</u> but do not say so to Edy — & let us see the result of the Exam = I meant her to go back until July or August -- -- but <u>must</u> I decide in a hurry? please wait a little - unless of course <u>you</u> will not have her back - in that case you wd. tell me — but you love the c<u>hi</u>ld both of you I know, for you have proved & in spite of her defective nature, you see the good of her -

I shd be better pleased if she wd start from Berlin on Thursday the 20th, or Friday 21 - <u>Not</u> on the 22nd it is leaving it too late. She seems to wish to come with <u>Elfrida</u>, & perhaps it wd be better than travelling alone - Anyhow please <u>telegraph</u> me when she starts, & pray see that she wears old **w a r m** things, & extra underclothing to keep her warm on the journey - her "spats" on her feet & her waterproof handy to be got at - <u>Very</u> warm - & do <u>not</u> give her a lot of money - she spent 40 marks last journey on nothing at all = This is <u>not</u> because I am <u>mean</u>, but because she must learn the value of money = Dearest Anna you are a darling, & when you come to stay with me for a month, I will tell you so - Keep Edy to early bed the last two or 3 nights before her journey it will rest her - I am so excited at her coming home - God bless you all - With much love & gratitude

Yours ever
Nellchen =

Ellen Terry may have dwarfed Edy, criticized her and hovered over her, but her surviving letters are free of the rage with which she excoriated Gordon Craig in the same years: Edy had no manhood to betray. Christopher's notes to the Memoir quote snippets from the "wise, tender, yet at times unsparingly critical letters" Edy received from her in Berlin: "Tell me something of how you like your life, and of the music and drawing—whether you think you'll get on well in these two things with your two new masters, and which you like best—*not* the personality of either of 'em, but let's hear of their attainments, and their teaching powers" (quoted in *Memoirs*, 194). Christopher writes that these letters "ought to be published some day" because they "show Ellen Terry as she was when the chameleon element in her nature, which made her swift to take the colour and form of some subjective image in another's mind, was passive" (*Memoirs*, 193); at the last, though, she seems to have added to her bonfire Ellen Terry's letters to her daughter, for the originals have proved impossible to locate. We have only Christopher's account of Edy's rueful comment on re-reading them: "If I could have done all Mother advised me to do, been all she wanted me to be, I should now be a very splendid and wise woman" (quoted in *Memoirs,* 194). Unlike Ted, who was bruised beyond repair by his mother's exhortations, Edy embraced the best self Ellen Terry tried to make for her.

The few who knew her thought she was indeed "a very splendid and wise woman," but she made herself neither student nor musician. In the nineteenth century, these disciplines required of women the gall and guile of combatants; trained on her mother's evasions and transfigurations, Edy could not begin the battle. Rheumatism may have relieved her even from the attempt, but centuries of male dominance probably daunted her as well. Christopher St. John's biography of Ethel Smyth publishes a letter from Virginia Woolf speculating about the crushing odds against female musicians in the years Edy considered becoming a pianist: "My own longing in reading your article is to escape the individual [Woolf writes to Ethel Smyth]; and to be told simply, plainly, objectively, 'in 1880 there was not a single woman in an orchestra; there was not a single teacher to teach women harmony; the expense of going to Berlin was 165 pound ten; eight women were educated partly by 1891; in 1902 Wood took five women violinists into his orchestra' "; and so on.

Edy needed no statistics to see that a woman needed more than art and hard work to succeed at music: she had to prepare for perpetual, and probably futile, battle. Ellen Terry had learned on her pulses the distortions of false roles, but she had never confronted institutionalized discrimination in the world outside the theater: if all instruments and public stages were withheld as a matter of course, one could not play even bad roles with spirit. Edy saw professional life with searing plainness, but her talent at seeing was the only one she trusted. Depressed and discouraged, she left Berlin, displaying her stiff and painful fingers as an excuse. Music became as fitful, as hauntingly elusive and private, as the rest of her identity. Clare Atwood, a painter who moved into Priest's House during the First World War, remembers Edy furtively leading an orchestra: "She was not beguiled into being [a musical] executant, except in one charming particular. Sometimes, rather rarely, when she was lying on her sofa, playing a Patience and listening to a B.B.C. concert, you might, if you were very still, hear Edy whistling like a lovely bird. She would lead the orchestra, slightly anticipating the beat, and those notes, so ghostly and so true, made one hold one's breath. One had, however, to be very careful to be seemingly unconscious of her obligato, unheard save by the very few" (Adlard, 141–42).

The roads beyond the theater were too strenuous, too sad. Edy was pained by her mother's representation of woman's condition, but the formidable reality of oppression shriveled her. Apathetically, she joined the family firm and became an actress. In 1890, when she was twenty-one, she joined the Lyceum, the year after Teddy had taken refuge in its shelter after failing at school. Her identification with her spoiled, incompetent little brother depressed her further. She had no heart to take on the mighty stage name her mother had given her; she refused to remember having chosen it herself. As Ailsa Craig, swallowed in her extravagant dress, she is a woebegone sight. She was swallowed in her mother as well: from her Lyceum days up to her death, Edy's life became inseparable from her mother's will and needs. Ellen Terry was all her sustenance, all her doom. In the year she began to act, she began despite herself to hate the mother she could not part from.

Photograph of Edith Craig as Ailsa Craig. *Reproduced by permission of the Harry Ransom Humanities Research Center, University of Texas, Austin.*

As she walked dutifully through secondary roles in the 1890s, Edy began to manage Ellen Terry, even to mother her. She wrote her letters, escorted her to theaters, dinners, and parties or was offered up as a pallid substitute for her, learned people's names on her behalf, and handled insistent fans; as she performed her backstage tasks, she emitted a hostility, sometimes even a ferocity, the charming Ellen Terry was unable to release. Edy was becoming her mirror-self, as Kate had been so many years before, but this time Ellen Terry was caught in goodness, leaving the wicked role for Edy. By the time of *Captain Brassbound's Conversion,* they were fixed in the roles the Lyceum had assigned them. Allan Wade, a young actor in *Captain Brassbound* who later appeared in Edy's suffrage plays, remembered his first impression of the mother and daughter:

> Miss Terry in the theatre meant that Edy was there also, taking care of her, seeing that she arrived on time, arranging or designing her costumes, trying to ensure that she rested and conserved some of her energy for her Jubilee Performance which was to take place late in April. One might almost have thought that the roles of mother and daughter had been reversed—and the "daughter" was by no means easy to control. Miss Terry, coming down from her dressing-room to the first floor, would, in the kindness of her heart, stop to chat with anybody she met—stagehand, dresser, understudy—there was always something to say. She had discovered, how I don't know for I certainly never told her, that I had been a subscriber, some years earlier, to Gordon Craig's magazine *The Page* which he had illustrated with his own woodcuts, and so I became for her "a friend of Teddy's" —though actually it was many years later that I first met him. "Oh, yes—you are a friend of Teddy's; I heard from him last week." "Come *on,* Mother," Edy's voice would be heard from the stage-door. "Oh, that's Edy," Miss Terry would say with an even sweeter smile. "I mustn't keep her waiting!" And then, perhaps, she would meet somebody else coming up from the stage below and have another little talk. To my interested observation Miss Craig, as I then thought of her, seemed genial, a little brusque in speech, and certainly a very dominant personality. (Adlard, 67–68)

Edy's appearance of acerbic dominance was her revenge on a mother who had gotten inside her, who had taken away the savor of the prizes and the sweetness of the struggle that gave life to women outside the theater. Ellen Terry tried to find jobs for her, as she had done for Ted, but like Ted Edy was prickly, not a useful actress at all. Shaw tried in vain to explain to Ellen Terry the paralyzing weight of a powerful parent: "She wants an opening ten times more than if she had no mother. Do you remember—or did you ever hear of—the obscurity of Mozart's son? An amiable man, a clever musician, an excellent player; but hopelessly extinguished by his father's reputation. How could any man do what was expected from Mozart's son? Not Mozart himself even. Look at Siegfried Wagner. Ellen Terry's daughter! Awful!" (16 April 1897. *A Corr.,* 136)

Ellen Terry could not imagine what powerful parents meant. Her own resilient family had enhanced, not engulfed her; mother and father were roles she cast people in at will. She had never believed in herself as a mother; once she was no longer fallen, it came to seem a poor part into which she put too much intensity because, after the Lyceum forbade her to feel powerful, her children offered her the only license she was allowed. She had never felt the oppressive, the ubiquitous family presence whose burden Shaw knew so well and tried to lift from the indolent Edy.

Shaw's interest in Edy was her one victory in her thankless role of her mother's understudy and double. When he got Edy cast in the Charringtons' company as Prossy in his *Candida* and Mrs. Linden in *A Doll's House,* he was kind but frank about her listlessness in rehearsals. She had inherited the weight of her mother's mantle, but she could never, Shaw implied, be an expansive actress of her mother's vintage: "Her voice is quite her own. But she needs to work and use her head a good deal; for she is like a boy in her youth and virginity, and cannot fall back on 'emotional effects' which are really only the incontinences of a hysterical and sexually abandoned woman, but which pull a great many worthless and stupid actresses through leading parts of vulgar drama. So she will—fortunately for herself—get nothing cheap" (29 July 1897. *A Corr.,* 171).

Shaw could not know it, but the budding St. Joan he saw in Edy was the spectral boy her mother might have played had she not been educated into womanliness. But Edy could sustain her cool boy-presence only offstage. She did manage to play an animated Prossy once *Candida* opened, but she was too clear-eyed to believe in Ailsa Craig. Edy faded out of acting because she was, as she put it, "audience-shy," a malaise that shadowed all her work. She knew from watching her mother all the things audiences had the power to make one be.

Ellen Terry transmitted her worry to Ted, who had escaped from the Lyceum to tour on his own. She even contemplated for Edy a girl's traditional career, one that had never before crossed her mind: the vocation of falling in love. But in 1894, she did not like to consider Edy's love too closely.

> Edy is enough to make one daft. I think she will <u>not</u> <u>work</u> at <u>anything</u>! She has an astonishing "Study" I shd like her to do <u>somewhere-anywhere remotely</u>-? the 2 parts of <u>Nan</u> in "Good for Nothing"—& <u>Margery</u> in Cousin Joe piece=

Possibly by the time she had done it <u>for a month</u> she might develop the part into a rather remarkable performance. Meanwhile she is studying <u>Emilia</u> in Othello - but altho' she wd <u>look</u> <u>magnificent</u> in it, it requires a <u>great deal</u> of the knowledge of the <u>Art</u> of acting to <u>even</u> <u>get through</u> with it—I cant tell you how beautiful she looks in the first dress of Jessica—Superb—but (by way of not <u>dashing her</u> <u>efforts</u>) (the dear old thing) I've <u>not</u> let her know how <u>very</u> far she <u>is</u> <u>at</u> <u>present</u> from thefaintestideaofknowinghowto<u>actthe</u>part,&Imustbeg<u>youdon't</u>tell <u>her</u>.

She can be <u>taught</u> I think, but she's lost at sea, without a Pilot = & then worst of all, the <u>whole thing</u> seems a supreme joke to her, & she wont <u>study</u> to <u>better</u> the thing she is doing—

Meanwhile she is <u>awfully happy</u> & very sweet—but perhaps by doing <u>Joke</u> parts (like Nan) she will find her vocation =

—You shd see her in the last act of the Merchant—Like a big jolly awkward school-boy = She's <u>good</u> in the bit at the window—As she says—"<u>Then</u> the water is <u>between</u> them" [the lovers]—!! I wish she'd fall in love—with a <u>boot</u> black—But why do I say that, since she is very happy & as merry as a school boy!

Edy did not want to play joke parts, or any parts at all, and so, to oblige her mother and escape her as well, she fell in love. It proved to be not at all what Ellen Terry wished.

The Lyceum's 1895 American tour was taut with bad feeling from the outset. Ten years earlier, at the zenith of her power and hope, Ellen Terry had snatched Teddy out of school to receive America; he had, as usual, thrown its glory away. When Edy finally became part of a Lyceum tour, she joined a company in disarray. In relentlessly newfangled America, the Lyceum was a loved memento of the theatrical past: the wave had crested and the end was near. While clinging to the home she had beautified, Ellen Terry brought with her tokens of the forces that would destroy that home. *The Man of Destiny*, Shaw's Napoleon play, was in her luggage; she was to woo Irving into producing it, at which she failed wretchedly. She was determined to stage another experimental assault from the enemy camp: *Godfroi and Yolande*, a macabre little play by Irving's son Laurence, in which Ellen Terry stepped out of her lovable type to play a charismatic leper. The "filthy leper play," as May Webster persisted in calling it, irritated Irving even more than Laurence did himself; his leading lady's advocacy seemed to him perverse. He kept aloof from Ellen Terry throughout the tour. His mind was already discarding his theatrical wife; Eliza Aria, with her singleminded loyalty, would soon take over that role. The *Cymbeline* projected for the next season had the coloration of an apologetic farewell to an Ellen Terry who could neither leave Henry Irving nor cleave to him. In the same way, her own children clung to her angrily, dragging her down because they could not make lives separate from hers. When, on the way to Memphis, a flood threatened to swamp the company's special train, the danger promised an exhilarating release from the fraught atmosphere within the elegant cars.

Ellen Terry's family as well as her theater was threatening to come apart. In 1895, Ted was testing on his wife May his skill at founding families and abandoning them: his mother received clearer and clearer warnings that she would find a discarded wife and two children waiting for her support when she returned from America. Teddy thought he was playing his father, but the joy, the freedom and beauty Godwin had given were beyond his self-absorbed imagination; now, with Ted's debts and his cast-off families in her keeping, she could never recover the free life that had given him birth.

As her world closed in on her, she learned that her sister Floss had died. The dear, sunny girl had never minded about the theater: she *was* the loving woman Ellen had acted so persuasively. Powerful, dutiful Sarah had been dead for three years; Kate and Marion, the remaining sisters, envied Ellen and would be glad to see her down. On her return to Liverpool, she learned that Ben had also died during the tour. Her father was the last, perhaps the only, person who had loved her; his death took too much away for her to talk about. Now there was no one to tell her to be her finest self; no one but her strong, competent daughter. All things were torn away; Edy could not go.

But Edy, too, had abandoned her on the tour. Ellen Terry never knew whether Edy's defection had been the cause or the consequence of the other frictions and betrayals that eroded the company. When her letters to Gordon Craig are not lashing out at his failures, they are uncharacteristically querulous and fearful. At first, she refrains from mentioning Edy: "I've written to Pinero, & asked him to look after me next=just one play of his before I end up. What bundle of ~~crimes~~ ~~follies~~ weaknesses can he keep for me to portray I wonder. Not jealousy. Not ambition=I can't do either of these — Now 'Drink' I shd. have rather liked to tackle—lightly & funnily="

Her nervous attempt to meet the future by becoming modishly wicked carries an oblique confession: she might not be able to "do" jealousy or ambition, but she could certainly suffer them, and she was. Over and over, she told reporters that she loved the public, who merely loved her back again, but fear was eating away even the pretense of that love: "We are going through a bewildering time —This moving from place to place & seeing so many would be friends—kind folk who overpower us with favors & who cannot understand that it must be that we are more to them than they to us. Who go night after night & get to know us & care for us — It is quite distressing." Gradually, she moves from the distress without to the shakiness within. Her New Year's wish is a prayer for direction: "For myself I could wish for a few more <u>fixed ideas</u>—beliefs—for I'm a <u>wobbler</u> — & a waverer— & a dreamer - & I'm old & shd be wiser — & I <u>feel</u> young! & weak = It's a fine world, but there are I think a few too many people in it who are <u>ignorant</u>— & I'm one of 'em."

When he was trying to pry his dead mother out of Edy's control, Gordon Craig would take this letter as Ellen Terry's admission of indifference to woman's suffrage, but the vote was not a burning issue in 1895. Certainly it was far from Ellen Terry's mind, and from Edy's as well, on the American tour. The need to please that galvanized her inveterate love of play found Ellen Terry wobbling between the old theater and the new, between freedom and need, between triumph and pathos. Above all, that new year, she wobbled between union with Edy and a suppressed impulse to let her go, as she had been let go as a girl in times that looked sterner, but were in some ways more tolerant, than the confused, emancipated 1890s. In the spring, when Edy withheld herself after Floss had died, Ellen Terry's sorrow finally erupted in a letter to her son that was heavy with slashes and deletions:

> Edy is going through a new & very strange phase = She will, she <u>must</u>, learn before long that it is an impossibility to go through this world (with any graciousness) taking all, & giving nothing. . . . I have scarcely <u>seen her on this</u> tour = & when I <u>most</u> of all wanted her she avoided me like the plague!!! . . . I <u>hoped</u> she <u>might be</u> in love! - but she scouts the idea - & it wd be a frightful chancery — she'd possibly - probably - want to go away again. I think she has a terrific "temper" which she keeps pretty tight hold upon. Yet she's sweet enough for <u>me</u> at all events = At her <u>worst</u> & tryingest I dote upon her- but she can **d o w i t h o u t** everybody so **a p p a l l i n g l y** (or rather she <u>thinks</u> she can, poor little girl =) If she has an idea in her head that <u>she'd like to live alone</u>, why doesn't she tell me? Practically, since we've been touring, she has been away all the time! & as I scarcely see much of Henry except in the confounded theatre, it's a precious good thing for me that I have Nannie Held with me.

Edy *was* in love, or so she and others claimed later on. At any rate, she was trying to play the only role that would allow her to leave a mother who, as she floundered in her roles, was coming to identify her own thwarted boundlessness with Edy's best good. Ellen Terry continues:

> It wd be, I think, a <u>very bad thing</u> for her & for me too, if she were not with me - (unless of course she married happily.) . . . One night in an awful passion (I've never seen such an exhibition from her but twice before in her life) she told me she loathed every friend I had in the world except Stephen [Coleridge]!!!—

she was livid from rage & then (when I had half died through the night from
the puzzling over her temper) the next morning she appeared fresh as a daisy, &
with a careless "good morning darling," & the normal salute, which is the greatest
extent to which she exercises her "duty" to me, & which with her means nothing,
she tripped down to breakfast & eat a good meal= When she gets ill & I have
her with me she gets her old sweeter self - I'm pretty tired - & after all my life
working I want things to go smoothly - they'll have to—or I shall break down.
. . . What concerns me is she looks so ill when she's away from me= — I have
hoped against hope she would care to try to improve herself for the stage—but
her lisp gets worse & worse & is really a terrible defect=

Separations, both incipient and actual, were beating down her buoyancy: her
own from Henry, Ted's from May, the new, socially aware theater from
the old grand one, the dead from the living. Edy was threatening her with
one parting more than she could bear. She may have known too that the pain
would be wasted, since Edy, like Ted, was doomed to love no one but herself.

Edy had tried to make a career apart from her mother; her will, not she, had
failed, and so she turned to respectability. In 1895, love still guaranteed a girl's
escape from home, and so Edy fell in love—though the young actor Sidney
Valentine was a safely married man. Margaret Webster provides the fullest
account of Edy's aborted romance:

> She fell deeply in love with Sidney Valentine, who was married. When Ellen
> Terry found out, she reacted with violence. She crushed the incipient romance as
> mercilessly as if she had been Father Moulton-Barrett [the tyrannical father of
> Elizabeth Barrett] in person. She threatened to send Edy home to England at once.
> It was an understandable way for a mother to behave, especially for this particular
> mother; but it did nothing to help Edy. With extraordinary lack of perception,
> she proceeded to make matters worse. She was, at this time, carrying on a mild
> flirtation with Frank Cooper, the handsome if slightly wooden actor who played
> such parts as Bassanio and Macduff. She would bring him back to supper after
> the performance and insist that Edy should stay up—or get up, if she had not been
> playing herself that night—in order to chaperone her. Mother and daughter both
> talked to Ben and May, who were, of course, powerless to help. Edy remained
> in the company and did as she was told. No one ever spoke of the episode again.
> (Webster, 175–76)

At some point Ellen Terry summoned Gordon Craig's highly unstable authority
against Edy's flight. Obediently, after they had returned to England, he wrote
his sister a muddled, affectionate letter:

My dear dear Edy do let me help you about <u>things I</u> could do so much better than Mother or another. Dreams are nothing - & are best banished & impossible realities come to be dreams. Don't let whoever advises you, I mean :-----: dont let him, her, or it, advise you selfishly Bring out the best side of -----'s nature & let him advise you into what is best for <u>you</u>=

    I speak as I feel & know through experience. For once in my life I have thought more of others than myself & things are smoother & more sane & safe than before: !!! **C a t a s t r o p h e   f o l l o w s** when one thinks selfishly about such things in spite of one self. You & -----: <u><u>must</u></u> not lead each other toward catastrophe. A woman can draw out of a man this unselfishness but the man must be the one to decide it &, <u>as it were, freely.</u> Of course in these matters no one allows others to know better than themselves but others may be allowed to influence one: so let me influence you - for I am not like Mother who only thinks of <u><u>you</u></u> & <u><u>me</u></u> & not of other outside persons for whom we may (<u>may not</u>) have love. I know your ideal is in some one person very good & proper but make your ideal <u><u>be</u></u> ideal. After all it is possible: & then the dream was worth the dreaming.

                    I've found it so =

                    Bless you old girl =

Edy had no ambition to draw unselfishness out of a man; she was trying to make a life for herself in the most acceptable way she knew, having withdrawn from the bolder ways. But she was as halfhearted about falling in love as she had been about school, about the piano, about acting. Many years later, with scarcely more conviction, she would repeat her performance: she enjoyed watching its effect. Falling in love showed her her power of throwing her mother into chaos. She would use that power later on. It was more potent than her love.

    Edy was excused from the summer tour of the English provinces, but Ellen Terry, of course, was not. According to the Websters, it was on this tour that her behavior became disturbing:

> Ben shared lodgings with Frank Cooper, with whom Nell had begun a mild flirtation during the American tour. He realized that it was assuming more serious dimensions. Presents would arrive for Cooper, with a card "from an admirer" in that unmistakable handwriting. The landlady would come to tell him that "a lady" was waiting downstairs in a carriage. Nell would "drop in" to look at an oil painting Cooper was doing, or he would announce casually that he was going out after the show "to see a friend." Nell took a childish delight in all this transparent intrigue. But Ben, who loved her, resented the jokes in the company, the sidelong smiles and what he felt to be the cheapening of her stature. "Degrading," he called it.
>
>   The morale of the company was not improved, and even Irving grew angry. "She called H. I. 'Frank' the other evening all through some supper till he got

perfectly furious." But you could never tell whether she was being mischievous or merely absent-minded. "She's been so funny tonight. She's immensely keen on a fly she saved from drowning in the water-bottle and which she insists follows her about from her sitting-room to her bedroom and has written to Sir John Lubbock about it and means to capture it tomorrow and take it to Manchester! But she was very fascinating and most entertaining." (Webster, 183–84)

No doubt the smiling company enjoyed what they saw as the sexual desperation of an aging actress, without knowing that they were watching one of Ellen Terry's most finely subtle (if uncontrolled) performances. Her flamboyant self-display over the married actor Frank Cooper was a parodic mirror of Edy's earlier, equally embarrassing pursuit of the married actor Sidney Valentine on the American tour. Her airy disclaimer to Bertha Bramly both masks and reveals her association of herself with Edy, an association that hints at their coming, consuming marriage, not to actors, but to each other: "No – I fear I can't snap up Frank Cooper (!) and marry him, for he happens to have a wife – and she's nice too – so he can't 'cut her throat with a bar of soap' – She is a jealous little lady too, but *not* of me – and I'm fond of her. They marry me to every man I act with – 'She acts so naturally' they say – 'it must be real' – Silly-fool-Asses!!! Mrs. Finch Hatton told me a few days since that my Edy was engaged to be married – I knew nothing about it but as Edy is away I sent her congratulations!!! She thought it very polite of me but knew nothing about the matter" (quoted in Manvell, 250–51). Ellen Terry was beginning the drowning which so many had prophesied for her so long ago, the drowning from which she was so outrageously excited about saving the fly. Intermittently, in 1897, she was drowning in Edy.

When Edy joined a South African tour in 1898, she made her final, half-hearted attempt to leave, but she was merely deferring her destiny. She had never repudiated the truth of her mother's lament to Shaw:

As to Edy becoming an actress I feel sure she can become something better than the best actress in the world. The difference between Edy in Manchester and Edy in Africa (oh, my heart is in my boots as I realize it) is this. If she is in any real difficulty she always sends to me, or comes to me, and we pick up her ends together. But when she is in Africa! Oh Lord, whom will she go to? And if she is ill too, she gets better quicker with me than with anybody. It's not jealous thought, all this. (I'm "made that way," with no inside Hell) and if someone should go to her and forgetting self for ever so short a time (as I'm able to do, just because I love her) then she would be healed, but there is not very much love wasting about, and folk like Edy dont get it just at the right moment. (13 April 1898. *A Corr.,* 223–24)

But when Edy bolted toward what she claimed was love, her mother had pulled her back. Ellen Terry did have an inside Hell, and "the Edy-devil," as she sometimes called her daughter, was its most intimate inhabitant. It was time for them both to live there. Edy made a garden for it, and arranged memories of her mother's past, restoring the role she had lost with her childhood: in the final phase of her life, Ellen Terry lived at the center of a community of women who played men's parts.

In 1896, they had met the woman who could take on the roles no man had been able to manage: creator of an Ellen Terry who would fit the new century, husband to Edy, and priestly presence who would sanctify the marriage between mother and daughter. Christabel Marshall was the daughter of the Victorian novelist, Emma Marshall. She was drawn to illegitimacy, claiming quite falsely that she herself was born out of wedlock; *Hungerheart*, her autobiographical novel, dignifies its heroine with muddled genealogical intrigue. In 1896, Christabel had just moved to London from Oxford; she was writing her first novel while working as secretary to Lady Randolph Churchill and her son Winston. According to *Hungerheart*, she had loved women stormily, if spiritually, since her childhood: thus, she reasoned, she must have the soul of a man. In *Hungerheart*, she names her fictional self "John"; when, several years after meeting Edy, she converted to Catholicism, she changed her name to Christopher St. John.

Many lesbians of that period gave themselves men's names, but few recreated themselves as saints. Christopher was possessed by sainthood. In *Hungerheart*, John realizes her vocation at the climax of her spiritual development, and cries ecstatically: "I want to be a Saint!" Having renamed herself after John the Baptist, Christopher needed a messiah whose presence she might proclaim. Ellen Terry stepped forward.

Ellen Terry was far more comfortable with Edy and Christopher's union than she had been at the idea of Edy's marriage: Christopher's sundry accounts make it clear that Ellen Terry deliberately brought them together. To the day of her death and beyond it as well, she presided over their life together: unlike most homosexual couples at the turn of the century, Edy and Chris were not outcast from family, but welded to it. For both of them, moreover, Ellen Terry was the primary beloved. Christopher had an embarrassing speech impediment that made her still more painfully earnest than she was by nature; the awkward young writer knew nothing about the theater when Ellen Terry, to whom she had written passionate letters, invited her into her dressing room during a performance of *King Arthur*. There, she caught a glimpse of her idol's "double": Edy in a Guinevere costume, about to stand in for her fidgety mother during the pageant. Three years later, Christopher was suddenly invited to visit. Edy had returned from her year in South Africa and was performing her former tasks as apathetically as ever. One of them was receiving worshipful women. She was sewing when Chris arrived; holding out her hand, she pricked the awed guest with her needle. "Cupid's dart," Christopher remembered, "for I loved Edy from that moment" (Adlard, 19). If she didn't, they both loved Ellen Terry, who could make them love each other.

In 1899, they took a flat together; in 1900, Ellen Terry bought her Farm at Smallhythe and gave Edy and Chris the closest and prettiest of the cottages. Unlike Gertrude Stein and Alice B. Toklas, who were to become so modishly daring in the 1920s, or the doomed female lovers in Radclyffe Hall's *The Well of Loneliness,* Edy and Chris never aped the exclusive roles of conventional heterosexual marriage: "I used to wonder which was the husband and which was the wife in the *ménage!*" Christopher wrote about the parallel relationship in *Hungerheart* (219). For both Edy and her mother, husbands and wives were curious, unnatural identities for lovers to assume. During World War I, when Ellen Terry was declining beyond knowledge, the painter Clare Atwood (who renamed herself "Tony") moved into their small cottage to become the crucial third party, preserving their community from shrinking into a couple. But as their maker, child, and idol, Ellen Terry could never leave them. Edy's "separate *ménage* with me, far from separating [mother and daughter], brought them into a closer relationship," Christopher wrote (Adlard, 29). It was in fact Edy's union with Christopher that made her union with her mother indissoluble.

Ellen Terry showed no conventional disapproval of Edy's and Christopher's household; with her purchase of the Farm and its adjacent cottages at Small-hythe, she absorbed her life delightedly into theirs. She is unlikely to have read the tomes of sexologists like Richard von Krafft-Ebing and Havelock Ellis, who at the end of the century were writing luridly about love between women as a dangerous disease; the shunning of female couples made fashionable by the new pseudo-science of sexology was as distant from Ellen Terry as the nervous taboos of her own girlhood had been. Few Victorians of her generation had regarded lesbianism with loathing, because few were certain of what it was. For Ellen Terry at the end of the Victorian age, it looked like an expansive and piquant new role that might free one from the brutality and jealousy of the love she knew. It was her son, not Edy, whose love brought ruin. Edy would force on her no helpless wives, no sobbing mistresses, no draining grandchildren. Above all, Edy would be there, always. There were to be no more losses.

"Edy is here," Ellen Terry wrote to Shaw from Smallhythe in 1904. "Did I tell you she is my right hand, and still growing to be my left hand, and happy as a schoolboy all the while? I fear to be too happy in her—I try to be quiet with it all. She has a cottage of her own here and we visit each other every day!"

(14 June 1904. *A Corr.,* 296). Ellen Terry rejoiced in having made a world that would keep her daughter, and Edy rejoiced in that world; as time went on, she came to believe that it was she who had made the Smallhythe community for her mother. As Ellen Terry's right hand and her left hand, Edy was not free, but she began to grow strong, for when Christopher came, her work took form: Edy began to appreciate the significance of theatrical costumes. Like her grand-mother Sarah, Edy was always sewing; now she saw that costumes had their own life, one that was stronger and more durable than human character. Ellen Terry had learned her very nature from the costumes they gave her; now Edy might form the clothes that determined women's beings.

At the same time that Ellen Terry was subsidizing Gordon Craig's opera productions, she set Edy up in an atelier. It was no more lucrative than her brother's work, but it gave Ellen Terry deeper pleasure, because she understood and identified herself with it. Writing to the designer of James Barrie's plays to promote her daughter's new career, she merges herself with Edy's work as she never did with Gordon Craig's: "I see you are going to design 'The Admirable Crichton.' Now the Artist generally chooses who shall carry out his designs by <u>making</u> the dresses. Do choose <u>Edy & me</u>!! <u>We</u> are Craig & Co. [She gives the address of the atelier] Allow me to recommend us strongly! Edy will make everything for my new play which I do in the Spring. Who is so intelligent as—<u>Craig & Co</u>.? & well you know it!" The formal advertisement for Craig & Co. sported a Gordon Craig drawing of a little bonnet. Enhanced by defining family and by Christopher's solid adoring presence, Edy began to reveal what she had always seen so clearly.

The atelier was too uncommercial to survive, but costumes were always the heart of Edy's theatrical vision: they epitomized the self-transforming power she sought to elicit. Edy was not a mere costume designer, any more than Gordon Craig was a mere set designer: like the Irving they had both studied, Edith and Gordon Craig required Napoleonic control over all aspects of production, or their visions would wilt unrealized. But the towering planes of Gordon Craig's sets exterminated the people who were the essence of Edy's theatrical world; for her, all human identity came from clothes, not from the settings that imposed their own dwarfing life on the actors.

She had begun her work on the Lyceum's fraught American tour, on which she designed the single production of Laurence Irving's *Godfroi and Yolande.* Back home, in 1899, Henry Irving placed in her charge the costumes for Sardou's *Robespierre,* one of his last and least successful productions. Looking back to her Lyceum days as May Webster, Dame May Whitty recalled how, through costumes, Edy "could transform the commonplace into something magical"

(Adlard, 51). As she grew older, her respect for the power of design became, like Godwin's, religious in its single-mindedness. Sybil Thorndike, who worked in Edy's Pioneer Players in the 1920s, eulogized her as a wizard: "I never remember her wanting new designs—she'd turn over a bit of old junk in the theatrical clothes basket—pick out bits here—bits there—and suddenly make a whole—the same with scenery and furniture. Literally she could use anything —old curtains as draperies—chair covers—she could transform into things unlike themselves" (Adlard, 81). For her, costumes were transfigured people. She refused to have them cleaned, so that the experiences that made them what they were might remain present. She lent Sybil Thorndike her mother's precious Lady Macbeth dresses with the proviso: "We won't have them cleaned, as they are now beautifully supple, and will almost play a part by themselves" (Adlard, 82).

She had seen her mother become what she wore. Young Harry's peg-top trousers had acquired totemistic significance as the essence of the boy-self Ellen Terry's life, her times, her own supple character, had forced her to discard. Edy shared her awareness of the magical power of costumes over character with a generation of feminists who were reconsidering everything in female life that men had called "natural." Cicely Hamilton, the penetrating social analyst whose *How the Vote Was Won* and *A Pageant of Great Women* Edy staged for the Actress' Franchise League, used clothes as a moral touchstone for women's deformation by society. Her *Marriage As a Trade* elevates the wisdom of unfallen children who have not yet been inculcated into gender codes; for them "sex was still a matter of garments." For Cicely Hamilton's generation, gender, seen truly, remained a matter of garments. In 1908, the year before *Marriage As a Trade* appeared, Ellen Terry's *The Story of My Life* was published. Suffused with the collaborative presences of Edy and Chris, *The Story of My Life/Ellen Terry's Memoirs* is steeped in regret for a lost, unfallen child, the cross-dressing Ellen Terry whose costumes maim her into womanliness. The actress's enforced adjustments and private embarrassments become paradigms of controlled female development in a society that un-makes its women.

Virginia Woolf's special mission was to recast the belligerent insights of her generation of women into irresistibly elegant language. Her *Orlando* weaves her contemporaries' vision of the power of clothes into a witty peroration on gender, its roles, and its transforming possibilities:

> The change of clothes had, some philosophers will say, much to do with [the imposition of modesty upon Orlando]. . . . Thus, there is much to support the view that it is clothes that wear us and not we them; we may make them take

the mould of arm or breast, but they mould our hearts, our brains, our tongues to their liking. So, having now worn skirts for a considerable time, a certain change was visible in Orlando, which is to be found even in her face. If we compare the picture of Orlando as a man with that of Orlando as a woman we shall see that though both are undoubtedly one and the same person, there are certain changes. The man has his hand free to seize his sword; the woman must use hers to keep the satins from slipping from her shoulders. The man looks the world full in the face, as if it were made for his uses and fashioned to his liking. The woman takes a sidelong glance at it, full of subtlety, even of suspicion. Had they both worn the same clothes, it is possible that their outlook might have been the same too.

Woolf's Orlando, whose clothes recompose his ardent manhood into female subtlety and suspicion, resembles the Ellen Terry Edy conceived. Edy's vision formed itself in the short-lived atelier that, like Gordon Craig's vast designs, mattered less as a practical reality than as a contagious cultural idea. Learning from her mother the power of costumes over being, recreating that mother and offering her to the world in the Memoir she helped conceive, Edy helped teach her generation about the making and the deformation of a woman. Ellen Terry was acting less and less. To the uninitiated, she was melting into an innocuous old dear; but through Edy's understanding she performed once again an exemplary role on behalf of watching women. Edy grew brave once she began to use in her work the lessons of her mother's life.

But she did not settle into that work easily or willingly. Around 1904, when Ellen Terry confessed to Bernard Shaw, "I fear to be too happy in her," the twenty-five-year-old Edy made one last abortive break for autonomy: she fell in love with her brother's collaborator with the Purcell Operatic Society, Martin Shaw. The entire cast of her life quickly brought her to heel. Ellen Terry objected to his disfiguring birthmark; the shocked Christopher attempted suicide in the best melodramatic manner. After saying her final "no" to her destiny, Edy settled where her mother had placed her, and thrived there.

Edy was fiercely mistrustful of men as lovers and husbands, opening her heart only in the world of women she had been born to; nevertheless, falling violently in love was the only protest she could conceive against the enclosures her mother wove around her life. Chris was understandably shattered by her sudden obsession: nothing in the Edy she knew had prepared her for it. *Hungerheart* describes her feelings, luridly but justifiably: "One horrible moment . . . A bomb hurtling through the serene air of my Paradise, exploding with a noise of devils' laughter, tearing up immemorial trees by the roots, laying waste the greenery of hope and faith—then filth, stench, corruption—then nothing, no suffering even—nothing" (226). *Hungerheart* suggests that after "Sally" destroys their idyll and kills "John's" sense that she is loved, things are never again the same. In the novel, Sally's love for a man is a wanton assault on happiness. But unlike Ellen Terry's Edy, Christopher's Sally has no brother.

Edy fell in love with Martin Shaw just after *The Vikings,* at the time Gordon Craig expatriated to Berlin. Ellen Terry's short, catastrophic management of the Imperial Theatre had been her last desperate bid to keep Teddy; through it, she lost both her son and her savings. After the Imperial's first and last season, Edy and Chris joined Ellen Terry on a provincial tour intended to redeem her management's losses; they produced *The Merchant of Venice, Much Ado,* and Heijerman's *The Good Hope* in Christopher's translation, conspicuously omitting *The Vikings.* Edy returned home to see that the cherished mother she had at last won away from her brother was heartbroken, impoverished, and defeated, burying herself for longer and longer periods in a dark world of her own. Once again it was her job to restore what her brother had destroyed. In 1904, Martin Shaw must have come to her as the image of the brother who had deserted her, who deserted all women, who let everyone down, to receive only coddling and acclaim in return. Martin Shaw restored the brother she wanted not only to punish, but to become. Gordon Craig's dashing, irresponsible exile illuminated her own life in its smallness. Never could she do what he had done; never again would they be friends. Ellen Terry would never understand that Edy's incomprehensible dream of marrying Martin Shaw was her last desperate attempt to consummate her mother's wish for a union between the girl and the boy in her own household, in her repertoire of roles, and in the society that told her what to be. Edy stayed home; and Ellen Terry's household, like the world outside, fractured into a war between women and men.

In 1907, at a time when militant young actresses were organizing on behalf of woman's suffrage, Ellen Terry took one final wicked revenge on Edy for her dream of flight. As she had done when she chased Frank Cooper, she parodied her daughter's desperate rush at a man: she married the handsome, simple actor, James Carew. The women responded with fury, as they had done when Edy tried to defect. Jim was a pedestrian actor, but Ellen Terry cast him in complex roles. In part he was a consoling cushion against her failure to please Shaw; he was also, as Martin Shaw had been for Edy, an inadequate substitute for the much-missed Gordon Craig (she wrote later of this much younger man: "He is a child" [*Memoirs,* 277]); the mock-child was also her adult escape from the children Gordon Craig was showering on "Granny." But the most devastating effect of Ellen Terry's last marriage was the chance it gave the actress to take an actress's revenge: she humiliated Edy by becoming her. It was her pleasure to hurt people by mimicking them, as she had mimicked Fred onstage when he was a clumsy boy. Edy had behaved like a fool with Sidney Valentine in 1895; Ellen Terry had swooped upon Frank Cooper in a broad parody of her daughter. Now, in 1907, she hurt Edy by becoming the dizzy girl who wanted to marry Martin Shaw. But Ellen Terry *did* marry James Carew, and so she flaunted her power.

The marriage lasted two years, during which communication ceased between the Farm and Priest's House. Ellen Terry played Edy's scandalous fantasy to consummation, and that was too much to bear. Most people outside Edy's circle laughed at her rage, but her betrayal was real: in bringing her together with Christopher, in buying Smallhythe, Ellen Terry had pledged herself to Edy and her women. No marriage could bind as closely as the one she had made with her daughter. And as Edy predicted, Jim departed after two years; Ellen Terry had made her point, and she could face the future. After the violent fights had ended, Chris quoted the admissions of the strange spouses: "I felt I could not live alone," Ellen Terry told her after the end. "Afterwards, I thought it better to live alone, apart from Jim, for we do not suit each other. We are better, and happier apart, and now we *like* each other very much" (*Memoirs,* 286). The fond, accommodating Jim agreed: " 'How wise Edy was,' James Carew said to me [Chris] after Ellen Terry's death. 'If I had had a place of my own, I should never have quarreled with Nell. The only way to get on with her was not to live in the same house' " (*Memoirs,* 285).

In essence, no one had ever lived in the same house with Ellen Terry: they had told her where to live and what to play, then sat back to imbibe her life. Playing an old woman alone, she was free to become what she had always been in her heart. Now she could play for herself alone, she could watch, she could even manage. More successfully than she had done at the Imperial, she had set the scene and selected the cast. She settled into her life on the Farm and her job of studying and quietly controlling Edy's world.

Ellen Terry, Edy, and Chris all retained London flats, but Smallhythe was the world they had conceived and made. Even today, it is a pocket of eerie stillness in the Kentish countryside. At the turn of the century it was haunted, as Ellen Terry herself was, by spectral drownings: the drowsy marshes of the former port city evoked images of the sea that had capriciously receded. Edward Burne-Jones described Ellen Terry's favorite countryside in the Five Ports region with an eye that imagined drowned doubles: "Yes, I know Winchelsea and Rye and Lympne and Hythe—all bonny places, and Hythe has a church

it may be proud of. Under the sea is another Winchelsea, a poor drowned city
—about a mile out at sea, I think, always marked in old maps as 'Winchelsea
dround.' If ever the sea goes back on that changing coast there may be great
fun when the spires and towers come up again" (quoted in *Memoirs*, 238). Edy's
friend Eleanor Adlard described Smallhythe itself as a land only provisionally
present: "The sea is now out of sight but never out of mind, and in some future
century it may return, lap up the Marsh and make a port again at Smallhythe"
(Adlard, 144).

Ghosts of floods, dreams of floods, intensified the quiet. When Edy transformed the Farm into the Ellen Terry Memorial Museum, making a monument
out of a home as deftly as she had made exotic costumes out of bits and scraps,
E. V. Lucas found Smallhythe impossible to describe for the *London Times*
without invocations of the water's return: "For many years now I have been
hearing of the village of Smallhythe in Kent—how in past times, not so far
distant, it was a harbour, and how, although now you can see nothing but sheep
and lambs and green grass and a few trees, ships once sailed from the sea right
up to this point, either to load or unload their goods for Tenterden, the nearest
big town and a wool centre: famous to-day for its wide street and its church
tower high on the ridge, but then amphibiously important. . . . earthy as the
village on the edge of the marshes now is, the imaginative eye does not find
it too difficult to envisage the old scene of water traffic."

Ellen Terry's imaginative eye saw in the marshes her own drowned doubles:
a poor girl's corpse that diverted her parents, now themselves dead and indifferent, while she devoured life in the country with Edward. She saw the drowned
Ophelia she had grown famous by becoming. As she sank between memory and
imagination, she saw her little replica Deirdre Craig, drowned in the Seine in
1913, and her beloved Laurence, "my Irving boy," drowned in 1914 in the wreck
of the *Empress of Ireland*. So many had drowned for her. It was right that she
should make her only real home among marshes that had risen from the sea and
lay dreaming of the sea's return. She sank into her own country, relieved at
having rescued her daughter from the fighting world and restored her to the
land that had given her birth.

Edy belonged in the country not only because she had been born there, but
because of what she was. The nineteenth century hallowed women who loved
each other when they retreated to nature and built shrines to purity. In 1778,
a century before Ellen Terry made herself into a myth by joining the Lyceum,
the twenty-nine-year-old Lady Eleanor Butler eloped with thirteen-year-old
Sarah Ponsonby to the Welsh countryside; for the next fifty years, "the Ladies
of Llangollen" made themselves famous for the sacredness of their loving

retirement. As long as it withdrew from the world, romantic friendship among women was, like nature itself, a temple that uplifted tarnished men. One of the many poetic testimonials to the Ladies sanctified the pastoral retreat their union allowed the world to contemplate:

> While ambition exults in her storm-beaten dome,
> Like the tower on your Mountain that frowns o'er your home
> With tranquil seclusion, and friendship your lot
> How blest, how secure, and how envied your cot!

Edy's death inspired a similar pastoral elegy. Her anonymous "old neighbour" did not commemorate Edy as a lover, but she did consecrate her as "heart of this place." The corporate speaker is a voice within the pastoral landscape, not a yearner for it from without. She immortalizes Edy on behalf of

> we, who loved as you
> This coign of England, this same green and blue,
> High thought, the poet's line, the quiet life
> Whose only warfare is a buskined strife.
> (Adlard, 14)

By 1900, when Ellen Terry bought Smallhythe as a retreat for herself, Edy, and Chris, women as a group were demanding economic power in the "storm-beaten dome" of the marketplace. Women who loved each other were no longer solacing presences beyond the world, but defiant antagonists within it. Their "cot" was no longer decked in ennobling images of renunciation, but in male sexologists' new, ideologically charged language of contamination and disease. With her instinct for manipulating cultural mythology, Ellen Terry clothed Edy in the consecrating pastoral imagery that had made culture heroes of the Ladies of Llangollen, rescuing her from the supposedly emancipated age that had begun to stigmatize lesbians as poisonous outcasts. Edy's friend Radclyffe Hall was to write her scandalous *The Well of Loneliness* in protest against a culture that was making pariahs out of women whose friendships had exalted beholders only fifty years earlier; but Edy's setting preserved her from the persecution Radclyffe Hall laments. Making Priest's House, her mother's gift, bloom with her garden, Edy let Chris drape their union in sanctifying religious imagery. Radclyffe Hall's Stephen Gordon might have seen herself as a monster only the ugliest clinical language could name, but Edy let the reverent Christopher solemnize her as a saint. With the wry enjoyment of her mother at the Lyceum,

Photograph of Edith Craig and Ellen Terry. *Reproduced by permission of the Furness Collection, Van Pelt Library, University of Pennsylvania.*

Edy accepted her apotheosis and blossomed into it.

The Ladies of Llangollen and their ennobled kin sanctified Ellen Terry's estate, but Smallhythe had more equivocal, local, guardian spirits. The Bidden-den Maids were Siamese twins who had lived in the Five Ports region in some legendary past. To this day, they are part of the local iconography because of their refusal to be separated: when one was dying, the healthy sister chose to die as well, rather than allow doctors to cut her free. If, in their guarded seclusion, Edy and Chris assumed the sanctity of the Ladies of Llangollen, Edy and her mother became the Biddenden Maids. They too did not separate for

Photograph of Edith Craig and Ellen Terry in old age. *Ellen Terry Memorial Museum, Smallhythe Place. Courtesy of the Trustee of the Ellen Terry Estate.*

death: Edy would not let them. After 1928, she resurrected her mother by turning the Farm into the Ellen Terry Memorial Museum and its adjacent barn into a theater where, through the Second World War, Shakespeare was performed every year on the anniversary of her mother's death. She is said to have become eerily like the blind Ellen Terry after 1928, taking on her groping mannerisms in the same mystic spirit with which Ellen Terry became Edy when she wanted to punish her. When Edy was old and ill, she held herself alive to see her mother's First Centenary Celebration in 1947; a few days after the service at St. Paul's, she let herself die. No great man, not Watts, Irving, or Shaw, molded Ellen Terry's identity at the end. It was the Biddenden Maids, local, obscure, female divinities, who gave the last great cultural command Ellen Terry received and responded to.

Mother and daughter were twinned, but they had never been alike. Chris first saw Edy floating by in a Guinevere dress, playing her mother's double, but Edy declared her separateness when she pricked Chris with her needle. The power of Ellen Terry and Edy over each others' identities did not erode their distinctiveness, but played with it. In the photograph on page 398, Ellen Terry seems to engulf the young Edy from behind, diverting backward with quasi-mesmeric power her daughter's piercing and saddened eyes. As she did in life, Ellen Terry both clings to Edy and towers over her. Their pose makes nonsense of the illusion they generated later on, that Ellen Terry was short, while Edy was tall (Holledge, 112): the large, lanky girl had been educated into appearing small, while shielding her daughter from her own brutal lessons in shrinking.

When they were regal old women together, Edy did tower over her inward-

Sketch of the Baroness "Jimmy" Overbeck by Edward Gordon Craig.

turned mother. She turns on Ellen Terry the powerful intensity she had once directed outward, at the camera; her mother seems simultaneously to shrink under that gaze and to remain alive because of it. As she does in many photographs, Edy exposes unself-consciously the powerful hands she inherited from Ellen Terry. Sybil Thorndike had never seen Ellen Terry's hands, but she was in awe of Edy's: "her hand gave me suddenly a jump, realizing beauty. To me, it was like seeing the da Vinci hands for the first time, or a chord of Bach—putting me in a place where I was able to grasp and convey the meaning myself. Her hands were extraordinarily expressive—not the conventional beauty hand, but strong, worker-shaped, and flexible" (Adlard, 80). Ellen Terry's hands were still more powerful than her daughter's, but as the photograph on page 399 shows, she kept them clenched and hidden to the end.

Despite their insatiable love for each other, their ways of loving women were as different as they could be. Ellen Terry knew no boundaries between herself and the women who drew her, while Edy's community thrived on separateness, not passionate kinship. Their icon was not the womanly actress, but the seditious, cross-dressing child they had never seen. At the turn of the century, fashionable women played Ellen Terry's forbidden role: they wore men's ties and trousers and adopted men's names. Even Gordon Craig, so rigorous about the boundaries of gender when he raised his own Teddy and Nelly, traveled to France in 1901 with Edy's cross-dressing friend, the Baroness "Jimmy" Overbeck, relishing the consummate boy she played throughout their holiday.

For Edy's community, the game was more than a carnival release: its theatricality kept the community alive. In deference to Edy their leader, to whom they had given the nickname "the Matka," the self-named Christopher and Tony dubbed themselves "the Matka's boys" (Steen, 325). Still adored for womanliness, Ellen Terry lived in semi-retirement among ghosts of the transvestism that had galvanized her childhood in the old, unrespectable days. Aping bourgeois taboos, the theater had forced it underground to the semi-respectability of music halls and burlesque: in the 1890s, Vesta Tilley used the license of the music halls to mimic men in more sharply satiric style than the legitimate theater allowed. In society, though, women aped men with stylish impunity through the First World War. Thereafter, the "mannish woman" was branded a pathetic grotesque, but she had been a declaration of defiance at the turn of the century, announcing, as Edy's costumes did, the power of clothes to make new, unafraid women. Radclyffe Hall's first novel, *The Unlit Lamp,* celebrates a generation of "active, aggressively intelligent women, not at all self-conscious in their tailor-made clothes, not ashamed of their cropped hair; women who did things well, important things . . . smart, neatly put together women, looking like well-bred young men." Shaw, a careful student of Edy's community and others like it, imagined his St. Joan announcing her glorification through the transforming power of clothes: "I am a soldier: I do not want to be thought of as a woman. I will not dress as a woman. I do not care for the things women care for" (Act I, scene iii). But for Ellen Terry, her daughter's life and her own cherished memories needed no canonization to authorize them. When she saw Rudolph Valentino's *Blood and Sand* shortly before she died, she entertained a vision of herself the Lyceum had forced her to deny: that of a female Romeo. She mused about Valentino: "If I were going to play Romeo, I should come here every night and study that man. *That's* the way to stand under the balcony!" (*Memoirs,* 329). Edy's world, the unnatural prison so many of her friends deplored, restored to the old woman the child's birthright.

The roles of Edy and her friends dramatized not so much their love for each other as their individually transformed natures. The Ladies of Llangollen made themselves into icons of renunciation; their counterparts at the beginning of the twentieth century imagined themselves as soldiers of a visionary metamorphosis. Their men's costume was their boundary, making them unique, discrete, honed for war, not for absorption into each other. In the 1980s, a decade that has returned to conventional femininity, claiming to loathe both theatricality and military discipline, a militant lesbian declares: "I hate games! I hate role-playing! It's so ludicrous that certain lesbians, who despise men, become the exact replicas of them!" (quoted in Newton, 7).

But in the 1890s, whether they were lesbians or not, militant feminists dreamed of war, not of love, a war that would produce millennial transformations of self and society. Theatricality was placed in the service of the grander mobility Emmeline Pethick-Lawrence describes: "We read, discussed, debated and experimented and felt that all life lay before us to be changed and moulded by our vision and desire." Just before the Great War swept woman's millennium away, Vera Brittain wrote in her diary of the same gloriously impending change: "The reading of *Romola* . . . has left me in a state of exaltation! It is wonderful to be able to purchase so much rapture for *2s. 6d.!* . . . It makes me wonder when in my life will come the moments of supreme emotion in which all lesser feelings are merged, and which leave one's spirit different for ever-more."

Edy became a warrior in art. The suffrage plays and pageants she staged for the Actress' Franchise League put all her wit and impertinence, all the spectacular resources of Lyceum visions, in the service of the woman's cause. Her dreams, like those of her generation, were of war, of lonely exaltation, of metamorphoses too grand for the mergings of romance.

Like her mother in the early days, Edy was a self-styled outcast who acted her culture's dreams. From the Boer War to World War II, wars, war fever, and military escalations defined the period of her adulthood. Her vision of herself as a warrior set her against her age's official pieties while acting out its myths of military glory. In 1942, in the middle of World War II, a member of her band commemorated the great days by honoring Edy's seventy-third birthday with a soldier's ode. Once again, Edy reflected in her obscurity the embattled world outside her pastoral:

> Your Birthday, Edy dear, deserves an Ode
> Written in times when wit was all the mode.
> But since we've left those stately days behind
> Be to my Muse's faults most kindly blind.
> So with no more ado she wants to say
> Stars also danced upon *your* natal day.
> Throughout your life you've thrown your soul and heart
> Into the maelstrom of the Actor's art.
> "We few, we happy few, we band of brothers,"
> Know indeed well, perhaps more than others
> What you have stood for in our modern Stage,
> How you have fought—when trash was all the rage
> To give the Public shows that they could bite upon
> On Sunday evenings, when fine plays you'd light upon.
> The Pioneer Players—need one introduce her?
> Who the guiding star? who the Producer?
> Who did the office of Lord Chamberlain plague
> To license some rare play? why, Edy Craig!
> Some people timid grow as they grow older,
> Dear Edy, you from year to year grow bolder.
> All through your life you've championed many a cause
> Because the flame burned bright, not for applause.
> And now, when others' leaves are sere and yellow,
> You're still the very devil of a fellow!
> "Time marches on", cuts down the weak and weedy
> "Time marches on", but never on with Edy.
> Breathless, old Time stands still, for you, you Dynamo!
> (I only wish my Muse could find a finer mot)
> With which to hail our dear "Napoleon Boney"
> And her Lieutenants, Christopher and Tony.

Solemn, prayerful, and devout, Christopher St. John was above all the staunch "lieutenant" her mother had found for them both. As a self-named John the Baptist, the mission on which she collaborated with Edy was the redemption of Ellen Terry from the prison of her own charm, forging her into a woman who would inspirit a militant generation. Christopher St. John became Ellen Terry's last great creator. In a time when advanced women saw themselves at war with men for their very existence, Christopher's redemption of both Edy and Ellen Terry was that of the spiritual warrior, not the romantic lover.

As a lover, Christopher was devoutly impersonal: she was aroused by transcendence, not absorption. In 1911, she wrote for Edy a fifty-page love missal, *The Golden Book.* Edy is its catalyst for a series of speculations on God and the exalted service He requires. The beloved is addressed in the third person, as "Edy," or "she." Only when she is asleep does she assume a physical presence: "My darling often talks as if she were unhappy because she could not do more for me. It is like her to feel that way; but she should not feel it. Once, when she went to sleep with her head on my shoulder, I thought to myself 'That is about all I can really do for her—put my arm round her while she rests her dear grey head on me.' But it did not make me unhappy to feel it; I suppose because I know that, just as I want herself and not her services, so all she wants is the same from me."

This high-minded impersonality is a portal to a nobler world "because to love very greatly is to understand something of eternal life" (*GB,* 40). Love is justified only as it aspires beyond itself:

> I was reading to-day a translation from St. Juan de la Cruz; & when I came to this I read it over & over again and wrote it down for Edy; because it was something that, through loving her, I had found for myself was true:
> "When love is purely spiritual as it waxes stronger, so also does that of God, and the more we dwell on it in our memory so much the more do we cherish that of God and the more it makes us long for Him; the growth of one keeping pace with the growth of the other."
> It seems to me that when I think of Edy it is nearly always with a little prayer; not a conscious one, perhaps, but a feeling as if I tried to turn my face to God for her. (*GB,* 42–44)

As Edy grew older and stronger, she threw all her religious energy into her work; it is difficult to imagine her participating in Christopher's quest for transcendence through love. There are glimpses of her in *The Golden Book* laughing like her mother at her partner's solemnities. But Chris's ecstasies and evasions seem to have granted Edy the privacy she needed to become her own woman at last: Christopher would never engulf her as her mother had done, or demand that Edy play her double. Edy may not have turned her face to God through Christopher, but through her she found it easier to face the world, and she was content.

Edy and Chris lived together at Priest's House until their deaths, but they separated over the years: when Ellen Terry's mission was fulfilled, they may have found there was little left to say. *Hungerheart,* Christopher's autobiographical novel, was published in 1915, four years after Edy was given *The Golden Book;* it celebrates a radically different sort of love. There is no consummation in a loving retreat with Edy ("Sally"); it ends on an unresolved note of sexual torment and denial. John, the protagonist, has as little sexuality at the culmination of her spiritual odyssey as she does in adolescence: "The hunger I had to find someone to love burnt me more with every inch that was added to my stature. It was *to love* I yearned more than to *be loved,* and I was entirely free from sexual instincts" (p. 88). John divides her soul from her body with a rigidity only the most moralistic of Victorians would have endorsed: "Men and women are not animals. Therefore they can never be happy when they are indulging the passions of animals. Their infinite souls must wake when the effects of the drug of pleasure have passed off. What a terrible melancholy there is in human love, however sweet its appearances!" (p. 191).

The love described above is heterosexual, but despite the imminence of lovers' eternity in *The Golden Book,* in *Hungerheart,* John's affair with Sally is as ephemeral as the other delusions the "drug of pleasure" brings. The wound of Sally's abortive attempt at marriage never heals. Like Christopher, John goes to Rome for her conversion, but unlike her, she does not return to Sally after two years. She directs her hunger to two vague but passionate episodes with women, then assuages it at last in her worship of the Virgin and her pure friendship with an all-wise and saintly nun. Her journey's end lies among women whose worship a hallowed Church licenses.

Hungerheart includes a curiously sour and dismissive portrait of Ellen Terry, one that repudiates Christopher's public allegiance. When John meets the great actress Louise Canning, she is overcome by a disappointment the novel never corrects:

> Neither that night nor at any time did she understand me in the least. A thought persisted in my heart that I was disappointed in her, although I kept it inactive with ardent assurances that I was not! The thought did not rise because she looked older and less beautiful than I had expected to find her. Although I could see in her face the traces of the years that had passed, I was not shocked. It was wonderful too how, as she sat at her mirror, she recomposed the illusion of youth with the aid of the little pots and bottles of ointments and washes and powders with which

the table was covered. Although she was too fat—I admitted it—her body was still a miracle of grace, still able to obey the dictates of her ever youthful heart. Her vitality, out of which she could have fed fifty ordinary natures, and still have had enough left to dazzle and fatigue those round her and to defy the threats of time, seemed to me superhuman.

I sat in the corner of the dressing-room, feeling like a timid bather in a buoyant sea, as the waves of her exuberant temperament broke over me. It seemed to me that she was all temperament—that heart and soul and intellect in her were all submerged in something which was all of them and none of them. In this vast temperament I detected an Olympian quality. I was reminded of the gods and goddesses in Lemprière's Classical Dictionary, in whom the noble and the trivial, the fine and the base, the generous and the mean, were inextricably mixed up. Louise Canning seemed always to be making harlequin leaps in her conversation: it required some mental agility to follow her; and if you had anything to tell her, you had to be very patient, for she was as slow in grasping a point as she was quick in making one. (pp. 212–13)

By 1915, Christopher had edited the first edition of Ellen Terry's *The Story of My Life,* arranging the actress's "harlequin leaps" into a rounded, dimensional portrait. But *Hungerheart* has only summary disapproval; both Louise Canning and her daughter Sally fade out of the action after John's pilgrimage to Rome and presumptive higher things. *Hungerheart* repudiates the reverent soldier-lover and literary henchman, anticipating the penitent who, on the threshhold of death, burned the papers entrusted to her. *The Golden Book* had quoted for Edy a line from William Morris's *Earthly Paradise:* " 'Cast no least thing thou loved'st once away'—and I like it still. It seems to me, sometimes, that no ideal that inspires humanity is ever really outworn; with new times it takes on a new form—that is all. Behind the deadest of all letters there was once the spirit that gave life; . . . I suppose it is because of that tendency in me that many forms do not seem so dead to me as they do to other people—art forms, for instance, or forms of expression" (*GB,* 46–47).

Edy would have been justified in construing these tender words as a promise that her own letters and her mother's would partake of the eternity Christopher claimed to know so well. But *Hungerheart* saw the true ending. In the journey of Christopher's renouncing life, eternity alone had power. At the last, it was Christopher's punishing eternity that burned the illusions Ellen Terry created, in which the actress had believed with all her soul.

Catholicism gave Christopher a God who would affirm spirit's ascendancy, but the hunger for that ascendancy was not hers alone: it gave faith to a generation of feminists. Like male disguise, the triumphant spirit insured the integrity and boundaries of the body: anger, sexual love, the appetite for victory and power, all purged themselves out of physical life. The perfect control toward which feminists aspired was the self-cleansing of soldiers who consummate their mission in death, not love. When, between 1906 and 1914, Christopher forged from Priest's House the self of Ellen Terry's Memoir and wrote *The Golden Book* for Edy, thousands of women were imprisoned in the war for suffrage, which had become bloody and holy at once. Passionate separateness inspired a congregation of prisoners who sanctified themselves in dreams of martyrdom. In Martha Vicinus's analysis: "[The prison that was their goal] was also their community, created through the fiery spirit that bound them together, despite fear, physical weakness, and long days spent in isolation. Going to prison was the self-transforming act that would alter not only the actor (the prisoner) but also the public. Isolated, yet united with fellow prisoners, the lonely martyr became . . . both the flame and the burnt offering, the self-fulfilled and the self-sacrificed" (Vicinus, *IW*, 268). Like Christopher, these spiritual warriors were inflamed by burnt offerings. They had no wish to be lost in each other: their isolated unity was their power to ignite millennial transformations.

Ellen Terry had learned only herself: unaware of the holy warrior's self-immolating discipline, she twinned herself not only with Edy, but with all the women she cared about. As a child she played her proper sister's sly mirror reflection; from then on she approached other women as reflections of herself, fleeing them when she frightened herself, pursuing them when she was on the verge of vanishing. Gordon Craig claimed, rightly, that men had offered her freedom from the prison of herself. He saw only loss and bondage when Edy's women shielded her from men's eyes in her last years: "Few people [i.e., few men] were allowed to see her. All she needed was freedom and the free passage to her of all those who cared to see her realize her old self" (*ETSS*, 190). But if men had tempted her with an impossible freedom, women bestowed identity, not only by adoring her, but by becoming her.

She poured out affection, but in her own way she was as distant a lover as Edy and Christopher. Unlike them, though, she took women into herself. Christopher cared only for heavenly ascent, but Ellen Terry lived in cozy intimacy with symbols of her friends. She explained her own brand of Catholicism to Elizabeth Winter:

> I am wearing a rosary made up of beads — a simple bead from each of my friends — <u>will</u> you send me one? & wd. "W. W." [William Winter] send me one do you think? — Don't be horrified when I tell you I already have 59, & that each one stands for a person I love dearly & I have reason to think loves me! A wide

liker!? - I suppose it is dreadful to think of 59 friends represented by a token &
many to come! I tell my beads, & bless my beads every day — & I am much
distressed there are 2 I cannot put a name to!!! Jet beads - Coral - Amber - Ivory
- turquoise - wood - "gold - silver - lead" —Crystal - Malachite - Bone - Emerald
- Pearl - & on it goes = . . . What an unconscionable length this scrawl!! & all
self — S e l f—Forgive me—

Ellen Terry's "rosary of friends" was her way of incorporating those she loved
into her own capacious being, blessing them by absorbing them into her private
symbolism. Transmuting loved ones into gold, silver, and lead, crystal, amber,
and ivory, grants them the glorified status of the pictorial actress: they too are
animate yet translated into the mystic half-life she bestowed on her favorite
flowers and jewels. She described this transfiguration to a jeweler who had sent
her his catalogue: "I delight in learning anything about Opals = They seem
to me to be spirit jewels — & I have the same feeling about some flowers —
the Orchid for example - - seems to me more - - living than other flowers="

Others' life is dearest to her when it radiates from within the inanimate. She
loves when she creates the glowing, imaginary life she gives to the characters
she plays. She wore men as well as women on her rosary, but the men she knew
could only beckon her to freedom and then deny it: she could wear them as
beads, but she was forbidden to incarnate them. She loved women, or hated
them, because she imagined they were like her: she could make them part of
her privacy as she did her beads. When she accepted them, she let them grow
into her as her characters did.

Her long correspondence with Audrey Campbell, which began around 1887
and faded with Audrey's marriage in 1912, is the drama of Ellen Terry's
intimacy with women. The Audrey Campbell the letters create is a warm, close,
cosily physical presence whose identity fluctuates with Ellen Terry's own transformations. Her tenderness would have no place in Christopher St. John's stern
religiosity, but unlike Christopher's Edy, the Audrey to whom Ellen Terry
writes never comes forth as a separate person.

Audrey Campbell was not a professional actress. Two writers identify her as
Ellen Terry's understudy. As Edy did offstage, she played Ellen Terry's double:
it was her job to become the actress at need. Christopher's more extended
account of Audrey Campbell does not call her an understudy, though it makes
her in a more sinister sense Ellen Terry's double: she was "an enthusiastic
amateur actress, and a plant of 'vigorous habit' in Ellen Terry's herbaceous
border of friends. After Ellen Terry left the Lyceum and formed a company
of her own to tour the provinces Miss Campbell joined it. [This is the 1903 tour

which Edy and Chris helped manage in order to recover the losses of Ted's *Vikings*.] She made no other professional appearances on the stage, married in 1912, and died tragically (drowned in a pond near her Surrey home) in 1926, two years before the death of Ellen Terry" (*A Corr.*, 98). In ways beyond her actual, Ophelia-like death, Audrey Campbell became one of Ellen Terry's drowned doubles. She drowns in letters as she did in life, under the force of Ellen Terry's passionate identification.

There is no trace of this overwhelming empathy in the letters Ellen Terry wrote in this period to Shaw and Gordon Craig. The letters to Audrey Campbell range more freely than the letters to men—they abound in passionate responses to books, places, politics, her own incipient blindness, the state of the world, topics she seemed less easy in discussing with men—and they also use more freely the language of love. She could no longer identify herself with men; her love for Audrey and for other young women was a spilling-over of her questing, sensuous need to become other selves. In Ellen Terry's generation, when most women were segregated economically and emotionally, it suited patriarchal ideology to sentimentalize an encompassing and empathic love among women that social historian Carroll Smith-Rosenberg characterizes as paradoxically "both sensual and platonic." By the time Edy came of age, women were fighting for a life beyond mere privacy and emotion; suddenly their unions looked dangerous; the role of lesbian was becoming discrete, stigmatizing, and consuming. Ellen Terry saw nothing but delightful tenderness in her feelings for Audrey Campbell, yet the sort of easy, expansive intimacy she claimed was becoming branded as pathological. The physicality of such an intimacy frightened the new experts in love; but its boundlessness carried deeper, less exclusively sexual dangers than official guardians of morality could comprehend.

The letters to Audrey "wobble" as persistently as Ellen Terry claims her mind did, particularly in regard to women. "I do loathe female company perpetually =", she wrote in 1904, a year in which she was doing her best to keep Edy perpetually by her side and away from Martin Shaw. Like all the women to whom Ellen Terry felt close, Audrey herself lives in these letters primarily through the actress's wavering reflections of her own decomposing identity.

She elicits Audrey's help in creating these reflections: "What do you think the Press think of 'the New Woman'?" she asks in a letter that simultaneously denounces the "unnatural and impossible" ideas of her feminist disciple Lawrence Alma-Tadema. She casts about for ways of imagining younger, freer women. The same letter begins by praising the self-creation of her "Dearest Duck Chuck" in words she will appropriate to praise herself: "I was so surprised by your letter & at first thought you so weak - - - - - -- but now (thinking of it) I know how <u>strong</u> you are, <u>to consent</u> to be so weak=" Her Memoir adapts this tribute to her own Desdemona: "Some nights I played it beautifully. My appearance was right—I was such a poor wraith of a thing. But let there be no mistake—it took strength to act this weakness and passiveness of Desdemona's. I soon found out that, like Cordelia, she has plenty of character" (*Memoirs*, 161). Watching Audrey act her womanhood teaches her how to value her own performance. Like the beads she makes of her friends, Audrey moves effortlessly into her own self-creation.

Audrey becomes not only Ellen Terry, but an image of both the formidable new woman and the acquiescent old one. Her letters about the business of womanliness—beauty, love, and marriage—shift as mercurially as her feelings do. When she feels fat, she taunts Audrey: "Well my pet, & are you still as happy & <u>as fat</u> as ever! I am! but mine is a <u>different</u> fat - the fat of age <u>sticks on</u>; yours comes & goes = ". Brooding about Henry, she broods about Audrey's love life as well:

> Well, & have you anything going on there, where you are? Any "Romance"? George Meredith says of Romance—"The young who avoid that region escape the title of Fool at the cost of a celestial crown"—
> Well — <u>per</u>haps yes— but they escape other ills also = Henry will be here until about next Thursday <u>week</u>="

Two weeks later, presumably just after Irving's departure, she is blunt, imperious, and tense: "You are what is called 'getting on,' & a girl shd be married at 25, so you have not time to lose = You wd cease to think of me for some time, but it wd be all right in a little time again, & if there's yr 'mate' trotting about the earth somewhere I wish you may get him!!"

Audrey has not come to heel three years later, and Ellen Terry, who as Irving's stage wife finds herself cast in bad parts, celebrates spinsterhood:

> ----**B l e s s** you—you **v i v i d** girl=

> You'll alter when you marry— & be unhappy (not his fault <u>always</u>—only sometimes —) & make him unhappy〰〰〰 (only sometimes!) but you'll <u>have to do it</u>—

With Ellen Terry guiding her, Audrey had good reason to wait to marry until she was forty-two; when she did so, Ellen Terry was too infirm to offer more than congratulations. In 1894, though, if Ellen Terry could not make marriage look attractive, she continually forced on Audrey the romance that was seeping out of her own life: "Bless you my little Audrey—take care of yourself, & encourage a love affair!! No other happiness believe me="

Ellen Terry's own love in these letters is warmer, more intimately physical, than in her loving letters to Shaw or Gordon Craig. Audrey is a cozily physical presence, not, as her daughter would become for Christopher, a conduit to the hereafter: "I send you a kiss on the tip of your small nose = & a blessing on your soul & body." To Audrey alone, she reaffirmed her girlhood belief that soul and body were blessed and the same. Elsewhere, she leaves her "with a kiss upon yr darling duck of a peach-cheek," and with "blessings on your fuzzy-wuzzy head." The Audrey these letters create is in some ways a "wobbly" figure, but if she lacks Gordon Craig's vivid coherence, her body is intensely, joyfully alive: "Well good night my Audrey dear. I wish I could see your dear pink soft lovely cheeks for a few moments, & get a sweet kiss & hear your voice & then I shd be happy=". "Good night my sweet little Audrey - Enjoy your beautiful self beautifully, & be sure I love to hear from you=" Only in these letters do we catch an echo of the intense sensuous delight of the young, acrobatic Ellen Terry who dreamed that love was art and her body was art's source. After she left Harpenden, only through her understudy could she enjoy her beautiful self beautifully. Eventually, even this oblique benediction was withdrawn.

For as the years go on, the letters erupt in sudden outbursts of rage for unspecified sins. When Ellen Terry excoriates Gordon Craig, she makes his flaws quite clear, but Audrey magnetizes her fury not so much for what she does as for the shameful thing she is:

Really my patience gives way—I entreat you if you can only come & express loathing of me, as you did this morning, not to come at all = You are quite outrageous & lack self government and gentle behaviour — I am not in the position of some idle girl or woman having nothing to do, instead I shall always be found to be a busy person everlastingly being called upon for my time, to some good end, by a great many people, but always happy to see those I love if they are the happier for being with me, & can settle happily down to their work or occupation with me—but you are so wonderfully exacting—so dictatorial, so unyoung lately to me that you distress, annoy, & anger me & I pray you not to come to me until you are in a more reasonable frame of mind—You will end by making your lovers hate you in the end —

I am yr lover for one —
I don't hate you **Yet**

She softens on the last page: "I hope when the new year has grown up a little you will come to me & be 'your own sweet self' -- Perhaps you have worries that I know nothing of? I've many that <u>you</u> know nothing of!—Believe in the ever love of yr <u>Nell</u> — " She heads this final page: "<u>I wish you the Sun & the Moon</u> = 31 Dec. 1900 ="

It is impossible to deduce the dreadful thing Audrey has done; she may only have provided too clear a mirror for a woman who herself had become exacting and dictatorial as she faced a vacant future and her own increasing lack of self-government.

As time went on, her Audrey became more wicked and obstreperous still:

> If I don't see you for <u>a long</u> time I may forgive you yr mad uncontrol of last week — I never cd <u>forget</u> it = At present the mere <u>thought</u> of you excites & irritates me — & I fear I am near breaking down —
>
> It appears a bit of the stage staff were outside my dressing room door that day, & the absurd stories there are in the theatre - I had hoped you wd not write — however you do — most airily! I can not see it quite in that light myself — I have <u>never</u> "left off caring" for any one I have loved ∿∿∿∿ but you have pressed me harder than most. It makes me ill to even write this to you =

Such bursts of despairing rage alternate with letters in the ordinary, affectionate style. This rage has none of the clarity of her anger at Gordon Craig in the same years (which she never dared direct at Shaw): it is as suffusing, intimate, and boundaryless as her love. It is impossible to tell where Ellen Terry leaves off and Audrey Campbell begins: as with an actor playing a character, the fervor of empathy knows no divisions.

Her marriage to James Carew in 1907 gave her anger a temporary outlet. Not Edy alone, but all her woman friends, tried to quench her obsession with this mediocre, embarrassingly young, actor; finally, she could with justification denounce women and thrust them out of her life. When Audrey Campbell tried to give advice, Ellen Terry wrote grandly: "The friend who <u>dictates</u> to one about what <u>other</u> friends one <u>may</u>, or may <u>not have</u>, becomes a nuisance --- I shd think it simply <u>grotesque</u> if <u>I</u> did such a thing!! = & I cannot allow it in another to be anything but a strange lack of good taste = It is an outrage when the <u>dictation</u> is persevered in = E.T."

Loftily ignoring her own dictatorial advice to Audrey over the years, Ellen Terry tried in one wrench to free herself from the women, the understudies, the doubles, in whom she saw herself magnified, sometimes delightfully, other times darkly and dangerously. But she wrote to Audrey with humble contrition when Jim, like the other men, failed to rescue her from reflections: "Of course my darling I know it all the while = — but anyhow I have now my own life to make & one had best be mostly alone making it.

> Love from
> Yr ever the same
> Old Frump="

She was "mostly alone" in that after Jim, there was no man in the house, but to the end of her life, she was surrounded by women who extended and explained her. As Christopher celebrated the life she called "mostly alone": "Ellen Terry spent the last 20 years of her life literally in single blessedness, having been adored by many men, and always having come back to herself in the end. Not a man was present when she passed out of this world" (*A Corr.*, 311). At Smallhythe she "came back" to a self that was multiply refracted: it lived in all the women who redeemed, imprisoned, tormented, and recreated her until she died and passed into them entirely.

From the beginning of the twentieth century, this expansive woman lived as the icon, muse, and double of the withheld, soldierly tribe that gathered around Edy and Christopher. Ellen Terry formed and fed herself through every particle of life. Inspired by Edy, Christopher made it her mission to give that malleable force a local habitation and a name suitable for the new century. She succeeded where Shaw had failed. Unlike him, Christopher never became famous. Only a community of women appraised the Ellen Terry who emerged out of the wreck of the Lyceum, but the Ellen Terry Christopher catalyzed is the woman who has come down to us, for it is Christopher's Ellen Terry who lives in words: without *The Story of My Life* (particularly with the acute, combative commentary Edy and Chris added in 1932), the *Four Lectures on Shakespeare* (which Ellen Terry toured in England, Australia, and America between 1910 and 1921), the Shaw letters, and the rich archive at the Ellen Terry Museum at Smallhythe, the actress would have vanished with the audiences who made her. The Ellen Terry Virginia Woolf wrote about is an inextricable part of Edy Craig and Christopher St. John's ideology, just as the young girl in "Choosing" is indistinguishable from G. F. Watts's peculiarly dark pastoral vision. Edy and Christopher in no way manipulated or distorted the woman they perpetuated: from the time of her first partnership with Kate, Ellen Terry needed another's catalyzing presence to take possession of herself. She was neither weak nor an empty vessel, but a woman so abundant that she required an accompanying artist to release the self that was fittest to live at that time.

The self Christopher catalyzed never became famous. Like all of Edy's women, it thrived in a subterranean, semi-professional world, while Irving's Ellen Terry was moving vacantly through the public imagination as the adored ghost of a dear. Irving's Ellen Terry was identified mainly by the grandchildren who kept mysteriously appearing; her explosions of rage and disorder were hidden. But once *The Story of My Life* appeared, even uninitiated women sensed a darker, fiercer Ellen Terry simmering in "Granny."

Aimée Lowther was not in Edy's set, but she had read the many saccharine articles along the lines of "What is the Subtle Charm Possessed by Woman-kind?" (*Philadelphia Inquirer,* 14 January 1900), which invariably quoted Ellen Terry as a chirpingly feminine authority; she had also read *The Story of My Life.* Grafting the two public women together, she wrote a parody unmasking the violent anger and the rage for power that fed Ellen Terry's vaunted adorable-ness. In "WHAT CONSTITUTES CHARM - an illustrated interview with Miss Ellen Terry," Aimée Lowther juxtaposes the darling with the woman Edy and Christopher lived with and served:

"Yes, I know that I am very charming," said Miss Ellen Terry, "a perfectly delightful creature, a Queen of Hearts, a regular witch!" she added thoughtfully, at the same time projecting a pip of the orange she was chewing, with inimitable grace and accurate aim into the reporter's eye.

"You know, at all events, that you have charm?" I said.

"What do you think, you idiot! I exercise absolute power over my audiences —I cast over them an irresistible spell—I do with them what I will—I am omnipotent, enthralling—and no wonder!" I looked at her across the table, wondering at so much simple modesty.

"But feeling your power, you must often be tempted to experiment with it," I ventured.

"Yes, now and then I am," replied Miss Terry. "Once, I remember, when I was to appear as Ophelia, on making my entrance and seeing the audience waiting breathless—as they always do—for what I was going to do next, I said to myself, 'You silly fools, you shall have a treat tonight—I will give you something you will appreciate more than Shakespeare!' Hastily slipping on a false nose which I always carry in my pocket, I struck an attitude and turned a somersault. Ah! the applause, the delirious, intoxicating applause. That night I felt my power, that night I knew that had I wished I could have held them indefinitely!" [Nose and somersault aside, this is only a delicate heightening of the Memoir's account of a triumphant mad scene in Chicago.] . . .

At that point, Miss Terry's little grandchild, who was playing about the room, began to howl most dismally.

"Here is a little maid who was a charmer from her cradle," said the delightful actress, picking up the child and playfully tossing it out of the third floor window. Seeing me look relieved, though somewhat surprised, she said merely:—"I have plenty more of them at home and they are all charming, every one of them! If you want to be charming you must be natural—I always am. Even in my cradle, I was quite natural. And now, please go. Your conversation bores me inexpressibly, and your countenance, which is at once vacuous and singularly plain, disagrees with me thoroughly. Go! or I shall be sick!"

So saying, the great actress gave me a vigorous kick which landed me outside her room, considerably shaken and entirely under the spell of her matchless charm.

Aimée Lowther's parody is based on the finely tuned self-parody Ellen Terry perfected over the years. The dear self rests uneasily on the volcanic self Edy and Chris drew upon. The power, the ambition, she continually denied, her rage against her son's multiple desertions and the all-loving role he forced on her, are perceptible presences in a Memoir that is not simply an account of an actress's achievements, but an anatomy of a woman's adaptation to her roles. Aimée Lowther's mock-interview is acutely aware of the dissonant kinship between the woman who is written about and the woman who writes.

Christopher St. John did not ghostwrite *The Story of My Life* and the *Four Lectures on Shakespeare,* any more than she did Ellen Terry's letters to Shaw. Earnest, abstract, and often lumbering, her own prose is in a different voice from the mercurial, often stinging style of the woman whose literary henchman she became. By her suggestive, expectant presence alone, Christopher created the woman who wrote the Memoir and the Shakespeare lectures as consummately as Watts created Ophelia, or Henry Irving his womanly actress. Through the medium of Christopher St. John, Ellen Terry honed the anger and rebellion that had never died into a new woman who was nobody's mother and nobody's child. Like saints and great men, Christopher's Ellen Terry stood at last alone.

When she gave her Shakespeare lectures, she wore flowing robes of crimson, white, or gray, according to the subject of the discourse; she was slender once more now that her banqueting days were over, and she turned back to the simple aesthetic costumes in which Godwin had taught her to love herself. Her lectures were not brazen and brilliant, like Fanny Kemble's readings; Ellen Terry did not declare herself through Caesar, Hamlet, or Shylock. She did read men's parts, but she wove her trespass into her encompassing ruminations on idiosyncratic topics that were dear to her: "The Children in Shakespeare's Plays," "The Triumphant Women," "The Pathetic Women," "The Letters in Shakespeare's Plays." As Christopher arranged the lectures from Ellen Terry's dictation, Shakespeare's verse is absorbed into Ellen Terry's consciousness: she no longer plays Shakespeare, but becomes him, letting glimpses of characters and fragments of verse spill out of her capacious mind.

Christopher reveals a godlike, infinitely creating presence. This abbess-like Ellen Terry, narrating a Nativity play Edy staged for the Pioneer Players, stands at the heart of Edy and Christopher's collaboration. Solitary, grand, and stately, she is an inspirational, even a priestly, presence, the source of both wisdom and art. From her power all things come.

The format of Ellen Terry's lectures has intimations of a grand transformation: the ruminating actress turns herself into a female Shakespeare. *A Room of One's Own* evokes the martyred figure of Shakespeare's witch-like sister Judith, who in Virginia Woolf's myth kills herself at the crossroads because she incarnates "a heat and violence" forbidden in women. But even in the 1880s, the essential femaleness of Shakespeare and his plays was an enticing literary idea, one that Ellen Terry embodied and, in her ten-year career as a lecturer, exalted. Frank Harris's idiosyncratic books exploited the idea of Shakespeare's femaleness, but in 1884, a novel appeared that was far more disturbing, though it seemed conventional: William Black's popular *Judith Shakespeare: A Romance.* Black's Judith is Shakespeare's daughter, not his sister. She is illiterate, hoydenish, powerfully imaginative, and, like Woolf's icon, witch-like in her subversive reverence. She adores and undermines her omnipotent father: she gives away his manuscript of *The Tempest,* allowing it to be pirated, then suffers in her guilt a penitential illness that leaves her sweetly loving, but helpless and infantilized. Her suicide is more appealingly feminine than that of Woolf's Judith Shakespeare, but it is equally, and chillingly, successful. Moreover, Black's presentation of William Shakespeare from the perspective of his disenfranchised daughter turns the sweet swan of Avon into a terrifying, if benevolent, paterfamilias, wrenching bardolatry into patriarchy. His female Shakespeare, an outsider in culture, vulnerable and disruptive, makes us reappraise the kindly Bard in a manner anticipating Virginia Woolf's mad martyr who lies dead for men's sins at the crossroads.

Ellen Terry's library at Smallhythe includes several books revising Shakespeare from the perspective of female characters who become the hidden composers of the plays. Mary Cowden Clarke's *The Girlhood of Shakespeare's Heroines* had already given each heroine an independent life before she assumed her role in Shakespeare's play, but once the play began, she was swallowed in its preordained design. Gordon Bottomley's *King Lear's Wife* (1915), *The True Ophelia: and Other Studies of Shakespeare's Women,* by an Actress (1913), and Lillie Wyman's *Gertrude of Denmark: An Interpretative Romance* (1924) all reorient the plays themselves around female perspectives. Like Tom Stoppard's

Rosencrantz and Guildenstern Are Dead (1976), they throw a wicked light on heroes by seeing them through the eyes of trammeled and silenced subordinates.

Graham Robertson claims that Ellen Terry longed to play Hygd, King Lear's wife (*Letters,* 78), but Hygd became another of her unacted parts. In Gordon Bottomley's play, Hygd dies humiliated by the unfaithful Lear. "Women are not meant for happiness," she tells her loving daughter Goneril, "a virgin huntress" who vows to keep faith with her mother by bringing her father down when the time comes. When women's loyalties to each other come into play,

Ellen Terry narrating a Nativity play for Edith Craig's Pioneer Players. *Billy Rose Theatre Collection, New York Public Library at Lincoln Center, Astor, Lenox and Tilden Foundations.*

virtue and vice, comedy and tragedy, change their names. *King Lear* becomes a different work entirely when we imagine martyred women lying behind the scenes, composing its brutal reversals.

Edy had already claimed to Ellen Terry that Shakespeare, her all-inclusive divinity, had left mothers and daughters out of account: "How many times Shakespeare draws fathers and daughters, and how little stock he seems to take of *mothers!* Portia and Desdemona, Cordelia, Rosalind and Miranda, Lady Macbeth, Queen Katherine and Hermione, Ophelia, Jessica, Hero, and many more are daughters of *fathers,* but of their mothers we hear nothing. My own daughter called my attention to this fact quite recently and it is really a singular one. . . . if there are mothers of daughters at all, they are poor examples, like Juliet's mother and Mrs. Page. . . . I often wonder what the mothers of Goneril, Regan and Cordelia were like! I think Lear must have married twice" (*Memoirs,* 162). Gordon Bottomley's mother-centered revision restored the silenced characters to Shakespeare's stage, imagining a single mother for King Lear's daughters who is sufficiently rich in suppressed and silenced power to reform a patriarch's tragedy in a woman's image.

The True Ophelia recreates *Hamlet, Macbeth,* and *The Merchant of Venice* through the consciousness of Ophelia, Gertrude, Lady Macbeth, and Portia. In the same years, Gordon Craig was reinventing Shakespeare's women as avenging furies, but in *The True Ophelia* they are the sole centers of plays deformed by a nineteenth-century theatrical tradition that heard only speechifying men. *Gertrude of Denmark* is devoted exclusively to Hamlet's mother, another of Ellen Terry's unacted, imagined parts. It begins by citing Ellen Terry as its inspiration. "Oh, didn't Shakespeare know a lot about us women!", she is supposed to have said to the author. Ellen Terry responds to Lillie Wyman's claim by placing a demure little "oh!" in the margin.

"Was it in a dream or a reverie that Gertrude of Denmark came and begged me to tell her story to the world?" Wyman goes on rhetorically (p. 1). Gertrude's story tells a revised *Hamlet,* as profoundly transformed as *King Lear* was in the revision of his abused queen. Gertrude marries Claudius out of selfless motives, to insure her son's succession, but she finds with him a more equal marriage than Hamlet's patronizing, paternalistic father was capable of. In his frenzied self-absorption, Hamlet himself is neither princely nor sweet: "Hamlet was a monstrous egotist, who could question all things in the Universe, himself included, but who could not see the answers to his questions, because his egoism imposed itself like a tangible substance between the eyes of his mind and everything in the Universe, not excluding himself" (p. 222). Gordon Craig's Moscow Art production had elevated Hamlet into the brooding mind of his play, but when the women Ellen Terry inspired restored the queen's authority, the tragic hero shrank into silliness and his play metamorphosed into Shavian irony: only a mother's wisdom knows the story.

Ellen Terry's Shakespeare lectures were staged so that the plays England worshipped found their center and their germinating source in the mind of a regal woman. She defined the heroines as she did her own performances, by the yardstick of power, not compliant womanliness: comic and tragic, good and evil, became manifestations of triumph and pathos, the unorthodox categories by which she measured her own evolving life. She did not force the public to see her as a man; she merely assumed male roles easily and at will. "The Children of Shakespeare" allows her to resurrect the pert little boys of her beginning, as well as some, like Robin in the *Falstaff* plays, she had never acted as a child. At least once, at the Hampshire House Club in 1909, she performed in a transvestite context: on the same bill in which she lectured on "The Letters in Shakespeare" and read Portia's mercy speech, two female acting students played Hamlet and Horatio. The lectures' format allowed her not only to reclaim her boy-roles, but to assimilate them into the stately persona Chris imagined for her. Christopher's conception allowed her to be male and female at once. It denied her only the union of body and soul.

Like the suffragists who starved themselves in prison for the glory of the Cause, the Ellen Terry of the Shakespeare lectures achieved transcendence at the cost of her sensuality. In Christopher's published version, the lectures withhold only the role Irving and Shaw withheld as well: that of Cleopatra, whom Ellen Terry played only by indirection in Sargent's brilliant portrait of her Lady Macbeth. In the published lectures, Ellen Terry dismisses Cleopatra by moralizing about her shallow wantonness. Only in manuscript does she celebrate, through Cleopatra, the soul in the body's life: "In Cleopatra [Shakespeare] draws the woman whose character, life & trade are one & all the 'grand amoureuse,' as the French aptly & delicately say—in Cleopatra, he refines sensuality of its grossness, he drags the nobility out of poor passion. As Antony dies in her arms—her words!—" She goes on to quote the great eulogy to magnitude, whose crowning lines she had borrowed in her diary to commemorate Irving's death: "And there is nothing left remarkable/Beneath the visiting moon." Christopher St. John restored many of Ellen Terry's lost roles, but like her other makers, she denied her idol the sensuous and supreme audacity through which she might have become the maker of herself.

Like the forbidden Cleopatra, Ellen Terry was a woman "whose character, life & trade were one." Edy and Chris arranged them in a harmony as intricate and enduring as their generation could imagine. The Ellen Terry of the Shakespeare readings was incomprehensible to many who had loved her at the Lyceum —William Winter found the lectures trite and irritating, clearly wishing she would retire decorously if she could no longer act decorously—but younger women found in these lectures the goddess they needed. In the years Gordon Craig was reinventing his mother as avenging demon and little woman in turn, Edith Craig found in her own reinvention the inspiration that brought her work to life at last.

Ellen Terry was often exalted as the mystic model from whom Shakespeare's women were drawn, but in Christopher's imagination she was King Lear, with Edy cast as Cordelia, the teller of corrosive truths: "To one as ebulliently expressive as Ellen Terry, her daughter's Cordelia-like abstention from the demonstrations of admiration and affection lavished on her by adoring friends of both sexes must often have caused pain" (*A Corr.,* 194). Chris goes on to say that, Lear-like, Ellen Terry came to understand Edy's fealty, but she had always understood her daughter too well. Above all, she understood Edy's need for her own animating presence, without which her child fell into sloth and despair at the world's animosity. It was Cordelia she never understood, though in 1892, she had played her at the Lyceum in an ambitious but poorly received production. On the margin of her script, next to Cordelia's refusal to play the flattering role in which Lear casts her, Ellen Terry wrote in her largest letters: "FOOL."

She tried to force honesty on her son, for he was a man: women could tell their truths only through the way they played their roles. Edy's irreverent plainspeaking was a foolish risk: life would have been less formidable had Edy consented to play life's games. Since Edy would not consent, Ellen Terry built for her a play-world at Smallhythe, keeping herself within it for Edy to draw upon. And Edy did draw on her, boundlessly. While she was reinventing her mother's life, a theater she could work in took shape: through Ellen Terry's indirections, she found her own direction, becoming a leader in a theater of protest that stood out against everything in the age that had made her mother what she was.

Julie Holledge makes the dramatic claim that the militant suffrage movement was born in Manchester in 1905, on the evening Henry Irving died in Bradford (p. 121). While Irving expired, Annie Kenney and Christabel Pankhurst staged a flamboyant demonstration at a major Liberal meeting. Their arrest galvanized the messianic rising of women that felt at the time like a grand transforming wave, cleansing the world. A year later, a suffrage demonstration interrupted Irving's solemn memorial service at Westminster Abbey; *Hungerheart* claims that Edy was converted at the moment she saw the women outside the Abbey. If so, she cast herself as the mediator between the patriarchal pomp of the theater Irving made and the political, communal energy of a theater he could never have imagined. She became an active member of the Actress' Franchise League, a radical organization founded in 1908 that devoted itself to theatrical propaganda. In 1909, Edy staged for the AFL two plays by Cicely Hamilton: *How the Vote Was Won* and *A Pageant of Great Women.* Her apprenticeship in the AFL was as powerfully formative as Ellen Terry's equally unorthodox apprenticeship in Watts's studio. May Webster, who chaired the AFL, described to her daughter its professional as well as political impact: "Actually, the League was performing an educational function of much wider scope, though its members did not know it at the time. Women playwrights emerged to write the necessary plays and pageants, or to ghostwrite other people's speeches. Women organized performances, directed them, stagemanaged them, attended to the box office, made up the accounts, handled the publicity. For the first time, they became more than just actresses; they learned everything there was to know about how to run an organization or a stage. Out of this grew such enterprises as Edy Craig's Pioneer Players, which pioneered many things women take for granted in all the entertainment professions" (Webster, 249).

Like Edy's community at Smallhythe, the AFL released women from the roles men wrote. For this reason, it thrived only as an invigorating alternative to the theatrical mainstream. *How the Vote Was Won,* a witty fantasy about a general strike of women, was produced in the interstices of the cast's regular professional commitments. Irving's perfectly run autocracy would have acknowledged nothing in common with Edy's freewheeling production. Her company was itinerant by definition, with a continually changing cast for each engagement; its fluidity created an interplay between stage life and everyday existence that the single-minded Irving would never have allowed. But Edy found her medium in this deprofessionalization of theatricality. "It was like a continuous review," Jane Comfort remembered of *How the Vote Was Won;* its changing casts and inconstant production conditions gave the play a potential open-endedness that fed the protean self, the continual and mighty changes, in which the suffrage movement placed its faith.

A Pageant of Great Women, whose climax was Ellen Terry's appearance as herself, was Edy's greatest success for the AFL. Since it was on a continuing tour to suffrage societies around the country, the production was as fluid and flexible as it could be. Life determined art: local suffrage societies provided plausible-looking members to incarnate Cicely Hamilton's Learned Women, Artists, Saintly Women, Heroic Women, Rulers, Warriors, and so on. There were no perceptible boundaries between women's lives and their stage roles: the pageant depended not on actresses' professional accommodations to men's visions, but on the women who placed their beings at the service of Edy's transfiguring arrangements, which themselves lent their power to the Cause. One role was always a problem: "The extreme popularity of Joan of Arc was on more than one occasion a source of real unpleasantness, when Edy had to deal firmly with some lady of entirely unsuitable appearance who, by sheer determination or the pulling of strings had got herself cast for the part" (Cicely Hamilton in Adlard, 43). Shaw watched with interest ordinary women as well as professional actresses battling to play the sort of disruptive, cross-dressing woman Henry Irving and his fellow actor-managers had barred from the respectable stage. Edy's theater, on the face of it so ephemeral and impromptu, subordinating beauty and even professionalism to the Cause, was recreating a new-old heroine the West End could use and might even, once again, learn to love.

At the peak of the suffrage movement, stage and street were inseparable. The banners, the demonstrations, the violent confrontations that forced police, jailers, and courts into predetermined roles in the suffragist scenario, had taken on the ritual, predictable excitement of Victorian melodrama. In political theater, though, actors and audience were one. The leaders of the movement flourished on the revolutionary stage: they were wizards at self-presentation. Fifty years after the elation had subsided, Christopher St. John quoted Max Beerbohm's informed appraisal of Christabel Pankhurst: "Let me emphasize first that she is a most accomplished comedian. Do not suspect me of a cheap sneer. The description is but part of the truth about her. But it is the part with which I as a dramatic critic am mainly concerned. She has all the qualities which an actress needs, and of which so few actresses have any. Her whole body is alive with her every meaning" (quoted in *Ethel Smyth,* 147). As "arranged" by Edy Craig, Cicely Hamilton's suffrage plays epitomized the heroic theater in the streets which set the stage for new and nobler arrangements in the world at large. Both outdoors and on stages, suffrage theater recapitulated Edy's mother-inspired pastoral at Smallhythe: it provided a model for the social transformations women's communities could ignite and produce.

Edy's political theater, fluid, alive, incorporating its audience's lives, militant, like her costumes, in its visionary awareness of transfiguration, realized many of her brother's ideas. Gordon Craig too imagined himself directing a theater that mirrored political life. His revered Mussolini seemed like an Irving reborn: both were leaders who promised to elevate and preserve what was fine, abolishing the coarse and crass. He too saw himself purging and purifying a theater that would become society. But Gordon Craig could not bear a capacious stage. He wrote to I. Gollancz during World War I:

> If democracy stands for *levelling down,* then Art and Democracy can never live in the same country. I always thought Democracy was what Greece once meant by it . . . that is to say a very aristocratic thing.
>
> It is no doubt true that other lands are able to boast an equal disrespect and disregard of their natural noblemen, their artists, great and small; but there seems to be no reason why England should struggle to be first in such a race. While every Englishman must love England, to love this England is impossible.

Edy was as aristocratic and exclusive as her brother, but as an artist she found her method by leveling down: when she extended her stage to disenfranchised women of all sorts, her theater came to life. She worked Irving's genius for spectacle and grand design into her own populist vision that absorbed the silenced members of her audience. On her own ground, she made the transformations her brother talked about so often, so persuasively, and so impractically.

On the face of it, suffrage theater repudiated everything Ellen Terry stood for. Her Lyceum role had barred her from the socially conscious Ibsen cult that had inspired suffrage drama. From afar, she had encouraged Janet Achurch (the first Nora in *A Doll's House*) and Elizabeth Robins (the first Hedda), but they were worlds apart. She wrote to that effect a pained letter to Elizabeth Robins, an elegy for a dream of union that seems to have been written from behind bars:

> I was just frightfully convulsed with pain when you called on Sunday & could not see you. The beautiful dream I had a couple of months since that—(what use in telling dreams?—but it was of our acting together) The dream is only a dream & will not turn out true after all = I'm always coming to see you, & all my moments are taken up in doing little things, & I've none of myself for myself & what I want to do = My best friends are in the cold & I'm freezing. [She signs her name.]
>
> I'll tell you my pleasant dream when we meet. 24th. yes - It's too late now —(at least for the present-)
>
> And I shd have liked it so very much =

Elizabeth Robins's popular *Votes for Women!,* which opened at Shaw's Court Theatre in 1907, began the suffrage drama within which Edy found her idiom: in her artistic association with Elizabeth Robins as in myriad other things, the daughter realized the mother's forbidden dream. Even Edy's reliance on amateur and semi-professional actresses had its genesis in Ellen Terry's seditious tricks: to general disapproval, she had let debutante and society girls walk on at the Lyceum, thereby freeing respectable girls to act. Ellen Terry's frustrated attempts to expand her roles and open her theater to the stultified lives of its audience pointed Edy's way. In turn, after 1910, Edy gave her mother work in her own semi-professional productions. The "leveling down" Gordon Craig shunned so fastidiously from abroad gave new life to Edy, her theater, and the mother who had made the dreams of both brother and sister.

In 1911, Ellen Terry's lectures were winning her love all over again. Despite the overweening connotations of Christopher's staging, she was still patronized as "the perennial adolescent Terry" who delivered her words with "the smiling artlessness of a child" (*Indianapolis Star,* 26 February 1911). But in the same year, another theatrical event made the press explode in horror. An issue of the *New York Review* that cooed with reverence for Ellen Terry's Shakespeare lectures screamed simultaneously: "LONDON SHOCKED BY LEWD PLAY GIVEN BY SUFFRAGETTES." The denunciation continued in smaller type: "Votes for women's cause injured by a drama so coarse in theme and so perverted in moral that many prominent ladies withdraw their support." The lewd drama was Margaret Wynne Nevinson's *In the Workhouse,* staged by Edy's new company, the Pioneer Players. By 1911, Edy was playing with gusto her mother's wicked mirror reflection.

The Pioneer Players was a subscription society, not a full-fledged company. Subscribers were guaranteed a certain number of seats for each production; performances were given only on Sunday nights. As with Edy's AFL players, the Pioneers rehearsed and performed in addition to other, regular employment: they did so out of love, for neither actors nor crew were paid. The grand Lyceum had possessed its employees; the Pioneers company worked voluntarily in tribute to Edy and her vision. As at the AFL, women controlled all aspects of production, doing work forbidden on the West End. Edy's advanced, challenging, powerful company was, for many women, a dream of employment realized.

In the Workhouse, which shocked so many Londoners, was typical of Edy's early productions in that it was concerned only peripherally with suffrage and associated legalities, dwelling instead on more intimate issues that determined women's actual lives, such as marriage, prostitution, and work. *In the Workhouse* boldly ignored single working women, to whom philanthropic Victorians had loved to condescend, to expose the discrimination against that supposedly privileged class of women, wives. The blunt decision of a working–class woman illuminates by implication the crippled lives of her pampered sisters. In the climactic scene, Lily, the heroine, chooses not to marry so that she may keep her earnings and her children. Her decision is Shavian, but her bald language is not: Edy did not want her actors to sound cleverer than the audience. Lily delivers her closing speech to her illegitimate baby: "I think we won't get married, my pet! Better keep single, I says, after what we've heard tonight. What I've heard tonight is a lesson to me. I'll not get married, not I. Just look at Mrs. Cleaver, an honest married woman. All 'er 'usband 'as done for 'er is to bring 'er and the kids to the 'ouse [the workhouse], and now they say she can't even go out to earn her living. Then look at Pennyloaf, free, rich, and prosperous and the kids 'er own. The bad 'uns wins my pet! Vice triumphant, I say!" (quoted in Holledge, 128).

Vice was triumphant indeed, for Ellen Terry had once made the choice of "Workhouse Lily": the illegitimate baby to whom these words were addressed might have been Edy herself. For her sins, Ellen Terry was adored and lauded as a paragon of womanly charm, while Edy was vilified for staging a play that translated her mother's silent decision into a curtain speech. Ellen Terry knew the truth; Cordelia was a fool for plain speaking; but it was Edy's mission to tell the stories of the silenced, and her mother had been silenced as effectively as the poor wise cockney.

In 1912, the Pioneers gave a forum to Jess Dorynne, the actress for whom Gordon Craig had left his wife, deserting her in turn when she became pregnant, to his mother's symphonic but ineffective fury. For the Pioneer Players, Jess turned her humiliation into political allegory: her companion plays, *The Surprise of His Life* and *Nellie Lambert,* feature heroines who transcend marriage. Her first play, in the tradition of *In the Workhouse,* is a rousing rejection of wifely dispossession; in the second, Nellie Lambert marries a bigamist and a cad because she is destitute, but "instead of committing suicide like any self-respecting melodrama heroine, [she] joins a suffragette procession determined to find freedom with her sisters" (Holledge, 130). Under Edy's generalship, Jess Dorynne wrote herself into roles Gordon Craig's degrading script had not conceived: she transmuted their affair by bringing it under her own, imaginative control, rewriting life to take the choice and the transcendence it had forbidden.

Gordon Craig had never liked the Pioneer Players. The year before Jess's play was produced, he wrote loftily to Ellen Terry of the unlovely reality Edy welcomed to her stage:

> Edy had a success last night – but I detest the turning *performances* into an excuse for delivering attacks on Censors & things.
> That surely could be kept to the journals or books etc. The performance itself &

the theatre is, or should be, surely too good a time & place to be disturbed by rows.

So Henry Irving might have claimed, but in her own idiom Edy was truer to Irving's legacy than her brother was: unlike Irving, she allowed into her theater voices from the streets, but like his Camelot, her propaganda and pageants served an ennobling dream. The communities of her stage had nothing to do with the technology that was invading the theater's humanness. At their best, they performed a dream of the human estate where community and glory were one, and each actor had the power to play out her elected destiny. In Edy's theater, the leading actors were women, but they were closer to Irving's kings and cardinals, devils and saints, than Gordon Craig's marionettes would ever be. In their small compass, the Pioneer Players, like the imperial Lyceum, allowed audiences to imagine that their lives were grand.

As an artist, Edy used all the human material she could find. As time passed and suffrage fever was diverted to the grimmer war abroad, the Pioneer Players changed as well: women still ran the theater, but the plays raised questions of patriotism and pacifism, organization and trade unionism, that involved the lives of men as well. The Players did stage stunning productions of Susan Glaspell's *Trifles* (1919) and *On the Verge* (1925), but after the war, the majority of its plays were by men. Feminists regretted Edy's abandonment of women, but the Pioneer Players remained vital by broadening their scope, and Edy strengthened herself when she brought male as well as female visions into her little empire. Like Virginia Woolf's *Orlando*, like Ellen Terry at her rarest, Edy made her imperial vision male and female at once, transcending in imagination the boundaries of the separatist world in which she lived.

Edy used everyone and everything she could find, but like Henry Irving and Gordon Craig, she was no democrat: she learned her role from Victorian actor-managers, ruling her productions absolutely. When, at the AFL, the suffrage committee challenged her primacy, she had no scruples about fighting them for her power, achieving the autocracy her brother insisted on in vain. She avoided the established theater and it avoided her. Even a woman-run organization like Lilian Baylis's Old Vic found her will to power threatening: "she would upset the staff," Baylis explained (Adlard, 25). Rule mattered more to her than success: "Perhaps it was a fastidiousness, a demand for perfection and complete control—qualities that could hardly be satisfied in the commercial theatre. No one could say that she was lazy—but she was a born director and so possibly the habit grew of moving pawns" (Harcourt Williams, in Adlard, 49). Her brother too needed to move pawns, but Edy's pawns were living men and women, while in the years when the Pioneers flourished, Gordon Craig was withdrawing into an imperial community of one, with the models, the screens, and the puppets, no living eye but his own confronted.

Increasingly, Edy modeled herself on the Henry Irving whose own model had been Napoleon. Her nickname swelled from the diminutive "Edy" to "Boney." Only military metaphors were sufficient to define her. Margaret Webster remembers "Edy in a barn or a little parish hall, marshalling her forces with equal generalship, swift in tactics, brilliant in strategy, making magic too with a couple of headlamps from an old car and a few women from the village" (Adlard, 56). In 1920, when financial peril struck the Pioneers, the *Illustrated London News* ran a plea on behalf of their "master and pilot," Edy: "For years she has stood at the head of affairs; she built the ship; she manned it; she stood firm at the tiller in fair weather and in storm, and now there is grave peril" (10 July 1920).

Between the Acts, Virginia Woolf's last novel, is our most haunting and suggestive, if elusive, evocation of Edith Craig. Woolf's mannish, imperious Miss La Trobe, whose pageants of women travesty England's history to exalt it, incarnates the eccentric determination with which the woman artist forges miracles. An outcast, half-seen and alone, hiding behind trees but furtively controlling the more visible players, Miss La Trobe, like Edy, wields an anti-professionalism that is triumphant and pathetic at once. She too is master and pilot of a ship: "Wet would it be, or fine? Out came the sun; and, shading her eyes in the attitude proper to an Admiral on his quarter-deck, she decided to risk the engagement out of doors." Miss La Trobe is more rootless and despised than Edy, who was an expansive ruler of her bounded world, but like Edy she fabricates on the margin of the recognizable stage the saving remnant of a collective vision that is a touch of healing sanity in danger.

Women could vote, some of them at least, but the suffragists lost their millennial war: men still ruled, and in the 1920s a generation of scarred young women danced to men's tunes. Still, Edy and her friends who had come of age in the 1890s dreamed themselves into becoming soldiers and soldierly leaders. In her own way, Edy had fought the great war her brother evaded; she had earned her Napoleonic title. She was in command, not of models, but of a few men and women.

Her few appreciators celebrate the life within her living pictures. In 1899, when she designed the costumes for *Robespierre,* the *Chicago Times Herald* ran an interview with her in which her mother did most of the talking. Like her daughter, but in aesthetic, apolitical language, Ellen Terry explained costuming as "the connecting link between painting and acting." But the reporter did not

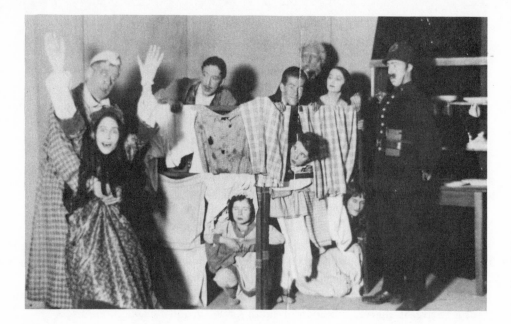

Through the Crack, staged by Edith Craig for the Pioneer Players, mid-1920s. *Reproduced by permission of Rackstraw Downes.*

Through the Crack, staged by Edith Craig for the Pioneer Players, mid-1920s. *Reproduced by permission of Rackstraw Downes.*

let Ellen Terry steal the scene. He understood Edy's designs, and gave her the appreciation she worked for: "Her pictures are made, but not with the brush. They are living, palpitating pictures" (25 February 1900). In 1920, the *Illustrated London News* praised "her predominant gift" in similar terms, as one that emphasized "not merely the creation of the picture, but its vitality." Gordon Craig had killed Irving's realizations, turning them into non-human exercises in pure design. Less fashionably, Edith Craig brought Irving's living pictures to realized life.

These photographs of *Through the Crack,* a children's play Edy staged for Sunday matinees in the mid-1920s, display the vital pictorialism that makes Edy's designs so like, yet so unlike, her brother's. His medium is masses; hers is people. In the apparent chaotic delirium of farce, her actors fall into dynamic patterns seemingly of their own accord: like that of Woolf's arranging Miss La Trobe, her generalship hides itself because it never suppresses the vitality it molds, finding the pattern that lies latent in her mobile ensemble. Unlike the Lyceum, no hierarchy of stars organized Edy's company: there were only bodies, centers of energy, bringing their energy to the pattern of the whole. Her costumes took life from the bodies they clothed, and bestowed in turn transformed identities; in the same way, her kaleidoscopic stage designs compose living forms into ever-new arrangements without seeming to violate their expansive identities. In the same way as she arranged Ellen Terry's dynamic, contradictory life into autobiographical documents, Edy arranges her actors without seeming to restrain them. Such an art is even more ephemeral than a garden or a dress; it is hard to find aesthetic theories that will fit it; but it aims to let its actors speak, and its audiences act. It molds its human material without telling it what to be. Within its regal assumptions, it is warmly democratic.

Edy's abundance and Gordon Craig's abstractions were equally antithetical to the commercial theater that had formed and adored Ellen Terry: born to its prizes and promises, neither could survive, psychically or artistically, within it. Both wanted only new worlds to conquer. While they were imagining those worlds, Kate's grandson John Gielgud became Ellen Terry's visible heir: from the beginning of his career, Gielgud has responded with flexible delight to the mutating trends within the entertainment world. He writes about his two prickly cousins graciously but with some friendly befuddlement; he remembers above all the chaos of Edy's stage world, the solitude of Gordon Craig's. Like all her contemporaries, he diagnoses Edy as "too managing to be tactful or popular. . . . Many theatre people admired and respected her, though they were somewhat wary of allowing her too much reign for fear of upsetting her collaborators. She was unlucky to have lived at a time when women were not greatly trusted with leading positions in the world of theatre (except as actresses) and in consequence she always had a good deal of suspicious resentment to contend with."

But the Edy in whose Nativity play he appeared at the beginning of his career proved, in her generous disorder, to be the opposite of managing. He remembers a stage more crowded and cluttered than the house, with himself as one of three shepherds in danger of choking on Edy's abundance. They had been directed to eat before seeing the Star in the East:

> We proceeded towards the footlights, where we sat to begin our speeches, to find, to our dismay, that slices of delicious soft bread, hunks of cheese, and apples had been realistically provided in our haversacks. These, rashly crammed into our mouths, made our enunciation almost unintelligible. However we hastily finished our lines (and our food) and progressed gingerly towards the doors at the back of the stalls, only to find them locked impenetrably against our exit. So we had to walk back along the ramp the way we had come, and sneak as unobtrusively as we could round the characters on the stage who were already engaged in playing another scene. (pp. 35–36)

Gielgud appeared in a special charity matinee, not a regular Pioneers performance: no doubt the Nativity play was more chaotic than usual. But the dismay of Edy's impeccably professional cousin points to the unorthodoxy of her determination to crowd her stage with life—the food, the displaced shepherds, the wandering extras—that the theater traditionally filtered out. Privately austere and withheld, Edy made her stage a bounty, cramming on it and, at her best, arranging lovingly the quirks and contradictions that generally hid in exile.

Gielgud writes generously about Gordon Craig's books and inventions, but he neither appeared in Craig's productions nor saw them. He had met Edy in the early 1920s; in 1930, while playing Prospero at the Old Vic, he met Gordon Craig, who had been invited to London to design the opening production for the new Phoenix Theatre: "Craig treated me somewhat patronizingly at this first meeting. He said, 'I felt we ought to get to know each other, as you seem to be quite popular here in London.' He went on to say that he had rushed from the Old Vic in horror after seeing only the opening scene of The Tempest, though Harcourt Williams, who had directed the production, was one of his old friends and fellow actors. . . . I was naturally very hurt by his airy dismissal of Lilian Baylis, the Vic, and all it stood for. Naturally, too, my vanity was piqued that he had seen so little of my own performance" (p. 37). Instead, he talked about his own designs for the Phoenix, which never materialized onstage.

As an old man with no promises left to keep, Gordon Craig was kinder to his triumphant cousin, but in the beginning he was clearly unnerved by the brilliant young man who was a Terry. Edy absorbed John Gielgud into her cluttered, vital world, which was large and rich enough so that her golden cousin would not shatter it; her brother never could. After Ellen Terry's death, Gielgud played in benefits for the Memorial and in birthday matinees at the Barn Theatre. Gordon Craig would have none of any of it.

Edy might not have been successful in her family's terms, but unlike the majority of women, she had power and her proper work. When, in 1925, the Pioneer Players disbanded at last, she became a leader in the Little Theatre movement, staging productions at York, Leeds, Letchworth, and Hampstead. While the commercial theater was settling into London's West End, Edy continued her mother's tradition, now becoming quaintly anachronistic, of provincial tours: bred in an inveterately itinerant theater, Edy never abandoned the unstylish, enthusiastic, audiences of the north. While London actors were settling down and living sedately, like other people, Edy's Little Theatre groups kept her mother's gypsy days alive.

As Edy expanded, Ellen Terry deteriorated, moving almost altogether into the sphere of Edy's generalship. Edy had found her style from making her mother without betraying her contradictory vitality; she had learned to arrange productions from arranging Ellen Terry. She had made of her mother an inspirational goddess for women, one few men understood, one who gathered into her grandeur the antinomies of male and female, tragedy and comedy, pathos and triumph. Having played Britannia for Irving, Ellen Terry became for Edy a more heroic and fearful personification, one who embodied, like Virginia Woolf's Orlando, the promise of infinite capacity, transcending the limitations of gender, of nation, and of Age.

After World War I, Edy, who thought she knew her mother's infirmities, could not face the fact that Ellen Terry could no longer do the Shakespeare readings: she needed the goddess her own imagination had made. After Ellen Terry's death, Edy hired Eleanor Adlard's companion, an American actress named Florence Locke, to continue the lectures. She wore an ornate Elizabethan costume instead of aesthetic Victorian robes, and was more brazen altogether than Ellen Terry. Florence Locke was another species of woman, but by that time Edy could not work without worshipping. She and Chris had begun to appear at rehearsals in friars' robes. Edy was not religious in Chris's way, but work had grown into her religion, one that needed a towering goddess to bless it.

Her mother remained alive, not in Florence Locke, but in her place. She had left half her capital, not to Gordon Craig, but to Elena and to Teddy and Nelly in trust; Edy received the other half outright, along with Smallhythe. Home was her mother's last gift, a home Edy could transform into the theater that would give her, at last, complete control. She controlled her estate with flair. With imperceptible alteration, the Farm became the Ellen Terry Memorial Museum, now a National Trust property, a rare immortality for an actor to receive. In the early years of the Memorial, Edy was a relentless fund-raiser. Survival was assured when J. P. Morgan sent a generous contribution, the same J. P. Morgan whose support Gordon Craig had demanded that his mother obtain for his short-lived school. Once again, Gordon Craig had talked, but Edy had done. The Farm became Ellen Terry's last and most lasting stage; the Barn, and then the entire countryside, became a theater of Edy's own.

Until the Second World War, Edy staged an annual Shakespeare production in the Barn; she also headed a subscription company that produced rare, esoteric plays. As her life centered increasingly around Smallhythe, she turned to pageants, drafting local residents with the same pitiless fervor out of which Wordsworth had made his *Lyrical Ballads*. Like Wordsworth's shepherds, the actors in her pageants embodied the art of her daily life, while London actors had to travel sixty-five miles to appear in Sunday productions at the Barn. The Barn had become a shrine. Wilfrid Walter wrote reverently after a Barn performance: "I always think of you as the guardian angel at the source of pure drama. It's a real & lasting inspiration to play at the Barn & to have something to do, however remotely, with the lovely spirit of Ellen Terry."

The Barn was for Sundays; at best, it reverently refreshed actors from their real work. Inevitably, like Gordon Craig in Italy, Edy at Smallhythe isolated herself from the public life her mother had gloried in. Sir John Gielgud writes frankly: "The yearly performances in the Barn at Smallhythe were always something of a chore I felt bound to appear at, and I watched [Edy and Chris] gradually growing older and more eccentric as the years went by." Edy lived more and more in the world she had made. The Barn was a fragile bridge to London; the pageants continually blessed daily existence. They made the union Edy had worked for since her days with the suffrage theater, destroying the barriers between actors and audience to show the shapes of art that inhered in everyday life. Through their ritual, their rootedness in the country, their tenderness toward a stately past, Edy quietly embraced the memory of her father.

He had named her after Eadgyth, daughter of Godwin, Earl of the West Saxons; the shy mystical artist in her had always been Godwin's daughter. Her earliest memories were of transfigured daily life, when she pattered in her kimono through the lovely Japanese rooms he had designed for Fallows Green; her pageants were her tribute to his house and his vision. The only work she produced on the West End was John Fletcher's seventeenth-century pageant, *The Faithful Shepherdesse;* in 1885, Godwin had staged the same pageant for his Pastoral Players. In it, he had played a friar, "and then only to be able to be unobtrusively present during the scene" (Harbron, 176). To summon that unobtrusive presence, Edy wore friars' robes to the rehearsals of her own pageants. Nontheatrical residents of the Hythe mobilized under her command as she transformed them into personifications of English history, literature, or theater. In a gentler key, Godwin's Pastoral Players had paid tribute to the art he and Ellen Terry had made from the heart of the country. Edy's pageants embraced her father's prayer for perfection.

Ellen Terry remained a city creature even in old age. Smallhythe was a retreat as Harpenden had been, not the real life of which art is made. But father and daughter turned at the end of their lives to the countryside as the source of authentic theater. Gordon Craig ceaselessly and fruitlessly invoked his father's spirit. Edy, with no fanfare, simply did what their father had done, and thus met in her fashion the man she had always known.

Clare ("Tony") Atwood was the last saving painter in Ellen Terry's life. When she moved into Priest's House, the actress was nearly bankrupt: she had flung her finances into helpless disarray by secretly, compulsively, giving money and treasures away. Tony made a budget. Even more providentially, her presence saved the fractious community from collapsing inward upon itself; she brought to it the strengthening power of the outsider. In this late photograph of a soldierly colony that stiffly refrains from touching each other and retains its contour through its differences, Edy, Christopher, and Tony represent a unit of quiet survivors. Tony not only invigorated the household, but, through her portraits, created Ellen Terry as a type of old woman as suggestively as G. F. Watts had created the young girl. Her portraits of Ellen Terry (1923) and of Edy (1943) show us, too, the extent to which mother and daughter took on each others' natures as time passed.

Strong and monastic, Ellen Terry has become the patron saint of a feminist generation. Her powerful composure eschews the mobility of the dynamic, imprisoned maiden Watts loved and helped create; there is no trace of his grotesque Ophelia's witch-like spell. Nor can we picture this massive woman snatching power with the frenzy Sargent saw in her Lady Macbeth, for Clare Atwood's Ellen Terry is a power in herself. She radiates; never would she fidget. Grandly serene, she has absorbed the rich life that the mobile girl and the immobilized woman longed for just beyond the frame. In this last portrait, Ellen Terry has no need of a world outside of her composition.

Edy, in contrast, eyes the viewer with the challenging stare of her childhood; she is not, like her mother, at rest. She is about to shift position; clutter surrounds her; her avid look searches out more life, more things, to add to her messy bed. Like the young Ellen Terry—but unlike Clare Atwood's—Edy is restlessly aware of the world beyond the frame. She has neither stability nor completion; innumerable objects and figures could be added to Atwood's open composition. As Clare Atwood paints it, Edy's world spills over like her plays, while Ellen Terry seals herself in monumentality.

Edy took her late-blooming vigor from her mother. Sometimes, as Margaret Webster recalls, she did so cruelly, as when she included Ellen Terry in her

Clare ("Tony")
Atwood, Christopher St.
John, and Edith Craig.

all-star matinee at an experimental theater in Hampstead: "Once I was able to smuggle myself into a rehearsal of [Portia's] Trial Scene, but it was not at all what I had expected. Ellen Terry was evidently disconcerted by the tiny, flat stage and the absence of footlights. Her sight was failing and she wore thick, heavy glasses. You could tell that she looked toward a voice rather than at a face and that she was nervous about getting too close to the edge of the stage. She seemed to have trouble in hearing the cues. Her own lines came hesitantly, and she continually asked for 'the word.' Edy, probably nervous on her mother's behalf, grew extremely irritable and shouted at her, as well as at the other actors. Everyone was embarrassed and unhappy. I crept away" (p. 273).

There was a dark, deforming side to the mothers and daughters whose stories Shakespeare refused to tell, and to the transforming potential of women together. Shaw was always boundlessly interested, suggesting to Christopher after Edy's death: "You ought to write a history of that *ménage à trois*. It was unique in my experience" (Adlard, 32). But Christopher never wrote the history of an experience that was her own, and not Shaw's at all. The experience was Edy's as well, but Edy never wrote about herself: her mission had been the freeing of her mother, not the declaration of herself. More subtly and surprisingly than the women from the streets whose unspeakable stories Edy arranged, the pioneers too had been silenced.

Ellen Terry was equally reticent about the Smallhythe community, but she had tried to evade it by so many routes—as she had evaded all her life the women she could not distinguish from mirrors—that it was as if she sensed her death among watching women. In the end, despite all the melodramas she had played so well, no man would rescue her.

Clare Atwood, *Portrait of Ellen Terry*, 1923.

Clare Atwood, *Portrait of Edith Craig*, 1943.

Child

PUZZLEDOM Ellen Terry's moving description of her last meeting with Henry Irving pays homage to the hero's death her own role forbade. Their partnership had been dissolved for three years when, in 1905, she visited his Wolverhampton hotel to play what both knew was a deathbed scene:

I found him sitting up in bed, drinking his coffee.

He looked like some beautiful grey tree that I have seen in Savannah. His old dressing-gown hung about his frail yet majestic figure like some mysterious grey drapery.

We were both very much moved, and said little.

"I'm glad you've come. Two Queens have been kind to me this morning. Queen Alexandra telegraphed to say how sorry she was I was ill, and now you—"

He showed me the Queen's gracious message.

I told him he looked thin and ill, but *rested*.

"Rested! I should think so. I have plenty of time to rest. They tell me I shall be here eight weeks. Of course I shant but still—. It was the rug in front of the door. I tripped over it. A commercial traveller picked me up—a kind fellow, but damn him, he wouldn't leave me afterwards. He wanted to talk to me all night."

I remembered his having said this, when I was told by his servant, Walter Collinson, that on the night of his death at Bradford, he had stumbled over the rug when he walked into the corridor [of his hotel].

We fell to talking about work. He said he hoped that I had a good manager . . . agreed very heartily with me about Froman, saying he was always so fair— more than fair.

"What a wonderful life you've had, haven't you?" I exclaimed, thinking of it all in a flash.

"Oh yes," he said quietly . . . "a wonderful life—of work."

"And there's nothing better, after all, is there?"

"Nothing."

"What have you got out of it all? . . . You and I are 'getting on,' as they say. Do you ever think, what you have got out of life?"

"What have I got out of it?" said Henry, stroking his chin and smiling slightly. "Let me see. . . . Well, a good cigar, a good glass of wine—good friends." Here he kissed my hand with courtesy. Always he was so courteous; always his actions, like this little one of kissing my hand, were so beautifully timed. They came just before the spoken words, and gave them peculiar value.

"That's not a bad summing-up of it all," I said. "And the end. . . . How would you like that to come?"

"How would I like that to come?" He repeated my question lightly, yet meditatively too. Then he was silent for some thirty seconds before he snapped his fingers—the action again before the words.

"Like that!"

I thought of the definition of inspiration—"A calculation rapidly made." Perhaps he had never thought of the manner of his death before. Now he had an inspiration as to how it would come.

We were silent for a long time. I thought how like some splendid Doge of Venice he looked, sitting up in bed, his beautiful mobile hand stroking his chin.

I agreed, when I could speak, that to be snuffed out like a candle would save a lot of trouble. (*Memoirs*, 261–62. All ellipses ET's)

Ellen Terry admired in Irving what she admired in death itself: its consummate theatricality, which her own death missed. She was not to "save a lot of trouble" by being "snuffed out like a candle": she died slowly, clamorously, embarrassingly, bit by bit. She died at Smallhythe, the only home she had ever conceived, while Irving was granted the death of their itinerant trade:

I know it seems sad to some that he should have died in the entrance to an hotel in a provincial town with no friend, no relation near him. Only his faithful and devoted servant Walter (whom, as was not his usual custom, he had asked to drive back to the hotel with him that night) was there. Yet I feel that such a deathbed was more fitting for such a man than one where friends and relations weep.

Henry Irving belonged to England, not to a family. England showed that she knew it when she buried him in Westminster Abbey. (*Memoirs*, 263)

Ellen Terry was not buried in the Abbey. After she left Irving's orbit, she belonged less and less to England, more and more to her family. She died neither grandly nor appropriately, but in the lingering, ordinary Victorian fashion: her own bed became her deathbed, and friends and relations wept around it. She played her death as she had played her life, heightening and transfiguring her culture's familiar images. By dying in the known way, she brought to her deathbed more cruelty, loss, and terror than Irving could imagine when he died in the sudden, rootless manner of a tragic hero who had made the world his stage and his audience his family.

As her mind and her eyes faded into Edy's control, she learned a helplessness she had never known before. As she remembered her childhood, she had had the power to make an attic prison blaze with glory; now the glorifying eyes shrouded out vividness, and the imagination that had found deliciousness in terror was full of ugly devils. She passed from guardian to guardian. Graham Robertson was the most soothing and maternal. Sharp-tongued, tyrannical Edy, who lived to keep enemies at bay, let herself be hated for showing the rage that was flooding over her charming mother. Only underlings and intimates saw that rage: it poured over James Carew during their short marriage, and over trusting female doubles like Audrey Campbell; it mortified the servants who came and went with increasing rapidity, until employment agencies blacklisted Ellen Terry, the actress everybody loved.

At one dark time around 1924, Edy and her women drew the wrath of the Terrys on their head by attempting to institutionalize Ellen Terry. Fred, outraged, demanded that his sister remain at Smallhythe; Gordon Craig wrote furious letters from Italy, insisting that his mother could never be ill: she was only playing, and would be herself instantly if she were allowed to see men. Finally "Barney" (Hilda Barnes), the last companion and nurse, withstood the mother's invective and the daughter's terror: she would watch Ellen Terry at home.

Edy let her own diagnosis die with her as outsiders denounced her as heartless, incompetent, or greedy. She had seen an Ellen Terry no one else would look at, who was her creature alone. As always, Edy would not or could not tell what she had seen. Her community of women prided itself on having extracted the real Ellen Terry from her phantasia of pleasing selves; they watched reverently, waiting for her to play the new part that would transform womanhood. But when that new part finally erupted before her eyes, Edy could no longer watch. She had her mother and it seared her, but with Barney's help, the idyll of home played itself out to the end.

Until what Ellen Terry repeatedly called the "madness" of the Great War elicited her own madness, she evaded Smallhythe, with its mirror reflections and its ghostly drownings, through an incessant series of tours. The tours were both animating and necessary, for after the catastrophe at the Imperial, she was never financially secure. Her far-flung, solitary tours, so different from the pompous Lyceum progresses, were a bracing exposure to dynamic and unprotected places. From within Irving's beautified Camelot, the English provinces had seemed dreary and deadly: "But Manchester - Liverpool ---- oh, I dread them - the rush — & the hardness — the unlovliness [sic] of it all! —" But in Edy's company, after the Lyceum and the Imperial had collapsed, provincial life looked vigorous and new:

> I am on tour (of the English Provinces) which began last September & ends the end of this month = You will be glad I'm certain to hear that it is a <u>real success</u> - for this time last year I lost ---- through one misfortune & another, just <u>everything I had</u> in the way of money, but now I am <u>picking it all up again</u> fast as may be — !! in fact I am the most successful of all the touring companies!! — <u>I am delighted,</u> for I act Shakespeare mostly, & have a very nice clever Company of young people (<u>no</u> one so old or so ugly as myself) the man who acts with me looks much older than he really is, & I am looking much younger lately than I have looked for many years. I'm made a grand fuss of everywhere, & <u>best of all</u> my Edy is with me & is <u>very</u> happy & <u>very</u> busy, & is my right hand - & my left = The provincial audiences are deeply serious in their love of Shakespeare, & not flippant as they are nowadays in London = ... The <u>stuff</u> that's talked about "what the people want" — I've done my best to freshen up all the — <u>illustration</u> — of the dear old plays, & my young people are clever & comely. Good singers — all new pretty dresses — & <u>one</u> <u>beautiful</u> scene of Ted's — all this please the people. & they <u>Love</u> me — &, they, <u>come</u>!! I am really fortunate in so many ways =

The world beyond Irving's empire was associated in her mind with Edy, with youth, and with the life that flourished on the margins of power. In 1910, she took her Shakespeare lectures to an America Irving had never shown her, writing to Stephen Coleridge from the *Oceanic*: "The first time I am making this long journey <u>alone</u>— & I feel strange." Two months later, "on the Train —Montana to Illinois=", she sent six tiny postcards to Graham Robertson. On them, in minute writing, she transmitted the vertigo and elation of her solitude in eerie landscapes:

> Do you love me <u>very</u> <u>much</u> now that I am very far away from you?
>
> All amongst the Ice & Snow— I do you -- -- "& <u>twenty</u> such"—! Only— only—there <u>aren't</u> twenty--- I'm thinking about you— & Binkie— & yr Mother — & Edy & Jim— & Edward (& Edward—) & Henry— & the work— & the <u>Moon</u> - & I just adore <u>all</u> & Every— I can't help it = The wonder of this journey! All ice & snow & brightest Sunshine— & last night the Moon on it all— all white — white— nothing else— & I <u>wished</u> from my soul that <u>I</u> was nothing else— Well— --. No good wishing. Think of me at my best— You are all "best"! Give my love to all the dear Doggies & to the garden & to the Moon= & to you, & say I <u>do</u> want to come & see you again = These pretty Jap cards (spoiled) are from Luny-Mooney
>
>   <u>Nell</u>

On her late tours, Ellen Terry saw countries from which success had shielded her. Her discovery of the exotic and the vast inspired her to embrace the living and the dead, the past and the present, and especially, the extinguishing moon that was guiding her into old age. Irving's Britannia came to recognize herself in unreclaimed places, though eventually, their strangeness no longer exhilarated, but shattered her.

In 1914, with the world on the brink of war, she bravely took her Shakespeare lectures to Australia, that most far-flung of continents. In her good days, Australia had seemed beyond the pale of rational life. She had used it in the 1890s to reproach Gordon Craig's lofty dismissal of theatrical conditions in England: "You are quite right in saying 'What are <u>notices</u>—? Nothing'= = A strange change is coming over <u>criticism</u>-&, <u>luckily</u>, the public is not led <u>nor ever will</u> <u>be</u>, by the press. <u>Discernment</u>, & <u>discrimination</u> the critics have not--but the public (English)-oh yes=They <u>may</u> for a <u>little while</u> take the <u>wrong thing</u>, & think it the <u>right</u>, but they <u>never pass over</u> the <u>right</u> thing=If I thought otherwise you & I wd be off to Australia tomorrow, & that is <u>not</u> a fine field for <u>ones own</u> self-improvement." But despite all the love the critics and the public had poured on her, she went off to Australia alone with Shakespeare when she was sixty-six.

Before war was declared in August she broke down. Christopher claims that her eyes and heart gave way together, but her addled letters to Graham Robert-

Atwood's thankless task to restrain Ellen Terry's whimsical charities, but hordes of mendicants sprang up for every one that was banished. The less Ellen Terry was told that she had, the more she tried to give. What motivated her perverse generosity in her last, depleted years?

She gave money and things as she had been trained to give herself: freely, recklessly, and on demand. Schooled, like all performers, in the art of self-abandonment, she gave away her inanimate self—the money she had earned, the treasures she had lived with—with the same bravado that led her to invest her identity in other peoples' visions. The particular wickedness with which she gave was, like her fooling at the Lyceum, an oblique demand for freedom and power. Spending rather than husbanding her wealth propelled portions of herself beyond the limiting boundaries of her life; when she gave to others, as when she translated them into beads on her rosary of friends, she incorporated their identities into her own. Forbidden to be everything she was, Ellen Terry spread herself around the world and enlarged her being through dispensing money and property.

After the Lyceum collapsed, her vice of giving grew into a frenzy. Her impassioned investment in Teddy and the Imperial broke her heart, but it did not teach her caution: after the catastrophe of 1903, giving was her most reliable self-affirmation. Until the shattering Australian tour of 1914–15, insecurity galavanized her into continual work, allowing her to recapture some of her early mobility. Between 1903 and 1913, she was frightened of the future and the potential abyss of the present, but she was experimenting, learning, extending herself into the new century, discovering lives that were not grand, work that was not imperial. Her giving had saved her from settling into retirement. When the mists descended and she became increasingly absorbed into Edy's women, her accelerated, foolish giving was, like her pranks at the Lyceum, a subversion of her role. Feminist ideology was declaring that money might make women free; Ellen Terry's mad bounty mimed the actress's unspeakable awareness that money, like a woman's very being, was simply nothing at all.

Feminists who came of age in the 1890s were painfully aware of the socially enforced poverty of women without protecting men. Barred from lucrative professions (with the rarefied exception of the arts), women were herded into underpaid service jobs and told they were fulfilling their selfless natures. Even women who married well were forbidden financial independence: until 1881, a married woman might own neither her inheritance, her property, her earnings, nor her children. Economic discrimination forced women to fulfill their ambitions by attaching themselves to wealthy men: for most, marriage was the only allowable highly paid profession. Insurmountable poverty, not nature or God, made women cringing and clinging; once they were free to compete economically, their very beings would change.

In the impoverishing society of Victorian England, Ellen Terry and a few other actresses stood out as triumphant exceptions to the financial dreariness of women's condition: they were not only visible, but visibly wealthy. Edy's circle scrutinized her for the economically inspired transformations Cicely Hamilton prophesied in *Marriage As a Trade:* "When—if ever—the day of woman's complete social and economic independence dawns upon her, when she finds herself free and upright in a new world where no artificial pressure is brought to bear upon her natural inclinations or disinclinations, then, and then only, will it be possible to untwist a tangled skein and judge to what extent and what precise degree she is swayed by those impulses, sexual and maternal, which are now, to the exclusion of every other factor, presumed to dominate her existence. And not only to dominate, but to justify it" (pp. 24–25).

For Cicely Hamilton and many of her associates, economic parity was more fundamental even than suffrage. When she and Edy began to work together at the Actress' Franchise League, she assumed that feminism came naturally to the daughter of a highly paid actress: "Had she not taken it for granted from childhood that a woman's interests could reach beyond the home, since her mother was artist and breadwinner?" (Adlard, 38). For women bred to ladylike loftiness, the centrality of money was a brave discovery. Woolf's *A Room of One's Own* weaves Cicely Hamilton's unwomanly emphasis on financial power into words of pithy grace: "Of the two—the vote and the money—the money, I own, seemed infinitely the more important" (p. 37). Woolf's seductive desideratum for women to achieve the freedom of spirit art demands—"five hundred pounds and a room of one's own"—had the authority of a truth no one had dared articulate. The vote that had come with such suffering was a mere prelude to that final happy ending.

Ellen Terry had had a room of her own, and far more than five hundred pounds, from the time she left Harpenden. Still, she had forfeited her comic mobility, she had dwindled, at the Lyceum, into a wife, she had lost her power when she failed to please. When, in her last years, she was encompassed by feminist spectators, she gave and gave what little she had, declaring in her own way that she was not free. She threw money away defiantly to proclaim her own poverty of spirit, from which five hundred pounds and a room of her own had not redeemed her.

For Christopher, who would never understand acting or the theater, this strain of self-despair made Ellen Terry a saint. Paying homage to her "Dearest and most blessed lady," she did not see that that too was a role one might play.

Ellen Terry's appropriation of Christopher's own life was Heaven's benediction: "You have given me the best, the most superb gift of my life in Edy. So my worship of you as the most wonderful of all women is steadied and deepened by the gratitude of a saved soul to its redeemer." With resonant humility, she signed herself: "Christopher (your ghost.)"

After Ellen Terry died, Christopher transferred her worship to her neighbor, Vita Sackville-West. The grand, bisexual inspiration for Woolf's *Orlando*, Vita inherited in Christopher's reverent imagination Ellen Terry's infinite capacity to become all things: "But I don't think of you as a woman, or as a man either," she wrote in her love-journal to Vita. "Perhaps as someone who is both, the complete human being who transcends both." She allowed her imagined Vita an eroticism she forbade Ellen Terry, who had evolved over the years into a surpassingly holy ghost. As Christopher understood it, her retreat into the spiritual ministrations of Thomas à Kempis was a retreat from performance as well: "That chameleon quality in Ellen Terry, which made it easy for her to take the form and colour of any image of herself she saw in another's mind, was affected by age. Those who had idolized their own image of her were perhaps never fully conscious that the disparity between it and the old Ellen Terry, which distressed, or annoyed, or alienated them, according to their temperament, was due to the fact that she had lost the power, and perhaps also the desire, to identify herself with the image" (*Memoirs*, 319). In the image Christopher made, Ellen Terry became a saint because she stopped acting at last.

On Christmas Day, 1925, she played the holy ghost at a Christmas party in Edy's London flat. Frail, erratic, living mostly on "another Planet," she returned to bless Edy's company for the last time. As Velona Pilcher, one of the guests, recalls:

> Her health drunk, the jokes failing, the last Christmas crackers popped, she at last said good-night and went to bed. A little later the guests began a gramophone dance round the deserted dinner-table to a tune from Whiteman's Band. Around and around they went, absurdly, not very gracefully, the paper caps wilting foolishly on their heads . . . when suddenly in the doorway swayed a silver figure, wrapped in a long loose cloak of snow-white fur. The head was high, flung back defiantly from the bent body; the white hair haloed it, and waved, as it moved, to the rhythm of the record. One poised hand beat the beat, posed like an Angel Gabriel, making the sign annunciate, and as the little group of earthly dancers fell back in a sort of fear from this dream whose sleep had been disturbed, and stood struck still before this pre-Raphaelite figure, drawn back into life by music and mirth, Ellen Terry began to dance. Silently once around the table, she danced—

slowly, stately, delicately, pouring beauty from her bones, bearing her years like a burden of long-stemmed lilies, moving like a blossom of snow blown down to its rest on the ground—and thus silently passed again out at the door. (Quoted in *Memoirs*, 332)

But Ellen Terry was only playing the Angel Gabriel: she had never claimed that she came from Heaven. On Christmas, she made a holy sign; on other nights, she danced to the moon in her garden. These dances disturbed Edy, but men remembered them. Graham Robertson celebrated the Ellen Terry who was "a daughter of the night, happy in its shadow and mystery and loving the moon with a strange ecstasy which I have never met with in another" (WGR, *Life Was Worth Living*, 143). She wrote to him accordingly: "My Moon delights me ever as keenly as when I was young— it is shining like mad tonight & sends its love to you along with mine." Her grandson Teddy never forgot being rapturously awakened to share the full moon: when he was an old man, the moon remained his grandmother. Ellen Terry's moon dances celebrated an ancient divinity Christopher's church could not accommodate: they were pure and pagan rites, sexual and proud, trammeled by no humility or solemnity. Once again, Ellen Terry evaded her holy role.

Graham Robertson claimed that Godwin had introduced her to the moon when they lived together in the country. But on the nights she was mad, Ellen Terry danced to a moon brighter than Harpenden's: it was the Lyceum's moon, which Godwin may have designed, and it had shone on Tennyson's *The Cup*. In *The Cup*, she had been Camma, Artemis's priestess; before a colossal statue of the goddess, she had poisoned the lustful villain Irving and herself. *The Cup* had taught her to worship a grand woman by singing to the power of the moon:

> Moon on the field and the foam,
> Moon on the waste and the wold,
> Moon bring him home, bring him home,
> Safe from the dark and the cold,
> Home, sweet moon, bring him home,
> Home with the flock to the fold—
> (*The Cup*, Act I, Scene ii)

The moon, and the goddess she stood for, had determined men's destinies in *The Cup*. Dancing in the garden, Ellen Terry paid homage to her own power in a time into which Tennyson had initiated her, before men came to rule. Dancing to the moon, she was no longer Christopher's "dearest and most blessed lady," but a blasphemous acolyte of an unblessed female power who had ruled dangerously. The church had expelled her; no church could hold her.

Edy did her best to subdue Ellen Terry's more disruptive visions, for she knew that Ellen Terry's wavering imagination determined her physical condition: "She was not blind, as has been stated, but anything that disoriented her affected her eyesight" (*Memoirs*, 316). To outsiders, the power within her apparent helplessness had never seemed greater. To the young actress May Agate, her blindness conveyed a magnitude the theater could not hold:

> I remember her sitting on a couch, tailor-fashion, in some loose, multi-coloured kimono, row upon row of beads around her neck, and calling me over to sit beside her that she might, with her powerful hands, turn my head sideways for her tired eyes to study. How she loved the theatre, "the stage-door, the smell of grease-paint", as she told me rather wistfully, for she had almost retired now. But in spite of this youthful enthusiasm I felt the presence of an exceptional brain behind those lovely sightless eyes—a brain which did not altogether bespeak the theatre—she might, I felt, have been a great painter or writer.

In 1913, when she had begun to deteriorate, Shaw was more outspoken: in a letter Christopher withheld from *A Correspondence,* he determined that this consummate professional had grown too powerful for any stage. The power of old age consigned her to the marginality in which her children were thriving. He repudiated that power with appropriate awe when she begged for work:

> You fill me with concern—with dismay. What am I to do or say? It's as if Queen Alexandra came to me and asked me to get her a place as cook-housekeeper, except that I'm not in love with Queen Alexandra. Nobody dare have you in a cast; *you'd* knock it all to pieces. A tiny yacht may throw its mast overboard and end its day quietly and serviceably as a ferry boat; but a battleship cant do that; and you are a battleship. What parts are there that even the most callous youngster who never saw you could offer you in the ordinary routine of theatrical commerce? Matrons at £15 a week or less. And then the agony of learning a part, and being hustled by a producer, and finally overwhelming everyone on the stage by dwarfing them and mopping up every scrap of interest and attention in the house! Can you wonder that we all recoil, and say "She would be splendid in it"; and then get some estimable mouse who would give no trouble and spread no terror? (9 November 1913. Quoted in Manvell, 283)

In her last years, the illness no one named intensified the terror her allure had always held: she had grown too powerful for any role, though she was never powerful enough to deny all roles. She played sanctity, she danced to the moon, she slid in and out of herself, but finally, she could only send lonely messages from her remote world. She left Edy a note: "The days are so short— I wake in the morning—I meet a little misery - I meet a little happiness. I fight with one, I greet the other— my strength is all gone - this day is gone— As to writing to the many friends who write to me - impossible."

Obligingly, Edy appropriated her mother's handwriting and eventually, her voice as well. In 1928, the BBC staged a program in honor of Ellen Terry's eightieth birthday (it was really her eighty-first); a special microphone was installed for her at Smallhythe. Christopher wrote a gracious speech which Edy became her mother to deliver: "Edy, who was greatly moved by her mother's inability to act her part in this last public scene, had some difficulty in reading the message in a steady voice, but she understudied Ellen Terry so well that many listeners wrote to tell her they could hardly believe it was not Ellen Terry herself speaking" (*Memoirs,* 336). Upstairs, a mad Ellen Terry towered once again over her assigned role: "I recall as the most poignant moment in my life hearing the mad scene from 'Hamlet,' with Fay Compton as Ophelia, downstairs [on the radio], while upstairs the fair Ophelia of 1878, now a distraught old woman, 'bound upon a wheel of fire, that mine own tears do scald like molten lead,' was playing Lear" (*Memoirs,* 335).

Today, somebody would give Ellen Terry's long illness a name. She would probably not be sequestered with it upstairs, in a torturing parody of the locked attic where her memories began; she would be discussing it on the radio and on television. But as she lived with it in her time, it took on the shape of all the secret illnesses of her life. She had always been too large, too avid and scattered, for her roles, and now there were no roles; Mr. Watts and the others had always said she would be mad; she had always seen too hungrily, too clearly, and now her eyes were taken away; she was always at her most lovable drowning, and now she had done it. Edy dutifully became her as she sank. Her last letter, written in the last month of her life, needed Edy in order to communicate at all. In a hand eerily like Ellen Terry's at its most controlled, Edy wrote a dry explanation to Ben Webster: "I've been talking to Mother about your trip to South Africa & that you will have to give up helping her with her affairs & this letter is the result. Its the only letter she has written in the last six months= I want to thank you too - <u>very much indeed</u>= I know how hard it has been for you during the last month or two & I appreciate yr attitude= Mother says 'give Bennie my love.' " She enclosed a penciled card from Ellen Terry:

> Dear Ben=
> Thank you

<u>Thank</u> you   so
~~much~~ for all you cd
have donne for me
God be with you -
& bring you
     annd
bring you to us all—safely
     baack
3 cheers for you
—& yours

                  fromm
                  Yrs
                  <u>Ellen Terry</u>

     Hip hip
     Harrah!!!!!

Like the Victorian she was, Ellen Terry pulled herself up from the "depths of down-ness" to make her last written words a cheer.

D E A T H   She was not altogether Victorian: Victorians loved to die or to imagine themselves doing so. Victorian fiction feeds on deathbed scenes, which grant good and evil characters alike a protracted luster life rarely allows. While they live, the plot hurries them along, but all the time in the world is theirs to die in. When death rejects them, stalwart heroes like Emily Brontë's Heathcliff or Dickens's David Copperfield refresh themselves by miming the magnificent consummation that makes the humblest of mortals briefly a star. The epilogue to *Asolando* (1889), which Robert Browning composed as his own epitaph, invokes neither extinction nor debility. Dying gives the poet a chance to gird his energy and boast of his vigor. Like Ellen Terry's, Browning's last written words are a cheer:

> No, at noonday in the bustle of man's work-time
>   Greet the unseen with a cheer!
> Bid him forward, breast and back as either should be,
> "Strive and thrive!" cry "Speed,—fight on, fare ever
>   There as here!" (ll. 16–20)

But Browning cheers the unseen and his own manly fortitude in its company; Ellen Terry cheered her friend, helper, and colleague on his way to South Africa.

Death's specter threw her back on life. Stylishly, she cheered her friends into the unseen, but she did not want to die herself, onstage or off. She put all her vigor into her life. What life forbade her to spend, she flung into mad channels, playing in imagination such impossible roles as Hamlet or King Lear, giving her money away, exploding into cadenzas of rage. She hoarded none of her energy for her death.

Nothing about Sarah Bernhardt was more Victorian than her virtuoso on-stage dyings; Sarah's gorgeous death raptures were part of the inhumanity Ellen Terry found both alienating and intriguing. Ellen Terry had spent herself in the service of great men, which Bernhardt would never stoop to do, but unlike Bernhardt, she did not live to die. Ellen Terry greeted only the visible with a cheer. She cherished the lives of her dead friends, not their deadness; she never understood the nineteenth-century cult of a glorifying death that gave existence its only intensity.

As the consolations of formal religion waned, the process of dying became passionately interesting to Victorians. God's providence, the eternal dominions of Heaven and Hell, assumed the poignant unreality of stage sets, and so only death, not the hereafter, remained to give magnitude to daily life's littleness. *In Memoriam A. H. H.,* Tennyson's long lament for a dead friend, finds life's richness in the mourning process: dying vicariously at great length, the speaker loses his mystic grasp of ultimate questions when time reconciles him to life. "Crossing the Bar" (1889), Tennyson's rich epitaph for himself, summons death in images of bounty, of water full to overflowing:

> Sunset and evening star,
>   And one clear call for me!
> And may there be no moaning of the bar,
>   When I put out to sea,
>
> But such a tide as moving seems asleep,
>   Too full for sound and foam,
> When that which drew from out the boundless deep
>   Turns again home.
>
> Twilight and evening bell,
>   And after that the dark!
> And may there be no sadness of farewell,
>   When I embark;

For tho' from out our bourne of Time and Place
        The flood may bear me far,
I hope to see my Pilot face to face
    When I have crost the bar.

Tennyson's poems, the elaboration of deathbed scenes, the drawn-out mourning rituals in which survivors enacted an ornate living death, all vindicate a scant and thwarted existence by the grand transformations of the ending. Compared to the opulent vision of ultimate revelations in "Crossing the Bar," Ellen Terry's dying is a simple violation by scantness and negation: "The days are so short — . . . my strength is all gone – this day is gone—" Ellen Terry died old and venerated, but hers was not the death of a Victorian sage. She was no vehicle of revelations beyond "our bourne." For the woman and the actress, there was no beyond, but only her many lives. Her past held the only intensity she could imagine, and that past died long before she did. Her death was merely one last deprivation.

Her favorite obituary cry, "there was none like him — none," is a lament with no conceivable consolation. In "Crossing the Bar," the speaker submerges his identity in a flood of cosmic plenitude, but the lives Ellen Terry found worthy of mourning cannot be absorbed or recalled: extinction is the only destiny worth their specialness. Before she actually died of a stroke on July 21, 1928, Ellen Terry had earned her own epitaph: a life unlike any other had gone. It died first in her memory, which lost her in old age; she had begun by forgetting her lines, and she ended forgetting herself. In her last years she scribbled ruefully in her notebook: "[Bishop] Ripon told me— memory is a very delicate organ & resents distrust." Hers had been distrusted for too many years. As Edy had taken over her eyes, her voice, her handwriting, her judgment, becoming her right hand and her left, so as the arranger of her mother's Memoir, she took on her memories as well. Edy alone prevented Ellen Terry's life from being quite lost.

In the theater as well, Ellen Terry was gone and there would be no one like her, for no women's lives would play themselves out entirely on the stage. By 1928 stage children were learning their cutely subordinate place. Protective legislation dictated that they be properly educated; their rehearsal hours, and thus their roles, were scaled to wholesome dimensions. No child would doze through all-night rehearsals or imbibe her identity from the theater alone; above all, no child would incarnate the theater's transforming principle, becoming in turn male and female, old and young, comic and tragic. They would conform to acceptable types. Even the great emancipator Shaw associated stage children with child laborers and other helpless victims; he never imagined that they might be vehicles of supranatural mobility. His review of *The Club Baby* is an enlightened attack on their very existence:

> The utter worthlessness of the sentiment in which our actors and playgoers wallow is shewn by their readiness to take an unfortunate little child who ought to be in bed, and make fun of it on the stage as callously as a clown at a country fair will make fun of a sucking pig. . . . Sir Matthew White Ridley is at present receiving £5000 a year, partly at my expense, for looking after the administration of the laws regulating the employment of children. If a factory owner employed a child under the specified age, or kept a "young person" at work ten minutes after the specified hour, Sir Matthew would be down on him like five thousand of brick. If the factory owner were to plead that his factory was producing goods of vital utility and the rarest artistic value, the plea would not be listened to for a moment. In the name of common sense, why are speculators in Club Babies and the like to enjoy illegal and anti-social privileges which are denied to manufacturers? . . . I suggest to the Home Office that a rigid rule should be made against the licensing of children for any new entertainment whatsoever. (7 May 1898. *Shaw's Dramatic Criticism*, 291–92)

By 1928, Shaw's peculiar morality dictated to theatrical convention as autocratically as Irving's spectacle had done in the 1890s. Never, under his dispensation, would stage children be anything other than adorable, sheltered distractions. Never would they extend eerie promises of becoming all things. As Ellen Terry diminished into a real child for the first time, the stage child she had been with terror and joy died irrecoverably.

With the death of Ellen Terry's childhood came the death of the mobile old woman she had fought to remain until her final deterioration: her protégées were too wise to put themselves at the mercy of a theater that discarded aging women ruthlessly. Lena Ashwell, who adored Ellen Terry and owed her career to her, vowed not to remain an actress beyond her physical prime. She threw her best energies into management when faced with the sad example of her aging idol. Her autobiography takes a bleak view of Ellen Terry's last itinerant years: "If she had succeeded [as manager of the Imperial] it would have been a triumph for England; but at sixty-five she was on one-night 'stands' giving a lecture-tour in America. Almost all the histories are tragic of those who devote their lives to art."

The heady, moony postcards Ellen Terry wrote to Graham Robertson as her train plunged through the brightness of the American West would have had no magic for Lena Ashwell. Politically and economically, she searched for "wider vistas" than the theater could promise. The gallantry of unprotected age drew only her loving pity:

> So I was feeling full of gloom, when into my room suddenly there danced Ellen Terry. Gracious, radiant, to me the most beautiful woman I have ever seen because it was not her face only, or her figure, but her soul that had such loveliness. Almost blind, alone, stripped of all the luxury and care which had for so long been hers; courageous, undefeated, young, she hugged me and said: "What do you think of me, Lena? Sixty-three, and on one-night stands." As if a one-night stand, that most horrible of all experiences, were a command performance. She came to the dress rehearsal [of the play Ashwell was producing], which lasted nearly all night, and kept on saying: "Nelly, you must go home, you must go home," and still she stayed, so interested, and alert and gay. (Ashwell, 174)

So many actresses who had learned from Ellen Terry were demanding protection, not experience. In the future older women, like children, would no longer be abandoned to the theater to learn themselves. There would be other schools to inculcate justice, social awareness, self-interest; their amply changing beings would be sheltered from audiences' love, fears, and needs; they could rest in one identity. In this wiser theater children would not, on cue, grow startlingly old; aging women would keep their dignity, but they would have no dangers to keep them "interested, and alert and gay." When Ellen Terry died, a complete stage life died with her. Women might be stars for fragments of their time, but no woman's life would learn and tell itself from childhood to old age on the stage. Actresses might be happier, but they would never again play themselves fully. There could be none like Ellen Terry when she died.

Clemence Dane defined her role in her final, imprisoned years: "Ariel in the tree" (*Memoirs,* 311). Dying crystallized the role she had played all her life, that of energy held captive, mobility cramped and confined. Future actresses would be protected, but they would lose Ellen Terry's knowledge of the energy prisons could forge. Because she had been captive in her life, the captivity of death was unimportant. When Mabel Malleson's husband died, she had sent a revealing consolation: "I can never think of Death sadly — worse is to lose those we love by some dishonour — That is the worst isn't it?"

When she had forfeited her comedy, she had lived through her own loss. By becoming the changing women others saw, she abandoned herself to a dishonor that was inseparable from her art and from the age that shaped that art. Such a confusing triumph was more momentous than the most beautifully staged death. Her own lifelong performance gave her no mighty revelations, but it did allow her to see that all women were artists, even those whom nobody applauded. In quiet appreciation, she left her mother with a variant of the obituary she reserved for her heroes. Her epitaph to Clement Scott places the obscured Sarah Terry in the company of Edward Godwin, Henry Irving, and Eleonora Duse: "There is no one left in the world now who is just the same as she was." Every woman's life requires the art Ariel perfected in his tree. The magnitude of such an imprisonment dwarfs anything death might do.

The power and primacy of life determined Ellen Terry's relationship to the dead. She mourned her sister Florence by becoming her, imbibing Florence's feelings across what Tennyson called "the bar," and using them to color her own reproach to Teddy: "I wonder whether, when we are dead, we are conscious of our own forgetting us, bit by bit, more and more, as the months go by. . . . I'm *alive*, but feel that in regard to you and yours, I feel you are forgetting all about me" (quoted in Prideaux, 212). As early as 1885, when she was called to the deathbed of Charles Kelly/Wardell, her second husband, she denied death's authority and graced her husband's corpse with all her intensity of play: "When I went upstairs I could not feel it was Charles, but I had the strangest wish to rehearse Juliet there by the bed on which he was lying!" (quoted in Steen, 185). She hoped for no face-to-face meetings across the bar; she preferred to pull her dead back to her. No imaginable afterlife could compete with her stage life, intensified as that had been by its recurrent imprisonments.

As far as she tells us, she never crossed the bar: she instructed her mourners to confront death as she had done, by flinging themselves back on life. In her copy of Thomas à Kempis's *The Imitation of Christ,* Edy and Barney found after her death lines by William Allingham, a minor Pre-Raphaelite poet who had preceded Graham Robertson at Sandhills, her restored Paradise:

> No funeral gloom, my dears, when I am gone;
> Corpse-gazings, tears, black raiment, graveyard grimness.
> Think of me as withdrawn into the dimness,
> Yours still, you mine. Remember all the best
> Of our past moments, and forget the rest.
> And so, to where I wait, come gently on.

She had written underneath these lines: "I should wish my children, relatives and friends to observe this when I die. E. T." (*Memoirs,* 345).

And so Edy staged her most popular pageant: a gaily dressed crowd, singing hymns, transported a coffin with a pall of shimmering gold from Smallhythe to the crematorium in Golders Green. Local farmers, "good and faithful toilers of the earth," paid homage: "haymakers with their rakes and pitchforks, shepherds with their crooks and sheep-dogs" (*Memoirs,* 347). Magical reconciliations prevailed: for the duration, brother and sister loved each other again. Gordon Craig was so moved by Edy's presence that he blurted out: "We must have more occasions like this." For a day he had found his real sister and was free from the need to fabricate sisters in art. The gaiety, the singing, the mingling of social classes, the ringing church bells (they were forbidden to toll), the shining summer weather, gave Ellen Terry her *As You Like It* at last. She may not have met her Pilot face to face if she did cross the bar, but she became for a day her own Pilot, steering her life to final harmony.

AFTERLIVES   But the pastoral funeral was play. It did not heal the divisions that had torn and stimulated her. Edy and Ted perpetuated her internal war between male and female roles, fighting in books and newspapers for possession of their mother's memory. Edy, who had overseen her long helplessness, championed a triumphant Ellen Terry, while Gordon Craig, whom her power had terrified all his life, wrote sentimentally about his pathetic little mother who wanted only to love. Poetic tributes by her acolytes Lawrence Alma-Tadema and Graham Robertson define the woman's Ellen Terry and the man's, who warred through the next generation. In "To Ellen Terry," Lawrence Alma-Tadema celebrates a victorious creating power:

> Dear and beloved! What giving of dull gold,
>   Or roll of praise, or chronicle of fame,
>   Can pay the debt we owe? Thy radiant name
> Shines on our hearts: when thine and ours are cold,
> How shall the child who knew thee not be told
>   Of Shakespeare's women, quickened in the flame
>   Of their surpassing sweetness, that became
>   New star-born visions, one yet manifold?
> Fact and desire, the day and the day's dreams
>   Lie sundered: but thy life-long glorious part
> It was to make things true, and that which seems
>   Beshade what is. Thy gift was to the heart,
>   Therefore the heart in richest gladness gives
>   An unmatched love, that ripens and outlives.

In this sonnet, Ellen Terry's created life prevails over time and loss; but Graham Robertson's poignant "Dream-Lady" has power only to make desolation when she fades away:

> Ah, Ellen Terry (name that seems to chime
> Along the echoing glades of Fairyland),
> Fill us again the draught of Beauty. Stand
> Where all the world may see you, and with rhyme
> Low-lilted, and with speech of face and hand
> Give us our Dream, bring back the Golden Time!
> (*Letters*, 208)

Two Ellen Terrys, a triumphant and a pathetic, wrestle in these poems, just as they do in the reminiscences of Edy and Ted: they kept alive the warring selves she had learned to be. For the next generation as for her own, Ellen Terry epitomized woman's possibilities: what she had been, the future might become. Eventually, as happens so often, the mighty Ellen Terry faded when Edy's generation died, leaving the helpless loving charmer to flicker in theatrical memory via Gordon Craig's descendants. Withdrawn into the dimness, Ellen Terry continued to obey her times.

She died with no message beyond directions for the pageant of her funeral, a funeral which, like *As You Like It* itself, reconciled opposites only as long as it held the stage. Only Edy and her women were present to interpret her as she died, and they claim that she ratified the bond with her daughter that had sustained her life. Christopher tells the story: "Her hand gripped mine; it was searching for something. I knew for what, when it reached my thumb. Edy had a peculiar square thumb. 'The murderer's thumb' it has been called in jest. It was by the thumb, Ellen Terry knew she could tell whether the hand on hers was Edy's. Edy was the one she wanted to give her a hand in her extremity, and with a strong powerful gesture of disappointment, she pushed my hand away" (*Memoirs*, 341).

Edy came as she always did to help her mother die: "During those hours, Edy sat by the bed constantly, holding that beautiful, still expressive right hand. The left one was powerless, motionless. The face had not been much changed by that cruel blow from Nature. But the breath of life was changed. It came more and more painfully as the dawn approached. The hand, gripping Edy's, moved from finger to finger, and with a last effort the voice, not miraculously clear and loud now, but thick and indistinct, spelt out on those fingers the word 'Happy,' 'H-a-p-p-y' over and over again" (*Memoirs*, 343). In Christopher's account,

Ellen Terry's death is a tribute to her daughter and a pledge that she dies as she has lived, as Edy's woman.

But Edy was not her only child with murderer's thumbs: Gordon Craig had them as well. They had both inherited Ellen Terry's eerily large, powerful hands, hands she hid throughout her life, though her children displayed their odd beauty proudly. Coincidentally, Ted was in London when Ellen Terry had her stroke; he had seen her, though he would not join the women's deathwatch. Ellen Terry's death spoke no more distinctly than her suggestive performances had done. She may have died deluded, thinking her son had returned to take her hand, assuring her last chimerical saving male of how h-a-p-p-y he had made her, obliterating Edy's jealous love once more at the last. Her son might have triumphed at her deathbed through his very absence, as men had done so often in her life. She pledged herself as she died, but we shall never know to whom.

It is pleasant to imagine that Ellen Terry figuratively grasped her own hand as she died and was happy to feel its largeness, its murderer's thumbs, the power that had always shamed her. "All her life lay in those strange, fine hands," Gordon Craig would write. Realizing their wonder for the first time, she went off into the mist as William Allingham had directed, waiting to be joined there.

Notes

INTRODUCTION:
THE ACTRESS EVERYBODY LOVED

p. 3 *"Not without tears"*: London Times, 13 June 1906.

p. 3 *"Queen of England"*: Lady of Fashion, 12 April 1906.

p. 4 *Always come:*

For an account of nineteenth-century alterations in theatrical design, see especially George Rowell, *The Victorian Theatre, 1792–1914,* 2d ed. (1956; reprint, Cambridge and London: Cambridge University Press, 1978), pp. 1–29.

p. 4 *Of theatrical London:* For a complete history of Drury Lane, see Brian Dobbs, *Drury Lane: Three Centuries of the Theatre Royal, 1663–1971* (London: Cassell, 1972).

p. 5 *"If you please"*: Manuscript of Ellen Terry's jubilee address, The Arnold Rood Collection, New York City. Hereafter cited as ET jubilee MS.

p. 5 *"National susceptibilities"*: Dublin Daily Express, 24 March 1906.

p. 6 *" 'Shouldn't I?' "*: The Tribune, 17 March 1906.

p. 6 *"Wondrous Ellen Terry"*: Quoted in J. C. Trewin, *The Edwardian Theatre* (Totowa, N.J.: Rowman & Littlefield, 1976), p. 14.

p. 6 *"Very proud"*: Quoted in an unidentified clipping, file 184, Henneke Archives of the Performing Arts, University of Tulsa. Hereafter cited as "Henn, Tulsa."

p. 6 *"Without a parallel"*: London Times, 13 June 1906.

p. 7 *"Ellen Terry's Beatrice"*: London Times, 13 June 1906.

p. 7 *And prostitute:* See Christopher Kent, "Image and Reality: The Actress and Society," in *A Widening Sphere: Changing Roles of Victorian Women,* ed. Martha Vicinus (Bloomington and London: Indiana University Press, 1977), p. 95. Hereafter cited as Vicinus, *A Widening Sphere* or Vicinus *WS.*

p. 8 *"Take hold of"*: Henry James, *The Tragic Muse* (1890; reprint, New York: Harper & Row, 1968), p. 150.

p. 8 *"Anthony Hope"*: Roger Manvell, *Ellen Terry* (New York: G. P. Putnam's Sons, 1968), p. 299. Hereafter cited as Manvell.

p. 9 *"Wheels go round"*: ET jubilee MS.

p. 10 *"Bath Buns"*: *Ellen Terry's Memoirs,* with a preface, notes, and additional biographical chapters by Edith Craig and Christopher St. John (1932; reprint, New York: Benjamin Blom, 1969), 281. Hereafter cited in the text as *Memoirs.* The first edition was published under the title *The Story of My Life.*

p. 11 *Votes for women:* See Julie Holledge, *Innocent Flowers: Women in the Edwardian Theatre* (London: Virago Press, 1981), p. 51. Hereafter cited as Holledge.

p. 14 *"We love?"*: Edward Gordon Craig, *Index to the Story of My Days: Some Memoirs of Edward Gordon Craig, 1872–1907* (New York: The Viking Press, 1957), pp. 287–88. Hereafter cited as *Index.*

p. 14. *"Getting at it"*: Quoted in Edward A. Craig, *Gordon Craig: The Story of His Life* (New York: Alfred A. Knopf, 1968), p. 198. Hereafter cited as EAC.

p. 14 *"I'm not!"*: To Audrey Campbell, 26 March 1906, UCLA Library, Special Collections. Hereafter cited as UCLA.

p. 15 *"Eloquent for me"*: ET jubilee MS.

p. 15 *Nose and chin:* Ellen Terry's witchlike self-caricature on a photograph of herself in *The Cup* is in the Arnold Rood Collection.

p. 15 *"Nobody like you"*: Manuscript, Harry Ransom Humanities Research Center, University of Texas at Austin. Hereafter cited as HRHRC.

p. 16 *"In the sun"*: Virginia Woolf, "Ellen Terry" (Jan. 1941), in *Collected Essays,* vol. 4 (London: The Hogarth Press, 1967), p. 67.

p. 17 *"Everybody loved"*: Obituary headline, *The Sphere,* 28 July 1928.

p. 18 *"Of a drama"*: Quoted in Michael R. Booth, "Pictorial Acting and Ellen Terry," *Shakespeare: The Victorian Stage,* ed. Richard Foulkes (Cambridge: Cambridge University Press, 1986), p. 80.

p. 19 *"Eloquence itself"*: W. Graham Robertson, *Life Was Worth Living: The Reminiscences of W. Graham Robertson* (New York: Harper & Brothers, 1931), p. 54. Hereafter cited as WGR, *Life Was Worth Living.*

p. 19 *"Present medium"*: Martin Meisel, *Realizations: Narrative, Pictorial, and Theatrical Arts in Nineteenth-Century England* (Princeton, N.J.: Princeton University Press, 1983), p. 30. Hereafter cited as Meisel, *Realizations.*

p. 21 *"Size and strength"*: George Bernard Shaw, *Complete Plays with Prefaces,* vol. 1 (New York: Dodd, Mead, 1963), pp. 710–11.

p. 21 *"In a trice"*: Edward Gordon Craig, *Ellen Terry and Her Secret Self* (London: Sampson Low, Marston [1931]), pp. 113–14. Hereafter cited in the text as ETSS.

p. 21 *"My dear!"*: Isadora Duncan, *My Life* (New York: Boni & Liveright, 1922), p. 181.

p. 22 *Voluminous sleeves:* William Weaver describes Duse's effect in *La Gioconda* in *Duse: A Biography* (New York: Harcourt Brace Jovanovich, 1984), p. 214. Hereafter cited as Weaver.

p. 23 *"Against it"*: Max Beerbohm, "Duse at the Lyceum," 26 May 1900, in *A Selection from Around Theatres* (Garden City, N.Y.: Anchor Books, 1960), pp. 46–47.

p. 24 *"They love"*: *The Athenaeum* (8 April 1876), 510.

p. 24 *"Nugget of power"*: Morris Carnovsky with Peter Sander, *The Actor's Eye* (New York: Performing Arts Journal Publications, 1984), pp. 25, 103.

p. 25 *"Better than them":* To W. Graham Robertson, 8 August 1909, Huntington Library, WR 591.

p. 28 *"Nor docile":* Sarah Bernhardt, *Memories of My Life* (1908; reprint, New York and London: Benjamin Blom, 1968), p. 240.

CHAPTER 1: STAGE CHILD

p. 30 *Social sobrieties:* For a complete account of the changing social status of the Victorian actor, see Michael Baker, *The Rise of the Victorian Actor* (Totowa, N.J.: Rowman and Littlefield, 1978). Hereafter cited as Baker.

p. 32 *"front of me":* Lillian Gish, with Ann Pinchot, *The Movies, Mr. Griffith, and Me* (Englewood, N.J.: Prentice Hall, 1969), p. 16.

p. 33 *"Bolton-le-Moors":* Edward Stirling, *Old Drury Lane: Fifty Years' Recollections of Author, Actor and Manager* (1881). Quoted in J. C. Trewin, *The Pomping Folk in the Nineteenth-Century Theatre* (London: J. M. Dent, 1968), p. 45.

p. 37 See Sandra M. Gilbert and Susan Gubar, *The Madwoman in the Attic: The Woman Writer and the Nineteenth-Century Literary Imagination* (New Haven: Yale University Press, 1979).

p. 37 *"half imp":* Charlotte Brontë, *Jane Eyre* (1847; reprint, Middlesex: Penguin Books, 1966), p. 46.

p. 40 *"spluttering and adenoidal":* J. C. Trewin, *Mr. Macready: A Nineteenth-Century Tragedian and His Theatre* (London: George G. Harrap & Co., 1955), p. 138.

p. 40 *"apostolic inspiration":* Souvenir program of Charles Kean's *A Midsummer Night's Dream,* 1856. Henn, Tulsa.

p. 41 *"ease and spirit"; "I ever saw":* Quoted in Morton N. Cohen, "The Actress and the Don: Ellen Terry and Lewis Carroll," in *Lewis Carroll: A Celebration,* ed. Edward Guiliano (New York: Clarkson N. Potter, 1982), pp. 4–5.

p. 43 *An average girl . . . "means for the end":* See Joan N. Burstyn, *Victorian Education and the Ideal of Womanhood* (New Brunswick, N.J.: Rutgers University Press, 1984), pp. 30–48. Burstyn's clerical quotation is on p. 121.

p. 45 *"my head":* Quoted in Constance Wright, *Fanny Kemble and the Lovely Land* (New York: Dodd Mead, 1972), p. 127. Hereafter cited as Wright.

p. 45 *"unpoetical craft":* Quoted in J. C. Furnas, *Fanny Kemble: Leading Lady of the Nineteenth-Century Stage* (New York: Dial Press, 1982), p. 319. Hereafter cited as Furnas.

p. 46 *"horrors!":* ET annotation to Charles Hiatt, *Ellen Terry and Her Impersonations,* Ellen Terry Memorial Museum, Smallhythe Place. Hereafter cited as Hiatt.

p. 47 *"as it was in me?":* 5 December 1897. The Arnold Rood Collection.

p. 48 *"& alive":* To Mr. Courtney, n.d., from King's Row, Chelsea. The Arnold Rood Collection.

p. 48 *as Shakespeare:* For a colorful and full account of the continuing centrality of theatrical spectacle, see Michael R. Booth, *Victorian Spectacular Theatre, 1850–1910* (London: Routledge & Kegan Paul, 1981).

p. 49 *"precious stones"; "paradise feathers":* William W. Appleton, *Madame Vestris and the London Stage* (New York: Columbia University Press, 1974), pp. 171, 178. Hereafter cited as Appleton.

p. 49 *"Under contract":* Aljean Harmetz, *The Making of "The Wizard of Oz"* (New York: Alfred A. Knopf, 1977), p. 107.

p. 50 *"An assemblyline"*: Quoted in Andrea Darvi, *Pretty Babies: An Insider's Look at the World of the Hollywood Child Star* (New York: McGraw Hill, 1983), p. 6.

p. 50 *"Choice meat"*: Quoted in *People* Magazine (12 Nov. 1984), 116.

p. 50 *"Playing boy"*: Laurence Olivier, *Confessions of an Actor: An Autobiography* (1982; reprint, Middlesex: Penguin Books, 1984), p. 24.

p. 51 *"And man"*: "The Sleeping Beauty in the Wood," Hoblitzelle Theatre Collection, HRHRC.

p. 52 *Stunted archness*: For Jean Davenport and the Infant Phenomenon, see Eric Wollencott Barnes, *The Lady of Fashion: The Life and Times of Anna Cora Mowatt* (New York: Charles Scribner's Sons, 1954), p. 246.

p. 55 *"Talked of"*: Quoted in *The Dickens Theatrical Reader,* ed. Edgar and Eleanor Johnson (London: Victor Gollancz, 1961), p. 339. Hereafter cited as Edgar and Eleanor Johnson.

p. 56 *Queen Christina*: See Betsy Erkkila, "Greta Garbo: Sailing Beyond the Frame," *Critical Inquiry* 11 (June 1985): 595–619.

p. 56 *Of Harlequin*: See David Meyer, "The Sexuality of Pantomime," *Theatre Quarterly* 4 (Feb.-Apr. 1974): 55–64.

p. 56 *"Her eighties"*: See H. Philip Bolton, *"Bleak House* and the Playhouse," *Dickens Studies Annual* 12, ed. Michael Timko, Fred Kaplan, and Edward Guiliano (New York: AMS Press, 1983), pp. 81–116.

p. 57 *Burlesque relations*: For Ellen Terry and Nellie Farren, see WGR, *Life Was Worth Living,* pp. 210–17.

p. 57 *Of both actresses*: See Margot Peters, *Mrs. Pat: The Life of Mrs. Patrick Campbell* (New York: Alfred A. Knopf, 1984), pp. 248–51. Hereafter cited in the text as Peters.

p. 57 *Her own Juliet*: See Wright, pp. 24–25, and Furnas, pp. 449–50.

p. 58 *"Not a man"; "a company"*: Quoted in Charles E. Pearce, *Madame Vestris and Her Times* (n.d.; reprint, New York and London: Benjamin Blom, 1969), pp. 55, 168.

p. 59 *"Singularly original"*: Quoted in Edgar and Eleanor Johnson, 309–10. William Kleb, "Marie Wilton (Lady Bancroft) as an Actress," *Theatre Survey* 20 (May 1979): 43–79, gives a full account of Marie Wilton's career.

p. 60 *"Of the plays"*: Martin Meisel, *Shaw and the Nineteenth-Century Theatre* (1963; reprint, New York: Limelight Editions, 1984), p. 95. Hereafter cited as Meisel, *Shaw.*

p. 60 *"Better man"*: Sir Squire Bancroft quoted in Marie and Squire Bancroft, *The Bancrofts: Recollections of Sixty Years* (1909; reprint, New York: Benjamin Blom, 1969), p. 340.

p. 62 *Families consumed*: See Kathleen Tillotson, *Novels of the 1840s* (1954; reprint, Oxford: Oxford University Press, 1961), p. 55.

p. 63 *male prerogatives*: The most illuminating accounts of costumed and cross-dressed women in the nineteenth century are Helene R. Roberts, "The Exquisite Slave: The Role of Clothes in the Making of the Victorian Woman," *Signs: Journal of Women in Culture and Society* 2 (spring 1977): 554–79; Lillian Faderman, *Surpassing the Love of Men: Romantic Friendship and Love between Women from the Renaissance to the Present* (New York: William Morrow, 1981), pp. 1–61; Sandra M. Gilbert, "Costumes of the Mind: Transvestism as Metaphor in Modern Literature," *Critical Inquiry* 7 (Winter 1980): 391–417; and Susan Gubar, "Blessings in Disguise: Cross-Dressing as Re-Dressing for Female Modernists," *The Massachusetts Review* (autumn 1981), N.P.). These astute discussions of female costumes, chosen or imposed, barely mention women in the theater.

p. 65 *Far-reaching fears*: For an analysis of risks the comic heroines do not take, see Clara

Claiborne Park, "As We Like It: How a Girl Can Be Smart and Still Popular," in *The Woman's Part: Feminist Criticism of Shakespeare*, ed. Carolyn Ruth Swift Lenz, Gayle Greene, and Carol Thomas Neely (Urbana: University of Illinois Press, 1980), pp. 100–116.

p. 65 *Constraints of gender:* See, for instance, Carolyn G. Heilbrun, *Toward a Recognition of Androgyny* (New York: Alfred A. Knopf, 1973), pp. 28–34, and Irene G. Dash, *Wooing, Wedding, and Power: Women in Shakespeare's Plays* (New York: Columbia University Press, 1981).

p. 65 *Male costumes mortifying:* Russell Jackson, " 'Perfect Types of Womanhood': Rosalind, Beatrice, and Viola in Victorian Criticism and Performance," *Shakespeare Survey* 32, ed. Kenneth Muir (Cambridge: Cambridge University Press, 1979), pp. 15–26. Hereafter cited in the text as Jackson.

p. 66 *"As Imogen":* William Winter, *Shadows of the Stage*, 3d ser. (New York and London: Macmillan, 1895), 291.

p. 67 *"Of course not":* ET to Edward Gordon Craig, 20 August 1901, HRHRC.

p. 68 *Sexual identity:* Marguerite Coe, "Sarah and Coq," in *Bernhardt and the Theatre of Her Time*, ed. Eric Salmon (Westport, Ct.: Greenwood Press, 1984), p. 79.

p. 69 *"Could be changed":* The Tribune, 17 May 1911.

p. 69 *"Polly Pan":* To Pauline Chase, n.d. [1907?]. Ellen Terry Memorial Museum, Smallhythe Place. Hereafter cited as ETMM.

p. 71 *"Its lessons":* Lewis Carroll, "Stage Children," *The Theatre* (2 Sept. 1889): 114, 116.

p. 71 *"Run his course":* Quoted in Annie Clark, *Lewis Carroll: A Biography* (London: J. M. Dent, 1979), p. 237.

p. 72 *"Possible effect":* Charles L. Dodgson, "Theatre-Dress," manuscript bms Eng. 718.11, Houghton Library, Harvard University.

p. 73 *"And bestiality":* George T. M. Shackelford, *Degas: The Dancers* (New York: W. W. Norton, 1984), p. 66.

p. 73 *"Me inside"; "and a dangerous":* Charles Dickens, "Gaslight Fairies," *Household Words* (2 Feb. 1855): 25, 27.

CHAPTER 2: A MARRIAGE IN ART

p. 76 *"in-law":* E. G. Craig, *Ellen Terry and Her Secret Self,* p. 67.

p. 77 *to thirteen:* See Deborah Gorham, "The 'Maiden Tribute of Modern Babylon' Reexamined: Child Prostitution and the Idea of Childhood in Late-Victorian England," *Victorian Studies* 21 (spring 1978): 353–79.

p. 78 *"person's head":* Quoted in Manvell, 35.

p. 102 *"of her day":* T. Edgar Pemberton, *Ellen Terry and Her Sisters* (London: C. Arthur Pearson, 1902), p. 101. Hereafter cited as Pemberton.

p. 83 *have existed:* David Loshak, "G. F. Watts and Ellen Terry," *Burlington Magazine* 105 (Nov. 1963): 476–85, is the definitive account of this strange love story. Loshak brushes rumored conspirators away, insisting that Watts was his own man. Hereafter cited as Loshak.

p. 84 *in her charge?'* Loshak, 479, insists in the face of Watts's evident passivity that "to think Watts was a man who allowed others to run his life is seriously to misread his character."

p. 84 *"forces of nature":* G.K. Chesterton, *G. F. Watts* (Chicago and New York: Rand McNally, n.d.), pp. 70–71.

p. 85 *"loves and hates":* Quoted in Elizabeth French Boyd, *Bloomsbury Heritage: Their Mothers & Their Aunts* (London: Hamish Hamilton Ltd., 1976), p. 10. Hereafter cited as Boyd.

p. 85 *of her art:* Quoted in Virginia Woolf, introduction to *Victorian Photographs of Famous Men & Fair Women by Julia Margaret Cameron* (Boston: David R. Godine, 1973), p. 18.

p. 86 *"to another":* The *Times,* 3 October 1910. Quoted in Boyd, p. 31.

p. 86 *"toward the tomb."* Quoted in Wilfred Blunt, *"England's Michelangelo": A Biography of George F. Watts, O.M., R.A.* (London: Hamish Hamilton, 1975), p. 62. Hereafter cited as Blunt.

p. 89 *was losing:* Leonée Ormond, *George Du Maurier* (University of Pittsburgh Press, 1969), pp. 87–88.

p. 90 *"was talking":* To W. Graham Robertson, October 1894. Huntington Library.

p. 91 *"if you wished it":* George Eliot, *Middlemarch* (1870; reprint, Boston: Houghton Mifflin, Riverside Editions, 1956), p. 8.

p. 92 *"a little Latin":* Marguerite Steen, *A Pride of Terrys: Family Saga* (London: Longman's, 1962), p. 100. Hereafter cited as Steen.

p. 93 *"decided tomboy":* Mrs. Stirling, quoted in Blunt, pp. 111–12.

p. 93 *Cupid costume:* According to Edy and Chris, this story "may be apocryphal." *Memoirs,* p. 52.

p. 94 *"were its source":* Elizabeth G. Gitter, "The Power of Women's Hair in the Victorian Imagination," *PMLA* 99 (October 1984): 936.

p. 99 *Isle of Wight:* Manvell, 335, quoting Edward Anthony Craig.

p. 100 *"loveliness of nature":* *Letters from Graham Robertson,* ed. Kerrison Preston (London: Hamish Hamilton, n.d.), 323, 316. Hereafter cited as WGR, *Letters.*

p. 101 *Cameron flutters:* Virginia Woolf, *Freshwater: A Comedy* ed. Lucio P. Ruolto (1923; reprint, New York and London: Harcourt Brace Jovanovich, 1976), p. 68. Hereafter cited as *FW.*

p. 103 *usable identity:* See Doris Janet McReynolds, "Images of the Theatre in Victorian Literature" (diss., University of Minnesota 1970), p. 131. Hereafter cited as McReynolds.

p. 106 *in women:* See Sally Mitchell, *The Fallen Angel: Chastity, Class, and Women's Reading* (Bowling Green, Ohio: Bowling Green University Popular Press, 1981), pp. 153–54; and McReynolds, p. 101.

p. 108 *"with little variation":* Quoted in Nancy Vickers, "The Mistress in the Masterpiece" in *The Poetics of Gender,* ed. Nancy K. Miller (New York: Columbia University Press, 1986), pp. 22–23.

p. 109 *"old frump":* To Audrey Campbell, 4 July 1904. UCLA.

p. 110 *"seems cheerful":* Edward Gordon Craig to Edith Craig, 19 February 1915, HRHRC.

p. 113 *"beautifully! E. T. =":* ETMM.

p. 116 *if she chose:* Loshak, 484, suggests that Watts drew away from her when he discovered that she was not a pliable child, but a woman as strong-willed and masterful as his patron.

p. 116 *"picture things":* Quoted in [Stephen Coleridge], *The Heart of Ellen Terry* (London: Mills & Boon, Ltd., 1908), p. 43.

p. 117 *"in you":* ETMM.

p. 118 *"your letter":* ETMM.

p. 118 *"never shall"; "personal contact":* ETMM.

p. 122 *"Ellen Terry's hair":* Quoted in Morton N. Cohen, "The Actress and the Don: Ellen Terry and Lewis Carroll," *Lewis Carroll: A Celebration,* ed. Edward Guiliano (New York: Clarkson N. Potter, 1982), p. 2.

p. 124 *"sincere regards":* 27 March 1876. *The Letters of Lewis Carroll,* ed. Morton N. Cohen with the assistance of Roger Lancelyn Green, 2 vols. (New York: Oxford University Press, 1979), I, 245.

p. 125 *"my letter?"*: 9 June 1894. *Letters* II: 1025–26.

p. 125 *"go alone"*: 24 April 1894. *Letters* II: 1020–21.

p. 125 *"won from her"*: 9 June 1894. *Letters* II: 1025.

p. 126 *"generous* kindness": 13 November 1890. *Letters* II: 812–13.

p. 126 *"the chapter"*: 26 May 1894. Fales Collection, Bobst Library, New York University.

p. 126 *"unusual sensation = "*: 11 January 1893. Fales Collection, Bobst Library, New York University.

p. 128 *"and her husband"*: 12 April 1894. *Letters* II: 1015–16.

p. 128 *"see them—"*: 3 March 1911. Furness Collection, University of Pennsylvania.

p. 129 *"Wonderland = Nellen"*: The Arnold Rood Collection.

p. 130 *"them together"*: *London Times*, 2 Sept. 1867. Quoted in Pemberton, 116–17.

p. 131 *"too long delay'd"*: 7 June 1867. Folger Library.

CHAPTER 3: LOVE AND THE HEART OF THE COUNTRY

p. 132 *"my side"*: 22 June 1866. Quoted in Manvell, p. 63.

p. 133 *"saying goes"*: Clement Scott, *Ellen Terry* (New York: Frederick A. Stokes, 1900), pp. 68–69.

p. 135 *"domestic life"*: Laurence Irving, *Henry Irving: The Actor and His World* (New York: Macmillan, 1952), p. 147. Hereafter cited as LI or LI, *MI.*.

p. 136 *"my former self"*: For a full analysis of Garrick's abridgement, see Irene G. Dash, *Wooing, Wedding, and Power: Women in Shakespeare's Plays* (New York: Columbia University Press, 1981), pp. 32–64.

p. 137 *in kimonos*: See Dudley Harbron, *The Conscious Stone: The Life of Edward William Godwin* (1949; reprint, New York: Benjamin Blom, 1971), p. 82. Hereafter cited as Harbron.

p. 139 *their trade*: See Michael Baker, *The Rise of the Victorian Actor*, pp. 98–99.

p. 139 *shadow on them*: For a discussion of the actress's march to respectability, see Christopher Kent, "Image and Reality: The Actress and Society," in Vicinus, *A Widening Sphere*, 94–116.

p. 139 *to grow*: For more about the power of fallen women over the Victorian imagination, see Nina Auerbach, *Woman and the Demon: The Life of a Victorian Myth* (Cambridge, Mass.: Harvard University Press, 1982), pp. 151–84.

p. 139 *"worse than death!"*: Ellen Wood, *East Lynne* (1861; reprint, New Brunswick: Rutgers University Press, 1984), p. 237.

p. 140 *"were small"*: ETMM.

p. 141 *"found drowned"*: See Tom Prideaux, *Love or Nothing: The Life and Times of Ellen Terry* (New York: Scribner's, 1975), p. 73. Hereafter cited as Prideaux.

p. 144 *no particular work*: John Stokes, *Resistible Theatres: Enterprise and Experiment in the Late Nineteenth Century* (New York: Barnes and Noble, 1972), p. 36.

p. 146 *particular "truth"*: *Index*, pp. 14–15.

p. 147 *may have been Godwin*: Manvell, p. 68. E. A. Craig, *Gordon Craig*, p. 37, claims that she went with her lifelong friends, the Casella sisters, and their parents.

p. 148 *"leagues apart"*: Edward Gordon Craig, *Ellen Terry and Her Secret Self*, p. 63.

p. 148 *"wood for ever!"*: *Memoirs*, p. 31. ET's ellipsis.

p. 148 *"in the Trianon"*: Madeline Bingham, *Henry Irving: The Greatest Victorian Actor* (New York: Stein and Day, 1978), p. 137. Hereafter cited as Bingham.

p. 149 *"Bath there"*: Undated fragment of a letter signed "Ellen Carew." ETMM.

p. 149 *"in another"*: WGR, *Life Was Worth Living*, pp. 140–43.

p. 196/199 *by drowning:* Martin Meisel discusses the frequency with which fallen women drown in theatrical melodrama in *Realizations*, pp. 138–39.

p. 154 *"to be burnt"*: 4 July 1894, HRHRC.

p. 160 "taught *her*": ETMM.

p. 161 *"real love"*: EAC, p. 60. "Edward ever," *Letters from Graham Robertson*, p. 208.

p. 161 *"queer old Frump!"*: 23 December 1886. ETMM.

p. 161 *"thing, isn't it?"*: 2 December 1887. UCLA.

p. 161 *"the holy of holies"*: 30 December 1890. The Huntington Library.

p. 162 *"battered ="*: The Huntington Library.

p. 162 "sense less": 2 October 1878. Quoted in [Stephen Coleridge] *The Heart of Ellen Terry* (London: Mills & Boon, Ltd., 1908), p. 15.

p. 163 *"splendid!!!"*: 8 September 1892. The Players Club, New York City.

p. 163 *"we all adored ="*: December 1889. UCLA.

p. 164 *"now & again"*: 25 November 1895. UCLA.

p. 165 *"poisonous weed"*: Charles Reade, *Peg Woffington* (Boston: Ticknor and Fields, 1853), p. 296.

p. 167 *"in his regard"*: Charles Reade, *The Wandering Heir* (Boston: James R. Osgood, 1873), pp. 142–43.

p. 169 *"in the theatre"*: Laura Hain Friswell quoted in McReynolds, pp. 97–98.

p. 171 *"were not pleased"*: Billy Rose Theater Collection, Lincoln Center Library for the Performing Arts, New York Public Library.

p. 171 *"the main land"*: Edward W. Godwin, "The Architecture and Costume of 'The Merchant of Venice,' " 1875; reprint, *The Mask* 1 (1908–9), p. 94.

p. 171 *"of South Kensington"*: William Archer, *Henry Irving, Actor and Manager: A Critical Study* (London: Field & Tuer, n.d.), p. 101. Hereafter cited as Archer.

p. 173 *"is always unerring"*: Henry James, *The Scenic Art. Notes on Acting & the Drama: 1872–1901*, ed. Allan Wade (New York: Hill and Wang, 1957), pp. 143–44.

CHAPTER 4: OUR LADY OF THE LYCEUM

p. 175 *"at Lyceum"*; "Your *Hamlet"*: ETMM..

p. 176 *or both:* See Bingham, p. 19, and Manvell, p. 103.

p. 177 *"by a Pre-Raphaelite"*: Max Beerbohm, *More Theatres: 1898–1903* (New York: Taplinger, 1969), pp. 565, 367.

p. 180 *"rescued Ophelia"*: Madeleine Bingham, *Henry Irving*, pp. 133–34. Bingham embellishes Marguerite Steen's account (Steen, p. 183).

p. 181 *of Victorians:* Manvell, pp. 247–48, presents a series of arguments against a consummated love affair.

p. 181 " *'Let me serve!' "*; *"of empire"*: Christopher St. John, *Ellen Terry* (London: The Bodley Head, 1907), pp. 38, 43.

p. 181 *female juvenile:* See Joseph Donohue, *Theatre in the Age of Kean* (Totowa, N. J.: Rowman and Littlefield, 1975), 73. Hereafter cited as Donohue.

p. 182 *"to loathing"*: T. Edgar Pemberton, *Ellen Terry and her Sisters*, pp. 167–68.

p. 182 *"well then"*: ETMM.

p. 183 *"suffer in the play"*: In *Our Corner*, October 1885. Reprinted in *Shaw: The Annual of Bernard Shaw Studies,* ed. Stanley Weintraub, vol. 4 (University Park, Pa., and London: Pennsylvania State University Press, 1984), pp. 11–12.

p. 186 *"keep her place":* Gordon Craig, *Henry Irving* (New York and Toronto: Longmans, Green, 1930), p. 98. Hereafter cited in the text as *HI.*

p. 188 *"considered equals":* Quoted in Laurence Irving, p. 66.

p. 188 *arm of Empire:* For an account of the Victorian theater's progress toward respectability, see George Rowell, *The Victorian Theatre: 1792–1914,* pp. 75–102.

p. 188 *"in theatre-land":* *The Bancrofts, Recollections of Sixty Years,* pp. 33–34.

p. 189 *"promotion into glory":* Martin Meisel, *Realizations,* p. 228.

p. 189 *"in a church":* Bram Stoker, *Personal Reminiscences of Henry Irving,* 2 vols. (New York and London: Macmillan, 1906), II, 68.

p. 195 *"pictorial terms":* Michael R. Booth, "Pictorial Acting and Ellen Terry," p. 83.

p. 195 *"every tone":* WGR, *Life Was Worth Living,* p. 55.

p. 195 *"when he was on the stage":* Preface, *Ellen Terry and Bernard Shaw: A Correspondence,* ed. Christopher St. John (New York: G. P. Putnam's Sons, 1931), p. xxiv. Hereafter cited in the text as *A Corr.*

p. 196 *"he speaks his part":* Henry James, *The Scenic Art: Notes on Acting and the Drama: 1872–1901,* ed. Allan Wade (New York: Hill and Wang, 1957), p. 139. Hereafter cited in the text as *SA.*

p. 196 *"actor and manager":* Michael R. Booth, *Victorian Spectacular Theatre: 1850–1910,* p. 120.

p. 201 *"had eluded her":* Margaret Webster, *The Same Only Different: Five Generations of a Great Theatre Family* (New York: Alfred A. Knopf, 1969), p. 171. Hereafter cited as Webster.

p. 201 *"drawing room mantelpiece":* *Shaw's Dramatic Criticism (1895–1898),* ed. John F. Matthews (New York: Hill and Wang, 1959), p. 183.

p. 202 *"as it does":* William Archer, *Henry Irving, Actor and Manager,* p. 29.

p. 202 *"well content":* 26 May 1895, HRHRC.

p. 203 *"I do believe!!!!!":* 3 June 1887. UCLA.

p. 204 *"try to do it":* ETMM.

p. 204 *"or sexual fulfillment":* Helen Heineman, *Restless Angels: The Friendship of Six Victorian Women* (Athens, Ohio: Ohio University Press, 1983), pp. 159–60.

p. 205 *"sick of it":* 3 October 1889, UCLA.

p. 205 *"be insisted upon":* To Elizabeth Winter, n.d., Folger Library.

p. 205 *"much of him!":* To Audrey Campbell, 24 August N.Y., from Edinburgh, UCLA.

p. 205 *"I have met":* To Elizabeth Winter, Jan. 1889, Folger Library.

p. 206 *"I want!!!!!":* 29 September 1893, ETMM.

p. 206 *"he just won't!":* 6 April 1897, ETMM.

p. 207 *"I do – for him":* To Mabel Malleson, 19 October 1905. Folger Library.

p. 207 *"get thinner":* 26 January 1888, HRHRC.

p. 208 *"and get left!":* Quoted in Edward A. Craig, *Gordon Craig: The Story of His Life,* pp. 91–92.

p. 210 *"from Eleanora?":* 20 May 1907. Huntington Library.

p. 211 *"signing a cheque!!":* 3 January 1908. Folger Library.

p. 211 *"is the fact":* To Mr. Copleston, 18 March 1889. Folger Library.

p. 211 *"second letter":* To Mr. Mead, April 19–?. Folger Library.

p. 211 *"on Sunday":* 28 November 1884. Folger Library.

p. 212 *"frightfully busy":* To "my dear old Mildred," n.d., Folger Library.

p. 212 *"write to her a line":* 1900. Houghton Library, Harvard University.

p. 212 *"the general company":* 17 April 1889, UCLA.

p. 212 *"is provoking!":* 23 July 1888, UCLA.

p. 212 "not to *sleep":* ETMM.

p. 214, p. 215 "look *at her"; "& Humourous":* HRHRC.

p. 215 *or be cruel:* See Alan Hughes, *Henry Irving, Shakespearean* (Cambridge and London: Cambridge University Press, 1981) and Edward M. Moore, "Henry Irving's Shakespearean Productions," *Theatre Survey* 17 (November 1976): 197–98.

pp. 216 *"very base":* Unless otherwise indicated, all annotations from Ellen Terry's scripts are in the ETMM.

p. 216 *"longer a boy":* 10 August 1897. Folger Library.

p. 217a *"name with you":* 25 December 1888. Players Club.

p. 217 *"thus—or thus":* 23 December 1907. UCLA.

p. 217 *"or defeat":* 10 June 1889. Folger Library.

p. 217 *"now* always": August 16, ?. ETMM.

p. 218 *"these numbers":* 3 April 1915. Huntington Library.

p. 218 *"my wits":* n.d. ETMM.

p. 219 "machine *is E. T.":* 28 July 1893; 9 December 1898; after September, 1899. HRHRC.

p. 220 "Cleopatra": ETMM.

p. 220 *"life of womanhood":* Henry Giles, *Human Life in Shakespeare* (Boston: Lee & Shepard, 1868), p. 24. Hereafter cited in the text as Giles.

p. 221 *"more than mortal":* Henry Curling, *Shakspere; the Poet, the Lover, the Actor, the Man. A romance.* 3 vols. (London: Richard Bentley, 1848), III, 2–3.

p. 221 *"womanhood are holy":* Ellen Terry, *Four Lectures on Shakespeare* (London: Martin Hopkinson, 1932), p. 151.

p. 222 *"heart of Shakespeare":* Peter Raby, *Fair Ophelia: Harriet Smithson Berlioz* (Cambridge and London: Cambridge University Press, 1982), p. 69. Hereafter cited in the text as Raby.

p. 222 *"with them all":* Quoted in Jack Hamilton, "Ellen Terry: Genius Offstage and On," *Players Magazine* (February 1948): 102.

p. 222 *"after all":* To Mr. Hill, n.d. Folger Library.

p. 223 *"wot rot!":* To Charles Coleman, 11 March 1902. Tucker-Coleman Papers, Swem Library, College of William and Mary.

pp. 223 *"silly ladies"; "foolish women":* "Stray Memories," *The New Review* 23 (June, 1891): 503, 504.

p. 223 *"FLETCHER (England)":* ETMM.

p. 223 *"tenuous Juliet":* Betita Harding, *Age Cannot Wither: The Story of Duse and d'Annunzio* (Philadelphia and New York: J. B. Lippincott Co., 1947), p. 103.

p. 226 *"Beatrice and Benedick":* Russell Jackson, " 'Perfect Types of Womanhood': Rosalind, Beatrice and Viola in Victorian Criticism and Performance," p. 21.

p. 227 *"read Gratiano":* 8 February 1889. HRHRC.

p. 317 *"Alas!":* ETMM.

p. 318 *"in every place":* To Dr. Furness, 1894. Furness Collection, Van Pelt Library, University of Pennsylvania.

p. 318 *"Fidèle":* Paula S. Berggren, "The Woman's Part: Female Sexuality as Power in Shakespeare's Plays," *The Woman's Part: Feminist Criticism of Shakespeare,* ed. Carolyn Ruth Swift Lenz, Gayle Greene, Carol Thomas Neely, pp. 28–29.

p. 319 *"hope and supplication":* The Atheneum (26 Sept., 1896), 428.

p. 232 *"had ever seen"*: Oscar Wilde, *The Picture of Dorian Grey* (1891; reprint, Middlesex: Penguin Books, 1949), p. 87.

p. 234 *"she replied sweetly"*: Margot Peters, *Mrs. Pat: The Life of Mrs. Patrick Campbell,* p. 237.

p. 235 *"But I shouldn't—"*: 1 January 1894. Huntington Library.

p. 235 *"around the states"*: 8 May 1900. Huntington Library.

p. 236 *"a little worse!"*: Folger Library.

p. 236 *"that's all right"*: To William Winter, 29 August 1889. Folger Library.

p. 236 *"you as yourself"*: To Ada Rehan, n.d. Rare Book Room, Van Pelt Library, University of Pennsylvania.

p. 237 *"what he painted"*: Annotation to Charles Hiatt, *Ellen Terry and Her Impersonations,* ETMM.

p. 237 "OPHELIA": n.d. HRHRC

p. 237 *"one of yr best"*: 9 September 1898. HRHRC.

p. 241 *of a new dispensation:* For an analysis of mermaids and other hybrid women in Victorian cultural mythology, see Nina Auerbach, *Woman and the Demon: The Life of a Victorian Myth.*

p. 243 *"his death"*: *Undine,* by De La Motte Fouqué, adapted from the German by W. L. Courtney (London: William Heinemann, 1925), p. 132.

p. 244 *"end act II"*: Alfred C. Calmour, *The Amber Heart: A Poetic Fancy in Three Acts* (London: Nassau Stream Press, 1888), p. 38.

p. 247 *"part,' she meant"*: Virginia Woolf, *Between the Acts* (1941; reprint, New York: Harcourt Brace Jovanovich, 1969), p. 153. First ellipsis VW's.

p. 248 *"and civil servants"*: Richard Findlater, *The Player Queens* (New York: Taplinger, 1977), p. 164.

p. 248 *"odious in a man"*: Sarah Bernhardt, *Memories of my Life,* p. 342.

p. 249 *"perfect than man's"*: Quoted in E. A. Reinhardt, *The Life of Eleonora Duse* (1930; reprint, New York and London: Benjamin Blom, 1969), pp. 64–65.

p. 251 *"LADY MACBETH!!!"*: To Clement Scott, n.d. [1888], Huntington Library.

p. 253 *"resolution and courage"*: Frank Harris, *The Women of Shakespeare* (New York: Mitchell Kennerley, 1912), p. 180.

p. 254 *"written by a man"*: Quoted in Mary S. Hartman, *Victorian Murderesses* (1977; reprint, Pocket Books, 1978), pp. 87–88.

p. 254 *"charm him"*: ETMM.

p. 254 *"sexual contrast"*: Joe Comyns-Carr, "Macbeth and Lady Macbeth: An Essay," (London: Bicklers & Son, 1899), p. 13.

p. 254 *"as men generally are"; "supports him in it"*: F. A. Leo, *Shakespeare Notes* (London: Trübner & Co., 1885), pp. 72, 77.

p. 256 "Queen!": ETMM.

p. 259 "Fire!": 31 December [1888]. Huntington Library.

p. 260 *"stuffy day too!"*: n.d. Folger Library.

p. 260 *"I'll be temperate"*: n.d. Folger Library.

p. 263 *"self-authorizing kingship"*: Elliot L. Gilbert, "The Female King: Tennyson's Arthurian Apocalypse," *PMLA* 98 (Oct. 1983): 877.

p. 361 *"something Shakespearean"*: Gordon Craig, *Two Letters on Macbeth* (1928). Reprinted in *Craig on Theatre,* ed. J. Michael Walton (London: Methuen, 1983), p. 179. Second ellipsis EGC's. Hereafter cited in the text as "Walton."

CHAPTER 5: MOTHERHOOD AND MODERNISM

p. 267 *"I think not"*: ETMM.

p. 271 *"made much of her"*: Joseph Hatton, *Henry Irving's Impressions of America* (1884), quoted in Manvell, p. 175.

p. 272 *"helped a bit"*: "Nelly's House - The Theatre Itself," unpublished manuscript, HRHRC.

p. 272 *"so exactly"*: Gordon Craig to Edith Craig. 12 October 1928. HRHRC.

p. 272 *"he praiseth her"*: Isabella Beeton, *The Book of Household Management* (London: S. O. Beeton, 1861), p. 18.

p. 273 *made them*: Edward A. Craig, *Gordon Craig: The Story of His Life*, p. 92.

p. 276 *"like a child!"*: ETMM.

p. 279 *"you and I"*: Alice Comyns-Carr's *Reminiscences*, quoted in Manvell, p. 225.

p. 280 *"grow old"*: Clement Scott, *Ellen Terry* (New York: Frederick A. Stokes Co., 1900), p. 1.

p. 281 *"not 'pass' "*: Ellen Terry to Elizabeth Winter, December, 1886. Folger Library.

p. 282 *"by the way!!"*: Ellen Terry to W. Graham Robertson, April 15, 1899. Huntington Library.

p. 283 *"mad at myself—"*: Ellen Terry to W. Graham Robertson, September 6, 1906. Huntington Library.

p. 284 *"lad the better"*: Ellen Terry to Gordon Craig, 3 December 1888. HRHRC.

p. 285 *"getting on!!"*: Ellen Terry to Edward Anthony Craig, 1 July 1919. Folger Library.

p. 285 *"Kate comes back"*: Ellen Terry to Nella Casella, n.d., The Arnold Rood collection.

p. 289 *at the same time*: For a full account of Ellen Terry's relationship to Shaw, see Margot Peters's *Bernard Shaw and the Actresses* (New York: Doubleday, 1980). Hereafter cited in the text as Peters, *Shaw*.

p. 429 *"cat nature again"*: *Letters from Graham Robertson*, edited and with an introduction by Kerrison Preston (London: Hamish Hamilton, 1953), p. 234. Hereafter cited as *Letters*.

p. 295 *"in 1900"*: Margot Peters in *Shaw*, p. 272, speculates plausibly that Edy transmitted this wounding remark.

p. 297 *"it's over"*: Quoted in William Weaver, *Duse: A Biography*, p. 109.

p. 300 *"clever & interesting"*: To Audrey Campbell, 14 November 1901. UCLA.

p. 300 *Henry James,* Summersoft: manuscript, HRHRC.

p. 301 *"likely to foster"*: Max Beerbohm, *Last Theatres: 1904–1910* (New York: Taplinger, 1970), p. 243. 26 March 1906.

p. 302 *"from Eleanora?"*: To W. Graham Robertson, 20 May 1907. Huntington Library.

p. 303 *"time has wings"*: To Maurice Magnus, 14 January 1909. Folger Library.

p. 303 *of acting*: See James A. Barish, "Antitheatrical Prejudice in the Nineteenth Century," *University of Toronto Quarterly* 40 (summer 1971): 296.

p. 304 *"their dinner"*: Quoted in *Gordon Craig on Movement and Dance*, ed. Arnold Rood (New York: Dance Horizans, 1977), p. xxi.

p. 307 *"with his hammer"*: Edward Gordon Craig to Edith Craig, c. 1898. UCLA.

p. 308 *"a living spirit"*: Edward Gordon Craig, *On the Art of the Theatre* (Chicago: Browne Bookstore, n.d. [c. 1911]), pp. 84–85.

p. 309 *of religious ritual*: See Christopher Innes, *Edward Gordon Craig* (Cambridge and London: Cambridge University Press, 1983), p. 24.

p. 310 *to happen next*: Quoted in *"Your Isadora": The Love Story of Isadora Duncan and Gordon*

Craig, ed. Francis Steegmuller (New York: Random House and the New York Public Library, 1974), pp. 379–80. Hereafter cited as Steegmuller.

p. 310 *"very much trouble":* Ellen Terry to Mr. Wilkinson, 1 February 1883. Folger Library.

p. 311 *"Oh, I'm tired":* To Bertha J. Bramly, 1885. ETMM.

p. 311 *"cannot be [?].":* Ellen Terry, diary entry, 6 October 1886. ETMM.

p. 312 *"later on-":* Ellen Terry to Gordon Craig, 17 November 1887. HRHRC.

p. 312 *"does it too":* Ellen Terry to Gordon Craig, 10 May 1888. HRHRC.

p. 312 *"& you will!":* Ellen Terry to Gordon Craig, 15 July 1888. HRHRC.

p. 313 *"Darling good bye":* Gordon Craig to Ellen Terry, 21 October 1888 [ET's date]. UCLA.

p. 314 *"school of experience": Woodcuts and Some Words* (1924). Quoted in *Craig on Theatre,* ed. J. Michael Walton, p. 10.

p. 314 *"it is no art": A Letter to Ellen Terry* (1908). Quoted in Walton, p. 80.

p. 315 *"in this work":* Quoted in Arnold Rood, "E. Gordon Craig, Director, School for the Art of the Theatre," *Theatre Research International* 8 (spring 1985): 15–16.

p. 317 *"to one point":* Ellen Terry to Elizabeth Winter, January 1889. Folger Library.

p. 318 *"so far-":* Ellen Terry to Gordon Craig, 5 June 1890. HRHRC.

p. 319 *"Mr. Craig":* Margaret Webster, *The Same Only Different: Five Generations of a Great Theatre Family,* pp. 177–78.

p. 323 *"shadow of her son": HRHRC.*

p. 324 "as Hamlet!!": Ellen Terry to Gordon Craig, 10 October 1894. HRHRC.

p. 325 *"or something?":* Edith Craig to Edward Gordon Craig, 1894. UCLA.

p. 325 *"built out":* Edith Craig to Gordon Craig, n.d. HRHRC.

p. 325 *"criticize oneself":* Ellen Terry to Gordon Craig, 1894. HRHRC.

p. 326 *"yr. BRAINS":* Ellen Terry to Gordon Craig, 27 May 1889. HRHRC.

p. 326 *"just Perfect!!":* Ellen Terry to Audrey Campbell, 8 August 1894. UCLA.

p. 326 *"T. & M. but----":* To Audrey Campbell, 24 February 1896. UCLA.

p. 326 *"you & yours":* Ellen Terry to May Craig, 1894. HRHRC.

p. 327 *"name you'll get":* Ellen Terry to Gordon Craig, 3 November 1897. HRHRC.

p. 327 *"come to know it":* To Gordon Craig, 22 August 1899. HRHRC.

p. 327 *"on first nights":* To Gordon Craig, 3 April 1901. HRHRC.

p. 327 *"trouble rather":* To Gordon Craig [Fall 1896?]. HRHRC.

p. 328 *"Explain to Jessy":* To Gordon Craig, 4 April 1899. HRHRC.

p. 328 *"admirable of her":* To Gordon Craig, 22 August 1899. HRHRC.

p. 330 "Mother-": To Gordon Craig, 16 May 1901. HRHRC.

p. 331 *"That's something":* To Gordon Craig, 20 August 1900. HRHRC.

p. 332 *"not work together":* To Gordon Craig, 22 January 1900. HRHRC.

p. 332 *"try with Egil!":* The Vikings at Helgeland, Act II. *The Collected Works of Henrik Ibsen,* trans. William Archer, vol. 2 (New York: Charles Scribner's Sons, 1906), p. 41.

p. 334 *"it could be":* Gordon Craig to Ellen Terry, 8 March 1903. *Marked "not sent":* UCLA.

p. 334 *"so like a man?":* Ellen Terry to Gordon Craig, 7 February 1902. HRHRC.

p. 335 *"artistic success only":* Ellen Terry, diary entries, 16, 22 April 1903. ETMM.

p. 335 *"led Miss Terry":* Max Beerbohm, *More Theatres: 1898–1903* (New York: Taplinger, 1969), p. 562. 25 April 1903.

p. 339 *"upon the strand":* All material about Graham Robertson is taken from Kerrison Preston's introduction to *Letters from Graham Robertson,* pp. ix–xxxi.

p. 341 *"West of the Moon"*: Graham Robertson, "Ellen Terry, First Fairy," *The Mask* 2 (1909–10): 4.

p. 341 *"as now"*: Gordon Craig, "A Letter to Ellen Terry from her Son," *The Mask* 1 (August 1908): 111.

p. 342 *"I pray you don't!"*: Ellen Terry to Ella Casella, n.d. The Arnold Rood Collection.

p. 342 *"East wind I guess!"*: Ellen Terry to Bessie Campbell, n.d. Folger Library.

p. 342 *"tired as I am"*: To Audrey Campbell, 27 June 1896. UCLA.

p. 342 *"to get dead"*: To Mr. Mosher, 5 May 1900. Folger Library.

p. 343 *"produce no remedy"*: Gordon Craig to Edith Craig, 1897. HRHRC.

p. 343 *"break down"*: Ellen Terry to Gordon Craig, 15 April 1896. HRHRC.

p. 343 *"cheerful temperament!!"*: Ellen Terry to Graham Robertson, 8 January 1903. Huntington Library.

p. 343 *"I'm ill anyway"*: To Audrey Campbell, 26 March 1906. UCLA.

p. 343 *"brain I think"*: To Audrey Campbell, 27 August 1907. UCLA.

p. 344 *"Bacon - Please"*: To Graham Robertson, 14 May 1912. Huntington Library.

p. 345 *"losing her reason"*: Unidentified clippings, Billy Rose Theater Collection, New York Public Library at Lincoln Center.

p. 345 *"frightfully thin!"*: To Mabel Malleson, 27 February 1919. Folger Library.

p. 347 *"leaves me at present"*: To Graham Robertson, 9 October 1914. Huntington Library.

p. 347 *"buds so poor"*: Gordon Craig to Ellen Terry, 1910–11. HRHRC.

p. 348 *"never grows old"*: *Cincinnati Tribune*, 21 May 1911.

p. 348 *"more at present"*: Gordon Craig to Ellen Terry, 5 June 1908. HRHRC.

p. 349 *and a lawsuit*: For an account of Gordon Craig's influence on Tree's *Macbeth*, see Michael Mullin, "Strange Images of Death: Sir Herbert Beerbohm Tree's *Macbeth*, 1911," *Theatre Survey* 17 (November 1976): 125–42.

p. 349 *"of a camera!"*: D. W. Griffith, around 1914. Quoted in Lillian Gish (with Ann Pinchot), *The Movies, Mr. Griffith, and Me* (New Jersey: Prentice-Hall, 1969), p. 130.

p. 349 *"do you say"*: Gordon Craig to Edith Craig from Berlin, 1904. HRHRC.

p. 350 *"they deserve"*: Gordon Craig to Ellen Terry from Munich, n.d. UCLA.

p. 350 *origin of theatre*: Ellen Terry, *The Russian Ballet*, with Drawings by Pamela Colman Smith (New York: Bobbs-Merrill, 1913).

p. 350 *intensifying virulence*: See *Gordon Craig on Movement and Dance*, ed. Rood, pp. 78–84.

p. 350. *"to the Art"*: *The Mask* 1 (1908–9): 104–5.

p. 351 *"father's body—murdered"*: Gordon Craig quoted in *Theatre Arts* (July 1926), n.p.

p. 351 *"of his imagination"*: "Transcript of a conversation in French, taken down in Russian, 24 April 1909, on the stage of the Moscow Art Theatre." Quoted in Eugene K. Ilyin, "Gordon Craig's Mission to Moscow," *Theatre Arts* (May 1954): n. p.

p. 352 *"to my scenery"*: Isadora Duncan, *My Life* (New York: Boni and Liveright, 1927), pp. 180–81.

p. 352 *"its source"*: Private conversation with Stella Bloch, 1984.

p. 356 *"indulge her public"*: Gordon Craig, "On Signora Eleonora Duse," *Life and Letters*, Desmond MacCarthy, ed., 1 (Sept. 1928), 293–94.

p. 357 *"speak of him"*: Gordon Craig, "Untitled Essay on Ellen Terry, Isadora Duncan, Eleonora Duse, 1928 Sept. 26." Unpublished manuscript, HRHRC.

p. 360 *"beautiful* and *clever?"*: E. V. Lucas, *Ellen Terry's Bouquet*. Manuscript, Folger Library.

p. 362 *"appetite for joy"*: Kenneth Tynan, "Visit to the Past" (1956). Reprinted in *Curtains* (New York: Atheneum, 1961), p. 142.

p. 363 *"will kill me"*: *Edward Gordon Craig: The Last Eight Years—1958–1966: Letters from Ellen Gordon Craig,* ed. and with an introduction by Edward [Anthony] Craig (Gloucestershire: The Whittington Press, 1983), pp. 19, 44. Hereafter cited as *The Last Eight Years.*

p. 363 *"live with him"*: Ellen Gordon Craig to Arnold Rood, 25 October 1972. The Arnold Rood Collection.

p. 364 *"told to do"*: Edith Craig to "Jack" [John Martin Harvey], Feb. 4, n.y. [during the German occupation of Paris]. The Arnold Rood Collection.

CHAPTER 6: EDY'S WOMEN

p. 366 *"sharpened extremely"*: *Edy: Recollections of Edith Craig,* ed. Eleanor Adlard (London: Frederick Muller, Ltd., 1949), p. 79. Hereafter cited as Adlard.

p. 368 *"producing everything"*: Quoted in Julie Holledge, *Innocent Flowers: Women in the Edwardian Theatre,* p. 162.

p. 369 *"was Ellen Terry"*: Virginia Woolf, "Ellen Terry" (1941), *Collected Essays,* IV (London: The Hogarth Press, 1967), 72.

p. 370 *"vision and desire"*: Quoted in Martha Vicinus, *Independent Women: Work & Community for Single Women, 1850–1920* (Chicago and London: University of Chicago Press, 1985), p. 81. Hereafter cited in the text as Vicinus, *IW.*

p. 370 *"forgive me"*: Edith Craig to George Bernard Shaw, 18 October 1931. HRHRC.

p. 371 *"that's Sandhills"*: Ellen Terry to W. Graham Robertson, 9 November 1917. Huntington Library.

p. 372 *"the same [?] knee"*: Edith Craig to Anna Hollaender, ca. 1890. Folger Library.

p. 373 *in 1960:* Holledge, p. 118; private conversation with Molly Thomas, curator, Ellen Terry Memorial Museum, Smallhythe Place.

p. 374 *"to be hurt"*: Quoted in Ellen Craig, p. 43.

p. 373 *"very regretful"*: Ellen Terry to Mr. Malleson, 13 Sept.-- n.y. Folger Library.

p. 373 "ought *to know"*: Ellen Terry to Gordon Craig, 9 April 1887. HRHRC.

p. 376 *"tries again="*: Ellen Terry to Gordon Craig, 25 July 1889. HRHRC.

p. 376 *snickering men:* See Vicinus, *IW.* p. 150, for a student's description of Girton's lonely bleakness in the 1880s.

p. 376 *"beef and prunes"*: Virginia Woolf, *A Room of One's Own* (1929; reprint, New York: Harcourt, Brace, & World, 1957), pp. 17–18.

p. 377 *"that's all="*: Ellen Terry to Edith Craig, n.d. ETMM.

p. 378 "Nellchen=": Ellen Terry to Mr. and Mrs. Alexis Hollaender, n.d. Folger Library.

p. 376 *"his orchestra"*: 8 June 1933. Quoted in Christopher St. John, *Ethel Smyth: A Biography,* with Additional Chapters by V. Sackville-West and Kathleen Dale (London: Longmans Green, 1959), p. 229. Hereafter cited in text as *Ethel Smyth.*

p. 383 *"as a school boy!"*: Ellen Terry to Gordon Craig, 12 November 1894. HRHRC.

p. 384 "lightly *& funnily="*: Ellen Terry to Gordon Craig, 3 November 1895. HRHRC.

p. 384 *"one of 'em"*: Ellen Terry to Gordon Craig, 28 December 1895. HRHRC.

p. 386 *"terrible defect="*: Ellen Terry to Gordon Craig, 15 April 1896. HRHRC.

p. 387 *"old girl ="*: Gordon Craig to Edith Craig, to Gravesend, Kent, 29 June 1896. HRHRC.

p. 387 *than her love:* Manvell, p. 305, follows Steen, p. 250, when he claims that Edy tried to achieve "a normal love affair" (as he calls it) when she fell in love, on the Lyceum's *1890* tour, with the hunchbacked Joe Evans, an American painter whom Ellen Terry befriended. Margaret Webster's account, published after Manvell's biography appeared, resolves the confusion about the date of Edy's love story and its object. The warmth with which Ellen Terry wrote to Joe Evans and Edy about each other throughout the 1890s makes it particularly improbable that catastrophic love had passed between them.

p. 389 *"a Saint!":* [Christopher St. John], *Hungerheart: The Story of a Soul* (London: Methuen, 1915), p. 293.

p. 391 *"know it!":* 18 October 1902. HRHRC.

p. 392 *"of garments":* Cicely Hamilton, *Marriage as a Trade* (New York: Moffat, Yard, 1909), p. 84.

p. 393 *"same too":* Virginia Woolf, *Orlando* (1928; reprint, New York: Harcourt Brace Jovanovich, 1956), pp. 187–88.

p. 396 *"water traffic":* E. V. Lucas, "The Ellen Terry Memorial," *Sunday Times,* 10 May 1936.

p. 367 *"your cot!":* Quoted in Elizabeth Mavor, *The Ladies of Llangollen* (1971; reprint Middlesex: Penguin Books, 1983), p. 93.

p. 397 *and disease:* See Lillian Faderman, *Surpassing the Love of Men: Romantic Friendship and Love Between Women from the Renaissance to the Present* (New York: William Morrow, 1981), p. 240.

p. 402 *"young men":* Quoted in Esther Newton, "The Mythic Mannish Lesbian: Radclyffe Hall and the New Woman," *The Lesbian Issue: Essays from "Signs",* ed. Estelle B. Freedman, Barbara C. Gelpi, Susan L. Johnson, Kathleen M. Weston (Chicago and London: University of Chicago Press, 1985), p. 13. Hereafter cited as Newton.

p. 402 *"for evermore":* 27 April 1913. Vera Brittain, *Testament of Youth* (New York: Macmillan, 1937), p. 52.

p. 403 *"Christopher and Tony."* From "Sally," n.d. UCLA.

p. 404 *"same from me":* Christopher St. John, *The Golden Book,* p. 50. Manuscript, UCLA.

p. 408 *"Forgive me—":* Ellen Terry to Elizabeth Winter, ca. 1904. Folger Library.

p. 408 *"other flowers=":* 27 July 1891. Folger Library.

p. 408 *Ellen Terry's understudy:* EAC, p. 56, and Holledge, p. 108.

p. 409 *"and platonic":* Carroll Smith-Rosenberg, "The Female World of Love and Ritual" (1975); reprinted in *Disorderly Conduct: Visions of Gender in Victorian America* (New York: Alfred A. Knopf, 1985), p. 55.

p. 409 *"so weak=":* Ellen Terry to Audrey Campbell, 6 September 1894. UCLA.

p. 410 *"Thursday week=":* 11 August 1890. UCLA

p. 410 *"get him!!":* 26 August 1890. UCLA.

p. 410 *"have to do it—"* 20 December 1893. UCLA.

p. 411 *"believe me =":* 30 October 1894. UCLA.

p. 412 *"write this to you =":* 8 June 1905. UCLA.

p. 412 "E.T." 26 April [1907?]. UCLA.

p. 413 "Old Frump=": 19 March 1908. UCLA.

p. 415 *"matchless charm":* New York *Evening Telegram,* 1909.

p. 416 *at the crossroads:* For Woolf's use of Black's *Judith Shakespeare,* see Jane Marcus, "Liberty, Sorority, Misogyny," in *The Representation of Women in Fiction,* ed. Carolyn G.

Heilbrun and Margaret R. Higonnet (Baltimore and London: Johns Hopkins University Press, 1983), pp. 78–79.

p. 417 *when the time comes:* Gordon Bottomley, *King Lear's Wife & Other Plays* (London: Constable, 1920), p. 13.

p. 418 *in the margin:* Lillie Buffum Wyman, *Gertrude of Denmark: A Romance* (Boston: Marshall Jones, 1924), p. 1. ETMM. Hereafter cited as Wyman.

p. 419 *Hamlet and Horatio:* Program, Hampshire House Club, 3 June 1909. Folger Library.

p. 419 *"visiting moon":* Ellen Terry's manuscript quoted in Betty Bandel, "Ellen Terry's Foul Papers," *Theatre Studies* 10 (May 1969), 49.

p. 422 *learn to love:* Stanley Weintraub's "The Genesis of *Joan*" lists myriad medieval sources for Shaw's saint, while ignoring the iconography of the feminist theater that flourished before his eyes. See *The Unexpected Shaw: Biographical Approaches to G. B. S. and His Work* (New York: Frederick Ungar, 1982), pp. 181–93.

p. 423 Gordon Craig to I. Gollancz, 15 March 1916. Folger Library. Ellipsis EGC's.

p. 423 *"so very much=":* Ellen Terry to Elizabeth Robins, n.d. Fales Collection, Bobst Library, New York University.

p. 424 *employment realized:* See Julie Holledge, *Innocent Flowers,* for a complete account of Edith's Craig's career, the achievements and repertoire of the Pioneer Players.

p. 426 *"disturbed by rows":* Gordon Craig to Ellen Terry, 1911. UCLA.

p. 427 *"out of doors":* Virginia Woolf, *Between the Acts* (1941; reprint, New York: Harcourt, Brace Jovanovich, 1969), p. 62. For intimations of Edith Craig in Miss La Trobe, see Jane Marcus, "Some Sources for *Between the Acts,*" *Virginia Woolf Miscellany* 6 (Winter, 1977), 1–3.

p. 430 *"contend with":* Sir John Gielgud, *Distinguished Company* (New York: Doubleday, 1972), pp. 33–34.

p. 433 *"of Ellen Terry":* Wilfred Walter to Edith Craig, May 31, 1938. UCLA.

p. 433 *"years went by":* Sir John Gielgud to Nina Auerbach, 11 November 1984.

CHAPTER 7: CHILD

p. 441 *"of it all!":* To Elizabeth Winter, 20 April 1889. Folger Library.

p. 441 *"so many ways":* To Elizabeth Winter, 2 May 1904. Folger Library.

p. 441 *"I feel strange":* 19 October 1910. *The Heart of Ellen Terry,* p. 67.

p. 442 *"Luny-Mooney Nell":* To Graham Robertson, 18 December 1910. Huntington Library.

p. 442 *"self-improvement":* To Gordon Craig, 6 August 1890. HRHRC.

p. 443 *"horrors seem true":* 27 December 1914. Huntington Library.

p. 443 *"that yet":* 2 May 1904. Folger Library.

p. 443 *"Wot Rot":* To Graham Robertson, 9 November 1917. Huntington Library.

p. 444 *away from the stage:* Unidentified clipping, Billy Rose Collection, New York Public Library at Lincoln Center.

p. 446 *"blessed lady"; "(your ghost)":* 17 June 1902; 27 June 1902. ETMM.

p. 447 *"transcends both":* Quoted in Victoria Glendenning, *Vita: A Biography of Vita Sackville-West* (New York: Alfred A. Knopf, 1983), pp. 252–53.

p. 448 *"along with mine":* 18 November 1918. Huntington Library.

p. 449 *"painter or writer":* May Agate, *Madame Sarah* (1945; reprint, New York: Benjamin Blom, Inc., 1969), pp. 193–94.

Chronology of Significant Dates

1837. Ben Terry sees the celebrated juvenile actress Jean Davenport.

1838. Ben Terry and Sarah Ballard elope.

1844. Birth of Kate Terry.

1847. Debut of Kate Terry.
Birth of Ellen Terry.

1851. George Frederic Watts moves to Little Holland House, the home of his patrons the Prinseps.

1856. Debut of Ellen Terry as Mamillius in Charles Kean's production of *The Winter's Tale.*

1857. Ellen Terry plays the good fairy Goldenstar, and then the bad Dragonetta, in the pantomime "The White Cat."

1858. Ellen Terry is acclaimed as Prince Arthur in *King John.*
Marie Wilton is acclaimed as the boy Pippo in H. J. Byron's burlesque, "The Maid and the Magpie."

1859. Charles Kean's company disbands.

1859–60. Ben Terry takes Kate and Ellen on tour in *A Drawing-Room Entertainment.*

1862. Ellen Terry in Bristol, where she plays an embarrassingly exposed Cupid in "Endymion."
Ellen Terry meets George Frederic Watts; she and Kate pose for his painting, "The Sisters."
Ellen Terry meets Edward William Godwin.
Kate Terry's performance in Sardou's *Nos Intimes* wins her London stardom.

1864–65. Ellen Terry's marriage to George Frederic Watts.

1864. Ellen Terry meets Lewis Carroll (Charles L. Dodgson), who photographs the Terry family.

1865. Publication of *Alice's Adventures in Wonderland.*
The Bancrofts produce T. W. Robertson's domestic comedy, *Society.*

p. 450 *"impossible":* Undated fragment, ETMM.

p. 451 *"Harrah!!!!!":* July 1928. Billy Rose Theatre Collection, New York Public Library at Lincoln Center.

p. 453 *"resents distrust":* ETMM.

p. 454 *"lives to art":* Lena Ashwell, *Myself a Player* (London: Michael Joseph, Ltd., 1936), p. 82.

p. 455 *"isn't it?":* 9 April, n.d. Folger Library.

p. 456 *"as she was":* To Clement Scott, 6 March 1892. Huntington Library.

p. 457 *"ripens and outlives":* Reprinted in *Literary Digest,* 11 August 1928.

1866. Henry Irving's first London success in Dion Boucicault's *Hunted Down*.
Ellen Terry travels to Paris.

1867. Ellen Terry joins the Wigans' company, where she and Henry Irving star in *Katherine and Petruchio*, Garrick's adaptation of Shakespeare's *Taming of the Shrew*.
Kate Terry retires from the stage to marry Arthur Lewis.

1868. Ellen Terry runs off to the country with Edward William Godwin.

1869. Birth of Edith Craig; Godwin designs a house for the family in Harpenden.

1871. Henry Irving's first performance as Mathias in *The Bells*.

1872. Birth of Edward Gordon Craig.

1874. Charles Reade persuades Ellen Terry to return to the London theater, where she stars in his plays, *The Wandering Heir* and *It's Never Too Late to Mend*.
Henry Irving plays an acclaimed Hamlet with the Batesons' company.

1874–75. Godwin's thirty-two articles, "On the Architecture and Costume of Shakespeare's Plays."

1875. Ellen Terry's acclaimed Portia in the Bancrofts' production of *The Merchant of Venice* is enhanced by Godwin's aesthetic designs.
After leaving the home he shares with Ellen Terry, Godwin tries and fails to kidnap Edith Craig.

1878. Ellen Terry's debut as Olivia in W. G. Wills's adaptation of *The Vicar of Wakefield*.
Ellen Terry's debut as Ophelia and as the leading lady of Henry Irving's Lyceum.
The American actress Ada Rehan becomes the leading lady of Augustin Daly's company.

1878–1881. Ellen Terry's marriage to Charles Wardell.

1880. Ellen Terry's debut as Beatrice to Charles Wardell's Benedick in *Much Ado About Nothing*.

1881. Tennyson's *The Cup* produced at the Lyceum with Godwin as production consultant.

1883. Ellen Terry's children take the name of "Craig."
First American tour of Irving's Lyceum company.

1884. Gordon Craig joins the Lyceum's second American tour as Joey the gardener's boy in *Eugene Aram*.

1884, 1885. Godwin produces *As You Like It* for the Pastoral Players.

1884–88. Edith Craig attends Mrs. Malleson's school, where she is groomed for Girton College, Cambridge.

1885. Death of Charles Wardell.
Faust produced at the Lyceum.

1886. Death of Edward William Godwin.

1887. Charles Charrington produces Ibsen's *A Doll's House* in London with Janet Achurch as Nora.
Ellen Terry stars in *The Amber Heart* at the Lyceum.

1887–1912. Ellen Terry's correspondence with Audrey Campbell.

1888. Gordon Craig is expelled from Heidelberg College in Berlin.
Edith Craig moves to Berlin to study music.
Macbeth produced at the Lyceum.

1889. Gordon Craig joins the Lyceum company.

1890. Edith Craig joins the Lyceum company.

1891. Publication of George Bernard Shaw's *The Quintessence of Ibsenism.*

1892. Death of Sarah Terry.

1892–1922. Ellen Terry's correspondence with George Bernard Shaw.

1893–97. Gordon Craig's marriage to May Gibson.

1894. Gordon Craig's debut as Hamlet.

1895. Henry Irving knighted.

Oscar Wilde sentenced to imprisonment for acts of gross indecency.

George Bernard Shaw writes *The Man of Destiny* for the Lyceum company.

Edith Craig falls in love with Sidney Valentine on the Lyceum's American tour.

Death of Florence Terry.

Death of Ben Terry.

1896. Christopher St. John meets Ellen Terry and Edith Craig.

Ellen Terry stars in *Cymbeline* at the Lyceum.

1897. Edith Craig joins Charles Charrington's company, playing Prossy in Shaw's *Candida* and Mrs. Linden in *A Doll's House.*

Johnston Forbes-Robertson plays an acclaimed Hamlet with Mrs. Patrick Campbell as Ophelia.

Publication of Bram Stoker's *Dracula.*

1898. Henry Irving begins the love affair with Eliza Aria that will last until his death.

Henry Irving relinquishes the management of the Lyceum to a syndicate.

After Arthur Lewis declares himself a bankrupt, Kate Terry returns unsuccessfully to the stage.

George Bernard Shaw marries Charlotte Payne-Townshend.

Edith Craig travels to South Africa with Mrs. Brown Potter's company.

1899. Edith Craig and Christopher St. John take a London flat.

Edith Craig designs the costumes for Sardou's *Robespierre* at the Lyceum.

1900. Ellen Terry buys the Farm at Smallhythe; Edith Craig and Christopher St. John share Priest's House.

1900–2. Gordon Craig collaborates with Martin Shaw on three acclaimed if uncommercial productions: Purcell's *Dido and Aeneas* and *The Masque of Love,* and Handel's *Acis and Galatea.*

1902. Gordon Craig elopes with Elena Meo.

Termination of Ellen Terry's association with the Lyceum company.

1903. Ellen Terry assumes management of the Imperial Theatre, where Gordon Craig produces Ibsen's *The Vikings.* Ellen Terry appears to be miscast as the fierce warrior Hiördis.

1904. Gordon Craig exiles himself from England.

Beginning of the love affair between Gordon Craig and Isadora Duncan.

With the assistance of Edith Craig and Christopher St. John, Ellen Terry and her company at the Imperial tour the English provinces.

Edith Craig falls disruptively in love with Martin Shaw.

Death of George Frederic Watts.

1905. Death of Henry Irving.

Ellen Terry's debut as Lady Cicely Waynflete in George Bernard Shaw's *Captain Brassbound's Conversion.*

Publication of Gordon Craig's *The Art of the Theatre.*

1906. Ellen Terry plays Hermione in Beerbohm Tree's production of *The Winter's Tale*.
Ellen Terry's jubilee.
Gordon Craig designs Ibsen's *Rosmersholm* for Eleonora Duse's company.

1907. Elizabeth Robins's production of *Votes for Women!* opens at the Court Theatre.

1907–9. Ellen Terry's marriage to James Carew.

1908. Publication of Ellen Terry's *The Story of My Life*.
The Actress' Franchise League founded.

1909. Edith Craig produces Cicely Hamilton's *How the Vote Was Won* and *A Pageant of Great Women* for the Actress' Franchise League.

1910–21. Ellen Terry reads her *Four Lectures on Shakespeare* in England (and English music halls), Australia, and America.

1911–25. Edith Craig heads the Pioneer Players.

1912. Gordon Craig produces *Hamlet* at Stanislavksy's Moscow Art Theatre.

1913. Drowning of Deirdre Craig.
Publication of Ellen Terry's *The Russian Ballet*.

1913–14. Gordon Craig founds a school of theater at the Arena Goldoni in Florence.

1914–15. Ellen Terry breaks down while touring Australia at the outbreak of World War I.

1915. Ellen Terry is operated on for cataracts, but is nearly blind thereafter.
Anonymous publication of Christopher St. John's *Hungerheart*.

1916–22. Ellen Terry appears in five forgettable films.

1923. Virginia Woolf writes the first version of *Freshwater*.

1925. Ellen Terry is designated Dame Grand Cross.

1928. Death of Ellen Terry.

1928–39. Edith Craig heads the Barn Theatre at Smallhythe.

1930. Vita Sackville-West moves to Sissinghurst, near Smallhythe.

1931. Christopher St. John publishes the correspondence between Ellen Terry and George Bernard Shaw.
Publication of Gordon Craig's *Ellen Terry and Her Secret Self*.

1932. Edith Craig and Christopher St. John publish an annotated, expanded version of Ellen Terry's *The Story of My Life* (under the title *Ellen Terry's Memoirs*), glossing the autobiography with their own commentary.

1933. Virginia Woolf meets Edith Craig and Christopher St. John.

1935. Virginia Woolf writes the second version of *Freshwater*.

1941. Publication of Virginia Woolf's "Ellen Terry" and *Between the Acts*.

1947. Death of Edith Craig.

1957. Death of Elena Meo.
Nelly Craig moves to Gordon Craig's home in Vence.
Publication of Gordon Craig's *Index to the Story of My Days*.

1960. Death of Christopher St. John.

1966. Death of Gordon Craig.

List of Works Cited

I. CULTURAL AND PERFORMANCE HISTORY.

Agate, May. *Madame Sarah.* 1945. Reprint New York: Benjamin Blom, 1969.

Appleton, William W. *Madame Vestris and the London Stage.* New York: Columbia University Press, 1974.

Ashwell, Lena. *Myself a Player.* London: Michael Joseph, Ltd., 1936.

Auerbach, Nina. *Woman and the Demon: The Life of a Victorian Myth.* Cambridge, Mass.: Harvard University Press, 1982.

Baker, Michael. *The Rise of the Victorian Actor.* Totowa, N.J.: Rowman & Littlefield, 1978.

Bancroft, Marie and Squire Bancroft. *The Bancrofts: Recollections of Sixty Years.* 1909. Reprint New York: Benjamin Blom, 1969.

Barish, James A. "Antitheatrical Prejudice in the Nineteenth Century." *University of Toronto Quarterly* 40 (summer, 1971): 277–99.

Barnes, Eric Wollencott. *The Lady of Fashion: The Life and Times of Anna Cora Mowatt.* New York: Charles Scribner's Sons, 1954.

Beerbohm, Max. *Around Theatres.* New York: Taplinger Publishing Co., 1969.

Beerbohm, Max. *More Theatres: 1898–1903.* New York: Taplinger Publishing Co., 1969.

Beerbohm, Max. *Last Theatres: 1904–1910.* New York: Taplinger Publishing Co., 1970.

Beeton, Isabella. *The Book of Household Management.* London: S. O. Beeton, 1861.

Berggen, Paula S. "The Woman's Part: Female Sexuality as Power in Shakespeare's Plays." In *The Woman's Part: Feminist Criticism of Shakespeare,* edited by Carolyn Ruth Swift Lenz, Gayle Greene, and Carol Thomas Neely, 17–34. Urbana: University of Illinois Press, 1980.

Bernhardt, Sarah. *Memories of My Life.* 1908. Reprint New York and London: Benjamin Blom, 1968.

Black, William. *Judith Shakespeare: A Romance.* 3 vols. London: Macmillan, 1884.

Bolton, H. Philip. "*Bleak House* and the Playhouse." *Dickens Studies Annual* 12: 81–116. New York: AMS Press, 1983.

Booth, Michael R. *Victorian Spectacular Theatre, 1850–1910.* London: Routledge & Kegan Paul, 1981.

Bottomley, Gordon. *King Lear's Wife & Other Plays.* London: Constable & Co., 1920.

Boyd, Elizabeth French. *Bloomsbury Heritage: Their Mothers & Their Aunts.* London: Hamish Hamilton Ltd., 1976.

Brittain, Vera. *Testament of Youth.* New York: The Macmillan Co., 1937.

Brontë, Charlotte. *Jane Eyre.* 1847. Reprint Middlesex; Penguin Books, 1966.

Burstyn, Joan N. *Victorian Education and the Ideal of Womanhood.* New Brunswick, N.J.: Rutgers University Press, 1984.

Calmour, Alfred C. *The Amber Heart: A Poetic Fancy in Three Acts.* London: Nassau Stream Press, 1888.

Carnovksy, Morris, with Peter Sander. *The Actor's Eye.* New York: Performing Arts Journal Publications, 1984.

Carroll, Lewis. "Stage Children." *The Theatre* (2 Sept. 1889): 115–17.

Carroll, Lewis, [Charles L. Dodgson]. "Theatre-Dress." Unpublished manuscript. Houghton Library, Harvard University, Cambridge, Mass.

Clark, Annie. *Lewis Carroll: A Biography.* London: J. M. Dent & Sons, 1979.

Coe, Marguerite. "Sarah and Coq: Contrast in Acting Styles." In *Bernhardt and the Theatre of Her Time,* edited by Eric Salmon, 67–89. Westport, Ct.: Greenwood Press, 1984.

Comyns-Carr, Joe. "Macbeth and Lady Macbeth: An Essay." London: Bicklers & Son, 1899.

Curling, Henry. *Shakespere; the Poet, the Lover, the Actor, the Man. A romance.* 3 vols. London: Richard Bentley, 1848.

Darvi, Andrea. *Pretty Babies: An Insider's Look at the World of the Hollywood Child Star.* New York: McGraw Hill, 1983.

Dash, Irene. *Wooing, Wedding, and Power: Women in Shakespeare's Plays.* New York: Columbia University Press, 1981.

Dickens, Charles. "Gaslight Fairies," *Household Words* 11 (10 Feb. 1855): 25–28.

The Dickens Theatrical Reader, edited by Edgar and Eleanor Johnson. London: Victor Gollancz, 1961.

Dobbs, Brian. *Drury Lane: Three Centuries of the Theatre Royal, 1663–1971.* London: Cassel & Co., 1972.

Donohue, Joseph. *Theater in the Age of Kean.* Totowa, N.J.: Rowman and Littlefield, 1975.

Erkkila, Betsy. "Greta Garbo: Sailing Beyond the Frame." *Critical Inquiry* 11 (June 1985): 595–619.

Eliot, George. *Middlemarch.* 1871. Reprint Boston: Houghton Mifflin, Riverside Editions, 1956.

Faderman, Lillian. *Surpassing the Love of Men: Romantic Friendship and Love Between Women from the Renaissance to the Present.* New York: William Morrow & Co., 1981.

Findlater, Richard. *The Player Queens.* New York: Taplinger Publishing Co., 1977.

Fouqué, De La Motte. *Undine,* adapted from the German by W. L. Courtney. London: William Heinemann, 1925.

Furnas, J. C., *Fanny Kemble: Leading Lady of the Nineteenth-Century Stage.* New York: Dial Press, 1982.

Gilbert, Elliot L. "The Female King: Tennyson's Arthurian Apocalypse." *PMLA* 90 (Oct. 1983): 863–78.

Gilbert, Sandra M., and Susan Gubar. *The Madwoman in the Attic: The Woman Writer and the Nineteenth-Century Literary Imagination.* New Haven: Yale University Press, 1979.

Gilbert, Sandra M. "Costumes of the Mind: Transvestism as Metaphor in Modern Literature." *Critical Inquiry* 7 (Winter 1980): 391–417.

Giles, Henry. *Human Life in Shakespeare.* Boston: Lee & Shepard, 1868.

Gish, Lillian, with Ann Pinchot. *The Movies, Mr. Griffith, and Me.* Englewood Cliffs, N.J.: Prentice Hall, Inc., 1969.

Gitter, Elisabeth G. "The Power of Women's Hair in the Victorian Imagination." *PMLA* 99 (Oct. 1984): 936–53.

Glendenning, Victoria. *Vita: A Biography of Vita Sackville-West.* New York: Alfred A. Knopf, 1983.

Gorham, Deborah. "The 'Maiden Tribute of Modern Bablyon' Re–examined: Child Prostitution and the Idea of Childhood in Late-Victorian England." *Victorian Studies* 21 (Spring 1978): 353–79.

Gubar, Susan. "Blessings in Disguise: Cross-Dressing as Re-Dressing for Female Modernists." *The Massachusetts Review* (Autumn 1981).

Hamilton, Cicely. *Marriage As a Trade.* New York: Moffat, Yard & Co., 1909.

Harding, Betita. *Age Cannot Wither: The Story of Duse and d'Annunzio.* Philadelphia and New York: J. B. Lippincott Co., 1947.

Harmetz, Aljean. *The Making of "The Wizard of Oz."* New York: Alfred A. Knopf, 1977.

Harris, Frank. *The Women of Shakespeare.* New York: Mitchell Kennerley, 1912.

Hartman, Mary S. *Victorian Murderesses.* New York; Schocken Books, 1977.

Heilbrun, Carolyn. *Toward a Recognition of Androgyny.* New York: Alfred A. Knopf, 1973.

Heineman, Helen. *Restless Angels: The Friendship of Six Victorian Women.* Athens, Ohio: Ohio University Press, 1983.

Ibsen, Henrik. *The Vikings at Helgeland,* 1858.

Jackson, Russell. " 'Perfect Types of Womanhood': Rosalind, Beatrice and Viola in Victorian Criticism and Performance." *Shakespeare Survey* 32: 15–26. Cambridge: Cambridge University Press, 1979.

James, Henry. *The Scenic Art. Notes on Acting & Drama: 1872–1901,* edited by Allen Wade. New York: Hill & Wang, Inc., 1957.

James, Henry. *The Tragic Muse.* 1890. Reprint New York: Harper & Brothers, 1968.

James, Henry. *Summersoft,* 1895. Manuscript, Harry Ransom Humanities Research Center.

Kent, Christopher. "Image and Reality: The Actress and Society." In *A Widening Sphere: Changing Roles of Victorian Women,* edited by Martha Vicinus, 94–116. Bloomington and London: Indiana University Press, 1977.

Kleb, William. "Marie Wilton (Lady Bancroft) As an Actress." *Theatre Survey* 20 (May 1979): 43–79.

Le Gallienne, Eva. *The Mystic in the Theatre: Eleonora Duse.* 1965. Reprint Carbondale: Southern Illinois University Press, 1973.

Leo, F. A. *Shakespeare Notes.* London: Trüber & Co., 1885.

McReynolds, Doris Janet. *Images of the Theater in Victorian Literature.* Diss., University of Minnesota, 1970.

Marcus, Jane. "Some Sources for *Between the Acts.*" *Virginia Woolf Miscellany* 6 (Winter 1977): 1–3.

Marcus, Jane. "Liberty, Sorority, Misogyny." In *The Representation of Women in Fiction,* edited by Carolyn G. Heilbrun and Margaret R. Higgonet, 60–97. Baltimore and London: The Johns Hopkins University Press, 1983.

Mavor, Elizabeth. *The Ladies of Llangollen.* 1971. Reprint Middlesex: Penguin Books, 1983.

Mayer, David. "The Sexuality of Pantomime." *Theatre Quarterly* 4 (Feb.-Ap. 1974): 53–64.

Mazer, Cary M. *Shakespeare Refashioned: Elizabethan Plays on Edwardian Stages.* Ann Arbor, Mich.: UMI Research Press, 1981.

Meisel, Martin. *Shaw and the Nineteenth-Century Theatre.* 1963. Reprint New York: Limelight Editions, 1984.

Meisel, Martin. *Realizations: Narrative, Pictorial, and Theatrical Arts in Nineteenth-Century England.* Princeton and London: Princeton University Press, 1983.

Mitchell, Sally. *The Fallen Angel: Chastity, Class, and Women's Reading.* Bowling Green, Ohio: Bowling Green University Popular Press, 1981.

Newton, Esther. "The Mythic Mannish Lesbian: Radclyffe Hall and the New Woman." In *The Lesbian Issue: Essays from "Signs,"*: 7–25. Chicago and London: University of Chicago Press, 1985.

Olivier, Laurence. *Confessions of an Actor: An Autobiography.* 1982. Reprint Middlesex: Penguin Books, 1984.

Ormond, Leonée. *George Du Maurier.* Pittsburgh: University of Pittsburgh Press, 1969.

Park, Clara Claiborne. "As We Like It: How a Girl Can Be Smart and Still Popular." In *The Woman's Part: Feminist Criticism of Shakespeare,* edited by Carolyn Ruth Swift Lenz, Gayle Greene, and Carol Thomas Neely, 100–116. Urbana: University of Illinois Press, 1980.

Pearce, Charles E. *Madame Vestris and Her Times.* n.d. Reprint New York and London: Benjamin Blom, 1969.

Peters, Margot. *Bernard Shaw and the Actresses.* New York: Doubleday & Co., 1980.

Peters, Margot. *Mrs. Pat: The Life of Mrs. Patrick Campbell.* New York: Alfred A. Knopf, 1984.

Raby, Peter. *Fair Ophelia: Harriet Smithson Berlioz.* Cambridge and London: Cambridge University Press, 1982.

Reade, Charles. *Peg Woffington.* Boston: Ticknor & Fields, 1853.

Reade, Charles. *The Wandering Heir.* Boston: James R. Osgood & Co., 1873.

Reinhardt, E. A. *The Life of Eleonora Duse.* 1930. Reprint New York and London: Benjamin Blom, 1969.

Roberts, Helene R. "The Exquisite Slave: The Role of Clothes in the Making of Victorian Woman." *Signs: A Journal of Women in Culture and Society* 2 (Spring 1977): 554–79.

Rowell, George. *The Victorian Theatre, 1792–1914.* 2d ed. 1956. Reprint Cambridge and London: Cambridge University Press, 1978.

Shackleford, George T. M. *Degas: The Dancers.* New York: W. W. Norton, 1984.

Shaw, George Bernard. "Dramatic Criticism in *Our Corner,* 1885–1886." In *Shaw: The Annual of Bernard Shaw Studies* 4, edited by Stanley Weintraub, 5–32. University Park and London: The Pennsylvania State University Press, 1984.

Shaw's Dramatic Criticism (1895–1898), edited by John F. Matthews. New York: Hill & Wang, 1959.

Shaw, George Bernard. *The Man of Destiny,* 1895.

Shaw, George Bernard. *Captain Brassbound's Conversion,* 1899.

Shaw, George Bernard. *St. Joan,* 1924.

Smith-Rosenberg, Carroll. "The Female World of Love and Ritual." 1975. In her *Disorderly*

Conduct: Visions of Gender in Victorian America, 53–76. New York: Alfred A. Knopf, 1985.

Stokes, John. *Resistible Theaters: Enterprise and Experiment in the Late Nineteenth Century.* New York: Barnes and Noble, 1972.

Tennyson, Alfred Lord. *The Cup,* 1881.

Tillotson, Kathleen. *Novels of the 1840s.* 1954. Reprint Oxford: Oxford University Press, Oxford Paperbacks, 1961.

Trewin, J. C. *Mr. Macready: A Nineteenth-Century Tragedian and His Theatre.* London: George G. Harrap & Co., 1955.

Trewin, J. C. *The Pomping Folk in the Nineteenth-Century Theatre.* London: J. M. Dent & Sons, 1968.

Trewin, J. C. *The Edwardian Theatre.* Totowa, N.J.: Rowman & Littlefield, 1976.

Vicinus, Martha. *Independent Women: Work & Community for Single Women, 1850–1920.* Chicago and London: University of Chicago Press, 1985.

Vickers, Nancy J. "The Mistress in the Masterpiece." In *The Poetics of Gender,* edited by Nancy K. Miller, 19–41. New York: Columbia University Press, 1986.

Weaver, William. *Duse: A Biography.* New York: Harcourt Brace Jovanovich, 1984.

Weintraub, Stanley. "The Genesis of *St. Joan.*" In *The Unexpected Shaw: Biographical Approaches to G. B. S. and His Work,* 181–93. New York: Frederick Ungar Publishing Co., 1982.

Wilde, Oscar. *The Picture of Dorian Grey.* 1891. Reprint Middlesex: Penguin Books, 1949.

Winter, William. *Shadows of the Stage.* 3d ser. New York and London: Macmillan & Co., 1895.

Wood, Ellen. *East Lynne.* 1861. Reprint New Brunswick, N.J.: Rutgers University Press, 1984.

Woolf, Virginia. Introduction, *Victorian Photographs of Famous Men & Fair Women by Julia Margaret Cameron.* Boston: David R. Godine, 1973.

Woolf, Virginia. *Orlando.* 1928. Reprint New York: Harcourt Brace Jovanovich, 1956.

Woolf, Virginia. "A Room of One's Own." 1929. Reprint New York: Harcourt, Brace, Jovanovich, 1957.

Wright, Constance. *Fanny Kemble and the Lovely Land.* New York: Dodd Mead & Co., 1972.

Wyman, Lillie Buffum. *Gertrude of Denmark: A Romance.* Boston: Marshall Jones Co., 1924.

II. Ellen Terry, Her Family, and Her Associates.

Edy: Recollections of Edith Craig, edited by Eleanor Adlard. London: Frederick Muller, Ltd., 1941.

Archer, William. *Henry Irving, Actor and Manager: A Critical Study.* London: Field & Tuer, n.d.

Bablet, Denis. *The Theatre of Edward Gordon Craig,* translated by Daphne Woodward. London: Eyre Methuen, 1981.

Bandel, Betty. "Ellen Terry's Foul Papers." *Theatre Studies* 10 (May 1969): 43–52.

Bingham, Madeline. *Henry Irving: The Greatest Victorian Actor.* New York: Stein & Day, 1978.

Blunt, Wilfred. *"England's Michaelangelo": A Biography of George F. Watts, O.M., R.A.* London: Hamish Hamilton, 1975.

Booth, Michael R. "Pictorial Acting and Ellen Terry." In *Shakespeare and the Victorian Stage,* edited by Richard Foulkes, 78–86. Cambridge: Cambridge University Press, 1986.

Chesteron, G. K. *G. F. Watts.* Chicago and New York: Rand McNally & Co., n.d.

Cohen, Morton N., ed., with the assistance of Roger Lancelyn Green. *The Letters of Lewis Carroll.* 2 vols. New York: Oxford University Press, 1979.

Cohen, Morton N. "The Actress and the Don: Ellen Terry and Lewis Carroll." In *Lewis Carroll: A Celebration,* edited by Edward Guiliano, 1–14. New York: Clarkson N. Potter, 1982.

[Coleridge, Stephen.] *The Heart of Ellen Terry.* London: Mills & Boon, Ltd., 1908.

Craig, Edward Anthony. *Gordon Craig: The Story of His Life.* New York: Alfred A. Knopf, 1968.

Edward Gordon Craig: The Last Eight Years—1958–1966: Letters from Ellen Gordon Craig, edited and with an introduction by Edward [Anthony] Craig. Gloucestershire: The Whittington Press, 1983.

Craig, Edward Gordon. "A Letter to Ellen Terry from her Son." *The Mask* 2 (August 1908): 109–11.

Craig, Edward Gordon. *On the Art of the Theatre.* Chicago: Browne Bookstore, ca. 1911.

Craig, Edward Gordon. *Two Letters on Macbeth.* 1928. In *Craig on Theatre,* edited by J. Michael Walton, 177–79. London: Methuen, 1983.

Craig, Edward Gordon. *Henry Irving.* New York and Toronto: Longmans, Green, & Co., 1930.

Craig, Edward Gordon. *Ellen Terry and Her Secret Self.* London: Sampson Low, Marston & Co., 1931.

Craig, Edward Gordon. *Index to the Story of My Days: Some Memoirs of Edward Gordon Craig, 1872–1907.* New York: The Viking Press, 1957.

Gordon Craig on Movement and Dance, edited by Arnold Rood. New York: Dance Horizons, 1977.

Duncan, Isadora. *My Life.* New York: Boni & Liveright, 1922.

"Your Isadora": The Love Story of Isadora Duncan and Gordon Craig, edited by Francis Steegmuller. New York: Random House and the New York Public Library, 1974.

Gielgud, Sir John. *Distinguished Company.* New York: Doubleday & Co., 1972.

Godwin, Edward W. "The Architecture and Costume of 'The Merchant of Venice.' " 1875. *The Mask* 1 (1908–9): 75–80; 91–95.

Hamilton, Jack. "Ellen Terry: Genius Offstage and On." *Players Magazine* (Feb. 1948).

Harbron, Dudley. *The Conscious Stone: The Life of Edward William Godwin.* 1949. Reprint New York: Benjamin Bloom, 1971.

Hiatt, Charles. *Ellen Terry and Her Impersonations: An Appreciation.* London: George Bell & Sons, 1898.

Holledge, Julie. *Innocent Flowers: Women in the Edwardian Theatre.* London: Virago Press, 1981.

Hughes, Alan. *Henry Irving, Shakespearean.* Cambridge and London: Cambridge University Press, 1981.

Ilyin, Eugene K. "Gordon Craig's Mission to Moscow." *Theatre Arts* (May 1954).

Innes, Christopher. *Edward Gordon Craig.* Cambridge and London: Cambridge University Press, 1983.

Irving, Laurence. *Henry Irving: The Actor and His World.* New York: The Macmillan Co., 1951.

Loshak, David. "G. F. Watts and Ellen Terry." *Burlington Magazine* 105 (Nov. 1963): 476–85.

Manvell, Roger. *Ellen Terry*. New York: G. P. Putnam's Sons, 1968.

Moore, Edward M. "Henry Irving's Shakespearean Productions." *Theatre Survey* 17 (Nov. 1976): 195–216.

Mullin, Michael. "Strange Images of Death: Sir Herbert Beerbohm Tree's *Macbeth*, 1911." *Theatre Survey* 17 (November 1976), 125–42.

Pemberton, T. Edgar. *Ellen Terry and Her Sisters*. London: C. Arthur Pearson, Ltd., 1902.

Prideaux, Tom. *Love or Nothing: The Life and Times of Ellen Terry*. New York: Scribner's, 1975.

Letters from Graham Robertson, edited by Kerrison Preston. London: Hamish Hamilton, n.d.

Robertson, W. Graham. "Ellen Terry, First Fairy." *The Mask* 2 (1909–10): 3–5.

Robertson, W. Graham. *Life Was Worth Living: The Reminiscences of W. Graham Robertson*. New York: Harper & Brothers, 1931.

Rood, Arnold. "E. Gordon Craig, Director, School for the Art of the Theatre." *Theatre Research International* 8 (Spring 1983): 1–17.

St. John, Christopher. *Ellen Terry*. London: The Bodley Head, 1907.

St. John, Christopher. *Hungerheart: The Story of a Soul*. London: Methuen & Co., 1915.

St. John, Christopher, ed. *Ellen Terry and Bernard Shaw: A Correspondence*. New York: G. P. Putnam's Sons, Ltd., 1931.

St. John, Christopher. *Ethel Smyth: A Biography*, with Additional Chapters by V. Sackville-West and Kathleen Dale. London: Longmans Green & Co., 1959.

Scott, Clement. *Ellen Terry*. New York: Frederick A. Stokes, 1900.

Steen, Marguerite. *A Pride of Terrys: Family Saga*. London: Longman's, 1962.

Stoker, Bram. *Personal Reminiscences of Henry Irving*. 2 vols. New York and London: The Macmillan Co., 1906.

Terry, Ellen. "Stray Memories." *The New Review* 23 (June 1891).

Terry, Ellen. *The Russian Ballet*, with Drawings by Pamela Colman Smith. New York: The Bobbs-Merrill Co., 1913.

Terry, Ellen. *Ellen Terry's Memoirs*, with a Preface, Notes, and Additional Biographical Chapters by Edith Craig and Christopher St. John. 1932. Reprint New York: Benjamin Blom, 1969. (This is a later, annotated edition of Terry's *The Story of My Life*.)

Terry, Ellen. *Four Lectures on Shakespeare*. London: Martin Hopkinson, 1932.

Tynan, Kenneth. "Visit to the Past." 1956. In *Curtains*. New York: Atheneum, 1961.

Webster, Margaret. *The Same Only Different: Five Generations of a Great Theater Family*. New York: Alfred A. Knopf, 1969.

Woolf, Virginia. *Freshwater: A Comedy*, edited by Lucio P. Ruolto. 1923. Reprint New York and London: Harcourt Brace Jovanovich, 1976.

Woolf, Virginia. *Between the Acts*. 1941. Reprint New York: Harcourt Brace Jovanovich, 1969.

Woolf, Virginia. "Ellen Terry." 1941. In *Collected Essays*, vol. IV. London: The Hogarth Press, 1967.

III. MANUSCRIPT COLLECTIONS AND THEATRICAL ARCHIVES.

The Arnold Rood Collection; Henneke Archives of the Performing Arts, The University of Tulsa; UCLA Library, Special Collections; Harry Ransom Humanities Research Center, the University of Texas, Austin; the Henry E. Huntington Library; the Ellen Terry Memorial

Museum and Library, Smallhythe Place; the Houghton Library, Harvard University; the British Museum and Library; the Fales Collection, Bobst Library, New York University; Tucker-Coleman Papers, Swem Library, College of William and Mary; the Furness Collection, University of Pennsylvania; Rare Books Room, Van Pelt Library, University of Pennsylvania; the Folger Shakespeare Library; the Players Club, New York City; the Billy Rose Theater Collection, New York Public Library at Lincoln Center.

Index